AF669674

STUDIES IN THE ORIGINS OF BUDDHISM

BY THE SAME AUTHOR

- Foundations of Indian Culture (2 Vols.)
- Life and Thought of Śaṅkarācarya
- Bauddha Dharma ke Vikāsa Kā Itihāsa
- Apohasiddhi
- Nyāyabindu
- The Meaning and Process of Culture
- Mūlya Mīmāṁsā
- Agnibīja
- Kṣaṇa aur Lakṣaṇa
- Sravanism and Indian Culture
- R.K. Jain Memorial Lectures on Jainism
- Bhāratīya Prampară Ke Mūla Svara
- Jaina Political Thought
- Dimensions of Ancient Indian Social History
- Vision and Symbolic Forms

STUDIES IN THE ORIGINS OF BUDDHISM

Govind Chandra Pande

MOTILAL BANARSIDASS PUBLISHERS
PRIVATE LIMITED • DELHI

3rd Reprint: ***Delhi, 2013***
Fourth Revised Edition: Delhi, 1995
First Edition: Allahabad, 1957

ISBN: 978-81-208-1016-7

MOTILAL BANARSIDASS
41 U.A. Bungalow Road, Jawahar Nagar, Delhi 110 007
8 Mahalaxmi Chamber, 22 Bhulabhai Desai Road, Mumbai 400 026
203 Royapettah High Road, Mylapore, Chennai 600 004
236, 9th Main III Block, Jayanagar, Bengaluru 560 011
Sanas Plaza, 1302 Baji Rao Road, Pune 411 002
8 Camac Street, Kolkata 700 017
Ashok Rajpath, Patna 800 004
Chowk, Varanasi 221 001

Printed in India
by RP Jain at NAB Printing Unit,
A-44, Naraina Industrial Area, Phase I, New Delhi–110028
and published by JP Jain for Motilal Banarsidass Publishers (P) Ltd.
41 U.A. Bungalow Road, Jawahar Nagar, Delhi-110007

PREFACE TO THE FOURTH EDITION

The continued interest of my readers has encouraged me to bring out this fourth edition which has been updated where necessary but the work remains substantially unaltered. Buddhist studies have been progressing all over the world, a progress which has been noted in several bibliographical surveys in recent years among which Prof. Nakamura's *Indian Buddhism* (Delhi, 1987) deserves special mention. Nevertheless, much of the ongoing research is centred on the publication, translation or interpretation of post-canonical texts as understood within the several 'national' traditions of Buddhist scholarship as it obtains today. To the older national orthodoxies of Buddhist interpretation have been added new directions, provided by recent ideologies or methodologies. However, one may be permitted to state that neither orthodoxy, whether Southern or Northern, nor ideology, whether Marxist or positivist ought to be allowed to hinder the pursuit of historical truth.

The earlier historical-critical work on Buddhism extending from Oldenberg to Miss I.B. Horner was based on the recognition of the relative antiquity of the Pali canon and its unique value for the understanding of early Buddhism. The significance of this fact, however, has been sometimes disputed, overlooked or minimized in the light of the counter claims one finds in the northern traditions. These traditions depend for the most part on Chinese and Tibetan translations of Indian originals which are almost wholly lost. Some fragments of canonical texts in Sanskrit or Prakrit have undoubtedly been discovered but they are tantalizingly few. Ancient Chinese translations too are not so literal as the much later Tibetan ones. Under the circumstances, it cannot be gainsaid that the best clue to the history of early Buddhism still continues to lie in the Pali canon.

Since the Buddha allowed his followers to remember his teachings in their own tongues, it must have facilitated the development of the canonical tradition in diverse dialects in diverse sects. That it is only the Pali canon of the Theravādins which has been fully preserved is, thus, only a historical accident but nevertheless it does make that canon a unique window from which to glimpse the life and teachings of the Buddha.

This is not to say that Theravāda is to be regarded as original Buddhism or that the Pali canon is to be identified with *Buddhavacana*. But this does mean that any enterprise which aims at discovering the *Buddhavacana* must specially turn to the intimations to be found in the Pali canon. References and quotations in later Mahāyānic literature do indicate many *sūtras* or *paryāyas* which could be part of *Buddhavacana* but this only confirms the value of the Pali canon in which most of these may still be found. The few attempts which have been made to compare the canonical texts in Pali with Chinese translations or Sanskrit fragments show that ordinarily these texts existed in differently ordered collections and while they had a generic similarity of theme, intent, concepts and environmental background, occasionally some of the versions go on to make substantial additions and significant alterations. Thus the Instructions to Kātyāyana illustrate essential identity between different versions while the Sūtra of the Great Decease shows much reworking.

A comparison of the Pali and non-Pali versions of the texts helps to exclude substantial portions of the canon such as the *Abhidharma* as sectarian and hence as post-Buddhic. If the sects arose in the second century A.B., the basic canonical texts which do not have any specific sectarian bias should belong to the first century A.B. They too, however, would represent the interpretative and elaborative monastic traditions of the age, not unalloyed *Buddhavacana,* to reach which the only way is the critical examination and stratification of the canonical texts as available in their most ancient and complete collection in Pali. Orthodoxy, whether of faith or of traditional Pali scholarship, should not be allowed to hinder this task.

The methodological approach of the present work steers clear of all orthodoxies, whether of traditional Pali scholarship or of Japanese or Tibetan scholarship. It is true that the relative antiquity of the Pali canon has been questioned by several students of Chinese, Tibetan and Japanese sources, just as the authenticity of the Mahāyāna *sūtras* was questioned by Hīnayānic schools in the remote past. These arguments, however, do not seem to sufficiently reckon with the non-sectarian and pre-Aśokan character of the first and second *piṭakas* except for several texts of the *Khuddaka Nikāya*. An important consideration in this context is the view one takes of the date of Buddha's *nirvāṇa* as also of the history of the Buddhist Councils. There has been recently a revival of the older view which dated Buddha's *nirvāṇa* in the fourth century B.C. on the ground that it occurred a century before the Second Buddhist Council, which is held to have taken place in the time of Aśoka. This tradition apparently confuses Aśoka with Kālāśoka Kākavarṇi and is adequately contradicted by the Ceylonese tradition which places Aśoka's coronation 218 years after the *Parinirvāṇa*. The attempts to determine the date of Buddha by using a chronology of material development based on considerations of archaeological evidence are far too hypothetical to decide the narrow difference of a mere century in days when changes in material life occurred over long periods in an insensible manner. The archaeological evidence is in any case too ambiguous to permit any precise social chronological inferences. The social ethos of the earlier parts of the canon does not need to be necessarily placed in the Mauryan Age which itself cannot be regarded a sudden break from the past.

Similarly there have been attempts to link the rise of

Buddhism with certain social and economic changes such as the rise of agriculture, trade and towns or the break up of the older clans of *gaṇas* by the emergence of a caste society. A definite correlation between Buddha's teachings or early Buddhism and such socio-economic conditions, however, is not only without sufficient evidence but also no plausible causal connection has ever been shown between them. It is only within the context of some kind of social determinism springing from a materialistic philosophy of history or a *positivistic* sociology that such attempts to explain spiritual doctrines or movements can have even *prima facie* plausibility. Buddhism did not arise as the particular voice of a social group or interest and it would be misleading to describe it as primarily a movement of social protest or dissent. It was a new discovery of moral and spiritual truth relevant to the eradication of existential suffering and thus appealed to all mankind equally. As the proclamation of Truth it was a universal message. One could doubtless be sceptical about such claims but such scepticism would itself presuppose an alternative and inevitably speculative or dogmatic theory about religion. The present work seeks to confine itself to an objective historical-critical appraisal of evidence.

The basic idea of the Brāhmaṇa-Śramaṇa dichotomy has been generally approved by competent scholars though their detailed explanations have naturally been diverse. There has been some more discussion about the concept of *nairātmya* in early Buddhism and at least some critical scholars have lent their support to the view that it would be misleading to construe *Anattā* as a simple denial of all spiritual or transcendental reality underlying the notion of the Self. It may be reaffirmed that that would not only contradict the evidence of the earliest texts but also introduce grave contradictions within the structure of Buddhist doctrines.

Some more researches have been done on the history

and doctrines of the early Schools but they do not affect the conclusions of the present work. They have, however, been evaluated by the author elsewhere in detail.

I must specially acknowledge my gratefulness to my friends Dr. Bhikkhu Pāsādika and Rev. S. Rinpoche who have helped me to stay abreast of the fast moving current of Buddhist scholarship.

To my publishers, Messrs Motilal Banarsidass Publishers Private Limited, I am beholden for their continued interest in the work.

Rama-navami, 1993 G.C. PANDE

Allahabad

PREFACE TO THE SECOND EDITION

In preparing the present second edition I have corrected some slips which had inadvertantly crept into the first edition and taken note of the significant and relevant publications since 1957 when the first edition of this work had been published. My conclusions and arguments, however, remain unchanged and hence the second edition remains substantially identical with the first.

I am grateful to my colleagues Dr. S.K. Gupta and Dr. S.N. Dube who have helped me in revising the work for the second edition. I am similarly grateful to my students Mrs. Nilima Vashishtha and Shri V.M. Diwakar.

That the second edition of the work has been prepared at all is above all due to the persistent interest of M/s Motilal Banarsidass. Had they not goaded me over several years the work might never have been completed.

4-4-1974 G. C. Pande
Jaipur

PREFACE

Much has been written on early Buddhism and yet the need of a fresh study of the subject can hardly be gainsaid. Mrs. Rhys Davids has raised the all-important question: what was the original message of Buddhism? This pointed query has rudely disturbed the almost settled composure of Buddhist scholarship. As soon as it is admitted that the original mandate of Buddhism might have been something different from what it is traditionally reported to have been—and tradition is not unanimous—we are forced to adopt a more critical, a more historical outlook towards our texts; and the adoption of this New Approach, of which Mrs. Rhys Davids has been the pioneer, at once necessitates a re-study of the problems of Buddhist origins.

At the very outset we have to realize that even the earliest available collections within the Buddhist canon are of uncertain date and heterogeneous contents. Mrs. Rhys Davids has drawn attention to the fact that the Nikāyas do not preach a uniform set of doctrines. It will be seen that they contain within themselves the seeds of multiform growth. From what we know about the Chinese Āgamas it appears safe to draw a similar general conclusion about them. A historical approach to ancient Buddhism, therefore, most certainly entails the stratification of the Nikāyas and the Āgamas. The task is attempted with reference to the Nikāyas in Chapters I—VII.

There is, again, an additional reason for a fresh study of the subject. The discoveries in the Indus Valley have revolutionized our perspective of the foundations of Indian religion and culture. They have shown that a civilized non-Vedic culture once existed in prehistoric India. This invalidates the common assumption that all higher thought in India existing before Buddha must necessarily have had a Vedic origin. In fact, civilization in India, as elsewhere, has been a composite creation. Numerous races and cultural communities have met and struggled and mingled in the long history of Indian culture which has progressed through the synthesis of diverse conflicts. It seems desirable to review from this standpoint the development of Vedic religion and culture and of the social and intellectual tendencies of the Age of Buddha and Mahāvīra. The task is here attempted principally in Chapters VIII–IX.

Although a great deal has been written on the life of Buddha, it still remains a desideratum to correlate his life and quest, experience and mission, with his teachings. This task is attempted in Chapter X.

There has been much controversy over the "correct" interpretation of such points of Buddhist doctrine as Pratītyasamutpāda and Nirvāṇa. Now the ancient canonical texts are themselves not quite agreed on these points, which is intelligible enough since the texts in question are spread over a considerable period of time. The "original gospel" assumed various forms in the course of its development and was soon grown over by them to the point of obscurity. It appears that unless the ancient Buddhist ideas are analysed clearly with reference to their historical or genetic relationship it will hardly be possible to trace firmly their original foundations. This task is attempted in Chapters XI–XIII.

The last two chapters attempt a brief analysis of certain historical problems arising out of the early development of Buddhism.

The present work is, thus, designed to consist of a group of organically connected historical studies relating to the origins of Buddhism. It is the doctrinal rather than the institutional aspect of Buddhism that is mainly considered. The subject-matter is for the greater part of a literary and religio-philosophic character, but the treatment is intended to be primarily historical.

The approach has been mainly through the Indian sources of Buddhism. Chinese and Tibetan sources have also been utilized as far as possible, though not from the original languages. The present work is substantially identical with a thesis of the same title which was approved in the University of Allahabad for the Degree of Doctor of Philosophy in 1947. The arrangement of material has been altered, and necessary modifications have been made in the light of subsequent study and reflection.

My deepest debt is to Pt. K. Chattopadhyaya, Reader in Sanskrit, University of Allahabad, who supervised my research work and has guided me all along. I am profoundly grateful to the authorities of the University of Allahabad viz., Sri B. N. Jha, Vice-Chancellor, Dr. B. R. Saksena, D.Litt., Dean of the Faculty of Arts, Sri K. L. Govil, Registrar, Dr. B. P. Saksena, Ph.D., Professor of History, and Sri G. R. Sharma, Head of the Department of Ancient History, Culture and Archaeology, who have made the publication of the present work possible.

It is regretted that owing to haste some misprints, which mostly do not affect the sense, have escaped proof-reading. Except for some obvious omissions of diacritical and punctuation marks, these have, however, been indicated in the list of errata at the end.

I am thankful to Sri Brij Nath Singh Yadav, M.A., D.Phil., for his help in the preparation of the Index. I am also thankful to Sri H. P. Ghosh, Manager, Indian Press, and Sri K. P. Dar, Press Manager, for their helpful co-operation in the printing of the present work.

G. C. Pande

CONTENTS

PART I

STUDIES IN EARLY BUDDHIST SOURCES

PART II

STUDIES IN THE HISTORICAL AND CULTURAL BACKGROUND OF EARLY BUDDHISM

PART III

STUDIES IN EARLY BUDDHIST DOCTRINES

PART I

STUDIES IN EARLY BUDDHIST SOURCES

CHAPTER I

THE BUDDHIST CANON AND ITS CHRONOLOGY

The Buddhist Canon.—In spite of the differences of language, place, dogmatic preferences, verbal variants, and the divisions of the canon, one can still speak of a "Canon of the Hīnayāna" divided in two Piṭakas. The only redaction of this canon which we possess in its entirety and in an early Indian language is the Pali redaction.[1]

The Abhidharma and its versions.—The relative lateness of the Abhidharma Piṭaka is manifest. It probably grew out of the Mātikās[2] and is found in only two schools—Thèravāda and Sarvāstivāda.[3] The Pali Abhidhamma consists of seven works—Dhammasaṅgaṇi, Vibhaṅga, Puggalapaññatti, Dhātukathā, Paṭṭhāna, Yamaka, Kathāvatthuppakaraṇa. The Sarvāstivāda Abhidharma also consists of seven works—Jñānaprasthāna, and the six Pādaśāstras. The six Pādaśāstras in their traditional order (which is a little different from that of Nanjio) are[4]: 1. Saṅgītiparyāyapāda, 2. Dharmaskandha, 3. Prajñaptipāda, 4. Vijñānakāyapāda, 5. Dhātukāyapāda, 6. Prakaraṇapāda. According to tradition the Abhidharma too represents the words of

[1] La Vallée Poussin, Opinions, pp. 30f.

[2] Winternitz, History of Indian Literature II, p. 166.

[3] The Dharmaguptas and the Kāśyapīyas are also supposed to have had an Abhidharmapiṭaka (see EMB II, 163, 165) but they were subsects of the Sarvāstivāda group. The Pañca-Mātuka of the Mahāsaṅghika canon may refer to the Vinaya (Ib., pp. 55-56).

[4] Rosenberg, Die Probleme, p. 271.

Buddha.[5] This opinion is, however, belied by the fact that the two Abhidharmas teach quite different doctrines. Takakusu tells us: "Comparing the two sets of Abhidharma works as far as accessible to me, I do not find anything in form or in matter which could lead us to suppose that they were the same, though they treat as a matter of course, of more or less similar subjects."[6] Perhaps the most striking resemblance is to be noted between the Puggalapaññatti and the Saṅgītiparyāyapāda as both follow the Aṅguttara method. But the contents of the two do not correspond.[7] It appears that the Abhidharmas are in fact a systematization and development of the doctrines of the sūtras along sectarian lines.[8] Their growth belongs to the post-Nikāya period.[9]

The Vinaya and its versions.—The Vinaya is available in the following versions: the Vinaya of the Theravādins in Pali, portions of the Vinaya of the Mūlasarvāstivādins in Sanskrit contained in the Gilgit Manuscripts (ed. Dr. N. Dutt), and in Tibetan and Chinese translations (in the latter, not in its entirety); the Vinayas of the schools of Sarvāstivādins, Dharmaguptas, Mahīśāsakas and the Mahāsaṅghikas in Chinese translation.[10] Besides, fragments are available in Sanskrit which clearly belonged to or were associated with the originals of some of these Vinayas.[11] At least eighteen of the narratives in the Divyāvadāna "sont

---

[5] Minayeff—Recherches, p. 14. fn; Wassiljew—Der Buddhismus I, p. 115; Aṭṭhasālinī—p. 23f (Nāgarī Edition, Poona 1942).

[6] JPTS. 1905, p. 161.

[7] Ib., p. 162.

[8] Cf. Glasenapp, ZDMG. 1938, 408-13.

[9] See below.

[10] Wassiljew—op. cit. I, p. 97. cf. Frauwallner, The Earliest Vinaya, p. 11, pp. 172 ff.

[11] Winternitz—op. cit. II, p. 283, fn. 1.

autant de fragments ayant fait jadis partie du Vinaya Piṭaka des Sarvāstivādins."[12] These are the Avadānas —1, 2, 3, 4, 5, 6, 7, 13, 19, 21, 23, 24, 25, 30, 31, 35, 36 and 38. Similarly is the Mahāvastu connected with the Vinaya of the Mahāsaṅghikas.[13] A Sanskrit version of the Prātimokṣa of the Mahāsaṅghikas has been edited by Dr. Pachow and Sri Ramakanta Mishra in JGRI X pts. 1-4. The Prātimokṣa of the Mūlasarvāstivādins too is available in Sanskrit.[14]

As to the relationship of these Vinayas, it is now an established fact that the Prātimokṣa is practically the same for all the sects.[15] But the agreement is supposed to extend to the Vibhaṅga and even the Khandhaka.[16] Fragments have been discovered at Koutcha which correspond to portions of the Mahāvagga;[17] and Beal remarks on the close resemblance that exists in the order of representation between the Pali and Mahāsaṅghika Vinayas where the Mahāvagga is concerned.

It appears that the diversity of the Vinaya redactions is a later growth based on an originally common stock of rules.[17a]

Corresponding to the DN, MN, SN and AN of the Pali canon there exist in Chinese translation the DĀ, MĀ, SĀ and the EĀ.[17b] Several suttas of the Nikāyas occur in the Chinese Tripiṭaka in separate translations

---

[12] Huber—B. Lecole Fr. 1906. p. 1.

[13] Ib. p. 3.

[14] IHQ 1953. Recently published are G. Roth, *Bhikṣuṇi-Vinaya*; Jinananda, Abhisamācārikā.

[15] Cf. JA. 1913—Nov-Déc. pp. 467, 549; JA. 1912 Jan-Févr. p. 103; JRAS—1862 pp. 407 ff; ZDMG. 1898. p. 645; Cf. Winternitz loc. cit. Also Dr. Pa-Chow's partly published thesis—Comparative Study of the Prātimokṣa.

[16] ZDMG 1898 pp. 647f; cf. Wassiljew op. cit. p. 19.

[17] Finôt—JA. 1911. Nov-Déc. 619-25.

[17a] Cf. Winternitz—loc. cit. For a recent reconsideration of the Vinaya see, Dr. G.S.P. Misra, *The Age of Vinaya*.

[17b] Nanjio, Catalogue, Columns 127-37.

also.[18] Further, fragments of various sūtras of the DĀ (Saṅgīti-sūtra, Āṭānāṭiya-sūtra), of the MĀ (Upāli-sūtra, Śukasūtra), of the SĀ and the EĀ, have been found in central Asia.[19] Finally, various Buddhist Sanskrit works like the Ab.k, Ak.V. MK and MK.V, contain quotations from these Āgamas. The Divyāvadāna makes frequent mention of the Āgamacatuṣṭayam.[20]

About the relationship of the Chinese Āgamas and the Pali Nikāyas, Anesaki tells us "The materials of both are pretty much the same but the order of arrangement is strangely different."[21] "The deviations, in matter, though usually inconsiderable, are sometimes interesting."[22] Prof. Akanuma has compared the Āgamas with the Nikāyas in his work—"The Comparative Catalogue of Chinese Āgamas and Pali Nikāyas," (1929). His main conclusions have been summarized by Prof. N. Dutt.[23] All the suttas of the DN with the exception of the Mahāli, Jāliya, and Subhasuttas are contained in DĀ, with a few in the MĀ. The DĀ contains two extra suttas. The order of suttas is very different in the two collections.[24] Of the 152 suttas of the MN only 19 are omitted in the MĀ viz., Cūḷasāropama (No. 30), Mahāsaccaka (No. 36), Sāleyyaka (No. 41), Verañjaka (No. 42), Kandaraka (No. 51), Jīvaka (No. 55), Kukkuravatika (No. 57) Abhayarājakumāra (No. 58), Apaṇṇaka (No. 60) Tevijjavacchagotta (No. 71), Ghoṭamukha (No. 94), Caṅki (No. 95), Vāseṭṭha (No. 98), Saṅgārava

[18] Ib. Columns, 138 ff.

[19] Winternitz. op. cit p. 234 fn. 3 Waldschmidt has edited *Catuṣpariṣat*, *Mahāvadāna* and *Mahāparinirvāṇa*.

[20] Divyāv. pp. 77, 331, 333.

[21] JRAS. 1901 p. 895.

[22] This with ref. to the MN. (Ib. 897).

[23] EMB II. p. 125 ff.

[24] See chap: Early and Late in the DN, where it is suggested that the Pali order is probably more authentic.

(No. 100), Pañcattaya (No. 102) Kinti (No. 103), Sunakkhatta (No. 105), Anupada (No. 111), Bhaddekaratta (No. 131). The MĀ contains 222 sūtras, 82 of which correspond to the suttas in the AN, 10 to suttas in the SN, 9 to those in the DN and the rest to suttas in the MN. The MĀ has, further, a few stray suttas corresponding to passages in the SN, Theragāthā, Therī?, and Vin (Mvg.).[25].

The SĀ, as it exists in Chinese, is divided into 50 sections and incorporates a large number of suttas of the AN and a few of the other texts. There are a few sūtras which have no parallels in Pali. The Sagāthavagga of the two collections has much in common, but not the Nidānavagga; the 8th and 9th chapters of Nidāna viz., Samaṇabrāhmaṇa and Antarapeyyāla are wanting in the Āgama, while the first and fifth chapters (Buddha and Gahapati) show marked differences. In the same section, Abhisamaya. Dhātu and other Saṃyuttas are almost passed over in the Āgama, but there is much agreement in the following five Saṃyuttas: Anamatagga, Kassapa, Lakkhaṇa, Opamma and Bhikkhu. In the Khandhavagga of the Āgama the following Saṃyuttas are wanting: Okkantika, Valāha, Vacchagotta, and Jhāna. In the Saḷāyatana-vagga the following are absent: Mātugāma, Moggalāna, Asaṅkhata, Sammappadhāna, Bala and Iddhipāda, while major portions of the Magga, Indriya and Sacca are omitted.[26]

The EĀ and AN have very little in common. This is partly due to the fact that a large number of the suttas

[25]EMB. loc. cit.; see below—"Early and Late in the MN". For a recent study of the Madhyamāgama, see Thich Minh Chau, *The Chinese Madhyamāgama and the Pali Majjhima Nikāya*. Prof. Bapat contests the thesis of the work—*Satkari Mookerjee Felicitation Volume*, pp. 1 ff.

[26]EMB. II. loc. cit. see below chap. Early and Late in the SN; Cf. Huber's review of Pischel's Bruchstücke des Sanskritcanons . .in B. L'ecole Fr. 1904. 473-'4. It appears that the SĀ contains suttas corresponding to MN. 1. 497, and AN 1. 185. cf. Lévi in Tóung Pao V. p. 299 quoted by Dutt. op. cit. p. 127.

of the AN are included in the MĀ and the SĀ. The Pali text is much more extensive than the Sanskrit and it seems that the two collections grew independently of each other. The following are more or less common to both. Samacitta (I. pp. 61-9), Devadūta (I. pp. 132-50), Brāhmaṇa to Loṇaphala (I. pp. 155-258), Cakka (II. pp. 32-44) Muṇḍarāja (III. pp. 45-62) Nīvaraṇa (III. pp. 63-79), Āghāta (III. pp. 185-202), Devatā to Mahā (III. pp. 329-420) Avyākata to Mahā (IV. pp. 67-139), Gahapati (IV. pp. 298-35), Savitta (V. pp. 92-112), Upāsaka (V. pp. 176-210), Jānussoṇi (V. pp. 249-73), and Anussati (V. pp. 328-58). This however is not an exhaustive list for there are stray agreements in other sections.[27]

In the absence of a detailed and exhaustive comparison between the Pali and Chinese sūtras it would appear very hazardous to comment on the relationship between the two. However, the fact of general similarity in contents appears to be as clear as that of difference in grouping and arrangement. That both the sets of collections go back to a common original is apparent. Winternitz concludes that they "were compiled from the same materials, but were arranged in different ways in different schools."[28]

The quotations from the Āgamas in later Buddhist Sanskrit works find in many cases their parallels in the Pali Nikāyas. Poussin thus states that "la haute antiquité des suttas Pali est confirmée par la temoignage des sources sanscrites."[28a] He points out that the Ak. V. contains parallels to SN. III. 25, Ib. 159, AN IV. 70—4; Similarly MK has passages corresponding to SN. III.

---

[27] EMB II. loc. cit.

[28] Op. cit. p. 235.

[28a] JA. 1902 XX. p. 237.

142, Ib. 138. Dr. Vaidya points out that Mk. XV, 7 seems to refer to SN. II, 172.[29] Some further parallels are noted below.[30]

A fifth Āgama or Nikāya does not appear to have been recognized by schools other than the Theravāda.[31] The Pali Khuddaka Nikāya is itself of a miscellaneous character with variable contents.[32] However, the Sanskrit canon is known to have included texts called Udāna, Dharmapada, Sthaviragāthā, Vimānavastu and Buddhavaṃśa, and corresponding to the Pali texts of the same titles.[33] Further, the Chinese Tripiṭaka contains texts corresponding to the Aṭṭhaka and Pārāyaṇa sections of the Sn. and the It.[34]

According to Rockhill "The Udānavarga contains 300 verses which are nearly identical with verses of Dharmapada; 150 more resemble verses of that work; 20 are to be found in the Suttanipāta; and about the same number are very similar to parts of the same book." Thus more than half of Udānavarga is found in works of the southern canon.[35] La Vallée Poussin identifies many more verses and says that Dharmatrāta—the translator of the Udānavarga—has utilized the whole of the Udāna, prose and verse.[36]

According to Lévi[37] the Dhp. is represented in the Chinese collection by four works—1. Fa-Kiu-King,

---

29 Études—p. 21.

30 See infra.

31 Dutt op. cit., p. 128; cf. Winternitz op. cit., p. 236, fn. 2.

32 See below Chap. III.

33 Winternitz loc. cit.

34 For a comparison of the Chinese and Pali versions see below Chap. III.

35 Rockhill—U. Vg.

36 La Vallée Poussin—JA. 1912 Mars—Avril—p. 312.

37 JA. 1912—Sept.-Oct., p. 203ff.

2. Fa-Kiupi-Yuking. 3. Tchóu-Yao-King, and 4. Fa-tsi-yao-song-king. The first was translated in 224 A.D. but was not a literally faithful translation. Dharmapada was then already in circulation in China. Of the 39 sections of the first only 26 belonged to the original translation. The Pali text also has 26 sections. The order of verses is quite different but the rubrics are disposed in the same order. The second was translated by two Śramaṇas between A.D. 290—306 and is based on the first. The third was translated in A.D. 398-9, and is a veritable Aṭṭhakathā. The fourth dates from the end of the 10th cent. A.D. and is a revision of the third by an Indian monk.

Lévi's detailed comparative study of the Apramādavarga in the various redactions of the Dhp. shows close similarity with occasional differences.

The chronology of the canon, esp. the Nikayas.— According to Buddhist tradition, the Vinaya and the Sutta Piṭakas were compiled immediately after the death of Buddha in the First Council held at Rājagṛha.[38] The question of the historicity and nature of the First

[38] The sources for the First Council are:

(i) Pali—CV.XI, which is the earliest of the group & from it are derived the traditions preserved in the Ceylonese chronicles and Buddhaghosa's commentaries.

(ii) Sanskrit—short notices in the Mvu and the Mañjuśrīmūlakalpa.

(iii) Chinese—the Vinayas of the Mahīśāsakas, Dharmaguptas, Mahāsaṅghikas and the Sarvāstivādins; Kāśyapasaṅgītisūtra (tr. A.D. 148—70); Aśokāvadāna (tr. c. 300 A.D.); Mahāprajñāpāramitāśāstra (tr. A.D. 402—5); Parinirvāṇa-sūtra (tr. A.D. 290—306); account of the compilation of the Tripiṭaka and of Tsa Tsang by Kāśyapa and Ānanda after the Nirvāṇa of Buddha in the Kingdom of Magadha, on the north of the town of Saṅkāśya (the work is in Chinese verse, dated between 317 and 420); comy. on the 1st Chap. of the EĀ (see Dutt—EMB. I, pp. 326ff).

(iv) Tibetan: Buston's History of Buddhism; Tārānātha's History of Buddhism.

Council has been the subject of keen debate among scholars for over half a century.[39] All the sources—Pali, Tibetan and Chinese--have been tapped and discussed threadbare. Oldenberg believed the First Council to have been a pure fiction, mainly on the ground that the Mahāparinibbānasutta gives the motive but not a word about the session of the Council.[40] Franke expressed the same opinion arguing that Cv. XI—XII constituted the only independent source of the tradition and were themselves no better than concoctions based on the Mahāparinibbāna sutta.[41] Jacobi had already answered Oldenberg reasonably by saying that it was not really necessary for the Mahāparinibbāna sutta to go out of its way to describe the Council.[42] Further, it has been suggested recently [43] that Cv. XI—XII originally formed part of the Mahāparinibbāna sutta. That Cv. XI—XII form a kind of appendix to the Cv. and could not have originally belonged to it, is very probable.[44] Further, Cv. XI begins abruptly unlike any other chapter of the Cv. It commences in the same way as the Mahāparinibbāna sutta and is closely allied to it in contents.[44a] Finally, a work entitled Saṃyuktavastu

[39] Minayeff op. cit., p. 25ff; Oldenberg—Introduction to the Vin. I, XXV—XXIX; ZDMG. 1898, pp. 613—94; Poussin IA. 1908, pp. 1-18; 81-106; Franke—JPTS 1908, pp. 1-80; R. C. Majumdar, Buddhistic Studies (ed. B. C. Law), pp. 26—72; Finôt—IHQ 1923, pp. 241-6; Obermiller. Ib., pp. 781-4; Dutt op. cit., p. 324ff. The volume of Przyluski—Le Concile de Rājagṛha—deals with all the traditions available in Chinese and Tibetan.

[40] Cf. ZDMG. 1898, 613-32.

[41] Op. cit.

[42] ZDMG. 1880, 184ff.

[43] Finôt & Obermiller—1. c; Dutt. op. cit., p. 337f. Dr. Dutt points out that the argument really holds with reference to Cv. XI only.

[44] See Winternitz op. cit., p. 25 & fn. 2.

[44a] Cf. Bauddha Dharma Ke Vikas Ka Itihās, pp. 161-62.

(Nanjio, 1121), the Vinaya of the Mūlasarvāstivādins, contains the account of both Parinirvāṇa and the Councils. It is thus not impossible that Cv. XI and DN. 16 formed originally a continuous narrative. It is, however, not clear why the Theravādins should have in that case separated the two. Perhaps they felt that Cv. XI had greater affinities with Cv. XII than with DN. 16.

But although it may no longer be plausible to regard the first Council as pure fiction, its nature and work remain uncertain. According to Minayeff, the account of the First Council contains two clearly distinguishable parts, of which the one speaking of the compilation of the canon is much later, being, in fact, posterior to the rise of the sects.[45] Prof. Poussin would regard the Council as an enlarged Pātimokkha assembly.[46] According to Prof. Dutt,[47] the motive of the Council was to determine the 'Khuddakānukhuddakāni sikkhāpadāni', the abrogation of which was sanctioned by Buddha just before his passing away. The account of the recitation of suttas by Ānanda is a later engrafting upon the account of his Pārisuddhi, which was then, except for the Dharmagupta Vinaya, shifted from its proper place, i.e., before the recitation of the texts.

That the huge mass of the Vinaya and the Sutta Piṭakas was "recited" in the First Council is, of course, manifestly impossible. A beginning in the direction,

[45] Op. cit., pp. 35-6. He points to the disagreement among the sources over what exactly was redacted in the First Council—Ib., p. 29. Dr. Dutt details the works supposed to have been redacted at the Council according to the various sources. Op. cit., pp. 333-4. Some sources speak of the redaction of the Abhidharma even—Minayeff, op. cit., p. 30.

[46] EMB I, 339.

[47] Op. cit., p. 339f.

however, might have been made quite naturally, but lack of certain evidence makes any pronouncement on the subject difficult.[48]

The years following the Parinirvāṇa appear to have been marked by a process of growth both with respect to the rules of discipline as well as with respect to doctrines. The Saṅgha grew in wealth, membership and complexity of organisation.[49] The original teachings must have left room for interpretative divergences, and the Theras in the various communities would act not only as the transmitters of tradition but also as commentators. Buddha himself is supposed to have discouraged the habit of regarding his actual words as sacrosanct and to have forbidden their "Sanskritization" and chanting after the Vedic manner.[50] This must have added to the swiftness with which the original

---

[48] Cf. Winternitz, op. cit., p. 7. Also, Mrs. Rhys Davids—Buddhism, p. 213 (H. U. L.).

[49] Cf. Ib., p. 26.

[50] Majjhima sutta 139 which condemns bias in favour of particular Janapada-niruttis and Saññās; Cv. V. 33, of which Senart gives the parallel versions from the Vinayas available in Chinese of four schools (JA. 1915 Mai-Juin, 441 ff). The Dharmagupta and Mahīśāsaka Vinayas speak of Śiṣṭabhāṣā only; the Sarvāstivāda and Mūla° Vinayas introduce "Chanting". Senart opines that perhaps at that time intonation was integral to correct speech. According to the Pali Aṭṭhakathā "putting in chandas" signified Sanskritization after the Vedic manner (Winternitz II, p. 603); Buddha permitted his teachings to be put down in "one's own speech" (Sakanirutti). Aṭṭhakathā takes it to mean Māgadhī (Winternitz II, p. 602) cf. La Vallée Poussin, Opinions, p. 36.

It appears that Buddha did not want his teachings to be fixed in any learned language but wished them to circulate in different local dialects. One may recall that Asoka followed a similar policy. It is thus that we have, for instance, the Prākṛta Dhammapadā found in Central Asia. Pali is probably one of these ancient dialects—the dialect probably of Central India or N. Deccan (see App. I).

message would get embedded in scholastic growth which followed several conflicting directions.

The crystallization of the divergent tendencies within the community in the shape of definite schism appeared, we are told, by the end of the first century A.B. The history of the schism is considered later,[51] but for our present purposes it is only necessary to observe that the state in which the canon was at the time of Saṅghabheda is difficult to ascertain. The minuteness, however, of the Ten Points at Vaiśālī or the Five Points of Mahādeva argues for a more or less well developed canon. Further, the period of a century will not appear to be too small to account for the extent of ideological development in the Nikāyas.

In the Nikāyas, in spite of variety and even discrepancy, there is a general impression of homogeneity.[52] Occasional controversies in interpretation are recorded, and though Saṅghabheda is feared,[53] it is not assumed as an actuality, except perhaps at a very few places.[53a] From the Kv. and the Ab. K. it is evident that the contending parties differed, not with respect to their scriptures, but only in their interpretation. It follows that the scriptures, which are mostly the Nikāyas[53b] go back to a period when the sects were, in important doctrinal matters at least, as yet one. Further, had not this been the case it would be difficult to account for the presence

[51] See Chap. XV.

[52] Cf. Keith—BP., p. 21.

[53] See Dutt—EMB. II, p. 7ff.

[53a] Thus DN. III, 133 which says "Abhabbo (Arahā) Navaṭhānāni Ajjhācaritum" may have in mind the points of Mahādeva. Similarly, SN. IV, 325 may have in mind the Vajjian heresy of the Second Council (Cf. MN, p. 372, Nāg. ed.).

[53b] This is apparent from Index I of Points of Controversy, (pp. 401-4).

of clearly Pudgalavādin texts within the Pali version of the Nikāyas.[53c] Also, it should be noted that from the standpoint of doctrinal evolution, the stage of thought reflected in sectarian controversies is later than that common in the Nikāyas. The former is maturer and more decided; besides, partly at least, it represents the continued further development of some of the latest trends visible within the Nikāyas. The Nikāyas, thus, appear to reflect the first and earliest period of the history of Buddhist thought when the Saṅgha was, in appearance at least, doctrinally one.[53d] It has, of course, to be remembered that particular versions of the Nikāyas may be expected to contain much editorial retouching, addition, and even expurgation.[53e] The problem will become more determinate were we to trust the Pali account of the Third Council, according to which the last of the Abhidharma works—the Kv. was composed by Tissa in that council held in the reign of Aśoka.[53f] The Kv. quotes from the Dhs. and Vbh. and refers to the contents peculiar to Paṭṭhāna. It does not quote from Dhātukathā and Puggalapaññatti, and has no direct reference to Yamaka, although like that work it uses 'vokāra' for 'khandha'. As to the other two piṭakas, "all, even the Vinaya, are for its compiler (s) 'Suttanta' just as we would say, not Leviticus, or Luke, or King John, but the Bible, Shakespeare."[53g] If then the Kv. belonged to the 3rd cent. B.C., the Nikāyas would have

[53c] See Chap. on Nirvāṇa.

[53d] Cf. N. Dutt—Aspects of Mahāyāna—pp. 146-7.

[53e] See Chaps. on Stratification.

[53f] The tradition is found only in the Aṭṭhakathās and the Ceylonese chronicles. See Debates Commentary, pp. 1-7 (tr. B. C. Law for the PTS).

[53g] Mrs. Rhys Davids—Points of Controversy; cf. Sakya, p. 365. Cf. Dr. S. N. Dube, 'The Date of Kathāvatthu', East and West, March-June 1972

to be placed at the latest in the first half of the 4th cent. B.C. Minayeff argued that the Kv. apparently referred to the Vetulyakas and hence could not be pre-Christian.[54] To this Rhys Davids answered that the name actually occurred in the commentary on Kv.[55] Mrs. Rhys Davids has suggested that the Kv. was not composed en bloc. It has a "patchwork-quilt" appearance, which is explained if we suppose that each kathā was framed as a new heresy gained importance and was then added to the memorial stock.[56] That the whole of Kv. does not belong to the same stratum follows clearly from the fact that the first debate of the book—Puggalakathā—has some marked linguistic peculiarities. It uses "Ke" for "Ko", "vattabbe" for "vattabbo" "vattabbaṃ", and "se" for "so"[57] It appears thus possible that the whole of the Kv. did not exist in the 3rd cent. B.C. On the other hand, it is probable that the first Kathā derives from a Magadhan text of Aśoka's times.

The very fact of the Third Council has been denied.[58] The more plausible opinion seems to be that the Third Council did take place, although it was a sectarian affair.[59] Aśoka, it is true, does not directly refer to the Council,[60] yet Dr. Bhandarkar seems to be right in thinking that some of his inscriptions appear to presuppose some such event.[61] That Aśoka is not

[54] Op. cit., p. 82.

[55] Dialogues (DN), pt. I, Preface: Cf. Oldenberg in ZDMG 1898, pp. 632-43.

[56] Intr. to Points of Controversy.

[57] Sakya, p. 359; JRAS 1929, pp. 27ff.

[58] See Dutt, op. cit., II, pp. 265-6; Keith BP, pp 18-9.

[59] Ib. Also, Mrs. Rhys Davids—Buddhism (HU) loc. cit.

[60] Minayeff, op. cit., p. 75.

[61] Aśoka, pp. 96-102 (2nd ed.).

clearer over the Council may be explained by the supposition that he was not as intimately connected with the council as the Pali tradition would have us believe.[62]

It is thus not improbable that some parts at least of the Kv. were composed in the time of Aśoka. Apart from the frequent and direct references of the Kv. to the Nikāyas, stylistic and doctrinal considerations alone should suffice to place the greater part of the Nikāyas prior to the composition of the Kv. The major portion of the Nikāyas, thus, appears to have certainly existed in the 4th cent. B.C.[63]

The relation of Aśoka to Buddhism has been the subject of much debate,[64] but it is clear that at places his rescripts show striking verbal similarities with the Nikāyas,[65] and although all the texts referred to in the Bairāṭ edict have not been satisfactorily identified, it is undeniable that Aśoka must have been familiar with a large number of Buddhist texts or Dhammaparyāyas which were regarded as the words of Buddha and some at least of which were identical with those found in our Nikāyas.[66]

An examination of the Bhārhut and Sāñchī inscriptions shows that "some time before the second century B.C. there was already a collection of Buddhist texts, which was called 'Piṭakas' and was divided into five 'Nikāyas', that there were 'suttas' in which the 'Dhamma' . . . . was preached, that some of these agreed with those

[62] Cf. Dutt, op. cit., II, pp. 269-70.

[63] Cf. Rhys Davids—loc. cit.

[64] Thus, see Hultzsch C. I. I. I; D. R. Bhandarkar—op. cit., Chap. III; Dutt, op. cit., II. Chap. XIV; Minayeff—op. cit., p. 77; Mrs. Rhys Davids—Buddhism, p. 226ff (H.U.L. 1934) etc. etc.

[65] Winternitz, op. cit., p. 16, fn. 1.

[66] Cf. Bhandarkar, op. cit., p. 89ff; Winternitz, op. cit., Appendix III; Keith, op. cit., p. 17.

contained in our Tipiṭaka, and that Jātakas of exactly the same kind as those contained in the Tipiṭaka, already belonged to the stock of Buddhist literature. . ."[67]

Finally, we are told that in the first century B.C., the entire Pali Tipiṭaka was written down in Ceylon.[68] The Nikāyas would then go back to the 3rd century B.C. at least.

The evidence for ascertaining the chronology of the canon, of which the Pali version is still available in its entirety, is, thus, small, but it may be asserted that the growth of the Nikāyas falls between the 5th and the 3rd centuries B.C.[69] The fact that the Nikāyas take but slight notice of the issues contested by the earliest sects certainly suggests that they had practically reached completion in the 1st century A.B.[70] The silence of the Vinaya over the third Council suggests that it had reached completion in the 1st two centuries A.B.[71] The silence of the canon over Aśoka, which contrasts so strongly with later tradition, is also significant in this respect and suggests its antiquity.

---

[67] Winternitz, op. cit., pp. 17-8.

[68] Ib., pp. 8, 617; Malalasekara–DPPN. II, pp. 817-8.

[69] It may be remembered that AN. III, 57 speaks of King Muṇḍa at Pāṭaliputra, Cf. C. H. I. I, p. 195.

[70] Rhys Davids concludes that the Nikāyas were put together out of older material at a period about half way between the death of the Buddha and the accession of Aśoka (Ib) Cf. La Vallée Poussin, Opinions–39.

[71] Cf. Minayeff, op. cit., p. 17.

CHAPTER II

THE STRATIFICATION OF THE NIKĀYAS: PROBLEMS AND METHODS

The Problem.—The Nikāyas or the Āgamas are admittedly of prime importance for the study of early Buddhist doctrines, but they are collections of early as well as late sūtras differently ordered and edited in their different versions.[1] The stratification of the sūtras thus appears a sine qua non of future progress in the direction of discovering ancient Buddhism.[2] Oldenberg, in his introduction to the P. T. S. edition of V. P. I. and again in the introduction to SBE. XIII (in collaboration with Rhys Davids), has indicated the probable course along which the growth of the Vinaya took place. The Pātimokkha[3] and part at least of the liturgical formulae embedded in the Khandhakas[4] form the earliest stratum. The old commentary, wholly philological and exegetical, and containing nothing of a legendary or quasi-historical nature,[5] constitutes the next stratum. The traditions of this latter character, together with what we may call Notes on the Rules, were, in the third stage, amalgamated to the Text and the old commen-

---

[1] See Mrs. Rhys Davids—Sakya; Buddhism (H.U.L.); What was the Original Gospel in Buddhism? etc.

[2] Cf. N. Dutt—EMB I, Preface.

[3] The Bhikkhunī-Pātimokkha is patterned on that for the Bhikkhus (Winternitz, op. cit. II, p. 24); and the "Sekhiyā Dhammā" are merely rules of etiquette, and, besides, vary in the various versions of the Vinaya. (Ib., p. 23 fn. 5; also JRAS, 1862, p. 409).

[4] Of these it is difficult to sift the earlier from the later. The Upasampadā Kammavācā may be indicated among the earlier ones (see SBE XIII, p. XIX).

[5] Ib., p. XVII.

tary.[6] The last two books of the Cv. are still later,[7] and the Parivāra is the latest of all.[8] Thus, starting from a small and definite nucleus, the Vinaya has reached its present form in at least five stages. The investigation into the Kammavācās, it may be observed, is as yet rudimentary; and it appears that merely literary criteria are not sufficient for their stratification. It is the history of the material and organisational growth of the Saṅgha that must supply the main test. Those suttas in the Sutta-piṭaka, which relate to Vinaya, can also be of help here.[9]

The narratives in the Vinaya Pitaka.—Again, though the ad hoc character of most of the narratives is patent, yet it has been admitted that they do contain some genuine history as well.[10] The fragments relating to Buddha's biography will be considered later.[11] As a whole, however, the question needs further investigation, especially in the light of the Northern versions.[12]

Oldenberg on the Sutta Pitaka.—From this picture of the evolution of the Vinaya to pass on to Dhamma in the way in which Oldenberg does, appears, however, without much justification. He supposes, on the ana-

---

[6] Ib., XVII.

[7] Cf. Winternitz, op. cit., p. 25 fn. 2 (The fact that section X of Cv. has been added for the benefit of the Nuns fits in very well with its having been the final chapter once).

[8] SBE XIII, p. XXIV; cf. Winternitz, p. 33 also.

[9] On the relative priority or posteriority of the two Piṭakas, opinions are as yet quite fluid (see Winternitz, p. 21 fn. 3). The problem, in fact, must be sub-divided as to the separate relations of the constituents of the two Piṭakas and solved in detail. It will only then be possible to make a general and yet accurately qualified statement.

[10] SBE XIII, p. xx; Winternitz, p. 27, 28.

[11] Infra, Ch. X.

[12] Cf. Takakusu—Int. Cong. Or. 1899. Tome 2, pp. 11-32 (A comparison of the Chinese and Tibetan Vinayas).

logy of the liturgical formularies, that the earliest expression of the Dhamma must have been in dogmatic paragraphs consisting of such formulae as the Four Noble Truths, the Twelve Nidānas etc., and barren of all narrative details.[13] The analogy does not hold, because, whereas institutional rules from their very nature demand the order and coherence of systematic expression, and lend themselves easily to a formular mode of statement, the case is just the reverse where the profounder truths of religion and philosophy are concerned, especially where these are of a more or less mystical character. Originating in inspired vision, they not unoften find, particularly in earlier times, contemporary concepts inadequate to their originality, and at first express themselves quite nebulously, taking frequently the aid of myth. Formulae, technicalities and system appear relatively later with the growth of the "School", of controversies, change in linguistic habits under the new impact, and, very often with the failing of inspiration.

These arguments are, indeed, not brought forth to prove that the evolution of Buddha's Word must have been along these lines. It is only intended to point out how hazardous is the analogy on which Oldenberg has thrown out his suggestions as to the probable development of the Sutta-Piṭaka.

The Sutta Pitaka: T. W. Rhys Davids, and Dr. B. C. Law.—On this subject, however, the work of Rhys Davids is more important. According to him the four Nikāyas "had been put together out of older material at a period about halfway between the death of the

[13] SBE XIII p. XII.

Buddha and the accession of Aśoka."[14] The course of the evolution is thus summarized: (1) The simple statements of the doctrine now found in identical words recurring in two or more of the present books—the stock passages or suttas.[15] (2) Episodes (not of doctrine only) similarly recurring. (3) Books quoted in the present books but no longer existing separately—the Sīlas, the Pārāyaṇa, the Octades, the Pātimokkha, etc. (4) Certain poems, ballads, or prose passages found similarly recurring in the present anthologies, or otherwise showing sign of greater age. (5) The four Nikāyas, the Sutta Vibhaṅga and the Khandhakas. (Approximate date 100 A.B.) (6) Sutta Nipāta, Therīgāthā, the Udānas the Khuddaka-Pāṭha. (7) The Jātakas (verses only), and the Dhammapada. (8) The Niddesa, the Iti-vuttakas, and the Paṭisambhidā. (9) The Peta- and Vimāna-Vatthu, the Apadānas, and the Buddhavaṃsa. (10) The Abhidhamma books, the latest of which is the Kv., and the oldest, perhaps, the Dhammasaṅgaṇi.[16] Dr. B. C. Law argues similarly, but with important differences (see his History of Pali Literature I. 42).

---

[14] C.H.I. I. 195.

[15] Some of these appear to have been called "Pariyāyas" or "Dhamma°", which has a more general meaning than "Sutta". "Pariyāya" occurs in the Nikāyas and is used by Aśoka—cf. DNI. 46; II. 93; III. 115; MN. I. 445; AN. I. 65; IV. 63; AN. V. 288, 291; very often the "Pariyāya" had a special name—thus Brahmajāla—DN. I. 46; Dhammādāso DN. II. 93; SN. V. 357. Sokasallāharaṇa AN. III. 62; Ādittapariyāyo SN. IV. 168; Lomahaṃsana MN. I. 83.

[16] Ib. 197; Buddhist India p. 188 has a similar list but with differences—*It requires the stock passages to occur in all the books; it does not have "etc.," under 3; *stage 4 as marked above is absent; *the Suttavibhaṅga and the Khandhakas are later than the four Nikāyas and also the texts entered above under 6; Cariyāpiṭaka occurs under 9 and the earliest of the Abhidhamma books is supposed to be the Puggala-Paññatti. The asterisked differences are quite important.

The test from vocabulary.—Further, Rhys Davids explicitly states the importance of the test from vocabulary, of "words used in one sense in the older strata of the literature and in another sense in the later strata (Abhiññā, anāgāmin, abhidhamma, ogha, etc.), new words introduced to modify or supplement ideas in older works (Dukkaṭa, dhutaṅga, etc.) and new words formed to express new ideas."[17]

Criticism.—The stock-passages and suttas, however, themselves belong to diverse strata. Their formation seems to have taken place in at least three different ways. Sometimes they represent very old sayings remembered unaltered or with very little alteration.[18] At others, a number of variant old versions seem to have received a single and late standardized form.[19] And in many cases the stock-passages are simply late formulae.[20]

In oral transmission mnemonic conveniences play a large part, and the reduction of the variety of expressions is clearly helpful in this respect. Besides, tradition as well as internal evidence prove that there was much "editing" of the texts; consequently the significance that attaches to recurrent identical passages in written literature is much lessened in this case. The only safe conclusion that can, in general, be drawn from them is about the upper limit to the composition of the larger texts within which they occur, provided they do not happen to be later additions to these.

Again, the books that once existed independently but no longer do so now, though undoubtedly earlier

---

[17] Dialogues of the Buddha III, p. ix.

[18] e.g., the small text "attadīpā viharatha—etc."

[19] Cf. Mrs. Rhys Davids—JPTS 1924-'27, pp. 244-45.

[20] e.g., "Abhikkantaṃ bhante abhikkantaṃ bhante etc." occurring at the end of many sermons (Thus DN. Suttas, 2-4).

than those in which they are referred to and also to the composition of the Nikāyas as a whole, do not yet form, among themselves, a single stratum. Whether the four Nikāyas were completed within the first or the first two centuries A.B., is considered in another chapter.[21] The "Itivuttakas" appear to have been placed too late.[22] The test from vocabulary is indeed important, but it is in most cases dependent on the view taken of the evolution of ideas in early Buddhism. In this respect Mrs. Rhys Davids' work is of paramount importance.

The work of Mrs. Rhys Davids.—According to her "early Buddhism is not to be learnt in a few formulae": "Eightfold Path", "Four Truths", "Three Marks" and the like; that "it is a discerning of....'fragments' as it were left-in in a surrounding structure of 'doctrine'."[23] She starts from the hypothesis "that world religions show a More of some kind in man, but never a Less."[24] She discovers that Gotama taught the doctrine of Man as Willer becoming better or worse along the way across the worlds. And in support of this she has collected together many "fragments" from the Nikāyas.

Winternitz has pointed out that Mrs. Rhys Davids assumes too much,[25] and Keith rightly complains that she relies a great deal more than warranted on what is already an obsolescent psychology. Besides, her "fragments" are mostly too short and ambiguous to be at all conclusive. And yet, after her work, the facts of inter-

[21] Chap. I.

[22] Cf. Winternitz, op. cit., p. 91. The point is considered in detail below.

[23] Buddhism (in the Home University Library; revised edition), pp. 8-9.

[24] Ib., p. 10.

[25] Visvabharti, N. S. May, 1936.

polation, elaboration and expurgation in the suttas can hardly be ignored.[26] And also, it is clear, that "the growing vogue of the coenobitic monk and his peculiar ideals, and the growing vogue of the study of mind, of mental procedure"[27] must be taken into account in rediscovering "the main fact about the old world view of man" whatever that might have been. In other words, increased "negativist" emphasis[28] and scholastic analysis and classification must be accepted, for purposes of stratification, as late characteristics.[29]

The Sutta Pitaka and other workers.—Apart from the "excursions" of Mrs. Rhys Davids, the "stratigraphy" of the Nikāyas does not seem to have attracted much attention.[30] Dr. Keith roundly declared it an impossibility.[31] According to Franke, the Dīgha N. is a unitary literary composition,[32] and the Majjhima "mindestens in groszen und ganzen das einheitlich, in Zusammenhang verfasste Werk eines Schriftstellers ist."[33] The groundplan of the former, according to him, is "der Nachweis,

[26] Cf. "Kenāpyadhyāropitānyetāni sūtrāṇītyabhiprāyaḥ" (AKV. Fol., 337 cited in Minayeff—Recherches...., p. 226); "sūtrāṇi ca bahūnyantarhitāni mūlasaṅgītibhraṃśāt" (Ib., p. 222).

[27] Buddhism, (HUL) loc. cit.

[28] Cf. JPTS 1924-'7. Contra—Wassiljew—Der Buddhismus Vol. I, p. 89.

[29] The particular conclusions of Mrs. Rhys Davids will be considered below, as occasion arises.

[30] Cf. "Rien n'a été fait pour déterminer les <<strates>> chronologiques des Ecritures pâlies" (La Vallée Poussin—Bouddhisme: opinions sur l' histoire de la dogmatique. 4th ed. avant—propos. p. viii).

[31] Buddhist Philosophy, p. 21; but contra I.H.Q. 1936 where he not only thinks the method of Mrs. Rhys Davids sound but himself with Schayer, unearths the traces of "earlier doctrines" in the Nikāyas.

[32] Z.D.M.G. 1913, p. 410.

[33] Ib., 1914, p. 474.

dasz Gotama Buddha, der Erhabene, ein Tathāgata (so gegangene) sei, d.h. dasz Gotama selbst den in D. II. 40. 97 vorgeschriebenen Heilsweg zur Erlosenden Erkenntnis zurückgelegt habe."[34] A certain homogeneity of ideas and style, of course, cannot be gainsaid, but the similarities of words, phrases and paragraphs pointed out by Franke, are not sufficient to prove his thesis which takes an inadequate notice of the differences. To explain this "identity-in-difference" we must resort to the hypothesis that the Nikāyas are frequently 'edited' texts embodying doctrines deriving from a common source.[35]

Directly opposed to Franke's is the view of Prof. Bapat.[36] He discovers three different literary strata in the Dīgha. The whole of the first volume is placed in the first stratum, and the argument is thus stated: "This Sutta (the Sāmaññaphala) forms the basis of all the subsequent suttas, except the last one, in the first volume, and serves the purpose of a common factor, thus indicating that almost the whole of the first volume must have been put together in its present form."[37] The point that seems to have been proved is the posteriority of most of the suttas of the first volume, in their finished form, to the Sāmaññaphala text.

Whereas this first stratum is marked by simplicity of teaching and the conception of Buddha as human,[38] the third stratum (indicated mainly in the third volume) compromises him on the subject of miracles, mentions

[34] W.Z.K.M. 1912, p. 199.

[35] Cf. Winternitz, op. cit., pp. 54-55. Some more particular conclusions of Franke are considered below.

[36] In A.B.O.R.I. VIII, 1926, pp. 1-16.

[37] Ib., p. 4.

[38] Ib., p. 7.

the Metteyya Buddha, shows a great love of "Purāṇic" legends as also the beginnings of Tantric literature and employs the "Aṅguttara-form" in the last two suttas.[39] It must be remembered, however, that the antiquity of Tantric beginnings in Buddhism is uncertain.[40] Also, the "Aṅguttara-form" by itself does not indicate lateness. Numerical considerations in literary arrangement were not unknown in pre-Buddhist times. In the "family books" of the Ṛgveda, the hymns within the deity groups are arranged according to the diminishing number of the stanzas contained in them. Thus in the second book the first group of Sūktas, addressed to Agni, begins with one containing sixteen stanzas but ends with one containing only six. The first hymn of the next group, addressed to Indra, has twenty-one, whereas the last has only four stanzas.[41] Again, if we consider the total number of hymns in each of the Books, from the second to the tenth, we get the following sequence 43, 62, 58, 87, 75, 104, 103, 114, 191—which is on the whole progressive. Further, the fact that the first and the last Books have the same number of hymns is also not without interest. If we turn to the AS., we find that in the first book, out of thirty-five, thirty hymns contain four stanzas each; in the second Book the hymns are as a rule of five stanzas each, these accounting for twenty-two in a total of thirty six; in the third Book out of thirty-one hymns thirteen contain six stanzas each; and in the next Book the majority, of hymns (twenty one out of

[39] Ib. p. 16.

[40] Cf. Bloomfield's remark on a similar problem, though in a different context—"The tenth book——contains a great deal of material, especially of an Atharvaṇic sort, which is undoubtedly foreign to the main theme....But why must all such material really be of more recent date....? (JAOS. Vol. XXI p. 43).

[41] Cf. Macdonell—A Vedic Reader—p. XIV.

forty) have seven stanzas each.[42] The "ekottara-principle" is clearly visible here. In the Brāhmaṇas, again, objects are grouped as Kins (Bandhus) if they can be imagined to be in some way the examples of the same number.[43] Despite its occasional obscurantism this practice may be looked upon as the beginning of classification, especially of a numerical character. This becomes significant if we reflect that the Aṅguttara form is nothing but a certain progression of numerical groups.

Besides, the fact that this form occurs in non-Buddhist writings as well seems to indicate that it developed out of a common literary antecedent.[44] Thus it is possible that it may have appeared quite early in the history of Buddhist literature, which is not to say that it was not used later.

Since, however, the main test of any scheme of stratification must be its consistency with the whole of evidence,[45] all these attempts obviously suffer through being fragmentary. That is, of course, hardly avoidable in the present state of our enquiry; and besides, their value lies in as much as they add to our stock of the observed peculiarities of style—early and late. It is only when this stock reaches a certain degree of fulness that a more or less complete stratification of the texts would be practicable.

---

[42] Cf. Winternitz op. cit. I. p. 121. [43] Cf. Tait. Up. 1-7.

[44] e.g. in the Jaina Ṭhāṇaṅga and Samavāyaṅga, and some texts in the Mbh. Vide Winternitz. II. p. 65 fn. 1., where it is also pointed out that this very numerical method is employed in some riddles and litanies of other peoples as well cf. Śatapatha Bra—1.5.4. 6-11.

[45] Cf. J. E. Carpenter's remark in another but similar connection. Referring to Gospel criticism he says "....its success depends on the elements selected for judgment....and the range of considerations admitted to influence the result". (The Bible in the 19th Century 1903. p. 220).

Criteria of Stratification.—The evolution of the Nikāyas falls between the age of the Upaniṣads and that of the Abhidharma and other Buddhist sectarian literature. This provides us with a general sense of direction in trying to discover what is early and what is late in the Nikāyas. The growth of monastic learning and of philosophical analysis and controversy led to increased complexity, subtlety and system in the realm of ideas, till the message of Buddha was converted into a stupendous scholastic philosophy.[46] At the same time the spread of Buddhism among the people led it to imbibe many elements of popular religion and helped the apotheosis of Buddha.[47] Pari passu with this orientation in doctrinal change there was a corresponding change in the style of expression which tended to lose simplicity and spontaneity and poetic vigour in favour of dry-as-dust abstract scholastic formulae.[48] Linguistically, too, the change may be seen in the use of new technical terms and in the development of new technical senses for old words.[49]

This is a very brief indication of some of the general criteria which may help us in stratifying the Nikāyas. The following remarks of Carpenter about the Gospel may be applied, mutatis mutandis, to our present context—"Most of the problems which they (the Gospels) suggest, can be solved, so far as solution is possible

---

[46] Cf. Rosenberg "Das Studium des alteren Buddhismus musz mit den in der Sammlung des Abhidharma enthaltenen systematischen Traktaten beginnen d.h. mit der sogenannten Literatur der<<Kirchenväter>>—und nicht mit den Sūtra" (Die Probleme der buddhistischen Philosophie p. ix. This is a veritable modern defence of the ancient Vaibhāṣikas.

[47] Cf. Louis Renou—The Civilization in Ancient India, p. 28.

[48] Cf. Winternitz—History of Indian Literature II. pp. 68-70.

[49] Cf. Rhys Davids—Dialogues of the Buddha III. p. ix.

at all, only with their own aid,—by the comparison, that is to say, of the materials which they offer us. The history of Gospel-criticism is in reality a history of this process; and its success depends on the elements selected for judgment, on the skill with which they are displayed before the critical verdict, and the range of considerations admitted to influence the result."[50] Like the Gospel, the Nikāyas "grew up in the dark; and their history can only be recovered in the form of a series of conjectures to account for the facts which they exhibit."[51]

Trends in the style and purpose of Metaphysics.— (a) *The state of doctrinal evolution*[52]: Within the Nikāyas there appears to have been a steady growth of metaphysical interest resulting in increasing enumeration, classification and definition. At first it seems to have concerned itself mainly with the collection, explication and harmonizing of the Master's sayings, but, as fresh problems emerged, it engaged itself more and more with further analysis on its own part, and, in the light of the new results, constantly reinterpreted the older dogmas. Rival interpretations sprang up and though attempts were made at co-ordinating them into coherent systems, only a few became standardized and the rest were condemned as heresy. This rise of sectarianism had a "retrospective effect" too as the sects not only composed new literature, but also tampered with the old one.[53]

---

[50] J. E. Carpenter—The Bible in the Nineteenth Century, (1903). p. 290.

[51] Ib. p. 303.

[52] For an excellent exposition of the meaning and process of doctrinal evolution in general, see Newman, Development of Christian Doctrine, Chaps. I and V; also Marin-Sola, L'Evolution homogène du Dogme Catholique, Tome I pp. 24ff.

[53] See Supra.

Side by side with metaphysics there was also the growth of a systematic Buddhist theology.[54] The number and classes of gods multiplied, one of the causes being the discovery or the adoption into the Buddhist fold of new mystic states or trances communicating with divine worlds.[55] Cosmological myths, in spite of the tradition which represents Buddha condemning these as futile "speculation"[56] flourished and indirectly served to discredit the gods.[57] Alongside it the attitude towards the miraculous underwent a significant change.[58]

The Rise of Buddhology.—But the most far reaching theological trend was the apotheosis of Buddha. The idea of a Being incomparably superior to all creatures, including gods, and from time to time incarnat-

---

[54] Its points of contact with Vedic theology and mythology appear in general confined to Brahmā (whose nearest Vedic equivalent would be the much too nebulous Prajāpati) and Brahma-loka, Yama and Pettivisaya (for Māra, see infra), Inda (Sakka belongs to the Budd. mythology then being built up cf. PTSD on 'Inda'; Dial. II. 294-298), Gandhabbas and Accharās. "Prajāpati" is mentioned only in the formula "devā sa—indakā sa brahmakā sa pajāpatikā" (PTSD) ; on Soma, Vāyu, Pajjuṇṇa and Varuṇa see Buddhist India p. 235. The ideas on hell are much nearer to the Purāṇas. On the whole the independence of this mythology is manifest, and it must have taken some time to develop.

[55] Another was the infiltration of the deities of local cults, esp. among the "Bhumma-Devas" (earth-gods) and the "Nāgas" (cf. Mahāsamaya and ātānāṭiya). As Rhys Davids remarks "the idea was to reconcile the people to different ideas. The actual consequence was that the ideas of the people thus admitted, as it were, by the back-door, filled the whole mansion" (Budd. Ind. p. 220). Mythology did not leave uninvaded even the citadel of Abhidhamma, which is shown by the fact that the third Section of Vibhaṅga (Abhidhammic) contains considerable mythological material (cf. Winternitz II. p. 168).

[56] e.g. in the Brahmajālasutta.

[57] Cf. the Aggañña Sutta. Whether Brahmacarya was possible for gods became a hotly debated point among the sects.

[58] Contrast the attitude in the Kevaṭṭa Sutta and the Pātimokkha with that in the Pāṭika Sutta.

ing, actually or apparently,[59] according to a fixed norm (Dhammatā) solely out of compassion, is without a previous parallel. It is quite foreign to the earliest texts and must have developed gradually. The degradation of the concept of the Arhant[60] was the other aspect of the change, which was principally responsible for the first rent in the garment of the Saṅgha.[61] The mention of previous Buddhas (like Sikhī),[62] of Future Buddhas (like Metteyya), of the "Bodhisatta", of the Pacceka-Buddha, of the "birth miracles" and the narrative of the life of the Buddha as governed by "Dhammatā"—these, then, emerge as late characteristics. The change that came over the concepts of "Saddhā" and of "Omniscience" is also significant in this respect.[63] Similar is the great extension of the practice of Thūpa-worship, which though undoubtedly ancient, came to acquire a quite exceptional importance for later Buddhists.[64] There was also the growth of the physiognomical dogma of the thirty-two "Mahāpurisalakkhaṇas".[65]

---

[59] See infra.

[60] Cf. Rhys Davids' introduction to the Pāṭikasutta in the Dialogues.

[61] See last Chap.

[62] In a general sense, of course, it is quite common to find Prophets referring to their spiritual predecessors and Buddha too might have done so. The theory of the Previous Buddhas, however, goes considerably beyond that. According to Mrs. Rhys Davids the idea of a Buddha was then "in the air." Kindred Sayings I. p. I. (fn).

[63] See below.

[64] The raising of tumuli over the dead is a widespread primitive practice. (Mitra, PI. pp. 301 ff; Macdonell, VM. p. 165; RS. VII. 89. 1). The anct. meaning of Thūpa goes no further—See PTSD. cf. Vin. iv. 308; Jāt. III. 56.(cf. Budd. Ind. p. 80). The non-discovery of pre-Aśokan stūpas is, however, significant, and indicates that the Buddhists took to them rather late. Cf. V.S. Agrawal, *Bhāratiya Kalā*, pp. 156-57.

[65] These are called lokāyatamahāpurisalakkhaṇas and, again, declared a Brahmanic doctrine (see Ambattha Sutta for example).

The general ideological trend.—The result of this section may be summarised in the statement that an increase in the number, extent, subtlety and frequency of the theological and metaphysical "enumerated groups" may be considered a sign of lateness.

(b) *The state of literary evolution*: In general, an older style is revealed by its striking simplicity, spontaneity and earnestness. It is often found in short texts although these short texts are frequently found embedded in larger ones. They are either dialogues reminiscent of the Upaniṣads,[66] but marked by a gentle, almost Socratic irony and sometimes more sustained reasoning;[67] or they are brief sermons, concerned not so much with philosophical niceties as with spiritual practice;[68] or more rarely, they are fragmentary biographical narratives.[69] In most cases they are sun-lit by apt similes and parables (both covered

The Brahmanic sources, however, are curiously silent.

At least two of the Marks have been sought to be traced to the influence of sculpture—those ref. to jālahatthapādo and uṇhīsasīso (see Foucher's L'Art gréco-boudhique du Gandhāra).

It is interesting to note that Sn. 1019, 1021 and 1022 refer to only 3 Lakkhaṇas. Cf. N. H. Samtani, The Arthaviniścaya Sūtra, p. 283.

[66] e.g., compare the Sāmaññaphala° with Bṛ. IV, I. See Winternitz, II, p. 37 fn. 1., also Ib., p. 76. Here, for example, is a text quoted in Ak. V. (Sphutārthā) I, p. 17 which is obviously very near to the Upaniṣads—"Uktaṃ hi Bhagavatā—Pṛthivī bho Gautama kutra pratiṣṭhitā. Pṛthivī brāhmaṇa abmaṇḍale pratiṣṭhitā. Abmaṇḍalam bho Gautama Kva pratiṣṭhitam. Vāyau Pratiṣṭhitam. Vāyurbho Kva pratiṣṭhitaḥ. Ākāśe pratiṣṭhitaḥ. Ākāśam bho Gautama kutra pratiṣṭhitam. Atisarasi brāhmaṇa. Ākāśam brāhmaṇāpratiṣṭhitamanālambanamiti vistaraḥ". In style and expression and orientation of intellectual quest this is to be scarcely distinguished from some Upaniṣadic passages, e.g., Bṛ. Up. III, 6; III, 8.

[67] Cf. Winternitz, II, pp. 69-70.

[68] e.g., MN. Sutta 61.

[69] e.g., MN. Ariyapariyesana sutta.

by Pali Upamā). Indeed, quite a number of these can be looked upon as having originated with Buddha himself,[70] who apparently was as fond of them as Jesus.[71] This fits in with the non-learned character of much of his audience,[72] the inspired and original character of his message[73] and the state of literary development in his times.[74] The parables are not merely illustrative and argumentative but also didactic, so that they frequently contain a positive teaching. Indeed some of these figures later became technical expressions.[75] This parabolic style was, however, superseded partly by the growth of greater precision and abstraction in expression and partly by the growth of edifying myth richly burdened with anecdotal trappings. Of course, late similes and parables are by no means rare, but they show a tendency to be lengthy and drawn-out to the minutest details, e.g., the comparison of the eight qualities of the ocean (Cv. IX, 1; 3f) or of the five kinds of monks in their relationship to women (Puggalapaññatti V, 3).[76]

---

[70] Cf. Winternitz, Loc. cit.; Sakya, pp. 313ff.

Mrs. Rhys Davids' interpretations are, however, quite arbitrary.

[71] Cf. "....the naturalness, the lucidity, and the aptness of his (Jesus') parables place them in a class by themselves" (ERE IX, p. 630).

[72] Which must have, for the greater part, consisted of wandering mendicants, khattiya clansmen and merchants (see Chap. on Life).

[73] See Chap. on 'Life of Buddha'.

[74] The Upaniṣads, it is well-known, make use of simile and connected figures to expound philosophical and mystic ideas, e.g., Ch. VI 6ff; Bṛ. IV. 3. 19, etc.

[75] Cf. Winternitz, op. cit., p. 74.

[76] In view of the fact that the method of answering an opponent by comparisons is hardly Abhidhammic (Kv. resorts to it rarely if at all) is it possible that the author of the "Milindapañho" took his cue from the Pāyāsirājañña Sutta?

In response to the needs of scholastic controversies and of the inculcation of dogmatics among the novices, a dry-as-dust catechistical style came into being. The "Vedallas" are a prominent example of this class. Pari passu emerged the commentarial style, illustrated by the "Vibhaṅgas".[77] The suttas calling themselves "Veyyākaraṇas" (otherwise, it is difficult to decide whether they are Veyyākaraṇas or not) should also perhaps be considered to have been similarly motived.[78]

There was also a considerable development of what may be called the "Purāṇic", or perhaps the "Mahāyānic" style. It is characterised by its wealth of narrative and descriptive material, by its predominantly mythological character, by its, to say the least, benevolent toleration of miracles, by exaggeration in numbers (of years, followers, converts, distances etc.) and in the epithets of praise and blame, and at places, by a marked change of taste.[79] Those suttas which exhibit a form akin to that of the "Jātakas" may be adduced as examples of this style,[80] e.g. MN. Sutta 81.

(c) *Interpolation*: Many suttas reveal patchwork. That is not surprising in view of the fact that they were transmitted down long and independent lines of reciters steeped in later ideas, formulæ and interpretations, never had a single standard linguistic expression, and

[77] These are not "purely philological-exegetical" as acc. to Oldenberg the commentarial core of the "Vibhaṅga" in "Vinaya" is.

[78] e.g. Brahmajāla.°

[79] Cf. Rhys Davids's introductory remarks to the Pāṭika Sutta, Dialogues, III.

[80] As to the "Parittās" they might have been used in certain popular circles quite early, but it must have been only gradually that they attained to that importance and recognition which is accorded to them in the Dīgha and the Khuddakapāṭha.

underwent probably more than one editorial revision.[81] The progress of doctrine has, thus, left behind its en-registrations on many of the ancient texts. They are not confined to interpolations and appendages. Many times the old texts are merely "retouched", for example made tidier in expression through the substitution of a looser statement by a more compact formula; or lists of adjectives are lengthened or cut down, or conventional beginnings or endings added. Most of these are cases of old texts unconsciously brought up-to-date. More serious is the assimilation of variant versions into new compositions, though they are sometimes left just jux-taposed.

Thus late expression may be consonant with early ideas and isolated late features may be found in an other-wise early text. For other reasons also too great a de-mand should not be made on consistency.[82] And as Bloomfield observes, in another connection, "at least the following caution ought to be observed; before throwing out we ought to know the reason why the redac-tors placed these extra materials where we find them."[83]

An interesting class is formed by those suttas (parti-cularly in D.N. II) which have Mahā prefixed to their titles and these appear to have reached their present bulk through the elaboration of shorter originals.[84] One result of the analysis of discrepancies which result from the confused jostling of old and new elements, is that

[81] Cf. Chap. I.

[82] Cf. the remark of C. Gore "Naïve records of personal ex-periences all the world over, which are quite credible on the whole, are still not drawn up with such precision as to stand minute cross-questioning" (Jesus of Nazareth p. 189 H.U.L.).

[83] J.A.O.S. Vol. XXI, p. 44.

[84] Cf. the Satipaṭṭhānasutta and Mahā°; cf. Bhārata and Mahā°.

sometimes we are able to glimpse sayings of an "unorthodox" character[85] i.e. sayings as are opposed to the established beliefs of the editors.

(d) *Vocabulary and other linguistic features* : Lutoslawski in his work on Plato's Logic has given great precision to stylometric methodology.[86] That procedure has the advantage of mechanical applicability, but it depends for its success on such extensive linguistic statistics as are simply not available in the field of Pali studies. The PTS dictionary is the best effort in the direction, but it does not list all the occurrences of a word, and treats the meaning historically in a few cases only. In any case, our situation is different from that of Lutoslawski, for we are after all not concerned primarily with the study of a particular person's style reflected in his choice and arrangement of words, in which case only, their comparative average frequency in texts of equal extent could be made the basis of further inference. For our purposes, words are just milestones in certain trends of semantic evolution, not the indicators of personal idiosyncracy. Unfortunately, uncertainty besets many of our word histories, which have, in any case, not been comprehensively worked out. At places, again, the possibility of interpolation makes a semantic test hazardous.

Below is a list of the words which through change in their meaning or importance indicate the age of the compositions in which they occur. It does not include wholly post-Nikāya terms such as, appanā, āvajjana, bhavaṅga etc., and omits such terms as Dukkaṭa, Duṭṭhulla etc., which are of "stratigraphic" significance for the Vinaya alone—

[85]e.g. SN. III 130.

[86]See Lutoslawski—op. cit., pp.66-72; 146-151. There has been considerable development in Stylistics in recent years but whether it has provided a reliable stylometry for contexts such as the present, is still a debatable issue—Cf. John Lyons, *New Horizons in Linguistics*, pp. 185 ff. Besides, the remarks on Lutoslawski above apply with even greater force to computer stylometry.

Ajjhattacintin.—The word is rare: PTSD has only two references, Sn. 174 and 388. Later on Ajjhatta became just the counterpart of what is Bahiddhā and preoccupation with either was condemned. Previously, however, Ajjhatta seems to have been commendatory. Similar is *Ajjhattarata*—Dn. II. 107; Sn. 263; Dh. 362; Ud. 64; A.N. IV. 312. Cf. Ātmaratiḥ—Ch. Up. VII-25-2 (Ajjhattasanti—Sn. 837—may also be noticed).

Paccatta, attan, anatta, attabhāva, attadīpa, °saraṇa. See *infra* on the problem of Self (Chap. XII).

Attha.—Mrs. Rhys Davids has pointed out that as a word for the summum bonum it tended to fall into disuse (see e.g. The Original Gospel....pp. 79—80).

Anāgāmin.—"....in the oldest passages referring to these four stages (of spiritual progress) the description of the third does not use the word a° (D.N.I. 156; II. 92, III. 107, M.N. II. 146) and a° does not mean the breaking of bonds but the cultivation of certain specified good mental habits....At It 96 only three stages, the worldling, the anāgāmin and the arahant; and the saṃyojanas are not referred to. It is probable that already in the Nikāya period the older, wider meaning was falling into disuse" (PTSD). It may be added that in many old passages the place of anāgāmin is occupied by "Opapātika" which occurs in a more general meaning in the Jaina canon, as also in the report of some heretical doctrines in the Nikāyas e.g., in the Sāmaññaphala sutta.

In view of this gradual growth of the theory of spiritual stages, it is likely that the terms Antarāparinibbāyin, upahacca°, sasaṅkhāra°, uddhaṃsota, and akaniṭṭhagāmin are also late, since these presuppose a fivefold classification of the anāgāmin.

Anusaya.—In the older texts the word usually occurs absolutely, without mentioning the cause or direction of bias. So Sn. 369, 545; M.N. III. 31 etc., or in the triplet adhiṭhnābhinivesānusayā S.N. II. 17; III. 10. etc. Later on its content is schematized in variant lists; and finally these govern the connotation of the word. It may be noted that among the sects the problem of the nature of 'Anusaya' and its relation to 'pariyuṭṭhāna' (used quite generally in the Nikāyas e.g. M.N. I. 18) and 'citta' assumed great importance.

Anussati (6)—A list of subjects to be kept in mind.

Apadāna—in the sense of 'sublime life history', appears late (See PTSD).

Appamāda, uṭṭhāna, parakkama, nikkama, viriya, Ārambha, and possibly Purisakāra are so closely interwoven with the Zeitgeist of the 6th century B.C. that emphasis on them must have been early.

Ababa, and abbuda (as also Roruva and Avīci) which are the names of hells or hell-periods, are possibly late.

Abhiññā has an earlier general meaning, and a later one referring exclusively to the six supernormal psychical powers (see PTSD).

Abhidhamma which would seem to mean "about Dhamma" i.e., expository to it, and not "special Dh."

Abhivinaya.—Must have come in familiar use only with the growth of an exegetical literature.

Abhibhāyatana.—in its specialized signification of the eight stages of mastery over the senses may be late.

Amata.—As a frequent expression for the summum bonum it is obviously nearer the upaniṣadic 'Gedankenkreis' than the other end of the Nikāya period.

Arahant.—Its meaning suffered a degradation (see Dialogues II Intr. to Sutta 14).

Aviha.—appears late. It stands for the 12th of the 16 Brahma-worlds—S.N. I. 35, 60; A.N. I. 279 Puggala° 17. Other words like ābhassara, subhakiṇha, manopadūsika, khiḍḍā° etc. appear similarly late. These belong to a mythology that was built up in independence of the Vedic tradition and must have taken time.

Āyatana.—already found in the upaniṣads though it became extremely important in abhidharma. It must have, therefore, on the whole, tended to increase in frequency and technicality. And we do find quite a number of diverse āyatana groups or schemes; rajassāyatana in Sn. 406 is quite general. Vimutti° in D.N. III. 241, 279 is more specialized; the six āyatanas are still more so; and the 8 abhibhāyatanas as well as the 10 Kasiṇa° are possibly later still. Āyatanakusalatā (D.N. III. 212) shows not only the growth of technicality but also of abstraction. Notice also āyatanika S.N. IV. 126.

Ārammaṇa—closely allied to the above in meaning, and like it, became very popular later in psychological discussions.

Āsava.—In the earliest texts it seems to have a quite general signification; then, for long, it denotes a set of three evils, which is later increased to four.

Inda.—See above.

Indriya.—Owing to its popularity groups multiplied till at Vbh. 122 sq. we have a list of 22 indriyas. Of these the last three appear late (the order as given in PTSD).

Upadhi.—At first it is used quite generally, and even where specified, means no more than material encumbrances like property etc. At the close of the Nikāya period, however, we find it systematized into a set of ten—(See PTSD).

Upādāna.—It begins with a general signification, but is later dogmatized in a set of four-Kāma°, diṭṭhi°, sīlabbata° and attavāda° D.N. II. 230; M.N.I. 51. 66; S.N. II. 3; V. 59 etc. Jaina "Āyāṇa" may be compared.

Ogha.—Used at first in a lively figure, it was for some time interpreted with a certain amount of latitude. A.N. III. 69 speaks of Kāmogha. Sn. 945 identifies ogha with gedha while S.N.I. 126 has five oghas. "Towards the end of the Nikāya period we find, for the first time, the use of the word in the plural and the mention of the four oghas identical with the four 'āsavas' see D.N. III. 230, 276; S.N. IV. 175, 257 V. 59, 292, 309; Nd. 159; Nd. 178" (PTSD).

Kappa (Mahā°) defined as consisting of four asaṅkheyya° viz. saṃvaṭṭa° saṃvaṭṭaṭṭhāyi°; vivṭṭa° and vivaṭṭaṭṭhāyi°, as in A.N. II. 142, appears much more elaborate and schematic than the saṃvaṭṭavivaṭṭa° of D.N.I. 14 or It. 15.

Kilesa.—"Its occurrence in the Piṭakas is rare; in later works very frequent..." (PTSD). Now the first statement at least, does not apply to upakkilesa which would seem to represent the earlier usage.

Khandha.—The three (increased to four a little later) dhamma° are reminiscent of "trayo dharmaskhandhāḥ.... (Ch. Up II. 2. 3. 1). On the other hand, the scheme of the 5 upādānakkhandhas is much later. It assumes a full-fledged theory of Anatta, and a conception of Viññāṇa which has travelled far from its original form. Starting from the simple distinction between kāya or rūpa and viññāṇa (citta), psychological analysis in the Nikāyas arrived at this subtler conception through an intermediate stage. And this result was itself superseded in the Abhidharma stage (see below).

Gavesana.—An early word according to Mrs. Rhys Davids. Coomarswamy in his review of her book "What was the original gospel in Buddhism?" remarks, "It would have been helpful to point out that the very word for way (Maggo: Dht. p. 298 has gavessati=maggana) derives from mṛg. to 'hunt' especially in the sense of track' " (JAOS 1938, p. 680).

Cakkavattī dhammiko dhammarājā cāturanto.—According to R. Chanda "probably post-Aśokan" (Mem Arch Sur. of India, No. 39 p. 16; cf. Bhandarkar, Aśoka, p. 236). This is unlikely, for how, then, explain the utter silence of the Piṭakas about Aśoka? Besides, there are other instances of the early Buddhist tendency to replace many popular or Brahmanic ideas by "counter-ideas". On the growth of the idea of King of Righteousness see Rhys Davids-Hibbert Lectures, p. 129ff.

Ñāṇavatthūni: Forty-four in S. N. II. 56 ff. discussed in extenso in Vbh. 306—44.

Taṇhā.—"The figure is a strong one, and the word Taṇhā is found mainly in poetry, or in prose passages surcharged with religious emotion. It is rarely used in the philosophy or the psychology. Thus in the long Enumeration of Qualities (Dh.) Taṇhā occurs in one only out of the 1366 sections (Dhs. 1059), and then only as one of the many subordinate phases of lobha" (PTSD). One may compare Ch. up. "apipāsa eva sa babhūva" (Ch. Up. III. 17. 6). It appears one of the central figures used by Buddha himself, and became less frequent as scholasticism grew.

Thūpa.—See *supra.*

Daṇḍa.—In the sense of violence (to creatures) appears an early usage and occurs frequently in verse, and is strongly akin to the Jaina usage.

Diṭṭhi.—Came to acquire later the very special meaning of heresy.

Dukkhatā.—The term occurs in Ch. up. VII. 26. 2. cf. D.N. III. 216; S.N. IV. 59; V. 56. Dukkha-dukkhatā is purely Buddhist.

Devayāna.—Sn. 139; D.N. I. 215. An Upaniṣadic and rare expression; hence early.

Dhammatā tathatā, dhammaṭṭhitatā, and dhammaniyāmatā: may be late on account of their great abstraction. Nirodhadhammatā (S.N. IV. 217) is similar. So is "Idappaccayatā". But cf. Bṛ. Up. IV. 1 where similar abstractions are used Prajñatā, Priyatā, Satyatā, Anantatā, Ānandatā and Sthitatā. Thus the issue remains uncertain from a linguistic approach. See below on Pratītyasamutpāda and Dhamma.

Dhamma.—The "doctrine" is Dhamma, because it proclaims the Norm that lies behind things; and since it is through the mind that the abstract norms behind sensible things are apperceived, dhammas are the objective counterpart of "Mano". This second meaning seems to have mediated in the progress of the meaning of dh. from "the Norm behind things" to the "things" themselves.

Dhātu.—Another of the much-used words like Āyatana and Indriya, and, like the former, of importance in Abhidharma. Its popularity betokens a strong analytical quest, which sought to reduce things to their ultimate elements, and thus we have kāma°, amata°, nirodha° and even nibbāna°.

The distinction between *nītattha*, and *neyattha* (e.g., A.I. 60) belongs to the age of sectarian controversies.

Parovara.—Found only in Sn. 353, 475, 704, 1048 and 1148 (PTSD). One may compare the Upaniṣadic usage. Probably early.

Paccekavasavattin. D. N. II. 261 Pacceka-Brahman—S. N. I. 146. Pacceka-Sacca—A. N. II. 41; V. 29.	These show a tendency which became very prominent later.

Pacceka-Buddha, e.g., M.N. III. 86; S.N. I. 92; Ud. 50.

Pajāpati.—See above.

Padhāna.—The more general earlier usage elaborated and crystallized in the sammappadhānas. The formula of the four padhānas as Saṃvara, Pahāna, Bhāvanā and Anurakkhanā as detailed in the Saṅgīti sutta seems to represent a still more precise and elaborate stage.

Parikkhāra.—The conception of the seven Parikkhāras of samādhi is an obvious improvement on the formula of eightfold path.

Parittā.—See above.

Parissaya—has a meaning which is the exact opposite of the Jinist meaning.

Purisa, °puggala, puggala.—While the first is the usual Upaniṣadic word, the third word is the usual one in Abhidharma. The second appears a transitional makeshift. Are the reasons for this introduction of the new word to be sought in the growth of the Anatta doctrine, which disliked purisa on account of its old associations? Already in the AN "Puggala" has reached pre-eminence; on the other hand, the only undoubtedly early use of the word appears to be in the "Sāmaññaphala sutta" where, however, it appears juxtaposed to satta.

Bodhisatta.—has been discussed above and would appear to be late.

Magga.—Mrs. Rhys Davids has suggested that it was not originally eightfold. The formula of the tenfold, at least, is clearly an elaboration. (The Tikapaṭṭhāna has twelve constituents—see PTSD).

Viññāṇa.—Originally the "More-than-Body" which in its *patiṭṭhita* state was the mutable transmigrant; later it came to mean almost exclusively "sense-perception" (this latter meaning has its beginnings in the latest Upaniṣadic texts) which is its status in the full-fledged five khandha theory.

Vedalla.—See above.

Saṃyojana.—Originally a general meaning in which the metaphor is clear. Later it was elaborated into diverse lists.

Saṅkhāra.—From a somehow 'conative' meaning (cf. the three saṅkhāras; abhisaṅkhāra) it came to have a very extended use and became very important later. A clearly late instance of its use is S.N. III. p. 87.

Saññā.—used loosely and in forming many lists, some of which are the obvious elaborations of others. (See PTSD).

Satipaṭṭhāna.—The usual scheme of four has come about through the elaboration of the simpler Sati or "mindfulness"—(See Chap. on Way).

Sahassī Lokadhātu.—D.N. I. 46; A.N. I. 228. Implies developed mythology (cf. M.N. III. 101).

Suññatā M.N. III. 111; Kv. 232. Shows abstraction and pronounced negativism. Great importance later. °Paṭisaṃyutta A.N. I. 72=III. 107=S.N. II. 257.

From the side of linguistic morphology even fewer data are available. Geiger distinguishes four stages in

Pali linguistic development,[87] of which only the first two are relevant to the present enquiry: 1. The language of the Gāthās i.e., the metrical pieces. It is of a very heterogeneous character, containing many archaic speech-forms which are distinguished from the old-Indian forms only phonologically. Fausböll[88] has pointed out that Sn. contains many old Vedic forms of substantives and verbs in the plural, such as Samūhatāse, Paccayāse, Paṇḍitāse, or Carāmase, Sikkhisāmase; the shorter Vedic plurals, as Vinicchayā and Lakkhaṇā for Vinicchayāni and Lakkhaṇāni; shorter instrumental singulars as mantā, pariññā, lābhakamyā,—for mantāya, pariññāya, lābhakamyāya; Vedic infinitives as vippahātave, uṇṇametave, sampayātave; contracted forms, such as, ātumānam, suvāmi, suvānā as well as archaic forms like sagghasi (=sakkhissasi), pāva or pāvā (Pavadati), pavecche (=pavesseyya), sussaṃ (=suṇissāmi), daṭṭhu (=disvā), paribbasāno (=parivasamāno), avocāsi, ruṇṇena, uggahāyanti.

2. The language of the canonical prose, which is more homogeneous than that of the gāthās. The archaic forms diminish in number and frequency, while the use of the new formations is no longer accidental or arbitrary as in the oldest period of the language, but is governed by more rigid rules.

Considerations of metre can also be useful occasionally, though the stratigraphy of metres has itself to be established at the same time.[89a]

(e) *Geography*.—According to Thomas the expansion of geographical knowledge towards the south and the west indicates a relatively later character of the reports.[89] In the DN. and MN. introductory sections generally mention the Kāsīs, the Kosalas, the Aṅgas, the Magadhas,

---

[87] Pali Literature and Language (tr. by Batakrishna Ghosh, pp. 1-2).

[88] In his intr. to SBE X (tr. of Sn). Quoted by Bapat in his ed. of Sn. (p. XXVIII).

[89] Life, pp. 13-14. [89a] Cf. Warder, *Indian Buddhism*, p.14.

the Kurus, the Vajjis and the Mallas. The Janavasabhasutta, however, also mentions, the Cetis and the Vaṃsas to the west of Prayāga, the Kurupañcālas, north west of the Kosalas, and still further west the Macchas and the Sūrasenas.[90] This list of twelve is extended in the AN.[91] to sixteen by the mention of the Assakas of South, the Avantīs north of the Vindhyas, and, in the extreme north, the Gandhāras and the Kambojas.[92] The Godāvarī is mentioned only in the introductory verses of Pārāyaṇa.

An "extension" of geographical knowledge, however, is difficult to prove. Even in the 6th century B.C. Kosambī had political connections with Avantī[93] and presumably with the adjacent states to the north-west;[94] and traders plied the caravans along the great highways to the North and the West. Again, Rhys Davids argues[95] cogently for the great antiquity of the Aṅguttara list of the Sixteen Powers. as also for the gāthās.

"Dantapuraṃ Kaliṅgānaṃ Assakānañca Potanaṃ.|
Mahissatī Avantīnaṃ Sovīrānañca Rorukaṃ||
Mithilā ca Videhānaṃ Campā Aṅgesu māpitā|
Bārāṇasī ca Kāsīnaṃ ete Govindamāpitāti.||[96]

---

[90] DN. II. p. 200.

[91] AN. I. 213; IV 252, 256, 260.

[92] Cf. also Thomas—Hist. of Budd. Thought p. 5.

[93] Budd. Ind. p. 4ff. That one of the queens of Bimisāra-Khemā hailed from "Madda in the Punjab" seems to be based on no better evidence than that of the Thig. A, and the Apadāna (see C.H.I. I. p. 183 & fn. 4).

[94] e.g. cf. C.H.I. I. pp. 213-214.

[95] Ib. pp. 172-173.

[96] Ib.

It appears, therefore, that it is hardly permissible to trace a successive growth in geographical knowledge from the DN. and MN. to AN.

It, however, stands to reason that there was a geographical extension of the Buddhist Saṅgha, and it must have taken place along the trade routes. Warlike relations between Avanti and Magadha, shortly after Buddha's death[97] may have retarded just as well as promoted the westward movement of the Buddhist monks. The materials, unfortunately, for reconstructing the pre-Aśokan geographical growth of the Saṅgha appear to be inadequate (see the last chapter).

Some sermons are reported to have been delivered at Madhurā and Avantī. These are, however, always attributed to some of the apostles, and in some cases, it is expressly stated that they were delivered "shortly after Buddha's death". We may suppose that true for all sermons of the class. It appears unlikely that Buddha himself frequented much the region to the west of a line that may be drawn from Sāvatthī to Kosambi, although some suttas report Buddha preaching among the Kurus.[98]

Some suttas speak of Buddha at 'Ālavī',[99] the location of which is uncertain (Is it the same as the later Aṭavī?) but those which speak of the "Kukkuṭarārāma" at Pāṭaliputta[100] (they do not introduce Buddha) may with some confidence be regarded relatively late.

---

[97] MN. III p. 7.

[98] e.g. the Mahānidāna sutta or the Mahāsatipaṭṭhāna sutta or AN. V. p. 29.

[99] e.g. AN. IV. 216, 218; I. 136.

[100] Do not these assume that there was a Vihara at Kukkuṭārāma?—In which case, may we suppose it to be the same as is reported by tradition to have been built by Aśoka? (Contra—Rhys Davids in C.H.I. I. p. 189).

Finally, a sutta in MN.[101] speaks of the 'yonas' as having only two classes (Vaṇṇas)—freemen (Ariyo) and slaves (Dāso). Whether it points to an Ionian commercial colony in India is uncertain.[102] Even if it is pre-Alexandrian, which is possible though not probable. it may most certainly be regarded relatively late.

F. Political and Social:

The political data have been fully considered by Rhys Davids. They belong almost wholly to the age contemporaneous with Buddha. The Kosala sam. of the Sn. speaks of the familiar relations of Buddha with the king of Kosala, and mentions the war between Pasenadi and Ajātasattu. It may be noted that the relations between Buddha and Ajātasattu appear just the opposite of those established at the end of the Sāmaññaphalasutta which may, therefore, be regarded later than the bulk of the Kosala sam. (The relations established in the Sāmaññaphala° apparently continued to the end, as is indicated by the Mahāparinibbāna). Again, MN. III. 7 speaks of Ajātasattu as fortifying his capital, Rājagṛha in anticipation of an attack by Pajjota of Avantī. This is supposed to have been shortly after Buddha's death. The only other reference to a political event which can be definitely placed in the years following Buddha's death is that referred to in AN. III. 57—63. We are told here how the thera Nārada consoled a king Muṇḍa at Pāṭaliputta, who was overwhelmed with grief at the death of his wife Bhaddā. It may be noted that Nārada simply redacts a sermon delivered by Buddha on a similar occasion. The chronicles tell us that a grand-

---

[101] MN sutta 93.

[102] cf. D. R. Bhandarkar-Asoka pp. 30-32.

son of Ajātasattu was named Muṇḍa and began to reign about the year 40 A.B.[103]

This is almost as much help as we get from the political data.

On the social side several monographs have been no doubt, written[104] but they all attempt to reconstruct a synoptic picture mainly on evidence of a "composite" character, which is drawn principally from the Jātakas and then freely combined with that found in the Nikāyas and the Vinaya. A detailed comparison of this evidence with the Brahmaṇic and Jinist sources still remains a desideratum. Since, however, the curve of the social history of Pre-Aśokan India at least can only be traced with reference to a time axis of relatively longer periods, it is unlikely that it will throw much light on the problem of Nikāya stratification. The most important considerations in this respect must relate to the history of the Saṅgha.

Prose and Verse.—On the basis of the oft-occurring sutta on 'Future Dangers' (Anāgatabhayāni)[105] Winternitz concludes that "the poetical pieces were not at first generally recognised, that their claim to be regarded as sacred texts was contested and that they were only later on combined into a Nikāya, namely the Khuddakanikāya."[106] Now although this particular text has been recommended by Aśoka, its authenticity is, for several reasons dubious. In the first place, it purports to be a prophecy, and prophecies are at once suspect as compo-

---

[103] See C. H. I. I. p. 189 and fn. 3.

[104] Rhys Davids, Buddhist India; Mrs. Rhys Davids in JRAS and C.H.I. I. Chap. VIII; Fick-Die Gliederung etc. R. L. Mehta. Pre-Buddhist India.

[105] e.g. AN-III. 107.

[106] Op cit II. P. 77.

sitions concocted after the event. And the truer and more wonderful they are, other things remaining the same, the greater must the suspicion become. Now it does seem remarkable that Buddha should have foreseen the great rise of verse and heresy within the Saṅgha. Again, this sutta speaks of monks as "*Abhidhammakathaṃ* Vedallakathaṃ Kathentā" and of the "Suttantā Tathāgatabhāsitā. . . .*lokuttarasuññatapatisaṃyuttā*".

The use of the underlined words suggests that the sutta belongs to a relatively late date in Nikāya history, and very probably represents the hostile reaction of the Abhidhammists to the other more popular trend within the Saṅgha. In any case to conclude from the sutta in the way Winternitz does is to invest it with more significance than warranted. That is, of course, not to contest the late and unstable character of the fifth collection as a whole.[107]

Cv. V. 33, is important in this context; a study of the four parallel versions of the text as given by some other sects,[108] however, suggests that the prohibition there is not against the use of verse as such but rather against "sanskritization" and chanting after the Vedic manner.

---

[107] Ib. fn. 3:—The Buddhists of Burma include in it four additional texts, while the Siamese edition of the Pali canon has eight of them missing: Vimāmavatthu, Petavatthu, Theragāthā, Therī°, Jātaka Apadāna, Buddhavaṃsa and Cariyāpiṭaka.

According to the Dīpavaṃsa v. 37 the mahāsaṃgītikas did not recognize the Paṭisambhidā, the Niddesa and a part of the Jātaka. The Khuddaka Nikāya as a whole does not appear in the Chinese Āgamas. Further the Divyāvadāna makes frequent mention of the Āgamacatuṣṭaya only (pp. 17, 331, 333); cf. Oldenberg in ZDMG. 52, 654ff.

[108] On the basis of their report by Senart in JA 1915 Mai-Juin 441ff.

On the other hand, it must be remembered that verse is a greater conserving medium and in oral transmission likely to be more conservative than prose. Besides, in our texts where prose and verse occur together, it is impossible to say in general whether the one or the other is older.[109]

In short, the verse-form is in itself of no stratigraphic significance. The Sn. and the Dh. contain quite a number of verses which are far from being distinctively Buddhist. These are either popular riddles, or of a gnomic or generally ascetic character. From a consideration of their content alone such verses are not stratifiable, and often the ancillary apparatus adopted here is also not fine enough to classify them.

Further, the difficulty of marking out interpolations and additions is much greater in verse since the suddenness or obscurity of transition from one verse to another is not incompatible with their forming an original unity, and the absence of short external sections makes the task of discovering the originally independent units of the composition an extremely hard one.

[109] e.g. in the Sagāthavg of the SN, Ud. and It.

CHAPTER III

THE STRATIFICATION OF SUTTA-NIPĀTA ITIVUTTAKA AND UDĀNA

Suttanipata (Sn.) and the Chinese Agamas.— According to Anesaki[1] no Chinese version of Sn. as a whole can be traced, but the "Aṭṭhakavagga" may be identified with No. 674 of Nanjio: "Sūtra spoken by Buddha on the fulness of meaning"—which was translated about the beginning of the 3rd century A.D. (According to Nanjio between 222—280 A.D.). It contains sixteen texts or stories in which verses are incorporated; and the agreement of the verse portion with Pali is perfect.

Now "it is just the Aṭṭhavagga which happened to be preserved in the fragments"[2] discovered from E. Turkestan by Stein; and what is more, the outstanding difference between the Pali and the Sanskrit version is the existence of prose narratives prefixed to the verses of the several vargas of the latter.[3] And Hoernle comes to the "unavoidable" conclusion "that the Sanskrit text is a translation from some vernacular....original; and that the translator, observing the absence of an introductory narrative, himself supplied that narrative, and pointed out the exact place where he came to the translation of the verses of his original text."[4] May not the

[1] JPTS 1906-'7, pp. 50-51.

[2] Hoernle JRAS. 1916, p. 709.

[3] Ib., p. 718. In the text the only discrepancies of any importance are these: For Pali verses 839-840 there must have been a much shorter text in the original for the Sanskrit translation; and there could have been only one verse for Pali 841-842 (Ib., p. 720).

[4] Ib., p. 719.

prose of the Chinese translation be similar in character and thus a later, almost commentarial, addition to the verse?

Prose and Verse.—In this connection it may be noticed that Franke regards the prose of Sn. as representing a later stratum than the Gāthās.[5] And Fausboll holds all the prose passages to be later additions.[6] It appears, however, that in regard to this problem one must be a "Vibhajjavādin" and not an "Ekaṃsavādin". In sutta 4, the prose sequel at any rate contains what is undoubtedly a late stock-finish—it recurs in suttas 7, 10, 19, 30, 31, 32 (with relevant additions) and 35, and is equally frequent in the other Nikāyas. In sutta 10 the verses are in the 'riddle-dialogue' form and do not stand in need of the prose preface. In sutta 17 the verses, in spite of different contents, have a somewhat similar form and hence receive a prose preface closely resembling that in suta 10. The verses in sutta 35 contain within the framework of the dialogue the necessary narrative also, and it is possible that the prose in the beginning is a later addition. The suttas 6, 7, 16, 19, 24, 26 and 31 can do very well without the brief prose with which they commence. Nor are the prose portions of sutta 32 at all necessary for comprehending the essential verse. And the possibility of the prose being a merely conventional addition in these cases is strong, although it is hard to clinch the argument. In sutta 29, on the other hand, the prose has as much claim to be regarded as authentic as the verse, which in the next sutta seems to take the preceding prose for granted as is also the case in sutta 33. In suttas 36 and 38 both the prose and verse can stand

[5] ZDMG. 1909, 1.

[6] Winternitz, II, p. 98.

independently. In fact in these suttas the verse is always introduced thus "Idaṃ avoca Bhagavā, idaṃ vatvā Sugato athāparaṃ etad avoca satthā." But it is impossible to say which is earlier.

The antiquity of the Atthaka and Parayana vaggas. —It appears that Pārāyaṇa vagga also occurs in the Chinese Tripiṭaka,[7] the Saṃyuktāgama of which contains, besides, the Megha and the Kokāliya suttas.[8] Further the Khaggavisāṇa, the ᵓabbajjā, the Padhāna, the Nālaka and the Sabhiya suttas find their counterparts, in some cases almost word for word, in the Mahāvastu and the Lalitavisatara.[9]

It is, however, only with reference to the Aṭṭhaka and Pārāyaṇa vaggas that we can, on external evidence alone, assert their extreme antiquity. Mahāvagga V, 13 speaks of the recitation of the Aṭṭhakavaggikas, and the same story recurs in Ud. V. 6 which has "soḷasa aṭṭhakavaggikas."[10] Divyāvadāna (really a part of the Mūlasarvāstivādavinaya as translated in Chinese and Tibetan) has developed the episode into a "petit roman" and relates the recitation of Ud. Pārāyaṇa, Satyadṛsṭi, Śailagāthā, Munigāthā, (Dulva adds Sthaviragāthā and °āgāthā) and the Arthavargīya sūtra.[11] The Sarvāstivāda Vinaya, preserved only in Chinese (the Chinese title=Daśādhyāyavinaya) agrees closely with it, but has the recitation of Pārāyaṇa and Satyadarśa only.[12] The

[7] Ib., 92 fn. 3.

[8] Bapat's ed. of Sn., p. xxx.

[9] Ib. Since the names of the sutta in Sn. do not seem to have been rigidly fixed, and many of them are known to have alternative titles (Ib. XVIII) may it not be that the Chinese counterparts of many other suttas of Sn. may yet be discovered?

[10] Lévi—JA. 1915—Mai-Juin, p. 403.

[11] Ib., 405.

[12] Ib., 407.

Mahīśāsakavinaya in Chinese (entitled Pañcādhyāya-vinaya) recites the Koṭikarṇa story after the manner of the Pali Vinaya. It speaks of the "sūtra des Seize Section de Sens" (The Chinese term—arthavarga).[13] The Dharmaguptavinaya, available in Chinese alone, and closely allied to the above mentions the recitation of the "Seize Phrases de Sens" (Arthapada). The Mahāsaṅghikavinaya differs most; it has Pūrṇa and Śroṇāparānta for Kātyāyana and Avantī, but speaks of the recitation of "Aṣṭavarga."[14]

The Koṭikarṇa history, thus, must have early formed a part of the canon, and it already presupposes the Aṭṭhakavagga. Again, the Dharmagupta enumeration of the contents of the Kṣudrakāgama in the Rājagṛha saṅgīti places "Arthapada" and "Dharmapada" side by side.[15] It may be noted that SN. III. 12 refers to the Aṭṭhaka by name.

Pārāyaṇa is mentioned twice in AN. II. 45, III. 399 and 401. So in S. II. 49. Sarvāstivāda vinaya mentions it among the "grands sūtras", in pursuance of a theme which is identical with Mahāvagga (Pali III. 5. 9); and occurs also in the Varṣāvastu of the Mahīśāsakas, Dharmaguptas, Mūlasarvāstivādins and Mahāsaṅghikas. The actual list, however, is given only in the Sarvāstivāda vinaya.[16] But in one passage the mahāsaṅghikavinaya speaks of the Pārāyaṇa and Arthavarga together,[17] and so does the Abhidharmamahāvibhāṣā.[18]

The internal evidence too points towards the antiquity of the Aṭṭhaka and Pārāyaṇa and has been in a general way indicated by Fausböll.[19] He points to the

[13] Ib., 408.
[14] Ib., 411.
[15] Ib., 415.
[16] Ib., 421-422.
[17] Ib., 422.
[18] Ib., 424.
[19] Int. to the Tr. of Sn. in SBE X, pp. xi-xii.

archaic and relatively obscure character of the language[20] of the Aṭṭhakavagga, and, on the ideological side, states "we see here a picture not of life in monasteries but of the life of hermits in its first stage. We have before us not the systematizing of the later Buddhist church, but the first germs of a system."[21]

The strata in Sn.--But whereas the Aṭṭhakavagga and the Pārāyaṇa undoubtedly represent the earliest stratum in Sn., it appears, in contradiction to Fausböll, that the Mahāvagga as a whole belongs to the latest stratum, while the suttas of the first two Vaggas have, in general, an uncertain status.

The title of the "Aṭṭhavagga" presents a difficult problem. In Lévi's survey whereas the Mahīśāsaka and Dharmagupta Vinayas have Arthavarga and Arthapada respectively, the heterodox sect par excellence—the Mahāsaṅghikas—have Aṣṭavarga. Sanskrit sources like the Divyāvadāna, the Ab. k. or the East Turkestan fragments already referred to, have Arthavarga in favour of which Lévi decides. That looks very unlikely, for while it is easy to see how Aṭṭhakavagga could have been mis-sanskritized as Arthavarga—there are other instances of wrong Sanskrit renderings—the reverse is difficult to explain. "Artha" becomes in Pali regularly "Attha" except in the compounds Aṭṭhapatti and Aṭṭhakathā where it means "meaning" (See PTSD). Indeed, that is how the Mahīśāsaka and Dharmagupta Vinayas seem to understand it, but with little cogency, since Artha in Arthapada or Arthavarga is best taken in the same sense in which we have Atthābhisamaya, Atthapatti, Paramattha etc. Besides, how otherwise explain the entry of

[20] See supra, Chap. II. It may be mentioned that there is a notable increase in the *v.* ls in the last two vaggas of Sn.

[21] loc. cit.

'Ka' in Aṭṭhaka? Finally, and this clinches, the vagga actually contains a group of four Aṭṭhakas (so called in the text) each consisting of eight verses.

This is of great significance. The Aṭṭhakavagga reveals a definite plan of arranging the suttas. We begin with one containing six verses; then follow octades, after which the sequence of the total number of verses in the suttas is as follows:--

10, 10, 11, 13, 14, 16, 17, 20, 20,[22] 20 and 21. This striking progressive order shows clearly that the present Aṭṭhakavagga is the product of careful editorial activity. (It is also noteworthy that both the first and the last suttas of this vagga speak of the Parissayas). It appears that like the Family Books of the Ṛgveda, the four Aṭṭhakas form a closely connected nuclear group to which the other suttas were editorially added.

The nuclear Atthakavagga.—The "Aṭṭhaka-group" has a distinguishing unity of metre, language, subject-matter and style of expression. Each of the four Aṭṭhakas consists of eight verses in a mixture of Indravajrā and Upendravajrā.[23] Considering the extent of these Aṭṭhakas, they show, even within the Aṭṭhakavagga, a greater use of archaic forms than the other suttas. In the Guhaṭṭhaka occur cutāse (verse 3), avītataṇhāse (v. 5) Vineyya (v. 7) and Pariññā (v. 8); the next has Pāvā which occurs twice (v. 3), ātumānaṃ (Ib), and niccheyya (v. 6); the Suddhaṭṭhaka has Pāvā (v. 2),

[22] Metrical variation ought to be noted.

[23] The metrical scheme of the sixteen suttas in the Aṭṭhakavagga is as follows :—

1. Anuṣṭubh; 2-5. Upajāti; 6. Vaitālīya (loosely); 7. Anuṣṭubh; 8-9. Upajāti; 10. Anuṣṭubh; 11-13. Upajāti; 14. Mixture of Anuṣṭubh and Vaitālīya; 15. Anuṣṭubh; 16. First half Anuṣṭubh, second Upajāti.

vadānaṃ (Ib), sitāse (v. 4), and gahāya (Ib);[24] and the Paramaṭṭhaka has paribbasāno (v. 1),[25] samuggahāya (v. 2) and Paṭicchitāse (v. 8). On the other hand, the following Jarāsutta of 10 verses has hardly any marked ancient form: Tissametteyya of similar extent has, however, sikkhisāmase (v. 1) sutvāna (Ib), caritvāna (v. 3), and vippahātave (v. 4)Pasūra°haṣ vadānā (twice-v. 1. & 2), sagghasi and sampayātave (both in v. 11) in 11 verses: Māgandiya has disvāna (v. 1), niccheyya (v. 3), vinicchayā (v. 4) and anuggahāya (v. 5) in 13 verses. After this though the length of the suttas increases much, only the Kalahavivāda°, Cūlaviyūha° and Mahāviyūha° have marked archaic forms to show.

In expression the Aṭṭhakas are more involved and obscure than the other suttas.[26] The very frequent occurrence of Nara and Jantu in them is also significant. and peculiar. The use of Guhā in the Guhaṭṭhaka is reminiscent of Kaṭha up.

The state of ideas, again, is perhaps the earliest to be found in the canon. Man-Nara Jantu–is bound and tormented in the world (Bhavo, loko) by pleasures (Kāma) and desire (Taṇhā, chando). Instead of the later formula of Paṭiccasamuppāda we have such simple statements as "(Kāmā. . . . icchānidānā bhavasātabaddhā. . . ." (Guhaṭṭhaka-v. 2), or the implication in v. 778 that desire (Chanda) springs from contact (Phassa). Egoism (Mamāyita) and Saññā–which is the wordly counterpart of Paññā (see vv. 847, 779, 792),–must be abandoned. So must all speculation (Diṭṭhi) and en-

[24] Is the Nirassajanti of v. 4 in this Aṭṭhaka the result of a confusion between Nirassanti and Nissajjanti?

[25] Is it connected with "Paryavasyati"? Cf. the expression Ditthiparibbasāno° in Cūḷa° and Mahāviyūha°?

[26] Cf. Fausböll. loc. cit.

cumbrance (upadhi). Avoiding the extremes (ubhesu antesu vineyya chandaṃ) and grasping nothing, not even individuality (Attaṃ pahāya anupādiyāno—800) a man attains to a state which is neither the self nor the non-self (Attaṃ nirattaṃ na hi tassa atthi—787), which is beyond all limitations (sīmātigo—795) and all mental and merely moral processess (Diṭṭha, suta, muta, ñāṇa, and sīlavata; where there is not the slightest mental construction: "Pakappitā natthi aṇū pi saññā"—802), and which means a peace (Santi, Abhinibbuti—783) that has neither the taste of pleasure nor is distasteful (na rāgarāgo na virāgaratto—795).

The rest of the Atthakavagga. Sutta no. 44, which **immediately succeeds the fourth Aṭṭhaka, goes out of its** way to incorporate in the last verse the conclusions of suttas 41 and 42. Sutta 49 develops the theme of v. 773 and we are here nearer the formula of Paṭiccasamuppāda. The Mahāviyūha appears to be a slightly more elaborate version of the Cūḷaviyūha.

Conclusion about the Atthakavagga.—On the whole, however, the ideological difference between the various suttas in the Aṭṭhakavagga is too small to permit a definite stratification within it, but it must be remembered that from the literary standpoint the Aṭṭhakavagga is not homogeneous.

The Parayana vagga.--It has already been mentioned that tradition closely connects the Aṭṭhaka and Pārāyaṇa vaggas. It is noticeable in this connection that just as the Aṭṭhaka has sixteen "suttas" so the Pārāyaṇa has sixteen "Pucchās". Its language shows occasionally old forms like Saṅkhātadhammāse (56.7), Sutvāna (twice in 60.1 & 2 also in 66.7), vajju (61.8), samaṇabrāhmaṇāse (four times in 62) Daṭṭhu (66.3), Disvāna (77.2).

In 58.6 occurs the rare, and possibly old, word Parovarāni. It is similarly rare for Buddha to be addressed as "Sakka" and even "Brahmā" (60, 3 & 5; 61.1) and "Samantacakkhu" is here suggested by "Sakka"—it has not as yet become dissociated and independent.

Sutta 63 of four verses is composed in the "gāyatrī" metre, which is rare if not unique. Though on a much more metaphysical level than the Aṭṭhakavagga, its doctrinal position is, on the whole, not much different. Its clearest exposition is found in sutta 61, which, taken in conjunction with the other suttas in the vagga, yields a picture somewhat as follows:—

Viññāṇa or consciousness as manifested in the individual, ceases in the highest experience (Paramavimutti cf. 61.4) but of what remains neither being nor non-being can be predicated. We have here a transcendentalism which is in danger of being misunderstood as Nihilism.

It may be noted that Nāmarūpa (at one place Nāma kāya 61.6) is a frequent expression in this text, but there is not the faintest suggestion of its interpretation in terms of the "khandhas" which find no mention. Its psychological analysis is exhausted in the tetrad "Diṭṭhasutamutaviññāta" (63.3) "Viññāṇaṭṭhiti" is yet used in its general and unformulized meaning (68.3). In the description of "Aññāvimokkha" in 68.2-3 we have the materials for the later formula of the fourth Jhāna.

The sixteen "Queries" may thus be placed in the same stratum as the Aṭṭhakavagga, though they are, perhaps, slightly later.

Conclusion about the Parayana.—The Vatthugāthās are, however, a definitely later addition. They show a knowledge of the south which is exceptional in the Nikāyas, are written in a fluent narrative style reminiscent of the Mbh-ballads (mark, for instance the verses 5—8), seem to use Abhiññā in the sense of miraculous powers, assume a fully developed theory of the Thirty-two Marks, and serve the merely commentarial purpose of furnishing a narrative setting to the "Queries" which in no wise depend upon it.[27] It is possible that the epilogue entitled "Pārāyaṇasutta" is also a later addition.

Mahavagga.—Though it is true that the Pabajjā— and Padhāna suttas find very close parallels in **Mvu.** II. 198ff and Ib. II 238ff (also LV.XVIII) respectively, and present the Buddha-legend in a form much less developed than many suttas of **DN** and **MN**, still as Winternitz has stated, it is impossible to place them in the earliest Nikāya stratum. The incident in the Pabbajjāsutta can hardly be regarded as historical and seems to have been invented "for the greater glory" of Buddha. The Padhanasutta is almost a continuation of it, but seems to stand in need of intermediate prose narrative to explain the change of speakers. Besides, it glories in an excess of asceticism, which is quite in contravention to Buddha's own mandate (sāsana). Much of the simplicity of these poems is to be attributed to their being good poetry.

The long and straggling *Sabhiyasutta* (cf. Mvu III. 394ff), which gives fanciful etymologies for Samaṇa and Brāhmaṇa, belongs to a still later stage in as much as it refers to sixty-three Sramaṇic dogmas.

The *Selasutta* (M. sutta 92-II. 146ff) can hardly be

[27] Cf. "The Mahāpurisalakkhaṇas....are in Sn. 1022 attributed to Bāvari (i.e., the "Babylonian"), and clearly point to the late origin of the vatthugāthās as well as to Babylonian influence" (W. Stede-Afterword to PTSD. p. 202. fn. 3).

earlier since the theory of "Thirty-two Marks" plays a central rôle in it, and Buddha is described as the supreme Dhammarāja, with Sāriputta as his commander.

The *Kokāliyasutta* (occurs in the Chinese Saṃyuktāgama—see supra) belongs to the same or even later stratum. For the relatively light sin of criticizing Sāriputta—Moggalāna, the monk Kokāliya dies miserably and, what is more, is condemned to a hell, the duration of which is simply inconceivable. We are given a series of ten hells, which are described in gruesome detail. Here is, in fact, a type-sutta for the extreme Purāṇic style.

Of the *Nāḷakasutta* (parallels in Mvu. & Lal. Vist), the first half consisting of the Vatthugāthās is, at any rate, from a late stratum. Buddha's birth is a great event for the gods, and Buddha himself is called "Bodhisatta". Besides, Asita is described as "Lakkhaṇamantapāragu" which may refer to his knowledge of the Thirty-two Marks. These, it may be remembered, are often described as "Mantesu āgatāni."

Finally, the *Dvayatānupassanā-sutta* is doubtless late. It introduces a dichotomy within the formula for the Four Truths, uses "Upādisesa" and "Anāgāmitā" technically, seems to distinguish between Cetovimutti and Paññāvimutti, and describes eleven Paccayas of Dukkha which include all those that occur in the Paṭiccasamuppāda except Nāmarūpa, Saḷāyatana, Bhava, Jāti and Jarāmaraṇa. In short, it evinces considerable dogmatic and analytical development.

Conclusion about the Mv.—Thus of the twelve suttas of the Mahāvagga seven appear definitely late, the term late comprising two strata; the first consisting of suttas 27 and 28, and the second of the other five.

The Rest.—Some of the remaining suttas of the Mahāvagga and the first two Vaggas embody the Buddhist protest against the social and sacrificial ideas of the Brāhmaṇas. They portray what may be termed the Brāhmaṇa-Śramaṇa conflict. To this class belong the Vasala°, Brāhmaṇadhammika°, Sundarikabhāradvāja°, Māgha° and Vāseṭṭha suttas. Except for the last, these suttas appear similar and are less dialectical than similar ones in DN and MN and the exception mentioned is actually found in the latter collection. They do not aim so much at confuting logically the theory of the Brāhmaṇas as at presenting a truer conception of the "Vasala", the "Brāhmaṇa" etc. They partake more of the nature of ethical sermons than of polemics. The Brāhmaṇadhammikasutta is partly an attempt to convince the Brāhmaṇas of the Buddhist ideal by representing it as having been followed by the ancestors of the Brāhmaṇas themselves, and partly an outcome of the tendency to imagine ideal visions of the future as having been actually realized in the past (since to go back to the past appears easier). This latter tendency is also followed in the Aggaññasutta of DN but receives there a much more developed and mythological treatment.

These suttas thus represent the earlier stages of a distinct genre in Buddhist writing; but it seems impossible to correlate, with any degree of certainty, the steps in this particular trend with those in the general ideological evolution of the Nikāyas.

Sutta 3 is apparently inconsistent with developed communal life among the Buddhist monks. Its use of the terms Attha and Parissaya, which later on practically disappeared in favour of "āsava" and "anusaya", also suggests the possibility of it being early. So does the use of Sneha more than Sineha (see PTSD). It describes the state of the fourth Jhāna without mentioning it by name. The five "āvaraṇas" (nīvaraṇas) are, however, presupposed as a technical expression. Also, its use of "ñāṇa" is different from that in the Aṭṭhaka— and Pārāyaṇa-vaggas.

Suttas 1 & 2 are not far removed in point of ideology and diction. The former uses samūhatāse and paccayāse (1.14 & 15) and the latter carāmase and bhavāmase (2.15). Besides, both these are written in the same metre, and have the same number of verses. It is likely that they have common authorship.

As already suggested the central five verses of sutta 4 are possibly nuclear in character. At any rate, they expound a lively parable of spiritual cultivation, which seems to belong to the same stage of development as the parable of the spiritual car (Dhaṃmayāna) in SN. It is quite innocent of any formulae, and may be placed in the earliest stratum. For the goal it uses the expressions Yogakkhema, Amata, and Sabbadukkhā (Pamutti).

Sutta 5 has much to say on the "maggo" but nowhere speaks of it as eightfold or tenfold, which argues for its earliness.

Sutta 12 has been recommended by Aśoka.[28] It uses the forms anuppavecche (12.20 & 3), muninaṃ (12.2) and atitariya (12.13); and the old term Rajo.[29] For the goal it has the expressions Santipada (12.2) and Paramattha (12.13); the fact that whereas Muni occurs in evey vese, Bhikkhu is seen only in the last one, may also not be without significance. It delineates the ideal

---

[28] See D. C. Sircar—Select Ins. I. p. 78, fn. 2.

[29] See the account of Jainism below, Chap. X.

of the solitary hermit meditating in the forest, and the total impression that one gets after perusing it resembles that resulting from the Aṭṭhakavagga. It may be placed in the same stratum.

Sutta 14 regards the prohibition of meat-eating as only symbolical of good conduct. With this may be compared the early Buddhist reinterpretation of such terms as Brāhmaṇa, Vasala, Yañña, Aggi, Vedagū, Arahant and Āhāro. This reveals a process of transvaluation in progress. In the MN,[30] however, the authors are eager to refute the Jinist charge of meat-eating levelled against them. This would appear to represent a later stage, since Buddha is reported to have partaken of "sūkaramaddava" and a development in the reverse direction goes against general probability. The present sutta, therefore, may be considered earlier than MN (loc cit).

The short uṭṭhānasutta (no. 22) is singular for its earnestness and power. It is reminiscent of Kaṭh.[31] It describes Pamāda as Raja and in its spirit of Kiriyavāda certainly belongs to the earliest Buddhism. The composition too may be early.

Sutta 24 addresses Buddha as Sakka (24.3) and calls him "Samantacakkhu, Sakko va devānaṃ sahassanetto" It describes the Ariyadhaṃma as Parovara (24.11) and explains Taṇhā as Nāmarūpa—(24.13). It looks early.

On the other hand sutta 13 (—Khuddakapāṭha VI) is the solitary example of a Parittā' in Sn. It pays homage to the Three "Jewels", speaks technically of the 8 Puggalas, the Ariyasaccas, the 6 Abhabbaṭṭhānāni (13.10), the 4 upāyas of vippamutti (Ib) and refers to

[30] Sutta 55.

[31] Kaṭh. 3. 14.

the theory of "Na te bhavaṃ aṭṭhamaṃ ādiyanti" (13.9). It clearly belongs to a late stratum, although it appears less developed than the similarly purposed Āṭānāṭiya sutta of the DN.

Of the remaining suttas it does not seem possible to assert anything except that sutta 20 gives the impression of earliness—for its "Inda" is the most venerable of gods; it develops a lively "upamā" (in the Pali sense) of "crossing the river" and concludes "āññāya atthaṃ paṭipajjamāno viññātadhammo so sukhaṃ labhethāti" (30.8).

Concluding table :

(*a*) *Early*	*Late*
The Aṭṭhakavg. (the 4 Aṭṭhakas appear earlier than the rest).	Suttas 27-28, 32-33, 37 (Vatthugāthās), and 38.
The Pārāyaṇavg. (minus the Vatthugāthās; Pārāyaṇa-sutta may also be late).	(Suttas 27-28 may be earlier than the rest).
(Suttas 1-3, 5, 12, 14, 22 and 24 appear early and may belong roughly to the same stratum as above).	Sutta 13 also appears late and may belong to the same stratum as above.

The rest uncertain.— (b) Suttas, 4, 7, 19, 30, 31 and 35 form a distinct class. Sutta 20 may be early.

Itivuttaka.—According to Watanabe[32] a collection of It, translated by Yüan Chwang about 650 A.D. exists in the Chinese Tripiṭaka. The scheme of its contents is indicated thus:—

I. Ekadharmakhaṇḍa	1.	sūtras	1—12
	2.	,,	13—24
	3.	,,	25—47
	4.	,,	48—60
II. Dvidharmakhaṇḍa	1.	sūtras	1—12
	2.	,,	13—24
	3.	,,	25—36
	4.	,,	37—50

[32] JPTS 1906; pp. 44-49.

III. Tridharmakhaṇḍa	1.	sūtras	1–13
	2.	,,	14–25
	3.	,,	26–28

The Pali scheme, on the other hand, may be represented thus:—

I. Ekakanipāto	1.	Pāṭibhogavaggo	suttas	1–10
	2.	Dutiya°		11–20
	3.	Tatiya°		21–27
II. Duka°	1.	Paṭhamo vaggo		28–37
	2.	Dutiyo°		38–49
III. Tika°	1.	Paṭhama°		50–59
	2.	Dutiya°		60–69
	3.	Tatiya°		70–79
	4.	Catuttha°		80–89
	5.	Pañcama°		90–99
IV. Catukka°				100–112

Fourth Nip. of doubtful authenticity.—The most striking difference is the absence of the 4th Nip. in the Chinese. It is noteworthy in this connection that at least four suttas of this Nipāta occur identically in the AN also—sutta 101=A.4.27; s. 105=Ib. 9; s. 108=Ib. 26; s. 111=Ib. 12. Furthermore, sutta 100 repeats after the third sentence the prose of sutta 98 which seems to have been suggested merely by word consonance. Sutta 102 in its prose portion describes the formula of the Four Truths, and its verses seem to distinguish three stages in the highest spiritual release—Āsavakhaya accompanied by Vimuttiñāṇa.[33]

It is, however, not unambiguous in its expression (shall we read the fourth line after the first?).[34] Sutta 103 has the same theme. Its last verse seems to distinguish between Cetovimutti and Paññā.° The next sutta instead of the earlier triad of Sīla, Samādhi and

[33] Cf. Mrs. Rhys Davids, Ind. Psy., p. 264.

[34] Cf. the similar and more coherent version in the verses of sutta 62. Have we a garbled borrowing in sutta 102?

Paññā, has the pentad of these plus Vimutti and° ñāṇa-dassaṇa, which is the scheme that occurs as a rule in the last books of the AN. The verses in sutta 105 seem to have been taken over from the sutta 15—they harmonize much more with the spirit and diction of the prose there. Sutta 109 presupposes considerable dogmatic development: it considers the 6 Ajjahttika—āyatanas and the 5 'Orambhāgiya-saṃyojanas' and well-known technicalties. Sutta 111 appears to use "khandha" in the later technical sense of the five Khandhas. The next sutta adds to Diṭṭha, suta, muta, and Viññāta, three other terms viz. Patta, Pariyesita, and Anuvicarita.

It appears, thus, that the fourth Nipāta is, as a whole, not only doctrinally more advanced than the rest of the It, but also partly depends in its composition on the preceding suttas and the AN. This taken in conjunction with its total non-appearance in the Chinese It. certainly points to it as having the character of a later addition.

The Third Nip.—Another point that emerges from the tables given above is the very regular and schematic arrangement of the suttas in the Pali Tika Nipāta. Now Watanabe informs us that whereas the Pali suttas of the first two Nipāta are almost all found in the Chinese, three fifths of those of the third are not.[35] Against this, of course, it has to be remembered that the third part of the Chinese is apparently defective since the regular "uddāna" fails to occur at its end, and also that the Chinese version of the suttas is in general more elaborate than the Pali one and appears later.

The internal evidence of the Pali version does not throw any certain light on the "stratigraphical" position

[35] loc. cit.

of the 3rd Nipāta. Its first two vaggas are, however, on the average, considerably shorter than those of the next two vaggas. Also, the prose in suttas 50-67 follows the same mode of enunciation, which strengthens the general impression of their closer unity.[36] Further, some, at least, of the suttas of the last two vaggas of the 3rd Nip. may with some certainty be regarded "late". Suttas 70 and 71 treat the theme of 64-65 in greater detail. Sutta 73 seems to take sutta 51 for its starting point. Sutta 74 speaks of the "Three Refuges". Suttas 82-83 describe the occasions on which the gods shout (Devasaddo niccharati). Sutta 90 advocates faith in the "Trinity" and speaks technically of "Yadidaṃ cattāri Purisayugāni aṭṭha purisapuggalā."

It is thus likely that the third Nipāta has earlier and later elements, the latter being principally represented in the last two vaggas.

The first two Nip.—The suttas of the first two Nipātas belong, in general, to the same stratum. The suttas 1-6 resemble each other obviously in prose and in verse so closely that they must be considered for all purposes a single group. They use "Anāgāmitā" in its general "pre-technical" meaning, and employ such forms as luddhāse, duṭṭhāse, mūlhāse, which are extremely rare in the It. This suggests that this is a very early group.

The suttas 7-13 are indistinguishable from the previous group as far as the verse portion is concerned. The prose has a different form but one which is common within this group. The next two suttas belong to the earliest ideological stratum. The former equates

---

[36] The prose and verse portions of the sutta 63 have nothing in common.

—Nīvaraṇa=Avijjā=Moha=Saṃsārahetu. It uses Nīvaraṇa pre-technically, and represents the earliest form of the Paṭiccasamuppāda. The latter sutta pictures man (Puriso) as wandering through the worlds—through this station and that (Itthabhāvaññathābhāva) accompanied by his Thirst alone. The two suttas are similar in form and complementary in content.

The suttas 16-17 are obviously a unity, the one dealing with the best internal and the other with the best external means of spiritual progress. The former describes the supreme goal as Anuttara yogakkhema and Uttamattha.

The demarcation of the 3rd vagga of Nip. 1 from the 2nd is just as arbitrary as that of the 2nd from the 1st. In either case the last and the first suttas are closely interdependent. It is likely that these divisions which follow no other principle than that of grouping ten suttas together are later introductions.

The prose of sutta 22 in which Buddha grandiloquently recounts his previous divine births is possibly later than the verse where we have Dāna, Samacariyā and Mettacitta for the Dāna, Dama, and Saṃyama of the prose. The difference is considerable.

Sutta 23 advocates Appamāda as the sole means to Atthābhisamaya, both diṭṭhadhammika and samparāyika. This has suggestions of earliness. The next sutta, on the other hand, belongs ideologically to exactly the same stage of development as the Ratana sutta of the Sn.

Sutta 25 (Sampajānamusāvāda) may have formed the original for the first part of the Cūḷarāhulovāda of the MN.

In sutta 27 (Mettabhāva°) it is noticeable that of the similes adduced only the first really fits in. The point to be illustrated is how "opadhikāni puññakiriyāvatthūni—mettāya cetovimuttiyā kalaṃ nāgghanti solasiṃ." The first simile is the transparent and very natural one of the stars and the moon. The second is "just as the autumn sun shines forth, dispelling all darkness from the sky." The relation between a lesser and higher virtue is, however, not that of darkness and light. The third simile speaks of the "osadhitārakā" shining in the morning, and has no reference whatever to any counterpart, similar or dissimilar. Again, if the following verses have any authentic reference to a simile, it is to the first one only. It is thus obvious that there has been a later addition to the prose text. Of such forced additions there are other examples in the Nikāyas.

In the second Nipāta the verse portions of the suttas 30-31 are less tolerant and more dogmatic than the corresponding prose.

The verse in sutta 38 has two distinct and unconnected divisions; the second occurs in MN and is more relevant there.

In sutta 43 the verse has six lines arranged in two groups of three each, and since each consists of eight syllables the metre may be supposed to be a variety of Gāyatrī. Ideologically also it leaves no doubt of the positive connotation of "Nirodha" which is described as "Santaṃ atakkāvacaraṃ dhuvaṃ ajātaṃ asamuppannaṃ asokaṃ virajaṃ padaṃ (then, nirodho dukkhadhammānaṃ saṅkhārūpasamo sukhoti)." In sutta 44 there seems to be a difference between the idea of the prose and of the verse. Both distinguish between Sa-upādisesa and Anupādisesa Nibbānadhātu but according to the former the second also appears attainable during life: "Tassa *idheva*—sabbavedayitāni anabhinanditāni sītibhavissanti ayaṃ vuccati......anupādisesā nibbānadhātu," while according to the latter "Anupādisesā pana samparāyikā yaṃhi nirujjhanti bhavāni sabbaso" (which is to be considered in contrast with the previous line: Ekā hi dhātuidha ditthadhammika saupādhisesā bhavanettisaṅkhaye)." According to the prose the distinction between the two Nibbutas lies in the fact that after Anupādisesa, experience is freed from all hedonic tone. This appears the earlier version since the view advanced in the verse is the one that became standard later. The earliness of the prose is also suggested by the fact that it speaks categorically of just five and not six senses.

Conclusion.—The It. thus reveals at least two, if not three strata, of which the earliest is represented principally in the first two and a half Nipātas and the latest in the fourth.

Udana.—Winternitz points out that the utterances are, "as a rule, older than the narratives into which they are inserted......"[37] The stories contained in many of the suttas are very simple and sometimes even inappropriate "to the pathos of the utterances themselves."[37] This appears quite correct, and what is more, not only do the verses and the prose introductions form two distinct but also the only two distinguishable strata within the Ud. The verses are in style and ideas quite homogeneous and show many signs of earliness. Metrical irregularities are not uncommon but they only strengthen the impression of antiquity. At places archaic forms occur but they are very rare:—Esāno 13.1; lapetave 21.1; sutvāna 38.1; and laddhāna 50.1. The language is, on the whole simple, clear, fluent and not without a

[37] Op. cit. II. pp. 85-86.

certain force. It is reminiscent of the Dhp. rather than of the Sn.

Of technicalities and formulae the verses are quite innocent, and yet they are, in most cases, more than merely moral or ascetic exhortations of a general character. They are, on the whole, distinctly Buddhist, but seem to belong to a pre-scholastic stage.

The prose introductions, on the other hand, serve generally the commentarial purpose of indicating the occasion of the particular udāna. In some cases the prose narrative has the flimsiest of connections with the following verse and in certain others none. Besides, in a few instances their lateness is manifest from their contents. The probably genuine and early prose is extremely rare.

The wholly mechanical arrangement of the Ud. contra-indicates a historical growth as among the various vaggas.

Vg. 1.—The first or 'Bodhivaggo' can be much more suitably named the 'Brāhmaṇavaggo' as nearly all the verses contain "Brāhmaṇa" as the vital word in them. In the prose introductions to the first three suttas, which also occur in the Mahāvagga (Vin.), the full formula, of the Paṭiccasamuppāda is concisely stated in both forms (the general and the detailed) and orders ('anuloma' and 'viloma'). The final verses are, on the other hand, of a much more general character. They simply speak of "Dhammapātubhāva."[38] Suttas 4-9 are concerned with the true conception of "Brāhmaṇa" and in every case the prose appears to be the result of ad hoc invention. In sutta 10 the prose has as much independence as the verse, but they are connected all the same. The

[38] See below.

former beside the interesting narrative has a short and rather obscure sermon. It becomes, however, intelligible if placed by the side of the more explicit first sermon of the MN. The first line of the verse occurs in the DN and the following two lines resemble very strongly Kaṭh.[39] Besides, there is a homily on these verses contained within the Ud. itself (sutta 71). These are undoubtedly very ancient.

Vg. 2.—The next vagga (Mucalindavagga) is better renamed "Sukhavagga" since all the verses in it are concerned with contrasting worldly and non-worldly happiness. In the first two suttas the prose has little relevancy to the verse, and in the next two ones it is ad hoc. In the following two suttas two different incidents are narrated to lead to the same moral contained in the final verse (the first line of which differs in form in the two suttas). In the other suttas of the vagga also, except shtta 18, and perhaps s. 20 (cf. v.7.1.) the prose has the general appearance of having been built upon the verse. In sutta 18, however, it dominates and the verse is of the nature of a short and pointed moral following from it.

Vg. 3.—In vagga 3 the verse of the first sutta has a very archaic appearance—it uses the form "lapetave" and its dhunamānassa purekataṃ rajaṃ" reflects the same idea as the "Dhona" of the Duṭṭhaṭṭhaka in the Sn. The expression "Sabbakammajaha" too is uncommon, and accords more with the Jinist than with the Buddhist emphasis. Whereas the verses of the suttas 22-24 vary but little, the corresponding prose narratives have little in common. The case is similar with the suttas 27-28.[40] In sutta 29 the expression Asippajīvī in the verse occa-

[39] Kaṭh 5-15.

[40] On sutta 27 see Winternitz II. p. 86.

sions a long list of the industries in the prose. In sutta 30 the form of metrical construction is quite unusual; and, more important, it speaks of only two "taṇhās", bhava-and vibhava°, instead of the usual three.

Vg. 4.—In the fourth vagga, the first sutta has a relatively long prose sermon employing the Aṅguttara form and connected but little with the final verses. The prose of sutta 34 illustrates the verse at the end by means of a very fanciful narrative. In the next sutta the verse may well have formed an original part of the prose. The same relation is possible in sutta 38, which relates the well known story of the Paribbājikā Sundarī. Sutta 40 appears a variant of the preceding sutta; its verse portion is a part of that of the latter, and the prose is brief and non-descript.

Vg. 5.—In vagga 5, the first sutta forms an integral whole and recurs in SNI. Its view of Attā as the dearest is reminiscent of Bṛ. up. The next two suttas belong to the other end of the scale, and presuppose a well developed Buddhology—the former describes how the mothers of the Boddhisattas must be shortlived, and the latter recounts an event contemporaneous with the Paccekabuddha Tagarasikhin. The very long sutta 45 has by way of verse two brief lines at the end, couched in metaphorical language and wholly irrelevant to what precedes. The prose details the eight miraculous qualities of the ocean and the Dhammavinaya.

Sutta 46 has already been considered in its various versions.[41] It is plainly later than the collection of the sixteen Aṭṭhakavaggikas, and yet belongs, as Lévi has pointed out, to the earlier rather than the later parts of the canon. In sutta 48 a story relating Devadatta's

[41] In connection with Sn.

schism has been prefixed to a verse which just states that it is easy for the good to do good and vice versa.

Vg. 6.—Of vagga 6, the first sutta recurs in the Mahāparinibbānasutta. It depicts Buddha as a vain magician who resorts to oblique hints in order to be requested to live longer. The next sutta partly occurs in SN I. pp. 77-9. The verse it has at the end is quite irrelevant to the preceding prose. The sutta which follows is an organic whole and contains the famous parable of the blind men and the elephant. It expresses Buddha's opposition to Ekaṃsavāda so well, correlating it with his Abyākatavāda, that it is difficult to resist considering it as old as Buddha himself. It stands on the same level as the parable of the poisoned arrow,[42] to which it is a valuable supplement.

The list of the Diṭṭhis mentioned in sutta 54 is extended in the next two suttas, which have an identical prose prefaced to variant verses. Sutta 59 is a typical instance of the ad hoc prose (see Winternitz, loc. cit.) Sutta 63 of the next vagga offers another equally patent instance. So does sutta 64. Sutta 67 is even less convincing. The author of the prose of sutta 69 seems to have grossly misunderstood the final verse, which intends "water" in no more than a merely figurative sense. Sutta 70 is a flagrant instance of the prose-verse unconnectedness.

In suttas 71-74 the introductions are negligibly brief and nondescript. In sutta 71 there is no verse; instead, there is a short prose homily on the final verse of sutta 10.[43] The suttas 73-74 too have no verse, the

---

[42] MN. Cūḷamāluṅkyaputta°.

[43] Winternitz (loc. cit.).

central text of the one occurring in it, and of the other in MN.[44]

The Cunda-sutta, which recurs in DN.s.16, contains the "unorthodox" report of Buddha's partaking of "sūkaramaddava" at the place of Cunda. The two verses beginning "Cundassa bhattaṃ bhuñjitvā etc." belong to the earliest stage of that genre which culminated in Aśvaghoṣa's Buḍdhacarita. The next sutta also forms part of DN.s.16, but beside the prophecy about the future of Pāṭaliputta it contains the miracle of crossing the river Gaṅgā; and both these, especially the latter, must be considered of dubious authenticity.

The identical prose preface to the suttas 79-80 is clearly based on the final verses, which however must be understood with reference to the similar utterances in the Pārāyaṇa vagga of the Sn.

Conclusion.—The verses of the Ud. thus represent a homogeneous early stratum while the prose is for the greater part later, and more heterogeneous.

[44] Sutta 144.

CHAPTER IV

EARLY AND LATE IN THE DĪGHA-NIKĀYA

Dirghagama and Dighanikaya.—The Chinese Dīrghāgama (No. 545 of Nanjio's Catalogue) contains thirty sūtras instead of the thirty four of Pali. After a comparison of these, Nanjio concludes that six of the former collection "seem not to be given in the Pali text, or at least with different titles."[1] These are: (5) on the four castes'; (11) 'on the Ekottara (dharma)'; (12) 'On the Trirāśi (Dharma)'; (15) 'on (the city) ö-tho-i-(?)'; (17) 'on the pureness (of practice)'; (30) 'on the record of the world.' On the other hand, the following ten suttas are missing in No. 545 (Dirghāgama): (6) Mahāli°; (7) Jāliya°; (10) Subha°; (17) Mahāsudassana° (but found in the Madhyamāgama);[2] (22) Mahāsatipaṭṭhāna°; (24) Pāṭika°; (27) Aggañña°; (29) Pāsādika° (30) Lakkhaṇa°; (32) Āṭānāṭiya°.

Nanjio, however, adds that on a minuter comparison some of these may still be found.

Now, according to Rāhula Sāṅkṛtyāyana[3] sūtra 5 of the Chinese corresponds to the Pali Aggañña, sūtra 15 to the Pāṭika, and sūtra 17 to the Pāsādika° and, from the other side, No. 22 of Pali is supposed to correspond to No. 98 of the Madhyamāgama; and No. 30 of DN to No. 59 of the latter collection (i.e., MĀ). Nanjio gives the title of this No. 59 as "on the thirtytwo characteristic

[1] Catalogue Column 137.

[2] Acc. to Anesaki—"The Mahāsudassana is incorporated entire in the Mahāparinibbāna à propos of the reference to the Sudassana story in the M.P.s. 5. 42." (JRAS 1901 p. 896)

[3] Intr. to the Hindi tr. of the DN. (Published Sarnath, 1936)

marks," and that appears to confirm this last identification.

According to Lévi[4] also Dīgha No. 29=Dīrgha Ā.17. Further, he proposes to equate one of the "grands sūtras" listed in the Sarvāstivādavinaya with the Mahāli° and Jāliya° of Pali. Moreover, according to him, though the Āṭānāṭiya is not found in the Dīrghāgama it must have formed a part of the Sanskrit collection as it is reckoned in the "grands sūtras" in the middle of the sūtras of the Dīrghāgama.[5]

Of the three sūtras of the Dīrghā°, untraced in Pali none it seems can be very early. Nos. 11-12 follow the Saṅgīti° and the Daśottara° and their titles also indicate their Aṅguttara form. As to No. 30, it appears from Nanjio's description to treat of cosmography and cosmogony in twelve chapters!

Thus all the suttas of the Pali Dīgha can be evidenced in the Āgamas, though not necessarily in the Dīrgha—That only suggests the conclusion that the division between the DN and the MN was not a watertight one, which is very plausible otherwise also. These two collections appear to have been made out of a not very dissimilar material along the rough test of the size of the suttas. Consequently a certain difference of opinion between the sects as to the exact position to be assigned to a particular sutta in this or that collection is easily intelligible.[6]

The order of Suttas in D.A. and D.N.—The difference in the order of the suttas that the Pali and the

---

[4] J.A. 1915, Mai-Juin. 421ff.

[5] Ib.

[6] Cf. the accusation levelled against the mahāsaṅghikas by the Mahāvamsa: p. 28f.

Chinese collections show within particular collections is however more serious.

According to Franke[7] the order of the Chinese Dīrghāgama almost suggests a deliberate attempt to remove the appearance of similar words and thoughts in the neighbouring suttas. He is inclined to attribute greater originality to the Pali than to the Chinese order, and advances the plausible argument that the latter makes 'Brahmajāla' the 21st sutta while in the Saṅgītisutta of the Cv, according to both the Pāli and the Dharmagupta canons, (Oldenberg Z. D.M.G. Vol. 52 653) it is represented as the first. It may be added that the testimony of the Dharmagupta canon is of particular value since the translator of the Dīrghāgama—Buddhayaśas—is also the translator of the Dharmaguptavinaya (Nanjio 1117) and the Dharmaguptaprātimokṣa (N.115g) beside that of the Ākāśagarbhabodhisattvasūtra (N. 68). If then the original of the Chinese Dīrgha too belonged to the Dharmagupta sect,[8] its present order is all the more discredited.

The order of the Pali sutta-groups seems to show roughly the historical phenomenon of later writings being added to earlier ones since the third and second books of the Pali DN are on the whole recognizably later than the first one.[9] Now, in the Chinese collection apart from the fourth varga which contains a single long cosmological sūtra in twelve sub-chapters and appears apocryphal, the first two vargas seem to have, on the whole, later material than the third. And the reason is that the first vagga of the Pali DN corresponds strongly to

[7] ZDMG 1913 (409f).

[8] Cf. Rāhula Sānkṛtyāyana, loc. cit.

[9] See Bapat's analysis already ref. to above; and Winternitz, II, p. 35.

the 3rd Vagga of the Chinese. All the ten sūtras of the latter are found in the former, the three extra suttas of which are absent from the whole of the Chinese DĀ. The order of the sūtras within the varga is, however, very different in the two. The Chinese order is much less intelligible than the Pali one. It breaks, for instance, the obvious sequence of the Ambaṭṭha, Soṇadaṇḍa and Kūṭadanta-suttas by the arbitrary interpolation of the Brahmajāla. The first and second vargas of the Chinese, on the other hand, show much less community with the 2nd and 3rd vargas of Pali, if taken separately. Chinese I contains only four suttas, whereas Pali II has ten, though it is noticeable that all the four of the former collection are out of the ten of the latter. One other interesting feature is that there are in these two vargas four groups of adjacent suttas such that they are adjacent in Pali also. These are Chinese 3-4; Pali 19-18: Chinese 5-6. Pali 27-26: Chinese 17-18; Pali 29-28: Chinese 9-10: Pali 33-34. The reversal in order in the case of the first three groups may be noted.

The relative solidarity of that group of suttas which forms the first book of the Pali collection is also apparent in the Chinese version, which seems to have preferred to add to them by placing the other suttas before rather than after them.

This division of the DN into two literary strata, however, does not carry us very far because of important exceptions and also because of the pervasive editorial activity which the collection evidences. Besides, the accurate formulation of comprehensively valid strata is impossible so long as the analysis in detail of particular suttas and doctrines is not carried much beyond the stage in which at present it rests.

Sutta 1: its late features.—The very first sutta makes the difficulties in the way of a clear-cut stratification apparent: it is a long and unitary composition, full of repetitions. It elaborately enumerates in a systematic manner sixty two speculative theses (Vatthus). The formular expressions appear long fossilized. Many of them recur identically in other parts of the canon. The Buddhists have here developed cosmological speculations of their own, which are in the same state as in the Pāṭika-suttanta. Further, the majjhima° and mahāsīlas are clearly inflated forms of the cūla°. The "eel-wrigglers", it is possible, have been made to vascillate over more problems than they ever knew: the list of these problems appears to have attained its present length through the mechanical addition of further items taken over from other contexts.

Contra-Indications.—But jostling by the side of these late features there are contra-indications too. The Brahmajāla, along with the Sāmaññaphala, is one of the two suttas which are explicitly mentioned in the canonical tradition of the first council.[10] It was separately translated into Chinese even before the full Dīrghāgama had been so rendered (Nanjio on 554). According to Watanabe "it (d. 554) corresponds with slight differences to the Pali Brahmajāla".[11] This shows the great repute in which the sutta was held. It makes not the slightest mention of the five khandhas or the Anatta doctrine, or even the Bodhipakkhiya dhammas. Above all, it represents the Paṭiccasamuppāda, not in its standard but in one of the earlier forms.[12] Its vehe-

[10] Vin II. p. 287.

[11] Quoted by Poussin in JRAS 1903, p. 583.

[12] See infra.

mence against holding to any speculation (Diṭṭhi) is reminiscent of the four Aṭṭhakas in the Sn, as also the expression—"Taṇhāgatānaṃ paritassitavipphanditameva" (e.g. DN.I. p. 48 Nāg. ed.; cf. Sn. sutta 49.v.5 "Passāmi loke pariphandamānaṃ pajaṃ imaṃ taṇhāgataṃ bhavesu"). Finally, many of the speculations detailed here are quite primitive and do seem to go back to very early times.

Conclusion—A late composition out of early material.—It appears thus that we have here a case not dissimilar to that of the First Sermon. In its present form it is a late composition, but it has been compiled out of ancient material. Diverse reports about the heresies in the times of the Master and condemned by him have been reduced to a single systematic and formular shape. That the previous variant versions disappeared after this standardisation is hardly to be wondered at. In this context it is significant to note that the sutta calls itself at the end a "veyyākaraṇa". It is a scholastic exposition, no doubt, but based on much older traditions.

Sutta 2—The various versions.—The second of the suttas mentioned explicitly in the conciliar tradition already referred to, was also translated into Chinese independently as well of the Dīrghāgama.[13] From a perusal of the English rendering of part of these in an appendix to Rockhill's Life of the Buddha (pp. 255-259) it appears that these show a confusion of names, which is comparable to that in similar reports in the Aṅguttara.[14] As to the Tibetan version in the Dulva, Rockhill states that it is very similar to the Pali sutta; only it looks

[13] See Nanjio............593.

[14] See below, Chap. on AN. Thomas-Life—p. 130; cf. P. V. Bapat—The Śrāmaṇyaphala Sūtra and its different Versions in Buddhist Literature—IC 1947, pp. 107ff.

much confused on doctrinal points.[15] This growth of confusion about the names of the rival teachers contemporaneous with Buddha, which is evidenced not only in the Chinese and Tibetan translations but also within the Pali Nikāya itself (e.g., in the AN), seems to have resulted from the indifference of latter-day monks to the merely historical data contained in the reports of the "Diṭṭhis". It may be this tendency which cuts out all such encumbrances from the Brahmajālasutta, and, instead, treats us with a merely logically constructed "net" of sixty-two "views".

Early features of the Sutta.—All this goes to enhance the impression of antiquity made by the Sāmaññaphala°, which is not only clearest in this respect, but in which the enumeration of the heresies follows organically from a context reminiscent of Bṛ. IV. I. Oldenberg's suggestion of an imitation here of the Upaniṣadic setting[16] is quite unwarranted. The situation described in the Pali sutta could well have resulted as naturally from the multiplicity of contemporary teachers plus the philosophical interest that king Ajātasattu is reported in the sutta to have had, as the one in the Upaniṣad did from the similar interest of Janaka in a not very dissimilar atmosphere of thought-ferment. Since there seems to be no reason to doubt this obvious explanation of the partial resemblance in form of the two texts, a resort to the hypothesis of literary borrowing is hard to justify.

Both the sections of the sutta—that relating to heretical doctrines and that to the "Sāmaññaphalas"—recur in identical formulation at many other places in the

[15] See Rockhill, op. cit., pp. 95-106.

[16] Quoted Winternitz, II, p. 37 fn. 2. Prof. Bapat conclusively establishes the authenticity of the historical setting of the Sāmaññaphala sutta (see IC, loc. cit.).

canon, especially the second, which occurs in all the subsequent suttas except the last one of the first vagga of the DN. From this we cannot, indeed, conclude that the whole of that vagga forms a single stratum,[17] although it certainly does emerge that suttas 3-12 of the DN in their present form presuppose the prior existence of the Sāmaññaphala°. It is, of course, not impossible that there once existed independently a text containing only the list of the "Sāmaññaphalas" to which the present sutta of that title and the other suttas mentioned above are equally indebted. But there is no direct evidence whatever to support this supposition.

The leading emphasis of the sutta is on the practice of spiritual life, though it contains incidentally a good deal pertaining to theoretical beliefs. Man is conceived as a complex of 'Kāya' and 'Viññāṇa'.[18] This represents a perceptibly earlier stage of analysis than the doctrine of the Five Khandhas, of which there is no mention here. It will be incorrect to suppose that there is no occasion for mentioning that doctrine, since, according to the context just referred to, the Bhikkhu, after he has attained to mental purity and quietude, proceeds to the attainment of 'Knowledge-vision' (Ñāṇa-dassana) and thus realizes his own nature as kāya-cum-viññāṇa, and, now, if the doctrine of the five khandhas were the ruling dogma about the nature of man, this opportunity should clearly have been availed of in order to mention it. The omission becomes all the more glaring if we remember that the enthusiasm of those who held the theory of the Five Khandhas was for some time so great that they insisted upon introducing it even where the

[17] Cf. Bapat. ABORI 1926, p. 4.
[18] See DN. I, pp. 87-88 (Nāgari ed.).

excuse for doing so was slight. Besides, between the view of man as Kāya-plus-Viññāṇa and the view of him as a complex of the Five Khandhas in its standard interpretation there is a clear gulf fixed by the difference in the meaning of viññāṇa. In the former it is "consciousness as individualized through embodiment", in the latter it is 'perception regarded as one of the four aspects of empirical consciousness.' This reflects not only increased psychological analysis but also a changed epistemological standpoint.

In form also the sutta shows early traits: it is a dialogue containing a sermon enlivened by "similes" (Pali-upamā) and free from exaggeration. It is true that it describes the Four Jhānas in a formular and schematic form, but it has to be remembered that the doctrine of 'Jhāna' probably belonged to the original mandate itself and consequently must have engaged the attention of system-makers very early. Besides, within the four prose Nikāyas, at any rate, an earlier stage of this doctrine is hardly to be found. The same remarks apply to the formula of the three vijjās although it must be remembered that the present sutta does not contain the exact formula.

Some late features.—Moreover the sutta as it is cannot be considered quite free from "interpolation". Like the preceding sutta it contains the lengthy threefold "Moralities", and these, it has been suggested by Rhys Davids, formed once an independent text. Our present sutta perhaps contained originally a reference to the 'Cūḷasīla' alone which may have been later replaced by its amplified version.

Para 83 of the sutta (in the Nāgari ed., para 99 of the PTS ed.) contains a conventionalized phraseology in which the convert-to-be expresses his reaction to the sermon and the desire to betake himself to the Three Refuges. As to when this formula came into existence it is difficult to pronounce with any degree of certainty, but it appears likely that when it did, it was added on to previously existing suttas as a convenient finish.

Finally, the description of 'Āsavakhaya' is suspect. The simile that follows illustrates the attainment of discrimination between a 'pure' principle and impurities really external to it. This resembles the picture of Sāṅkhya 'Prasaṅkhyāna'. The actual description, on the other hand, only speaks of the knowledge of the Four Truths (which are repeated with the substitution of "Āsava" for 'dukkha') and of the consequent emancipation from the Āsavas. Of any discriminative insight in the sense indicated above there is no talk. It appears therefore that the repetitive section of the Four Truths has usurped the place of the original reference to the dawn of Paññā or Vijjā. That there was such a reference is also supported by the fact that DN. s. 8. subsumes the last 'Sāmaññaphala' in the Paññāsampadā. Suttas 3 and 4 subsume it under Vijjā and Paññā respectively. It., (Sutta) 99 also speaks of "Puna ca paraṃ—Bhikkhu āsavānaṃ Khayā anāsavaṃ cetovimuttiṃ paññāvimuttiṃ diṭṭhéva dhamme sayaṃ abhiññāya sacchikatvā upasampajja viharati* ayamassa tatiyā vijjā adhigatā hoti avijjā vihatā vijjā uppannā tamo vihato āloko uppanno. . . ." At many other places also there is reference to the three vijjās, with the last sāmaññaphala as the third 'vijjā'. Further the conception of 'Āsava' as threefold is not its earliest conception. Nor was avijjā at first regarded as

*This occurs in DN. 6 also (DN. Pt. I. P. 181 Nāg. ed.).

merely one-third of the whole evil This also argues against the earliness of para 81 (Nāgari ed.=para 97 of the PTS ed.).

Sutta 3-5.—Suttas 3-5 are closely interconnected in subject and style, and all presuppose the sāmaññaphala.° They are long unitary compositions and full of anti-Brahmanic polemic. Compared to the similarly purposed suttas in SN I and Sn, they are more developed, being longer, more aggressive and more dialectical. In the first (i.e., D.N. 2) the theory of the Thirty-two Marks is well-established. There is supernatural intervention in favour of Buddha who himself displays miraculous powers in order to convince a Brāhmaṇa about the two Marks not visible normally from the outside. The 'sāmaññaphalas' are divided into 'caraṇa' and 'vijjā. This corresponds to the 'sīla-paññā' dichotomy of the next sutta.

DN. 4 speaks only of the "Lokāyatamahāpurisalakkhaṇas" while there is no reference to the number 32. The next sutta is in this respect similar. Unlike the preceding two, however, it is directed not against caste but against sacrifice, and it achieves its purpose not through disputation but through offering a figurative and ethical reinterpretation of the idea of sacrifice, taking the aid of a Jātaka-like tale in doing so.

Of the three suttas, thus only the second (DN. 4) is free from miracle and myth; it is likewise the most logical. Since, however, the correlation between the growth of the miraculous, of the Jātaka-form and of 'dialectics' among the early Buddhists is as yet a quite uncertain subject, it is impossible to attempt a minuter stratification as between these three suttas.

DN. 6.—DN. 6 describes the true purpose of "Brahmacariya" as "Cetovimutti-Paññā°", and not the attainment of miraculous powers. This sounds an early note. The use of "opapātika" for "anāgāmin" is concordant with it, though the use of the expression "three Fetters (saṃyojanas)" as if it were a well known technicality indicates that we are not dealing with a text belonging to the earliest stratum. This is confirmed by the bare enumeration of the eightfold way. It occurs at a place where the "sāmaññaphala" series might have been expected. Both serve the same purpose of grouping together spiritually helpful practices, though the latter considers them primarily as means to progressive ends. It is not suggested that the formula of the 'Eightfold Path' has here ousted an original reference to the "Sāmaññaphalas" though that is not impossible—but only that unlike the latter the antiquity of the former is dubious. It appears to be one of the many attempted systematizations of the more or less general directions of Buddha relating to the Way.

Jaliya Sutta.—To DN. 6 is tacked on at the end, the Jāliya sutta without any relevancy whatever. And this other sutta itself suffers from confusion. Instead of answering the problem raised by Jāliya, Buddha is made to digress into the "Sāmaññaphala" text, thus very aptly illustrating himself, as it were, the gibe of Ajātasattu "Ambaṃvā puṭṭho labujaṃ vyākareyya" (DN. 2)!

The original continuation appears to have been lost. Can it be recovered elsewhere in the canon? It is worth recollecting here that the present sutta is one of the few not traceable in the Chinese Dīrghāgama.

Sutta 8.—In sutta 8 Buddha refutes the charge of condemning all asceticism, of which he explains his own conception; the cultivation of friendliness (mettacittaṃ) and the attainment of Freedom (cetovimutti, Paññā°). It is noteworthy that almost throughout DN. I. the talk is of Vimutti and not Nirodha. At this point Acelakassapa (Buddha's addressee) asks him to explain the three "Sampadā" and so we have the sāmaññaphala text repeated. The following two paragraphs appear to have been suggested by paras 6—12 (both in the Nāgari and PTS eds). That they portray Buddha as very vainglorious is a further argument for their lateness. Finally, it may be noticed that this sutta mentions both the Eightfold Path as well as the Sāmaññaphala series, which is not divided into three grades-sīla°, citta°, and Paññā-sampadās.

DN. 9.—Composite.—DN. 9 is a lengthy patchwork showing at least two clear strata. The first belongs to the stage of the Sāmaññaphalasutta. The second adds to it three "arūpa-vimokkhas". (The treatment of this very topic of "Anupubbanirodha" is still more elaborate in AN.). It appears that this section was added on to an already existing sutta, for that will also explain the addition of para 22, which goes beyond the stage of thought reflected in the sāmaññaphala°, and that in this way: the first version of the sutta contained reference to the Olārika° and Manomaya Attās only—as is the case in the Sāmāññaphala°. With the inclusion and growth of the prestige of the "arūpavimokkhas" (the two very highest of which Buddha is reported to have turned down as useless during his "quest") in the Buddhist fold, the conception of the "arūpī saññāmaya Attā" also became important. The later

---

* Unless otherwise stated the ref. for the first two volumes of DN. is to the Nāgarī ed.

redactor, who was familiar with it, finding it missing in the older sutta interpolated it and furnished the answer of the corresponding query by a mechanical adaptation of the answer in the previous two paras. The sutta according to all expectations should end in para 31 (Nāg. ed.) where not only is the sermon ended but the chief addressee is also satisfied. It is continued, however, partly as a zealot's reaction to the disrespect shown to Buddha by the Paribbājakas in the preceding para and partly as an attempt to meet their objections better—Buddha had only said that he did not answer certain problems because they were irrelevant to spiritual perfection. That, however, is no satisfactory answer to one who wants to know just those very problems. The answer now added is that they are indeterminate (Anekaṃsika), although indeterminacy is established by no better means than an appeal to the previous answer:—a proof of the lack of much originality in the redactor. It is not impssible that Buddha himself had given this answer at a different place, whence it has been adapted here.

Then follows a reconsideration of the whole problem of Attā. This section seems to use, however, two ancient upamās—that of the Janapadakalyānī,[19] ridiculing those who talked more than evidence warranted; and that of the transformation of milk, establishing an unchanging identity behind changing appearances. Now the drift of the second 'simile' is clearly "un-Buddhistic" and so we have the corrective—

"Iti imā kho citta lokasamaññā lokaniruttiyo lokavohārā° paññattiyo yāhi Tathāgato voharati aparāmasaṃti!"

---

[19] Occ. also in the Tevijja°.

DN. 10.– DN. 10 is explicitly later than the death of Buddha. Ānanda arranges the Sāmaññaphala° under the three khandhas of Sīla, Samādhi and Paññā. This further analysis of the Sāmaññaph° may suggest the relative lateness of the sutta.

"Confusion" in D.N. 11.–D. N. 11. is actually composed of two independent suttas. The junction point is contained in para 13 (in PTS ed. 67). The "first" sutta (i.e., paras 1—12) explains Buddha's views on miracles. The extension of the connotation of the term "Pāṭihāriya" is comparable to the similar extension attempted with the terms "Brāhmaṇa", "Yañña", "Maṅgala", "Dāna", etc.

The abrupt transition to the next sutta is thus effected "Imāni kho kevaṭṭa tīṇi Pāṭihāriyāni mayā sayaṃ abhiññā sacchikatvā paveditāni Bhūtapubbaṃ Kevaṭṭa imasmiṇ yeva Bhikkhusaṅghe aññatarassa Bhikkhuno evaṃ cetaso parivitakko udapādi kattha nu kho ime cattāro mahābhūtā aparisesā nirujjhanti."[20]

This tacking on is similar to that in the Mahālisutta already referred to.

But whereas the whole of the first sub-sutta of DN. 11 belongs to the same early stratum, the second one consists of some very ancient verses at the end preceded by a late mythological preface (which describes an ascending hierarchy of fourteen classes of Buddhist gods) belonging to the class of "Tendenzschriften", its purpose being to make the gods confess their own inferiority to Buddha and themselves stress the folly of seeking refuge in anybody else except in him.

An examination of the final verses, moreover, shows that they too are not free from later addition. First we

[20] DN. I, p. 247 (Nāg. ed.).

have three lines of query[21] "Kattha āpo ca paṭhavī tejo vāyo na gādhati|
Kattha dīghañca rassañca aṇuṃ thūlaṃ subhāsubhaṃ
Kattha nāmañca rūpañca asesaṃ uparujjhati.||
Then follows the answer (Tatra veyyākaraṇaṃ bhavati): "Viññāṇaṃ anidassanaṃ anantaṃ sabbatopabhaṃ ettha āpo ca" etc. till "asesaṃ uparujjhati Viññāṇassa nirodhena etth'etaṃ uparujjhati."

The conception of Viññāṇa in the first of this second group of lines deserves to be noted; it is, so strongly reminiscent of the Upaniṣads. That in such a viññāṇa "Prapañcopaśama" should be sought, is easily intelligible. Now comes the last line which is not only unnecessary but flatly contradicts what precedes. And the situation is in no wise mitigated by the fact that the last line is in itself not late, since it occurs in verse 6 in the "Ajitamāṇavapucchā (Sn. Pārāyaṇavaggo).[22] There the meaning of Viññāṇa is different.[23] It is true that both these meanings of Viññāṇa—transcendental and phenomenal—are probably equally ancient. Buddha himself perhaps used the term ambiguously. But that the two usages should be juxtaposed in such a manner as to lead to the appearance of a flagrant contradiction is more than suspicious. The best ex-

[21] The transition from the prose to these is supplied in a manner that deserves to be noted. B. says that the question should not be asked in the manner in which it is done in the prose quotation above, but thus—as in the metrical lines that follow. One may pertinently ask: "Why? what is wrong with the prose formulation?" The only answer would seem to be: "Nothing. But the verses have to be brought in!"

[22] On Viññāṇa see below, where its two meanings are distinguished, and the explanation that Buddhaghosa offers to the present text is also considered.

[23] Cf. "Yattha nāmañca rūpañca asesamuparujjhati Taṃ te dhammaṃ idhaññāya acchiduṃ bhavabandhanaṃ." (SN. I. 35)

planation seems to be that the last line is a corrective appendix added by one for whom Viññāṇa had a purely phenomenal meaning.

DN. 12.—DN. 12 is a short lively dialogue with a "Socratic' turn. It reveals Buddha full of compassion for others and criticizing 'spiritual selfishness'. It mentions as well known technicalities the following:—The Sotāpattiphala, Sakadāgāmi, Anāgāmi and Arahatta. The use of "anāgāmin" suggests that it is later than DN. 6, which has "opapātika".

DN. 13—early.—DN. 13 is, barring repetitions, a medium-sized spirited dialogue, full of good-humoured irony and fittingly illustrated by upamās. Of these, that of the Janapadakalyāṇī has already occurred; the two new upamās are: of the river Aciravati and of the Andhaveṇī. The latter is placed among the "original" upamās by Mrs. Rhys Davids.[24]

The sutta draws a very vivid picture of Brāhmaṇic society and beliefs, just as we might expect these to have been in the 6th cent. B.C. Further, the character of Buddha stands out for its earnestness and independence of thought. He insists that Truth must be directly known, and declares a merely traditional belief quite inadequate.

Besides, the sutta is quite free from any late features. This strengthens the impression of earliness which it breathes in style and spirit.

It deserves notice that paras 6—7 (PTS ed., paras 9—10) suffer from some confusion. Buddha in para 6 asks his Brāhmaṇa visitors as to the point of their dispute. This is quite unnecessary in view of the fact that

---

[24]Sakya, p. 326.

the controversy has been already communicated to him in the previous para. Further, the next para (para 7) mentioning the diversity of ways propounded by the Brāhmaṇas asks if they all equally lead to salvation. So far right, but it now goes on to adduce an illustration *to prove that all ways do lead to the same end,* and then asserts as much explicitly. The Brāhmaṇas, thus, themselves answer their own problem, and in a way which might have been employed by Buddha himself! May it be suggested it was *Buddha* who pointed out that there could be more than one right way to the goal, although in fact there was not a single *Brāhmaṇic* way which could be called right? In the face of this common thrust the Brāhmaṇas would forget their mutual differences, thus leading to the discussion that follows.

As to the problem of the Peyyāla after para 75 (of the PTS ed.) there can be no doubt that that edition is in the wrong. For the correctness of the Burmese edition, the Nāgari ed. adduces convincing arguments (see DN. I, p. 283 fn Nāg ed.).

Second Vagga—Change of atmosphere (DN. 14).— With the very first sutta of the second Vagga a change in atmosphere is unmistakable. In DN. 14 the lives of the Buddhas follow an unvarying archetype; all their course is but the manifestation of eternal norms (Dhaṃmatā). Already the list of the Previous Buddhas has enlarged to six; and the thirty-two Marks of greatness are mentioned in detail. The title itself of the sutta "Mahāpadāna" suggests its lateness. The "apadānas" became a popular genre later on, but the very word, in this meaning, is not early (see PTSD).

Yet the sutta does not represent the latest stratum even within the four prose Nikāyas. Its description of the Paṭiccasamuppāda is less developed than that which became standard later.[25]

Though it uses the term Dhammatā it does not do so in connection with the Paṭiccasamuppāda. Further, instead of the twelve Nidānas (as in the Sutta in SN. II, which contains the standard form) it has only ten.

There is another circumstance that deserves to be noticed; on p. 28 (DN. II Nāg ed.) para 21 (Ib) ends thus—"Nirodho nirodho ti kho bhikkhave Vipassissa Bodhisattassa pubbe ananussutesu dhammesu cakkhum udapādi, ñāṇaṃ udapādi, paññā udapādi, vijjā udapādi, āloko udapādi." After this we have yet another para before the Bhāṇavāra ends, and it proceeds thus—"Atha kho bhikkhave vipassī Bodhisatto aparena samayena pañcasu upādānakkhandhesu udayabyayānupassī vihāsi: iti rūpaṃ etc. . . . Tassa pañcasu . . . . viharato na cirasseva anupādāya āsavehi cittaṃ vimucci." The implication is that "freedom" does not follow immediately from "knowledge". This is in direct contradiction to other more authentic reports of the doctrine; and is in itself quite untenable. The explanation would seem to be that we have here an interpolation by some over-enthusiast of the Five Khandha theory who, finding all reference to this doctrine missing in what precedes, thought it to append it here as a remedy.

The interpolative character of this para is proved by yet another fact. It is immediately followed by "Atha kho bhikkhave vipassissa bhagavato arahato sammāsambuddhassa etadahosi yannūnāhaṃ dhammaṃ deseyyanti" but then he reflects—"adhigato kho me ayaṃ

[25] Cf. "The oldest account (of the Paṭicca°) is found in the Mahāpadāna where 10 items form the constituents of the chain." (PTSD) But see below Ch. XI.

dhammo gambhīro duddaso....duddasam idaṃ ṭhānam yadidaṃ idappaccayatā paṭiccasamuppādo....." This implies the following sequence of events: the realization of Paṭiccasam°; the desire to preach it; hesitation. This sequence is however rudely broken by the intrusion of the para in question (para 22, p. 28 of DN. II, Nāg. ed.) according to which the Bodhisatta became a Sammāsambuddha not through the realization of the Paṭiccasam° (the culmination of which in the viloma order is reached in Nibbāna—see the quotation above "Nirodho nirodho ti kho,") but through the practice of the feeling of impermanence in the Five Khandhas! The paragraph, in short, is not only unnecessary and inconsistent but also breaks the natural sequence of the context.

DN. 15.—Composite.—It is possible that the suttas having Mahā prefixed to their titles have perhaps attained to their present bulk either through successive additions or the elaboration of shorter originals.[26] DN. 15 (Mahānidāna) presents an instance of the second class.

Para 1—22 (Nāg. ed.) constitute the first piece of the mosaic. Buddha disagrees with Ānanda when the latter describes Paṭiccasam° as "simple", and proceeds to explain it. In other words, the sutta represents a deliberate essay in philosophic interpretation undertaken to refute those who considered Paṭiccasam° "simple". This suggests a scholastic authorship, delighting in metaphysical subtleties. The use of the terms Adhivacanasamphassa and Paṭigha° point in the same direction. It is noticeable, however, that in the explanation of Nāmarūpa there is no mention of the Five Khandhas.

---

[26] Cf. Winternitz, II, p. 39.

There is a very unusual feature in this exposition of the Paṭiccasam°, and that is the digression in paras 9—18. This seems to embody an attempt to harmonize with the generally known law of Paṭiccasam° another form of it, developed along a different line. This other form has a part-parallel in the Sn. (Sutta 49).

In paras 21—22 Viññāṇa is explained as the transmigrating agent that takes on a new name and a new body. This dangerously soul-like character of Viññāṇa appears to have caused the addition of the next section in the sutta, comprising paras 23—32. It intrudes upon the previous section suddenly and without apparent relevancy. This is not to say that it is radically opposed to the former in idea; but there is an undoubted shift of accent. While the preceding "section" expounds Viññāṇa-cum-Nāmarūpa as coterminous with the phenomenal,[27] the present section directs attention to the utter transcendentality of "Attā". This difference comes out clearly in the last few lines of para 32 (with which the second section closes). These are manifestly patterned on the last lines of the preceding section (in para 22). Whereas these latter leave the matter at the level of the phenomenal, the former by a slight change focuss the whole attention on what lies beyond it. The second section, in short, is a supplement to the first.

Then follows a discourse on the Viññāṇaṭṭhitis which has no relevancy to the immediately preceding context. It appears to have been suggested by the fact (viññāṇapatiṭṭhiti) mentioned towards the end of the

[27] Ettāvatā kho Ānanda jāyetha vā jīyetha vā mīyetha vā cavetha vā, ettāvatā adhivacanapatho, ettāvatā niruttipatho, ettāvatā paññattipatho ettāvatā paññāvacaraṃ ettāvatā vaṭṭaṃ vaṭṭati itthattaṃ paññāpanāya yadidaṃ nāmarūpaṃ saha viññāṇena." (DN. pt. II, pp. 50-1, Nāg. ed.).

first section (i.e., in para 22) of which it is an elaborate and schematic development. It, however, goes beyond the purpose of the sutta into the attainment of liberation and furnishes the occasion for the detailing of the eight "vimokkhas".

The sutta thus shows the successive growth of a short and compact original. None of its pieces, however, can be counted among the earliest in the Nikāyas, nor yet among the latest.

DN. 16 —A veritable mosaic.—Of the mosaic character of the Mahāparinibbāna° there can hardly be any doubt. According to Winternitz,[28] very early there must have been a "sutta of the perfect Nirvāṇa" which in course of time, through interpolations and additions, became the present "Great sutta of Pari°". According to him those sections in which Buddha appears as a human being represent the authentic and earlier portion. Such are: the narrative of the illness which befell Buddha at Beluvagrāma; or the grief of Ānanda in the fifth section. The verses, too, which are scattered in the Sutta bear, according to him, "the stamp of the greatest antiquity". On the other hand, where Buddha works miracles like a demigod or a magician, and the concluding section which mentions the relics of Buddha and the erections of stūpas, are regarded as late.

Rhys Davids has exhaustively listed those passages of the sutta which occur in other parts of the canon also and concludes that full one-third of the sutta thus recurs.

The conclusions of Przyluski.—Przyluski has considered in great detail the various versions of the sutta.[29]

---

[28] loc. cit.

[29] See also Dr. W. Pachow: Comparative Studies in the Mahāparinibbāna-sutta and its Chinese Versions. (1946)

His conclusions are formulated in three groups: those relating to the Parinirvāṇa; those relating to the itinerary; and those about the funerary rites.

As to the first he finds that two Parinirvānasūtras are discoverable in the Sthavira-and Mūlasarvāstivādin canons—"l'un, très court, presque entièrement rédigè-en vers [Saṃyukta A (i.e. SĀXIII. 4, p. 59a, Col. 1) et saṃyutta pāli (I p. 158)], l'autre qui reproduit les stances du premier, mais en les encadrent dans de long developpements en prose (vinaya des mūlasarvāstivāda et mahāparinibbānasutta)."[30]

With regard to these we see "Saṃyukta Ā, est très voisin du texte de l'Avadānaśataka et du Dulva."[31] A comparison of these with the Pali version reveals that the most significant difference lies in the absence from the latter of the first verse by an anonymous Bhikkhu pronounced over the death of the master, and of the last two by Ānanda.[32] The first verse is of no doctrinal significance; as to the latter, Przyluski suggests that the omission is due to the changed ideas about the cremation of Buddha as a cakravartin, which was contradicted by the verses in question, since these represented Buddha as merely covered by "cīvaras"; hence they were suppressed.[33]

But it must be remembered "Dass Ānanda nicht zugleich mit dem Andern, vielmehr erst bei einer späteren Gelegenheit seinem Gefühle durch einem lyrischen Erguss Luft machte, wird im Avadānaśataka ausdrücklich gesagt."[34] It is therefore possible that these verses

---

[30] JA. 1918 t. XI, pp. 511-12. [31] Ib. p. 501.

[32] Ib., p. 508.

[33] Ib., p. 526.

[34] Speyer in ZDMG 53. 1899, p. 123.

have been omitted from the Saṃyutta version because they do not, strictly, belong to the context. Their non-appearance in the Mahāparinibbāna also, however, supports Przyluski's hypothesis.

The fact that in contrast to the Saṃyutta, the verses of Anuruddha are made to precede the utterance of Ānanda in the Dīgha, is, according to Przyluski, to be explained as a triumph of the theologians.[35] This appears quite likely, although Rhys Davids thinks it "scarcely possible."[36]

As to the itinerary[37] Przyluski traces three stages of its growth: 1. This belongs to the "ère de Rājagṛha." It was a narrative of Buddha's journey across Magadha, consisting principally of discourses arranged in decreasing numerical order: at Rājagṛha, discourse of 7 or 6 points; Pāṭaliputra—5 points; Koṭi—4 truths; Bhoganagara—three causes of earthquake. At Pāvā and near the river Kakutsthā "les deux transfigurations et les deux offrandes de nourriture". "Il n'était guerre alors question de Vaiśālī que pour mentionner le dernier regard jeté sur elle par le Maître et peut-être aussi la reception du Buddha par la courtisane Ambapālī."

2. The period of Vaiśālī owing to the spread of the faith in the Vṛji country.

3. Further northward spread of the faith and the entry of Śrāvastī in the narrative.

As to the funerary rites,[38] "Le cérémonial traditionnel indien a fourni la trame des rècits bouddhiques." This is true of the older records, the newer ones having

---

[35] Op. cit., p. 526.

[36] Dialogues—II, p. 73.

[37] JA. 1918. t. XII, pp. 455-56.

[38] JA. 1920. t. XV, pp. 53-54.

effaced some of the earlier features "C'est ainsi que des traditions relatives aux lamentations des pleureuses, aux lavagė du corpse, au cortege funèbre ont été peu à peu èliminées," and can only be restored from the traces left in some versions. On the other hand "Sur ce fond antique....apparaissent des ornements plus éclatants et plus moderns." They are taken from the ceremonial of kings and the efforts of the theologians to divinize the Buddha.

The main tendencies that were, thus, responsible for the elaboration of the originally plain and personal narrative of the last journey and death of Buddha may be thus indicated: the desire to interpolate later doctrines so as to give them the appearance of great authenticity (the very importance of the narrative made it the special victim of interpolation); the revision of the older text in the light of the newer apotheosis of Buddha.

An analysis of DN. 16.—To examine internally the Pali DN. 16[39] (Nag. ed.) 1—15: There is nothing against the meeting with Vassakāra and the sermon to the Vajjis having been historical.

6—11 of the six lists of Aparihāniya dhammas the first suits the occasion most. The lists appear to have been successively added merely in order to enhance their prestige, with the result that we have now a veritable cascade of them.

12—15 Itinerary notices, which cannot be checked on internal evidence alone.

16—17 Sāriputta praises Buddha,[40] and considers

[39] A detailed comparison with the Chinese Version will be found in Dr. W. Pa-Chow: Op. cit.

[40] This is not to be found in any of the Chinese Versions (Dr. Pa-Chow: Op. cit. p. 23).

that the only way to Enlightenment lies through abandoning the five Nīvaraṇas and cultivating the four Satipaṭṭhānas plus the seven Sambojjhaṅgas. This represents a particular interpretation of the "Way" and its very eagerness to establish its bonafides as unique may be considered suspicious.

18—25 Journey to Pāṭaligāma and a sermon to the householders there.

26—32. This contains the prophecy about the future greatness of Pāṭaliputta, and the dangers to it. This section could hardly have been added much before the Village of Pāṭaligāma actually attained such eminence as to become the capital of Magadha, an event which according to tradition took place in the reign of Kālāśoka (B.C. 392—365).[41]

33—34 The miraculous crossing of the Gaṅgā. This appears to have resulted from a misunderstanding of the final udāna "Ye taranti aṇṇavaṃ setuṃ katvāna visajja pallalāni/ Kullaṃ hi jano pabandhati, tiṇṇā medhāvino Janā ti//"

This contains no reference whatever to an actual crossing of any river.

II 1—3 Sermon on 4 Truths

4—5 Itinerary

6—7 B. explains the after life of many individuals

8—9 Dhammādāsapariyāya on faith in the Three.

10—11 to Vesālī

12—13 Short sermon on Sati and (sampajañña)

14—25 The well known story of Ambapālī. For an invention the story with its discomfiture of the Lic-

---

[41] See Fleet JRAS 1906 p. 670.

chavi noblemen would appear very unpolitic on the part of a growing church.

21—26 Buddha at Beluvagāma; his illness; and the sermon to Ānanḍa. Winternitz argues convincingly for its authenticity on the whole.

III. 1—51 The whole of the section appears to present a single very late stratum. Buddha is portrayed as harbouring the desire for further life, and made to throw out an oblique hint to Ānanda that if so requested he might exercise his miraculous powers to prolong his earthly stay. Ānanda, however, disappoints him,

and for this has to suffer rebuke soon after. Later, according to tradition, the theras again took him to task on this very account in the First Council. It was in all likelihood to strengthen their case against Ānanda that this section was inserted in the Mahāpari° which incidentally degraded Buddha himself to a level where he could harbour mundane longings, boast like a magician, and take to devious ways of expression.

The rest of the section accords with it. When Buddha yields to the temptation to die, there is a great earthquake. This is described as "Bhiṃsanako lomahaṃsano". May it not be that these adjectives have been suggested by the "gāthā" of Ānanda at the death of the Lord "Tadāsi Yaṃ Bhiṃsanakaṃ tadāsi lomahaṃsanaṃ Sabbākāravarūpete Sambuddhe parinibbuteti." (This is among those gāthās at the time of Parinibbāna the earliness of which has been demonstrated by Przyluski). This is supported by the probable lateness of the verse that follows. E. Muller quotes, and agrees with Windisch that the last pāda of this stanza (III § 10) which reads "Abhida Kavacamivattasambhavaṃti" is later than (Divyāvadāna, p. 208) "Abhinat Kośamivāṇḍasambhavaṃ" because the latter gives the better sense and suits the metre. (JRAS. 1913, p. 1089).

Buddha utilizes the occasion to enumerate a list of the 8 causes of earthquakes and follows it up by three other quite irrelevant and quite unconnected lists of "eights".

At the end, this section (III) purports to set down B's farewell speech recommending the seven lists that constitute the 37 Bodhipakkhiyas. Then follows the leave-taking and finally a few verses. It is a little remarkable that the words reported to be Buddha's last[42] should also have been uttered by him three months before his death. Is it not better to suppose that whoever composed this sermon thought to add to its appearance of authenticity by appending to it some acknowledgedly authentic words of the Master, forgetting the difference in context?

The verses at the end, on the other hand, appear much earlier. They show no trace of the existence as yet of any systematic dogmatics. In fact, they contain the sort of material out of which the latter must have developed. IV 2—3: whereas in DN I. we had the twofold or threefold lists of Sīla and Paññā or Sīla, Samādhi and Paññā, § 2 adds to it a fourth element—Vimutti, § 3 ascribes to Buddha verses which speak of him in the third person and explicitly describe him as Parinibbuta. These are obviously apocryphal. It may be noticed that §§ 2—3 have the same subject-matter. It is possible that § 3 versifies § 2. In §§ 7—12 Buddha preaches the

[42] i.e., Vayadhammā saṅkhārā appamādena sampādetha.

four "mahāpadesas" which seem to assume controversies over the authenticity and interpretation of sutta or vinaya, and the existence of the class of "Dhammadharā vinayadharā" 13—20 seem to contain, in contrast to the preceding, the very ancient narrative of B's dinner at the place of Cunda.

22—38 contain the justification for the title of the Bhāṇa-vāra—Āḷāravedalla".

39—43 take up the thread of narrative which is apparently broken by the previous sequence. This coupled with the fact that this latter (22—38) describes a miracle and shows Buddha as possessed of a very sensitive vanity, suggests its interpolative character.

V. 1—7 Presuppose the apotheosis of Buddha.

10—11 Buddha prescribes a cakravartin's treatment for his body after death.

12. The four classes deserving a Thūpa. Distinguishes between Sammāsambuddha and Pacceka°.

13—14 Ānanda weeps and Buddha consoles him.

15—Seems to imply the doctrine of Previous Buddhas.

16—Buddha praises the wonderful qualities of Ānanda

17—22 The past of Kusināṛā. The mallas come to see Buddha 23—30: The conversion of Subhadda—In 27 Buddha regards the Eight fold Path as the chief mark of his doctrine; with this contra 1. § 17; and III 50).

VI—7 The last moments. No late element discoverable here.

8—9 B. first climbs up to the Saññāvedayitanirodha, then comes to the first Jhāna; goes up again—this time only up to the 4th Jhāna, where he reaches "Perfect Nibbāna". One may ask why this tortuous procedure? The account varies greatly in some of the Chinese versions (see Pa-chow op. cit. 69).

10. Contains the verses which Przyluski regards as very ancient, but the accounts in the different Chinese versions all contradict each other. (see Pa-Chow loc. cit.)
11—28: closely interwoven with the mythical and the miraculous. Buddha appears as a veritable great deity.

DN. 17.—DN. 17 is an elaboration of DN. 16 V §§ 17—18.[43] Its lateness is further manifest from the detailed and gorgeous descriptions that it contains of the royal city, the 7 Jewels and the "Dhamma" palace. It also shows great exaggeration in numbers, and is not free from the miraculous.

Its Jātaka-form also suggests lateness, although it differs in several important respects from the Jātaka of the same name (No. 95 in Fausböll's edition).[44] It has no Paccuppannavatthu and differs radically in emphasis. According to Rhys Davids No. 95 serves to illustrate "Aniccā sabbasaṅkhārā" etc. Now the present sutta appears to be really addressed to the laity. It points out that king Suddassana got all his glory through the practice of the virtues of Dāna, Dama, and Saṃyama. And the implication is clear enough.

DN. 18.—DN. 18 is similar to the above in as much as it also is an elaboration of a portion of DN. 16 (II. 5—7). [45] It is permeated by the mythical and the miraculous. It mentions the four Iddhipādas, the three "Okāsādhigamas" (a rare set), the four "satipaṭṭhānas" and the three "aveccappasādas" And it mentions the eight elements of the Path in the form of "Samādhi" and its seven "Parikkhāras".

It is, therefore, in style as well as doctrine, late

[43] See Bapat ABORI 1926 p. 10.

[44] See Rhys Davids in intr to the tr of DN. 17 (Dialogues II).

[45] Bapat loc. cit.

DN. 19.—Prof. Bapat suggests unconvincingly that DN. 19 is based on DN. 18.[46] It appears that we have here an ancient non-Buddhist story preaching the "Karunajhāna" as the way to the direct realization of Brahmā, converted to Buddhist purposes. This is suggested by several circumstances: It contains some old-looking memorial verses which contain the name of "Govinda" (the hero). This suggests that the present composition takes as its point d'appui an earlier legend. Further, it is interested solely in Brahmā, which is hardly to be expected from a composition originally Buddhist. Even the introduction of all the four Brahmavihāras, which, it may be remarked, occurs first in the penultimate section of the story proper, appears the work of the adapter, who, it is possible, was responsible for other changes also.

The introductory and concluding portions of the sutta mention some specifically Buddhist doctrines. The former asserts the impossibility of two Buddhas being contemporaries in the same "Lokadhātu". The latter speaks of the "Eightfold Path" and uses 'Opapātika' for "anāgāmin" and in this it reminds one of DN. 6 which also mentions precisely these points.

DN. 20.—As to the next sutta, Rhys Davids states: The prologue has been preserved as a separate episode in the Saṃyutta I, 27. The way in which the list is fitted into the frame-work in our sections 4, 5 and 6 is very confused and awkward; and the grammar of the framework is inconsistent with the grammar of the list. It is highly probable therefore that the list itself, and also the epilogue, had been handed out as independent works in the community before our sutta was composed......

[46] loc. cit.

Our §§ 10–20 look very much like an improved and enlarged edition of the bare list in the Āṭānāṭiya."[47]

DN. 21.–Composite.–Rhys Davids calls DN. 21 an example of "Tendenzschriften written with the object of persuading the Kosala clansmen that they did not need to be in the least afraid, for their own gods were on the side of the reformation."[48] Winternitz advances the analogy of the sectarian Purāṇas and considers the sutta late.[49] Bapat comes to the same conclusion[50] on grounds of the mythological character of the sutta, and the secular character of the poem it incorporates, a fact which he interprets as a sign of decadence. It may be added that the sutta calls itself a "veyyākaraṇa" at the end.

On the other hand, there are undoubted indications of its earliness. It has been quoted by name in AN. Its title and the purpose and style of its second Bhāṇavāra are reminiscent of the "pucchās" in the Pārāyaṇavaggo of the Sn. The first series of questions and answers (DN. 21 II. 1–2) is closely similar to Sn. Sutta 49 (of the Aṭṭhakavagga) and contains an unusual development of the theory of "Nidānas". Otherwise also the answers to the queries do not suffer from hackneyed expressions and formulae.

It appears that while the late features of the sutta are mainly confined to the mythological, the early features are mainly confined to the dialectical portions of the sutta. Now it is noticeable that the former (the mythological portions) are found almost wholly in the introductory first Bhāṇavāra and the conclusion of the

[47] Dialogues, II. Int. to DN. 20.

[48] Op. cit. Int to DN. 21.

[49] Winternitz, II, p. 43.

[50] Op. cit.

second. And it is these portions alone that use verse. May it not then be said that we have here the case of an early short prose dialogue concerned with dogmatic points and not far removed from the Aṭṭhaka and Pārāyāṇa vaggas of the Sn. encased within a later, luxuriantly mythical prologue and epilogue?

Mahasatipatthana°.—The Mahāsatipaṭṭhāna° is like the Mahānidāna placed among the Kurus at Kammāsadamma. It consists of the Satipaṭṭhāna° of the MN, to which it adds a long term by term explanation of the Four Truths. This seems to account for the change of the title to Mahā°. That this appended explanation is late comes out from its use of the Abhidhammic dictionary style of definition, as also from its unusually detailed character.

As to the rest of the sutta, it is of some interest to notice that it uses the term "dhamma" in two different meanings. Following the introspection into "citta" the Bhikkhu is asked to examine with equal care the Dhammas and these are thus successively enumerated: (a) Five Nīvaraṇas; (b) Five Upādānakkhandhas; (c) Six ajjhattika and bāhira āyatanas; (d) Seven Bojjhaṅgas; (e) Four Ariyasaccas.

The meaning in a–c is the same, and closely related to "citta", that is to say, "Dhamma" is here used primarily as a psychological term. In d–e, however, the meaning becomes more ethical and dogmatic. In the first division the Bhikkhu is urged to become aware of the actual constituents of his being; in the second, to see whether he is following the right doctrine.

Though the sutta has the same function as the Mahānidāna°—to systematically elaborate an existing dogma—it is in this respect later than the former in that it represents the latest stage in the development of the doctrine of "sati" in the Nikāyas. It may also be noticed that whereas the Five Kh. doctrine occurs in the former sutta, it does not in the latter.

Payasisutta.—The next sutta has important bearings on the position of soul in early Buddhist belief. That a similar sutta occurs in Jinist literature[51] does not either prove that it has been borrowed thence or from an earlier source.[52] And in any case it must have met the approval of the editors, else we shall have to imagine too glaring an oversight.

DN. 24.—In DN. 24, I §§ 1—6 form a distinct section. Buddha is here opposed to miracles and, besides, the raison d'etre of the sutta—to rebuke Sunakkhatta Licchaviputta for his unworthy interest in "things superhuman (Uttarimanussadhammā) and "First Beginnings" (Aggañña)—ends here. In the succeeding portion of the sutta there is a complete change of spirit. Buddha is portrayed extremely eager to prove that he *had* shown miracles, till in II § 13 he is a veritable magician. Rhys Davids' remarks on the coarse humour of the sutta, which, he says, "would appeal more strongly to a music Hall audience or to school boys out for a holiday. . . . ,"[53] apply only to this second "magical-mythological" part of the sutta. This too, however, does not form a single whole, since in II § 21 there is an abrupt and unintelligible transition from a discussion of the 'Origins' (Aggañña) to that of the Subhavimokkha. This seems to represent an inorganic appendix for which oversight is probably responsible.

---

[51] See below.

[52] Cf. Winternitz, p. 44 Fn. 1.

[53] Dialogues III int. to D. XXIV.

DN. 25.—DN. 25 (Udumbarikasīhanāda) not only resembles DN. 8 (Kassapasīhanāda) in title, but deals also with the same subject—Asceticism true and false; only it is much more elaborate. Bapat's suggestion that the former is based upon the latter, and is younger, appears to be correct (op. cit., p. 11).

DN. 26.—In the next sutta, §§ 2—26 form a unified composition depicting the ideal of the righteous ruler, the fall and recovery of mankind, and the appearance of "Metteyya". These represent a late age in Buddhist speculation.[54] On the other hand, § 1 contains the recurrent sermon "Attadīpā bhikkhave viharatha" etc. And between § 1 and §2 no transition whatever is indicated. The last paragraphs §§ 27—28 revert with equal abruptness and elaborate § 1. Have we here the spectacle of a late composition in early wrappings.

DN. 27.—Purposing to subvert the Brāhmaṇic pretensions about caste, Buddha in DN. 27 begins at the very beginning—the origin of the world! This is in flat contradiction to his usual reticence about the beginnings (Aggañña), a circumstance which caused the apostacy of Sunakkhatta Licchaviputta. Further, where they tread on common ground its mythology resembles that of the previous suttas. Winternitz, therefore, appears right in assigning this sutta to a late stratum.

It may be noticed that the present sutta appears unique in the Nikāyas in that it prefaces the epithets Dhammabhūta and Brahmabhūta by two new ones—Dhammakāya and Brahmakāya (DN. III, p. 84).

DN. 28.—DN. 28 is the elaboration of a part of DN. 16.[55] Its first two paras are identical with DN. 16

[54] See Winternitz, II, p. 43.
[55] Cf. Bapat, op. cit., p. 14.

I §§ 16—17 (except for its additional first line, which is the last of Ib § 15). But Ānanda gives vent to his admiration for Buddha here by enumerating the various excellences (anuttariyas) of his teaching. As a result we have an exceedingly formidable list of the 7 Kusaladhammas, 6 āyatanapaññattis, 4 Gabbhāvakkantis, 4 Ādesanāvidhās, 4 Dassanasamāpattis, 7 Puggalapaññattis, 7 Padhānas (the Bojjhaṅgas), 4 Paṭipadās, Bhassasamācāra, Purisasīla°, Anusāsanavidhi, Parapuggalavimuttiñāṇa, 3 types of Sassatavādas,[56] Pubbenivāsānussatiñāṇa and the iddhividhās. It mentions in the main only such dogmas as relate to spiritual practice. It does not appear that much significance can be attached to its silences, for whether it aims at fulness is impossible to decide. It may be noticed that it uses in § 7 (DN. III, p. 105) the rare and significant word Viññāṇasota.[57]

DN. 29.—DN. 29 also contains quite a large and miscellaneous collection of already existing doctrinal points. Among others it systematically expounds the Pubbantadiṭṭhis and Aparantadiṭṭhis and details the thirty-seven Bodhipakkhiya Dhammas. It appears, therefore, that it cannot be regarded as very early.

DN. 30.—Sutta 30, which describes with great fulness the thirty-two marks of great men and contains a variety of metres, belongs manifestly to a very late stratum in the Nikāyas.[58]

Sutta 31.—Sutta 31, addressed to the laity and interpreting the six quarters "Buddhistically", does not contain any marked late features. It may be early.

Atanatiya.—The Āṭānāṭiya sutta, for the most part

[56] DN. 1 has four types.
[57] See Chap. on Nirvāṇa.
[58] Winternitz, II, p. 42.

in verse, is a "Parittā" or Protection-charm. It is much more mythological, and much longer than the 'Ratana' sutta of the Sn. which has the same purpose. It bows to the seven Buddhas, describes the retinue of the four mahārājas and then names the more violent yakkhas, some of whom are Vedic gods and sages! It clearly belongs to a late stratum.

The last two suttas.—Of the Saṅgīti—and the Dasuttara-suttas, the latter immediately follows the former even in the Chinese Dīrghāgama (Nanjio 545—suttas 9—10). Further it is more systematic than the former. It treats each numerical group from 10 stand-points and thus has exactly 100 items in all. It is much shorter and appears to be a systematic selection out of the Saṅgītisutta in which no principle of "in-or-ex-clusion" is discoverable.[59] It may be noticed that of the ten meshes of the classificatory net used in the Dasuttara, four are mentioned in the Mahāsaḷāyatana° of the MN.

These are the categories of the Pariññeyya, the Pahātabba, the Bhāvetabba and the Sacchikātabba.

As to the Saṅgīti° it is in the first place to be remarked that its preamble is divisible into two little connected parts, represented roughly by §§ 1—5 and §§ 6—7. The text itself attempts a full collection of the known points of doctrine, with no more system than assured by the aṅguttara form. The heterogeneous character of the contents is manifest. Similarly the haphazard nature of the listing is apparent from such a repetition as that of the five khandhas which are followed by the five upādāna khandhas.

In its completed form the list is undoubtedly very late. This comes out from its inclusion of such late

[59] Cf. Mrs. Rhys Davids: Original Gospel, Appendix.

groups of ideas as the four Oghas, the five Anāgāmins, the eight Abhibhāyatanas; the nine Anupubbanirodhas, and the ten Kasiṇāyatanas.

As to the problem of the 'Eighfold Path' raised by Mrs. Rhys Davids,[60] formulæ for that doctrine as well as for the 'Tenfold Path' do indeed occur in the Saṅgīti° though not as referring to the 'Maggo'. The first occurs as the 8 Sammattas and the second as the 10 Asekhadhammas. It appears that this should be interpreted to indicate, not that the sutta is prior to the formulation of the Eightfold or Tenfold Paths, but much posterior to it, when the idea had faded from the focus of scholastic interest. This happened in the Abhidhammic period. And it is relevant to remember that the Sarvāstivādins actually placed a text called Saṅgītiparyāya and resembling the Saṅgītisutta among the Abhidhamma texts.[61]

Conclusion.—N.B.—For the first two vaggas the reference is to the Nāg. ed., for the third to the P.T.S. ed.

EARLY	LATE	COMPOSITE	UNCERTAIN
Sutta 2 (§§81 & 83 may be later)	Sutta 1 (based on early material)	Sutta 8	Suttas4-5 (perhaps "late")
,,		,, 9	
		,, 11	,, 6-7 (6-defective ?)
,, 13	Sutta 3		
		,, 15	,, 10
	,, 12 (?)		,, 19
	,, 14 (earlier than S.2.1.1 ;	,, 16 [early§1.5 ;	,, 20
	,, s. 22 interpolated?)	§2.21-26;	,, 23
	,, 17	§4.13-20]	,, 31

[60] Original Gospel—App.

[61] See Takakusu JPTS 1904—5.

EARLY	LATE	COMPOSITE	UNCERTAIN
	Sutta		
	,, 18	§5.13-14;	
	,, 22	§6.1-7,10;	
	,, 24	Late §1.6-11;	
	,, 25	§26-32;	
	,, 26	32-34;	
	,, 27	§3;	
	,, 28	§4.7-12;	
	,, 29	§5.1-12;	
	,, 30	Uncertain-the	
	,, 32	rest]	
	,, 33	Sutta : 21	
	,, 34		

CHAPTER V

EARLY AND LATE IN THE MAJJHIMA–NIKĀYA

The grouping and order of suttas in the MN "unhistorical".—The authenticity of the groupings and arrangement of suttas in the MN is rendered suspect by the great difference which the Pāli and Chinese versions[1] show in this respect. The fact that in the Pali text each "vagga" contains just ten suttas (with the exception of the vibhaṅga°, which has twelve) and each "Paṇṇāsa" just five "vaggas" argues strongly for the mechanical, unhistorical character of its divisions and sub-divisions.[2] As to its arrangement of the suttas, it is clearly mechanical in the whole of the middle "Paṇṇāsa". The suttas have been here divided into "Vaggas" according to the class of persons who figure predominantly in them, which they do principally by playing the role of the addressee. Thus, the suttas in the "Gahapativagga" contain sermons and dialogues in which Buddha addresses householders, sutta 57 alone being exceptional. And it is similar with the following 'vaggas' in this "Paṇṇāsa". In the previous "Paṇṇāsa" too a similarly systematic grouping occurs in vaggas 3—4, the first containing only such suttas as are centred round an "upamā", and the next such as

[1] From Nanjio's Catalogue it appears that the MA contains a larger number of suttas than the MN, and that the former includes some suttas which are found in other Nikāyas in the Pali canon. Thus suttas 59, 66, 68 and 97 of the MĀ are found in the DN as Lakkhaṇasutta, Aggañña° (?), Mahāsudassana°, and Mahānidāna° respectively.

[2] Cf. Franke, ZDMG 1914, p. 474. The similarity of the neighbouring suttas led him to conclude: "M. mindestens im groszen und ganzen das einheitlich, im Zusammenhang verfasste Werk eines Schriftstellers ist" (l. c.).

are in pairs, e.g., Cūḷagosinga and Mahā°. The Vibhaṅgavagga in the third "Paṇṇāsa" forms a distinct unity in the sense that it contains suttas having a common characteristic form.

This suggests that the place and order of occurrence of the suttas in the MN[3] has not, in general, come about through any historical process of growth. It is largely, if not wholly, the work of the collectors.

The third Pannasa possibly later.—But there seems to be indicated the possibility of a significant exception. It may turn out that the third "Paṇṇāsa" contains on the whole more of later material than the first two "Paṇṇāsas". Certainly it contains the greatest number of such suttas as can with some definiteness be supposed "late".[4] Mrs. Rhys Davids remarks: "Whether or not it may be held to betray later compilation, nothing in these volumes, especially in the last, is so thrown into relief as the importance in Buddhist ethics of cultivating psychological analysis......of the last thirty-four suttas no less than fifteen are concerned with this question."[5] Although the beginnings of psychological analysis may go back to the most primitive Buddhism, its greatest growth and popularity must undoubtedly be placed much later, in the Age of the Abhidhamma. And this suggests that a concentration of psychological suttas harmonizes more with a later than an earlier compilation. And the same argument holds generally for the suttas in the Vibhaṅgavagga: although it is possible that Buddha might have adopted (especially as he grew old)

[3] The Pali version, which alone is referred to henceforth. For the Majjhima Paṇṇāsa the ref. is to the Nāgarī Edition by N. K. Bhagwat. For the rest, the ref. is to the PTS edition.

[4] See below.

[5] JRAS. 1902, p. 481.

the method of himself delivering only a short sermon, leaving it to be elaborated by one of the leading disciples, and this might account for the peculiar form of these suttas which are divided into an uddesa and a vibhaṅga,[6] yet it is much simpler to suppose this form to have been the result of a growing "commentarial" vogue, the vogue, that is, of systematically elaborating older texts and ideas. And it is important to remember that the uddesas in question furnish not so much short sermons for the vibhaṅgas to explain, as concise analytical abstracts of the latter. They appear like brief "arguments" that have been prefaced to longer texts for the convenience of understanding and remembering the latter.[7]

Classification of suttas into Early, Late, Composite and Uncertain.—On the whole, however, it is the individual sutta, and not any obviously detectable group of suttas, that must form the unit to start with in the stratification of the **MN**. But although a few suttas can be indicated as early and a few others as late, some appear "composite" in character, that is to say, show within them more than one literary stratum. This leaves out of account those suttas which, though unitary as compositions, nevertheless exhibit diverse ideological strata. Again, the very comprehensiveness of the classes "early" and "late" must, it may be supposed, conceal undetected —or rather unprovable "sub-stratum"—heterogeneity. At places this has been indicated. In contrast to the DN the number of "uncertain" suttas about the earliness or lateness of which it is impossible to pronounce with any definiteness, is very large. This is due partly

---

[6] For the two extra suttas of this vagga see below.

[7] For a further consideration of these suttas see below.

to their shortness, which hinders the concurrence of several distinct tests, and partly to their elusive generality and homogeneity.*

(*a*) *Early*:

Sutta 7 is significantly entitled Vatthūpama.° It begins by pointing out that just as a cloth to be coloured brightly must be purified of its dirt, so must the heart (citta) that has to move along the path of progress (Sugati) be purified of its upakkilesas. There are certain evil emotions and desires which are then mentioned. The list also occurs at other places in the Nikāyas. The purificatory process forms the following sequence:— Aveccappasāda — Pāmojja — Pīti — Passaddhi — Sukha— Samādhi. The formula occurs at many other places. The heart (citta) of the monk is now like a clean washed cloth or purified gold. No more does pleasant experience cause in him attachment. Then follows abruptly the stock formula of the four Brahmavihāras and its relevancy is hard to understand. After it occurs "So atthi idam, atthi hīnam atthi paṇītam, atthi imassa saññāgatassa uttariṃ nissaraṇanti pajānāti";[8] thus knowing he is released from the three āsavas and reaches the end of Brahmacariya. Again "vuccati. . . . bhikkhu sināto antarena sinānenāti "[9] This suggested to Sundarika Bhāradvāja the idea of inviting Buddha to an actual bath in the river Bāhukā considered sacred. Buddha exposes the hollowness of such superstitions and Sundarika is converted.

* For the Majjhima Paṇṇāsa the references are to the Nāg. ed.

[8] MN. I, p. 38.

[9] Ib., 39.

All the material of the sutta, except possibly the list of the upakkilesas, is early, and there is nothing in it that suggests lateness except perhaps the interruption of the Four Brahmavihāras.

Sutta 17—A short and utterly simple sermon on the kind of forest in which a monk should dwell, which, however, is quite mechanically repeated with reference to Gāma, Nigama, Nagara, Janapada and Puggala. This appears like spinning out.

The doctrinal assumption too of the sutta is no more elaborate than that "sati" and "samādhi" are the means to the attainment of "āsavakkhaya" and "anuttara-yogakkhema" for the sake of which the monk strives. Unlike later pictures of the doctrine, this places equal emphasis on the negative and positive aspects of the goal, the means to which are not set in any of the later formulae.

The sutta appears to belong to an age when the Buddhist monk was more a solitary hermit who meditated in the forest than the active member of a town-dwelling church. The implicit picture of the "Saṅgha" is nearer that in the Sn. than in the Vin.[10] It appears that it was this incongruity of the sutta with later conditions which led to the appendant sections with Peyyālas about Gāma, etc. This suggestion is supported by the following circumstances: Before the sermon, Buddha is represented as saying that he would deliver the "vanapatthapariyāya" and it would be quite remarkable indeed if he should actually proceed to deliver a sermon of which the "Pariyāya" on "Vanapattha" forms less than one-fifth. In other words, the aforementioned suggestion about the lateness of the sections relating to

[10] Cf. Fausböll's intr. to the tr. of Sn. in the SBE.

Gāma, etc., explains very well the title of the sutta, which is undoubtedly old since it is contained in the text itself.[11] And as already pointed out, there is a discernible cause for the appendage.

In any case, the earliness of the sutta is suggested by its simplicity in thought and style as also by the character of the external environment which it brings home to the reader.

It may be noted that the sutta uses the rare form "Anāpucchā".[12]

Sutta 24.—In a dialogue between Upatissa Sāriputta and Puṇṇa Mantāniputta the latter expounds the true purpose of the doctrine and points out how the various first views are but so many progressive stages to it. This is illustrated by the remarkable Rathavinīta comparison. That this was central in the sutta is indicated by the almost concurrent titles in the Pali and Chinese versions of it.[13] The comparison speaks of King Pasenadi as journeying from Sāvatthi to Sāketa by seven relays of chariots. This intimate and original simile has the appearance of being taken from life. That it should have occurred, in those days of short historical memory, to a latter-day monk does not seem very likely.

The doctrinal position of the sutta is in full agreement with this appearance of earliness. There is as yet no question of stereotyped formulae,[14] and unlike the later discussions between the monks[15] the subject of interest is not some technical nicety, an unresolved

---

[11] This does not assume anything about the authenticity of the introductory section.

[12] MN. I, pp. 106, 107.

[13] Anesaki—JRAS. 1901, p. 897.

[14] As in the catechetic dialogues between the monks.

[15] As, e.g., in the Vedalla suttas.

contradiction or a new problem demanding answer; it is, on the other hand, the central problem of what may be regarded as the true end of the religious quest.

Finally it may be noted that the sutta has been supposed to be one of the texts referred to by Aśoka.[16]

Sutta 29.—Sutta 29: It is a short earnest sermon which is closely allied in spirit to the sutta just discussed. It too seeks to distinguish the essence of Brahmacariya from the superficies, and like the other sutta has a central parable—that of a man seeking the essence of a huge tree and mistaking it for the outer bark, etc. It fits in very well with the present context and is closely intertwined with the main text.

At the end, the sutta summarizes itself neatly thus: "Iti kho bhikkhave nayidam brahmacariyaṃ lābhasakkārasilokānisaṃsaṃ, na sīlasampadānisaṃsam, na samādhi,° na ñāṇadassanānisaṃsaṃ, Yā ca kho ayaṃ bhikkhave akuppā cetovimutti etadatthamidam bhikkhave brahmacariyaṃ etaṃ sāraṃ etampariyosānanti."[17]

An earlier stage of the doctrine is difficult to imagine. Of course, older doctrines may occur in later compositions, but, then, the present sutta displays no late features whatever.

Suttas 29 and 30 compared.—The relation of this sutta (Mahāsāropama°) to the next sutta (MN. s. 30), which is Cūḷasāropama°, deserves notice. In spite of the title it is the following sutta which is the longer and more elaborate one. Both deal with the same subject and have the same summary at the end. It is possible that one is not the elaboration of the other but that both are two different versions of the same sutta. An impor-

---

[16] e.g., D. C. Sircar —Select Ins. I, p. 78 fn. 2.

[17] MN. I, p. 197.

tant addition in sutta 30 is its attempt to enumerate the states higher than Ñāṇadassana and these are set out as the "Jhānas" and the "Vimokkhas".[18] This clearly attributes an unusual meaning to the term Ñāṇadassana, which in the Sāmaññaphala sutta appears equivalent to "viññāṇassa (Kāyapaṭibaddhassa) dassanaṃ."[19] In later texts its meaning became more general but did not depreciate in estimation.[20] The present use therefore shows the term in a stage where it was either not yet adapted to Buddhist purposes, or, as is more likely, its usage fluctuated. It may be remembered that a deprecatory use of Ñāṇa occurs at places in the Sn (in the four Aṭṭhakas, for example).

Sutta 26.—Sutta 26 contains the first of the three closely connected biographical pieces relating to Buddha in the MN. It describes the days between the (Mahābhiniṣkramaṇa) and the conversion of the Pañcavaggiya Bhikkhus. The autobiographic form of the narrative distinguishes it from the other two main canonical accounts of Buddha's life, viz., DN. 16 and Vin (the opening sections of the Mvg.). This form, however, is probably to be regarded as an apocryphal contribution. The verses that appear in the narrative (MN. I, pp. 168—169; 171) seem to belong to the same genre of balladic biography as is also evidenced in the DN (Mahāparinibbāna°) and the Sn (Pabbajjā—and Padhāna suttas). The sutta has another similarity with DN. 16 and that is the separate occurrence of parts of it. The incident of (Brahmāyācana), for instance, occurs in SN.I.,

---

[18] By implication Ñāṇadassana has nothing to do with these, and represents a lower attainment.

[19] For a fuller discussion of the term see infra.

[20] Cf. Vin. IV, 26 (see PD).

and has been obviously utilized in the second Bhāṇavāra of the much later Mahāpadāna-sutta (DN. 14).

But, unlike the Mahāparinibbāna°, the present narrative shows no obvious late features. Further, an earlier form of this biographical tradition is not discoverable in the canon.

It is important to notice that whereas the purpose of the whole sutta is to explain the "Noble Quest" (Ariyapariyesana), which provides the occasion for the illustrative "reminiscences" of Buddha, the paragraph that begins on page 173 (MN. 1) treats abruptly of a different subject—how the Bhikkhu should avoid the five strands of sensuous desire (Kāmaguṇas). The last para ends with the realization by the Pañcavaggiyas that "Akuppā no vimutti, ayamantimā Jāti natthi dāni punabbhavo ti;" and this para suddenly begins "Pañcime Bhikkhave kāmaguṇā, katame pañca" etc. Further, this new section indicates its lateness by a schematic account of the nine contemplative stages. It may also be noted that it is much more closely connected—in subject-matter and simile—to the previous sutta (MN. 25) than to the present one. Is it possible that MN. 26 represents a "confusion" of two (once) different suttas—the Ariyapariyesana° and the Pāsarāsi?°[21] The wavering of the title would then be, incidentally, well explained.

The other two biographical suttas.—Of the other two biographical suttas of the MN, no. 36 is distinctly later than the one just considered. It belongs to an age when the "Bodhisatta" idea had come into existence.[22] The extreme exaggeration in which the sutta revels

---

[21] For this title see Papañcasūdanī—Part II, p. 163. (PTS ed.).

[22] Cf. Har Dayal—The Bodhisattva Doctrine in Sans. Buddh. Lit., p. 43.

while depicting the penances of Buddha may be noted. Of course, it is more than probable that during his "Quest" Buddha experimented with austere asceticism too, but that is not inconsistent with a tendency to exaggerate its severity among his followers owing to their eagerness to repel the charges of the Nigaṇṭhas. The present sutta itself contains an indication to that effect. Saccaka—the Nigaṇthaputta—suggests "Addhābhoto Gotamassa sāvakā cittabhāvanānuyogamanuyuttā viharanti no kāyabhāvananti."[23] Buddha answers by explaining the true nature of these two types of "culture" (Bhāvanā) and Saccaka is apparently convinced. But then Buddha does not stop here, but goes on to establish in great detail through an autobiographical narrative of how he had had an unrivalled experience of "Kāya-bhāvanā" in the ordinary sense as well. This overweening anxiety not to be considered "behind" in any sphere, it seems, is more consistent with the disciples than with the Master himself. And, as already pointed out, that it is a scholastic composition, can hardly be doubted in view of the fact that it uses the term "Bodhisatta".[24]

The last of the biographical triad in the MN.—sutta 85—is the fullest, since it combines the account of the Ariyapariyesana° which lacks the sections on asceticism and the "vijjās", and that of the Mahāsaccaka° which lacks those on Brahmāyācana et seq.

Of course, a direct borrowing is impossible to prove, but the use of the word "Bodhisatta" indicates that sutta

[23] MN. I, p. 238.

[24] The main part of *sutta* 100 consists of a repetition of the text on asceticism which occurs in this sutta. The two suttas are clearly not independent. It may be that both utilize the same stock text. The query at the end of sutta 100—Atthi devāti—also occurs in sutta 90, but B's mode of answering is quite different.

85 cannot be in any case much earlier than sutta 36. (Mahāsaccaka°).

All these three suttas have considerable similarity with the account in the Lalitavistara, the similarity at places being quite literal.[25] But owing to the uncertainty about the sources utilized in this latter work. this fact of similarity (or of the accompanying dissimilarity) cannot by itself be taken to indicate either the earliness or the lateness of these accounts.

Ambalatthikarahulovada.°—To come back to the "early" suttas—The Ambalaṭṭhikārāhulovāda° is simple and practical, beside being short. It is quite free from any formulae, although the description of "introspection"—Paccavekkhaṇa—afforded a splendid opportunity for their introduction, the doctrinal context being similar to that utilised in the Satipaṭṭhāna°.

It has been suggested that the specification—Ecā Lāghulovāde musāvādaṃ adhigicya Bhagavatā Budhena bhāsite"[26]—has been adopted by Aśoka in order to distinguish MN. 61 from among the several other suttas addressed to "Rāhula". That is possible; on the other hand, it has to be remembered that Aśoka shows no such care in the case of the other texts, e.g., Aliyavasāni. Now it is noticeable that the sutta contains two distinct sections, the first dealing with Sampajānamusāvāda and the second with Paccavekkhaṇa as the means to purify the actions of body, speech and mind. The two are not very closely connected, and in the present sermon the section relating to Musāvāda is the shorter and doctrinally less important one.

Is it not then possible that the specification was

[25] See Chap. on Buddha's Life.
[26] Aśoka's Bairāt Edict.

adopted by Aśoka, because he wanted attention to be particularly directed to the first of the two sections of the Rāhula sutta?[27]

Sutta 63.—Sutta 63 is the famous sermon to Māluṅkyaputta on the "Abyākatas". Māluṅkyaputta adopts an uncompromising and determined attitude, formulating the fundamental problem in a pointed manner: either Buddha should answer the queries raised, or honestly confess his ignorance. Buddha replies by means of the arrow-parable, which, in substance, is an appeal to expediency.

The nature of the problem, which Buddha must have had to face often enough, the simple and practical character of the answer, the centrality of the parable, all these support the impression of earliness which the sutta as a whole carries.

Sutta 71.—Sutta 71 is unusually short. Buddha disclaims all pretence to omniscience (after the Jaina manner), claiming as a substitute the knowledge of the "three vijjās". This doubtless belongs to an early stratum for the issue was, with the growth of apotheosis, soon involved in controversy, and even the least pretentious view which seems to find representation in MN. 90, went beyond the sutta under consideration.

Sutta 108.—Sutta 108 seems to contain a historical narrative setting; it claims to belong to a period shortly after Buddha's death, when Ajātasattu was threatened by Pajjota and Rājagaha was being fortified. Such settings are quite rare in the Nikāyas, and there seems to be no reason to doubt the veracity of the present one. Also,

[27] Cf. MN, 61 "se retrouve à peu près identique dans la collection sanskrite traduite en chinois (Madhyamāgama-sūtra 14 Tchoung A-Lan)." (Lévi—JA 1912, Nov.-Dec., 495).

the contents of the sutta are quite in line with the supposition that its compilation is not far removed in time from the events which it describes. Ānanda explains to the Brāhmaṇas Gopaka Moggalāna and Vassakāra—the Magadhan mahāmatta—that Buddha had not appointed any individual as his successor, and that consequently "Dhamma" alone was their Refuge (Paṭisarana). Dhamma is defined, not as sutta and vinaya, but as " (Yaṃ) Sikkhāpadaṃ paññattaṃ Pātimokkhaṃ uddiṭṭham."[28] Ānanda also recounts the ten "Pasādanīyadhammas" which include the more important "Sāmaññaphalas."[29] This summary of the "Dhamma" appears to belong to an age when the canonized literature and with it the central doctrines of the Buddhist community had not yet attained to any great elaboration. Besides, the fact that Buddha left behind him no individual as successor could have been a curiosity only while it was yet a novelty, and it could not have remained that much longer after Buddha's death, at least in the area about Rājagaha.

Sutta 144.—Sutta 144 relates the last moments of Channa, who commits suicide. That custom is an old one finding its parallel among the Jinists.[30] It is true that the sutta contains a section in catechistic style on the "Anattahood" of the senses, the sense-perceptions and the "sense-perceptible" objects. But that is far from being any certain indication of lateness. On the other hand, the following words of Mahācunda addressed to Channa seem to contain a quotation with a decidedly

---

[28] MN. III, p. 10.

[29] On the earliness of the Sāmaññaphala-list see remarks on DN. 2........

[30] See below.

archaic imprint "Tasmātiha, āvuso channa, idaṃ pi tassa Bhagavato sāsanaṃ niccakappaṃ manasikātabbaṃ; nissitassa calitaṃ anissitassa calitaṃ natthi; calite asati passaddhi,* passaddhiyā sati nati na hoti; natiyā asati āgatigati na hoti; āgatigatiyā asati cutūpapāto na hoti; cutūpapāte asati n'en'edha na huraṃ na ubhayamantarena es'evanto dukkhassāti."[31] The style of this passage may be compared with that of the passage in the Devadaha sutta[32] which summarizes the Jinist doctrine. Again, the following sentence of Buddha, who does not condemn the action of Channa,[33] is hardly harmonious with the Anatta doctrine as understood later—"Yo kho Sāriputta, imañca kāyam nikkhipati aññañca kāyaṃ upādiyati, tamahaṃ sa-upavajjoti vadāmi."[34]

Finally, the earliness of the sutta is presumptive in the sense that there is little intrinsic probability in an obituary sutta being composed de novo long after the death of the person concerned. Of course, that does not rule out the possibility of a "re-dressing" of older material.

(*b*) *Late*:

Sutta 8.—It presents a lengthy list of forty-four qualities to be practised, if true austerities (Sallekha) are to be followed. It is quite possible that we have here the inflated form of a previously existing less verbose and more pointed "Sallekhapariyāya" which attempted to distinguish the Buddhist discipline from current ascetic and mystic practices.

* The PTS. ed. places the comma after sati.

31 MN. III, p. 266.

32 Cf. also Ud., p. 8 (Nāg. ed.).

33 The moral issue which arises is similar to that faced by B. immediately after Realization.

34 Loc. cit.

Sutta 12.—MN. 12 or the Mahāsīhanāda° is as lengthy as it is exaggerated.[35] Sunakkhatta Licchaviputta casts aspersions on Buddha's supernormal powers and the Dhamma preached by him. This rouses Buddha to grandiloquent self-praise; he details the ten Powers (Balas) of the Tathāgata and his four Excellences (Vesārajjas), and then goes on to describe the knowledge that he possesses of the 8 Parisās, the 4 Yonis, and the 5 Gatis. After this he proves himself to be the Paramatapassī, the Paramalūkho, the Paramajegucchī and the Paramavivitto. He is even sensitive on the score of his age which is stated to be eighty and explicitly asserts his superiority in energy to several young men put together.[36] And he takes care to point out several times that anyone who disparaged him was as good as thrown intc hell.

In occasion and spirit this sutta resembles the Pāṭikasuttanta of the DN.[37] while with the Cūlasīhanāda° it has no more than titular similarity.

Sutta 28.—MN. 28 contains a sermon by Sāriputta in which he explains a very developed theory of the Five Khandhas. Man is regarded as an aggregate of impermanent matter and "dependent" phenomena. The four elements are described in great detail, and the conception of Viññāṇa is purely "epiphenomenal". It seems to use "ākāso" in the sense of empty space.[38]

The lateness of the sutta is confirmed by the fact

---

[35] With its description of B's asceticism compare that in sutta 36.

[36] With this contrast the humility apparent in a section of D. 16 whence the expression about the age as eighty seems to have been taken.

[37] Where the same person disparages B. on the score of miracles.

[38] MN. I, p. 190.

that it explicitly quotes from M 21[39] "vuttaṃ kho panetaṃ bhagavatā kakacūpamovāde: ubhatodaṇḍakenāpi ce bhikkhave corā acarakā aṅgamaṅgāni okanteyyuṃ, tatra pi yo mano padoseyya na me so tena sāsanakaroti."[40] There is another quotation in the sutta on pages 190—1 "vuttaṃ kho panetaṃ Bhagavatā: yo Paṭiccasamuppādaṃ passati so dhammam passati, yo dhmmaṃ passati...." (cf. "Yo bhikṣavaḥ pratītyasamutpādaṃ paśyati sa dharmam pasyati, yo dharmaṃ paśyati sa Buddhaṃ paśyati." Quoted in AK. V. III. p. 48). This time, however, the source is not specified. Sutta 32 suggests its lateness by containing the developed standardized list of the nine meditative stages,[41] as well as another of eight classes of gods.

Sutta 33.—The next sutta contains an elaborate comparison of the Bhikkhu with the cowherd, establishing no less than eleven points of contact. Buddha begins the sermon with "Ekādaschi bhikkhave aṅgehi samannāgato etc.[42] and the style is reminiscent of the AN. Further, in speaking of "bhikkhū....dhammadharā vinaya° mātikā°...."[43] the sutta implies that these three distinct classes had already come into existence, that is to say, it bespeaks a developed stage of canonical literature. Finally, it may be noted that the sutta lays a great stress on respect being shown to the "Elders": "Ye te bhikkhū therā rattaññū cirappabbajitā saṅghapitaro saṅghapariṇāyakā te atirekapūjāya pūjetā hoti."[44] Now Anesaki tells

[39] Which contains a most glowing description of the ideal of Mettā. It abounds in similes and parables. It is perhaps a very early sutta.

[40] Ib. p. 189.

[41] On the growth of this list see chap. on way.

[42] MN. I. p. 220.

[43] Ib. 221.

[44] Ib. P. 222, 224.

[45] JRAS 1901 p. 897.

us "In the chinese Āgamas the title (Thera) occurs, as far as I know, only thrice—the title Āyuṣman being used otherwise in such cases. Can we conclude either that the Chinese version is derived from traditions dating from an age in the history of Buddhism when the authority of the Theras was not yet solidified, or it descended from a school antagonistic to the authority of the orthodox Theras?"

Now it is important to notice that in sutta 108 of MN. Ānanda tells a Brāhmaṇa that the criteria of respect were furnished to them by the ten Pasādanīya dhaṃmas which Buddha had declared "Yasmiṃ no ime dhammā saṃvijjanti taṃ mayaṃ etarahi sakkaroma mānena pūjema, sakkatvā garukatvā upanissāya vihārama ...."[46] Of age, of "Therā....cirappabbajitā saṅghapitaro...." as the recipients of special honour, there is here no talk. It appears, therefore, that the authority of the "Elders" grew only gradually;[47] and was never recognized by all. The present sutta (MN. 33) openly ranges itself on the "authoritarian" side and thereby confirms the general picture of its lateness.

Sutta 35.—Sutta 35 contains a disputation between Saccaka—the Nigaṇṭhaputta—and Buddha in the midst of a Licchavi assembly. Buddha summarizes his position in the formula "Rūpaṃ bhikkhave aniccaṃ...... viññāṇaṃ aniccaṃ; rūpaṃ....anattā....viññāṇaṃ anattā; sabbe saṅkhārā aniccā, sabbe dhammā anattā, ti."[48] The doctrine of Anatta in the Five khandhas has

[46] MN. III. p. 11.

[47] The traces of a *"solitary hermit" stage* in the development of the saṅgha also supports it.

[48] MN. I. p. 230 The same summary by Assaji on p. 229; with it may be compared the other summary by him in the Mahāvagga: ye dhammā hetuppabhavā"etc. Both are marked by the same degree of abstraction and generality.

here come to occupy the central place in the Buddhist teaching and actually overshadows all else. This orientation suggests a mature scholastic age.

Saccaka Nigaṇṭhaputta is represented as implicitly accepting this fivefold analysis of the Purisapuggala, only asserting the "Attahood" of the khandhas. This even remotely fails to connect with what we know of the Nigaṇṭha views of soul and mind. Either, then, the whole situation is merely a literary device to reassert the banal catechism on the Three Marks as applied to the Five Khandhas;[49] or the redactor was so steeped in the latter theory that he could present nothing better than a very garbled version of the Nigaṇṭhaputta's view. The second alternative is in fact suggested by a closer examination of Saccaka's statement. He begins promisingly with the simile "Seyyathāpi bho Gotama ye kecime bījagāmabhūtagāmā vuḍḍhiṃ virūdhiṃ vepullam āpajjanti sabbe te paṭhaviṃ nissāya paṭhaviyaṃ patiṭṭhāya seyyathāpi....ye kecime balakaraṇā kammantā karīyanti sabbe pathvim nissāya paṭhaviyaṃ patiṭṭhāya...."[50] This at once brings before the mind the view that regarded Rūpa as the Nissaya or Patiṭṭhā of Viññāṇa. But what actually follows is much less coherent and to the point "Evameva...rūpattāyam purisapugalo rūpe patiṭṭhāya....viññāṇattā...."[51] These lines appear to have usurped the place of some more fitting sequel. There are other instances also of similar aggrandizement by the Five Khandha formula.

A final indication of the lateness of the sutta may be found in the fact of a Yakkha intervening on behalf

[49] Ib., pp. 232–233.
[50] Ib., p. 230.
[51] Loc. cit.

of Buddha in the dispute; such a miraculous occurrence is found in DN. 3 also.

Suttas 41, 42.—These are variants of the same sutta, the difference being confined to the names of the place and the persons in the preamble. The main sermon is exactly identical in the two. It synthesizes the two ideas of the threefold pure and impure action and the ten "sīlas" into a single scheme, thus offering a list of three types of mental, four types of vocal and three types of physical good and evil deeds. Its lateness, however, comes out much more clearly from the fact that it presents a hierarchy of twenty-five classes of gods, of which no less than eighteen are above the "Brahmakāyikas": This surely indicates a great anterior development of Buddhist mythology.

Suttas 43, 44.—Suttas 43-44 are the two well-known Vedalla suttas. They are concerned with the explanation of a series of technical terms in catechism style. The discussions take place in dry philosophical and dogmatic atmosphere, and involve essays in precise definition and fine distinctions, as for example, between Paññā and Viññāṇa.[51a] The whole presupposes considerable doctrinal development, and shows very clearly the tendencies of scholastic systematization. It is significant that Buddha is not a participant in either of the discussions, although in the second, he praises Dhammadinnā at the end.

Sutta 50.—Sutta 50 relates the interesting episode of Māra entering the belly of Mahāmoggalāna and being informed that he (the Māra) happened to be in a way the latter's (Moggalāna's) nephew. Mahāmoggalāna recalls how in the days of the Kakusandha

[51a] MN. I, 292–293.

Buddha, he had been the Māra Dūsī whose sister's (Kāḷi's) son the present Māra was. At the end occur a number of verses, which refer clearly to sutta 37, recalling the marvellous exploits of Mahāmoggalāna therein.[51b]

The sutta obviously belongs to an age when the memory of the apostles had been wholly covered over by the mists of myth. The mentioning by name of a previous Buddha also indicates lateness.

Sutta 64.—Its lateness is suggested by the fact that it distinguishes between Cetovimutti and Paññāvimutti "——Atha kiñcarahi ekacce bhikkhū cetovimuttino ekacce Paññāvimuttinoti."[51c] The rest of the sutta fits in with this impression since it explains the formula of the five "Orambhāgiya saññojanas" and details the first seven meditative stages (upto viññāṇānañcāyatana) as the way out; Ib. para 2 (Nāg. ed.) raises a very interesting problem which may be thus formulated: since the child's mental development is so immature,[51d] how can the "Anusayas" be said to apply to him? That they nevertheless do apply, is dogmatically asserted to be the case. An explanation, however, is not given; instead, the five saṃyojanas are expounded in the usual way. Now the implication behind the view would seem to be that the Anusayas are "cittavippayutta", i.e., the existence of immoral tendencies in a person is consistent with his unconsciousness of them. Some sects, we know, actually held this view. Has, then, an imperfect expurgation occurred here?

Sutta 75, which is long and straggling in its present form at any rate, appears late since it describes the

[51b] See II, 17–23, pp. 237–238 of M.I.

[51c] MN. pt. I, p. 107 (Nāg. ed.).

[51d] The text explains this immaturity in detail—cf. sutta 78.

early life of Gotama in a way which suggests that myth-making had already commenced to fill in the gaps in memory. The lines in question are "Tassa mayhaṃ Māgandiya tayo pāsādā ahesuṃ, eko vassiko, eko hemantiko, eko gimhiko, So kho ahaṃ Māgandiya vassike pāsāde vassike cattāro māse nippurisehi turiyehi paricāriyamāno na heṭṭhā pāsādaṃ ārohāmi.'[52]

The sutta, however, undoubtedly contains some early looking material, as, for instance, the charge of being a "Bhūnahu" against Gotama or the parable of the "Jaccandhas".

Sutta 77 is very long collection of miscellaneous elements which include those of the 37 Bodhipakkhiya dhammas, as well as the 8 vimokkhas, the 8 Abhibhāyatanas and the 10 kasiṇāyatanas. Very considerable dogmatic development is, thus, presupposed.

Sutta 81 relates a tale in which the Kassapa Buddha plays an important role, and thus indicates its own lateness.

Sutta 90 is a medium-sized unified work answering miscellaneous queries in the form of a dialogue between Buddha and King Pasenadi. Its interpretation of'Omniscience' is more scholastic than in sutta 71. It represents as a matter of fact the Sarvāstivādin view as against that of the Mahāsaṅghikas and the Vātsīputrīyas.[53] Further, it is interesting to note that it is much less liberal in its outlook on caste than sutta 84.[54]

Sutta 91 enumerates the thirty-two marks of great men, describes the ideal (which are at the same time patently conventional) ways of Buddha in everyday life.

[52] MN. Pt. 2, p. 175 (Nāg. ed.).

[53] MN. Pt. II, p. 331 (Nāg. ed.) cf. Ab K. volume VI, pp. 254–255.

[54] Contra Ib., p. 332 with p. 271.

Sutta 93.—deals with caste and looks less like a dialogue than a sustained literary essay full of scintillating polemic. Its reference to the "Yona-Kambojas" suggests its lateness.

Sutta 94.—describes the events which led to the building of an Upaṭṭhānasālā for the saṅgha at Pāṭaliputta by the Brāhmaṇa Ghoṭamukha. It closes with the sentence "Sā etarahi Ghoṭamukhīti vuccati."[55] It appears that the narrator is not dealing with contemporary events but rather relating an old legend, possibly eponymous in origin.

It may be noted that the sutta expressly refers to Buddha as Parinibbuta. Also, the categorical statement of Udena "Na kho no....kappati jātarūparajataṃ paṭigaṇhetuṃ ti"[56] is strongly reminiscent of the controversies that raged in the "second council".

In sutta 103 the doctrine is thus briefly and technically explained "Seyyathīdaṃ cattāro satipaṭṭhānā, cattāro sammappadhānā, cattāro iddhipādā, pañcindriyāṇi, pañca balāni, satta bojjhaṅgā, ariyo aṭṭhaṅgiko maggo".[57] The formulæ for the 37 Bodhipakkhiyā Dhammā have obviously become so well established that the need for explaining them was not felt.

Then, the sutta passes on to admonition in case "Siyaṃsū dve bhikkhū abhidhamme nānāvādā".[58] The Abhidhammic controversies only generally referred to, are of an interpretative character. This also indicates the lateness of the sutta.

The lateness of sutta 102 is suggested by several circumstances. It begins with a succinct statement of

[55] Ib. p. 373.
[56] Ib. p. 372.
[57] M. II. p. 238–'9 (PTS ed.).
[58] Ib. p. 239.

the argument of the sutta (uddesa as it is called), which, concerned like the Brahmajāla° with heterodox metaphysical speculation, reclassifies the usual five Aparantānudiṭṭhis into three. It has a greater number of "indeterminate" problems than the standard list, and all are here treated according to the fourfold dialectic. The present sutta therefore appears to be the result of a further scholastic activity over some of the material in the Brahmajāla.

Sutta 109.—presents a close scholastic analysis of the Five Khandhas in catechism style. What, however, is of great interest is the fact that a very pertinent objection to the Anatta-theory—why should the actions of the Anatta touch anybody?[59]—is raised but left unanswered. Instead, we have the banal catechism on the three Marks as applied to the Five Khandhas. This strongly raises the suspicion that the original sequel has been deleted and replaced by a sort of "panacea"—answer.

Sutta 111.—contains an unusually detailed psychological analysis of the nine meditative stages upto Saññāvedayitanirodha. Mrs. Rhys Davids points out the similarity of the style with that adopted in the Dhs.[60] Her statement that we have to regard it as an 'early' example of that style is true enough, but then it would be equally true to say that the style itself is late. Compared to the "abhidhammic" texts the present sutta may be early but its very resemblance to those writings suggests that it must be regarded as late when our quest is to find out the original mandate of Buddhism.

Sutta 112.—presents the spectacle of heterogeneous elements of different stages thrown together without the

---

[59] Ib. III. p. 19.

[60] JRAS 1902.

least regard for consistency. It has, *e.g.*, four different conceptions of viññāṇa: as one of the 5 khandhas, as one of the 6 dhātus, as the 6-fold perception, and as the counterpart of the body. The sutta appears in the nature of a collection of the doctrines which "tena bhagavatā jānatā passatā arahatā sammāsambuddhena sammadakkhātā",[61] and presupposes a considerable previous growth of these.

Sutta 115 declares him a learned monk (Paṇḍitobhikkhu) who is "dhātukusalo ca—āyatana°....Paticcasamuppāda°....ṭhānaṭṭhānakusalo ca...."[62] And then proceeds to explain (enumerate, rather) these with dogmatic terseness. At the outset comes the string of six groups of "dhātus": the 18 dhātus; the three groups of six dhātus; three dhātus; and two dhātus. The order of diminishing numbers may be noted. Then follows Paṭiccasaṃ° preceded by its general and abstract formulation.

As in the sutta considered above, it is mainly the state of doctrinal development reflected in it which suggests the lateness of the sutta. The prominence of dry-as-dust classification and enumeration harmonizes with this suggestion.[63]

Sutta 116 speaks of 500 Pacceka Buddhas as having dwelt in the Isigili hill of Rājagaha, and caps this statement by a remarkably long list of their names, both in prose and in verse.

---

[61] MN. III. p. 29. etc.

[62] Ib. p. 62.

[63] Cf. "Another feature suggestive of later workmanship is the exhaustive enumeration of categories of Dhātuyo put into the mouth of Gotama in sutta 115" Mrs. Rhys Davids JRAS 1902, p. 476.

Of sutta 102, she remarks that Gotama instead of waving aside speculation as was his wont analyses and criticizes it "more like a doctor of church than its founder" (Ib) See below.

Sutta 120 enumerates 25 classes of gods; it subdivides the Brahmās into sahasso°, dvisahasso°, ti°, catu°, pañca°, dasa°, and sata°, and speaks of the sahassīlokadhātu, pañca°, dasa°, and sata°. Mythological system-construction has advanced far indeed!

Sutta 123 describes a large number of "abbhuta-dhammas" which must accompany the ante-natal preparations and the final birth of a "Bodhisatta". The sutta obviously belongs to a period when the Buddha was a full fledged god, or rather, more, and his birth a miraculous descent of the divine.

Of **suttas 129–130** Mrs. Rhys Davids remarks that Gotama here treats of retribution in afterlife "with a picturesqueness worthy of a mediaeval prior or a village curé".[64] From this, according to Winternitz, it is not possible to argue for the lateness of these suttas, since it is possible that "even in earlier times a more popular conception of the doctrine of karman may have existed side by side with the purely philosophical one".[65] This possibility would have been indicated had Buddhism been like, say, the Vedic religion, which rising from comparatively primitive-popular conditions became gradually, along one line of its development, increasingly philosophical and esoteric. There it would be correct to argue, for instance, that the "Atharvaṇic" hymns of the 10th maṇḍala of RS, do not necessarily indicate lateness. Buddhism, however, started as the elevated message of a sublime spiritual personality addressed primarily to the purpose of Nibbāna. Its mystic-esoteric emphasis is plain from the beginning. The extent of lay following must have been to start with quite restricted, and that too, it appears, was confined mainly to the wealthy

[64] JRAS, 1902, p. 476.　　[65] Op. cit. II. p. 53.

and aristocratic classes. Of course, the humanitarian impulse[66] which the original message contained—the seed of an aspect of mahāyānism—must have in course of time resulted in the introduction and growth of a more popular and less esoteric side to Buddhism. This is not contested. But the point is, when did this aspect become important enough to produce such canonical literature as is represented in the suttas under consideration? It appears that this could hardly have happened in the earliest age of the history of Buddhist scriptural writings. Beside the general argument mentioned above, it may be urged that those suttas which are more or less clearly early, nowhere represent Buddha as inculcating a morality based on fear. His argument against sin does not appear to have been an appeal to hell fire.

It may be noted that the conception of hell torments is far from being very prominent in Vedic literature. The source from which the Buddhists drew in elaborating it, apart from an over-vivid imagination, appears to have been Jinist tradition.

Suttas 131—134 are built round the same "uddesa" which consists of four "gāthās" pertaining to the "Bhaddekaratta". In 131 which is entitled Bhaddakaratta sutta, Buddha after enunciating the Uddesa goes on into a vibhaṅga which construes the simple and quite non-dogmatic advice about looking with equanimity at the present and not running after the past or the future, to mean that one must never identify oneself with any of the five khandhas and then rejoice over it. It is clearly the case of a set of hallowed old verses interpreted exclusively in terms of a later dogma.

---

[66] These terms, however, must be understood with a certain reserve:—The doctrine of Mettā was originally much more "mystic" than "humanitarian".

Sutta 132, entitled Ānandabhaddekaratta°, shows Ānanda repeating the sermon; Buddha praises him and himself repeats it. In sutta 132, entitled Mahākaccāna-bhaddekaratta°, the monks forget the uddesa and vibhaṅga of the Bhaddekaratta and approach Buddha who enunciates only the uddesa and hence the Bhikkhus ask Mahākaccāna to supply the vibhaṅga. He complies with the request but we get a new vibhaṅga this time, which requests the Bhikku to see that the Viññāṇa is not ensnared in the senses and the sense objects. At the end Buddha commends the exposition. It is noticeable that the conception of Viññāṇa here is different from and earlier than that in the previous two suttas.

Sutta 134, "Lomasakaṅgiyabhaddekaratta", employs the expression "Bhaddekarattiyo gāthā". It has the same sermon as in 131-132.

In **sutta 135** Buddha is asked the cause of inequality among men, and he answers "Kammassakā, māṇava, sattā kammadāyādā kammayonī kammabandhū kammapaṭi-saraṇā, kammaṃ satte vibhajati yadidaṃ hīnappaṇītatā-yāti".[67] The Māṇava, however, is slow to grasp, and an explanation follows, which consists in showing how particular sins are visited with particular retributions. Now the main text occurs identically elsewhere also in the Nikāyas,[68] but followed by a different explanation. It appears, therefore, that it represents an ancient text on which the present sutta comments. The distinctive elevation of style of the fragment quoted above is notable.

Sutta 137 has the following uddesa "Cha ajjhatti-kāni āyatanāni veditabbāni: cha bāhirāni....: cha

[67] MN. III. p. 203.
[68] AN. III. 186: V. 288.

viññāṇakāyā veditabbā; cha phassakāyā....; aṭṭhādasa manopavicārā—; chattiṃsa sattapadā tatridaṃ nissāya idaṃ pajahatha. Tayo satipaṭṭhānā yadariyo sevati yadariyo sevamāno satthā gaṇamanusāsitumarahati. So vuccati yoggācariyānaṃ anuttaro purisadaṃmasārathīti. Ayamuddeso saḷāyatanavibhaṅgassa."[69] It is obviously nothing better than an abstract of the details that follow, and probably represents nothing more. The dogmatic enumeration and classifications which exhaust the sutta suggest its lateness.

It may be noted that the term satipaṭṭhānā is here used in a very unusual sense.

Suttas 141, 142:—It is on account of these suttas that the vibhaṅgavagga exhibits the anomaly of containing twelve suttas instead of ten as the other vaggas in the MN do. In form also these diverge most from the other suttas in the vagga. In sutta 141, Buddha tells the Bhikkhus "Tathāgatena...arahatā sammāsambuddhena Bārāṇasiyaṃ...dhammacakkaṃ pavattitaṃ...yadidaṃ catunnaṃ ariyasaccānaṃ ācikkhanā desanā paññapanā paṭṭhapanā vivaraṇā vibhajanā uttānīkaṃmaṃ."[70] He mentions these and asks the Bhikkhus to go to Sāriputta-Moggalāna for their better exposition. Then follows a term by term explanation by Sāriputta of the formula for the Four Truths. The prominence of the style of dictionary-definitions is quite marked. There can hardly be a doubt that this sutta is no more than an early commentary on the First Sermon.***

---

[69] MN. III, p. 216.

[70] The inappropriateness of this reference to self in grandiloquent third person tells its own tale.

*** It is worth noting that in this summary and comment on the First Sermon, no reference at all is made to the advice

Of the next sutta Mrs. Rhys Davids remarks that it makes Ānanda plead the cause of Gotamī a second time. and belongs properly to Vinaya. She seems to be quite right in regarding both these suttas as probably interpolated in the vagga.[71]

Sutta 143 is a curious jumble. It speaks among others of the 6 senses, Viññāṇa, samphassas, samphassajavedanās, dhātus (Paṭhavī...viññāṇa) the 5 khandhas, and of the viññāṇa as nissita or a° in all these elements. It thus has at least four conceptions of Viññāṇa: (1) as perception, in the group cakkhuviññāṇa, etc.; (2) as one of the six ultimate elements (Dhātus); (3) as the fifth khandha and (4) as an entity which is different from all the psychological factors enumerated but liable to be entangled in them. These various conceptions of Viññāṇa grew up in different contexts, and not all of them at the same time. Our present sutta accomplishes just a mechanical assemblage of the results of several independent inquiries, belonging to diverse doctrinal strata. The resultant incongruity comes out clearly in the expression which the sutta has to repeat more than once: "Viññāṇanissitaṃ viññāṇaṃ".[72] The soul-like character of this latter viññāṇa suggests, however, that the sutta is not without an ancient nucleus. This is supported by the fact that the sutta purports to describe the last hours of Anāthapiṇḍika. That a sutta relating to the death of that great patron of the saṅgha should have existed early, accords wholly with general probability.

---

about avoiding the two extremes. Is that because this part of the sermon has already been commented upon in sutta 139?

[71] JRAS 1902, p. 475.

[72] MN. III, pp. 259-260.

(*c*) *Composite*:

Sutta 3 contains a sermon by Buddha and then one by Sāriputa. The former in its two paragraphs contains two distinct divisions. The first is a short, extremely high-minded earnest sermon: Be my Dhammadāyāda, not Āmisa°. In its rugged directness, the repetitive ringing phraseology, and the very nature of its contents, it is strangely reminiscent of Aśokan rescripts. An example is afforded by its very first sentence: "Dhammadāyāda me bhikkhave bhavathamā no āmisadāyādā; atthi me tumhesu anukampā; kinti me sāvakā dhammadāyāda bhaveyyuṃ no āmisadāyādāti".[73] The fact that this first sentence recurs at the end of the paragraph in the form "Tasmātiha me bhikkhave dhammadāyāda bhavatha etc.," seems to indicate the end of the sermon, or at least of as much of it as was at all remembered later with any degree of faithfulness. The nature of the longer succeeding para points in the same direction. It seems to understand Āmisādāyāda quite literally illustrating it by a hungry Bhikkhu who, invited by Buddha himself to partake of the extra food in his (Buddha's) almsbowl in order to avoid waste, proceeds to do so. The condemnation of the Bhikkhu appears as unreasonable as bathetic. That Buddha should have proceeded to illustrate his pregnant opening words by so depressing an example and buttress it by a no more inspiring appeal to a type of asceticism which attaches great significance to denial in small matters, placing it above the plain dictates of commonsense, is hardly credible. It may be remembered that this type of unreasoning asceticism is quite opposed to the general attitude of Buddha on the subject, and is, moreover, specifically condemned in the

[73] MN. I. p. 12.

sutta that just precedes the present one, according to which hunger falls in the type of "āsavas" that are "Adhivāsanāpathātabbā".[74]

As to Sāriputta's sermon, the data are not decisive, but the fact that it introduces the formula of the eightfold path, and a considerable list of evil emotions and desires, which also occurs inorganically at the end of some sections in the AN,[75] seems to indicate its comparative lateness.

The first para of Buddha's sermon in the sutta may, therefore, be regarded as an example of the class of early fragments embedded in longer texts.

Sutta 22 is composed of several independent "subsuttas" (a) (MN. I. pp. 130-135) Buddha rebukes Ariṭṭha for misunderstanding him to the grievous extent of regarding sensual indulgence as permitted. To illustrate the delusive understanding of *the nine Aṅgas of the canon*—which are named—Buddha adduces the Alagaddūpamā after which the sutta as a whole has received its title. He concludes with the injunction "Tasmātiha bhikkhave yassa mẹ bhāsitassa atthaṃ ājāneyyātha tathā naṃ dhāreyyātha. Yassa ca pana.....na ājāneyyātha ahaṃ vo tattha paṭipucchitabbo ye vā panassu viyattā bhikkhū."[76]

Then follows abruptly a paragraph on kullūpamā, which, however, reveals its connection at the end "evameva kho bhikkhave kullūpamo mayā dhammo desito nittharaṇatthāya vo no gahaṇtthāya. Kullūpamaṃ, vo...ājānantehi dhammā pi pahātabbā, pageva adhaṃmā".[77] This "comparison" expresses in a force-

[74] MN. I. p. 10.
[75] e.g. AN. III. p. 278; 452.
[76] Ib. p. 134.
[77] Ib. 135. It is also ref. in sotta 38 Ib. pp. 260-261.

ful and original way an elevated idea. The section (a) as a whole, however, is doubtless late, since it speaks of the 9 Aṅgas of the canon.[78] It appears, therefore, that the Kullūpamā is within it an "early fragment" just as the statement of the Bhikkhus "Appassādā kāmā vuttā-bhagavatā bahudukkhā bahūpāyāsā, ādīnavo ettha bhiyyo aṭṭhikaṅkalūpamā kāmā vuttā..maṃsapesūpamā... (till) sappasirūpamā...",[79] appears to be the quotation, or a standardized summary of older doctrines. The sentence "Appassādā...ettha bhiyyo" and the "upamās" occur identically elsewhere also in the canon.

(b) (MN. I pp. 135-142) Then begins a little relevant, lengthy discourse on the "points of speculation" (Diṭṭhiṭṭhānas) in catechism style. It describes the six viewpoints about the Attā, applies the "three marks" to the five khandhas, defines a number of old terms that have now come to be technical, as, e.g., ukkhittapaligho, sankiṇṇaparikho etc.,[80] and has a para on "Na tumhākaṃ[81] which occurs as a separate sutta in SN. II & III, and which, according to Mrs. Rhys Davids, itself suffers from interpolation.[82]

The sutta is thus clearly composite, i.e., an assemblage of parts which are neither organically connected nor can all be supposed to belong to the same literary or ideological stratum.

Sutta 19, is also composed of independent sections. The first concerns the dichotomy of the Vitakkas with a view to better introspection. They are to be divided into two classes, one comprising Kāma°, vyāpāda° and

---

[78] Ib. p. 133.
[79] Ib. p. 130.
[80] Ib. p. 139.
[81] See Sakya—p. 325.
[82] Ib. p. 140-141.

vihiṃsā and the other their opposites; the relation of the Bhikkhu to those belonging to the former class should be as of the cowherd to his charge in early autumn, whose freedom from anxiety on its account in early rains illustrates the attitude to be cultivated towards the latter class. This alone has the claim to the title "Dvedhāvitakkasutta" proper. The advice, it may be noticed, is derived by Buddha from his own reminiscences of the days when he was only a "Bodhisatta".[83] This indicates that the sutta is late.

Then follows the stock-text from the first Jhāna to the attainment of the three Vijjās. It appears that in the narrative attitude our author forgot that it was not his purpose to describe the whole spiritual career of the Bodhisattva.

This is followed abruptly by an entirely independent section containing the parable of the deer (Migasaṅgha°").[84] It illustrates how Māra ensnares men by Nandirāga & Avijjā, opening for them the false eightfold path, and how the Tathāgata undoes his work by showing the right way. It closes with an earnest exhortation to the Bhikkhus to meditate.[85] The parabolic style of this section as also the simple and practical character of its teachings suggest in a general way its earliness. It is true that it contains a formula, but that is among the earliest evolved by the Buddhist community.[86] At any rate this appendent section is most probably earlier than the first which uses the term "Bodhisatta". As to why it came to occupy its present

[84] Cf. the Nivāpa sutta. [83] MN. I. 114.

[85] The lines "yaṃ bhikkhave satthārā karaṇīyam.... anusāsanīti" (Ib. p. 118) occurs elsewhere also e.g. in the AN. and the SN.

[86] See Chap. on Way.

place is difficult to explain. Perhaps two immediate suttas have become rolled into one.[87]

Sutta 38 (Mahātaṇhāsaṅkhaya°) has three distinct divisions: (a) MN. I, pp. 256-260. The first contains the very important criticism of Sāti by Buddha. Sāti thought that viññāṇa could be regarded as an identical, unchanging transmigrant "Tathāhaṃ Bhagavatā dhammaṃ desitaṃ ājānāmi yathā tadevidaṃ viññāṇaṃ sandhāvati saṃsarati anaññanti". Now, as will be seen more clearly later, since Buddha also believed in a transcendental viññāṇa to which the category of becoming was inapplicable, he very properly asks "katamantaṃ Sāti Viññāṇanti".[88] The answer of Sāti—"Yvāyam bhante vado vedeyyo tatra tatra kalyāṇapāpakānaṃ kammānaṃ vipākaṃ paṭisaṃvedetīti" showed, however, that he meant no more than the empirical self, which according to Buddha was completely analyzable into the contingent reactions of the senses and the mind (the 6th sense) to the corresponding objects and hence was constituted of elements in incessant transformation. And, pointing out as much in effect, Buddha consequently rebuked Sāti for his misunderstanding. Sāti did not realize that the consciousness that is unchanging is not individual, and the consciousness that is individual is not unchanging. His error lay fundamentally in supposing the viññāṇa 'an sich' to be the same as its particular manifestations and hence Buddha emphasized "Yaññadeva bhikkhave paccayam paṭicca uppajjati viññāṇaṃ tena teneva saṅkhaṃ gacchati. . ."[89] This is illustrated by the "fire-comparison"—"Seyyathāpi Bhikkave yaññadeva paccayampaṭicca aggi jalati tena teneva saṅkham gacchati:

[87] Cf. the Chinese version.
[88] MN. I, p. 258 cf. the remarks in PTSD (sub viññāṇa).
[89] Ib., p. 259.

kaṭṭham ca paṭicca aggi jalati kaṭṭhaggi tena saṅkhaṃ gacchati; sakalikañ ca paṭicca...sakalikaggi tv'eva" etc."[90] So are the Cakkhuviññāṇa, etc. To correct Sāti's "confusion" the emphasis is here laid not on the identical entity that lies behind the manifestations, but on the contingency, plurality and impermanence of these latter. It may be noted that in sutta 96 this very simile occurs but owing to the change in context with the opposite emphasis. Buddha there criticizes the Brāhmaṇic attempt to erect impassable barriers between one caste and another, and hence says: "Ariyaṃ khvāhaṃ, brāhmaṇa lokuttaraṃ dhammaṃ purisassa sandhanaṃ paññāpemi. Porāṇaṃ kho panassa mātāpettikaṃ kulavaṃsamanussarato yattha yatthéva attabhāvassābhinibbatti hoti tena teneva saṅkhaṃ gacchati, khattiyakule ce etc.,"[91] and then follows the comparison. Here the transcendental (lokuttara) essence that lies at the back of the accidents of individuality (Attabhāva) receives emphasis.[92] Both the aspects are as a matter of fact complementary, and it was an over-accentuation of the second that led to the later "Anattavāda".

(*b*) MN. I, pp. 261-265. Buddha had made reference in general to the concepts of Paṭiccasamuppanna and Āhārasambhava in (a); (b), therefore, takes the opportunity to explain in a dry catechistic style the later ideas

[90] Ib., p. 259. [91] MN. Pt. II, p. 391 (Nāg. ed.).

[92] It is the same in sutta 90, where a "fire-simile" is used to show that there is no difference in the emancipation attained through the different Padhāniyaṅgas "seyyathāpi, mahārāja, puriso sukkhaṃ sālakaṭṭhamādāya aggiṃ abhinibbatteya, tejo pātukareyya; atha aparo puriso....ambakaṭṭhamādāya.... udumbarakaṭṭhamādāya....siyā nu kho tesamaggīnaṃ nānādāruto abhinibbattānaṃ kinci nānākaraṇaṃ-acciyā accim, vaṇṇena vā vaṇṇaṃ, ābhāya vā ābhaṃ ti? No hetaṃ bhante...." (MN. pt. II, p. 333-334 Nāg. ed.). It may be remarked that in the Kaṭha a "fire-simile" is used to bring into relief the immanent unity of phenomena.

of the four Āhāras and the full grown formula of Paṭiccasamuppāda, incidentally correlating the two. The scholastic interpolator concludes irrelevantly: knowing thus the Bhikkhu will not run after Pubbanta or Aparanta, which brings into relief the Sandiṭṭhika character of Dhaṃma. (c) (M. I. pp. 265-270). This is the real Taṇhāsaṅkhayasutta. It contains a version of Paṭiccasamuppāda different from that in (b), and taking up the problem of bondage and misery through desire, which now emerges, suggests the practice of Sīla and the four Jhānas as the way out. Its earliness is indicated by its interpretation of Paṭiccasaṃ°;[93] by the fact that it contains only the (cūḷasīlas), and by the omission of the "arūpavimokkhas".

The sutta is thus clearly a composite of early and late strata.

In Sutta 60 the first twenty paragraphs (Nāg. ed.) contain the Apaṇṇaka sutta proper, the next three dealing with the totally irrelevant topic of four Puggala types in the Aṅguttara style. This latter section occurs identically, except for the change in names, in sutta 51 also. It seems difficult to explain the appendix except through some gross confusion in transmission.

Sutta 62 (Mahārāhulovāda°) shows interpolation, addition at the end, and resultant confusion. The history of the sutta may be reconstructed thus (ref. to the Nāg. ed., MN. Pt. I).

1. The original form: Para 1 (minus the last two and a half lines) followed by paras 3-12 constituted it. This is a sermon on distinguishing Attā from Rūpa which is then explained as the five Dhātus from Paṭhavī to Ākāsa. This suggests that Attā is implicitly regarded

[93] See below.

as the sixth dhātu or viññāṇa. And this receives support from the following circumstance: the result of cultivating the idea of Anattahood "Taṃ netaṃ mama, nesohamasmi, na meso attāti"[94] in the material elements, is said to culminate in the detachment of the "citta" from them.[95] Now the form of the Anatta-meditation shows clearly that it was a process of distinguishing and detaching the Attā from the material elements. Attā is, therefore, implicitly identified with Citta, and we know that at one time at any rate in the early history of Buddhism citta and viññāṇa were considered synonymous.[96] Attā is, therefore, conceived as viññāṇa here, in contradistinction to Rūpa, and this gives us the familiar early contrast between Kāya and viññāṇa.[97]

2. The last two and a half lines of para 1 were added to bring the sutta in line with the five khandha theory. Buddha had asked Rāhula "Yaṃ kiñci Rāhula rūpaṃ...sabbaṃ rūpaṃ netaṃ mama...yathā bhūtaṃ sammappaññāya daṭṭhabbanti". The interpolator makes Rāhula ask "Rūpameva nu kho Bhagavā, rūpameva nu kho Sugatāti?"[98] and by way of Buddha's answer adds "Rūpampi Rāhula, vedanāpi Rāhula... viññāṇampi Rāhulāti". Had the sermon belonged originally to the age in which the 5 khandha theory was rampant, it is hardly likely that Buddha should have made so serious an omission and left it to be pointed out by Rāhula. It may be remembered that the Buddha of that

---

[94] Op. cit. p. 88 etc.

[95] "Paṭhavīdhātuyā cittaṃ virājeti, āpo...." etc., which occurs at the end of paras 3-7. Paras 8-12 are still more explicit: "Paṭhavīsamaṃ hi Rāhula te bhāvanaṃ bhāvayato uppannā manāpāmanāpā phassā cittaṃ na pariyādāya ṭhassanti" etc.

[96] On this point see Chap. XII on Nirvāṇa.

[97] On the whole doctrine see Chap. XII on Nirvāṇa.

[98] Op. cit. p. 88.

age never hesitated introducing the full list of the 5 khandhas even quite gratuitously at times. Further, the sequel containing the original continuation, deals with the five elements of the Rūpakkhandha alone, and is silent about the other khandhas. Finally, if the suggestion mentioned above about viññāṇa is correct, this would introduce a patent contradiction.

3. The form of the exhortations "Paṭhavīsamaṃ Rāhula bhāvanaṃ bhāvehi Āposamaṃ..." etc., in paras 8-12 seem to have led on to para 13 which, with its "Mettāsamaṃ Rāhula bhāvehi—karuṇaṃ Rāhula.... asubhaṃ Rāhula...aniccaṃ Rāhula...", is, except for the last exhortations, little relevant to the context, and similarly led to para 14 on Ānāpānasati which, while concluding, reveals its utter irrelevancy "Evaṃ bhāvitāya kho Rāhula ānāpānasatiyā...te carimakā assāsapassāsa tepi vīditā va nirujjhanti." The sermon had intended to be an exhortation on the distinction of Rūpa from Attā![99]

4. To justify this last addition, para 2 was interpolated. After the exhortation by Buddha in para 1 it makes Rāhula go out and be asked by Sāriputta to cultivate Ānāpānasati. He comes back to Buddha and requests "Kathaṃ bhāvitā nu....bhante ānāpānasati kathaṃ bahulīkatā mahapphalā hoti mahānisaṃsāti".[100] Here follows the second para. Buddha in answer goes back to his own interrupted sermon, and reverts to the present query only when the reader, and one may suppose the listener too—well nigh forgets it! Para 2 is in fact a clumsy interpolation between para 1 and para 3ff, which patently breaks the thread of the sermon, and is only meant to justify the appendage of para 14.

99 Ib p. 94. 100 Ib. p. 89.

Sutta 66: (a) §§ 1-6 (Nāg. ed.) Udāyin praises Buddha for prohibiting meals and wandering for alms at night. Buddha points out how many disliked his insistence on small points saying "kimpana imassa appamattakassa oramattakassa adhisallikhitévāyaṃ samaṇoti",[101] whereas actually no tie sufficient for bondage was small enough to be neglected. He illustrated the point by the comparison of the Laṭukikā. Throughout there is a rare personal ring, and we seem to have before us an interesting trait of Buddha's character revealed—his insistence on thoroughness and detail.

(b) § 7—has an abrupt and little connected sermon in the Aṅguttara style on four Puggala-types. §§ 8-10 commence another sermon with equal abruptness on the five strands of sensuous desire and the nine stages of meditation. (b) is thus, apart from the appearance of unconnection and abruptness, ridden with numbers and formulas which, tog ther with the banality of its contents, places it in striking contrast to (a).

Sutta 139: Buddha begins by a short sermon, which is in a terse and lucid style reminiscent of the Tai up, and the Dharmasūtras..."Na kāmasukhaṃ anuyuñjeyya hīnaṃ gammaṃ...na ca attakilamathānuyagaṃ ...etc., te ubhe ante anupagamma majjhimā paṭipadā ...nibbānāya saṃvattati...névussādeyya na apasādeyya dhaṃmameva deseyya...ajjhattaṃ sukhaṃ anuyuñjeyya. Rahovādaṃ na bhāseyya. Sammukhā na khīṇaṃ bhaṇe. Ataramāno va bhāseyya, na taramāno. Janapadaniruttiṃ nābhiniviseyya, sāmaññaṃ nātidhāveyya."[102] This he declares "Ayaṃ uddeso Araṇavibhaṅgassa" and a detailed comment on each of the above injunctions

[101] MN. Pt. I. p. 119 (Nāg. ed.).
[102] MN. III. p. 230 (PTS ed.).

follows. This style of putting forth a brief thesis and then elaborating i is very unusual for Buddha, since few other instances of it are found in the Nikāyas. Besides, it is not exactly the case that Buddha here first states a point in short and then elucidates it in full; he is here made to deliver a whole sermon in a brief and forceful style first, declare it merely prefatory to his main purpose which is a laboured commentary upon it, and finally, deliver the comment itself! It seems only reasonable to suppose that the "Uddesa" represents an old text or series of texts on which the "Vibhaṅga" furnishes a comparatively later commentary.

Finally following the lead of Mrs. Rhys Davids,[103] a few early "fragments" may be pointed out from among some suttas, a general stratum-analysis of which is at present highly hazardous. In sutta 72 the doctrine of the impredicability of the emancipated mind (vimutta-citta) confuses Vacchagotta who like Maitreyī confesses "Etthāhaṃ bho Gotama aññāṇamāpādim, ettha sammohamāpādim". Yājñavalkya had saved the situation by taking recourse to a well-nigh agnostic epistemology. Buddha says "Alaṃ hi te vaccha aññāṇāya alaṃ sammo hāya Gambhīro hi ayaṃ vaccha dhammo duddaso duranubodho santo paṇīto atakkāvacaro nipuṇo paṇḍita-vedanīyo...".[104] Here is a clear appeal to mystic experience, which Buddha proceeds to explain by means of the very expressive fire-parable. When fire is extinguished, can it be said of it that it has vanished in this or that particular direction? Vacchagotta himself answers "Na upeti bho Gotama Yaṃ hi so—aggi tiṇakaṭṭhupādānaṃ paṭicca ajali tassa ca pariyādānā aññassa ca

[103] Cf. "Buddhism" (H. U. L.) pp. 67 ff

[104] MN Pt. II. p. 159 (Nāg. ed.)

anupahārā anāhārā nibbuto tveva saṅkhaṃ gacchatīti".[105] Buddha then points out "Evameva kho Vaccha yena rūpena Tathāgataṃ paññāpayamāno paññāpeyya taṃ rūpaṃ Tathāgatassa pahīnaṃ. . . rūpasaṅkhāvimutto kho Vaccha Tathāgato gambhīro appameyyo duppariyogāho seyyathāpi mahāsamuddo. . ."[105] This is closely paralleled by the answer given in the Upasīvamāṇava pucchā in the Sn. "Accī yathā vātavegena khitto (. .) atthaṃ paleti na upeti saṅkhaṃ. Evaṃ munī nāmakāyā vimutto atthaṃ paleti na upeti saṅkhaṃ. (Verse 6). . . . Atthaṃgatassa na pamāṇamatthi yena naṃ vajju taṃtassa natthi Sabbesu dhammesu samūhatesu samūhatā vādapathāpi sabbā" (verse 8.) The idea and style of expression are both similar, and the Rūpa of the prose seems to serve the same function as the Nāmakāya of the verse.

"Rūpa", however, suggested to our redactor the other 4 khandhas and he consequently repeated the prose lines quoted above with reference to them.

In sutta 72, §§ 5-7 (Nāg. ed.) and the first five and a half lines of § 8 thus appear to contain an early "fragment". The preceding sections are more or less conventional in style, and occur in substance in the Cūḷamāluṅkyaputta° which has already been discussed. The last nine lines in § 4 which introduce the 5 khandhas are, it may be remarked, uncalled for, and the pretext on which they are introduced is rather forced: Vacchagotta asks whether Buddha himself had any Diṭṭhigatas (this after Buddha had emphatically condemned them) and Buddha instead of saying "no," silently interprets the term Diṭṭhigata in a very unusual way (as equivalent to

[105] Ib. p. 160.

what has been seen or realized?) and speaks of the 5 khandhas!

In **sutta 75** occurs the parable of one who is born blind (Jaccandha), who not being endowed with the necessary sight is easily deceived in his quest of a white cloth. So is one who has not cultivated the Noble vision (Ariyacakkhu) liable to deception about Nibbāna. Nibbāna is here regarded as something to be directly realized, and the faculty which leads to it is considered ordinarily unavailable. It has to be known immediately but in an immediacy which is higher than that of the senses. This idea of the ariya or Dhamma-cakkhu as the means to Nibbāna is essentially a mystic idea, and found at other places also in the Nikāyas. However, in its later occurrences (within the Nikāyas), it underwent a certain degradation in meaning when it was no longer considered to lead to Nibbāna immediately.

In **sutta 107** occurs the parable of the way to "Rājagaha.[106] Buddha merely points out the way;[107] whether anybody makes progress along it or not, depends wholly upon him or her. Faith in the Tathāgata or, for the matter of that in Dhamma or Saṅgha, does not as yet make up even partly for the weakness of the individual. Nor is the path specified as eightfold. Actually, the whole of the sutta appears early. Spiritual progress according to it begins with right conduct and reaches its climax in or immediately after the fourth Jhāna. This is the path to which the parable applies. Not only is the theory of the path as eightfold in abeyance, but also of the "arūpajhānas" which were later accorded so important a position. The stage of doctrinal development in

---

106 MN. III. pp. 5-6 (PTS ed.).
107 "Maggakkhāyī. . . . Tathāgatoti" Loc. cit.

the present sutta roughly corresponds to that in the Sāmaññaphala°.

In **sutta 125** the novice Aciravata fails to convince the prince Jayasena that a Bhikkhu may attain to the pointedness of mind. He reports this to Buddha who remarks that the prince was too much engrossed in the senses to understand what could only be understood through freedom from them. He illustrates the point by two comparisons: the inability of the prince was similar to that of the untamed elephant in the sphere of the tamed, or that of the man standing at the foot of a hill to have the glorious vision of one on top of it. The second upamā, it may be noted, has the same underlying idea as in the "Jaccandha" parable of sutta 75. Further, it occurs briefly in the context of Buddha's enlightenment in sutta 26: "Sele yathā pabbatamuddhaniṭṭhito Yathāpi passe janataṃ samantato Tathūpamaṇ Dhaṃmamayaṃ sumedha Pāsādamāruyha samantacckkhu etc."[108] It is interesting to note that a very similar verse is quoted in the Yogabhāṣya (see below chap. XII).

Buddha then suggests to Aciravata that if he had employed these two upamās they might have proved effective against the prince. Aciravata, however, points out that he had never known them before. The sutta might have been expected to end here: instead, now follows a long parable detailing the stages through which a wild elephant is tamed, and then the corresponding "taming" of the Bhikkhu by the Tathāgata. This sequence perhaps represents the elaboration of the first of the two upamās referred to by Buddha.

(d) Uncertain :

The rest of the suttas of the MN. must at present be

---

[108] MN. I. p. 168 (PTS ed.).

regarded uncertain from the point of view of stratification. The following analysis will bring into focus some of the difficulties and problems that arise in an attempt to stratify them.

The very **first sutta** shows an opposition of indications and contra-indications with neither appreciably tipping the balance. Its psychological analysis is relatively rudimentary. It subsumes mental phenomena under the classes: Diṭṭha, suta, muta, and Viññāta.[109] This scheme is found at places in the Sn. also.[110] Later, as in [MN. Sutta 22] it was elaborated into Diṭṭha, suta, muta, ñāta; patta, pariyesita, and anuvicarita. Another early feature is the mention of Pajāpati apart from Brahmā which suggests that the former has not yet lost himself in the latter. On the other hand, it mentions, apart from Pajāpati and Brahmā, the divine classes of the Ābhassaras, the Subhakiṇhas and the Vehapphalas. It also speaks of the Abhibhū, which at many other places in the Nikāyas occurs merely as an adjective of Mahābrahmā. Finally, it mentions familiarly the four Arūpavimokkhas. Here is thus a mixture of early and late features, but none are strong enough to be at all decisive.

In the **second sutta** the difficulty arises from the fact that only doctrinal tests are applicable to it, and their exclusive use is apt to lead to a vicious petitio principii. Another difficulty in the application of doctrinal tests in the absence of any other clues is that of evaluating the "silences". The present sutta for example, speaking of Bhāvanā, mentions only the seven sambojjhaṅgas as its subject. That it is silent on this occasion about the other members of the Bodhipakkhiya Dhammas may or may not have a "stratigraphic" significance.

---

[109] MN. I, p. 3. [110] See PTSD in sub "Diṭṭha".

In **sutta 4** the difficulty arises from the fact that the main contents of the sutta—that "Bhayabherava" constitutes an impediment in solitary meditation for the impure alone—are too general to be classed in any particular stratum. The sutta doubtless contains the stock early description of the four Jhānas and the three Vijjās, but the relative chronological position of the whole to this part is quite uncertain. It may be a late text utilizing earlier stock passages, or it may be nearly contemporaneous with them.

In **sutta 5** the style suggests lateness. It consists of lengthy explanations exchanged between Sāriputta and Moggalāna, and uses the Aṅguttara form. Its contents, which deal with the concept of Aṅgana, show, however, no lateness whatever. It may be mentioned that the rather lengthy and unusual "upamā" mentioned by Mahamoggalāna at the end seems to be forced.

The doctrinal content of **sutta 6** which includes inter alia reference to the peaceful Arūpavimokkha, the 3 saṃyojanas and the oraṃbhāgiyasaṃyojanas, suggests that in its present form it could not belong to the earliest stratum. The form of the sutta, however, renders it peculiarly open to expansion through addition.

The emphasis that the sutta places on Samatha and Vipassanā suggests that it may have been among those which must have formed the basis of the Dārṣṭāntika sect.[111]

The first part of **sutta 14** (cūḷadukkhakkhandha-sutta) contains a critique of sense pleasure and the second, which does not explicitly indicate its relevancy to the query which led to the first but possibly is in-

---

[111] Cf. Ab. K., Vol. IV, p. 122 fn. 3.

tended as a corrective to its answer, contains a critique of the opposite theory—Nigaṇṭha asceticism.

Sutta 13 (Mahādukkhakkhandha°) appears an elaboration of the first part. **Sutta 14** itself is uncertain on account of the more or less stock character of its contents: they may belong to very early as well as to later strata.

Sutta 15, a sermon by Mahāmoggalāna, which closes with an exhortation to introspection (Paccavekkhaṇa), is too nondescript in contents and style to be stratified.

Sutta 16 in which Buddha speaks about the 5 cetokhilas and the 5 cetasovinibandhas is similar. It may be noted however that at the end it contains a section on the four Iddhipādas which is wholly irrelevant to the context but contains the simile of the 'brooding hen'' which is considered early by Mrs. Rhys Davids.

Sutta 18 contains a cryptic sermon by Buddha on Papañcasaññānidāna and its precise and technical explanation by Mahākaccāna. The fact that Buddha names seven "anusayas" seems to show that at the time the sutta was composed the doctrine already had a previous history.

Sutta 20, concerned with the psychology of mental control, is simple and practical. It describes five ways of restraining "vitakkas". This appearance of earliness is however rendered nugatory by the fact that the fifth and final resource against the 'vitakkas' is described to be the ascetic use of force—a procedure which Buddha is supposed to have condemned at other, more authentic, places.

Sutta 23 contains a popular riddle explained Buddhistically. Its mention of the 5 khandhas suggests that it could not be very early.

Sutta 25 contains the very elaborate Nivāpa parable. Partly similar shorter comparisons occur in other suttas. Perhaps it is a later composition suggested by these.

Sutta 27: the central sermon is concerned with describing the spiritual course through the Sīlakkhandha, the Jhānas, and the three Vijjās. The detailed narrative setting, however, indicates that the composition of the sutta need not be contemporaneous with the material it utilizes.

Sutta 32 consists of a parable to illustrate the five classes of monks—Arahā, opapātiko, sakadāgāmī, sotāpanno and saddhānusārī. The sutta obviously cannot be prior to the formula, the antiquity of which has not been investigated.

Sutta 37 (Cūḷataṇhāsaṅkhaya°) contains a very short but complete and lucid sermon delivered to Sakka. It deserves to be noted that within the sermon itself Sakka is invariably called Devānaminda *only*. It may be remembered that the word "Inda" went out of Buddhist use very soon. Then follows an account of the marvellous adventures of Mahāmoggalāna who wanted to make sure whether Sakka had really grasped the sermon or not. The sutta as a whole seems to belong to an age when the personal reminiscences of the apostles were lost in the haze of myth-making. The nuclear sermon may be earlier. It has, of course, to be remembered that the passage of saints from historical to mythical figures need not take much time. Finally, it may be noted that the contents of this sutta are clearly referred to in the Māratajjaniya sutta.

Sutta 39 describes the "Samaṇakaraṇa-dhammas" It is another example of those suttas the core of which is constituted out of the Sāmaññaphala text. These suttas do not appear to belong to an age much later than that of the Sāmaññaphala text. Besides, given the earliness of their doctrinal stratum, it does not seem very material if we cannot precisely determine the literary stratum of such suttas.

Sutta 40 also is concerned with what makes a Samaṇa. The treatment is quite different: asceticism does not make for Samaṇahood; what does so is the practice of the four Brahmavihāras. The earliness or lateness of the sutta is quite indeterminate since its doctrinal content, which alone throws any light on the problem, is not peculiar to any particular stage of early Buddhist dogmatic evolution.

Sutta 45 (Cūḷadhammasamādāna°) describes the four Dhammasamādānas. In effect, the sutta advocates the way of the four Jhānas,[112] in opposition to sensual indulgence or ascetic austerity. The idea is early but one which persisted with equal force later. As to its expression it may be noted that the sutta contains the comparison of the Māluvā creeper in detail. This is also utilized in brief in a poem in the Dhp. The literary relation between the two texts is, however, difficult to determine.

The next **Sutta**—Mahādhammasamādāna°—is lengthier but deals with the same subject. It, however, describes the best way to be the practice of the 10 sīlas. It is thus addressed more clearly to the laity.

Since the list of the 10 sīlas appears an elaboration of that of the 5 sīlas, it doubtless presupposes a certain previous doctrinal evolution.

Sutta 47 advocates a critical attitude towards the Teacher (Tathāgata is apparently used here in a general pre-Buddhist sense) and a faith based on sight ("...ākāravatī saddhā dassanamūlikā...").[113] There is

---

[112] It may be noted that the result of the 4th Jhāna is said to be heaven.

[113] MN. I. p. 320.

a curious disharmony between the prevailing idea of the sutta and its actual expression. Has an ancient sutta been editorially toned down?

Sutta 48 is more concerned with discipline than with doctrine. Its use of the abstract expressions Dhaṃmatā[114] and Balatā[115] suggest lateness.

Sutta 51: Buddha sermonizes to Pessa on the four types of individuals (Puggala), and after he is gone, decides to expand the sermon for the benefit of the monk (—vitthārena vibhajāmi. . .").[116] The way this explanation is tacked on to the main sermon suggests that it may be a later addition. In its contents, however, it is mainly based on two earlier stock texts: that containing the description of ascetic practices and that on the "Sāmaññaphalas".

Sutta 52 mentions Kukkuṭārāma at Pāṭaliputta and contains a sermon by Ānanda to Aṭṭhakanāgara. It describes the four Jhānas, the four Brahmavihāras and the first three Āruppas as the eleven "doors to immortality" (Amatadvāra).[117] The sutta has two unusual features: it describes only three Āruppas; and speaks of each of the "doors" as sufficient in itself. Also, its very "positive" approach to the summum bonum is reflected in the use of the expression—anuttarayogakkhema,[118], amata,[119] and Sotthi[120] (". . . .ekamekenāpi amatadvārena sakkuṇissāmi *attānaṃ sotthiṃ* kātuṃ"). The whole sutta may be contrasted with those which describe spiritual progress as lying through a sequence of nine cessa-

[114] Ib. p. 324.
[115] Ib. p. 325.
[116] MN. Pt. I. p. 5 (Nāg. ed.).
[117] MN. Pt. p. 16 (Nāg. ed.).
[118] Ib. p. 13 etc.
[119] Ib. p. 16.
[120] Ib.

tions (Anupubbanirodhas).[121] It plainly belongs to an epoch when the full list of the "Āruppas" was not yet firmly established.

Sutta 53 contains another sermon by Ānanda, though Buddha is present here. It describes the Sekho Pāṭipado and his progress to the highest goal, the whole course being dichotomized into "caraṇa" and "vijjā". This procedure resembles that in the Ambaṭṭhasutta (DN. 3). In connection with the three Vijjās the parable of the brooding hen is used.

The next sutta has two interesting features: (a) it contains a collection of seven comparisons (upamās) on the pursuit of the senses. May it be regarded as a culling together?

(b) Instead of describing the Jhānas it just says "yāyaṃ upekkhā nānattā nānattasitā taṃ abhinivajjetvā yāyaṃ upekkhā ekatte ekattasitā yattha sabbaso lokāmisupādānā aparisesaṃ nirujjhanti taméva upekkhaṃ bhāveti"[122] And then describing it as "anuttarā upekkhāparisuddhi" proceeds directly to the Vijjās. This silence, however, can only with hazard be taken as evidence of the still unsettled position of the Jhānas.

In sutta 55 Buddha refutes the charge that he knowingly partook of meat, although he saw no harm in it in case there was no reason even to suspect that the meat had been prepared for him. The main point was, as the succeeding sermon shows, not to wish harm to anybody. With this attitude may be compared that in the Āmagandha sutta in the Sn. There meat eating appears permitted without further reserve, and it is this freer

[121] For other examples of this stage see discussion in Chap. on the stratification of AN.

[122] Cf. MN. I, p. 367 (PTS ed.), MN. Pt. I, p. 32 (Nāg. ed.)

attitude that fits better with the partaking of Sūkara-maddava at the place of Cunda.

Sutta 56 is a long, literary composition on the conversion of Upāli, ending with an elaborate poem in praise of Buddha. The author of the sutta shows that he was well versed in the Jinist doctrines of which he describes an early form![123] This knowledge was possibly derived from older sources. There are, however, no means to ascertain the authenticity of the sutta more precisely.

Sutta 57 describes the four types of kamma, which may be compared with the Jinist Leśyās or the "abhijātis" of Gosāla.

In Suttā 58 Buddha refutes a trivial dilemma presented by Nātaputta. In its uncertainty it is partly similar to sutta 56.

Sutta 59 resolves the controversy between Udāyin and Pañcakaṅga Thapati about the number of Feelings (vedanās) by declaring both right in different contexts (Pariyāyena). Then follows a hierarchy of pleasures (sukha) which is little relevant.[124] It begins with the pleasure of the senses (Kāmasukha) and ends with the pleasure beyond idea and feeling (in saññāvedayitanirodha). Perhaps the harmonization of the first part and the systematization of the second are both scholastic contributions; perhaps not.

Sutta 65 is long with miscellaneous contents. It speaks of the formula of the various classes of the released from Ubhatobhāgavimutta to Saddhānusārī; *of the increase of Sikkhāpadas and the decrease in the number of*

---

[123] See Jacobi–SBE. 45. XVI-XVII.

[124] Contrast the "felicific calculus" in the Br., & Tait. Upaniṣads.

the Bhikkhus; of sundry other problems of discipline; and of the tenfold path. As Winternitz remarks, the sutta presupposes a certain previous history of the Saṅgha.[125]

Sutta 67 has two unconnected divisions: the first narrates how a large number of noisy Bhikkhus were expelled but later excused; while the second contains a short parabolic sermon on the Four Fears, enounced in the dogmatic style of the Aṅguttarasuttas. **Sutta 68** encourages righteous emulation, and contains the formular description of the Opapātika, the Sakadāgāmin, and the Sotāpanna.

In **sutta 69** Sāriputta advises a forest-dwelling monk. It is interesting to note that when in the Saṅgha, he is asked to observe proper courtesy, especially towards the Elders. Among other counsels, it may be marked, he is asked to concentrate on Abhidhamma and Abhivinaya, as on "ye te santā vimokkhā atikkamma rūpe āruppā. . . ."[126] The sutta seems to reflect the growing dominance of the town-dwelling saṅgha.

The point of **sutta 70** is that faith is necessary in the beginning and is addressed to those monks who placed overmuch reliance on self, and refused to accept anything that was not immediately obvious. It appears that they took their stand on the cliché that the Dhamma was Sandiṭṭhika and not Kālika.

The sutta describes the seven Puggalas: ubhato-bhāgavimutta. . . .saddhānusārī, and considers the first two no longer liable to fall. It may be noted that this thesis about the Arahant was the most important one contested in the first doctrinal schism.

---

[125] Ind. Lit. II, p. 53.

[126] MN. Pt. I, p. 143.

Sutta 73 summarizes the practice of Dhamma as consisting in the avoidance of evil (akusala), which is defined as the three (akusalamūlas) and the 10 (Micchāsīlas) and the cultivation of Peace and Insight (Samatha and Vipassanā). This emphasis recalls the Dārṣṭāntika sect.

Sutta 74 depicts Buddha as a thorough-going sceptic, who would not hold even the sceptical thesis itself.[127] The ideal monk viewing the body and the three feelings as non-self, is emancipated, and "Evemṃ vimuttacitto kho Aggivesana bhikkhu na kenaci saṃvadati, na kenaci vivadati, yañca loke vuttaṃ tena voharati aparāmasaṃ ti."[128] This sutta seems to represent an early strand of thought. It only expresses more logically and very uncompromisingly that opposition to holding any "opinion" (Diṭṭhi) which is found prominently even in the earliest texts, e.g., in the Aṭṭhakavagga of the Sn.

Sutta 76 seems to draw much of its material from the Sāmaññaphala sutta. It however presents the heretical doctrines without the historical accident of names, and grades them from the Buddhist standpoint into two classes: Abrahmacariyavāsas and Anassāsikabrahma°. Further it criticizes each doctrine with vigour, and confuses together the doctrines of Pakudha and Gosāla. Thus it goes beyond D. 2 in many respects and is probably later.

The section on the Arahant emphasizing that "Abhabbo so pañca ṭhānāni ajjhācarituṃ,"[129] has a covert reference to the sectarian controversies on the subject The following section which seems to be a comment on

---

[127] Ib., pp. 168-170.

[128] MN. Pt. II, p. 171 (Nāg. ed.).

[129] MN. Pt. II, p. 195 (Nāg. ed.).

the oft occurring expression "Khaye khayañāṇaṃ" must owe its existence to some special reason. It has interesting doctrinal implications. The ludicrously negativist character of the comparison may be noted.

The sutta, in short, carries many indications of its lateness.

In **sutta 78** the first sentence of § 4 finds its logical and immediate sequence in § 9. The intervening text forms an abruptly intruding complete whole which is an alternative answer to the view of Samaṇamaṇḍikāputta, although in its form of expression it is not apparently relevant. Either it is an interpolation, or § 9 is an appendics, to justify which was interpolated the sentence referred to above.

In **sutta 79** Buddha waiving aside the topic of Pubbanta and Aparanta proceeds to sermonize on doctrine by announcing the general formula of the Paticcasam. The interruption of Udāyin, however, turns the conversation into another direction. The following §§ 7-11 of the sutta are practically the same as the first five of the next sutta. After it, although both discuss the topic of happiness (sukha), there is a marked difference in treatment. In the former, Buddha says that the way to the absolutely happy world lay in the four Jhānas, although the Brahmacariya that he himself advocated had the different end of the three vijjās. The principal means are, however, again the same viz., the four Jhānas. In the latter (**sutta 80**) the corresponding text is much shorter and contains a contrast between Kāmasukha and Kāmagga°; whether the two suttas represent "variants" or not is problematic.

Sutta 82 is a vigorous and edifying tale which could belong to any stratum; the **next sutta** also is primarily a story but one exhibiting the Jātaka form. It mentions the 4 Brahmavihāras and the eightfold Path.

Sutta 84 expressly belongs to the period posterior to Buddha's death. It contains a sermon by Mahākaccāna at Madhurā delivered to "Rājā Madhuro Avantiputto"[130] on the perfect equality of the four castes, which is more liberal than the view attributed to Buddha in **sutta 90**.

Sutta 86 contains the legend of Aṅgulimāla, the authenticity of which remains an open question. In **sutta 87** Pasendi taunts Queen Mallikā with her blind faith in Samaṇa Gotama when she believes the latter's (Gotama's) cryptic paradox "Piyajātikā sokaparidevadukkhadomnassupāyāyāsā piyappabhavikā ti".[131] Finally, however, she succeeds in converting the king to her side. The general fact of Gotama's intimate relations with the court at Kosala appears historical,[132] but that affords little help in this particular case.

Sutta 88 reports a sermon by Ānanda to King Pasenadi on the three samācāras (Kaya,° etc.) It is too general to characterize any particular stratum.

The next sutta contains a praise of Buddha by Pasenadi. Here again as in the case of suttas 86-87 there is a general impression of basic authenticity which it is impossible to prove or disprove.

Sutta 92 which occurs in the Sn. also, speaks of the 32 marks of great men[133] and describes Buddha as Dhammarājā and Sāriputta as his Senāpati.[134] This tendency to effect comparisons between Buddha and the universal

---

130 MN. Pt. II. p. 268 (Nāg. ed.).
131 Ib. p. 310.
132 See Chap. on Buddha's life.
133 Ib. p. 354.
134 Ib. pp. 355-356.

monarch which is exhibited in other forms in DN. 16, appears to be only a stage in his apotheosis. The sutta appears late.

Sutta 95 §§ 1-6 are very similar to the introductory portion of DN. 5. The Thirty-two Marks are mentioned. Then follows a critique of the Brāhmaṇas who believed on faith, on tradition etc., and, finally, a unique sequence of stages leading to Saccānupatti. The distinction that is implicitly effected between Saccānupatti and Saccānubodha is far from clear.

Paradoxically enough, it may be noted, this Buddhist statement of spiritual means itself describes Faith as the basis of all else.

Suttas 96 and **98**[135] are earnest and eloquent critiques of caste. Such encounters must often have taken place in Buddha's own life time, and there is nothing whatever to suggest the lateness of these dialogues. They may be very ancient, at least in their substance. It is of course impossible to be positive either way.[136]

Sutta 97 gives the character and last hours of the Brāhmaṇa Dhānañjani and how Sāriputta preached to him the inevitability of retribution after death, and on another occasion, when Dhānañjani neared his end, the four Brahmavihāras as the way to the world of Brahmā. The sutta is as little significant in its contents as difficult to stratify.

In **sutta 99** Buddha in a dialogue with the Māṇava Subha confutes a number of Brāhmaṇic theories. The first declares the householder spiritually superior to the Pabbajita.[137] On this point Buddha declares himself a

---

135 Which occ. in the Sn. also.
136 Cf. Winternitz's remark on sutta 93—op. cit.
137 See below.

Vibhajjavāda. As to the five virtues helpful in the acquisition of merit,[138] Buddha points out that no Brāhmaṇic sage ever claimed to have had a direct acquaintance with them or their results, and consequently in advocating them the Brāhmaṇas were no better than a file of blind men.[139] This enrages Subha who voices Pokkharasāti's scepticism about man attaining to superhuman knowledge and vision. Buddha answers by the pointed parable of the blind man who denied what he could not see. Buddha then shows how the five virtues of the Brāhmaṇas imply a sixth viz., pity (Anukampā) and are really but aids to the cultivation of a mind free from all taints of violence.[140] Finally follows, after the parable of the village Naḷakara, instruction in the way to Brahmasahavyatā, which is comprised by the four Brahmavihāras.

This sutta reminds one forcibly of the Tevijjasutta (DN). Both have the Andhaveṇūpamā with the criticism it illustrates and the Brahmavihāras. In both Buddha claims to be particularly versed in the way to Brahmasahavyatā, criticizes the Brāhmaṇas in the same ironical, dialectical style, uses many short and illuminating parables and gives the same total impression of a powerful and earnest mind. It does not appear likely that the suttas could have been composed independently.

Sutta 101 is a fairly long (MN. II, pp. 214-288. P.T.S. ed), unitary composition (except that the frequent

---

[138] These are Sacca, Tapa, Brahmacariya, Ajjhena and Cāga Similar lists can be found in Bra. works.

[139] The upamā occ. at many other places.

[140] "Cittassāhaṃ ete parikkhāre vadāmi, yadidṃ cittaṃ averaṃ avyāpajjhaṃ tassa bhāvanāya" (MN. Pt. II. p. 421) (Nāg. ed.). Cf. Vyāsa on Y. S. II. 30, who states that all the varied rules of discipline are followed only in order to cultivate Ahiṃsā all the better.

stock section at the end beginning "Idha Tathāgato etc.," may be an inorganic appendix). It contains a carping critique of the Jinist theory of Upakkama or Padhāna. The first two pages of the sutta resemble the second part of the cūḷadukkhakkhanddha°[141] so much that they seem to be but variants of the same text. And since the opening sections of sutta 101 form the basis of what follows, the possibility is raised that that sutta is merely an elaborate version of part of M. 14 or some other similar text.

The opening summary of Jinist views "Yaṃ kiñcāyaṃ Purisapuggalo... dukkhaṃ nijjiṇṇaṃ bhavissatiti"[142] appears like a quotation. Its dogmatic and repetitive style affecting a great show of logical precision certainly finds ample illustration in Jinist works. But possibly it is a stock summary, deliberately imitating the Jinist style. The confusion patent in "kammakkhayā dukkhakkhayo, dukkhakkhayā vedanākkhayo, vedanākkhayā sabbaṃ dukkhaṃ nijjiṇṇaṃ bhavissatīti"[143] may have been intentionally introduced to give the Jaina doctrines an obscurantist taint. These several features are also shown by the other stock summary of the Jinist doctrines in the Sāmaññaphalasutta.

Sutta 104: The death of Nātaputta furnishes the occasion for a sermon on concord and discipline. It is not a little remarkable that the same event should have occasioned two other suttas as well—the Pāsādika° and the Saṅgīti° in the DN.

Sutta 105 recognized the growth of bogus Arahants, and admits that a monk who fancies himself an Arahā

---

[141] i.e., MN. I. pp. 92-93.
[142] MN. II. p. 44. It occ. identically in MN. 14: MN. I. p. 93.
[143] MN. II. p. 214.

may not always do so rightly. This indicates conditions such as led to the first doctrinal schism from which the sutta may not be far removed.

In sutta 106 the prominence attained by the arūpa vimokkhas has thrown into shade the older doctrine of "Ānañja" as the acme of spiritual progress.[144]

Sutta 110 purposes in the main to preach the 10 Sīlas.

Sutta 117: It begins with defining "Ariyo sammā samādhi sa-upaniso saparikkhāro" as that one pointedness of the mind (cittassa ekaggatā) which is the crown of the preceding seven aṅgas—Sammādiṭṭhi etc. In other words, of the elements of the Path, Samādhi is here given the focal position, the rest being regarded as merely contributory to it. These (as well as their opposites) are then defined, each element being considered twofold—as Sāsava, puññabhāgiya upadhivepakka; and as ariya, anāsava, lokuttara, maggaṅga. It is interesting to note that Sammādiṭṭhi in its second aspect is defined, not as the four truths (which is the usual practice). but as "Paññā paññindriyaṃ° balaṃ dhammavicayasambojjhaṅgo..."

From each of the elements (including sammādiṭṭhi!) it is declared, sammādiṭṭhi, °vāyāmo, °sati follow as consequences. Thus the description comes upto Sammā ājīvo. Then, instead of °vāyāmo being described similarly (which would have multiplied the sort of instance furnished by Sammādiṭṭhi) we are suddenly given the formula of the tenfold Path in the form" "Sammādiṭṭhissa—°Saṅkappo pahoti etc"——and told "Aṭṭhaṅgasamannāgota sekho pāṭipado dasaṅgasamannāgato arahā hoti". The idea is then elaborated. It is

[144] See Chap.....on Way to Nirvāṇa.

clear that the sutta represents a later doctrinal stratum than that represented by the first formulation of the eight-fold Path, into which it introduces many niceties of systematization, and to which it adds two further elements.

Sutta 121 (cūḷasuññata°): The end of spiritual effort is described as "Yathābhuccā avipallatthā pari-suddhā paramānuttarā suññatāvakkanti".[145] The path to it lies through successive meditational stages. It may be noticed that afer "Nevasaññānāsaññāyatana" the usual "Saññāvedayitanirodha" fails to occur, its place being taken up by "Animitto cetosamādhi". The sutta implies that the final beatitude (i.e., the final "Nihil") cannot be attained while the aspirant is yet living. Such a clear and outspoken adumbration of the esoteric aspect of the later Śūnyavāda is extremely rare in the Nikāyas.

The following Mahāsuññata° at first speaks of the Animitto cetosamādhi (without using that expression) but soon presents only loosely knit miscellanea.

Sutta 124 praises Bakkula and is too general for any stratification.

Sutta 126 regards the elements of the eight-fold Path as the only means of attaining beatific results; the absurdity of hoping for them while these are being violated is illustrated by a number of "comparisons".

Sutta 127 contains a scholastic discussion on various points, mainly theological, in which Pañcakaṅga Thapati, Anuruddha and Kaccāna participate. In style it resembles the Vedalla-suttas, and it is unlikely that it should be early.

Sutta 128 has two different and unconnected parts. In the the first, piqued over the monks who quarrelled among themselves, Buddha utters a number of gāthās,

[145] MN. III. pp. 108-109.

many, at least, of which occur in the Dhp. and the Sn. in very different contexts. In the second, Buddha points out the eleven Upakkilesas as responsible for the fleeting character of photistic appearances (abhāsas). He recalls his experience *as a Bodhisatta.* This clearly suggests the lateness of this part.

Sutta 140 contains a detailed and elaborate exposition of the six dhātus, and regards pure equanimity (upekkhā parisuddhā pariyodātā) illustrated by the 'gold-simile, as the chief means to Nibbāna. Although its elaborateness and the uddesa-vibhaṅga style suggest the lateness of the sutta, its ideas and the upamā it uses are early.[146] Besides, unlike some of the other vibhaṅga-suttas, it has a touching narrative framework, which, according to Winternitz gives the impression of actual events.[147]

In the central part of **Sutta 145** Puṇṇa, who was about to leave for Sunāparanta, is given a sermon on forbearance by Buddha who apprehended for him a hostile reception there. In spirit the sermon recalls the Kakacūpamovāda.

In **sutta 146,** Nandaka, who was at first unwilling, finally instructs the nuns in a catechism applying the three Marks to the senses, the sense-objects, the sense-perceptions and the resultant three types of feelings. The "lamp" and the "tree" similes are used to illustrate the contingent and impermanent character of Viññāṇa and Vedanā. The sutta is of uncertain stratum.

The following **sutta** makes Buddha himself catechise Rāhula similarly on the six senses, "sense objects", "sense-perceptions" and "sense-contacts". It may be

---

[146] See below.
[147] Winternitz, op cit.

remarked that this style of teaching harmonizes more with a doctor of a church expounding standardized dogmas to novices than with an inspired Pathfinder wishing to introduce a chosen disciple to higher mysteries. The style and contents of the sutta are quite incongruous with the promise "Tena kho paṇa samayena anekāni devatāsahassāni Bhagavantaṃ anubandhāni honti: ajja Bhagavā āyasmantaṃ Rāhulaṃ uttariṃ āsavānaṃ khaye vinessatīti".[148] The succeeding *"chachakkaka" sutta* describes the six sixes"=Ajjhattikāni āyatanāni—bāhirāni—viññānakāyā...phassakāyā...vedanākāyā...taṇhākāyā..."[149] with untiring monotony Each element, on account of its impermanence, is described as Anattā. The same idea is then repeated by way of describing the paths leading to the origin and destruction of Sakkāya. Then follows a section mentioning the three "Anusayas"—rāga°, Paṭigha°, avijjā°.

The whole sutta with its mechanical, "numerical", formular style suggests lateness of composition.

Sutta 149 (Mahāsaḷāyatana°) regards the five khs. and the groups that were later collectively called the 37 Bodhipakkhiya Dhammas as well established technicalities. This shows that it cannot belong to the earliest doctrinal stratum. The distinction that it effects between Pariññeyya, Pahātabba, Bhāvetabba and Sacchikātabba dhammas may have been a suggestive factor in the more detailed analysis of the Dasuttarasutta.

Sutta 150 is a short sermon on detachment from the senses and sense-objects; it offers little data for stratification.

Sutta 141 must be placed in the same stratum as sutta 149. It also speaks technically of the five khs. and

[148] MN. III. p. 278. [149] Ib. p. 280.

the (37 Bodhipakkhiya dhammas), and uses the scheme Pahīna, Pariññāta, Bhāvita and Sacchikata. It also shows its affinity to the suññatā-suttas by lavishly praising "Suññatavihāras". It categorically asserts "Mahāpurisvihāro hesa, sāriputta, yadidaṃ suññatā"?[150]

Sutta 152 contains trenchant criticism of the method of Indriya Bhāvanā, preached by the Brāhmaṇa Pārāsariya. Mrs. Rhys Davids remarks may be quoted. "To become morally strong, the student was not, as some taught (e.g. in sutta 152) to ignore sense experience, but to break it up into its constituent processes and resultants, so as to divert those complex impacts of the external world from kindling delusion and passion, and convert them into the cool judgements of the intellect."[151] The earnest, though common closing section, the style of distinguishing "Aryan" from vulgar practices, the frequent use of comparisons suggest the earliness of the sutta. The peculiar and cryptic way in which the doctrine of Pārāsariya is stated suggests that we have here the fading memory of some doctrine once actually held. The way in which it is criticized, sarcastically and briefly, but decisively seems to show a definite individuality behind it. This appearance may of course be due to good literary work. It is, however, noticeable that nothing definitely suggests the lateness or the apocryphal nature of the sutta.

---

[150] MN. III. p. 294.
[151] JRAS 1902 p. 481.

Conclusion

(A) *Early*	(B) *Late*	(C) *Composite*
Sutta : 7	Sutta : 8,	Sutta : 3,
	12	22,
17	28,	19,
24	33	38,
29 (cf. 30)	35,	60,
26 (cf. 36,85,100)	41/42 (variants)	62,
61,	43,	66,
63,	44,	139,
71,	50,	72,
108	64,	75,
140 (Possibly)	69 (Possibly)	107 (Probably to be classed as Early)
144	75,	
152 (Possibly)	76 (Possibly)	
	77	
	81,	
	90	
	91,	125
	93,	
	102	
	103	
	109,	
	111,	
	116,	
	120	
	123,	
	129,	
	130,	
	131-4,	
	135,	
	137,	
	141,	
	142,	
	143,	
	146 (Possibly)	
	149 (Possibly)	

(D) Uncertain.

The remaining Suttas.

CHAPTER VI

EARLY AND LATE IN THE SAMYUTTA-NIKĀYA

Samyuktagama and the Samyutta Nikaya. According to Anesaki[1] there are three versions of the Saṃyuktāgama in Chinese. The first dates from the 2nd century, and the second from the beginning of the 5th. These are both based on central Asian or North Indian originals. The third was translated between 435-493 and comes from the Jetavana Vihāra in Ceylon.

Anesaki points out[1] that "Der Sagāthavagga dieser drei Versionen enthält 318 sūtras, von denen 244 mit den Pali-Sagātha sutta übereinstimmen. An manchen Stellen stimmen die chinesischen Versionen mit den Texten des Theragāthā, Therīgāthā und Suttanipāta überein, da nämlich, wo die entsprechenden saṃyutta Stellen von diesen abweichen." The agreements and differences indicate a common source. But the third version seems to mix the two traditions—the North Indian and the Pali tradition.

Anesaki has a further interesting remark[2] to the effect that the word saṃyukta is found only in a later Chinese translation of a Pali Vinaya text. The Chinese title given in all the earlier works means literally 'miscellaneous' and indeed the texts, in their present form, have rather the features of miscellaneous collections than Saṃyukta, "bound together (according to subjects)."

This seems to be in relation to the Pali text, a serious difference. Another is implied in Nanjio's

---

[1] The 13th Int. Cong. of the Orientalists, Hamburg. Sept. 1902. Section II. A. p. 61.

[2] Ib. p. 62.

remark on No. 544—Saṃyuktāgama-Sūtra, which, he says is to be compared to the Saṃyutta Nikāya..."About half of this Sūtra is the same as or similar to Nos. 542, 543."[3] Although in the Pali version also some suttas are common between the SN. on the one hand and the MN. and the AN. on the other, this common element forms a very small fraction of the whole.

It appears that in contents as well as arrangement the Chinese collection of the SĀ. is much more miscellaneous than the Pali collection (SN.).

Distinctive features of the Sagathavagga. In the Pali, the first or Sagāthavagga is, on the whole, markedly different from the other four vaggas.[4] Whereas these latter treat, for the greater part, of points of metaphysics and psychology in a set formular style, the former is concerned mainly with the ethical regulation of conduct, events out of Buddha's life, and other much simpler but more picturesque material. The conspicuous part that verse and narrative play in the first vagga is in striking contrast to the very prosaic prose formulae which dominate the rest. Although quite a number of later pieces are to be found in the first vagga, yet, on the whole it has a greater proportion of early suttas than the other vaggas. These two divisions are, therefore, treated here separately.

Devata samyutta. Feer has suggested that "The Sagātha is properly a collection of verses which are supplied with their narrative commentary."[5] This assertion appears an overstatement. Within the Sagātha-

[3] Catalogue, p. 135.

[4] About the Sagātha, Mrs. Rhys Davids remarks "Nevertheless, the matter of them is of the stamp of the oldest doctrine known to us, and from them a fairly complete synopsis of the ancient dhamma might be compiled" KS. I. p. vii.

[5] SN. I. Int. p. xvi.

vagga, however, there is undoubtedly a class of suttas in which verse is central and most probably primary and which, therefore, needs to be treated separately. This is comprised mainly by the first or Devatāsaṃyutta where prose is either absent or functions merely as an introduction, and that too frequently very brief and monotonous, to the Gāthās.[6] These display, in origin and nature, a surprising variety. In some cases they have nothing specifically Buddhistic about them. In some others, originally non-Buddhist verse appears to have been adapted to Buddhist use. Specifically Buddhist compositions, of course, abound. Some verses are riddles in form; others are more plainly moral exhortations. It may be presumed that those verses which are unencumbered with formulae or reveal these in a yet incipient and fluid stage, are, in general, earlier than those in which ideas find a crystalline expression in technical formulae. Of course, it has to be kept in mind that other than chronological factors can account for the difference in style.

Devatasamyutta : As already suggested, it is on the whole a miscellaneous collection of verses belonging to diverse strata. Some distincion between these is possible.

***(a)* Early: SN. 1. 1. 1. 1:** "Ogha" is already more than an explicit simile, but its signification is as yet quite general.[7] The verse describes Buddha "Brāhmaṇaṃ parinibbutaṃ", with which may be compared the expression "Brahmabhūtatta."[8]

---

[6] The Devatā saṃ has much greater similarity to the verse anthologies of the Kh. N. than to the prose Nikāyas.

[7] Cf. PTSD on 'Ogha'.

[8] See Geiger, Dhamma und Brahman p. 5. Cf. Brahmabhūta MN. I. III; III, 195, 224; SN. IV, 94. AN. V. 226; It. p. 27 (P. T. S. ed.).

SN. 1. 1. 1. 2: It speaks of release from Saññā, Viññāṇa and Vedanā only. The omission of the other two khandhas (as also the absence of the word "Khandha" itself) is significant. Instead of Nibbāna it uses the expression "Sattānaṃ nimokkhaṃ pamokkhaṃ vivekanti."[9] Here the word Satta deserves to be noticed as much as the word Viveka. Salvation is implicitly conceived as the release of an individual through the realization of some fundamental distinction. With this may be compared the upamā illustrating "Āsavakhaya" in DN. 2.

SN. 1. 1. 2. 2: It regards "upadhi" as equivalent to the handicap of having worldly ties like family and property (cf. Sanskrit "Parigraha"; Upādhi has come to have so much of metaphysical association) Emancipation from it is declared to be the source of joy. With this may be compared the sentiment expressed in Sn. Dhaniya sutta.

SN. 1. 1. 2. 3: Like the previous sutta it consists of a popular verse and its Buddhist counterpart. The latter contains the assertion "Natthi attasamaṃ pemaṃ".[10] This is the same idea as finds a more forceful and explicit expression in the Mallikāsutta of the Kosala saṃ.[11] As Mrs. Rhys Davids has pointed out, Attā can hardly mean the ordinary individual self in this context. That would make the statement patently false, and although cynically-minded philosophical ingenuity may not be deterred thereby, it is difficult to imagine Mallikā, herself a mother and wife, uttering it in that case with enthusiasm.[12] Further, the idea is in expres-

[9] SN. I. p. 2.
[10] SN. I. p. 6.
[11] Ib. p. 75.
[12] Kindred Sayings I. p. 196 is. 1.

sion clearly reminiscent of Yājñavalkya.[13] The expression "Attakāma" also is suggestive of the upaniṣads. It is true that the two lines beginning "Evaṃ piyo etc.,"[14] suggest that Attā is to be contrasted with "Para" and hence to be taken to mean the individual. But it must be remembered that these lines (beginning evaṃpiyo etc.,) are not concerned with the explanation of the idea in the Sutta, which is effected summarily in the preceding two lines. They represent rather an afterthought, a moral drawn on the spur of the moment, and in such transitions a silent slide of the meaning from the special to the more general and usual is not impossible.

SN. 1. 1. 3. 3: contains the famous figurative query about the disentangling of a plait of matted hair, and its answer. It is in substance a short and simple summary of the doctrine. Its conception of Nibbāna "Yattha nāmañca" etc., finds a close echoe elsewhere too in the canon.[15]

SN. 1. 1. 3. 7: has the same conception of Nibbāna as above, which is expressed with considerable *verbal* resemblance.

SN. 1. 1. 4. 7: It uses a short "Upamā" which is suggestive of the Kaṭha-upaniṣad parable of the chariot. It speaks of Buddha as "Refuge" but is silent on the other two Refuges, which may be significant. It uses at least one clearly early form "gatāse"[16] and another which is unusual and possibly early-dakkhitāya.[17] Whether the prose of this sutta is as old as the verse is uncertain.

SN. 1. 1. 5. 6: It explains the means to salvation by utilizing the parable of the car (Yāna). The author

---

[13] Br. II. 4-5.
[14] SN. I. p. 75.
[15] Cf. Sn. 1037; DN. I. p. 223. See J.P.T.S. 1909 pp. 312-13
[17] SN. I. p. 26. [16] SN. I. p. 27.

speaks of "maggo", of "sati", and of "sammādiṭṭhi, and yet, shows no acquaintance with the formula of the Eightfold Path. It is relevant in this connection to note that a similar but more elaborate parable—of the Brahmayāna—occurs in the Maggasaṃyutta.[18] There the prose preface takes care to introduce the formula of the eightfold path. The parables group together a number of qualities and practices helpful in leading man spiritually onwards, and it appears that it was out of such more or less fluid material that the formulae relating to the way crystallized.[19]

SN. 1. 1. 6. 5-7: These consider that Man (Satto) on account of Thirst (Taṇhā) wanders through the world (Saṃsāra). There is a close resemblance here with It 1. 2. 5. The disharmony of these texts with the doctrine of Anatta as understood later[20] is manifest.

(*b*) **Late: SN. 1. 1. 1. 5-6:** Both these suttas answer certain queries in terms of various imprecisely specified groups of five. Dogmatics has been pigeon-holed so far in numerical groups that to refer to a particular dogma it is deemed sufficient to quote a certain number!

SN. 1. 1. 7. 10: identical remarks apply to it with equal force. It is the same with **SN. 1. 1. 5. 4.**

SN. 1. 1. 3. 1: speaks of Sakkāyadiṭṭhi without further explanation, which suggests that a technical reference is here intended.

In **SN. 1. 1. 4. 8:** The unusually long prose section has little relevancy to the verse that follows. Besides, the panegyric contained in it shows that the cult of Buddha" could not have been long in the offing. In **SN. 1. 1. 5. 10**

[18] SN. V, p. 6.

[19] For a fuller discussion see below.

[20] In the Sagāthavagga itself........cf. "Suddhasaṅkhārapuñjoyaṃ......" SN. I. 135.

=**SN. 1. 2. 3. 4:** (except for the prefatory line in prose of the latter) the cult of the previous Buddha is unmistakable as it refers summarily to a tale placed in the times of Kasapa (Buddha). The tale is found in detail in sutta 81 of the MN.

(*c*) **Uncertain:** To this class belong the remaining suttas of the Devatāsaṃyutta. They are usually too general to be placed in any particular stratum. Perhaps a detailed literary, linguistic and metrical analysis involving comparison with similar non-Buddhist verses may suggest a way to stratify them. **SN. 1. 1. 2. 6:** may be noted. It describes how the Noble Path may be "purified" (of the obstacles which cloud the vision). No reference whatever is made to its eightfold nature. This silence, however, may not be significant in view of the shortness of the text.

The rest of the Sagāthavagga

(a) Early **SN. 1. 2. 2. 3:** It has a verse prefaced by a conventional prose setting.[21] The verse reads "Bhikhūsiyā Jhāyi vimutta-citto Ākaṅkhe ca hadayassānupattiṃ Lokassa ñatvā udayavyayaṃ ca Sucetaso asito tadānisaṃsoti."[22] The expression "hadayassānupattim" is as remarkable as it is rare in the Nikāyas; and it is manifestly out of tune with the habitual pitch of the later wording for the spiritual goal. The use of this figure shows a dangerous predilection towards the Sakkāya heresy!

SN. 1. 2. 3. 6: The end of the world, lying beyond all change, is not to be attained through any sort of

---

[21] Which is the case with many other suttas also in this and some other saṃyuttas in the Sagātha.

[22] SN. I, p. 52.

motion. Nor indeed "appattvā lokassa antaṃ dukkhassa antakiriyaṃ vadāmi. Api khvāhaṃ āvuso, imasmiññeva vyāmamatte Kaḷevare saññimhi samanake lokāñca paññāpemi samudayañca nirodhañca nirodhagāminiñca paṭipadanti."[23] This sutta occurs in the AN. also.[24] It treats of the idea of transphenomenal Quiet in an unusual way, and clearly reveals a "subjectivist" bias. Its "Samanaka-kaḷebara" is but another expression for "Saviññāṇakakāya" which belongs to an earlier stage of analysis than the dogma of the five khandhas.

SN. 1. 3. (Kosala sam): We are told at many different and independent places in the Nikāyas[25] of the very friendly relations that existed between Buddha and Pasenadi—the king of Kosala. At more than one place Queen Mallikā is shown to have been equally (at one place, much more)[26] full of reverence for Buddha, who must have delivered more than one edifying sermon to his royal patrons and answered many of their problems and difficulties. Owing to the power and prestige of the King, Buddha's meetings with him must have left a particularly deep impression on early Buddhist Tradition. Of course, owing to the same reason the actual historical reminiscences must have been specially liable to receive fictitious—and that need not be always conscious—elaboration. When, therefore, the Kosalasaṃyutta claims to report dialogues between Buddha and the Kosalan king, we may expect a mixture of authentic and unauthentic material.

The doctrines preached are of a simple ethical character, which may be due to their earliness, or possib-

[23] SN. I, p. 62.
[24] AN. II. 48ff; IV. 430 (this may be a later version).
[25] For a discussion of the ref. see below.
[26] MN. II. 106ff.

ly to the fact that king Pasenadi was not metaphysically inclined. The rarity of formulae favours the former alternative. That would also very simply explain the relative abundance of "historical references" in these suttas.[27]

Some suttas, however, clearly belong to a later stratum. Such are SN. 1. 3. 2. 9-10. These together form the Mahyaka Jātaka (iii. 299) where a more graphic and detailed account is given.[28] The second of these suttas has the same title as the first and begins verbatim like it. Possibly it was suggested by the first sutta. Its lateness is apparent from the fact that it speaks of the Pacceka Buddha Tagarasikhi, of the Mahāroruvaniraya and of hundreds, of hundreds of thousands of years in hell.

On §§ 5-10 of SN. 1. 3. 2. 8: Mrs. Rhys Davids has the remark "This interpolated sutta on "Ānanda's proposition is given detached in S.V. 2. It is scarcely in place here." It may be noticed that ideologically too it appears more developed than the rest of the sutta which preaches quite generally about "appamāda" and the good effects of the example of a Kalyāṇamitta, whereas this one introduces the formula of the Eightfold Path (proficiency in the realization of which is declared to be the chief effect of having a kalyāṇamitta).

SN. 1. 4. 3. 3: The sutta describes the last days and death of the monk Godhika. Falling repeatedly from Sāmādhikacetovimutti he committed suicide. Buddha's attitude is, by implication, of acquiescence, as in the similar case of Channa reported in the MN. Paragraph 19 clearly indicates that viññāṇa was regarded as the

[27] See infra.

[28] Kindred Sayings I, p. 116 fn. 4.

transmigrating entity, and Nibbāna as its becoming "appatiṭṭha". This conception of viññāṇa is earlier than that in the theory of the five Khandhas in its standard interpretation. The sutta possibly echoes a historical event.

SN. 1. 6. 1. 1: consists of the "Brahmāyācana" which occurs with some difference in DN. 14 as also in the Ariya-pariyesana-sutta and the Bodhirājakumāra° of the MN. The nuclear psychological conflict may well be ancient and authentic although its present mythological presentation would appear to be later.

SN. 1. 6. 2. 5: occurs identically in DN. 16 and has been considered in that connection. There are three important differences here from the version in the Mahāparinibbāna°. The first is the difference in the order of the verses uttered by Ānanda and Anuruddha. This seems to have been well explained by Przyluski. The second is the non-mention of the Saññāvedayitanirodhasamāpatti in the Saṃyutta-version. This supports the suggestion already made that the section on the Arūpavimokkhas which is found in the description of Buddha's last meditative course is due to later interpolation. The third difference is closely connected with this. Ānanda in DN. 16 mistakes Parinibbāna and Saññāvedayitanirodha and Anuruddha has to correct him. This shows that at the time of the final redaction of DN. 16 the scholastic abilities of Ānanda were not rated very high, and this supports Przyluski's hypothesis. It may be noted that there is more than one Nikāya text which lends colour to Ānanda's mistake. (Cf. Chap. on DN.)

SN. 7. (Brahmana°) consists, as is the rule in the Sagātha, of short suttas in mixed prose and verse

In style and contents these are so similar that they must be placed in the same stratum. All narrate as their main theme the conversion of Brāhmaṇas who display openly their hostility and contempt for the Śramaṇa-Muṇḍakas. The Buddhist doctrines that find expression in these suttas are mostly such as oppose Brāhmaṇic social pretensions or try to replace their ritualistic bias by a more purely ethical outlook. These suttas are in harmony with the similar poetic and simple suttas of the Sn.,[29] and appear to represent an earlier stage of this genre, of which later examples are to be found in the similar suttas of the DN. and the MN. These latter are longer, more elaborate, more dialectical and much more aggressive in tone. It is no longer a Brāhmaṇa-Śramaṇa conflict but a more restricted Brāhmaṇa-Buddhist conflict, that is to say, the Buddhists have now come out before the Brāhmaṇas in their proper individuality and are no longer treated as merely one of the many Śramaṇa sects. Further, the Buddhists are no more content with moral suggestion and persuasion; instead, they take up the sharper weapon of dialectic. And this opposition did not abate in later times.

(b) Late: SN. 1.2.3.9: Towards the end of the Sutta, which is a panegyric on Sāriputta, four Upamās occur to illustrate how "the celestial retinue of Susīma ......while the praises of the venerable Sāriputta were being uttered waxed wondrous in diverse colour-tones.'[30] The fourth Upamā is that of the autumn-sun, which shines forth in the sky free from clouds. Now, whereas the first three similes have a more or less clear reference

---

[29] Kasibhāradvāja is common. SN. I. 213-15=Sn. sutta 10; Cf. also the Sundarikabhāradvāja.

[30] Tr. as in K. S.

to variegated scintillation,[31] the point of the fourth one is obviously the increase of brightness after the removal of obscuring factors. And that is precisely the sense in which it has been used at another place in the canon,[32] where it serves to illustrate the attainment of "Insight into Phenomena" (dhammacakkhu) after the purification of mind. This appears to have been the original sense in which the simile was employed, possibly by Buddha himself, who considers spiritual realization as a kind of vision or illumination.[33]

In the present context, then, the fourth "simile" represents a not very appropriate adaptation from texts belonging to an earlier stratum. Other instances of such misadaptation are not lacking in the Nikāyas, especially when a constellation of comparisons, gathered from different sources, was appended to illustrate some particular point.[34]

The relationship between the two end-verses of the sutta, which are on Sāriputta, and Theragāthās 1002-1003, which are attributed to him, is certainly very close, but it appears difficult to decide as to which is the original.[35]

SN. 1. 4. 5: (Mārasaṃyutta and Bhikkhuṇī°). That before the supreme spiritual crisis, Buddha was faced by some sort of temptation is plausible enough; but on account of its literary promise, the idea was exploited a good deal in Buddhist writings, and a veritable mythology was erected round the figure of Māra.[36] On the one hand, his conflict with Buddha supplied a motif to ballads bearing a heroic character; on the other, if any

---

[31] Cf. K. S. I. p. 89 fn. 1.
[32] AN. I. p. 242.
[33] Cf. chap. on Nirvāṇa.
[34] Cf. It. sutta 27.
[35] Cf. K. S. I. p. 89 fn. 3.
[36] See chap. on Life of Buddha.

practice or idea was to be condemned it was a simple device to make Māra its advocate. All this must have led to the obscuration of the genuine early traditions by a mass of later clouds. Thus in any given set of writings in which Māra figures, probability is in favour of a predominance of later pieces.

Māra's activity as revealed in these suttas falls generally into four classes: to frighten, to shake confidence and conviction, to tempt by worldly attraction, and to advocate false doctrines. The last most plainly indicates the lateness of some suttas. In SN. 1. 4. 2. 6., while Buddha sermonizes on the five upādānakhandhas, Māra tries to disturb the gathering by taking on the form of a bull, but is foiled by being recognised. In the next sutta he attempts to disturb a sermon on the six phassāyatanas. In SN. 1. 4. 2. 9. he vaunts of his power over the (18 dhātus). In S. 15 Māra mostly represents secular temptations, but in the last two suttas (9 & 10) he propounds metaphysical problems and is answered in terms of a fully mature "Skandhānātmavāda". It is noticeable that many verses of this Saṃyutta are found in the Therīgāthā as well.

SN. 1. 6. (Brahmasamyutta) 1. 2. When Buddha finally decides "Dhammaṃ......upanissāya vihareyyanti"[37] Brahmā points out how the same course was adopted by previous Buddhas, and would be adopted by Future Buddhas. The sutta also mentions the sequence from Sīlakkhandha to Vimuttiñāṇadassana°.

SN 1. 6. 1. 3: Brahmā himself tells the mother of Brahmadeva who had attained to arahatship that her son had reached beyond the gods (Atidevappatta) and an offering (Āhuti) to him (Brahmā) was sheer ignorance!

[37] SN. I. p. 139.

A clear instance of Tendenzchriften! In SN. 1. 6. 1. 4. the Brahmā Baka falls into the eternalist heresy and has to be rescued by Buddha. In the next sutta another Brahmā is shown to imagine his status unapproachably high, whereas it is found finally that many of the greater disciples even of Buddha could go higher at will (throughout physical height is implied!). In SN. 1. 6. 1. 6. two Paccekabrahmās demonstrate to Brahmā their superiority over him. In the next three suttas also Pacceka-brahmās figure. The last of these is unintelligible unless the narrative of the following sutta (SN. 1. 6. 1. 10) is kept in mind. This latter sutta recounts the dire consequences which the monk Kokālika had to face owing to his having slandered Sāriputta-Moggalāna. The prose portion of this sutta agrees closely with the Kokālikasutta of the MN., which, however, has a much greater number of verses. The sutta occurs in the AN. too.

SN. 1. 6. 2. 4. narrates a story of the time of the previous Buddha Sikhin.

(c) **Uncertain:** The remaining suttas and Saṃyuttas of the Sagāthavagga are not easily amenable to stratification. The generality of their contexts offers the main difficulty. A closer investigation, however, of Saṃyuttas VIII-XI will probably lead to better results. It is hardly possible, for instance, that SN. 1. 8. 7. should belong to the same stratum as SN. 1. 9. 1. The former lavishes elaborate praise on Sāriputta, mentions the three Vijjās and the six Abhiññās,[38] and distinguishes between Ubhatobhāgavimutti and Paññā°. The latter in a few simple and earnest verses asks the monk to shed from him, like a bird, the dust (Raja) of desire by means of resolute

[38] Cf. PTSD on the history of the ten Abhiññās.

effort (Padhāna) and mindfulness (Sati) in the forest. The language of these verses is as archaic as the sylvan atmosphere. The forms Bhavāsi, Sārayāmase and Vidhūnaṃ are used. Many such verses are to be met with in early Jinist poetry.[39]

The other Vaggas of the SN.

The later stratum: ideas. As already stated, these differ from the first vagga by the predominance of metaphysics and formular prose. At least two strata are discoverable within these. The first, which embraces the majority of the suttas, shows a remarkable homogeneity and is late. These are concerned with the statement, exposition and correlation of dogmatic formulae which along their several lines represent the highest peak of mataphysical evolution in the Nikāyas, ignoring, of course, the abhidhammic and commentarial works included in the Khuddaka. Such are the doctrines of Paṭiccasamuppāda with twelve "nidānas", the five khandhas, and the Āyatanas. As to the last or Mahāvagga, it is not impossible that the formulae contained therein and relating to spiritual practice, more so the ideas which they express, are probably earlier than the more abstruse metaphysical formulae of the preceding vaggas.

And Style: In style, the suttas of this group are typically scholastic. Usually they dispense with any narrative trappings. Commencing directly, they proceed to enumerate and (or) describe in detail all the elements of a formula, which may be done quite generally or from some special standpoint. Often the catechistic style is adopted. The result is enormous repetition and a surprizingly large number of suttas (for the whole

---

[39] Cf. Sk. 1-2-1-15.

of the S. 2889).[40] As a matter of fact, it will be wrong to regard these suttas generally independent. Considerable groups of them stand closely together, and were most probably composed together. Winternitz plausibly suggests that the tedious multiplication of suttas possibly originated in their use as religious exercises. Mrs. Rhys David's suggestion that the fact "that the varying suttas were collected from different sources, from different vihāras or even laymen" may have been a factor in their multiplication, has equal plausibility.[41]

Winternitz[42] draws our attention pointedly to the tedious repetitions which we meet here.[42] For example, the Saḷāyatana-Saṃyutta (XXXV) comprises no less than 207 suttas, speeches and dialogues on the six senses. With untiring monotony it is here demonstrated that sight, hearing, smell taste, touch and the mind (manas) are Anicea, and Dukkha and Anatta, and that the sense perceptions and the sense objects corresponding to the six sense organs are similarly Anicca, and Dukkha, and Anatta. Further, in the case of each sense-organ, and each corresponding class of sense-perceptions and sense-objects the whole series of assertions is repeated literally, and every assertion forms a sutta in itself.[43] In brief, this stratum is much nearer to Abhidhammic writings in its dry-as-dust formulized ideas and style than to Buddha. It is interesting to note that Burnouf actually thought by mistake that the "Nidānavagga" belonged "sans doute" to Abhidhamma.[44]

---

[40] Winternitz II. pp. 56-57. [41] Quoted Ib. 57 fn. 1.

[42] Winternitz, of course, intends describing all the suttas of the SN. in a general way. Actually the description applies to the late though dominating class of suttas in vaggas II-IV.

[43] Winternitz, op. cit. p. 56.

[44] Quoted by Feer in his Int. to the ed. of SN. II. p. XII. fn. 1.

The earlier Stratum: Side by side with these suttas are, however, found, the infrequent glimpses of earlier doctrines and a different style. These may, in the present state of inquiry be grouped together in a single 'early' class, although we should not expect a priori that these fragments should belong to the same epoch.

Its main ideas: These are either free from formulae or show them in the course of development. The idea of a "Mean" lying between extremes is at places prominent. Paṭiccasamuppāda in its standard form appears as the crowning synthesis of various incomplete attempts at causally explaining the genesis of misery. Attā sometimes appears much more a transcendental entity than a delusive appearance to be denied. Viññāṇa and Citta appear interchangeable, and are conceived as the mutable transmigrating "More-than-body". Vimokkha or Vimutti is the emancipation of this Viññāṇa-citta from phenomenal adjuncts (Patiṭṭhā, upadhi). Through further psychological analysis, however, the signification of Viññāṇa was narrowed to become merely one of the four aspects of mind (the "more-than-body") but even here the scheme of the five khandhas passed through a quincunx-stage before becoming a mere five-fold.

Some fragments lend support to Schayer's view about the existence of an earlier, non-psychological distinction between Rūpa and Dhamma, a distinction which may be described as that between the apparent form and the real norm.

The explanation of phasso as a "contacting of three" (Tiṇṇaṃ Saṅgati) appears a later interpretation of an earlier concept.

And Style: In style these fragments are a refreshing change. They are richer in narrative and often decked with parables and similes. Besides, they are not unoften "nuclear" in character, i.e., they appear sometimes as the original nuclei of suttas which in their present form must be regarded as appended and (or) interpolated. In the Nidānasaṃyutta and the similar bigger Saṃyuttas many originally independent suttas have been brought into a mechanical uniformity with the rest by the forced introduction of the leading formula of the Saṃyutta. In some cases the real continuation seems to have been thus blotted out, though in the main, what we have is just inorganic addition. These additions are generally quite monotonous and were perhaps due in some cases to editorial retouching at the time or (times) of collection. Part of the responsibility perhaps lies on the "reciters" who must have found it convenient to repeat the leading and frequent formula of the Saṃyutta with all the suttas, and found it quite inconvenient to preserve small variations which were no longer understood, or were even opposed to the standard doctrines as expressed in the completed formulae. Sometimes the character is nuclear only with reference to more elaborate other texts.

It is a striking fact that out of Vaggas II—V by far the greatest number of the earlier "fragments" occur in the second Vagga, after which they become increasingly infrequent. It may be stated generally that the older portions of the SN. show a concentration in the first two vaggas.

Nidānasaṃyutta

(a) **Late:** In this stratum may be placed the following classes of suttas: (i) There is first the class containing nothing or little else beside the bare statement of the fully evolved formula of Paṭiccasamuppāda. To this belong suttas 1, 3, 4, 10, 13-14, 16, 29-30, 49-50, 60, 71, 81, (these may be regarded as really one composition), and 82-93 (interdependent). The variation between these is small and insignificant, for instance, sutta 3 has the same contents as sutta 1, with the difference that the two sequences of the Nidānas—as leading to Samudaya and as leading to Nirodha—are called this time micchā-and sammā-paṭipadās respectively. In suttas 4-10 Paṭiccasam° is described as discovered by the seven Buddhas (cf. DN. 14, where the same subject is stated but the formula has only 10 Nidānas).

(ii) Then there is the class of suttas which contain in addition to the formula of the Paṭiccasam° some elucidatory elaborations of its elements also. Such are suttas 2 (a 'vibhaṅga' on sutta 1. It explains Nāmarūpa in the same way as the Sammādiṭṭhisutta of the MN. This is nearer to the later explanation of the term, according to which Nāmarūpa=Five khandhas than the explanation in the Mahānidānasutta in the D), 27-28, 33 (which, besides, expands the Nidānas into 44 Ñāṇavatthus by the application of the fourfold scheme—as in the 4 Truths—to eleven of them), 34 (it has 77 Ñāṇavatthus), and 51 (it contains an "Upamā" also).

(iii) Some suttas combine the formula of the paṭiccasam° with other doctrines and formulae: suttas 11-12—These combine the doctrine of the four sustenances with that of the Paṭiccasam°. To say that Kabaliṅkāra āhāra, Phassa and Manosañcetanā (food, sensation-feeling, and conation) function as sustenances (āhāras) for the phenomenal continuation (ṭhiti, patiṭṭhā) of Viññāṇa, is readily intelligible (cf. suttas 38 and 64: MN. 9, etc.). To turn Viññāṇa itself into an āhāra can be understood only as the product of a growing vogue of the "Anatta". Further since the theory of Āhāra has the same function as that of Paṭiccasam, viz., to explain the basis of phenomenal existence, the two represent actually two parallel answers to the same problem. Hence to apply the formula of Paṭiccasam° on to that of the Āhāras appears to be the product of an unseeing zeal for the former formula. The result is certainly confusion, for, of the four Āhāras sought to be explained in terms of the Nidānas, two recur literally in the explanatory chain of causes. These are Phasso and Viññāṇa; also, Manosañcetanā is in significance not much different from saṅkhāra. If a distinction is at all sought to be effected between the two, it is the former—equal to abhisaṅkhāra with its active emphasis?—that is more entitled to be called the cause. More precisely the causal relation between the two will be in this interpretation akin to that between the seed and the sprout; roughly, conative striving—sañcetanā—leads to mental Gestaltungen—Saṅkhāra—and these in turn to further striving. As already stated, Paṭiccasaṃ° was not in fact intended to explain the genesis of the Āhāras; rather, both were meant to explain the same fundamental fact, and had much in common.

The degradation of Viññāṇa into an "āhāra" leads inevitably to the difficulty raised by Phagguna in sutta 12, to avoid which recourse is had to a mode of expression that reduces the āhāra-formula into that for Paṭiccasam. Since the query begins with Viññāṇa, the preceding two terms, Saṅkhāra and Avijjā, do not occur in this version of Paṭiccasam°. Nāmarūpa seems to be implicit in the general expression Punabbhavābhinibbatti.[45] Sutta 35 takes up the same problem as sutta 12,

[45] SN. II, p. 13, cf. Mrs. Rhys Davids' Original Gospel, pp. 112-113.

but more systematically, and examines it with respect to all the Nīdānas. Sutta 36 is similar to it. Sutta 63 illustrates the four āhāras by grisly similes.

Sutta 20 describes Paṭiccasam° as "Dhammatā dhammaṭṭhitatā dhammaniyāmatā," independent of the Tathāgatas,[46] and goes on to stress the impermanence of all its elements, and explains its knowledge to be a corrective of preoccupation with how one has been in the past and the present and would be in the future. Sutta 21 combines with Paṭiccasam° the theory of the changefulness of the Five khandhas, while sutta 23 combines with it a rare "causal sequence of joy and happiness."[47] Suttas 41-42[48] introduce the Five fears (corresponding to the five sīlas) and the Four Sotāpattiyaṅgas. Paṭiccasam° is called the Noble Law (Ariyo ñāyo).

Finally, suttas 68 and 70 introduce the distinction between the Paññāvimutta and the Ubhatobhāgavimutta, the latter also applying the Three Marks to the Five Khandhas. (iv) Sutta 31, which quotes and explains a verse from the Ajitapañha in the Pārāyaṇa, is unlikely to be early.

(b) **Early:** The most striking group of suttas belonging to this stratum is that which contains the metaphysical doctrine of the Middle as the solution of some obstinate antinomies. The problems and the answers are, however, so briefly given that a precise statement of their implications presents many difficulties. Since these difficulties are more philosophical than textual, they are treated later.[49]

---

[46] SN. II, p. 25.

[47] K. S. II. VIII.

[48] Mrs. Rhys Davids regards "the refrain of assurance of ultimate salvation" in sutta 41 early, seeing in it "the triumph song of him who is leading the good life" (K. S. II, p. XI).

[49] See below.

The suttas belonging to this class are—15, 17-18, 24-26 and 46-48. In the case of all these, except suttas 25-26, the standard formula of Paṭiccasm, is found appended at the close of the sermons, apparently as the positive content of the doctrine of the Middle (Majjhena Dhaṃmo). Mrs. Rhys David's suggests that Paṭiccasam was a name given to this doctrine at a later date by the compilers of the Suttapiṭaka.[50] That is possible, but it is practically certain that the elaborate and stereotyped formula which the term Paṭiccasam° usually signifies, represents only the final shape which the Middle-doctrine, of which some earlier glimpses may be caught in these suttas, came to assume. The formula as such, therefore, must be regarded in the case of these suttas as a later substitution for part of the more fluid original continuation. Mrs. Rhys Davids advocates this conclusion in the case of sutta 18[51] and the arguments are generalizable to the other suttas of the class which are greatly similar in problem and answer.

In sutta 15 "nādhiṭṭhāti attānam eti" of § 6 presents undoubted difficulty. Mrs. Rhys David's remarks "Feer's text reads attā na me ti (wrongly divided in the text). The comy. reads attā meti. Either can be read consistently with the context." It is impossible to see how that can be done, since between the two readings there is a difference of full hundred and eighty degrees. Mrs. Rhys Davids accomplishes the feat by separating "nādhiṭṭhāti" from "attā na meti" and interpolating "who thinks."[52] This appears more change than can be justified. But why redivide Feer's text? and why not translate "(who) does not take up his stand upon it,

[50] K. S. II. p. v.
[51] K. S. II. p. X.
[52] Ib. p. 13. fn. 1.

(who) resorts to the self."[53] With this may be compared such texts as "attadīpā viharatha" etc. This, of course, goes against orthodoxy but in the pursuit of orthodoxy the comy., has to delete the very palpable particle 'Na'—a questionable procedure. Besides, "attānameti" need not mean any thing more startling than "takes a turn away from the objects of the world," and this is precisely what the preceding phrases mean.

This sutta is referred to in SN. also, which confirms its antiquity. Nāgārjuna quotes it and Candrkīrti assures us that all the sects accepted its authenticity.[54]

Sutta 17 contains another application of the Middle Doctrine. Sutta 18 has the same problem, but the answer shows an enigmatic divergence: instead of asserting the expected identity-in-difference of the person who sows with the person who reaps, it proceeds to assert the identity-in-difference of the person who feels with his feeling! The difficulty must have been noticed by the commentator who gets over it by taking Vedanā to mean Kāraka-vedanā.[55] Perhaps the sutta suffers from the 'confusion' of two different texts.

Sutta 24 too is concerned with the same problem, and the anwer again varies in form, but this time intelligibly. It is declared that 'sukha-dukkha' are 'paṭicca-

---

[53]Cf. Ib. p. 13.

[54] It is noted by Nāgārjuna—
"Kātyāyanāvavāde Cāstīti nāstīti cobhayam |
Pratiṣiddham bhagavatā, Bhāvābhāvavibhāvinā ||"
(MK. XV. 7)

Candrakīrti comments "Uktaṃ hi Bhagavatā Āryakātyāyāyanāvavādasūtre yadbhūyasā Kātyāyanāyaṃ lokostitāṃ vābhiniviṣṭo nāstitāṃ ca tena na parimucyate. . . .*Idañca sūtram sarvanikāyeṣu paṭhyate*". (The first sentence of the passage quoted by Candrakīrti agrees closely with "Dvayanissito'yam Kaccāyana loko yebhuyyena atthitañceva natthitañca"—SN. II. p. 17).

[55]K.S. II, p. 18, fn. 1.

samuppanna' and that is equated to "arising dependently on phassa (Phasspaccayā)". Ānanda is surprised at the depth of this single expression (pada) and for his benefit a new section is added containing the full formula of Paṭiccasasm°. The juxtaposition of older and newer strata is here apparent. Sutta 25 is similar to the preceding in problem and answer; only it adds avijjā and the three saṅkhāras as further paccayas. Sutta 46 revives the problem of sutta 17 and sutta 47 that of sutta 15. Sutta 48 adds to the antinomy of Being and Non-Being a wholly new one on ekatta and puthutta (one and many).[56]

Sutta 22 repeats sutta 21, and then adds a new sermon the central idea of which is expressed in the sentence "Tasmātiha bhikkhave viriyamārabhatha appattassa pattiyā anadhigatassa adhigamāya asacchikatassa sacchikiriyāya."[57] This second sermon, which has no organic connection with the first, appears early on account of its earnest tone, freedom from formula and a strikingly positive outlook towards the goal.

The sermon in sutta 37 begins by stating "Nāyaṃ bhikkhave Kāyo tumhākaṃ nāpi aññesaṃ purāṇamidaṃ kammam abhisaṅkhatamabhisañcetayitaṃ vedaniyaṃ daṭṭhabbaṃ."[58] Then follows the Paṭiccasam° formula for both the general and applied forms. Mrs. Rhys Davids states that here we have "an important saying with a genuine ring, but treated as incidental."[59] This

[56] The middle doctrine thus deals principally with these three problems:—

(a) Being and Non-being (Becoming):
(b) Identity and diff. in personal life.
(c) One and Many.

[57] SN. II. p. 29.

[58] Ib. p. 65.

[59] K. S. II. p. XI.

appears correct. The saying implicity rejects the extremes of personal identity and difference, and, instead, emphasizes the character of experience as a procession of suffering (Vedanā) contingent on previous Kamma which itself originates in desiring and striving (abhisaṅkhāra, abhisañcetanā). The saying is a clear expression of the doctrine of Majjhena Dhammo i.e., the oldest form of Paṭiccasam.

Sutta 61 with the monkey simile has important doctrinal implications on the nature of body, mind and self.[60] The formulae of Paṭiccasam° and the Five Khandhas have been appended to it.[61]

Sutta 62 is, for the first half, a repetition of the preceding sutta, but after the general formula of Paṭiccasam° it suddenly diverges into an altogether different sutta on the origin of the threefold feeling.

The ending, however, is the same for both. This seems to be another instance of that sort of "confusion" which sutta 22 exhibits. The second sermon on Vedanā, however, with its simile of two faggots of wood,[62] itself appears early.

The following suttas form an early class because they reveal the formula of Paṭiccasam° yet in the course of evolution.[63] Sutta 19 (The central doctrine: avijjānīvaraṇassa—bālassa taṇhāya sampayuttassa evamayam kāyo samudāgato Iti ayaṃ ceva kāyo bahiddhā ca nāmarūpaṃ itthetaṃ dvayaṃ dvayaṃ paṭicca phasso Saḷevāyatanāni //yehi phuṭṭho bālo sukkhadukkham paṭisaṃve-

---

[60] See below.

[61] See Mrs. Rhys Davids in K. S. II. p. XI. Also the Birth of Indian Psychology etc.

[62] On this simile see Chap. on 'Life of Buddha'.

[63] For a reconstruction of the evolutionary sequence see below.

diyati etassa vā aññatarena//)[64] Sutta 32 [on Sāriputta's declaration of his attainment of aññā, Buddha tests him by a catechism (was that the usual practice?). The Nidānas are taken back to Vedanā only]; Sutta 43 [the first part describes the causal chain of dukkha as extending from (Saḷāyatana) to Taṇhā; the second relating to Cessation (Atthaṅgama) brings forward the series upto Jarāmaraṇa]; Sutta 45 (wholly similar, but presents only the fuller version of 43. II); Sutta 44 (similar to it but with respect to Loka); Sutta 52 (the series from Taṇhā to Jarāmaraṇa as also the comparison of faggots and fire to illustrate upādāniyadhammas); Suttas 55-56 (same idea, with a different simile); Sutta 60 (similar to the above mentioned, but begins like DN. 15); Sutta 53 (similar to sutta 52 except that it substitutes saṃyojaniya for upādāniya and uses the different simile of the oil-lamp); Suttas 57-58 (similar to it, with a change in simile corresponding to that in sutta 55-56); Sutta 59 (it joins the motif and simile of suttas 57-58 to the idea in sutta 39); Sutta 65 (it describes the Bodhisatta's realization of the Paṭiccasam with ten "nidānas". It thus belongs to the same doctrinal level as the treatment in DN. sutta 14. It contains the important parable of the city. Mrs. Rhys Davids remarks: "And in the 'City' sutta, his way-showing and the ancient path of the good life reverberate as if he were himself yet talking to us".[65] One may compare the upaniṣadic parable of the return to Gandhāra); Sutta 66 (gives the unusual series dukkha <upadhi<taṇhā<piyarūpa-sāta°=sense objects); Sutta 67 (Paṭiccasam° with ten Nidānas; the last two Nāmarūpa-Viññāṇa are declared mutually dependent like "two

---

[64] SN. II, p. 24.
[65] K. S. II, p. XI.

sheaves of reeds leaning one against the other".)//[66]//A few suttas reveal an early conception of viññāṇa. These are suttas 38-40 (sutta 39 is more elaborate than sutta 38; and a step nearer the later formula of Paṭiccasam°. Part of sutta 40—Natiyā asati...nirujjhanti"—[67] occurs in the Channovādasutta in the MN.);[68] Sutta 64 (it inconsistently combines the idea of Viññāṇa as assuming a "Platform"—Patiṭṭhā—with that of the four Sustenances. The result is the unintelligible statement Viññāṇe ce—āhāre atthi rāgo patiṭṭhitaṃ tattha viññāṇaṃ virūḍhaṃ."[69] Originally perhaps the sutta spoke only of the first three 'āhāras' attachment in which was the cause of the patiṭṭhā of Viññāṇa.[70] The sutta has an important set of similes to illustrate this assumption of a basis or platform by Viññāṇa).[71]

Nidānavagga—the other saṃyuttas

The Abhisamaya-saṃ° reiterates the same idea with different comparisons in eleven suttas. The idea itself—"puggalassa abhisametāvino etadeva bahutaraṃ dukkhaṃ yadidaṃ parikkhīṇaṃ...appamattaka-mavasiṭṭhaṃ[72]—is too general to be stratified. The Dhātusaṃ° with its emphasis on Dhātu and the separateness of elements is clearly suggestive of the Abhidhamma and its "Dharma-theory", which is considered below.[73]

Suttas 1-10 are loosely connected, and were perhaps composed as a whole; only suttas 7-8 and suttas 9-10 appear "variants"—they differ only by the latter group

[66] K. S. II. 8.80.
[67] SN. II, p. 67.
[68] Cf. SN. III. 132ff; also Cf. Ud., p. 84.
[69] SN. II, p. 101.
[70] Cf. Sakya, p. 159.
[71] See Chap. on Nirvāṇa.
[72] SN. II, p. 133.
[73] Cf. K. S. II, p. XII.

having an additional detail about *lābhanānatta*. Suttas 11-12 introduce further dhātus; sutta 13 points out that the noble, the average and the low must have corresponding ideas. Suttas 14-29 have the same refrain "Dhātuso sattā saṃsandanti samenti".[74] Suttas 30-39 are on the four material dhātus.

Anamataggasam°—In the refrain "anamataggāyam bhikkhave saṃsāro pubbakoṭi na paññāyati avijjānīvaraṇānaṃ sattānaṃ taṇhāsaṃyojanānaṃ sandhāvataṃ saṃsarataṃ"[75] we seem to have "what is probably a real saying" with its forceful warning and the rare term "anamataggo."[76] It may be noted that the expression in this refrain is scarcely consonant with the doctrine of Anatta as understood later. Nāgārjuna quotes it in MK. XI. 1, as the saying of Buddha.[76a]

Kassapasam.° Suttas 5 and 11 seem to contain some actual reminiscences of Kassapa.[77]

The whole of the *Lābhasakkāra* saṃ° is built on the refrain "Dāruṇo lābhasakkārasiloko kaṭuko pharuso antarāyiko anuttarassa yogakkhemassa adhigamāya".[78] The refrain may be early.

Rahulasam° applies the "three marks" in a very mechanical and monotonous catechistic style to the senses, the sense objects etc., (a large number of dogmatic categories). It is most probably a late scholastic composition.

The suttas of the *Lakkhaṇasaṃ*° present but slightly differing variants on the same theme, which is of an un-

---

[74] SN. II. p. 154, etc. [75] SN. II. p. 178, etc.

[76] K. S. II. p. xii.

[76a] "Pūrvā prajñāyate koṭirnetyuvāca mahāmuniḥ.
Saṃsāronavarāgro hi nāsyādirnāsti paścimam."
(MK. XI. 1)

[77] See below.

[78] SN. II. p. 226, etc.

certain stratum. In the Opammasaṃ° each sutta illustrates some dogma by a "comparison". Sutta 1 appears possibly early since it contains an early doctrine (which is not to say it was not held later) with a fitting illustration. Sutta 7 appears late. It distinguishes between "Ye te suttantā Tathāgatabhāsitā lokuttarā suññatapaṭisaṃyuttā" and "ye pana te suttantā kavikatā"[79] which indicates a good deal of previous literary activity. The greater part of this sutta occurs as part of the sutta on Future Dangers.[80] The rest of the suttas are uncertain, which holds of the next saṃyutta except suttas 1. 3, 8-9 and 11 (the verses are irrelevant). These seem to echo actual recollections.[81]

Khandhavagga.—The first Saṃyutta (*the pervasive stratum*): By far the greatest part of the Khandh..saṃ° preaches a uniform doctrine in a uniform style. The variations are but slight. Suttas like 23, 25, 29, 35, 36 and 70 emphasize detachment in the Five Khandhas. Suttas 26-28, 60, 73-75 achieve the same effect by directing attention to their sweet first taste (Assāda) and bitter after taste (Ādīnava). Suttas like 5-6 point to their origin and decay. Suttas 30, 32, 37-38, 41-52, 71-72, 96-98 and 102 speak of their impermanence. Suttas 9-11, 2-21, 40-42, 49-55 (to which is appended the idea of 53-54) 59, 66-68, 76 (the verses at the end may be earlier), and 80 apply to them (the 5 Khandhas) the Three Marks in catechism style. Suttas 5-6 speak of them merely as "not mine". Apart from sundry elaborations there is scarcely any significant difference between suttas 43, 44 (defines Sakkāya in terms of the Khandhas, which are treated under the fourfold or catusaccika

[79] SN. II. 267. [80] See eg., AN. III. 107.
[81] See Chap. on the Life of Buddha.

scheme), 45-48, 50 (4-fould scheme), 56 (the Khandhas are explained and treated as catuparivaṭṭa), 57 (similar), 58 (distinguishes) between the Sammāsambuddha Tathāgata and the Paññāvimutta bhikkhu), 61 (Khandhas as on fire), 62, 63-65, 78-79 (with explanations of the Khandhas, and abstract terms for them—rūpatta, vedanatta etc.),[82] 81 (introduces other doctrines as well, including the 37 Bodhipakkhiyas), 93 and 99-100 (on the anamatagga refrain). Sutta 31 describes the khandhas as sin.

Kh. Sam° (contd.) Some unusual though late suttas.—Sutta 3 quotes from the Māgandiyapañha and sutta 4 from the Sakkapañha. Both these apparently belong to a comparatively later stratum.

In sutta 90 Ānanda quotes the sermon which occurs independently in SN. II. pp. 16-17. Suttas 91-92 are repetitions of Rāhula saṃ°—suttas 21-22.

Sutta 94 declares that the Tathāgata is, like the lotus in water, "loke saṃvaḍḍho lokamabhibhuyya viharati anupalitto lokenāti."[83]

Sutta 95 contains a constellation of comparisons to illuminate the hollow insubstantiality of the Khandhas. At the end occurs a poem of similar import in which "illusionistic" tendencies are plain, and which uses the term Santāna.[84] This sutta is most probably very late.[85]

Sutta 122 uses the term "Anāgāmin" technically, and thus indicates its lateness.[86] Sutta 136 describes the khandhas as but masses of glowing embers (Kukkula). It formed the leading text of the Kukkulavādin sect;

---

[82] SN. III. p. 87.

[83] SN. III. p. 146, cf. Kv. XVIII, 1.

[84] Cf. DN. III. 105: "Viññāṇasota".

[85] Some of the verses occuring at the end of this sutta are almost identically quoted by Candrakīrti in his comy., on MK. (MK. V. I. pp. 41-42.)

[86] See PTSD.

possibly it has been suggested by the Third Sermon at Gayā.[87]

The Puggalavādin sutta 22 is already well known;[88] sutta 106 has a similar implication. Sutta 89 has a most interesting debate between the Theras and Khemaka who takes up a position similar to that of the Puggalavādins. The Theras, worsted in argument, have managed to rehabilitate their position by tampering with the text of the record; they make Khemaka himself suddenly swerve into the orthodox fold, and give an irrelevant explanation of his own very real difficulties about the theory of Anatta.[89]

Khandha-sam (contd.) Some early fragments.—Mrs. Rhys Davids enthusiastically, and it appears rightly advocates the genuineness of the short and simple sermon by Buddha to Nakulapitā embeded in sutta 1 and the parable of the way embedded in sutta 84. Buddha's sermon in the former assumes only a simple Kāya-citta analysis of man.

Sutta 33 regards the khandhas as foreign to a man's self as the trees in the Jeta-wood. The emphasis here is clearly not on the rejection of the self but on the rejection of the non-self.[90]

Suttas 53-54 supply clear instances of editorial retouching and twisting. In sutta 53 the original sermon seems to have been to the effect that Viññāṇa was bound up in matter (Rūpa) through striving and delighting (Saṅkhāra and Nandī), with the disappearance of which it became free. This doctrine is similar to that found in some suttas of SN. II. In its present form the

[87] Vin. I. 34-5.
[88] See Chap. on Nirvāṇa.
[89] See Chap. on Nirvāṇa.
[90] K. S. III. pp. VI-VII.

sutta interpolates all the five khandhas in §§ 5-10, with the result that Viññāṇa now seems to divide itself from itself and lets this alter ego become its platform and bondage![91] How else can Viññāṇa find patiṭṭhā and ārammaṇa in "Viññāṇadhātu" itself? The addition of "Dhātu" cannot be taken as an intentional indication of a difference of meaning between Viññāṇadhātu and Viññāṇa, since this addition, confined to the interpolated part of the Sutta, comes merely from the frequency with which the word dhātu was used in later times (when the interpolation must have taken place). It has been added to Rūpa and Saṅkhāra also just to express these more after the scholastic fashion of the day.

Sutta 54 is similar to it except that it has an additional preface containing a significant simile, and that the interpolation of the five Khandhas has here invaded even that part of the sermon which is expressed in sutta 53 (this section now being expanded into four separate sections).

In sutta 82, which is on the whole very scholastic, a significant query is raised towards the end—"Anattakatāni Kammāni katamattānaṃ phusissanti"[92]—but is side-tracked by an irrelevant and banal catechism.

In sutta 83 Ānanda recalls a sermon of Puṇṇa Mantāniputta to the effect that the five khandhas serve as the reflecting surface for the Ego-feeling, or, in modern terminology, that self-consciousness is mediated by objects. The view is suggestive of the Sāṅkhya position that the Ego-sense is contingent on the delusive identity of cons-

[91] Mrs. Rhys Davids' interpretation is totally unconvincing. See Sakya, p. 325.

[92] SN. III, p. 103.

ciousness with the modifications of Intellect, which are related to it only as reflecting media. The sutta may contain some really ancient echo. Suttas 87-88, on the last moments of Vakkali and Assaji, may also contain some actual recollections. To Vakkali Buddha says: "alaṃ Vakkali kiṃ te iminā pūtikāyena diṭṭhena yo kho Vakkali dhammaṃ passati so maṃ passati."[93] A latter-day writer would hardly dare to compose the first of these two lines. Similarly realistic is Assaji's confession of a regret in sutta 88, § 13. And in both Attā occurs in the rare meaning of "conscience".

In sutta 101 the main sermon relates to Bhāvanānuyoga with respect to the 37 Bodhipakkhiyas. This is illustrated by the simile of the brooding hen, and the resulting freedom from the "saṃyojanas" by the simile of the boat-joints. This is probably a relatively early sermon.

Khandhavagga: the other samyuttas.—*Rādhasaṃ* is similar in idea and style to the preceding. Sutta 1 gives an interesting series with which may be compared those in MN. and the Indriyasaṃ°—sutta 42. All the three agree in distinguishing Vimutti and Nibbāna.

Sutta 11-46 are clearly not independent compositions.

Ditthisam° states with tiresome repetition that all the various Diṭṭhis spring from an ignorance of the true nature of the Five Khandhas.

Okkantikasam° lists a large number of objects. the knowledge of whose impermanence leads to Assurance (Niyāma). The ten suttas can scarcely be considered independent compositions.

Uppadasam° is concerned with the changefulness

93 SN. III, p. 120.

of those very objects which find mention in the previous saṃyutta.

Kilesasam° describes the same as "Upakkilesa".

Sariputta-sam°.—The first nine suttas were clearly composed as a whole, since they deal in succession with the nine meditative stages.

Sutta 10, which describes the encounter of Sāriputta with the Sucimukhī Paribbājakā, is in a wholly different and very realistic style. It probably contains the record of some actual meeting. Then follow saṃyuttas on the Nāgas, the Supaṇṇas, the Gandhabbakāyas and the Valahas or Valahakāyika deities. These are of an obviously popular character and origin. The suttas of the Vacchagottasam° differ but little, and seek to trace false doctrines to an ignorance of the Five Khandhas.

In the **Jhanasam°** the subject of Jhāna is treated in brief and mechanically constructed suttas dealing with the samāpatti, ṭhiti, vuṭṭhāna, kallita, ārammaṇa, gocara, abhinīhāra, sākkacca, sātacca, and sappāya of samādhi, as well as the combinations of these. It is clearly a late scholastic product.

Saḷāyatanavagga—the first Saṃyutta:

The greater part of the suttas in this saṃyutta is exceedingly uniform in style,[94] but from the standpoint of ideas a number of classes may be sorted out.

(*a*) Those suttas which speak of the senses (sense is throughout used to include mind, unless otherwise specified) and the sense objects only. (*b*) Those which add to these, sense-perceptions, sense-contacts (samphassa) and thence resulting threefold feelings (the usual

[94] According to Mrs. Rhys Davids this section is "markedly by and for the monks". K. S. IV, p. VII.

term in these suttas it may be noted is Vedayita, not Vedanā). (*c*) Those which introduce the formula "cakkhuñca paṭicca rūpañca uppajjati cakkhuviññāṇaṃ Tiṇṇam saṅgati phasso// phassapaccayā vedanā. . . ."[95] (and so with the other senses). This shows a further application of the terminology of Paṭiccasam°, and a perceptible change in the meaning of "contact". In suttas of group (b) "contact" is a bilateral affair between the senses and their objects. This feature comes out clearly in the simile of two faggots of wood, which sometimes illustrates it. Out of this contact result perceptions as well as feelings, but the one is not necessarily causal to the other; rather, both have their immediate source in the same sense-contact. In other words, consciousness, produced by the contact of the senses with the outside world, has from the very beginning cognitive as well as affective dimensions.

This situation changes in the suttas of group (c), where "contact" has become trilateral. It is, in fact, no longer merely a "contact" of the senses with the sense objects, but a complete, though solely perceptive, experience depending on which feeling originates. Perhaps the use of Phassa instead of Samphassa in these texts is not without significance.

(*d*) These suttas add to the senses, sense objects and sense perceptions, the further class of Viññāṇaviññātabbā dhammā (cakkhu°, etc.).

To (*a*) belong the suttas—1-23, 70, 71-73 (sense objects are not mentioned). 92, 94-95 (both have verses at the end, and are similar in contents), 96 (this gives an

---

[95] Cf. "cakṣuḥ pratītya rūpāṇi cotpadyate cakṣurvijñānam trayāṇāṃ sannipātaḥ sparsaḥ sparśasahajā Vedaneti vistaraḥ." (MK. V. III, p. 250.)

unusual interpretation of the term Abhibhāyatana and although Buddha is apparently the speaker, it quotes throughout "Parihānaṃ etaṃ vuttam Bhagavatāti"), 98 (similar except that the Abhibhāyatanas do not occur), 104 (Yogakkhemī pariyāya), 105 (the impermanent senses and sense objects are the cause of Sukha-dukkha), 108, 187-188 (sutta 187 declares that what the many-folk call ocean, is merely a mass of water; "cakkhu bhikkave purisassa samuddo tassa rūpamayo vego,"[96] and so with the other senses. The figure is strikingly unusual. Sutta 188 has the same fundamental idea and image), Sutta 189 (containing the lively comparison of the six sense objects with the six hooks of Māra—the fisherman), 143 (speaks of Chaphassāyatanas), 135 (similar) and 139-144 (three marks applied to the senses and sense objects).

To (b) belong Suttas 24-59, 62, 76-82, 84-86 [85 describes the world (loka) as void (suññā) because suññamattena attaniyena va], 89, 121 [The three Marks applied to the senses, etc......and "Yampidaṃ samphassapaccayā uppajjati vedanāgataṃ saññāgataṃ saṅkhāragataṃ viññāṇagataṃ."[97] Viññāṇa thus is a direct product of samphassa, not one of the three factors whose coincidence (saṅgati) constitutes samphassa. The sutta calls itself a veyyākaraṇa], 90-91, 99, 100, 101, 101-102 (use of the Jetavana simile; so also 137-138), 109-110 (suttas 191-192 treat of the same subject but illustrate it by means of simile and are lengthier, and more rational. In form they are dialogues between monks), 111-112, 122-123 (similar to 109-110), 124-126, 146-149, 151, 159-166, 167-186, 195 (=196. The term vedayita is not used); nor is adukkhamasukha spoken of).

[96] SN. IV, p. 175.

[97] SN. IV, pp. 106-7.

To (c) belong Suttas 60-61, 93 [a later version of 92 which belongs to class (a). It seems to speak by way of explanation "Yā imesaṃ tiṇṇam dhammānaṃ saṅgati sannipāto samavāyoayaṃ vuccati....cakkhusamphasso etc.],"[98] 106-107 (A clear attempt to correlate the analysis of perception to Paṭiccasam°. The first says "Tiṇṇam saṅgati/ phasso Phassa-paccayā vedanā//° Paccayâ taṇhâ ayaṃ dukkhassa samudayo."[99] The second is more elaborate and introduces the remaining series from Taṇhā to "Sokaparideva...upāyāsa"—Besides, it speaks of loka instead of dukkha) and 113.

To (*d*) belong Suttas 65—68 and 87.[100]

(*e*) Another class of suttas is formed in this saṃyutta by those in which the leading emphasis does not fall on the psycho-epistemology of the Āyatanas, and in which, at the same time, the other central theme is itself of too general a character to be amenable to stratification. Such are suttas 63, 64, 74, 75, 88,[101] 114-115, 120, 129 (on Dhātunānatta), 130 (Similar), 150, 152, 190, 194 (calls itself "ādittapariyāya"[102] and employs grim exaggeration), 198, 199 (The prose narrative appears to have been suggested by the verse at the end which occurs independently also),[103] 202, 203 and 207 (Cf. SN. I. 221), 153, 154, 155—158, 83 (Phagguna asked Buddha whether there existed a sense through which one might see "atīte buddhe parinibbute—chinnapapañce." The query has obvious and dangerous doctrinal implications, and is of course answered in the negative. Its form of expression however remains very peculiar); 133 (Is there any historicity in this very realistic narrative)?

---

[98] SN. IV, p. 68. [99] Ib., p. 86.

[100] Occ. in MN. also (Sutta 144).

[101] Cf. MN. Sutta 145.

[102] But diff. from the Third Sermon. [103] SN. I. 7.

The dividing line for this class is rather faint, and many of these suttas could well be regrouped under the preceding classes, just as some of the suttas of those classes could well be placed here. The present attempt is merely to invite attention to the existence of these groups. The few general conclusions drawn do not depend on the marginal cases.

Sutta 116 comments on a sutta, which occurs in SN. I. and AN. II. 46 in the light of the ruling Saṃyutta context and thus indicates its lateness. So does sutta 197 by collecting together a very large number of "comparisons" to illustrate the 4 mahābhūtas, 5 upādānakkhandhas, nandirāga, 6 ajjhatikāyatanas, sakkāya, Nibbāna, arahā, 4 oghas (this technical use by itself shows lateness),[104] aṭṭhaṅgikamagga and viriyārambha.

In sutta 193 Udāyi asks Ānanda "Yatheva nu kho... Ayaṃ kāyo bhagavatā anekapariyāyena akkhāto vivaṭo pakāsito iti pi ayaṃ kāyo anattāti sakkā evameva viññāṇam pidamācikkhituṃ desetum paṭṭhapetuṃ vivaritum vibhajituṃ uttānīkātumiti pidam viññāṇamanattā ti."[105]

Does it not suggest that Buddha himself had not as clearly emphasized the Anattahood of Viññāṇa and that this task was accomplished only by his followers, who like Ānanda here, confined the meaning of Viññāṇa to "Perception" and then demonstrated its contingency and hence Anattahood?

Salayatanasam° **(contd.).**—The following suttas appear early on grounds other than those relating to the evolution of the leading doctrine of the Saṃyutta: Sutta 69 (narrates the death of Upasena—Sāriputta's brother—by snake-bite; there would seem to be little reason for inventing the incident), Sutta 97 [defines the "appamāda-

[104] See PTSD. [105] SN. IV. p. 166.

vihārin" as one who is detached in the senses and sense objects. Through Pāmujja, Pīti, Passaddhi, Sukha and Samādhi he reaches the goal of Dhammapātubhāva. The sutta is not a merely mechanical composition along the saṃyutta context], Sutta 103 (Buddha quotes an enigmatic versified saying of Uddaka Rāmaputta, and interprets it along his own views. There does not seem to be any reason to doubt the genuineness of the quotation), Sutta 117 (B. recalling his Bodhisatta days delivers a short sermon in a quite individual style, and Ānanda comments upon it. As in the case of SN. III. sutta 1, or SN. IV sutta 116 (cf. also MN. Vibhaṅgavagga) so here an ancient fragment seems to have been exegetically elaborated; the sermon itself contains a doctrine which is certainly very old, and expresses it in a style reminiscent of the verses "yattha nāmañca rūpañca" etc.[106] The reference to Bodhisatta, however, indicates that even the main sermon, in its present form at any rate, cannot be very old. Or is it that an earlier and looser expression has been substituted by the more precise and technical "Bodhisatta"?[107]), Sutta 118 (Buddha gives a sermon to "Devānaminda"; Viññāṇa appears here, not as an impermanent epiphenomenally arising percept, but rather as the "soul" which gets attached to sense objects and grasps them), Sutta 119 (a variant of the preceding), Suttas 124-126, 128 and 131 (are similar), *Sutta* 127 (narrates how Piṇḍola Bharadvāja converted King Udena by convincing him how it was possible for even youthful monks to lead a life of perfect chastity if only they followed the eminently practical and profound precepts of the Master on the subject, which are ex-

[106] See supra.

[107] For such changes see comment on the "First Sermon" in SN. IV.

plained. The sutta breathes an air of reality, and there is nothing against its probable historicity).

Sutta 132 (recalls an encounter of Mahākaccāna with the Brāhmaṇa Lohicca and his pupils in the Avantis. Mahākaccāna addresses them in ancient-looking gāthās and finally wins them over. The atmosphere of Brāhmaṇa-Śramaṇa rivalry, the use of verse, and the simplicity of ideas assimilate the present sutta to those of the Brāhmaṇa-saṃ° in SN. I.), sutta 136 (The central part of the sutta consists of verses which occur in the Sn. also,[108] and have a rare profundity and elevation), sutta 145 (elevation), sutta 145 [essentially the same idea as in sutta 37 of the Nidāna saṃ, which is considered above; only, this time the fourfold scheme (of the truths) is applied, and the eightfold path is introduced. Besides, the present sutta has the ending "yaṃ kho bhikkhave satthārā karaṇīyaṃ etc." which occurs at a few other places also and carries with it a very strong impression of an earnest personal exhortation], Sutta 200 (consists of an unusual but striking and significant parable about Nibbāna and the means thereto. No formulae are assumed), sutta 201 (a practically identical variant of the preceding), Sutta 204 (contains two very significant parables; the first on the Judas tree—Kiṃsuka—has the same import as that in the parable of the blind and the elephant in the Udāna; the second or the city parable is still more significant for the reconstruction of the early phases of the doctrine, esp. as relating to Viññāṇa. This second parable, however, has little relevance to the point at issue, and appears like a fragment out of context).[109]

[108] Sn. V, 759-765.

[109] See Mrs. Rhys Davids—Sakya—p. 325; Chap. on Nirvāṇa.

Sutta 206 (here again while the first simile illustrates the process of effecting control over the mind and appears early, the second irrelevantly, though eloquently, compares "I" or "Mine"—mere words depending on the five psychophysical aggregates—with the sound of the lute which has no more substantiality and is equally contingent. The second simile clearly belongs to the same level of thought as the famous chariot parable of the Bhikkhuṇī-sam), Sutta 206 (contains the parable of the six animals of "diverse range and diverse pasturage").

***Salayatana* vagga: the other samyuttas.**—*Vedanāsaṃyutta*: (*a*) sutta 1-3, 5 and 7-14 speak with small material differences of the three Feelings. Suttas 23-28 apply to these the Fourfold scheme (as in the Truths). Sutta 24, it may be noted, recalls Bodhisatta days.

(*b*) Suttas 11, 15-20, 22, and 29 offer a much more penetrating and detailed analysis and classification of affective experience, especially of the gradual cessation of feeling in the course of meditative stages. Sutta 20 also occurs as part of sutta 19 which is found in the MN. too (see comments on it in that connection).

(*c*) Sutta, 4, with its bold assertion that there was no pātāla except physical suffering, is unlikely to be the product of scholasticism which was so steeped in the cosmography of after-life hells. The three verses at the end of sutta 6 appear especially early; beside the fact that they preach in a very simple and direct way the undoubtedly old doctrine of the affective neutrality of the wise, may be counted their omission of "dukkhamasukha" as a feeling. This, taken in conjunction with the statement of Pañcakaṅga Thapati in sutta 19, suggests that in the earliest utterances the prevailing mode was possibly of characterizing the world of feeling in two ways only—as pleasant and as painful—the attitude of neutrality with respect to feeling being considered the attitude of the emancipated. But the number of feelings soon increased to three and beyond. Sutta 21 is very unusual in its views on the doctrine of Kamma (see Chap. XI.).

Matugamasam°.—is the product of an ascetic tendency which can not be considered the distinctive characteristic of any particular epoch of early Buddhist history.

Jambukhadaka - sam° = Samandaka - sam°.—Sariputta defines a number of technicalities including "ogha".[110] Its lateness is manifest.

Moggalana-sam°.—Suttas 1-9 form a single compositional unit, and appear to have been suggested by Bhikkhusaṃ°.

Sutta 1. The insertion of Animitto cetosamādhi in the place of the more usual saññāvedayitanirodha may be noted. This reflects the growing vogue of suññatā. Suttas 10-11 are concerned in a mythological way with the marvellous other world contacts of Moggalāna. They can be hardly earlier.

Cittasam°.—The ten suttas built round the central figure of the householder Citta are too homogeneous in style to belong to different strata. Besides, the figure of Citta itself is remarkably individual and unifies the suttas closely. The lateness of the saṃ° is indicated by several facts: sutta 1 may be dependent on SN. IV 89, 107-8: sutta 5 seems to quote the verse from Ud. 75 § 5; many suttas e.g. no. 6, contain extremely scholastic, subtle discussions in the vedalla style; *whereas Buddha occurs nowhere in the Saṃ, the "therā Bhikkhū" are everywhere prominent.*

[110] See, PTSD on 'Ogha'.

Of the *Gāmaṇīsaṃ°* it may be noted that sutta 10 speaks of a controversy in the royal assembly (rājaparisā) as to whether "kappati samaṇānaṃ sakyaputtiyānaṃ jātarūparajatanti". Buddha emphatically answers in the negative. Such a doubt (as is implicit in the controversy) could easily have arisen in the minds of laymen during the epoch of the second council, when Buddhist practice on the subject was no longer uniform. And the present sutta may be a composition deliberately directed against the Vajjiputtakas.

Sutta 12 is long and straggling, and does not appear an organically unified composition. Its different parts are but loosely connected.

Asankhatasam°.—Suttas 1-11, dealing with the "Asaṅkhata" and the way to it, are really multiplications of the same sutta, differing only in the way that is advocated. It is noticeable that in suttas 5-11 the seven groups of Bodhipakkhiyadhammas are introduced in the numerical order of DN. 16 and not in the one followed in SN. V.[111] This numerical order is noticeable in suttas 1—4 also: the way according to sutta 1 is kāyagatā sati (one factor), acc., to sutta 2 it is samatha and vipassanā (2 factors), acc. to sutta 3, savitakko savicāro samādhi, avitakkavicāramatto samādhi and avitakko avicāro samādhi (3 factors)—and acc. to sutta 4 suññata samādhi, animitto°,[112] appaṇihito° (3 factors). These two facts, the identity of style and leading idea, and the arrangement of variations according to a definite plan suggest that this group of suttas (1-11) was composed as a whole and is late. This is confirmed by its inclusion of the three-

[111] Cf. Mrs. Rhys Davids' remarks on the two orders in her introd. to AN. V. pp. VI, X.

[112] In the text ('Avimitta" has been printed Ib. IV (p. 360).

fold classification of samādhi which is unusual in the Nikāyas.

Sutta 12 is composed of separate sections each of which is a repetition of the corresponding sutta above but with slight elaboration.

Suttas 13—14 are a collection of names for the final goal.

Avyakatasam°.—Suttas 7, 9—10 are distinguished from the rest by being free from any reference to the doctrine of the Five Khandhas. Suttas 9—10, besides contain definitely "early" doctrines,[113] the former also utilizing a simile.

Sutta 2, at the other end, appears particularly late; it carries the doctrine of "khandhānattavāda" to its logical extreme: since the Tathāgata is neither the khandhā taken individually, nor as taken collectively, nor yet anything apart from the khandhas, he is not to be got at even while living! And this is supposed to be the explanation of Buddha's silence about the fate of Tathāgata after death. One cannot help commenting that if this is true, Buddha could not have justifiably repudiated ucchedavāda (as he does e.g. in sutta 10) and all talk about a "via media" (Majjhena dhammo) is simply obscurantism. As a matter of fact, in §§ 13—21 of the present sutta we have a delineation of the non-existence of Tathāgata in life and after death which seems to leave little wanting. The central argument has been improved upon in the Kv.

The other suttas in this saṃyutta have the same general answer to the problem: all predication has the

[113] See below. With sutta 10 cf. sermon to Kaccāyana in SN. II.

khandhas for its subject, and Tathāgata after death is free from all khandhas.

It may be noted that sutta 1 uses the same ocean-comparison as occurs in the MN. Aggivacchgotta°.

Mahavagga.—Tedious repetitions abound in the Mahāvaggo. The Gaṅgā 'Peyyāla' and the subsequent vaggas (Appamāda, Balakaraṇīya, Esanā, Ogha) are common to the nine first saṃyuttas, and three "even of the saṃyuttas, the fifth (Sammappadhāna), the sixth (Bala) and the ninth (Jhāna) are nothing more than this very part, which can not be rehearsed wholly each time.[114]

The result is that the effect of homogeneity, which as far as doctrine is concerned is mainly confined within the separate saṃyuttas, is carried over into the vagga as a whole. Each of the Saṃyuttas takes over a leading idea and with but slight variations repeats it. This feature, which is found in the preceding saṃyuttas also, becomes so prominent here that any stratification of the suttas within this vagga becomes exceedingly difficult.

The first seven saṃyuttas of the vagga form, as distinguished from the rest, a connected group. This treats of the seven classes of Bodhipakkhiya Dhammas though they are not called as such.[115] The list occurs in other parts of the Nikāyas also, but apart from the order of the various groups within it, there is practically no variation. The formulae are always given in the same form, and it is doubtful if they underwent any considerable evolution to reach their present shape. At least little trace has remained behind of the anterior stages. It has even been suggested that these formulae were

---

[114] Feer, SN. V. pp. V-VI.
[115] See Mrs. Rhys Davids KS. V. p. V-VI.

preached by or compiled in the life time of the Master himself.[116]

In the first saṃyutta the verses in suttas 4 alone envisage a pre-formular stage of the way. These occur in SN. I. also. The verses at the end of sutta 34 are also free from formula, but though dealing with the subject of spiritual means have no specific concern with the way. It may be noted that the term Sambodhiyaṅga seems to occur here in a general significance.

Sutta 8 contains a Vibhaṅga on the formula of the eight-fold path. and is possibly later than the other suttas in the saṃyutta. In sutta 28 the elements of the formula are given in the form of "Sammāsamādhi sa-upaniso saparikkhāro." For the rest the suttas of the Saṃyutta are quite homogeneous.

In the next saṃ°. suttas 2, 3, 4, 52 and 53 contain beside the formula, explanations and comments also. Suttas 6, 23, 24, 30, 54, 55 and the vaggas 7—8 are the most striking instances of those suttas in this saṃ., which treat its leading doctrine in relation to other doctrines. The closeness of the relation between the Bojjhaṅgas and the Nīvaraṇas comes out especially. In saṃ°. 3 (of this vagga), suttas 6—8 are constructed around parables, while suttas 9 and 12 form part of DN. 16. Sutta 10 is an instance of the addition of explanatory elaboration to formulae.[117] This tendency is illustrated in

[116] For a discussion of the subject see below.

[117] Saṃ. 3: Sutta 13 admonishes Ānanda who is grieved at the death of Sāriputta. The introduction of the satipaṭṭhāna-formula is scarcely apt in the context. In fact §§ 10-11 both occur in other and more fitting contexts. Similarly the occasion of the present sutta as well as the admonition in § 8 are strongly reminiscent of DN. 16.... The mention of the list of five khandhas from sīla to vimuttiñāṇadassana also suggests lateness. In other words, there is not much in the sutta the genuineness of which is above suspicion. *(Contd.)*

saṃ.° 4 (of this vagga) by suttas 9—10 and 36—40 (these contain a formula different from the dominant one of the Saṃ). Sutta 42 of this saṃ° (4) is quite unusual in style. It constructs an ascending series of "Paṭisaraṇas" —from the senses to Nibbāna.[118]

As already mentioned, saṃyuttas 5—6 are merely repetitions of the Gaṅgā-peyyāla and the following three vaggas from the standpoint of the sammappadhāna and Bala formulae.

Of the **Iddhipadasam°** sutta 10 occurs in DN. 16. Sutta 11 gives an interpretation of the Iddhipādas different from that given by sutta 13 and it is supported by suttas 14 and 201 (which is called a vibhaṅga). In sutta 15 a Brāhmaṇa raises the pertinent objection" chandeṇa ca chandaṃ pajahissatīti netaṃ ṭhānaṃ vijjatīti" which does not seem to be satisfactorily answered by Ānanda.

The **Anuruddhasam°** deals with the four satipaṭṭhānas in the usual way, and the next saṃ° is just a repetition of the Gaṅgā peyyāla etc. with reference to the four Jhānas.

In **Anapanasam°** sutta 10 at first speaks of ānāpānasati in conjunction with Kāyānupassanā, vedanā° and citā° only. But the last paragraph introduces in the concluding sentences dhammānupassanā also and appears a later addition made to bring the sutta in line with later ideas.

Sutta 14 purports to give a speech by Buddha on the occasion of the passing away of Sāriputta-Moggalāna. The fact that §§ 6-9 of the present sutta are the same as §§ 9-12 of the preceding one shows that the two can be scarcely independent.

[118] Saṃ. 4: Sutta 49 is unique in speaking of three only of the usual group of 5 indriyas-Sati, Samādhi and Paññā.

In the **Sotapatti—sam°** sutta 21 has the appearance of being early on account of the ideas that it contains. Man is considered a compound of body and mind (citta) the former of which is left behind when the latter journeys to the World beyond.[119]

Saccasam°.On the important First sermon "Oldenberg was content to see nothing 'inorganic' in that version of the wayword, as against Deussen who did (Buddha 6th ed. 148n; Allgem. Gesch. der Phil. 1. 3., 138 156)."[120] Mrs. Rhys Davids agrees with Deussen "that there has been editing, but not regrouping of materials from other utterances."[120]

According to her there has been undoubtedly "a reduction of a discourse, remembered in *these* words by one listener, in *those* words by another, to a fixed wording," particularly of "those sayings which came to appeal most *forcibly to the monk*: Ill and riddance of Ill. . . ."

This is likely, but so much is certain that the sutta as it is cannot be regarded very early: (*a*) the section on the Four Truths comes suddenly upon the preceding one, and in fact contains a second, more comprehensive, summary of the doctrine with the result that the eightfold path is needlessly repeated. This repetition shows that when §§ 4—5 were composed there was as yet no intention of speaking of the "four truths", for, if that had been the case the sermon would most probably have begun with them and let the path come in its proper place.

(*b*) The version of the "four truths" mentions the

---

[119] See Chap. on Nirvāṇa. Cf. Mrs. Rhys Davids K. S. V. p. VIII.

[120] JPTS 1924-27 p. 244-'5.

Five Khandhas although it speaks of Taṇhā alone instead of the full formula of Paṭiccasam°.

(*c*) Koṇḍañña who is not spoken of in the beginning turns out to be the one who gets enlightenment at the end; this is surprizing and suggests some defect in the text.

(*d*) The sutta calls itself a "Veyyākaraṇa"[121] and speaks mythologically of the jubilation of the various classes of gods over it.

Sutta 31, with the lively figure of Siṃsapā leaves, is valuable as a corrective of DN. II. p. 100 "desito mayā dhammo anantaraṃ abāhiraṃ karitvā......"

(*N.B.*—(1) Those suttas which are proximate with respect to their contents are,in enumeration, placed together, (2) Sutta-groups are indicated by semicolons.)

I Sagātha vaggo—(a)Devatāsam.

Early: SN. 1.1.1.1.-2. Ib 1.1.2.2.-3, Ib 1.1.3.3, Ib 1.1.3.7 Ib 1.1.4.7, Ib 1.1.5.6. Ib 1.1.6.5-7.

Late: SN. 1.1.1.5-6, Ib 1,1.7.10, Ib 1.1.3.1., Ib 1.1.4.8, Ib 1.1.5.5.10 (= 1.2.3.4.)

Uncertain: The rest e.g. Ib 1.1.2.6.

(*b*)*Rest of Sagāthavg.*

Ealy: SN. 1.2.2.3., Ib 1.2.3.6., Ib1.3. (minus Ib 1.3.2.9-10, and Ib 1.3.2.8.§§5-10), Ib 1.4.3.3., Ib 1.6.1.1., Ib 1.6.2.5.

Late: Ib 1.2.3.9$_1$, Ib 1.4.-5, Ib 1.6.1.2-4, Ib 1.6.1.6, Ib 1.6.2.4.

Uncertain: The remaining samyuttas and suttas.

II. Nidānavaggo—(a) Nidāna Saṃ°

Early: Suttas 15,17-18,24-26,46-48; 22(§5ff); 37; 62; 19,32, 43,45,44,52,55-56,60,53,57-58,59,65,66,67;38-40,64.

---

[121] SN. V. p. 423.

Late: Suttas 1,3,4-10,13-14,16,29-30,49-50,69,71-81,82-93; 2,27-28,33-34,51 ; 11-12,35.-36,63,20,21,41-42,68, 70 ; 31.

Rest of Nid. Vg.

Early: Anamattagga Saṃ (refrain); Kassapa Saṃ (suttas 5 and 11). ·Lābhasakkāra Saṁ (refrain possibly) Opamma Saṃ (Sutta 1).

Late: Rāhula Saṃ ; Dhātu Saṃ (possibly).

Uncertain: The rest of the Saṃyuttas and suttas.

Khandha Vg.

Early: Khandha Saṁ : Suttas 1 (§4), 84 (§§ 26-30) 33, 53 (minus §§ 6-10), 54 (minus § 17), 83, 87-88, 101.

Late: The remaining Saṃyuttas and suttas.

IV. Saḷāyatana Vg—(a) Saḷāyatana Saṃ.

Early: Suttas 69, 97, 103, 117 (§§ 1-4). 118, 119, 124-126, 128, 131, 127 (?), 132 (?), 136 (verses), 145 200, 201, 204 (§ 7. §§ 8-9, the second parable being out of place)' 205 (§§ 4-5), 206 (possible).

Late: The rest, though divisible into several distinct and doctrinally interesting classes.

(*b*) ***Saḷāyatana Vg. the other saṃyuttas***: Vedanā Saṃ°, suttas 4 and 21 early ;

Mātugāma—uncertain ; Jambukhādaka° (= Sāmaṇḍaka)-late ; Moggalāna-probably late ; Citta°-probably late ; Gāmaṇī-uncertain ; Asaṅkhata -uncertain, Avyākata°-suttas 7, 9-10 early, sutta 2 late.

V. Mahāvagga. Magga Saṃ° Sutta 4 (Verses)-early ; Sacca-Saṁ° "First Sermon" (edited) The rest uncertain.

CHAPTER VII

EARLY AND LATE IN THE AṄGUTTARA NIKĀYA

Ekottaragama and the Anguttara Nikaya.—According to Nanjio[1] the Chinese Ekottarāgama (No. 543) consists of 52 chapters. In the Pali Aṅguttara,[2] on the other hand, there are 160 vaggas.[3] Again, according to Nanjio "........the sūtra has 'Evam mayā śrutam ekasmin samaye' 555 times, i.e. as many short sūtras collected." Hardy, on the other hand, remarks, "Now we learn from a versus memorialis, that there are 9557 suttas in the Aṅguttara, and, there are, in fact, at most about 2344 suttas in the Aṅguttara, as was known to Buddhaghosa in the fifth century A.D."[4]

This suggests that the Pali Aṅguttara has a considerably greater number of subdivisions than the Chinese Ekottara.

Authenticity of the 11th Nipata doubtful.—As to

[1] Catalogue of the Chinese Translation of the Buddhist Tripiṭuka, p. 133.

[2] The Manorathapūraṇī has the expressions "Aṅguttarāgama" and the "Four Āgamas" in place of "Nikāya". (Vol. I. pp. 1-2)

[3]

Nipāta	Vagga
I	20
II	17
III	16
IV	27
V	26
VI	12
VII	9
VIII	9
IX	9
X	12
XI	3
	160

the number of the main divisions, the AN. has eleven Nipātas; a passage from the Abhidharmakośavyākhyā, quoted by Minayeff, tells us "tathā hi ekottarikāgama āśatād dharmanirdeśa āsīdidānīm tu ā daśakād dṛśyata iti."[5] With this latter tradition agrees the fact that in the "summary of the contents, with a literal translation of the Chinese titles of the 52 chapters" given by Nanjio, the highest numeral referring to a doctrine-group is ten. This leads one to doubt the authenticity of the eleventh Nipāta in the AN. And when it is considered that this Nipāta contains the smallest number of vaggas and also the fact, as Hardy puts it, that "in the last Nipāta hardly anything original is found,"[6] this doubt deepens, and the possibility can scarcely be denied that the 11th Nipāta of the AN. may be of the nature of a comparatively later appendix.

A new trend in composition from the 6th Nipata onwards.—This leads one to a consideration of a prominent feature of the AN which has been very clearly stated by Mrs. Rhys Davids[7] "From the sixes, there is a beginning of making the requisite number out of two groups of three each." These are sometimes of opposites, of things somehow connected, e.g. 3 taṇhā's and 3 mānas. This is continued in the Sevens and in the Eights. In the Nines it becomes commoner, but the complementary lists—usually of 5 and 4—have sometimes no obvious connection. "Usually one is doctrinally much more important than the other e.g. 5 cetokhila's and 4 Satipaṭṭhāna's. And the latter is invariably put *after the former*."[7]

---

[4] AN V. prefare p. vi-vii.

[5] Recherches sur le Bouddhisme. [6] AN V. p. vii. fn. 1.

[7] What was the Original Gospel in Buddhism? p. 137.

The Nipātas from the sixth onwards, esp. Nipātas 9–11, cannot, however, be considered later than the preceding ones merely on account of the increasing use they make of this style of composing the suttas. Hardy's list of these "composite" suttas[8] indicates that but for a few exceptions their component groups do not occur as such in the previous Nipātas, on which, therefore, any obvious dependence of the authors of these "composite" suttas is negatived. Of course, dependence may still be a fact and reflect itself in a borrowing of ideas; but "borrowing" is difficult to prove in the case of these hort pointed texts.

The omission of certain "titular" groups.—Mrs. Rhys Davids has pointed out the striking failure of certain "important" numerical groups of doctrines to occur under their own title in the proper Nipāta of the AN.[9] Of Nibbāna and Vimutti it may be stated that although these were from the beginning important doctrines, they were not important as "ones", at least in the Nikāyas. Of the non-appearance of the Three Marks and the Three Refuges *as such* in the "threes", the best explanation seems to be that by the time the "threes" were closed these doctrines had not yet become important as such and hence were not mentioned as independent groups. The three marks, it may be noted, occur at most places in the Nikāyas not by themselves, but as applied to some other doctrinal group such as the Five Khandhas for example. The process of abstraction which gave to them an independent status appears to have taken place later.

---

[8] AN V. app. IV cf. also Ib. Preface p. vii.

[9] Prefatory note to the Index of the AN; JRAS 1935; App. to What was the Original Gospel of Buddhism?

Of the omission of the Four Noble Truths, the Five khandhas and the component groups of the list of the Bodhipakkhiya dhammas (including, of course, the Eightfold Way, but excluding the sambojjhaṅgas which occur among the Sevens) in the proper Nipātas and under the usual titles,[10] the explanation that is offered in the Prefatory Note to the Index of the AN by Mrs. Rhys Davids appears the most plausible viz.,—that the SN and AN are not independent compilations but that suttas relating to certain topics, which include the topics under consideration, were swept in and garnered in separate saṃyuttas of the former collection and were hence omitted as main titles from the latter.[11] A more detailed elaboration of the hypothesis is, however, bound to be largely speculative because of our ignorance of the precise way in which the compilations came to be what they are. In any case, a nice compartmentalization is too much to expect, and the fact that some of the Bodhipakkhiya groups occur quite frequently in the "composite" sutta of the 9th and subsequent Nipātas[12] does not invalidate the hypothesis. Besides, it is not unlikely that these suttas are relatively later.[13]

"Omission" and the Numerical order in the Ekottaragama.—A propos the omissions it may be noted that according to Nanjio the first sūtra of chapter 21 of the EĀ is "on the Triratna", while that of chapter 25 is 'on Catussatya" (so is the first sutta of chap. 27

---

[10] "The Four Truths occur among the Fours, but under the title, not of Ariya as elsewhere in the Nikāyas but of Dukkha and Loka." (AN. Index, p. VIII fr. 2).

[11] Ib. pp. vii-viii.

[12] The eight elements of the Way occur as part of a group of ten in the 10th Nip.

[13] Cf. Mrs. Rhys Davids—"What was the Original Gospel in Buddhism?" p. 143.

"Equally going (or treating?) of the four Truths"). It is, however, not clear whether these are the titles of the sūtras or merely summaries of their contents. Besides, from the summaries or titles given by Nanjio, the 52 chapters of the Chinese collection do not appear to follow the Ekottara order rigorously. Thus chapter 2 begins with a treatment of the "ten intense thoughts" chapter 14 with that of the five sīlas, and chapter 21 with that of the Triratnas; henceforth the numerals again rise to ten.

The difficulties in stratifying the Anguttara Nikaya.—The stratification of the suttas in the AN presents exceptional difficulties. The monotony of style is one, and the generality of contents is another. And throughout we meet with formulae which for the greater part show little variation.

Some special classes of suttas within it.—Quite a number of suttas preach simple virtues, and most of these were perhaps composed for the benefit of the laity. These are generally so non-distinctive that it is impossible to place them in any particular stratum. It is the same with suttas classifying the monks by means of various similes (of the royal horse or elephant, for example), or those condemning women. Similar is the large number of suttas relating to human types (classes of Puggalas).

Some suttas, however, such as those dealing with the varying lists of Saññās, Sīlas, Anusayas and Saññojanas are stratifiable, rather classifiable as preliminary to stratification, but solely on doctrinal grounds.

Some other suttas such as those dealing with the 8 Abhibhāyatanās should become stratifiable in case the history of the formulae they contain becomes clearer.

A large class of suttas dealing with the Tathāgata appears late since it shows the apotheosis of Buddha as already achieved or in the process of coming into being.[14] The most flagrant example is 4·127 which describes the miracles accompanying the birth of Tathāgata. In 4·118 Buddha is an object of worship and his life a type. In 4·36 he is considered a class by himself. The many suttas dealing with the Powers of Tathāgata form part of this class of suttas.

As a result it is with respect to very few independent suttas that any stratification can be attempted. And the conclusion seems unavoidable that the number of suttas in the AN which may be considered early is extremely small.

Considerations towards the stratification of some suttas of the AN.—Nipāta 1: is distinctive in the sense that the vaggas rather than the suttas constitute its real divisions. From this fact it results that the Nipāta is not a collection of as many independent "ones" as there are suttas in it. Nor are all the vaggas unified and independent. Vagga 4 is a continuation of vagga 3. The first two suttas of vagga 6 are a continuation of vagga 5, and should have, for the sake of system, belonged to it. Similarly, vagga 6 (suttas 8—10), vagga 7, vagga 8 (suttas 1—3) and vg. 9 belong to a single series. On the other hand, vaggas 24—26 present a miscellaneous and ununified appearance even within themselves.

Vaggas 5 (including the first two suttas of vagga 6) and 23 are distinctive, being completely unified within and containing really a single sutta each. Both are illustrated by apt similes and are free from formulae.

---

[14] Winternitz—History of Indian Literature II, p. 66.

The simile in vagga 5 occurs in DN. 2 also but its significance is much clearer here on account of the fact that the text is explicit on its view of the nature of "citta" These two vaggas, especially the first (vg. 5) appear early. They have no essential connection with the Aṅguttara-scheme, and might have occurred in the MN for instance.

Nipata 2: (Late).—Vagga 3—suttas 5—6 distinguish between "Neyattha" and "Nītattha" suttantas. This was a disputed point among the sects and could have arisen only after canonical literature had reached considerable extension.

Vg. 6. 1—4 compare the Tathāgata and Cakkavattin.

5. distinguishes between Sammāsambuddha and Paccekabuddha.

6—8 have been perhaps suggested by DN. sutta 16.[15] Two notable features of this Nipāta may be stated: Vg. 5 is wholly devoted to the same subject of the various kinds of Parisā; and vaggas 7—17 are much nearer to DN. sutta 33 than the rest, being just bare lists.

Nipata 3.—Sutta 21, which discusses the Saddhāvimutta, the Kāyasakkhi and Diṭṭhipatta, appears late since it uses the term "anāgāmin" technically for the third stage towards Arahatta.[16] In form, the sutta consists of a controversy between monks (Saviṭṭha, Mahākoṭṭhita and Sāriputta), followed by the question being referred to the Master who declares that each of the participants in the controversy had judged but partially ("ekaṃsena").

---

[15] Cf. (Āḷāravedalla). [16] AN. I, p. 120.
See "anāgāmin" in the Pali Dictionary of the Pali Text Society.

Sutta 32 quotes a verse from the Pārāyaṇa-Puṇṇaka-pañha, and two from the Pārāyaṇa-udayapañha. This suggests that it is at least later than the earliest stratum of texts in the Nikāyas; but this impression must be placed by the side of that given by the doctrines it teaches: there is a certain meditative stage (samādhipaṭilābha) such that "cetovimutti-Paññā-vimutti"* is attained in it and all egoism (ahaṅkārama-maṅkāramānānusaya) in body-mind (saviññāṇka-kāya) as well as in external objects is shed. The description of this meditative stage is apparently found in the quotation from the "Udayapañha", and it appears to be the same as was later formulized into the fourth Jhāna. The use of the Kāya-viññāṇa distinction (rather than of the closer analysis of the Khandhas) and the occurrence of no formula for any Jhāna suggest that doctrinally, at least, the sutta probably does not belong to the latest stratum in the Nikāyas. There is, of course, no impossibility in earlier doctrines occurring in later compositions![17]

The verses at the end of sutta 39 would be much more appropriate at the end of sutta 38 which is perhaps based upon them. In style these verses are reminiscent of the Padhānas in the Sn, and seem to represent an early balladic fragment relating to Buddha's life. The prose of sutta 38 contains a description of the luxury of Buddha's early life which included a set of three different palaces for the three seasons.[18] This suggests some previous growth of biographical legend for Buddha.

---

* Apparently not distinguished.

[17] The same verse from Puṇṇakapañha is quoted in AN. 4. 41, but the explanation given there is much more dogmatic and full of formulae.

[18] Cf. MN. sutta 75.

The prose of Sutta 39 explains the leading idea of sutta 38 in a more dogmatic style and without the narrative setting;[19] it is perhaps based upon sutta 38.

The verses at the end of sutta 40 are divisible into two: the first two verses, and the rest. The former are in a different and simpler metre, and contain an earnest, plain, brief and forceful admonition addressed directly (i.e. the addressee is put in the second person), while the latter is an indirect injunction in a more elaborate metre, and may well be a summary of the prose in the sutta.

Sutta 52 preaches self restraint (Saṃyama) but quotes verses preaching liberality. These verses occur in SN. I. also, and appear to be misadaptations here.

The two lines at the end of the sutta, printed as prose in the text,[20] are really verse, although the first two pādas are in a different metre than the next two.

Sutta 76 is a short discourse on "Bhava", illustrated by a parable which seems to contain very early views about the nature of Viññāṇa and Rebirth. The sutta appears early.

Sutta 80 is doubtless late since it presupposes a very considerable development of Buddhology and mythical cosmology.

Sutta 100 considers spiritual progress equivalent to the purification of mind ("citta") and illustrates it by the appropriate gold simile. Its general doctrinal position is the same as that of the Sāmaññaphalasutta. The view taken of the nature of citta, the presence of the apt simile, the emphasis on practice, and the absence of any feature belonging to a stratum later than that of DN. Sutta 2 suggest the earliness of the sutta.

---

[19] Cf. sutta 35; also MN. sutta 130. [20] AN. I. p. 155.

Sutta 101 uses the term "Bodhisatta", but there is nothing else in the Sutta to suggest its lateness.

Sutta 124 is unusual in its narrative. Buddha arrives at Kapilavatthu and not finding a rest-house (āvasatha) wherein to put up for the night, decides, on the recommendation of Mahānāma the Sakka, to stay at the hermitage (assama) of Bharaṇḍu (ka)[21] Kālāma, who is described as an old fellow student (Purāṇa sabrahmacārī) of Buddha's. Next morning Buddha describes to Mahānāma three types of Teachers, advocating the comprehension (Pariññā) of kāma only, of kāma and Rūpa only, and of these as well as of Vedanā. He then asks Mahānāma whether all of them had the same or different objects (Niṭṭhā). Bharaṇḍuka Kālāma suggests thrice that they had the same object in view. But Buddha contradicts him every time, and at this repeated discomfiture before Mahānāma, Kālāma is so upset that he leaves Kapilavatthu never to return.

The strange figure of Bharaṇḍu (Ka) Kālāma, his stranger reaction—for usually the opponents of Buddha humbly confess their error—the doctrine discussed, the absence of any monk accompanying Buddha—all these are unusual features.

Sutta 134 appears late because of the abstractness of its expression which suggests much doctrinal development. According to "Uppādā vā Tathāgatānaṃ anuppādā va Tathāgatānaṃ Ṭhitā vā sā dhātu dhammaṭṭhitatā dhammaniyāmatā sabbe Saṅkhārā aniccā.... (So—dukkhā—& anattā......)."[22]

Nipata 4.—Sutta 6 mentions the 9 divisions of the canon and hence assumes for it a previous development

---

[21] Both forms occur in the sutta.
[22] AN. I. p. 286.

which should be long enough for the analysis of its complexities to become crystallized into this formula.

Sutta 14 and 69 have the same final verse which speaks of four classes of "effort" (Padhāna): restraint (saṃvara), rejection (Pahāṇa), cultivation (Bhāvanā), and preservation (Anurakkhaṇā). The prose of both the suttas seeks to explain these four terms, but while that of sutta 69 speaks of the usual sammapadhānas that of sutta 14 brings in the Sambojjhaṅgas and the six saññās (aṭṭhika etc.) and is more elaborate. It appears that both are later than the verse, and between the two the prose of the sutta is later than that of sutta 69. The short sutta 16 (prose and verse) speaks of Rūpa, Vedanā, Saññā and Saṅkhāra only. The omission of Viññāṇa decisively indicates the earliness of the sutta, for had the doctrine of the five Khandhas become well established it is extremely improbable that we should have had anything less than the complete fivefold. Sutta 75 which speaks of the four aṅgas (Rūpa, Vedanā, Saññā and Bhava) appears to be about the same stage of development.

Sutta 455/46 on the "end of the world" (Lokassanto) occurs in SN. I. also and has been considered before.[23]

Sutta 180 says that a monk may assert having heard a Dhamma or Vinaya text directly from Buddha or from some particular community of monks or from some one or many theras who should be "Bahussutā āgatāgamā dhammadharā vinayadharā Mātikādharā....."[24] But the sutta goes on to counsel that before his statement is accepted as authentic the text in question must be looked

[23] Cf. also AN. 9. 4-7.
[24] AN. II. p. 169.

for in Dhamma and Vinaya. It is obvious that these already existed in the form of more or less fixed collections. The sutta, therefore, must be very late. It may be noted that the sutta describes Buddha himself as delivering the sermon during his stay at the Ānandacetiya in Bhoganagara. Does the cetiya derive its name from that of the famous apostle?

Sutta 189 seeks to classify the more important Sāmaññaphalas with reference to their means. It is noticeable, however, that instead of the four Jhānas it mentions the eight Vimokkhas as such. It seems to represent an isolated scholastic gloss.

Sutta 196 on the crossing of the flood" appears early in part. It is simple in ideas (i.e. free from formulae, technical expressions and metaphysics), lays stress on the purity and not the austerity of conduct, and is parabolic in style. The earliness of the apt simile comes out particularly from the fact that the Buddha in answering the questions of the two Licchavis who are his interlocutors, does not use the term "ogha" at all, but merely speaks of "river" (nadī). A later author composing a simile to illustrate the then technical term "ogha" would hardly have dared to depart as much. But §§ 7—10 are totally irrelevant and should have been placed in the Yodhājīvavagga.

Sutta 197 raises the interesting query whether we have here a historical tradition about Mallikā's ugliness.

Sutta 199 describes 36 Taṇhāvicaritas. Compared to the simple description of Taṇhā as Ponobhavikā etc., in apparently early texts this appears very much more elaborate, numerical, and systematic. Hence the sutta also appears comparatively late. The next sutta (200) is on the same level of thought.

Sutta 251 is in style similar to DN sutta 34, but uses a less elaborate scheme and is, of course, in length less than one-tenth of the latter.[25]

Nipata 5.—Sutta 49 purports to have been delivered to king Pasenadi on the death of queen Mallikā, but it is impossible to assert or deny its historicity. It is, as far as the contents go, a repetition of sutta 48. Sutta 50 is, again, the same sermon but this time delivered by Nārada at Pāṭaliputta to king Muṇḍa on the death of queen Bhaddā. The historical reference clearly shows its lateness.

Suttas 131—133 establish various similarities between the Tathāgata and the universal monarch. This would appear to belong to the same stratum of thought as is reflected in D. Sutta 16 which is undoubtedly late in its present form.

Nipata 6.—Sutta 34 describes how Mahāmoggalāna went to all the divine worlds upto that of Brahmā and learnt that without the three "aveccappasādas" the attainment of "sotāpatti" remained impossible. The marvellous, mythological, and tendentious character of the sutta, as well as its emphasis on faith*, especially in the church (Saṅgha) suggests its lateness.

Sutta 55 comprises two distinct parts: the first depicts Soṇa frightened of asceticism and tempted by the world; Buddha goes to him and by means of the very appropriate and famous simile of the lute shows to him the wisdom of moderation.[26] Soṇa follows the advice

[25] Cf. AN. Sutta 149.

* Which is expressed in a set formula.

[26] Cf. the short "sūtra of the 42 sections" which also uses the lute-comparison similarly. The sūtra is supposed to be the oldest Buddhist text of China and traces its origin to Kāśyapa Mātaṅga (see Acta Orientalia 1927 pp. 197-237, where the whole sūtra is translated into German).

and becomes an Arahant. This part of the sutta with its emphasis on the golden mean (or Majjhimā paṭipadā; this term is not used in the sutta which has "Samatā" instead)[27] and the bright illustration appears to embody an old text.

Soṇa comes to Buddha and says that an Arahā, freed from the Āsavas, is intent (adhimutta) on nekkhama, paviveka, Avyāpajjha, Taṇhakkhaya, upādānakkhaya and Asammoha. This is not strictly organic to the first part and may be later.

Sutta 60 appears late because it speaks of the Elders engaged in Abhidhammic debates (therāṇaṃ abhidhammakathaṃ kathentānaṃ) and Mahākoṭṭhita propounds in it a view about Jhāna and the "animitto cetosamādhi" which appears an isolated scholastic product. The next sutta in which the Elders guess the meaning of a riddle quoted from the Pārāyaṇa (Vuttaṃ bhagavatā Pārāyaṇe Metteyapañhe) and are finally enlightened by Buddha himself would also appeai to be late.

Nipata 7.—Sutta 50 in which Nandamātā recounts her wonderful qualities, speaks of the morning-recitation of the Pārāyaṇa and would appear to be not much removed in time from the sutta just referred to.

Sutta 54 has four unconnected divisions: (a) §§ 1—9: on how to avoid sleepiness; (b) § 10: sundry instructions mainly against "Uddhacca"; (c) § 11 (non-bracketted portion) a short sermon on Taṇhāsaṅkhayavimutti which is the same as is found delivered to Inda in Cūḷataṇhāsaṅkhaya sutta of the MN; (d) § 11 (bracketted portion) on the cultivation of merit; it involves much mythology and the comparison with the universal monarch.

[27] AN. III. p. 375.

Sutta 68 seeks to inculcate ethics by the threat of torment in hell delineated with exaggerated and too vivid flourishes. It can scarcely be considered a genuine utterance of Buddha. The sutta calls itself a veyyākaraṇa (AN. IV. 135).

Sutta 70—Buddha quotes a most vigorous sermon by a previous teacher Araka on the uncertainty and changefulness of life, illustrated by a string of lively similes. At the end Buddha exhorts the monks to engage unfailingly in meditation (Jhāyatha mā pamādattha)[28] so as not to repent afterwards. On the historicity of Araka it is impossible to pronounce. Though the sutta contains a common enough idea, it is quite unusual in style. With any numerical group of seven it has nothing whatever to do. Its brevity, simplicity, earnestness and use of short, apt similes suggest genuineness.

Nipata 8.—Sutta 12 on the conversion of Sīha Senāpati[29] has considerable similarity in style and subjects to the Upāli sutta of the MN. As in the case of the latter the internal evidence of the sutta is wholly consistent with its authenticity, but in the absence of independent confirmation it is impossible to argue for the historicity of the events narrated.

In sutta 82 Puṇṇiya asks Buddha the reason wherefore "Appekadā Tathāgataṃ dhammadesanā paṭibhāti appekadā na paṭibhātīti."[30] This query is unusual and the correct answer would seem to be the waywardness of higher visions and inspirations, or the mystery of Time in spiritual pilgrimage, which makes different times unequally valuable for imparting spiritual instruc-

[28] The ending is found at other places also.

[29] At another place in the AN Sīha appears as a Buddhist Upāsaka.

[30] AN. IV. 337.

tion. The actual answer in the text, however, is banal and bathetic "Saddho ca Puṇṇiya bhikkhu hoti" etc.

Nipata 9.—The brief sutta 14, which has a great deal in common with 8·83, seems to use 'Nāmarūpa' in the general and ancient sense in which it is used in the Upaniṣads and the Sn.[31] The style of the sutta too is reminiscent of such upaniṣadic dialogues as between Gārgī and Yājñavalkya. This suggests its earliness which is not contra-indicated.

According to sutta 44, one becomes truly a Paññāvimutta only in the Saññāvedayitanirodha, and sutta 45 asserts the same of the ubhatoghāgavimutta. This does not seem to recognise any such distinction between the two as is implicit at some other places in the Nikāyas, and hence possibly represents an earlier state of affairs when the term Paññāvimutti had not become degraded in meaning to just an intellectual comprehension of the Truths as distinguished from their full realization.

Nipata 10.—Sutta 2 converts the moral exhortation of sutta 1 into the statement of a natural law (Dhammatā) operative in independence of any will (cetanā). This transformation is readily intelligible in terms of a growing vogue of scholasticism which sought to replace the picture of an individual now progressing, now regressing, but always in pursuance of his own volitions, his own striving—about which one could at best state that such and such activities, being contributory to such and such ends (attha) should lead to such and such results (Ānisaṃsa) but could never dogmatise in the way one could about natural events—by

[31] "Kimārammaṇā Samiddhi Purisassa Saṅkappavitakkā uppajjantīti? Nāmarūpārammaṇā bhante ti" (AN. IV. p. 385). The use of the term "Purisa" is also suggestive of earliness.

the picture of certain sequences of mental phenomena progressing through inevitable stages towards good or towards evil, always regulated rigidly by necessary laws. In the eagerness to treat mind systematically, to give to psychological conclusions and ethical distinctions the form of necessary, objectively valid formulae, the more popular conception of mental events as bearing the imprint of the vagaries of an individual "minder" acting from behind the scenes was increasingly thrown into the shade, and. pari passu, a revision took place in the wordings of some of the older formulae also.

Sutta 26 quotes a verse from the Kumārīpañha (in SN. I.)—and by the sheer force of dogmatic assertion discovers in it a reference to the ten kasiṇas. Both the facts —of quotation, and of interpretation in favour of the ten kasiṇas—indicate the lateness of the sutta.

Sutta 27 may be described as a miniature of the AN. The fact that it is a collection of heterogeneous doctrines unified in the main only by the numerical scheme, does not seem to argue in favour of its earliness. Further, some of the doctrines mentioned are themselves late viz. those of the 5 Khandhas, 7 Viññāṇaṭṭhitis, and 8 Sattāvāsas. It is also noteworthy that none of the terms naming the doctrines (as e.g. the term Pañcupādāna kkhandhā) are anywhere explained in the sutta. They are treated as so many well known technical expressions.

Sutta 28 is similar in form, but more unified in contents and without any doctrines which may be described as late.

Conclusion.—The results of this investigation into the AN may be tabulated as follows (By far the greater part of the AN is here left out as uncertain. The classes

"Early" and "Late" are not homogeneous within themselves).

Early		Late	
I.	Vagga 5 and 23	II.	3.5-6
III.	Sutta 39 (verses at the and)	II.	6.1-8
III.	Sutta 76	III.	Sutta 21
III.	Sutta 100	III.	Sutta 32 (early in substance)
		III.	Sutta 38
		III.	Suttas 80,134
IV.	Suttas 16,45-6,75,196,251 (earlier than D. sutta 34 ?)	IV.	Sutta 6,14,180,189,199
		V.	Suttas 50 (later than king Muṇḍa) 131-33
VI.	Sutta 55 ("composite")	VI.	Suttas 34,60-1
VII.	Sutta 70	VII.	Suttas 50, 54 (perhaps composite), 68
VIII.	Sutta 12 (Possibly)		
IX.	Sutta 14	X.	Suttas 2,26-7
		XI.	The whole Nipāta

PART II

STUDIES IN THE HISTORICAL AND CULTURAL BACKGROUND OF BUDDHISM

CHAPTER VIII

REVIEW OF THE VEDIC BACKGROUND

The Significance of Pre-Vedic Civilisation.—Anthropology, philology, and archaeology reveal to us that from prehistoric times India has been the home of many races and cultures, whose conflicts have provided the principal challenge of her social history. The continuing vitality of Indian society has been ever dependent on the success with which she has responded to this challenge. Her cultural life thus displays from the most ancient times the character of a progressive synthesis, seeking unity in the midst of an unending and bewildering diversity, and peace and harmony in the midst of struggles and conflicts.

The discovery of Indus Civilisation has revolutionised our perspective of Indian cultural origins somewhat in the same way as the discovery of Aegean Civilisation revolutionised the perspective of Greek history. We can no longer regard the course of Indian history as the career of a victorious Aryan civilisation contaminated increasingly by the force of indigenous barbarism. On the contrary, the Aryan invasion of India must be regarded as "the arrival of barbarians into a region already highly organised into an empire based on a long-established tradition of literate urban culture."[1] This is a veritable Copernican revolution!

The remnants of the Indus Civilisation have been found over a large area extending from Rupar, at the

[1] Piggott, Prehistoric India, pp. 257-58.

foot of the Simla hills to Sutkagen-dor, near the coast of the Arabian Sea, 300 miles west Karachi.[2] Excavations at Rangpur, district Jhalawar, Saurashtra have left no doubt of their association with the Harappan tradition.[3] Thus, the Indus Civilisation can "claim a larger area than any other of the known pre-classical civilisations."[4] The chronology of this civilisation is still uncertain but it appears that it was fully developed in the time of Sargon of Agade who is now placed a little before 2300 B.C. Wheeler, thus, dates the Indus Civilisation between 2500 and 1500 B.C.[5] This, however, is impossible to accept because it leaves too little time for the evolution of Vedic culture. Nor can it be reconciled with the evidence of the Boghaz-köi inscriptions (c. 1400 B.C.) which seem to refer to Vedic Indian deities, not to the Indo-Iranian.[6] It seems that the Aryan Invasion of India can not be placed much later than 2000 B.C.[7] Now if we regard 2300 B.C. as the mean date in the career of the Indus Civilisation, which was then "in full flower", we get the period 2800 B.C.–1800 B.C. as the possible date of this civilisation. This will harmonize with the evidence of Archaeology, Vedic philology, Ancient Indian history, and ancient Near-Eastern history.

As to the relation between the Vedic and the Indus Civilisations, it is surely fantastic to regard the former as earlier than the latter or to ascribe the authorship of

---

[2] Wheeler, The Indus Civilisation, p. 2.

[3] Indian Archaeology, A Review 1953-54 pp. 6-7.

[4] Wheeler—loc. cit.

[5] Wheeler, op. cit., p. 4; Ib. pp. 84-93. cf. Piggott, op. cit., p. 211, 214 ff., 240-41.

[6] Winternitz I, p. 305. cf. The Vedic Age (ed. R. C. Majumdar) p. 204; CHI I, pp. 72-73. On Varuṇa as an Indian deity see below.

[7] On the date of the earliest hymns of the RS see Winternitz I, p. 310.

[7a] That the civilization ended about 1750 B.C., is now more or less certain, see Allchin, The Birth of Indian Civilization (1968) pp. 139-44.

the Indus Civilisation to the Aryans.[8] Sir John Marshall has conclusively shown that the Indus Civilisation was quite distinct from and earlier than the Aryan Vedic Civilisation.[9] Formerly, there seemed to be a wide gulf in time between the Pre-Vedic and Non-Aryan Indus Civilisation on the one hand, and the Aryan Vedic Civilisation on the other. But the tendency of modern Archaeological progress is to bridge the gulf between the two increasingly (See e.g., Indian Archaeology, A Review 1953—4 loc. cit.).

It has been suggested that the Indus Civilisation perished through the violence of insurgent Aryans. The Ṛg-Vedic references to the destruction of 'pur's have been taken to be references to the walled-cities and forts of the Pre-Aryans.[10] The fight of Indra with 'dāsas' and 'dasyus' is interpreted as the struggle of the Aryans against the Non-Aryans.[11] Piggott has even seen in Indra's exploit of releasing the waters a reference to the Aryan destruction of the bunds built to protect the Harappa cities from flood.[12] Pt. K. Chattopadhyaya has, however, conclusively shown that 'dāsa' and 'dasyu' refer to demons as traditionally understood, not to Non-Aryan human beings.[13] Indra as a god naturally fights against demons who are as naturally conceived to be foes of Rite, dark and mis-shapen, of strange speech, and

[8] Cf. The Vedic Age, pp. 194-95; L. Sarup in IC IV.

[9] Marshall, MIC. For a criticism of Dr. Sarup's view, see Pt. K. Chattopadhyaya, Presidential address in the Vedic Section of the Ninth AIOC, Trivandrum.

[10] Wheeler, op. cit. p. 90; Piggott, op. cit. pp. 261-63.

[11] CHI I, pp. 84, 86; Keith, RPV. I, p. 234; Macdonell, VM. p. 157; Piggott; loc. cit.

[12] Piggott, loc. cit.

[13] See Pt. K. Chattopadhyaya: Dāsa and Dasyu in the Ṛgveda (Proceedings of the Nineteenth International Congress of Orientalists held at Rome.)

evil. Their forts' and cities' are nothing but a poetic and fanciful representation of clouds in the interests of myth. Of course, it may be conceded that the Aryan invasion must have created for some time a picture of confused struggles and perhaps even the myth and fancy of the conflicts between gods and demons may contain an indirect and imaginative echo of a more actual and historical conflict. But it is clear that the RS contains no direct reference to the fight of the Aryan race against a dark-skinned', 'snub-nosed', aboriginal people called Dāsas and Dasyus. There is no doubt of the existence of a highly civilized non-Aryan people in India at the time of the Aryan invasion and of the conflicts which must have ensued between the two subsequently, but we do not on that account need to turn myth directly into history. The fact of the matter is that prior to the discovery of Indus Civilisation, the modern historians of India were inclined to picture her pre-Aryan inhabitants as dark and savage—very much like 'demons'!—so that in the description of demons they readily discerned their own picture of the pre-Aryan aborigines of India! As to the racial composition of the Indus Valley people it is difficult to generalize at present. They appear to have been a mixed population, including Proto-Australoids, Mediterraneans, and Mongoloids.[14] The description of the Indus Civilization as Dravidian, as is sometimes done,[15] does not seem to have any positive evidence in its favour as yet.

Of the high degree of material culture which these

[14]Wheeler, op. cit. pp. 51-52. Cf. S. K. Chatterji in The Vedic Age pp. 145 ff.

[15]S. K. Chatterji, op. cit. pp. 156-8; C. Kunhan Raja in History of Philosophy, Eastern and Western (Ed. S. Radhakrishnan)—p. 38. On the horse in the Indian civilization, see D. P.Agrawal, *The Copper Bronze Age of India*, p. 255; on the 'Cemetery H' people, see H. D. Sankalia in *Purātattva*, 1972-73, pp. 12 ff. At the Scandinavian Institute of Asian Studies an attempt has been made to decipher the Harappan script as a Proto-Dravidian Script.

Pre-Aryans possessed there is no doubt at all. Their attainments in the realm of spirit are, however, not equally known to us, mainly because of the paucity of written records and our ignorance of the script. But "paradoxically it would appear that the Indus Civilization transmitted to its successors a metaphysics that endured. whilst it utterly failed to transmit the physical civilization which is its present monument."[16] It is undeniable that some of the most important elements of the religious life of latter-day India go back to the Indus-Civilization. Among these may be mentioned the worship of a proto-type of Śiva, who is represented as Paśupati. Yogī, and perhaps Naṭarāja; of the Mother-Goddess, of the *pīpal* tree, and of the bull and some other animals associated with the gods.[17] Phallic worship and the great sanctity that has ever been attached to water in India may also go back to the Indus Civilization.[18] Most important, the definite occurrence of a cross-legged posture with the out-stretched palms placed on the knees,[19]

---

[16] Wheeler, op. cit. p. 95.

[17] Marshall, MIC I pp. 77-8; Mackay, The Indus Civilisation, pp. 96-7; Wheeler, op. cit. pp. 67, 83—4; Piggott. op. cit. pp. 201-3. Cf. my Meaning and Process of Culture.

[18] Mackay, op. cit. pp. 77-8, 85; Wheeler, op. cit. p. 83; Piggott. loc. cit. On the Śiśnadevas of RS. see Proceedings & Transactions of OC, Patna, 1930, pp. 501-2; K. Chaṭṭopādhyāya, Pravāsī, 37, 2, p. 559, fn. 2.

[19] Esp. on the three seals from the same site (see Wheeler, op. cit. p. 79), is represented the figure which Marshall identified with Paśupati (Marshall, op. cit. I. p. 70). Wheeler speaks of its "brooding, minatory power" (op. cit. p. 83) K. A. Nilakanta Sastri is sceptical of Marshall's identification, but admits the antiquity of Yoga, and adds that "the yogic posture....occurs also in a stutue of a male figure and in a small faience sealing where a deity in the same attitude is apparently worshipped by a kneeling nāga." (The Cultural Heritage of India II p. 22). See also the stone figure, apparently seated in a yogic posture, represented in Wheeler. op. cit. Pl. XVII A.

and the probable occurrence of what looks remarkably like the Śāmbhavī Mudrā[20] seem to suggest that the beginnings of Yogic practice in India may also belong to the Indus Civilsation.[21] The worship of gods in a personal and iconic form, as a kind of 'pūjā', has been traced back in India to pre-Aryan sources,[22] which ought to include the Indus Civilisation too. In the light of this pre-Vedic background it is clear that cultural development in the Vedic Age must be understood as a growing fusion of Aryan and Non-Aryan elements, which produced towards the close of the period a veritable revolution in religious ideas. After the initial stages of confused warfare, the distinction between the Aryan and the Non-Aryan must have been increasingly blurred, as the Aryans tended to settle down, through the almost inevitable process of racial miscegenation which is reflected in the growth of caste[23] and in the changes which came over the Aryan language.[24] Thus, in the later Vedic period the sense of racial separation and colour prejudice tend to disappear. The very collection and classification of the Vedas is now attributed to Vyāsa in whom the presence of Non-Aryan blood is beyond all doubt [25] It is interesting to note that the Br. Up. prescribes orthodox Vedic magic for obtaining a son having a dark com-

---

[20] Wheeler, op. cit. Pl. XVI. Śāmbhavī Mudrā is thus described "Antarlakṣyam bahirdṛṣṭirnimeṣonmeṣavarjitā." (cf. Gheraṇḍa–Saṃhitā. 3. 64). Wheeler doubts the yogic significance of the 'narrowed eyes'—(Wheeler, op. cit. p. 64)

[21] Cf. Pt. K. Chattopadhyaya: Pravāsī, Bhāga 37, Khaṇḍa 2, pp. 557 ff; R. P. Chanda, Indo-Aryan Races, pp. 99ff, 148ff.

[22] S. K. Chatterji, Vedic Age, pp. 160-1.

[23] See below.

[24] CHI I p. 110, S. K. Chatterji, op. cit. p. 157.

[25] Cf. S. K. Chatterji, Bhāratīya Āryabhāṣā Aur Hindi, pp 53-4. (Rajkamal, 1954)

plexion and red eyes,[26] which may be contrasted with the reference of Patañjali to the characteristic complexion of a Brāhmaṇa as fair and ruddy with blonde hair.[27] This racial mixture between the Aryans and the Pre-Aryans and the consequent creation of a composite society must have proceeded apace as the Aryans reached North-Eastern India in the later Vedic Age. Piggott says, "clearly after the first drastic Aryanisation of the Punjab some sort of modus vivendi was arrived at; if not there, eastwards in the Ganges Basin as the frontier receded eastward, and Harappa ideas permeated the religious thought of the Brāhmaṇas."[28] Śatapatha Brāhmaṇa contains a well-known reference to this eastward passage of the Aryans when they crossed the Sadānīrā and colonised Videha beyond Kośala, Sadānīrā forming the boundary between the two.[29] Videha soon became the centre of a mighty intellectual ferment as is clear from the glimpse we obtain of the age of Janaka in the Bṛ. Up., and from Buddhist and Jaina references. It seems thus that by the later Vedic Age the evolution of Aryan society and thought had reached a point where it felt the full impact of Pre-Vedic and Non-Aryan ideas. These ideas appear to have been represented by wandering ascetics and yogīs surviving from pre-Vedic times and called 'Munis' in Vedic literature and 'Śramaṇas' in the age of Buddha and Mahāvīra.[30]

[26] Bṛ. U p. 6. 4. 16: "Atha ya icchetputro me śyāmo lohitākṣo jāyeta, trīnvedānanubruvīta, sarvamāyuriyāditi, udaudanam pācayitvā sarpriṣmantamaśnīyātām īśvarau janayitavai."

[27] Mahābhāṣya on Pāṇini II, 2.6: "gauraḥ śucyācāraḥ kapilaḥ piṅgalakeśa ity enān apyabhyantarān brāhmaṇye guṇān kurvanti."

[28] Piggott, op. cit. p. 286.

[29] SB. 1.4.1.10-17.

[30] ṚS. X. 136.

Munis and Sramanas in the Vedic Age.—The Keśi-Sūkta of the ṚS[31]. delineates for us the strange figure of the 'Muni' who is described as long-haired, clad in dirty, tawny-coloured garments, walking in the air, drinking poison, delirious with 'Mauneya' and inspired. The reference is rare in the ṚS, and the description seems to show that the author was filled with a certain sense of wonder at the sight of the 'Muni' performing miracles, whom he ignorantly thought to be delirious. There can hardly be a doubt that the 'Muni' was to the Ṛgvedic culture an alien figure. As will become clear below, asceticism is directly opposed to the entire Weltanschauung of the ṚS. In the AB occurs another 'mad' muni-Aitaśa.[32] The TA. speaks of Śramaṇas who were called 'Vātaraśanāḥ'. They led a celibate life, could disappear at will and teach to brahmanas the way beyond sin.[33] The Tāṇḍ. B.[34] speaks of "Turo devamuniḥ", with which may be compared the "Airammadodevamuniḥ" who 'saw' appropriately enough the Sūkta on Araṇyānī in the ṚS.[35] The AS[36] too speaks of the divine Muni and the ṚS mentions Indra as the friend of the Munis,[37] and at another place refers to the 'shaking' of the Muni.[38] Tāṇḍ. B. again speaks of a place called 'Munimaraṇa,[39] and also speaks of the 'Yatis' as enemies of Indra.[40] Later, 'Yati' definitely meant an ascetic,

---

31 Cf. S. K. Dutt—Early Buddhist Monachism, pp. 51ff.

32 Vedic Index II. p. 167. Etaśa is mentioned as one of the seven "vātaraśanā munayaḥ" in connection with ṚS. X. 136.

33 TĀ. I. pp. 87; 137-8.

34 Tāṇḍ. B. II. p. 601.

35 ṚS. X. 146.

36 AS. VII. 74.1.

37 ṚS. VIII. 17. 14.

38 ṚS. VII. 56. 8.

39 Tāṇḍ. B. II. p. 96.

40 Ib. I. p. 208.

e.g., Muṇḍ. up. 3.2.6. ŚB addresses Tura Kāvaṣeya as Muni'.[41] It may be recalled that his father 'Kavaṣa-Ailūṣa' was driven out from the sacrifice on the Sarasvatī with the words "O, Son of a female slave, you are a rogue and not a Brāhmaṇa."[42] TĀ makes obeisance to the munis of Gaṅgā and Yamunā (Namo Gaṅgāyamunayor munibhyaḥ).[43] Discipline in the Āruṇaketuka necessitated poverty and begging, and a Bhikṣu Āṅgirasa is mentioned as the seer of ṚS X. 117. The word Śramaṇa occurs once in the Upaniṣads,[44] although the Muṇḍakopaniṣad has obvious reference to the shaven-headed ascetics who reviled the Vedas.

According to the Vedic Index, it would be unwise "to conclude from the comparative rareness of the Muni in the Vedic texts that he was an infrequent figure in Vedic times; he was probably not approved by the priests who followed the ritual, and whose views were essentially different from the ideals of a muni, which were superior to earthly considerations such as the desire for children and dakṣiṇās."[45] Thus, we can discern in the Vedic period, outside the strictly Vedic pale, wandering groups of ascetics sometimes styled as Munis who were "the precursors of the strange ascetics of later India."[46]

Fuller information about these Muni-Śramaṇas is to be had from early Jaina and Buddhist literature. Here they are placed by the side of the Brāhmaṇas but distinguished from them. The Brāhmaṇas are here

---

[41] ŚB. II. p. 1041. Śaṅkarācārya quotes a Śruti according to which the Kāvaṣeya seers did not see the point of Vedic study and sacrifice (comy. on BS. III. 4. 9.).

[42] AB. 8. 1.

[43] TĀ. I. p. 166.

[44] Bṛ. Up. 4. 3. 22. (See Mrs. Rhys Davids, Sakya p. 42.)

[45] Vedic Index II. pp. 167-8.

[46] Ib.

depicted as treating the Śramaṇas with scant courtesy, calling them 'muṇḍakas' and 'vasalas'. As late as the 4th cent. B.C. the Greeks noted the distinction between Brāhmaṇa and Śramaṇa, whom, still later, Patañjali described as eternal opponents.[47] The independence of the Śramaṇas from the Vedic tradition comes out also from a consideration of the early history of the Jaina faith. The analysis of the origins of Sāṅkhya and Yoga also shows that these were doctrines of the tawny-clad ascetics—the Kapilas, who were not indebted to the strictly Vedic tradition.[48]

"Śramaṇa" beliefs and practices are considered in detail in a subsequent chapter, but the general nature of the Śramaṇa world-view may be summarized here in order to see clearly its relationship to Brāhmaṇa thought. Practically all the Śramaṇa sects held towards the world an attitude of ascetic pessimism, disbelieved in a personal cause or creator of the universe, accepted a plurality of souls and an ultimate distinction between soul and matter, regarded the world of common sense as real and as due to one or more real factors at least partly independent of the soul, and consequently regarded as indispensable for salvation some form of strenuous practical discipline aiming at effecting a real alteration in the situation of things. We might loosely say that these Śramaṇas[49] were, in general, ascetic, atheistic, pluralistic and "realistic". The essential basis of this world-view seems to have been the idea of saṃsāra—of Karman and transmigration. This comes out clearest from a consi-

---

[47] Patañjali ad Pāṇini II. 4. 9.

[48] See below.

[49] See below.

deration of the earliest faith of the Jainas—one of the oldest surviving sects of the Munis!

We find, thus, that in the Vedic period there existed two distinct religious and cultural traditions—the strictly orthodox and Aryan tradition of the Brāhmaṇas, and, on the fringe of their society, the straggling culture of the Munis and Śramaṇas, most probably going back to pre-Vedic and pre-Aryan origins. Towards the close of the Vedic period, the two streams tended to mingle and the result was that great religious ferment from which Buddhism originated.

Śaṅkarācārya has observed that the Vedic religion is two-fold—Pravṛtti dharma and Nivṛtti-dharma.[50] The fact of the matter is that the orthodox Aryan Vedic tradition was in the beginning essentially Pravṛtti-dharma, but later on, partly through inner evolution and more through the influence of the Muni-Śramaṇas it developed Nivṛtti-dharma as a tendency within its fold. We propose to review the development of Vedic religion from this standpoint and analyse the fateful revolution which occurred within it in the later Vedic Age and led to important consequences for the subsequent development of Indian religion and thought.

The Evolution of Vedic Society.—We may begin by reviewing briefly the evolution of Vedic society. In the early Vedic period we find the Aryans settled mainly in the north-west of India. Their geographical horizon extends from the Kubhā in the west to Gaṅgā and Yamunā in the east. It is, however, the rivers of the Punjab which mark the principal scene of their activity. Particularly important is the region later called 'Brah-

[50] Comy. on the BG. Introduction.

māvarta' between the two divine rivers, Sarasvatī and Dṛṣadvatī. Later on, the region of Kuru-Pañcāla in western U. P. became the chief centre of Aryan orthodoxy. That remained so even when the Aryans, crossing the Sadānirā, had advanced from Kośala to Videha. As Fick has shown, even in the age of Buddha, the Brāhmaṇas looked to the north and the north-west for their inspiration. The region of Magadha was looked down upon as impure and the Licchavis were described as Vrātyas. It seems, thus, that the passage of the Aryans towards the east, particularly into the region of Bihar, was felt to be associated with the growth of heterodoxy. This harmonises well with the fact that Buddhism and Jainism both arose in this eastern area.

The early Vedic Aryans led a life of mixed pastoral and agricultural economy. The growth of the importance of agriculture was soon reflected in the sanctity which came to be attached to the cow who was declared 'aghnyā'.[51] Society was organised in villages or 'grāmas' and tribes or 'janas' ruled by kings with the assistance of the assemblies called 'sabhās' and 'samitis'. As the tribes settled down, the first territorial states or janapadas' came into existence. Side by side with this economic and political development, there was a growing division of labour in society. The rulers and the priests[52] were the two classes that first distinguished themselves from the mass of the people called 'Viśaḥ'. In the later Vedic period, a fourth class, the Śūdras comes into view. The predominance of the non-Aryan element

[51] Cf. C. H. I. I. p. 102. (A similar protest, it may be recalled, was lodged against cow-killing by Zoroaster in Iran).

[52] D. D. Kosambi suggests that "the Brahmans were associated with the rich pre-Aryan Indus Valley Culture". (JBBRAS. 1946. p. 41). Cf. Piggott. op. cit. p. 286.

in their composition can hardly be doubted.[53] Economically, they were the most primitive class and yet their recognition as a distinct caste is seen to come last in the evolution of Vedic social order. This suggests that their emergence represents, not a growing division of labour which led to the rise of a yet newer and more specialised functional class, but the entrance into the fold of Vedic society of a new people or community.[54] In the older period, miscegenation had been freer but by now social organisation was tending to become rigid,[55] and so, with firmer lines of social demarcation, that part of the community which was predominantly non-Aryan, particularly in its cultural traits, tended now to be segregated, and served as the general receptacle for any new non-Aryan tribes which, in the course of the expansion and settlement of the Aryans, might be socially amalgamated with them. This would also elucidate the otherwise inexplicably low status which is assigned to the Śūdras.[56] It is not necessary in this connection to appeal exclusively or even principally, to the sense of racial discrimination. The feeling of cultural difference is sufficient to account for the peculiar rules governing the status of the Śūdras. For example, it seems fairly clear that the 'Śvapākas' were held in abhorrence because of their custom of cooking dogs, as their name implies.[57]

---

[53] CHI. I. pp. 86, 128-9; Vedic Age, pp. 386-7, cf. Ghurye, Caste and Race in India, Ch. VII. Risley's theory suffers from undoubted exaggeration and fails as a general explanation of caste, but it does serve to bring out the significance of anthropometric data.

[54] Cf. R. P. Chanda, Indo-Aryan Races, p. 36.

[55] C. H. I. I. pp. 126f.

[56] See P. V. Kane, History of Dharmaśāstra II pt. I pp. 33 ff.

[57] JBBRAS. 1951. p. 183, fn. 6.

Further, the yogic idea of invisible influences emanating from every person and tending to uplift or corrupt others according to the character of their source, implies that to every cultural community corresponds a definite spiritual environment which is not the less real for its intangibility.[58] This naturally put a premium on the primitive and tribal taboos relating to food, physical contact etc., between persons belonging to widely different cultural groups.[59] The evolution of caste thus implies that Vedic society became gradually more complex and composite. It remained, however, almost wholly rural, and, even towards the close of the period, had not advanced much beyond the tribal stage. We have to note that it was at first an expanding, pioneering society exhibiting some of the characteristics of a frontier civilisation—its sense of insecurity and robust optimism, its premium on "success", and its reliance on religion as means unto that.[60] Under such circumstances, priests and warrior-kings were naturally in the fore and led society. Towards the close of the period, however, pioneering become a difficult task involving advance into the more inaccessible regions of the north-east and those beyond the Vindhyas. This period of decelerated pioneering was bound to witness a change in social perspective, the beginning of doubt about the bounty of Nature and its Gods, of pessimistic reflection. In these changing circumstances, the more thoughtful naturally felt the force of that pessimistic

---

[58] Cf. J. H. Hutton, Caste in India. pp. 181, 183 ff.

[59] Ib.

[60] Cf. H. J. Laski—The American Democracy Chap. I-II, where the psychological role of an expanding economy and a frontier civilisation are lucidly indicated.

weltanschauung which, as already indicated, was held and preached by the Muni-Śramaṇas.

Thus, just as Vedic society became increasingly mixed racially and culturally and changing from a vigorous colonizing and pioneering stage came to have the aspect of a complex society with an old tradition where men were beginning to doubt old ways and reflect over the meaning of life and seek new ways, Vedic religion evolved pari passu from the pre-eminence of gods and the happy co-operation of gods and men through sacrifice to a veritable "Götterdämmerung" and the jettisoning of Rite in favour of Right and Gnosis. Vedic religion advanced from pursuing the world to transcending it, from propitiating gods to seeking the Self. But this change was only beginning yet and affected only a few thoughtful persons. It came principally through the influence of the Munis, although changed material circumstances and the inner dialectic of thought prepared the way for it.

Gods and Men.—The older portions of ṚS constitute the chief source of information for the religion of the first Aryans in India. Our knowledge is consequently fullest about the beliefs of the priestly class.[61] There are traces also of a more popular religion for which, however, we must, in the main, go to the AS. The core of the priestly religion consisted in belief in many gods and a few goddesses who were worshipped, primarily for secular welfare, by means of prayer and food-offerings. Many of these gods represented the phenomena of nature.[62] The degree of their anthropomorphization

[61] Cf. Keith, RPV I pp. 55 ff.

[62] For the later conceptions of the Devatā-tattva in India see Yāska, Nirukta (Daivata-Kāṇḍa); BS. I. 3. 26-33 and

varied, and they did not possess, in general, sharply defined individualities. This has misled some scholars to recognize here a monotheism,[63] and others to advance the hypothesis of Henotheism or Kathenotheism.[64] Polytheism, in fact describes the situation correctly; only it has to be remembered that Vedic gods are not exclusive like the Baals,[65] or defined individuals as in the Olympian pantheon.[66] There also were Sondergötter,[67] and later some abstract deities. Pari passu, animistic beliefs held sway, as ever.[68]

Indra.—As already indicated the Indians of the ṚS were on the whole an active, warrior people engaged in struggle with the aborigines and among themselves but were, in the main, prosperous and contented with life. The character of the people is reflected in the tone of their great gods and, for the earlier period, in no case better than in that of Indra who is the victorious warrior, the jovial and human god, a great drinker and a mighty eater.[69] He is the most individualized and anthropomorphic of the Ṛgvedic pantheon, with the largest amount of mythology to his share.[70] He is gene-

---

Śaṅkara's comy. thereon; BG VII. 20-23; YS, I. 28; Ib. II. 44. where the Tāntrika conception of Devatā is foreshadowed. Cf. Sri Aurobindo's mystic interpretation of the Vedic Devatās—Hymns to the Mystic Fire. Foreword. (Second ed. 1952).

[63] See Schmidt—The Origin and Growth of Religion—pp. 172 ff. esp. p. 187. For a general criticism see Karsten—The Origins of Religion, pp. 179 ff.

[64] This theory of Max Müller has now been generally rejected—see Oldenberg, RV p. 102—fn. 1; Macdonell, VM p. 10 f; Keith, RPV—I, pp. 88-9.

[65] Cf. CAH I p. 200.

[66] Cf. Gilbert Murray—Five Stages of Greek Religion, p. 64.

[67] See Oldenberg, RV pp. 60-63; Keith RPV. I p. 64.

[68] Keith, RPV. I. pp. 71 ff.

[69] Keith RPV. I. p. 243.

[70] Cf. Ib. I. p. 124ff.

rally believed to have been a god of thunderstorm.[71] Pt. K. Chaṭṭopādhyāya, however, believes that Indra was originally the god of strength and war. The name is probably Indo-European;[72] the deity is clearly as old as the Indo-Iranian times, since the Verethraghna of the Avesta and the Vahagn of the Armenians are clearly the same as the Vṛtrahan of the ṚS.[73] Verethraghna is known to have been the god of victory.[74] As to the Avestan reference to the demon Indra, it occurs in fact only once, not twice, in the very late text of the Vendidad[75] and is not evidence for the state of affairs contemporaneous with the ṚS. The connection of Indra with war and might is plain in the ṚS.[76] and "Indriya" was even in early Buddhist texts, synonymous with "Bala".[77] The transmutation of Indra into a rain-god, effected within the ṚS, appears to have been the result of two facts: lightning—Vajra—was a symbol of strength and the storm-gods—Rudra, Maruts, Apāṃ Napāt—were considered on that account mighty. Indra clearly, being the mighty par excellence, must possess the Vajra. Further as the need of a war-god became less prominently felt, the other aspects of the war-god—Indra—were more attended to.

---

[71] Macdonell, VM. p. 54.

[72] See Jacobi (KZ. XXI.—p. 317) cf. the Celtic goddess Andraste—see Macculoch—The Rel. of the Anct. Celts pp. 41-2; John Rhys—Hibbert Lectures on the Origin and Growth of Rel. as Illustrated by Celtic Heathendom—p. 200.

[73] Oldenberg, RV p. 132; RPV I. p. 133.

[74] VM. p. 66.

[75] See Pt. K. Chaṭṭopādhyāya in Proc. & Transac. of the Fourth O. C. (Allahabad) Vol. II. p. 14 & fn. 1.

[76] See e.g. VM. p. 54. On the etymological connection of Indra with "manliness" see Jacobi—op. cit., pp. 316-9. On Vṛtra=Enemy see K. Chaṭṭopādhyāya op. cit. pp. 15-16.

[77] See Chap. on the Way to Nirvāṇa.

Surya, Agni and Brhaspati.—Sūrya, Agni and Bṛhaspati were other prominent gods of this period. The first two probably go back to Indo-European times.[78] Agni is closely connected with the home, with the ancestors and with sacrifice.[79] He is the priest among gods, and carried the righteous dead to their after-life abode in heaven.[80] Bṛhaspati is the god representing the power of prayer,[81] and as such very important from the priestly standpoint.

Varuna.—The ethical sublimity and the almost monotheistic tone of the hymns addressed to Varuna[82] have justly attracted the attention of scholars. The nature of this god has not been, however, satisfactorily explained. Some have proposed to see in him the moon-god,[83] while the more generally accepted opinion regards him to have been the sky-god.[84] Pt. K. Chaṭṭopādhyāya would interpret him as the Night-sun. The equation Varuṇa—Ouranos is, according to him, untenable since the two words diverge in two independent features—vowel sounds, and accent.[85] Varuṇa, in fact, is of the same form as the Ṛgvedic Dharuṇa, Aruṇa, etc., and appears to have been a purely Indian word. Similarity of characteristics is, further, no sufficient ground for connecting Varuṇa with Ahur Mazda.[86] The ṚS presents the real

---

[78] Cf. the words Helios and Sol with Sūrya; and, Ignis, Agni (Icelandic), and Ugnis (Lithuanian) with Agni.

[79] Macdonell, VM pp. 95 f.

[80] Ib.

[81] Ib. p. 101 f.

[82] e.g. AS IV 16.

[83] Oldenberg, RV pp. 189-90; Hillebrandt agrees. Ib. 189. fn. 2.

[84] VM. p. 27 f; RPV. I. p. 102.

[85] Cf. VM. p. 28; RPV. I. p. 100; Bloomfield defends the correctness of the equation vigorously—Bloomfield, RV p. 136f.

[86] Bloomfield, RV pp. 120 ff; ORV pp. 184 ff.

and close associate of Varuṇa in Mitra. The association is indeed so close as to warrant the supposition that the two are but aspects of the same fundamental deity, which can only be the sun. Now Varuṇa is found associated with the night also[87] which suggests the forementioned thesis. This would explain a number of other facts. The sun-god has ever been the guardian of morals, and since night and darkness have an obvious association with sin and crime, what would be more natural than to expect Varuṇa—the sun during the night to be the chiefest of the gods of righteousness? The connection of Varuṇa with water also becomes hereby transparent, for the sun sets in the west and the Aryans first knew the ocean to have been in the West.[88] This also explains how the "Vāruṇī dik" came to mean the West in later literature.

Further, there seems to be no force in the view that Varuṇa was ousted by Indra towards the end of the Ṛgvedic period.[89] The comparative silence of the tenth book of the ṚS about Varuṇa must be set by the side of the fact that in the seventh book, which also contains much late material, Varuṇa is prominent. In the Brāhmaṇas Varuṇa can hardly be said to have declined. He is there the most important figure where Prāyaścitta is concerned. That his functions became narrower and better defined illustrates a frequent enough form of historical development. One may compare the case of the Greek god Poseidon.[90]

---

[87] Cf. VM., p. 25; RPV., I. p. 97; see RS I, 115. 4-5.

[88] Cf. AS I. 33.2. which says plainly "Yāsāṃ rājā Varuṇo yāti madhye satyānṛte avapaśyan janānām". The reference clearly points to the setting sun.

[89] Cf. VM. pp. 65-6. The view was advanced by Roth and Whitney.

[90] See Cook-Zeus, I, p. 717 fn. 2.

The growth of moral consciousness.—Viṣṇu is another solar deity who became prominent towards the close of Ṛgvedic Age and in the Brāhmaṇas.[91] The increase in the importance of solar deities, in fact, suggests that the growth of moral consciousness represented a marked trend in the evolution of early Vedic religion.

The growth of abstract deities.—Another trend was the growth of abstract deities. Two classes can be distinguished within these: of those gods who are simply the personifications of abstract ideas, and of those whose names denote primarily either an agent or designate some attribute.[92] Of these the members of the first class at least are on the whole very late. The origin of Aditi is still obscure, but the hypothesis of Macdonell that it lies in the hypostatization of Aditi from such expressions as "Aditeḥ putrāḥ" appears to be plausible.[93] The goddess has no definite physical features; she is implored to grant freedom from guilt or sin and lent herself quite easily to mystical identifications.[94]

Viśvakarman is a Seer, a priest, our father. He is the highest apparition (paramā sandṛk), the dhātṛ and the Vidhātṛ.[95] He seems to have represented the One God, whose conception was then being evolved, in his architectonic aspect.

Later, Viśvakarman was expressly identified with Prajāpati, who is clearly adumbrated in the ṚS as the One God—the creator of heaven and earth, the first born and the sole lord of all.[96] He embraces with his arms the whole world and all creatures.

---

[91] Cf. VM. p. 37.
[92] VM. p. 115.
[93] Ib. p. 122.
[94] Cf. VM. p. 121; RPV I. pp. 215f.
[95] RS X. 81, 82.
[96] RS. X. 121.

Manyu, Kāma,[97] Śraddhā, Kāla, Skambha, and Prāṇa appear to have been other deified abstractions that came into being towards the end of this epoch.[98] Kāla is prominent in the Brāhmaṇas and still later in the Mbh.[99] Prāṇa too stands for the highest principle at places in the Brahmaṇas and in the Upaniṣads.[100]

Monotheistic and Pantheistic trends.—A marked tendency in the ṚS is the growing perception of unity between the various gods and the consequent rise of monotheistic and, more important, pantheistic ideas From the beginning it was clear that the gods, generally speaking, shared very much the same attributes of might light, goodness and wisdom. Frequently pairs of gods were formed,[101] and the attribution to the pair of the feats of either led naturally to the association of one god with exploits which were not his in the beginning. Another factor leading to the assimilation of deities was the similarity of the functions which they performed, though in their own ways.[102] The close connection in nature of the elements which the gods often represented strengthened the tendency to syncretism. Further, many of the important gods were easily seen to be the representatives of either the same elements or of different forms of the same elements. Along these lines and under the stress of the peculiarly Aryan genius of philosophical speculation the idea that the various

---

97 Cf. AS. IX. 2; XIX. 52.

98 VM. p. 120; RPV. I. p. 209.

99 Cf. Chap. on Religious conditions in the Age of Buddha. Cf. AS XIX. 53-54.

100 Set below.

101 VM. pp. 126ff.

102 Thus Agni repels demons by fire, but Indra performs the feat with the thunderbolt—RPV. I. 88.

gods were but aspects and names of the same God was increasingly realized.[103]

But philosophical speculation followed another direction too. In Greece as well as in India philosophy began in the same way—with cosmology. The two kindred enquiries were—out of what source has the cosmos sprung? And, who fashioned it? There is implicit in the one an evolutionist, in the other a creationist attitude. The primary object of search in the first case is Primordial Matter;[104] in the second, it is the Primordial Person.

In the ṚS the first enquiry is quite minor and ever subordinate to the second. The gods are often conceived architectonically.[105] They partake in the fashioning of the universe after the manner of the carpenter. It is then asked "what was the wood, what the tree out of which they fashioned heaven and earth?"[106] At one place the answer is given that the cosmos emanated in stages from the primal Asat through the power of Brahmaṇaspati.[107]

A pantheistic answer to the query is, however, clearly to be discerned at places in the ṚS. Thus the Nāsadīya sūkta traces the universe to the Original One, and the Puruṣasūkta contains explicitly the germ of the monistic idea later elaborated in Vedānta that the sentient principle is at once the material as well as the efficient cause of the universe.

---

[103] RS V. 3. 1-2; I. 164. 46; X. 114. 5; I. 89. 10; X. 121 esp. ṛc. 8: "Ye deveṣvadhi deva eka āsīt. . . ." It may be observed that the 10th ṛc of this sūkta is probably later than the rest since there is no "padapāṭha" corresponding to it.

[104] Cf. the Phusis of the early Greek cosmologists, and the Arché of Aristotle (cf. Burnet—Early Greek Phil. pp. 12-14).

[105] Cf. Macdonell, VM. p. 11.

[106] RS X. 31. 7; Ib. 81. 2, 4. [107] RS. X. 72; Cf. X. 82.

Eschatology.—The eschatological beliefs of this period appear[108] to have been few and vague. The doctrine of rebirth is unknown.[109] At death the body is doubtless destroyed but apparently not in any final manner; the righteous dead, with the assistance of Agni, Pūṣan and Savitṛ go to the heaven of Yama.[110] There with a perfected body they enjoy a very secularly imagined blessed existence in the company of the Fathers and the gods.[111] The wicked are either destroyed at death, or, what is perhaps more likely, fall in the subterranean abyss of darkness.[112] The soul is the breath—Prāṇa, Ātman, or life—Asu, or mind—manas.[113] Personal identity is apparently preserved in afterlife.[114]

On the conceptions about righteousness, the information is meagre. But to the most advanced ethical speculation of the times the ideas of truth and order seem to have appeared basic to morality.[115]

Ritual and its development.—The ritual was originally a simple affair.[116] It consisted of the addressing of hymns of prayer by a priest to a deity accompanied by the offering of food to him. But in the course of time complexity set in. Many varieties of sacrifices were invented, and the services of several priests became necessary. Details increased and the procedure tended to be rigid. This development benefitted the priests directly, and so we notice that the chief lines of evolution during

108 See VM. p. 165ff.

109 RPV. II. p. 570; VM. p. 166.

110 RS. X. 14-18.

111 RS. IX. 113; I. 154 where the germs of the later idea of "Goloka" may be discerned.

112 VM. p. 169.

113 Ib. p. 166.

114 Ib.

115 Cf. Bloomfield, RV. pp. 125-9.

116 On Ṛgvedic ritual cf. RPV. I. pp. 252-6.

the Middle Vedic Period are the growth of ritualistic practice and associated mythology. Incidentally the beginnings of several sciences were laid, and the Brāhmaṇas became a very self-conscious and proud caste.

The nature of sacrifice.—Anthropologists have interpreted the essential nature of sacrifice diversely—as ancestor worship, as gift offering, as a fertility rite, as communion with deity etc.[117] It seems possible to bring together some evidence in support of each of these from the Brāhmaṇas,[118] which show the sacrifice in a very complex stage of evolution. Originally distinct strands have become by now intricately involved, and a simple and categorical answer about the nature of middle Vedic sacrifice is apt to be one-sided and misleading.

Classes of sacrifices.—Traditionally the Śrauta sacrifices have been divided into Haviryajñas and Soma. The former consist of Agnihotra, Darśa-Pūrṇamāsa, the Cāturmāsyas, Āgrayaṇa, animal sacrifice, Sautrāmaṇī, and the Piṇḍapitṛyajña. Soma sacrifices are also divided into seven: Agniṣṭoma, Atyagniṣṭoma, Ukthya, Ṣodaśī, Vājapeya, Atirātra and Āptoryāma.[119] They are further classified into Ekāhas, Ahīnas and Sattras. Aśvamedha and Rājasūya were among the most important Soma sacrifices. Towards the end of the middle. Vedic period the construction of elaborate "citis" as part of some soma sacrifices seems to have come into prominence.

---

[117] See RPV. I. 257 ff.

[118] Thus the Piṇḍapitṛyajñas have an obvious connection with ancestor-worship, the practice of "Iḍābhakṣaṇa" clearly contains the idea of communion with deity, the Aśvamedha preserves traces of fertility rites etc.

[119] Gaut. Dh. S. VIII. 18. According to AB "Sa eṣa yajñaḥ pañcavidhognihotraṃ darśapūrṇamāsau cāturmāsyāni paśuḥ somaḥ" (quot. Kāt. Śraut. S. Intro. p. 30. Acyutagranthamālā) cf. ŚB. II. 184.

Agnihotra.—The nature and purpose of Agnihotra are much debated within the Brāhmanas. It is clearly recognized to have been at least partly intended as an aid to the rising sun.[120] It led to freedom from sin[121] and was the veritable ship to heaven.[122] The evening Agnyupasthāna was held by some to be primarily desirable for the sake of asking for gifts.[123] The sun was believed to enter the fire at evening,[124] and this occasioned much speculation.[125] The various elements of Agnihotra were symbolically interpreted,[126] while a Janaka is credited with having attempted to trace the working of Agnihotra in the atmosphere, heaven, earth, man and woman.[127] Agnihotra has here become an immanent objective principle which is to be philosophically comprehended.

Darsa and Purnamasa.—The New-moon and Full-moon sacrifices have been recognized as the Prakṛti of all other Iṣṭis.[128] Agni and Indra are the central deities in the former, while Agni and Soma are the main deities in the latter. The peculiarity of the conjunction of Agni and Soma has been noted.[129] Some appear to have believed that the New-moon offering helped the moon to be reborn and wax.[130]

Caturmasyas.—The seasonal character of the Cāturmāsyas is apparent. The Varuṇapraghāsa clearly brings

120 ŚB. I. p. 178; cf. TB. I. p. 40; cf. RPV. II. p. 318.
121 ŚB. loc. cit.
122 Ib. p. 190.
123 Ib. 191 f.
124 Ib. p. 178.
125 Ib. II. 1195f.
126 Ib. 1174ff.
127 Ib. 1196-7.
128 Kāt. Śraut. S. Introduction, p. 34.
129 Oldenberg, RV p. 439 fn. 2.
130 ŚB. I. 96-7.

out the connection of Varuṇa with sin offering.[131] The Śunāsīrīya is evidently an agricultural rite for ploughing.[132] At one place we are told that the Vaiśvadeva sacrifice leads to Sāyujya and Salokatā with Agni, Varuṇapraghāsa to that with Varuṇa, while Sākamedha takes one to Indra.[133] The meaning of the Āgrayaṇa Iṣṭi is transparent enough.

Pasu.—The animal sacrifice, though an integral part of the Soma sacrifice, may be performed independently also. The consumption of the Iḍā was doubtless important, but there is no question of the death and eating of a divinity.[134] The cruelty involved in the killing of the animal became noticed and the priests sought to mitigate it by mystical and quasi-magical operations.[135]

Sautramani.—The Sutrāmaṇī though classed as a Haviryajña in sūtras is perhaps more akin to the soma sacrifices.[136] It involves the offering of animals and surā. Hillebrandt regards it as a remodelled non-Brāhmaṇical rite, which is criticized by Keith as insufficiently evidenced.[137]

Pitryajnas.—In the case of the offerings to the dead the similarity between the domestic and the Śrauta ritual is marked.[138] Another fact clearly indicated is the difference of attitude towards the dead and the gods.

Soma sacrifices.—The soma sacrifices are chiefly remarkable for their complexity which reached enormous proportions in such sacrifices as Vājapeya, Rājasūya,

[131] RPV. II. 322.
[132] Ib. 323.
[133] ŚB. I. 250.
[134] See RPV. I. pp. 270 ff.
[135] e.g. ŚB. I. 379, 384.
[136] RPV. II. p. 352.
[137] Ib. pp. 353 f.
[138] Ib. p. 431.

and Aśvamedha. Vājapeya appears to have been originally a ksatriya rite for the sake of victory in war.[139] Iṣuprāsana, Ājidhāvana, Dundubhivādana and Madhugrahasamarpaṇa are perhaps the nuclear elements. Features like the Yūpārohaṇa appear to be later additions. The Horse-sacrifice shows clear traces of solar and fertility rites.[140] It might have originally celebrated the advent of the spring sun, the cause of fertility.

The philosophy of sacrifice.—The chiefest idea which the priests repeatedly stress is that of the majesty of sacrifice. Sacrifice is indeed identified with Viṣṇu[141] and with Prajāpati.[142] It is the nave of the universe.[143] It is essential for creation, and on it the gods depend.[144] It is almost lauded into a super-divine cosmic principle.[145] Its potency is incalculable,[146] and through its help the sacrificer was assured not only a celestial after-life, but[147] safety, longevity, progeny, prosperity and fame in this life.[148]

Morals and the values of life.—The fundamentally secular character of the values of the early Vedic age remains intact. One thought this world fair, and wished

[139] Cf. ŚB. I. 549-50 where two inconsistent views are juxtaposed, that Vājapeya is for the priest as Rājasūya is for the king, and again that the former is for the king as much as for the priest, leading the king to Sāmrājya.

[140] Cf. ŚB. II. 1343, 1355f; Keith, RPV. II. 346.

[141] TS VIII, p. 4630; TB. III, p. 1258.

[142] ŚB. I. 3. 30; TB. 1.7.1.4; AB. 7.4.1; TS. 1.6.10.

[143] TS VIII, p. 4630; TB. III, p. 1358.

[144] ŚB. I. 32; RPV. II. loc. cit.

[145] ŚB. I. 656; "Yajñapuruṣa" is the final essence (Rasa) of all creation—Ṣaḍ. B., pp. 141-2.

[146] Engaged in sacrifice one becomes more than man ŚB. I. 137; RPV. II. 454 ff.

[147] ŚB. I. 127; II. 797.

[148] ŚB. I. 116; Ib. 7; II. 1054.

the next to be fairer.[149] Kāma, Bhoga, Bhūti—these expressed values. Life, it was felt, had much to offer that was dear, and so one imagined even celestial existence after the same manner.[150] It was, however, now realized that abstinence in diet, and chastity were essential for spiritual vigour.[151] The touch of death polluted.[152] Sin is darkness, death. It is sometimes described as if quasi-physical[153] or a person.[154] It could be inflicted on another. But it was realized to be connected with deliberate volition.[155] One may be sinful at heart.[156] Confession[157] and penance did good. Truth was the greatest virtue as untruth was the greatest sin.[158] Gods were distinguished by truth, and it was perceived how difficult the ideal was for mortals.[159] Eyes were regarded the great source for the knowledge of truth,[160] although it was frequently emphasized that the gods love what is hidden. The theory of Four Obligations had been formulated.[161]

Change among gods.—Ad hoc mythology has grown, but the influence of the gods is declining due to a twofold cause: on the one hand, prayers and ritual acts are

---

[149] "Ayaṃ vāva loko bhadrastasmādasāveva lokaḥ Śreyān" (AB. I. 53). A utopian picture—ŚB. II. 1310-1.

[150] TB. III. 1245; Ib. 1385ff; Ib. 1418; TA. I. 98-9; ŚB. I. 134ff; Ib. I. 567; Ib. II. 783, 788, Cf. Oldenberg, WB., p. 101, TS. VI. 2493—Tānd. B. I. 16.

[151] TB. I. 55.

[152] TS. 6. 1. 1.

[153] Cf. TS. I. 198; TB. III. 1214; ŚB. I. 171, 178; Ib. 657-8.

[154] Cf. the role of Nirṛti—ŚB. I. 577, TB. I. 294, ŚB. II. 779.

[155] Cf. ŚB. I. 503.

[156] ŚB. I. 500.

[157] ŚB. I. 221.

[158] ŚB. I. 1; TS. 2.2.2.20; ŚB. I. 2; Ib. 168, 194.

[159] AB. I. 31.

[160] AB. I. 31, and Sāyaṇa's quotation from the Taittirīyas; Ib. 40; ŚB. I. 37.

[161] ŚB. I. 102.

increasingly regarded potent 'en soi'; on the other, the priestly tendency to discover underlying identities has led to the clear recognition of a supreme deity, usually called Prajāpati and often given an impersonal turn by being identified with Yajña.[162] Both in the Mīmāṃsā which followed the former line of thought and in the Vedānta, which evolved partly at least from out of the latter, "gods" play quite a subordinate role. The one makes the Word the source of all power,[163] the other an impersonal Absolute.

"Symbolism", Vidya, and Upasana.—It appears that alongside the growth of the practice of Agnicayana there was a great vogue of symbolic interpretation.[164] This was in fact the only way left to the priests along which they could offer an at least seemingly rational explanation of the ritual. It proved, however, to be a suicidal step, for, if the rite was really symbolical, was not knowledge of greater account than outward acts? If one grasped the idea behind a sacrificial act, where was the

---

[162] Agni as all the gods—TB. I. 387; TB. III. 1352-3; the various gods are only the rays of the supreme light which is Prajāpati or Indra—ŚB. I. 178, 401; Sūrya as Parā devatā (ŚB. I. 423); Prajāpati as father and mother—ŚB. I. 566. On Prajāpati see RPV. II. 442 ff, Ranade & Belvalkar, Creative Period 343ff. The highest point of this trend is reached in a way in the dialogue of Śākalya and Yājñavalkya where a systematic attempt is made to reduce the gods to a unity—ŚB. II. 1198-9.

It may be noted that the Brāhmaṇas several times speak of a class of gods called "Sādhyas". They are said to have antedated the other gods (Kāṭh. S. 279; AB. II. 585) and to have their realm above Devaloka—ŚB. I. 365. They are at one place interpreted as the Prāṇas (ŚB. II. 1057), at another as the givers of success (Kāth. S. 263). They however remain obscure cf. Mait. S. 285, TS. I. 378, AB. I. 275, 278, TB. I. 52.

[163] Cf. ŚB. I. 40: "Vāco vā idaṃ sarvaṃ prabhavati;" ŚB. I. 158. "vāgvai Brahman"; TB. III. 1258: "Brahma vai vācaḥ paramaṃ vyoma"; AB. I. 203 "Vāg hi Brahma".

[164] ŚB. I. 654 ff; Ib. 648; II. 1157 ff; II. 1005; Ib. 1043-5, Ib. 812-3; Ib. 865-6; Ib. 879, 891, 909; Ib. 1106-10; TB. III, 1426.

necessity of actually performing that act? Vidyā or the knowledge of the symbolic significances of sacrificial details became very important. It could secure to men the manifold results of the sacrifices[165] of which some purely symbolical varieties were invented.[166] What Vidyā could get for a man nothing else could.[167] "Knowledge", however, was not as yet purely intellectual or wholly dissociated from action. The given symbolic idea is often asked to be meditated upon. Thus "upāsanās" came into vogue, and the "Vidyās", greatly prized and zealously guarded,[168] came to have in time an esoteric aspect.[169] The esoteric interpretation of sacrifice reached its culmination later in the Tantraśāstra.

Brahmana-Eschatology and the origins of the theory of Transmigration.—The Upaniṣadic trends towards

---

165 TA. 509; ŚB. II. 1045, 1167, 1181; Ib. 1076, 1089, 1090; for one who possesses the requisite vidyā, the whole of life becomes Tapas—Ib. 1094 (cf. ch. up. 3.16-17).

166 Sāvitracayana (TB., pp. 1315 ff) is simpler and more symbolical than the Suparṇaciti of the ŚB. Nāciketāgnicayana is similar (TB., pp. 1355 ff). The Āruṇaketuka in which water is the only material used for "bricks" is still more abstract (TA. 2. ff). A compendious statement of the symbolism behind the various cayanas is found in TA. 83-5. cf. ŚB. II. 1105.

167 Vidyā superior to mere Cayana—ŚB. II. 1096; Ib. 1111; "Na haivaṃ taṃ lokaṃ dakṣiṇābhirna tapasānevaṃvidaśnuta evaṃvidām haiva sa lokaḥ"; cf. "(svādhyāyāt) Prajñā vardhamānā caturo dharmān brāhmaṇamabhiniṣpādayati" (Ib. 1186); "Manuṣyalokaḥ putreṇa—karmaṇā pitṛloko vidyayā devalokaḥ" (Br. up. 1. 5. 16); Sāvitra vidyā alone can lead to the knowledge of the self after death, not mere sacrifice (TB. III. 1348-9).

168 An instance is supplied by the narrative of Atyṃha Āruṇi and Plakṣa Dayyāmpāti—TB. III. 1335 ff.

169 Although most of the abstract symbolical cayanas are more or less esoteric, a few may even be designated mystical. Such are the Sāvitra and the Āruṇaketuka. The evidence in the case of the former is practically decisive since TB. III. 1339 ff purports to describe the experiences to which the Sāvitra science led some actual persons, and the experience of Devabhāga Śrautarṣa clearly belongs to the mysticism of the "audile" type.

pantheistic speculation and preference for knowledge to ritual action, thus, have fairly commenced in the last period of the Middle Vedic Age. Some scholars have seen in the eschatological speculations of this epoch the origin of the doctrine of transmigation as well.[170] This has been questioned,[171] and it appears, rightly. That there are no traces of the doctrine in the ṚS is practically certain[172] and that the usual attitude of the Brāhmaṇa-texts towards afterlife does in no way assume any such doctrine is also clear. *A careful examination of all the passages occurring in these works and bearing on after-life reveals the following general state of beliefs*: Future existence, at least of a blessed character, is assured to a man only through the correct performance of sacrifice. The sacrificer is reborn after death from the fire[173] into the midst of gods and enjoys an immortal existence[174] imagined after the manner of the life here. So far there is hardly any improvement over the beliefs of the previous age. However, the functions previously performed by the ideas of righteousness and divine favour are now practically replaced by that of the magical potency of the correctly performed sacrifice.[175] Ethical considera-

[170] Oldenberg, RV–563 ff; Oldenberg, LU–27 ff, 105 ff; Bloomfield, RV. pp. 252 ff; Creative Period–p. 82. The last two admit the likelihood of non-aryan influence.

[171] La Vallée Poussin–L'Inde jusqu'au 300 avant JC. pp. 282 ff; Cf. Garbe–ERE. XII. p. 434.

[172] Keith, RPV–II–pp. 570-1.

[173] ŚB. II. 1090; Ib. 1383; communication between Pitṛloka and Jīva° through fire; ŚB. I. 175, 188; cf. TB. 1344; AB. I. 151, 199.

[174] ŚB. II. 1208: "amūrvai rātrayo bhūyasaya iti"; ŚB. II–1050–immortal body after death through "citi"; AB. I. 197, 419, 420.

[175] It is only through a particular piece of sacrificial knowledge that one is born "with eyes" in the other world–ŚB. I. 94 (the implication perhaps is that otherwise one is born in dark-

tions enter but sparingly in the attainment and constitution of future existence. Imperfections in sacrifice, on the other hand, lead to defects yonder, so much so that by disturbing the sacrifice of another one may imperil his future life. At places sin is declared an obstacle to heaven but the defect could be remedied through sacrificial agency.[176] Sometimes it is felt that the quality of sacrifice should mean a difference in afterlife.[177] Thus one may gain to the world of and communion with a particular god and not another.[178] And though immortality is generally assured it is sometimes feared that only the heaven beyond or within the sun—to be attained through special ritual or ritualistic knowledge—may be really free from time and death.[179] Sometimes the deficiency of food is feared in the other world, the remedy

ness); ŚB. I. 120; Thrice is one born—Of the father, of the mother, and of the sacrifice—Tal. B. 92ff, (Cf. ŚB. II. 1139; Ait. Ā. 172-6). One sacrifices for the sake of Devaloka, and there is a way to the Gods and another to the Fathers—ŚB. I. 143; one sacrifices for the sake of Yamaloka—ŚB. I. 478; through agnicayana one is born yonder "as" "Hiraṇmaya"—ŚB. II. 1052; gods of the solar rays when pleased take one to heaven—ŚB. I. 423; knowing the Nāciketa fire one gets what one desires in wide, wide worlds (uruṣu ca varīyassu ca lokeṣu)—TB. III. 1292; "sakṛdiva hi suvargo lokaḥ" (TB. I. 299); to enter heaven it is necessary to please the Ādityas sacrificially—Mait. S. 61.

176 Sacrificial fire burns all one's sins and hence bestows prosperity and renown here, a meritorious world hereafter—ŚB. I. 170.

177 ŚB. I. 250-1.

178 TA. 156; Ṣaḍ. B. 42; TB. I. 234-6, 282; III. 1340, 1347-8; nine heavenly worlds—TB. I. 89; Kāṭh S. 300; Ib. 238: "Yathālokam".

179 See—ŚB. I. 189; ŚB. II. 1053, Ib. II. 1067, Ib. 1097; Ib. 1101; Ib. 1114-7; cf. TB. III. 1377; Ib. 1378 (cf. ŚB. I. 189); TB. 1382; for a criticism of the theory that the doctrine of Saṃsāra arose from the idea of Punarmṛtyu, see Poussin op. cit. 282-3. Ulukya Jānaśruteya exclaimed that the world of the sun was "immortal" (amṛta' and good enough for him; who knew about the world beyond the sun?—Tal. B. 6; Cf. Ib. 23-4.

being again of a ritualistic nature.[180] Rarely, the tone is sceptical—immortality belongs to gods alone; man can, at best, only hope for a long life in this world,[181] or who knows whether an after-life at all exists? It is best, therefore, not to hurry away from this world.[182]

To see the origins of the doctrine of transmigration in this 'Gedankenkreis' has slight plausibility. That doctrine indeed has ever been closely and essentially bound up with a number of other ideas without which it would be impossible. These are, the idea of the soul as something distinct from the body, immortal, and "pure" by nature; the idea of "Karman" as a more or less foreign and accidental factor which nevertheless entails a strict subjection to the laws of moral causality, and finally the idea that all worldly joys are worthless. When the Upaniṣads present us with the first undoubted instances of the doctrine of Saṃsāra, they do it in this developed form.[183] And it is in essentially the same form that the doctrine meets us in the earliest Jaina works and Orphic fragments.[184] In this very form has it ever since been held. Transmigration is unthinkable apart from belief in an innately immaculate and immortal conscious principle, recognition of the law of karman and a deep-seated urge for Mukti. Now our Brāhmaṇa texts entertain but shadowy and conflicting views about the soul which is ever conceived in close connection with the body and never thought to be naturally immortal.

[180] TB. III. 1339; Kāṭh. S. 230 cf. Hunger as death—ŚB. II. 112, death in after-life is just hunger—TB. III. 1289-90.

[181] Tāṇḍ. B. II. 519, 569; Kāṭh. S. 59; ŚB. I. 155, 167; cf. ŚB. II. 1054, 1067.

[182] TS. I. 196: "Nāsmāllokātsvetavyamivetyāhuḥ ko hi tadveda yadyamusmiṃ lokesti vā na veti".

[183] Bṛ. Up. III. 2. 13; IV. 4; 5; RPV. II. 573.

[184] See below. Cf. Keith—JRAS. 1909 569 ff.

Even the gods had a definite origin in birth and acquired their immortality through sacrifice.[185] Further they are ever dependent on food supplies from this world.[186] As to men, they survive death not by virtue of anything inherent in them but solely by virtue of being reborn from the sacrificial fire.[187] There is no reason whatever for death, taken in itself, not being final. Besides, it seems to be implied that in some mysterious fashion it was this body that was "put together" (sandhatte) through the agency of sacrificial fire in the future existence.[188] The idea of the essentially divine and immortal human soul appears to have been as foreign to the thought of the Brāhmaṇas as to that of pre-Orphic Greece.[189] In either case it seems to have entered as part of the doctrine of Saṃsāra.

It hardly needs as much argument to establish that the idea of an inflexible moral law extending far beyond the grave is quite beyond the ken of our priests of the Brāhmaṇa-books of this age.[190] And nothing leaps to the eyes more forcibly than the utterly mundane character of their Weltanschauung. They wished for future existence only as a glorified continuation of the existence here. Of Vairāgya, of Mukti as opposed to Bhukti, there

---

[185] ŚB. II. 1126. [186] ŚB. II. 1138.

[187] Yajña becomes the soul of the Yajamāna in the other world—ŚB. II. 1138-9, 1141; one is born "Āhutimaya"—ŚB. II. 1254.

[188] ŚB. I. 528; Ib. 391; Cf. TB. III. 1377: "Saśarīra eva svargaṃ lokameti"; cf. TB. I. 453-4; Ib. III. 1226; cf. Tāṇḍ. II. 446; Cf. Mait. S. 32; Kāṭh. S. 296. At places discarnate future existence is conceived but pantheistically (these texts may be quite late)—ŚB. II. 1074, 1088; future existence can only be discarnate—ŚB. II. 1090.

[189] Diff. between gods and men—ŚB. I. 652; Ib. II. 1048.

[190] "Karman" means to them simply "ritual act"—ŚB. II. 833; cf. ŚB. I. 109; the other-world is doubtless "made" (kṛta), but made by sacrifice—ŚB. I. 671.

is as yet not the slightest awareness. The conception of immortality—Amṛtatva—is just that of endless duration in a changeful world of sensuous enjoyment, which is nearer the conception of Saṃsāra than of Mokṣa.

It is thus impossible to see a linear and simple evolution from the Brāhmanic views regarding after-life to the theory of transmigration found at places in the Upaniṣads. We are left to the hypothesis of an influence ab extra, which has been indeed already advanced by Poussin and Garbe and partly accepted by Belvelkar and Ranade. The Brāhmaṇas with their ideas of death as a rebirth, their fervent quest for immortality coupled with the incipient fear of dying again or suffering through hunger in a world won by sacrifice, and the hope of a timeless world beyond the sun had induced no doubt a certain receptivity in the Vedic mind for the doctrine of Saṃsāra.[191] The sources of this doctrine must have been the Munis and Śramaṇas, already alluded to, who harked back to pre-Vedic times.[192]

---

[191] The following texts are possibly acquainted with the doctrine of Saṃsāra: Tāṇḍ. B. I. 105, 122, 123, 126, II. 126, 351, 378, 382, I. 214, 475-76; AR. II. 814; TR. III. 1289: TĀ. I. 34-37; Tal. B. 114; ŚB. II. 1332, 1193; TĀ. I. 23. If these passages could be regarded as earlier than those passages of the Upaniṣads wherein the doctrine of Saṃsāra is clearly presupposed, the theory of Oldenberg about the origin of the idea of transmigration in India would receive considerable support.

[192] Tylor considered the idea of transmigration a widely scattered primitive superstition (Primitive Culture II, p. 16) Cf. ERE XII, p. 426. Garbe declared that no primitive people conceived of afterlife as more than the immediate prolongation of human existence in animals and trees (Ib., p. 434). In Greece the idea of transmigration apparently came from Thrace (Rohde, Psyche, p. 347). It may be noted that there is an essential similarity between the Orphic and Pythagorean views on transmigration and the various Indian views on the subject (Cf. Op. cit., p. 342) of which the general character has already been indicated.

Upanisadic Thought.—The interaction between Vedic and non-Vedic thought seems to commence definitely in the period of the Upaniṣads. While the Brāhmaṇas witnessed the growth of Brahmavidyā as the "Science of Sacrifice", "the Upaniṣads witness its growth as the "Science of Self". There is a steady development of idealistic and monistic lines of speculation. Organically connected is the dominant Upaniṣadic view about the path to salvation. It is only the clear knowledge of reality that can emancipate the soul. Clear knowledge may, of course, require repeated consideration or contemplation primarily of an intellectual character, but it is knowledge that is emphasised as the means to the summum bonum, not action—a position which may be contrasted with that of early Jainism.[193] So far the Upaniṣadic doctrines are in the main a continuation and development of Middle Vedic thought. But when we suddenly come across at places in the Upaniṣads with belief in transmigration and an ascetic volte-face in fundamental values, it is plain that we have to do with Śramaṇa influence, of which the general character has already been indicated.

The doctrine of Karman and the priestly world: Moral Revolution.—The evident circumspection with which Yājñavalkya introduced Ārtabhāga to the idea of Karman clearly shows that the idea was new to the priestly world and its favourable reception in that circle a matter of doubt.[194] This is easily intelligible since the

---

[193] Śaṅkara, the great Vedāntic commentator, has, thus, clearly explained the distinction between Jñāna and Kriyā, and declared that the former alone can lead to Mokṣa, e.g., in his comy. ad BS. I. 1. 4.

[194] Bṛ. Up. 3.2 Schrader's contentions (ZDMG. 1910. 333-5) are unconvincing; see RPV. II, p. 574. Ārtabhāga takes his

law of Karman would be decidedly disadvantageous to the sacrificial priest. If the moral quality of an action solely and irrevocably determines the future, man becomes the captain of his destiny; the priest and sacrifice, then, cease to be indispensable. More serious, through sacrifice one hoped to win divine favour; but if the "acts" of a man were omnipotent, where, indeed, would divine favour be? And if the gods did not possess the power of independent grace, were not sacrifice and prayer useless? Further, the births of the gods had been spoken of; had, then, the gods a previous life? And if the divine status was an effect of karman, how could it be immortal? If the stay in heaven too was necessarily of a limited duration, was not one forced to turn the gaze elsewhere in order to find an answer to the quest for immortality—Amṛtatva?[195]

Such would be the anxious thoughts which the new theory of karman must have raised in the minds of the more thoughtful priests. It is clear that the full realization of the implications of the new theory is tantamount to a complete revision of the old Vedic eschatology. The acceptance of the theory of karman was, in course of time, destined to usher in a silent revolution.[196]

---

stand on an old Vedic idea—RS. X. 16. 3; VM. p. 166. Yājñavalkya explains the process and laws of transmigration more fully to Janaka in Bṛ. up. 4.4. 1-5. To the priestly assembly he puts a riddle on the subject—Ib. 3.9.28. cf. Kāṭh. up. 1.6.

[195] Muṇḍ. 1.2.12; ch. 8.1.6; Kaṭh up. 4.2. "dhruvamadhruveṣviha na prārthayante"; Bṛ. up. 1.4.15: "ya ātmānameva lokamupāste na hāsya karma kṣīyate", otherwise, "mahat puṇyaṃ karma karoti taddhāsyāntataḥ kṣīyata eva"; Cf. ŚB. I. 189: "ahorātre....sukṛtaṃ kṣiṇutaḥ...." Cf. Ib. II. 1089 Saṃvatsara as Mṛtyu.

[196] The following passages are chiefly relevant for the later upaniṣadic belief about death and afterlife: Kaṭh I. 5-6; Bṛ. 4.3. 37-38, 4. 1-2, 3-5, 9.7 Īśa 3. 9 ff. Kaṭh 3.7, 4.10, 5.6, 7, 6.16; Praśna

Jnana and Karman.—First as to the fate of sacrifice. An extreme section realizing the inefficacy of sacrifice to secure real immortality abandoned it completely.[197] Others, more moderate, sought to reconcile it with the newer vogue of "knowledge", and thus laid down the beginnings of "Jñānakarma-samuccayavāda".[198] The majority of the orthodox priests held on to the old belief with only a slight modification: Karman doubtless determined future; but were not sacrificial acts the most righteous of acts?[199] Besides, sacrifice was the very principle of life,[199a] of death and of the stages beyond death,[200] so that the proper comprehension of its mysteries and of the connected upāsanās might legitimately be expected to lead one to perfect peace, even eternity.[201]

Karman and Deity.—The position of the gods altered completely. They tended to become no more than the souls born in a certain station,[202] and subject

1.9 ff. 3.7, 10; Muṇḍ. 1.2. 9-12; Tait. 3.5; Ait. 2.4; Bṛ. 5.10.1.6.2: Ch. 4.15.5-8, 5.10.1-8, 6.9.3; Kauṣ. 1.2, 4. Cf. TA I. pp. 35-36.

[197] ŚB. II. 1111 "na tatra dakṣiṇā yanti nāvidvāmsastapasvinaḥ"; Muṇḍ. 1.2. 7ff; Ib. 3.1.8; ch. up. 8.1.6; Śvet. up. 6.4; ŚB. II. 1473; Kauṣ. up. 2.

[198] Īśa up. 2; Kena up. 4.8; ch. up. 2.23.1—but yajña is interpreted as Tapas; ch. up. 5.24; ŚB. II. 1090—immortal though discarnate future existence through Vidyā or Karman; the statements of the Īśa up. are interpreted by Vidhushekhara Bhattacharya to advocate Jñānakarmasamuccayavāda (Basic Conception of Buddhism. p. 6.).

[199] ŚB. II. 1361: "Pārikṣitā yajamānā aśvamedhaiḥ parovaram | Ajahuḥ karma pāpakaṃ puṇyāh puṇyena karmaṇā ||

[199a] Ch. up. 3.16-17; ŚB. II. 1094.

[200] Bṛ. up. 6.2; ch. up. 5.3-10.

[201] Kaṭh. up. 1. 170-18; 2.10 (where the second line flagrantly contradicts the first); cf. Ib. 3.2; Śāṅ. B. p. 24. ŚB. II. 1069-70, 1050-1; Tal B. p. 9. defines "Karmakṣitiraṃrtam....", ŚB. I. 84; cf. Ib. I: 246.

[202] Cf. ŚB. II. 825 where it is implied that the soul may have a human or a divine form (rūpa). Cf. Śaṅkara's comy. on BS. I. 3.28.

to the dominion of karman. Some of them were even conceived to be executive functionaries towards the operation of the laws of karman.[203] The one God is called at one place "Karmādhyakṣa".[204]

The opposition of karman and the divine freedom of grace was, however, revived at a higher level when the conception of a supreme deity became important. The line of solution which the upaniṣads show is to deny the ultimacy of the freedom of human will and say that the ultimate source of all karman is God.[205]

Amrtatva.—The conception of Amṛtatva tended to change from that of perpetual afterlife i.e. an unending continuation of this life, to that of eternal being or the absolute transcendence of empirical existence. The main factor in this progress was the realization that an afterlife which is built on the same ground pattern, motived and sustained by the same basic factors as this life, must, however beatifically conceived, share the essential features of all empirical existence—impermanence and finitude.[206] It is a great spiritualization of values that takes place, and it proceeds from the understanding that the fundamental need of man is not a utopian rearrangement of this world,[207] not a heaven however fine —but a transcendence of it:[208] that infinity and eternity —which alone can satisfy—are the precise negation of

[203] Ch. up. 4.15.5-6.

[204] Śvet. 6. 11.

[205] Kauṣ. up. 3.9; cf. Śvet. up. 3.12; also consider the implications of the theory of the Antaryāmin—ŚB. II. pp. 1468ff. Śvet. 1.12—Brahman as prompter (Preritṛ); Ib. 6.16.

[206] Kaṭh. up. 2.10: "na hyadhruvaiḥ prāpyate hi dhruvaṃ tat"; Kaṭh up. 1. pointedly elaborates the older conception of Amṛtatva and its newer critique.

[207] A Brāhmaṇic utopia—ŚB. II. 1310-11.

[208] Real satisfaction follows not the pursuit but the renunciation of Desire (Kāma)—Muṇḍ.—3.2.2.

this world.[209] Amṛtatva implies, not Āśis and Bhūti, but renunciation;[210] it is not the characteristic of life in a particular world, but the essential charateristic of the Ātman.[211] To obtain immortality one has only to know the self,[212] to turn back from the world.[213]

This attitude, however, is only partially and fitfully expressed in the Upaniṣads.[214] It is Buddhism and later Advaita Vedānta that were to express it most eloquently.

The Growth of Self-knowledge.—Meanwhile a mighty change had been coming over the conception of Ātman.[215] Many Brahmaṇa texts interpret the "Ātman" in terms of the body and there seems no reason to doubt that "Dehātmavāda" was at one time the dominant view.[216] But already in the ṚS Ātman is used in the sense of "breath, life"[217] and "Prāṇātmavāda" or the idea

---

[209] Ch. up. 7.24 on the new conception of infinity (Bhūman) which is called amṛta; Kaṭh up. 2.1-2; Śreyas & Preyas are radically different.

[210] Muṇḍ. up. 3.2.1; cf. ŚB. II. 1156, 1371; Bṛ. 2.4.1; 3.5; since bondage within Saṃsāra resulted from Kāma and Karman (Bṛ. 4.4.5) it was necessary to abandon them—Bṛ. 4.4.6-7; Kaṭh. 2.20; Muṇḍ. 3.1.5; Śvet. 1.11.

[211] Bṛ. up. 2.5.1.ff. Ib. 3.7.3; Ib. 4.3.12; Ib. 4.4.25; Ib. 5.14-8; Muṇḍ. 1.2.11; Ib. 2.2.5, 7.

[212] Bṛ. up. 4.4.14, 17; Kaṭh up. 6.14-15; Kena up. 1.2. Ib. 2.4; cf. Śvet. 6.6.

[213] Kaṭh. up. 4.1-2.

[214] The striking centinuation and persistence of old values is illustrated by ch. up. 8.12; Kena up. 4.9; ch. up. 8.2; Ait. up. 4.6. (5.4); Kauṣ up. 3.2.

[215] On the strength of the fact that the princes Ajātaśatru and Aśvapati never mention Brahman, Prof. Carlo Formichi infers a Kṣatriya opposition to Brahman (JDL. XV. p. 106). The Ātman theory, on the other hand, originated in the AS and received a rational and lay development (Ib. 103).

[216] Tāṇḍ. B. II. 430; Ṣaḍ. B. 82-4; Tāṇḍ. I. 124; 139, 140-1, 188, II. 124; AB. I. 85, 507; TB. I. 106, 107, 255; 463, II. 625, III. 1226; ŚB. II. 845-6, 864, 867, 878, 905, 045 (Ātman assimilates food), 947.

[217] VM. p. 166.

that it is the force animating the body rather than the body which is the real self, persisted throughout the Brāhmaṇas and is met with in upaniṣads. Its content, however, changes. The dependence of Prāṇa on food[218] and its connection with the length of life were early noticed.[219] It was recognized to be something contrasted with the body,[220] though pervading it,[222] and responsible for the motion of the limbs.[223] Often it is sub-divided variously and the chiefest Prāṇa identified with Ātman.[224] The subsidiary Prāṇas are connected with different parts of the body, and sometimes a rudimentary attempt is made to indicate a functional distinction between them.[225] The function ascribed to Udāna in some upaniṣadic texts is especially to be noted.[226] In these texts Prāṇa is implicitly connected with particular "nāḍīs" —a line of speculation which received much development later. The unity of the various Prāṇas was, however, kept in mind.[227] Sometimes Prāṇa is located in the heart.[228] It is identified with the "golden person",[229] with light.[230] In some texts, Prāṇa forms with Manas, Vāk, Cakṣus and Śrotra a pentad.[231] Vāk is declared to

---

218 ŚB. II. 948; TS. I. 198.

219 ŚB. II. 1269; Kāṭh. S. 292.

220 ŚB. II. 1050; Ib. 1082-3.

221 ŚB. II. 1069, Ib. 888-9.

222 AB. I. 156; ŚB. I. 79. ŚB. I. 58: fire as Prāṇa; Ib. II. 946; "Sarva evātmoṣṇaḥ".

223 ŚB. II. 865. 224 ŚB. I. 374-5.

225 Kāṭh. S. 286; Cf. TS. II. 726; Kāṭh. S. 129; Ch. up. 133.

226 Praśna up. 3.7, 9; ch. up. 3.13.5; cf. Ib. 5.23.2.

227 ŚB. II. 593. I. 262, 581.

228 ŚB. I. 387; See Chāgaleya up., where the conception of Ātman is that of an animating force—Four Unpub. Up. p. 11.

229 ŚB. II. 863.

230 ŚB. II. 885-6.

231 ŚB. II. 982; Ch. up. 2.7; Ib. 2-11. Ib. 3.18; Ib. 4.8; Tait. up. 1.7.

be a form of Prāṇa.[232] And though some texts call Manas the basis of Prāṇa,[233] according to others, the senses together with the mind have their ground in Prāṇa.[234] This latter view was apparently suggested by two observations: the senses and the mind function only while the body yet breathes,[235] and in sleep all faculties are suspended and apparently absorbed in breathing which alone continues unimpaired.[236] That is why Prāṇa is called Ever Wakeful,[237] and superior to all other functions (Karmans).

Prāṇa was easily identified with Air,[238] sometimes with Fire.[239] Prāṇa-vāyu is in some cosmological fragments made the Arché of all things.[240] At some places Prāṇa is identified with the principle of Intelligence (Prajñā).[241]

At other places, however, a distinction is effected and the superiority accorded to Vijñānātman.[242] The identification of the Ātman with consciousness or mind (Vijñāna, Prajñā, Prajñāna) is common in the Upaniṣads.[243] At some places it is believed that the Ātman

---

232 TB. I. 131; cf. ŚB. I. 50-1; cf. Ib. 652.

233 Kāṭh. S. 284-5; ŚB. I. 275-6; II. 1424: "Manovat prāṇānāmadhipatiḥ".

234 Bṛ. up. 1.3.1.5.21.

235 Kauṣ. up. 2.14.

236 ŚB. II. 1074; Tal. B. 84.

237 Tāṇḍ. B. I. 368.

238 ŚB. II. 975, 897; Tāṇḍ. B. I. 120; AB. 1.4.2.4; ŚB. I. 6, 581.

239 ŚB. II. 1074; cf. Ib. 1118.

240 Cf. ch. up. 1.11.5, Ib. 4.10.10.

241 Kāuṣ. up. 3.1.4.

242 Bṛ. up. 2.1.

243 Bṛ. 2.1.17; Kaṭh. 4.3; Bṛ. 4.3.7; ŚB. II. 1007 "Manomayo yaṃpuruṣaḥ"; Ait. up. 3. In one text (Bṛ. 4.4.2ff) Vijñāna is clearly the Saṃsārin. This is significant in view of the fact that in Buddhism it is vijñāna that functions as Saṃsārin. In later Vedānta too it is the Vijñānamaya-koṣa that is regarded as

attains to its real nature in the state of dream-consciousness.[244] At some others, self-consciousness is identified with the state of deep-sleep.[245] More rarely, it is realized that self-consciousness must be a unique "thing-in-itself", undeniable and yet impredicable.[246] The great paradox is perceived and stated—if consciousness implies the duality of subject and object, how is self-consciousness possible?[247] How may that be known which is the prius of all knowledge?[247]

This led to the last great development in the upaniṣadic ideas about the nature of self. The Ātman is,

---

the transmigrant and empirical self (e.g., BS. ŚB.—p. 335; Ved. Sāra., p. 5). Muṇḍ. 3.2.7 distinguishes Vijñānamaya from the Parāvyaya. Praśna 4. 9. distinguishes him from the Parākṣara. Tait. Up. 2.1.5. makes him one of the "kośas". Bṛ. 2.4.12 effects an apparent distinction between Mahatbhūta and vijñānaghana. Praśna 5.5 distinguishes a Jīvaghana from Parātpara puruṣa Ārṣ. Up. speaks of Mahāvijñāna (Four Unpub-Up., p. 17).

[244] Ch. Up. 8. 10.

[245] This is, e.g., the view of Ajātaśatru of Kāśī—Bṛ. Up. 2. 1; Kauṣ. 4; Bṛ. Up. 4.3.21 (Ib. 19) "Yatra supto na kañcana kāmayate na kañcana svapnaṃ paśyati" shows that the reference is to the state of dreamless sleep. Ch. Up. 8.3; Praśna—4.4. suggests that the reference is to the dream state Ib. 6. 8. 1-2 (cf. Praśna—4. 6) Ib. 8. 11. (Indra perceives the inadequacy of the view).

[246] Kaṭh. Up. 6. 12. 13; Kenā Up. 2.4. calls it Pratibodhavidita—different from knowledge and superior to ignorance (Ib. 1. 3). cf. Bṛ. Up. 4.4.13; Māṇḍ. invented the appropriate term "Turīya" which it described negatively and paradoxically (Māṇḍ. Up. 7, 12). That Māṇḍ. Up. is very late is undoubted; Walleser and Vidhushekhara Bhattacharya make it posterior to the Āgama Śāstra of Gauḍpāda (Der ältere Vedānta, pp. 5. ff; ĀŚ. XXXVIII-XLVII; RPV. II—503). Kaṭh. Up..5. 15. Muṇḍ. 2. 10—Śvet. 6. 14: the prius of all empirical knowledge is transcendental; ŚB. II. 1466; the dialogue between Uṣasta cākrāyaṇa and Yājñavalkya—the Ātman is immediate, though being ever the Subject it cannot be known as an object.

[247] Bṛ. Up. 2.4.14; Ib. 4.3.23ff; Ib. 3, 7, 23; Ib. 3.8.11; Kaṭh. Up. 5.14; Kena Up. 1.4.ff: The depths of the problem confounded Maitreyī and Mb. Sp. 219 attempts a clearer solution than that of Yājñavalkya.

but it cannot be described except negatively,[248] analogically,[249] paradoxically.[250] In it all opposites meet;[251] it escapes all opposites.[252] It is beyond thought and speech.[253] Silence is its most eloquent expression.[254]

Vedic ideas about the self, thus show a remarkably continuous progress from Dehātmavāda to Nirguṇātmavāda or Anirvacanīyā°.[255] It should be noted that on the psychology of waking consciousness, the Upaniṣads do not bestow much attention. The dynamic and functional idea of consciousness is not much developed in the Upaniṣads. There is little conception of consciousness as a volatile energy manifesting itself in functionings of diverse orders such as feeling or willing,[256] and

---

[248] Bṛ. Up. 2. 3, 6; Ib. 4.4.22; Tait. 2.7; Kaṭh. Up. 3.15; Ārṣ. Up. 11. 57-60 (Four Unpub. Up., p. 17).

[249] Ārṣ. Up. 11.57-58 (Four Unpub. Up., p. 17); Bṛ. 4.3.7.

[250] Kena Up. 2.1-3; Īśa Up. 4. Kaṭh Up. 1.2.21; Śvet Up. 3.19.

[251] Bṛ. Up. 4.3.22ff; Ib. 4.4.5; Tait Up. 2.6; Īśa Up. 5; Kaṭh. Up. 2.20; ŚB. II—p. 1458.

[252] Bṛ. Up. 3.8.8; Kena Up. 1.3; Īśa Up. 10.13; Kaṭh Up. 2.14; Śvet Up. 4.18.

[253] Kena Up. 1.3; Tait Up. 2.9; Kaṭh. 2, 8; Muṇḍ Up. 3.1.7.

[254] Cf. "Upaśānto' Yamātmā" quoted by Śaṅkara in his comy. on BS. 3.2.17; cf. ŚB. I. 162-3; "Sarvaṃ vai pūrṇaṃ.... sarvaṃ vā aniruktam...." ŚB. I. 3: "Anirukto vai Prajāpatiḥ"; I. 53; "Sarvaṃ vā aniruktaṃ"; I. 28; there is a "fourth" world beyond the three obvious ones, with regard to this fourth silence is desirable—"Tūṣṇiṃ caturtham"; I. 624: "Aparimitaṃ vā aniruktam".

[255] Tait 3. attempts a gradation of several of the identifications of the self and thus founds the famous Kośa-theory.

[256] Cf. ŚB. II. 1444-5, where the Ātman is analysed into the double triad of Vāk, Cakṣus and Ātman (here probably equal to Manas), and the corresponding Nāman, Rūpa and Karman: it is further stated that "Tadetattrayaṃ sadekamayamātmātmo ekaḥ sannetattritayam...." (1-2); the analysis of the person into Manas Vāk, Prāṇa, Cakṣus, & Śrotra is old and goes back to the Brāhmaṇas (see supra) on the relation of Manas and Vāk the priests were fond of dwelling. Vāk makes known what is in the Manas (ŚB. I. 536, 63). Vāk and Manas are essentially one (ŚB. I. 181). The latter is superior to the former being inde-

springing from diverse "fields"[257] as in seeing, hearing etc. Nor is the apparently epiphenomenal character of consciousness much investigated.[258] In short, a careful psychological analysis of empirical consciousness is quite lacking in the upaniṣads,[259] and the reaction came in the shape of Abhidharmic Buddhism which bestows the greater part of its attention on the classification and correlation of the elements of empirical consciousness.

Brahman.—Side by side with the progress in the conception of Ātman, there took place a development in cosmological speculation. Some found the arché of all things in water,[260] some in fire, some in air,[261] and

---

pendent (ŚB. I. 67) Manas directs Vāk (AB. I. 161, 248). *Manas* is connected with the heart (Mait. S. 292; ŚB. I. 300; II. 1099-1100, 919-840), is very quick (Kāṭh S. 205; ŚB. II. 1155; I. 560), the source of desires (Kāma: Tal. B. 59; Bṛ. up. 3.2.7. ŚB. II. 857), of reflection (Tal. B. 62; Manasā dhyāyati. TS. I. 244); and of sundry other ill-defined functions, (Bṛ. up. 1.5.3; TB. III. 1408; ŚB. I. 310). It is the chiefest form of Prāṇa (ŚB. II. 1077; II. 840—see above. Not the separate senses, but the Manas is the chief instrument of knowledge (Bṛ. 1.5.3). Attention is necessary to action (ŚB. I. 679).

[257] Gocara—Kaṭh up. 3.41; āyatana was the usual Buddhist term (on the upaniṣadic use of āyatana see Ch. 5.15, 7.24.2; Ib. 4, 1.3; Bṛ. 3.9.26; Ib. 4.1.2.7; 6.3.2; Praśna 1.10). Ārtabhāga and Yājñavalkya expound the doctrine of eight Grahas and corresponding Atigrahas viz., prāṇa—Apāna (Gandha), Vāk—Nāman, Jihvā—Rasa, Cakṣus—Rūpa, Śrotra—Śabda, Manas—Kāma, Hasta-Karman, Tvac-sparśa—Bṛ. 3.2.1-9, to Maitreyī Yājñavalkya expounds a more systematic analysis of the senses and their objects and functions—Bṛ. 2.4.11; Kaṭh up. 6.10, distinguishes between five jñānas, Manas and Buddhi; Kaṭh 3.3: Buddhi regulates the Indriyas through the Manas.

[258] Some texts note the dependence of mind on food. ch. up. 6.5.1.4; Ib. 6.6.1-2; Ib. 7.26.2.

[259] Sometimes a rudimentary analysis of mental states is attempted—Ait up. 3.2; cf. TB. III. 1315, 1316. cf. ch. up. 7. which attempts a gradation among manas, saṅkalpa, citta, dhyāna, vijñāna. . . .smara, āśā. cf. Oldenberg, LU. pp. 101-'2-fn.

[260] Tal. B. 57; ŚB. II. 1506; Ib. 1131; Ib. 658, 1110-1.

[261] See above.

some in Ākāsa.[262] Some sought the origin of all things in an undifferentiated state or chaos,[263] others in void,[264] and still others in neither sat nor Asat.[265] Sometimes a number of these ideas are combined[266] and a series of emanations constructed.[267] Usually a sentient principle is accepted as creator.[268] At first many gods or one god functioned as efficient causes.[269] though during the middle period the idea of one deity came definitely to the forefront.[270] At the same time the creator ceased to remain merely an efficient cause.[271] If the One God

---

262 Ch. up. 1.9, Praśna–2.2; Ch. up. 3.18.1.

263 ŚB. II. 1435; cf. TA I. 51: Asataḥ sadye tatakṣuḥ...."; cf. ŚB. I. 647 which equates Asat to Ṛsis or Prāṇa; Ib. II. 1120.

264 Ch. 6.2.1-2 (here Asat most probably means void); cf. ŚB. II. 780 "yadvai nāsti tadalakṣaṇam.." cf. Bṛ. up. 1.3.28: "Mṛtyurvā asat"; Ch. up. 3.19.1; Tait up. 2.6.1, 2.7.1; TB. I. 429-35: it is first stated "idaṃ vā agre naiva kiñcanāsī and then very curiously "tadasadeva sanmanokuruta syāmiti". Cf. the similar statement in Tait. up. 2.7.

265 Cf. RS X. Nāsadīyasūkta; ŚB. II. 1191-5 where "Manas" is made neither sat nor asat.

266 Tal. B. 53: Sat and Asat; ŚB. I. 647-50, quite a jumble; Ib. 666-9, similar Tait. up. 2.1.

267 The contradictions in upaniṣadic cosmologies were early noted and attempts have ever since been made to explain them —see Mbh. ŚP. 182-36; BS. 1.4.14ff; Creative Period pp. 339-41. All the cosmological passages in the upaniṣads are indicated in Creative Period p. 334.

268 Prājāpati is the usual designation of the creator in the cosmological texts of the Brāhmaṇa books—Tāṇḍ. B. II. 209, 419, ŚB. I. 92-3; Ib. 174, 656-9; II. 839; Tal. B. p. 46; on Hiraṇyagarbha as the one Deity—see AS. IV. 2; cf. AS. XIII. 3.

269 For the dominantly polytheistic stage see above. ŚB. I. 53; TB. I. 18; TA. I. 86-'9 (an inconsistent combination of Prajāpati creating out of himself and creation out of primeval waters).

270 TB. III. 1352-3; TA. I. 180-1; ŚB. II. 1095, 1100-1: Cf. Śāṅ—B. p. 18.

271 Bṛ. up. 2.1-20; Kauṣ—4.19; Cf. TS VII p. 3599: Prajāpati enters his creation out of love (Sāyaṇa—Preṇā—Premṇā); cf. ch. up. 6.3.2; ŚB. II. 1434: Ait Ā. 2.4.1; Praśna—1.4.ff. ch. 7.26.1.

created all things out of Himself the doctrine of Pantheism becomes asserted by implication. And as much was soon explicity asserted.[272] Pari passu is noticeable a great development of the very ancient tendency to identify ādhidaivika and ādhyātmika elements, culminating in the affirmation of the identity of the divine universal self with the individual self and thus came into being the doctrine of Ātmādvaita.[273] Its corollary of phenomenal illusionism is as yet not so clearly realized.[274] At the same time some texts are found to proclaim the doctrine of Brahmādvaita which differs from Ātmādvaita in verbal expression only. The word Brahman comes from the ritualistic expression brahman meaning prayer or mantra,[275] which the priests had during the Middle Vedic period extolled in so many ways and in such ex-

---

[272] Īśa up. 1: RS. X. 2-3; TB. III. 1322; ŚB. II. 1114-7—Vaiśvānara or cosmic person (cf. Ch. Up. 5. 11ff); ŚB. II. 1436. "Brahma vā idamgra āsīt"; Cf. Bāṣkala. up. verse 8ff; AS. II. 1. in spite of its great obscurity, is clearly pantheistic in import.

[273] Ch. up. 4. 10-15, where the Ātman is identified with various deities; Ib. 3.13: the light within is the light beyond the heavens; Kauṣ 4.1.19 (also Bṛ. 2.1.1-20) where Brahman is identified with various deities and persons, finally with the person in deep sleep; Ch. Up. 6. 9ff (Bṛ. 1.3.12ff; Ib. 1.5.5ff; Ib. 2.3. ŚB. II. 1455:; Ch. up. 6.9.ff; Bṛ. up. 1.4.10; Ib. 2.5.19; Ib. 4.4.12-25; Kaṭh 5.11; ŚB. II. 1453: "Brahma tamparādāt yonyatrātmano Brahma veda". The tendency is common in the Brāhmaṇas e.g., ŚB. II. 1074, 1077. Many texts emphasize the thorough immanence of Deity but are not necessarily pantheistic: Īśa—6-7; Kauṣ. 4.20; Śvet. 1.15; Ib. 4.16; on the other hand, some texts emphasize immanence with a clearly pantheistic import—thus Kaṭh. up. 5.9.ff.

[274] Thus though Īśa up. 6 is pronouncedly monistic, the next verse clearly regards creation as real; Ch. up. 6.1.3ff, 6.4.1.ff are among the rare texts implying "illusionism", cf. Kaṭh 4.11. Kath. up. 2. 19 declares the appearance of all changes and action in the Ātman to be mere ignorance.

[275] For the various interpretations of the term see Creative Period pp. 346-51.

travagant terms[276] that it finally came to have the meaning of First Principle.[277] Thus whatever entity the cosmological philosophers decided upon as the creator and sole principle of the universe that the priests could designate as Brahman. This enabled them to appropriate the whole of the Ātman-theory and stamp it with orthodoxy. The history of Brahmādvaita is, therefore, as far as its doctrinal content goes, the same as that of Ātmādvaita.[278]

The summum bonum.—The knowledge of Ātman became the supreme object of quest among the Upaniṣadic thinkers[279] owing to two convergent causes. On the one hand, it was felt that knowledge, bliss and power must reach their culmination in the Self. Since the Ātman was all, the knowledge of Ātman must mean the knowledge of all. Besides, the very essence of the Self was realized to be knowledge. Further, it was grasped that the final object of every desire is the Self.[280] All joys are merely wavicles out of the ocean of Ātmanic bliss.[281] Ātman being the sole beloved[282] communion

276 AS. X. 2; Ib. X. 8. ŚB. II. 1142; I. 5, 648; II. 892; TĀ. I. 141, 142, 152, 103, 89, II: 508-9; ŚB. II. 892, 1081, 1142, 1167; OLU pp. 47-52; Creative Period 351-4. AS. IV. 1 calls Brahman the source of Sat and Asat, who propped the earth, the atmosphere and the heavens.

277 Tait 3.1; Ch. 3.14.1; cf. BS. 1.1.2—"Janmādyasya yataḥ".

278 Oldenberg clearly and briefly indicates the distinction between his and Deussen's views on the relation of Brahman and Ātman thus "Deussen—stellt dieser Auffassung des Verhältnisses von Ātman und Brahman eine andere entgegen, nach welcher es sich nicht um zwei parallele Strömungen des Gendankens handelt, sondern, der Begriff des Ātman aus des Brahman durch eine blosze Verschärfung des subjektiven Moments, welches in ihm liegt, sich entwickelt hat" (Buddha p. 33 fn. 2).

279 Ch. up. 8.7.1.

280 ŚB. II. 1452; 1498-9.

281 SB. II. 1491; Tait. up. 2.8. curiously attempts a calculus of Brahmānanda (cf. Bṛ. up. 4.3.33).

282 ŚB. II. 1436: "Preyonyasmātsarvasmādantarataraṃ yadayamātmā..ātmānameva priyamupāsīta.."

with it was the highest rapture.[283] Attaining to the bliss of the Ātman one shed all desires[283a], all fears.[284] Finally, to approach the Self was to approach the sole source of all power.[285]

On the other hand, as has been mentioned, a great change had come over the eschatological perspective. Dissatisfaction with the world had grown. Life, here or in heaven, was ever subject to the sway of impermanence and the bondage of karman. Permanence and freedom were, therefore, eagerly sought and it was felt that only in the Ātman could they be had.[286] One knowing the Ātman crossed all sorrows[287] and was, indeed, raised beyond both good and evil.[288] Action touched him not.[289] Thus was formulated the ideal of "Jīvanmukti". After death the "Vidvān" obtains final release (Mokṣa) which is eternal.[290] The attainment of Brahmaloka seems to have meant the same thing although later tradition distinguished between them. But what was the way to the realization of the Self and the attainment of freedom from Saṃsāra?[291]

---

[283] Bṛ. up. 4.4.12; Kaṭh. up. 2.20; Tait. up. 3.10.5-6; Ch. up. 7.25.2; Bṛ. 2.1.19.

[284] Tait. up. 2.9. cf. Muṇḍ. 2.2.7 "ānandarūpamamṛtaṃ yadvibhāti".

[285] Kena up. 1.1-2; Kena up. 3-4; ŚB. II. 1468ff.

[286] The eternity and freedom of the Ātman constitute a cardinal principle in the Upaniṣads. Bṛ. 4.4.20, 22; Kaṭh. 2.18, 5.1; Śvet. 2.15; Muṇḍ. 2.1.2; Bṛ. 4.5.13. The freedom of the Ātman is criticized from a theistic standpoint—Śvet. 1.2, 8.10.

[287] Ch. up. 7.1.3 "Tarati Śokamātmavit"; Śvet. 2.14; Muṇḍ. 3.2.9.

[288] Tait. up. 2.9; Bṛ. up. 4.4.22; Ch. up. 4.14.3; Muṇḍ. 3.1.3.

[289] Īśa up. 2. "na karma lipyate nare"; Bṛ. 4.4.23.

[290] Kena up. 1.2; Ib. 2.5; Ch. up. 4.15.6.

[291] Kaṭh. up. 2.17; Ib. 3, 16; Ch. up. 8.13.1; Ib. 8.4.2; Ib. 8.3.2, Praśna 6.15. cf. RPV. II. 577; Bṛ. 4.4.23.

Vicara.—Intellectual effort is generally supposed to be sufficient. One listens to the wise and comprehends the true doctrine reflectively. Thus, having instructed Janaka, Yājñavalkya exclaims: "You have attained to Safety (Abhaya)."[292] Śvetaketu asks his father to repeat the instructions till he understands them.[293] The great Śaṅkarācārya thought this the right procedure to attain Brahmajñāna,[294] and his school holds that if the hearing of the "Mahāvākyas" does not lead to direct knowledge, reflection and meditation on them should be resorted to.[295]

Of course, the teacher must "know", and the student be properly "qualified". These reservations are already present in the Upaniṣads. The importance of the teacher is spoken of in the Kaṭh. up.,[296] Ch. up.[297] and the Śvet.[298] up. As for the student, he must have faith, practise Tapas and Brahmacarya and curb the senses.[299] "Introversion" is necessary,[300] and so is "catharsis".[301] It is stated that no one may hope to attain to the Self through intellect (Prajñāna) who does not possess the requisite moral and mental qualities.[302] Perhaps this defence of the necessity of a pure conduct was prompted by the existence of a class which emphasized the intellect exclusively. However, a special regulation of conduct

---

292 Bṛ. 4.2.4.

293 Ch. 6.5.ff.

294 e.g., Upadeśasāhasrī—p. 2.

295 Vidyāraṇya considers Vicāra necessary—Pañcadaśī. IX. 30; cf. "Taccāparokṣajñānaṃ tattvamasyādivākyāditi kecit. Manana-nididhyāsanasaṃskṛtāntaḥkaraṇādevetyapare." (Vedāntaparibhāṣā. p. 199.)

296 2.7-9; 3.14.

297 4.9.3; 6.14.2.

298 6.23.

299 Muṇḍ. up. 3.1.5; ŚB. II. 1496, Praśna. 1.15.

300 Kaṭh. up. 4.1; cf. Śvet. up. 3.18.

301 Kaṭh. up. 2.20; Muṇḍ. 3.1.8.

302 Kaṭh. up. 2.23; Ib. 3.7.

must have been known among some spiritual seekers at least, as the story of the Brahmacarya of Indra and Virocana suggests. Brahmacarya here takes on a new meaning which corresponds to the shift in the meaning of Brahman.[303] It is this newer meaning of Brahmacarya that is usual in early Buddhist literature.

Yoga.—Thus while many texts emphasize intellectual effort, and some indicate the necessity of regulated righteous conduct, others stress the need for Yoga and "Yogic" practices.[304] There are some implicit references to the control of breath,[305] and theNāḍīs are spoken of.[306] Concentration on some symbol esp. Om is recommended.[307] The "heart" is mentioned with evident mystic signification.[308] There are intimations at places

---

[303] See chap. on "Religious condition in the Age of Buddha" Cf. ch. up. 8.5.

[304] Kaṭh up. speaks of Adhyātmayoga (2.12), Yoga—which is defined as "sthirā indriyadhāraṇā" (6.11), and Yogavidhi (6, 18); Śvet. up. 1.2. speaks of "Dhyānayoga".

[305] Kaṭh. up. 5.3; Muṇḍ. up. 3.1.9; Śvet. 2.9. The theory of "Inner Agnihotra" as expounded in ŚĀ pp. 14-15 has a surprising kinship to the theory of "Ajapājapa". Both are based on the idea that one might be automatically performing a spiritual act with each breath.

[306] We are told that they are very numerous, very fine, proceeding from the heart or from the sun and of many colours. Entry of the soul into them means sleep. One of them goes up to the top of the head, and if the soul leaves the body at death along it, it is sure to attain to immortality—Kaṭh. up. 6.16; Praśna up. 11.3.6f; ch. up. 8.6; Bṛ. up. 4.3.20; Kauṣ. up. 4.19.

[307] Kaṭh up. 2.15-17; ch. up. 2.233 (cf. Tal B 10) Muṇḍ up. 2.2.3-4, Tait. up. 1.8; Praśna up. 5.1-5; Śvet up. 1.14; cf. Kaṭh 4.8; ch. 1.4.ff; Śaun. up. (Four Unpub. Up. pp. 20-22).

[308] Heart as the seat of the Puruṣa or Antarātman—Kaṭh up. 6.17 (cf. Śvet. 5.8-9 where the metaphysical status of this person is sought to be decided): as the seat of bondage—Kaṭh up. 6.14-16; as the source of the Nāḍīs (see ref. in 36.4); as the place where the mind should be concentrated—Śvet. up. 2.8. cf. Kaṭh 6.9; as containing the inner Ākāśa—ch. up. 2.12.9; Ib. 8.1. Tait. 1.6. on Hṛdaya cf. ŚB. II. 975.

of mystic experiences, of forms, colours, lights and sounds.[309] Instances of Morphism and Photism are mentioned. Ecstatic rapture inspires some passages.[310] Some texts display the "logophobia" of the mystic,[311] and others his love of paradox[312] and obscurity.[313] While at some places the vision of the self is said to follow the rapt contemplative gaze of the mind cleansed of its impurities,[314] there is at one place reference to the intensity of devotion,[315] and at another, it is asserted that the initiative in spiritual progress must come from the Ātman itself.[316] This is clearly the idea of Grace, which was to become so important later on.

The origins of Yoga.—The origins of Yoga present a difficult problem. In the first place it is not easy to decide what may and what may not be Yoga. In later times the term was applied to almost any method of spiritual discipline and became, consequently, quite amorphous. Modern writers by implicitly equating Yoga to Mysticism have added to the former all the vagueness of the latter. Thus, Hauer understands by Yoga all ecstatic practices, and by ecstasy almost any abnormal state of the mind.[317] Belvalkar and Ranade consider the leading purpose of Yoga to be the acquisition of "super-

---

309 Kaṭh up. 6.17; Bṛ. up. 2.3.6; Śvet up. 2.11; Muṇḍ. up. 2.2.9; ch. up. 8.4.2; Ib. 3.2.2-3; Ib. 3.13.8; Bṛ. up. 5.9.1; ch. up. 1.6.6; Śvet. up. 5.8.9; Kaṭh up. 6.17; TA. I. 183-5; cf. CSUP. pp. 348ff; Kaṭh up. 4.13; AS. X. 2.31-32.

310 Bṛ. up. 4.3.21; Ib. 2.1.19.

311 Bṛ. up. 4.4.21; Īśa up. 9; ch. up. 7.1.3.

312 See above.

313 TĀ. I. 102-5; ŚB. X. 1097ff; TĀ. I. 24ff; 55 (which contains a verse quoted by Vyāsa in his comy on YD. 4.31, but which nevertheless remains obscure).

314 Muṇḍ up. 3.1.8; Kaṭh up. 2.6.9.

315 Muṇḍ. up. 2.3. ("bhāvagatena cetasā").

316 Kaṭh up. 2.22.

317 Hauer: Die Anfänge der Yogapraxis—pp. 1-2.

natural" powers.[318] It is easy for these writers, therefore, to trace the origin of Yoga to primitive magical and religious practices which abound in parts of Vedic literature.[319] All rites aiming at "purification" or self-abnegation are considered "Yogic". Similarly all practices tending to bring about states of frenzied emotional excitement or else exceptional torpor are subsumed within Yoga.

This is a little unfortunate, and would have without doubt surprized Patañjali and Buddhaghosa who have, following much older tradition, described the Yogic states of consciousness so clearly. The tranquil and clear collectedness of consciousness is seen to be the essence of Yoga.[319a] Frenzy is here just as much out of place as coma. Nor has ascetic mortification any essential connection with Yoga.[320] Similarly, not all purificatory or ascetic practices can be called Yoga. The first appearance in Vedic literature of anything resembling Yogic practice is in those portions of the Brāhmaṇas and the upaniṣads which advocate meditative worship (upāsanā). It is generally of three types—Aṅgāvabaddhōpāsanā,[321]

---

318 The Creative Period. p. 405.

319 Cf. Garbe—ERE. XII. pp. 832-3; Oldenberg, LU. 259; Hauer is especially inclined to seek the origins of Yoga practice among the Vrātyas whom he considers to have been non-Brāhmaṇa holy men, with Rudra as chief deity, and wandering habits (Bhāratīya Anuśīlana—pp. 13ff; Die Anfänge etc. pp. 172ff). The main source for this view is AS. XV, which is full of obscurity. cf. RPV. II. p. 402.

319a See my article on "Patañjali's Interpretation of Yoga" in Mountain Path, 1967 pp. 213-16; also "Bedeutung des Yoga in *Yoga-Heute* ed. Von. Mangoldt, 1971.

320 This idea has been probably much assisted in its currency by the fact that Christian mysticism has ever been closely associated with ascetic practices. Cathartic practices are doubtless declared necessary in the YS. (2.1, 32) but they must not be too severe (Vyāsa on YS. 2.1) Buddha who was such an advocate of Jhāna condemned austerities (see below).

321 e.g., ch. up. 1.1.1.ff; Ib. 2.2.1ff.

Pratīko°,[322] and Ahaṃgraho°.[323] In any case the process is primarily of an intellectual character and there are only a few intimations of the attainment of any cognizable type of samādhi-consciousness. These are mostly confined to Kaṭh.[324] up., Muṇḍ. up[325] and Śvet up.[326] The lateness of these texts especially the last has been recognized.[327] They belong to the epoch when "Śramaṇic" elements had begun to be absorbed in priestly thought and are unlikely to be far removed from the time of Buddha.[328] Now it is undeniable that Yogic practices were common and ancient among the ascetics of the 6th cent. B.C. Buddha's teachers had attained to and *taught* the two highest Arūpasamāpattis. It will be admitted that having mystic or Yogic experiences for oneself is not the same thing as being able to guide others to have them. The former may occur to a certain extent even spontaneously and take the "mystic" by surprize, who may neither comprehend the true significance of his experience nor know the way thither. The sporadic, vague, and semi-poetic character of part of Upaniṣadic "mysticism" is suggestive of some such state of affairs. On the other hand, some passages in the Kaṭh and the Śvet. are more systematic.[329] May it not be suggested, then, that systematic yogic practice made its ap-

[322] e.g., ch. up. 3.18.1.ff.

[323] e.g., Īśa up. 16; ch. up. 4.11-15.

[324] Kaṭh 2.20; 3.13; 6.10ff.

[325] Muṇḍ.—2.2.7ff; 3.1.7. [326] Śvet. 2.14.

[327] Oldenberg, LU. pp. 203ff; Deussen, PU. p. 24: Keith, RPV. II. p. 502. ff.

[328] Cf. the similarities between the Muṇḍakopaniṣad and Jaina views claimed by Hertel—RPV. II. pp. 503-4. It may be noted that the condemnation in the Īśa up. of abandoning works and committing suicide becomes very significant if we take it against a Jaina or similar background.

[329] Kaṭh. 3.13; 6.7 ff; 6.18 speaks of "complete yoga technique" Śvet. 2.8.ff.

pearance in the Vedic circle owing to the influence of a Pre-Vedic tradition?

The origins of Sankhya.—Here we may examine the much debated problem of Sāṅkhya origins. According to Garbe,[330] the Sāṅkhya philosophy did not undergo in the course of its long history any essential modifications. We may thus take the classical Sāṅkhya of the Kārikās to represent in the main the original Sāṅkhya also. Further, the Sāṅkhya of the Epic and of the Upaniṣads is the product of a combination of this Sāṅkhya with Vedāntic ideas. Consequently, the Sāṅkhya was originally heterodox i.e., non-Vedic. Jacobi disagrees from Garbe chiefly in positing the existence of a "pre-classical" form of Sāṅkhya which differed principally from the classical form in being addressed to the masses rather than to trained dialecticians, in interpreting Satkāryavāda differently and in not having the theory of the threefold Pramāṇas so well developed.[331] Further from the similarity between the Sāṅkhya and the Jaina views regarding the nature of matter, the size of the individual souls, belief in karman and transmigration, the doctrine of Ahiṃsā etc. Jacobi argues that both these systems originated by degrees out of a common cultural and philosophical heritage.[332] Oldenberg sees the origin of Sāṅkhya in the Kaṭha and esp. the Śvet., and thinks that Epic Sāṅkhya, far from being a contamination of classical Sāṅkhya with Vedānta, represents, on the contrary, an independent line of development taken by original Sāṅkhya.[333]

---

330 Die Sāṅkhya Philosophie—pp. 3ff.

331 Creative Period—p. 417.

332 Die Entwicklung—pp. 24-5; on the argument about the size of the soul see Creative Period, p. 418—fn; cf. ERE VII, p. 465.

333 Oldenberg, LU. pp. 206ff. Cf. Belvalkar, Sri Gopal Basu Mallik Lectures, p. 81.

Inspite of Oldenberg, however, it does not appear to us plausible to contend for a Vedic origin of Sāṅkhya. Since the precise interpretation of Upaniṣadic and epic Sāṅkhya is a matter for controversy, the only proper procedure appears to be to start with "classical" Sāṅkhya. Its great conservativeness has been pointed out by Garbe, while the lateness of the Kārikās has been much exaggerated.[334] Now to this Sāṅkhya we can apply all the four general characteristics of "Śramaṇa" thought, viz., being ascetic, "realistic", pluralistic and atheistic.[335] This supports the suggestion of Jacobi that Sāṅkhya and Jainism must have evolved out of a common cultural and philosophical heritage. This milieu, we have seen, was distinct from the Vedic milieu.

This view receives powerful support from the fact that Bādarāyaṇa already declares the heterodox character of Sāṅkhya.[336] This was probably a traditional opinion. The Sāṅkhyas themselves give support to it in as much as they trace the origin of their doctrines to Kapila who was the first of those to become enlightened, and not to the Vedas.[337] As to Kapila it may be suggested that

---

334 According to Paramārtha's Life of Vasubandhu the latter composed a Paramārthasaptati (according to one tradition in the Vidyāmātrasiddhi, the prose comy. on the Suvarṇasaptati of the heretic also) in opposition to a work of the Sāṅkhya teacher Vindhyavāsa who learned his doctrines from a Nāga king Vṛṣagaṇa or Vārṣagaṇa but modified them greatly. This Vindhyavāsa is identified by Takakusu with Īśvarakṛṣṇa (B. l'éc. Fr. 1904, p. 58). This is the chief reason for regarding the Kārikās late. Takakusu's identification itself is, however, not based on any convincing arguments.

335 See supra.

336 BS. 1.1.5; Garbe. op. cit. p. 4.

337 Sāṅkhya Kārikā, 70; the saying of Pañcaśikha—"Ādividvānnirmāṇacittamadhiṣṭhāya etc."—quoted by Vyāsa in his comy. on YS. I. 25. The succession of teachers from Kapila to Īśvarakṛṣṇa is thus given in the Chinese comy. on the Sāṅkhya Kārikās:

the name is really eponymous having been derived from the Kapilas or the "tawny-clad".[338]

Let us briefly examine Upaniṣadic Sāṅkhya. In the first place it has been claimed that the conception of Pradhāna may be discerned in the following Upaniṣadic passages: Muṇḍ. 1. 1. 6-8; Ch. 6. 2. 1ff; Kaṭh. 3. 11. (Kaṭh. 6. 7-8 may depend on Kaṭh. 3); Śvet. 1. 8. 10, 4.5, 10. Of these Bādarāyaṇa and Śaṅkara have shown, and we think with justice, that neither the Akṣara of the Muṇḍ nor the Sat of the Ch. Up. can be interpreted as the Pradhāna, since they are seen to be conscious principles (see BS. 1. 1. 5-10, 1. 2. 21-23 and Śaṅkara's comy. thereon). Between the description in Kaṭh. 3 and the classical Sāṅkhya scheme of the Tattvas, however, the agreement in words and order of representation is too close to permit us to regard them as totally independent. Either, then, the Upaniṣadic account is a first form of the classical scheme, or it represents a Vedāntic attempt to swallow some Sāṅkhya terms and ideas. The latter hypothesis will explain what led our author to call the individual soul "mahān Ātman", and introduce an "Avyakta" between it and the supreme soul when, as is clear from Kaṭh. 3. 13, he did not at all need to do so. The former hypothesis, on the other hand, will commit us to a theistic Sāṅkhya believing in the unity of individual souls (cf. Kaṭh. 3. 12).

Kapila—Āsuri—Pañcaśikha—Ho-kia (Garga or Gārgya)——Yeou —leou—kia (possibly uluka)—Po—pó—li——Īśvarakṛṣṇa (B. L'Ec. Fr. 1904, p. 59).

The hostility of Sāṅkhya to Vedic teaching should also be noted—Sāṅkhya Kārikā, 2; Buddh. car. XII. 30 where Arāḍa Kālāma, whose doctrines greatly resemble the Sāṅkhya, condemns Vedic ritual as inefficacious (Anupāya).

[338] Cf. Garbe, op. cit. p. 3.

The Śvetāśvatara-passages clearly assume an acquaintance with the Sāṅkhya conception of Pradhāna, but seem to weave their knowledge into a pronouncedly theistic web.

Muṇḍ. 3.1.8-10 use Sattva and Citta synonymously while Kaṭh. 6.7. uses Sattva in the place of Buddhi (cf. Kaṭh. 3.11.). Ch. 7.26.2 also uses Sattva in the sense of Citta. "Ahaṅkāra" is used in Śvet. 5.8, and Praśna 4.8, but the import is not determinable precisely.

"Puruṣa" is a familiar figure in Vedic literature. In the Upaniṣads various conceptions are formulated about his nature. At the lowest he is identified with the image or the shadow (Bṛ. 2.1.9, 12); at the highest he is called Vijñānamaya (Bṛ. 2. 1. 16ff; Praśna 4.9) or Manomaya (Tait. 1.6.1). He is sometimes called Kartṛ (Praśna l.c; Muṇḍ. 3.1.3), and sometimes Akartṛ (Śvet 1.9). He is located in the eye, usually the right one, Kauṣ. 4. 17, 18; Ch. 1.7.5, 4.15.1, 8.7.4; Bṛ. 2.3.5, 4.2-3) or in the heart (Bṛ. 4.3.7, 5.6.1; TĀ II, p. 510). More than once his size—equal to the length of a thumb—is referred to (Kaṭh 4. 12, 13, 6.17, Śvet 5.8, 3.13 cf. Ch. 5.18.1). No attempt is visible to discriminate the Puruṣa from the mind; nor is a plurality of Puruṣas noticeable. The distinctively Sāṅkhya conception of Puruṣa is hardly to be encountered in the Upaniṣads.

According to Senart the distinction of the three Guṇas is ultimately traceable to the distinction between the three divisions of the universe—earth, atmosphere and heaven (JA. 1915 Juillet—Août 151ff). La Vallée Poussin agrees with him (L'Inde jusqu'au 300 a.J.C., p. 270) and so does Oldenberg (LU. 214-15). The idea has little to commend itself, for even in the Upaniṣads, apart from the Śvet. Up., the only text which may be said to show a knowledge of the Triguṇa theory is Ch. 6.2.ff. All things are here said to be but modifications of Tejas, Ap, and Anna, which are red, white and black respectively. A generic similarity to the Triguṇa conception is clear but there is no data to conclude more definitely (cf. BS. 1.4.8-10, and Śaṅkara's comments thereon).

Final Perspective.—We thus see that during the Upaniṣadic period there arose in a section of thinkers great dissatisfaction with the type of thought found in the Brāhmaṇas and later developed and systematized in Pūrvamīmāṃsā. These thinkers, grappling with the problem of the nature of ultimate reality, came finally to the conclusion that it was something inexpressible though its immediate experience was the summum bonum of human life. The ideal for which one must strive is the attainment of freedom (Mokṣa) from Saṃsāra, and Freedom is consequent on the "intuition"—'different from knowledge, above ignorance'—of the Ātman or the unique essence of all things.

Further, the Upaniṣads show that a synthesis has commenced between the Vedic and the non-Vedic streams of thought.

CHAPTER IX

RELIGIOUS CONDITIONS IN THE AGE OF BUDDHA

Social Being and Social Consciousness.—The sixth century B.C. was "an age of far-reaching religious reforming activity over the whole of the ancient world."[1] As in the Period of the Philosophers[2] in China and in the Age of the Sophists in Greece, there was a remarkable intellectual and religious ferment in India in this period. It was, as it were, an Age of Enlightenment for the human race. The materialistic interpretation of history[3] would attribute this change in human consciousness to a change in social being.[4] On the other hand, idealist historiography would see here an unfoldment of the spirit or the progress of thought through its autonomous dialectic.[5] It cannot be denied that by the side of intellectual and spiritual advance there also occurred important economic and political changes in the sixth

---

[1] CAH. III, p. 499.

[2] Cf. Fung Yu-Lan, A History of Chinese Philosophy, p. xvii.

[3] For which the locus classicus is to be found in Karl Marx's Preface to the Critique of Political Economy.

[4] For the correlation of philosophy and socio-economic change in the age of Confucius, see Fung Yu-Lan, op. cit., pp. 8-14. For the interpretation of ancient Greek thought from the point of view of social change, see G. Thomson, Aeschylus and Athens; F. M. Cornford, From Religion to Philosophy; B. Farrington, Greek Science.

For a treatment of the Age of Buddha from a materialistic point of view, see D. D. Kosambi, Ancient Kosala & Magadha (JBBRAS 1951). See also Atindranath Bose, Social & Rural Economy of Northern India, II, pp. 481-2.

[5] Which is the point of view commonly found in older histories of philosophy. Cf. Bury, History of Greece, p. 321. (London, 1906).

and the fifth centuries B.C. in China,[6] India,[7] and the mediterranean world,[8] which must have produced a sense of social distress and awakened the spirit of questioning. The experience of social change and suffering is undoubtedly connected with the quest of new pathways in religion and philosophy.[9] Social crisis, however, only indicates the need for fresh thinking without determining its nature. Social change is an "occasion" rather than a "cause" of spiritual change, providing its antecedent rather than logical reference.

Social Change in the Age of Buddha.—In India, the age of "migrations and settlement" was over, and the territorial element had attained preponderance over the tribal in the organisation of the state. The country was divided into a number of Janapadas which included monarchies as well as republics.[10] As in the "Period of the Contending States" in China,[11] a trial of strength was taking place between the monarchies,[12] and, what is

---

[6] See Fung Yu-Lan, loc. cit; Wu-ta-ku'n, Past and Present I; Latourette, The Chinese: Their History and Culture; Fitzgerald, China. [7] See below.

[8] See, e.g., Bury, op. cit., pp. 180 ff; CAH. V, pp. 16 ff; Cf. Thomson, op. cit., pp. 85 ff; G. C. Field, Plato and His Contemporaries, Pt. II.

[9] Cf. Toynbee, Civilisation on Trial.

[10] Cf. "This reminds us of the political situation at about the same period in Greece. We shall find a similar analogy, due to similar causes, in other matters also". (Rhys Davids in CHI I, p. 175). Cf. IHQ. March 1954, pp. 38-49, where a parallel is sought between the development of the Greek city-state and the Indian Janapada. Rhys Davids (Buddhist India), K. P. Jayaswal (Hindu Polity) and Ray Chaudhury (PHAI) sum up almost all that we know about these ancient states. See also V. S. Agrawal—India As known to Pāṇini. Cf. Wagle, Society at the Time of the Buddha, pp. 29 ff; Dr. M. R. Singh, A Critical Study of the Geographical Data in the Early Purāṇas, pp. 44 ff.

[11] 403-221 B. C. The state of Chin played the role of Magadha.

[12] Kośala had already absorbed Kāśī, and now Magadha, swallowing Aṅga, turned against Kośala, and ultimately we hear of hostilities between Magadha and Avanti.

more, between the monarchical and the non-monarchical forms of government.[13] The contest plainly showed the decline of republics,[14] the rise of absolutism,[15] and the growing success of Magadhan imperialism. These manifold political changes naturally provoked much discussion[16] and Political Science seems to have taken its birth in this period,[17] to reach its culmination a couple of centuries later in the Arthaśāstra of Kauṭalya.[18] The Brāhmaṇas advocated the ideal of the "Universal Ruler", which is reflected in the ritual of some of the sacrifices.[19] The Jainas protested against political violence,[20] while the Buddhists formulated later the ideal of the "Universal Moral Ruler", which the most famous monarch of ancient India tried to put into practice.[21] There was

---

[13]Thus Vidūḍabha attacked the Śākyas, and Ajātaśatru the Licchavis. For a new study of the republics, see Sharma, *Republics in Ancient India.*

[14]It has been suggested that an important reason for the decline of the gaṇa-rājyas was "the development of private as against tribal property, following conquest over aboriginal populations and the development of the tribe into an oligarchy" (JBBRAS, 1951, p. 186).

[15]Cf. "There are two concomitants of the new monarchical system. The internal is characterized by a standing army and permanent officials without tribal bonds, owing allegiance to the king alone.... The external development is conquest....The state as a mechanism of violence unconnected with and therefore hostile to tribal power has come into being...." (JBBRAS, 1951, p. 187). Cf. Ghoshal, *History of Indian Public Life*, Vol. II.

[16]Cf. K. V. R. Aiyangar : Some Aspects of Ancient Indian Polity, p. 62

[17]Cf. A.S. Altekar : Prācīna Bhāratīya Śāsana Paddhati—pp. 2 ff. Dr. A. D. Pant's Introduction to Beni Prasad's *Theory of Government in Ancient India* (1968).

[18]There are obvious Greek and Chinese parallels to this change, at about the same time, illustrating how similar causes tend to produce similar effects.

[19]Cf. K. P. Jayaswal: op. cit., pp. 195 ff; Beni Prasad, op. cit., pp. 49 ff.

[20]e.g., U. IX.

[21]Bhandarkar, Asoka, pp. 232 ff. cf. Rhys Davids, Hibbert Lectures, pp. 129 ff.

also much discussion about the origin of society and state, and about the strength and weakness of republics.[22] It has been suggested, though speculatively, that the political troubles of the age provided its more thoughtful and sensitive souls with incentive to withdraw from the world.[23]

The ruling class was comprised by the Kṣatriyas and their kinsmen, some of whom had nothing except their heredity to proclaim their aristocratic status in society. The kings hunted and made love[24] and waged wars of aggrandisement, and at the same time, some of them, like the European despots of the Aufklärung, patronised the new vogue of philosophy. The Kṣatriyas appear in this age as much the leaders of intellectual life as the Brāhmaṇas.[25] The Upaniṣads already mention royal philosophers, like Pravāhaṇa Jaivali of Pañcāla, Aśvapati of Kekaya, Ajātaśatru of Kāśī, and Janaka of Videha. Kṛṣṇa in the BG (IV. 1-2) speaks of the philosophical tradition of the royal sages, with which may be compared

---

[22] See Mbh. Śāntiparva (Rājadharma-section), and the Artha śāstra of Kauṭalya.

[23] Thus Toynbee places Buddha in the "Times of Troubles" of the Indic World—(A Study of History, III, pp. 270 ff). cf. JBBRAS 1951, p. 186.

[24] King Udayana furnishes the most notable example of the lighter side of royal life and was a favourite with poets and dra matists later on.

[25] Indeed, the hypothesis of a conflict between the two has been sometimes put forward and the Kṣatriyas have been credited with the leadership of a revolt against Brahmanical religion and social supremacy. It is, however, difficult to see any real class basis for such a conflict. Nor is there any definite evidence for the suggestion. The Kṣatriyas undoubtedly played an important part in the new religious movements which sprang from a conflict of philosophical and cultural standpoints as indicated above. There is no question here of a social, class conflict.

the reference to an exclusive Kṣatriya-Vidyā by Pravāhaṇa Jaivali in Bṛ. Up. (6.2.8).[26]

The growth of towns and commerce and the organisation of trade and craft into guilds make the social landscape of this age quite distinct from that of the preceding period. The emergence of money is noticeable and it must have involved critical changes in social life in its turn.[27] We hear of fabulously rich merchants like Meṇḍaka of Aṅga, Anāthapiṇḍika of Kośala, and Ghoṣaka of Kauśāmbī[28] and they patronized the new religious movements.

It is well known how the Protestant Reformation of the sixteenth century has been connected by some historians with the rise of capitalism and the middle class.[29] A similar correlation has been proposed for Jainism and Buddhism too,[30] but the suggestion remains merely speculative. There is no doubt, however, that the older Vedic gods and sacrifices were conceived in the midst of

---

[26] Cf. Tagore's A Vision of India's History (Reprinted separately by Visva-Bharati, 1951). Also, Rhys Davids, Buddhist India, p. 257.

[27] Cf. N. C. Bandopadhyaya: Economic Life and Progress in Ancient India I, pp. 240ff, 254ff, 285ff; CHI I, pp. 205ff: 210ff: D. R. Bhandarkar, Ancient Indian Numismatics (Lecture II), would trace the use of coined money back to the earliest Vedic period. A revealing illustration of the social changes and distress that follow the introduction of money-economy is furnished by the history of Japan in the seventeenth century—see G. B. Sansom, Japan, pp. 470ff. Apart from social instability and distress, the growth of money tends to make social thought impersonal and abstract (see Spengler, Der Untergang des Abendlandes II, p. 603ff) and leads to the 'reification' of social relations (see Paul M. Sweezy, The Theory of Capitalist Development, pp. 35 ff.). Recently there has been much discussion about what has been called the Second Urban Revolution, see Purātattva, 1972-73.

[28]Whose gift to the Buddha, the Ghoṣitārāma, has been recently uncovered by Archaeology—G. R. Sharma, *Excavations at Kauśāmbi.*

[29]e.g., Tawney, R. H., Religion and the Rise of Capitalism. Cf. Marx, K. Capital I, p. 51.

[30]JBBRAS, 1951, pp. 192-3; Atindranath Bose, loc. cit.

a rural and agricultural landscape.[31] In the atmosphere of town-life much of the symbolism of the older religion, derived from natural phenomena and pastoral and agricultural functions, would become dim, the gods less convincing, and the ritual obscure and even pointless. Nevertheless, it is well to remember that unlike Protestantism the Jaina and Buddhist movements were ascetic and monastic in character, without any tendency towards 'secularisation'. Besides, Jainism and Buddhism can hardly be looked upon as reforming movements.[32] And finally, it is difficult to be certain that money economy and capitalism had actually developed to such an extent in the age of Buddha as to justify the general and speculative reasoning indicated above.[33] Thus, although the patronage of many wealthy merchants for the Jainas and the Buddhists in this age is undoubted, we cannot see here any special class affiliations.

The Brahmanas and their religion. The Brāhmaṇas formed a proud caste[34] in this epoch and placed before themselves the ideal of a priest's and teacher's life with its pursuit of Vedic study and the performance of sacrifices.[35] In practice, however, many Brāhmaṇas were not priests; some of them were engaged in admi-

---

[31] It is worth noting that town life and its new economic conditions were distasteful to the Brāhmaṇas, see Bandyopadhyaya N. C., op. cit. p. 288; Ib. p. 305; CHI I pp. 237-8; Āpastamba, Dh. Sū. 1.32.21; Baudhāyana, Dh. Sū. II. 3.2.53; Vāsiṣṭha Dh. Sū. II. 40 (against usury).

[32] See below.

[33] Cf. Rhys Davids, Buddh. Ind. p. 50.

[34] Cf. Uttarajjhayaṇa, XII. 5.

[35] On some distinguished Brāhmaṇa teachers referred to in the Nikāyas, see N. Dutt, EMB I, pp. 27-8. On Brāhmaṇa sacrifices, see MN I. 343-44; SN I. 75; AN. IV. 41; DN. I. 127, 141 etc.

nistration, some were landlords and yet others were petty cultivators, and lowly serfs.[36]

The bigger Śrauta sacrifices could have played but a small part in the life of common people, for whom the essence of their faith must have consisted in the performance of a time-worn ritual, which, from the evidence of the Brahmanical Gṛhya—and Dharma-sūtras, appears to have been woven into the very fabric of their daily life. Unlike the Śrauta sacrifices, the system of domestic ritual did not meet with much opposition from the Jainas and the Buddhists, so that, much later, Udayanācārya could say that there did not exist any philosophy which rejected the Vedic sacraments from conception to the last rites of the dead even though it might declare these merely conventional.[37]

Brahmanical religion had long passed its "springtime phase", when it had been a simple harmony between gods and men.[38] Now a sharp contrast had developed between its prevailing tendency, which was formalistic, ritualistic, and at heart quite worldly, and the new departure of the Upaniṣads, which tended increasingly in an esoteric and ascetic direction. We have seen that in the Upaniṣads the doctrine of ritual act is often replaced by that of knowledge, and sometimes by that of theistic devotion; and at the same time the moral rather than the ritual component of action tends to be emphasized. In the Bhagavadgītā and the Śānti-Parvan of the

---

[36] Fick, Die soziale Gliederung......pp. 156 ff. DN. Sutta 16 speaks of Brāhmaṇa ministers. The Ambaṭṭha & Soṇadaṇḍa Suttas (DN) speak of Brāhmaṇas owning considerable estates.

[37] Ātmatattvaviveka, p. 417. (Chaukhamba Ed.), cf. AN. V. 263.

[38] Cf. BG. III. 10-16, which seem to describe the essentials of the old Vedic religion.

Mahābhārata this conflict and change of ideas receives a clearer and fuller expression. Ritualism is here seen definitely worsted in its struggle with ascetic renunciation and the creed of a life of virtue and devotion.[39]

There is thus no doubt that within the religion of the Brāhmaṇas there was a growing cleavage of ideas about the fundamental values of life, which resulted in the adoption of Mokṣa as the summum bonum in addition to the Trivarga. The scheme of the Caturvarga thus became completed, and the Vedic religion became truly a synthesis of Pravṛtti-dharma and Nivṛtti-dharma. This change found its social reflection in the formulation of the theory of the Four Stages of Life in the Dharmasūtras.[40]

Now, it has been held by many older writers that Buddhism and Jainism arose out of this anti-ritualistic tendency within the religion of the Brāhmaṇas.[41] We have, however, tried to show that the anti-ritualistic tendency within the Vedic fold is itself due to the impact of an asceticism which antedates the Vedas. Jainism represents a continuation of this pre-Vedic stream, from which Buddhism also springs, though deeply influenced by Vedic thought. The fashionable view of regarding Buddhism as a Protestant Vedicism and its birth as a Reformation appears to us to be based on a misreading of later Vedic history caused by the fascination of a historical analogy and the ignorance or neglect of pre-Vedic civilisation.

---

[39] See R. G. Bhandarkar, Collected Works, IV, pp. 3, 10; Belvalkar and Ranade, The Creative Period, pp. 443 ff.

[40] See below.

[41] R. G. Bhandarkar, loc. cit.; E. Hardy, Indische Religionsgeschichte, 58ff; Dutt, EMB I, pp. 13ff.

Popular Religion.—Man's religious faith expresses itself in harmony with his cultural environment. Hence the diversity of social conditions is reflected in the variety of religious life, and this phenomenon is particularly marked in India where the heterogeneity of cultural conditions has always been striking. Thus in India "the crudest animism and demonism still underlie the semi-philosophical and ethical concepts of the educated few;......the symbols of the higher thought are the awesome physical realities of the peasantry."[42] The Gītā[43] explains it by saying that faith follows the bent of men's minds; the 'Sāttvika' worship the Devas, the 'Rājasa' worship the Yakṣas and Rakṣas'as and the 'Tāmasa' worship the Bhūtas and Pretas.

The worship of the Yakṣas was widespread. The term is almost a popular synonym for Devatā[44] and there is much force in the view that Yakṣa-worship represents, on the popular level, a continuation of pre-Aryan religion.[45] The Yakṣas were spirits, often connected with trees,[46] and granted wordly desires, esp. progeny and wealth.[47] They have very often the character of local deities or patron saints,[48] though some of them seem to have been associated with cosmological functions too. They are specially connected with Yama and Śakra.[49] Sometimes they are malevolent, and even take possession of men's persons inducing in them symptoms of frenzy.[50] Yakṣīs sometimes appear to tempt

---

42 Wheeler, The Indus Civilisation, p. 83.
43 XVII. 3-4.
44 Coomarswamy, A. K., Yakṣas, Pt. I, p. 36.
45 Ib.
46 Ib., p. 32. 47 Ib., p. 36.
48 Ib., pp. 14 ff.
49 Cf. JBBRAS, 1951, p. 177.
50 Ib. Coomarswamy, op. cit., p. 21-2.

men, and resemble the Apsarases.[51] Some of the Yakṣas appear to have been gradually taken up in Brahmanical and Buddhist pantheons.[52] Not only did they satisfy the popular demand for readily propitiable deities who would grant fertility, they met the needs of the romantic imagination which peoples trees, and woods, old buildings and cross-roads with the denizens of invisible worlds, who can occasionally peep into human life after twilight and make it more picturesque. Besides, they provided an immense material for those more speculative minds who loved to build hierarchies of gods after gods. And finally they influenced the development of later Indian iconography and Tāntrika ritual.[53]

Besides the celestial gods and wood-land deities, the people worshipped various kinds of lowly beings like the shades of the departed, evil spirits, and various animals such as elephants, horses, cows, dogs and crows.[54] A vague and variable polytheism which merged imperceptibly into polydemonism constituted popular theology.

Popular festivals were held in honour of "Indra, or Skanda, or Rudra, or Mukunda, or demons, or yakṣas, or the snakes, or...... in honour of a tomb or a shrine, or a tree, or a hill, or a cave, or a well, or a tank, or a pond, or a river, or a lake, or a sea, or a mine."[55] "Brāhmaṇas and Śramaṇas, guests, paupers and beggars" were on such occasions entertained with food and gifts.

---

[51] Ib., pp. 13, 27.

[52] e.g., Kuvera and Vajrapāṇi—see Coomarswamy, op. cit., pp. 28 ff.

[53] Ib., pp. 24 ff.

[54] B. C. Law, India as Described in Early Texts of Buddhism and Jainism, pp. 195, 197-8, cf. BG. IX. 25.

[55] Jaina Sūtras I, p. 92. cf. MN I. 39. Jain, J. C., Life in Ancient India as depicted in the Jaina Canons—pp. 215 ff. Cf. Dr. V. S. Agrawal, Prācīna Bhāratīya Lokadharma.

Mixed company and liquor,[56] and rough crowd[57] were then not unknown. With this may be compared the "Samajjā" which is referred to in Buddhist literature, and which, originally at least, had a cult-significance.[58]

The soul was in popular belief a homunculus within man, an invisible being with vital and psychic functions, subtle and vaporous and vague like a shadow or dream—image or reflection.[59] It is important to remember that this represents a substantialistic and anthropomorphic conception of the self. It has been widely current in all ages and countries, and is found in the Upaniṣads also. It does not, however, exhaust the Upaniṣadic conception of Ātman, which advanced beyond the conception of an individual, substantial soul *animating* the body to that of the inconceivable, transcendental Self, the ground and prius of all being.[60] The word ātman thus stood in this age both for the 'soul', in its common conception, and for the 'self' of philosophers and mystics. This duality in the meaning of ātman was unfortunate because the Buddhists and some of their modern interpreters have generally taken 'ātman' to mean only the 'soul' of popular imagination and belief. They have thus found it easy to criticise. On the other hand, the philosophical ātmavādins have always been baffled by this denial. One may deny a particular con-

[56] Jaina Sūtras I, p. 94.

[57] Ib., pp. 95-6.

[58] See Pali Dictionary (PTS).

[59] See Rhys Davids, Budd. Ind., pp. 251 ff; cf. W. Ruben—"Materialismus in Leben des alten Indiens". Acta Orientalia, 1935, p. 143, which discusses the Pāyāsi suttanta of the DN. Pāyāsi's conception of the soul is that of Everyman.

[60] See above Chap. VIII; A. C. Mukerji in 'The Cultural Heritage of India', Vol. III, pp. 475 ff. (second edition).

ception of the self; how can one deny the very existence of the self? The Buddhist view of 'attā' is unintelligible with reference to the highest Upaniṣadic conception of ātman'. It becomes full of meaning, however, if it is taken in the light of popular belief on the subject.

The ideas of heaven and hell seem to have played an important part in popular eschatology. We meet with a very vivid conception of hell in Jaina literature, although such a picture is wanting in Vedic literature. The emergence and prevalence of the idea of Karma probably accounts for the difference.

The Rise of Asceticism.—By the side of this secular society and religion where ritual, wealth and dominion were the leading values and where life was spent in the pursuit of evanescent joys and in pleasing or fearing spirits, lay the world of wandering mendicants. The growth and spread of asceticism is, in fact, the most characteristic feature of the new religious life then springing up in north-east India.

Jacobi has suggested that the Brāhmaṇa ascetic supplied the common archetype which was copied by the Buddhists as well as the Jainas.[61] In support of this view is adduced the resemblance which both the Jinist and the Buddhist rules of discipline for the mendicant bear to those found in the law-books of Gautama and Baudhāyana.[62] In the first place, it must be remarked that the resemblances consist in the main of rules of a very general character; "the first four great vows of the Sannyāsin" for instance, may be said to belong to the

[61] Cf. Max Müller—Hibbert Lectures (p. 351); Bühler, tr. of Baudhāyana Dh. Sūtras (S. B. E.); Kern, Manual of Indian Buddhism; S. K. Dutt. Early Buddhist Monachism.

[62] SBE 22, pp. XXIII-XXX.

universal repertoire of asceticism.[63] In other words, if there was a borrowing, it was not so much of particular regulations as of the ideal of the ascetic. Now Jacobi of course believed that Indian asceticism originated in Brāhmaṇa circles and that "the germs of dissenting sects like those of the Buddhists and the Jainas were contained in the institute of the fourth Āśrama."[64]

The theory of the four Asramas not Pre-Buddhistic.—This supposition, however, is open to question. That the theory of the four Āśramas was well established in pre-Buddhist times is an assumption without proof. "The word Āśrama does not occur in the Saṃhitās or Brāhmaṇas."[65] The expression "atyāśramibhyaḥ" occurs in Śvetāśvatara up. VI. 21, but the Up. with its conglomerate and eclectic character,[66] reference to a contemporary thought-ferment, and relatively developed doctrine of Yoga and Theism, does not appear to be very early; whether it is earlier than Buddhism is not certain. Besides, the very expression "atyāśramibhyaḥ" seems to imply that mendicancy was as yet beyond the ken of the 'āśramas'.[67] According to Kane "perhaps the earliest reference to the four Āśramas though somewhat obscure occurs in the Ait. Br. 33.1. (Kinnu malaṃ kimajinaṃ kimu śmaśrūṇi kiṃ tapaḥ/ Putram brahmāṇa icchadhvaṃ sa vai loko vadāvadaḥ//)."[68] To see here a reference to the four

[63] In details differences are not wanting, e.g., see SBE 22, p. XXIV para 2; p. XXV paras marked 14 & 15; p. xxvi paras marked 18, 19 & 20; p. xxvii para marked 22.

[64] Ib. p. xxxii.

[65] Kane—Hist. of the Dh. S. II. pt. I, p. 418.

[66] Cf. Creative Period, p. 119.

[67] Cf. the view of Jaimini as quoted by Bādarāyaṇa, BS. III. 4.18, and the comy. of Śaṅkara thereon.

[68] Loc. cit. The son, it may be remembered, has always had

Āśramas appears quite speculative.[69] Kane admits that even in the much clearer reference of Ch. up. II. 23.1 there was as yet no clear distinction between the third and the fourth Āśramas.[70] This is supported by Muṇḍ. I.2.11. where "ye hyupavasantyaraṇye" and the "Vidv āṃso bhaikṣacaryaṃ carantaḥ" are apparently the same set of persons.[71] Mendicancy is also referred to in Br. III. 5.1. "Going forth" is referred to in Ib. IV.4.22 and in Ib IV.5.2., where it seems to follow the second Āśrama immediately. All these four references are connected with Yājñavalkya. Muṇḍ. (III.2.6.) too speaks of "Sannyāsayogādyatayaḥ śuddhasattvāḥ": but although these references show acquaintance with mendicancy, it is doubtful if a scheme of the four Āśramas is implied. The Dh. Sūtras are of an uncertain date and even the supposedly oldest of them, Gautama and Baudhāyana, appear to be, in their present shape, works of a "composite" nature, for the former mentions the Yavanas, giving

---

a great importance in the Vedic tradition. Without him one is not freed from one of the three debts which everybody inherits at birth (see Baud. II. 6.35.6). The theory of the Three Debts is already found in Brāhmaṇa literature (see above, Ch. VIII).

[69] Sāyaṇa, of course, states "āśramacatuṣṭayaṃ vivakṣitam" (AB,–IV p. 63 Ed. Sāmaśramī). He takes "mala" to refer to the second Āśrama; this is impossible for the following reasons:

(a) Why should one who advocates having progeny condemn the second Āśrama?
(b) Why should the second Āśrama be mentioned first?
(c) Only one who is ascetically minded may refer to the second Āśrama as "Mala".
(d) It appears much more plausible to take "Mala" to mean "dirt" or "dirty clothes" which were associated with the Munis. cf. "Munayo vātaraśanāḥ piśaṅgā vasate malā" (RS. X. 136).

[70] Kane, op. cit. p. 419; so, Ib. II. pt. 2. p. 930. Śaṅkara quotes an opinion on this text which declares "Sandigdhaṃ cāśramāntarābhidhānam" (Comy. on Brahmasūtras III. 4.18).

[71] Cf. Śaṅkara, loc. cit. II. 4.1. with udyāsyan for pravrajiṣyan.

them a fictitious origin in terms of the caste theory,[72] and as to the latter, the arguments of Hopkins appear convincing (vide C.H.I. I.p.249). The strongest argument for their earliness appears to be simplicity of the cultural picture found in them but it is obviously a rough indication. According to Hopkins, the Sūtras "cannot well be earlier than the seventh or later than the second century B.C."[73] It does not therefore appear to be safe to assume that the theories found in these sūtras were well established dogmas in Brāhmaṇa circles prior to the 6th Cent. B.C. and Jacobi has himself shown that the Jinists were in that century already an old and respected sect.[74] If, as Jacobi argues, the Sūtrakāras would have considered it opprobrious to borrow from heretics, the Jinists, it appears, would have thought the same. As a matter of fact, it is within the Brāhmaṇa circle itself that we find evidence of opposition to the so called fourth Āśrama.[75]

Brahmanas originally hostile to the "Fourth Asrama".—The passage already quoted from the Aitareya Brāhmaṇa may be considered in this light. The whole sacrificial tradition with its material values points in the same direction. It is true that, as witnessed by some of the latest upaniṣadic texts, (considering only the authentic Upaniṣads) there was towards the end of the later Vedic period a revolt against this tradition in some sections of the Brāhmaṇas themselves. But the very rarity of the report suggests the isolated and new-fangled character of this movement. At one place in the Nikāyas[76]

[72] Gaut. V. 21.
[73] CHI I. p. 249.
[74] Op. Cit.
[75] See S. K. Dutt, Early Buddhist Monachism, pp. 51 ff.
[76] MN. Sutta 99; Cf. AN. I. 168.

we find a prominent Brāhmaṇa criticising the "Pabbajjādhikaraṇa" as something alien and opposed to the "Yaññādhikaraṇa". Frequently in the Nikāyas the Samaṇa-Muṇḍakas are delineated in sharp opposition to the Brāhmaṇas, and it may not be without significance that the upaniṣad most vociferous in the denunciation of sacrifice and the advocacy of the "Fourth Āśrama" is entitled the "Upniṣad of the Muṇḍakas".

Baudhāyana, doubtless, refers to a Vaikhānasaśāstra but it dealt with the third Āśrama.[77] What is more significant is the information vouchsafed by him that "Aikāśramyaṃ tvācāryā aprajananatvāditareṣām/Tatrodāharanti/Prahlādirvai Kapilo nāmāsura āsa sa etān bhedāṃścakāra devaiḥ spardha-mānastānmanīṣī nādriyeta[78] (with this may be compared Gaut. I.3. 3. "Teṣāṃ gṛahastho yoniraprājananatvāditareṣām") Kapila may be merely eponymous for the Kapilas or the tawny-clad ascetics.

The first form of the four Asrama theory in the Dh. S.—That the theory of the Four Āśramas was not an old and settled theory in the times of the Dharmasūtras appears from the irregularity of the nomenclature adopted by them in this respect. Āpastamba speaks of Catvāra āśramā gārhasthyamācāryakulaṃ maunam

---

[77] "Vānaprastho Vaikhānasaśāstrasamudācāraḥ"—Baud. II. 6.16. Besides, this Vaikhānasaśāstra seems to have been connected with the Śramaṇas. Vās. IX. 10 speaks of the "Śrāmaṇakāgni" for which Gaut. I. 3.26 has "Śrāvaṇakāgni". Haradatta explains Śrāvaṇaka to be the Vaikhānasa Śāstra. Now, as Vas. (loc. cit.) suggests, Śrāvaṇaka is probably an error for Śrāmaṇaka. Thus Vaikhānasa Śāstra becomes Śrāmaṇaka Śāstra.

[78] Ib. II 6.29-30. cf. MN. I p. 902 where the Samaṇa Gotama is charged with being a "Bhūnahū" (Skt. Bhrūṇahā?) Was it because Gautama encouraged men to wander forth into the "homeless state"?

vānaprasthyamiti."[79] Gautama has Brahmacārī, Gṛhastha Bhikṣu and Vaikhānasa.[80] Vasiṣṭha lays down the classification—Brahmacārī, Gṛhastha, Vānaprastha and Parivrājaka.[81] Baudh. agrees with him.[82]

The entry of asceticism into the Vedic fold.—It appears that originally the Āśramas recognised in the Vedic tradition were the first two. Later on, possibly with the dawn of the age of the Upāsanās, the practice of repairing to the forests came into vogue. Perhaps the sanctity which primitive thought attaches to forests, trees and high places had something to do with the growth of this practice,[83] which in course of time grew into a veritable institution. All the while, outside the strictly Vedic pale, were wandering groups of ascetics, sometimes styled the Munis, of whom we have already spoken. When towards the close of the later Vedic period Brahmanic values had undergone a great change and some sections at least within the Vedic circle were willing to consider seriously that apparently pessimistic world picture which the doctrine of Saṃsāra entails. more friendly and more fruitful communion with these Munis or Śramaṇas appears to have taken place.[84]

In other words, the ideal of the ascetic appears to have come down to the Jainas and the Buddhists. not from the Brāhmaṇas, but from previously existing 'here-

---

79 Āp. II 9.21.1.

80 Gaut. I. 3.2.

81 Vās. VII. 1-2.

82 Baud. II. 6.14.

83 The injunction found in the Nikāyas "to meditate under the trees (Rukkhamūlāni)" may be noted in this connection. (see chap. on the Way) Buddha himself is traditionally supposed to have obtained Enlightenment while meditating under a tree (see Chapter on Buddha's life).

84 See above.

tical' ascetic sects.[85] As a matter of fact, the ascetic ideal was even then in the process of being absorbed by the Brāhmaṇas. The fact that the earliest doctrine of the Jainas is the doctrine of Saṃsāra with its practical corollary of asceticism and is hardly anything more, lends support to this view. And so does the fact that there are reasons to believe that the Jainas are much older than the sixth century B.C.[86]

The Origin of the Ascetic-Intellectual Movements of the 6th Cent. B.C.—According to Rhys Davids, the growth of wandering bodies of religieux, the Paribbājakas, was the result of an intellectual movement before the rise of Buddhism, which was in a large measure a lay movement, not a priestly movement.[87] It is difficult to understand how the wild growth of utterly unworldly ascetic bodies can be described as a lay movement. It is in fact neither priestly nor lay. It originated neither in Brahmanical reform nor in Kṣatriya revolt, nor in middle class convenience. The Śramaṇa movement was a world renouncing ascetic movement—classless and casteless. In its essential idea and spirit it has no special affinity with the attitude and interest of any particular social class.[88]

The adoption of the ascetic idea requires a firm faith in spiritual happiness and as firm a despair of material life. Its wide prevalence in a society bespeaks not only the acuteness of its religious consciousness but also considerable social distress. In practice, the ranks of the mendicants are filled not merely by ardent reli-

---

[85] Cf. S. K. Dutt. loc. cit.
[86] See below.
[87] Buddhist India, p. 159.
[88] See below.

gious souls but in the main by those whom despair of material life has driven into vagrant beggary.

It is easy to see how the age of Buddha provided both the necessary conditions of the rise of asceticism. It was an age of great spiritual vitality, when the clash of rival schools and sects and basic points of view fed the flame of spiritual quest. At the same time it was an age of frequent and bloody wars and of much economic change. These circumstances must have created a feeling of distress and despair in the minds of many. Thus when the circumstances were ripe the old seed of a continuing ascetic tradition from remote protohistoric times found a suitable soil and burst into flower.

Brahmana and Non-Brahmana ascetics.—The ascetics were divided into many classes.[89] The most marked cleavage was between the orthodox and the heterodox, or as the Kalpasūtra expresses it, between the "Bambhaṇnayesu" and the "Paribbāyayesu ṇayesu".[90] The Brāhmaṇa attitude was not so uncompromising towards secular life; it envisaged renunciation only after the proper fulfilment of social duties.[91] The difference of attitude towards caste must have been another dividing line between the orthodox and the heterodox. Orthodox opinion prohibits any one except a Brāhmaṇa or a Dvija from becoming a Parivrājaka,[92] while in the Buddhist saṅgha all the four castes merged like rivers in the ocean, renouncing their former names and lineage and were

[89] Rhys Davids, Budd. Ind. pp. 144-6; Jaina Sūtras I p. 128, fn. 1; Law, B. C., India as Described in Early Texts of Buddhism and Jainism, pp. 229-30. Dr. G. S. P. Misra, The Age of the Vinaya,

[90] Kalpasūtra I. 9.

[91] Cf. Uttarajjhayaṇa (XIV. 9): "Ahijja veye parivissa vippe putte pariṭhappa gihaṃsi jāyā | Bhoccāṇa bhöe saha itthiyāhiṃ āraṇṇagā hoha muṇo pasattha" ||

[92] Kane, op. cit. II pt. 2. pp. 942-6.

reckoned just as recluses.[93] Similarly, the difference of scriptures and the attitude towards them was another of the dividing lines between the "Brāhmaṇa" and "Śramaṇa" ascetics.[94] The orthodox view, again, frowned at any formal "renunciation" for women, while, as a matter of fact, they could and did join some of the heterodox ascetic orders.[95]

Hermits and Mendicants.—The victory of mendicancy over forest-dwelling was not won early within the Brahmanic fold. In the Mbh. we find that sylvan colonies preponderate over the peripatetics. Śaṅkarācārya quotes an opinion which tried to designate the mendicants and the hermits by the same term. He points out, however, that the hermits dwelling in the forest were distingnished by the practice of Tapas in the sense of physical austerities, whereas the wandering mendicants were characterised by the practice of self-control etc.[96] Actually, the real distinction which prevailed between the two in earlier times consisted in the fact that the hermits continued to perform Vedic ritual. while the mendicants gave it up. This distinction was important only for orthodox Brahmanical ascetics. Gradually, however, even for them Vānaprastha came to be regarded as merely a preparation for Sannyāsa. and fell into disuse.[97]

---

[93] F. L. Woodward: Some Sayings of the Buddha, p. 251. On the bars to admission into the Buddhist saṅgha, see EMB I. 281-2.

[94] Vas. (X.4) lays down:
"Sannyasetsarvakarmāṇi vedamekaṃ na sannyaset |
Vedasannyasanācchūdrastasmādvedaṃ na sannyaset" ||
With this contrast Uttarajjhayaṇa (XIV-12): "Veyā ahīyā na bhavanti tāṇaṃ".

[95] Kane, op. cit. II. pt. 2. pp. 945-6.

[96] Comy. on BS. III. 4.20.

[97] Kane, op. cit. II. Pt. 2. p. 929.

The Jatilas.—Brahmanical hermits dwelling in the forests and practising asceticism seem to have been styled Jaṭilas. They lived in large groups, had group leaders, engaged in austerities, tended fire, and performed sacrifices.[98] They were also called "Aggikā Jaṭilakā".[99] We are told they believed in action, in will: "Kammavādino ete Kiriyavādino".[100] They appear to have been colonies of the Vānaprasthas.[101]

Magicians and Quacks.—Some of mendicants appear to have practised a variety of quack 'sciences'—omens, dreams, physiognomy and the like, as they do even now.[102]

Peripatetics.—The Parivrājakas wandered alone, or banded themselves into communities under a spiritual leader—Satthā, Gaṇācariyo etc.[103] The details varied. Thus the Ājīvakas seem to have had a much looser organisation than the Nigaṇṭhas.[104] Buddha's institution of an order without a supreme head was a revolutionary novelty in this respect.[105] Like the wandering students of mediaeval Europe,[106] the Paribbājakas flocked around teachers, held the most diverse dogmas about salvation and energetically engaged in disputes. In some ways

---

[98] Vinaya Piṭaka I. 24-31.

[99] Ib. p. 71.

[100] Ib.

[101] Cf. Vas. IX. 1: "Vānaprastho jatilascīrājinavāsī". cf. Uttarajjhayaṇa (V. 21): "Cīrājiṇaṃ nagiṇiṇaṃ jaḍi saṅghāḍimuṇḍiṇaṃ | Eyāṇi vi na tāyanti dussīlaṃ pariyāgayaṃ ||"

[102] Uttarajjhayaṇa VIII. 13; XV. 7-10; Sūyagaḍaṃga 1.12. 9-10. cf. Vasiṣṭha. X. 21.

[103] e.g., Thāṇaṅga, 439.

[104] Cf. "The Jaina religious order with Mahāvīra as gaṇī. . . .and nine. . . .gaṇadharas. . . .was modelled on the republican constitution of the nine Licchavi or Mallaki clans." (Law, B. C. op. cit. p. 211).

[105] MN—Gopaka-moggalāna sutta cf. Jayaswal, K. P., Hindu Polity I. pp. 45 ff.

[106] Mrs. Rhys Davids, Sakya. p. 121.

they remind one of the Sophists[107] and of the wandering teacher-philosophers of Confucian China.[108] Nevertheless, unlike these, they were essentially mendicants who had renounced the world. They were intellectually active but with a spiritual seeking, and their purpose was to practise "Brahmacarya"[109] in the sense of "discipline for the realization of the Most High."[110] They had nothing of the secular and intellectual humanism of the Sophists[111] or of most of the Chinese philosophers.

'Brahmacarya' originally meant 'discipline' for Vedic study. As the meaning of 'Brahman' changed in the Upaniṣads, Brahmacarya came to have a new meaning in addition to the older one. It came to stand for the discipline which the quest of Brahman or the highest reality entails.[112] Following the distinction of Muṇḍaka between 'aparā vidyā' and 'parā vidyā', we may distinguish the two usages of 'Brahmacarya' as 'apara-Brahmacarya' and 'para°'. The Parivrājakas were concerned with Para-Brahmacarya only.

The leading vows of the Brāhmaṇa, Buddhist, and Jaina monks had a fundamental resemblance,[113] which was the result of a community of practical ideals. The Yoga sūtras[114] describe non-violence, truth, avoidance of theft, continence, and the renunciation of all property

---

107 Rhys Davids, Buddhist India, p. 141-2.

108 Cf. Fung Yu-Lan, op. cit. pp. 48 ff.

109 Cf. AN IV. 384 where several possible purposes of "Brahmacarya" are distinguished.

110 See below.

111 Cf. CHA V. pp. 377 ff.

112 Ch. Up. VIII. 7.2 ff; Praśna I. 1; Kaṭha. I. 2.15; Muṇḍaka. I. 2.11-12. cf. BS. I. 3.36 and the comy. of Śaṅkara thereon

113 See above.

114 II. 30-31.

as "great vows", universally binding. With difference of emphasis and interpretation in the different sects. these vows indicate the general pattern of ascetic endeavour through the ages in India. By adopting absolute chastity,[115] and poverty, the ascetics tried to rise above the bondage of physical drives and the egoistic limitations of family and property. By respecting the life and property of others, they signified that they were not anti-social. If they gave up the world of common social and economic relations, it was only for the fuller pursuit of Truth, which transcends the sphere of bodily appetites and egoism. They sought to transcend, not disrupt, social life. Indeed, having abandoned secular society, they themselves entered a new society based on spiritual relations. They became the spiritual sons of the Teachers whom they followed and participated in a spiritual fraternity, believing that man is not fundamentally a material being, driven by the instincts of 'production' and 'reproduction'.[116] He is essentially a spiritual creature striving after a goal not attainable in the kingdom of Man.

The ascetics aimed at obtaining 'purity' (Viśuddhi)

---

[115] Such was the importance of chastity that in course of time it came to be the principal meaning of Brahmacarya. There are, however, indications to the effect that there existed a school of thought which sought to attain spiritual happiness through material happiness. It is appropriately called "Śātavāda" or "Hedonism" (Technically, of course, it is *not* hedonism.) see Sūyagadaṃga I. 3.4.6; Aupapātika sūtra sect. 75 (quoted B. C. Law. op. cit. p. 229); Schrader, Über den Stand ....p. 54; MN Sutta 45. It might have been an ancient 'Tāntrika' view which saw ritual significance in sense enjoyment. cf. ṚS I. 179; Ch. Up. III. 17.3; BG. IV. 26 (second half); Kathāvatthu XXIII. 1.

[116] Cf. Vernon Venable, Human Nature: The Marxian View.

on which various theories were advocated[117]—Āhāra,[118] Saṃsāra, Upapatti, Āvāsa, Yañña, and Aggi-paricariyā. The means generally adopted were mortification of the flesh,[119] solitude, study and meditation. The dress, food, and habitation of the ascetics were rigidly regulated.

Dress and Appearance.—In dress and appearance the mendicants did not always present a prepossessing sight. Hariesabala is thus described by the Brāhmaṇas: "Kayare āgacchāi dittarūve kāle vigarāle phokkanāse Omacelaye paṃsupisāyabhūye saṅkaradūsaṃ parivariya kaṇṭhe//"[120] The outfit of the ascetic was of the simplest and the lowliest but varied among the different sects. Among Brahmanic ascetics it was usual to cover nakedness with a cloth; it might be washed and even dyed yellowish—red.[121] Sticks, a rope, a cloth for straining water, a water vessel and an alms-bowl were other permissible items.[122] In the case of the Buddhist monk, it appears that the list of the articles permitted to him became steadily enlarged. A perusal of the Kammavācās in the Mahāvagga and the Cullavagga indicates this. The Jinist gibe about the Buddhist monk's "luxurious" living was not, from the Jinist standpoint, wholly pointless.[123] He was, for instance, permitted the use of "foot-

---

117 MN. I. 80-2.

118 See below.

119 Cf. DN. I. Kassapasīhanāda sutta; N. Dutt. EMB I. 17 ff.

120 U. XII. 6. The rules about the keeping of hair varied among the different sects. The Jaṭilas as the name signified kept matted hair; the Nigaṇṭhas had the hair plucked out, while, as the term Muṇḍaka shows, the prevalent practice was to shave the head periodically. (cf. Vas. X. 6: Muṇḍomamaparigrahaḥ". This rule applies to the Parivrājaka: the Vānaprastha was supposed to remain Jaṭila—Ib. IX. 1).

121 SBE. 22 p. XXVI.

122 Ib. p. XXVIII.

123 See Minayeff, op. cit. p. 48, fn. 4.

coverings" in the open Ārāma, and also of a torch, a lamp, and a walking-stick.[124] Such a permission would hardly be imaginable in the case of an early Jinist monk. This difference between Buddhist and Jinist discipline was in the main caused by Buddha's rejection of harsh asceticism and the fact that the Buddhists formed from the very beginning an organised corporate body, which, with time, appears to have grown wealthier.

Though Mahāvīra himself followed the more rigorous Ājīvaka practice of going entirely naked, yet he permitted the Nigaṇṭhas to put on a single robe, which justifies the reference to them as "Ekasāṭaka" by Gosāla.[125] In a Buddhist passage, however, the Nigaṇṭhas are apparently distinguished from the Acelakas as well as the Ekasāṭakas.[126] The explanation of this discrepancy must be an actual discrepancy of practice in the matter of clothing among the early Nigaṇṭhas. The more rigorous followers of Mahāvīra, the "Jinakalpikas" and those Ājīvakas who continued to remain within the Nigaṇṭha fold[127] appear to have followed the principle of complete nakedness, while the rest, it appears, adhered to the less strict but older practice. Further, the rules about dress varied even among the same group of monks according to season. The Āyāraṅga, thus, permits a monk to have in winter from one to three robes, which however, must be worn unchanged, unwashed etc. With the advent of summer new robes may be begged, but less may be put on, so that even nakedness is permissible.[128]

---

[124] S. Dutt. Early Budd. Monachism p. 31.

[125] E. R. E. I p. 265. [126] SN. I. p. 78.

[127] Cf. Hoernle "Ājīvakas" in the ERE; also Cf. SBE. 22—p. XXVI.

[128] AN. I. 8.4, 5, 6.

The begging bowl was another article about which ascetic practice varied. The Ājīvakas regarded it impermissible, and were, hence, called "hatthāpalekhanas" but the Nigaṇṭhas differed. On the other hand, whereas the Ājīvakas considered it correct to take food to a sick brother in the householder's bowl, the Nigaṇṭhas feared therein the inadvertent destruction of life which the layman's bowl might contain.[129]

As to the food which the ascetic might use, practice again varied. The Brāhmaṇa ascetic was required to abandon all desires for sweet food, take only such parts of plants and trees as became detached spontaneously, and to avoid the destruction of seeds.[130]

The Ājīvakas permitted cold water, unboiled seeds and specially prepared food. The Nigaṇṭhas forbade all the three.[131] The Buddhist rules were in the matter

As to the kinds of cloth, permissible are "cloth made of wool, silk, hemp, palm-leaves, cotton or Arkatūla or such like clothes" (Jaina Sūtras I. p. 157). Of such cloth a young, healthy and strong monk may wear normally one robe, not two (Ib.) but a man should possess four raiments (the first to wear in the cloister, the second and third for out of door, the fourth for assemblies) (Ib). The dyeing or bleaching of cloth was forbidden (Ib. p. 164). Clothes not permitted were—of fur, of goats' hair, of blue cotton, of common cotton, of Bengal cotton of Paṭṭa, of Malaya fibres, of bark fibres, of muslin, of silk; (clothes provincially called) Desaraga, Amila, Gaggala, Phaliya, Kāyaha; blankets and mantles (Ib. p. 158). This last list is incidentally informative about what apparels were considered luxurious. An under and an upper garment were recommended if it rained hard (Ib. p. 302).

[129] ERE. I. p. 265.

Bowls of bottle-gourd, or wood, or clay were permitted (Jaina Sūtras I p. 168). A young, strong and healthy monk might take only one bowl (Ib). (According to the commentary this rule applied only to the Jinakalpikas etc. Ordinary monks could have a drinking vessel besides the alms-bowl—Ib. Fn. 2)

[130] SBE. 22—pp. xxvi-xxvii.

[131] ERE. I. loc. cit. The monk was to avoid "living beings, mildew, seeds, sprouts, flowers, eggs, layers, and moisture" (Jaina

again very liberal. Since the monks were permitted to accept invitations, specially prepared food is obviously permitted by implication. There is reason to suppose that even meat eating was not categorically forbidden.[132] Buddha, however, advised the monks to eat only once a day,[133] and "measure in eating" (Bhojane mattaññutā) was a frequently emphasized precept. The very contrast in which the rationality and moderation of the Buddhist attitude stand to the practice of the other ascetic sects so far as we know them suggests the extent to which extremism formed the prevalent gospel. Exaggerated attention to merely external details is another noticeable feature. In this connection it is interesting to note that one of Buddha's last declarations is supposed to have referred to the revocability of the lesser precepts.[134]

And yet in the account of the first council, and more so in that of the second, wrangling over small points is prominent. The achievement of "Purity" appears to have been one of the more widespread ideas among the Parivrājakas.[135]

Sūtras I p. 304). Similarly, he was not to accept as alms "flattened grains, grains containing much chaff, or half-roasted spikes of wheat etc. or flour of wheat etc., or rice or flour of rice "recognised as only once worked" (Ib. 89).

[132] As a matter of fact even the Jinist monk could accept meat in alms under certain circumstances, see Jaina Sūtras I. pp. 114-115.

[133] MN. Sutta 66.

[134] Mahāparinibbāna sutta (DN. sutta XVI).

[135] Cf. Ch. Up. VII. 26-2—"Āhāraśuddhau sattvaśuddhiḥ etc." The idea that pure food leads to mental purity seems ever to have had a great fascination for the Indian mind. The idea appears to have originated in philosophies like the Sāṅkhya which explained the fact of psychophysical interaction in terms of a "con-substantiality" of body and mind. cf. Ch. Up. VI. 5.1: "Annamaśitaṃ tredhā vidhīyate. . . .yoṇiṣṭastanmanaḥ." (Śaṅkara comments: Tataścānnopacitatvānmanaso bhautikattvameva, na Vaiśeṣikatantroktalakṣaṇaṃ nityaṃ niravayavaṃ cetigṛhyate").

Habitation.—The monks appear to have been predominantly eremitical. The natural canopy of a tree, or some deserted building, cemetery, caitya, or mountain cave furnished to them their lodgings.[136] But sometimes the laity arranged for special dwelling places.[137] Gardens or Ārāmas were also not infrequently utilised by the mendicants for their stay. The rules among the Brāhmaṇa ascetics appear to have been more stringent on the present subject than among the Jinists and the Buddhists.[138]

Rain retreat and uposatha.—Eremitical tendencies in course of time gave way to the coenobitic among the Buddhists as well as among the Jinists. The institution of the Rain-retreat appears to have been a contributory factor in this development.[139] It was certainly an institution common to the Brāhmaṇas, the Buddhists and the Jainas.[140] Originating in physical necessity, it appears to have come to acquire ceremonial significance.[141] The uposatha or periodical gathering of the community was another institution equally universal.

Intellectual Ferment.—Religious and philosophical beliefs were extremely diverse in the age of Buddha which appears to have been an age of thought-ferment.[142]

[136] Cf. Vās. X, 12-13 "Anityāṃ vasatiṃ vaset. Grāmānte devagṛhe śūnyāgāre vā vṛkṣamūle vā."

[137] Thus Queen Mallikā had set apart a place for the Paribbājakas—see Malalasekar DPPN II, p. 457.

[138] Cf. SBE 22, pp. xxv-xxvii.

[139] Cf. S. K. Dutt, op. cit., p. 123.

[140] Gaut. I 3. 12. "Dhruvaśīlo varṣāsu". With reference to the Buddhists and the Jinists the evidence is plentiful and well known.

[141] Cf. Dutt. Ib. 124.

[142] Belvalkar and Ranade, Creative Period, pp. 443 ff; Rhys Davids, Budd. Ind., p. 159; Schrader, Über den Stand....Contra, S. K. Dutt, op. cit., p. 47.

Schrader has already accomplished the task of culling together the relevant information from the various Jaina sources, although he does not distinguish the value of these texts according to their chronological position.[143] We have to remember that the later reports of earlier views are likely to have been inaccurate at times.

The Philosophies of Time.—The references to Kālavāda in the commentaries of the Nandī and the Āyāraṃga are undoubtedly late in view of their developed and systematic character. References from the AV and the Mbh., however, show that in some form the doctrines are earlier. That Kāla is in the Mbh. the "absolute höchste Prinzip"[144] should, it appears, be understood more as a poetic than as a philosophic utterance. Struck by the irresistible tragedy of time and impressed with a sense of Fatalism one spoke of time with awe and in superlatives. That sense of wonder which has been called the mother of philosophy expresses itself at first in more or less poetic forms and that is the stage, it appears, to which on the whole the "Kālavāda" of the Mbh. belongs.[145]

Svabhavavada.—"Svabhāvavāda" seems to have points of contact with Sāṅkhyan as well as Gosālian views. Like the former it seems to have recognised the

---

[143] See also G. N. Kavirāj; Theism in Ancient India, Sarasvati Bhavana Studies II 93 ff, who discusses the philosophical implications of some of the views referred to by Schrader.

[144] Schrader, op. cit., p. 24.

[145] Brāhmaṇa literature offers many imaginative-reflective utterances about time. Thus see Śat Brā I, p. 462 (ed. in the Acyutagranthamālā); Ib. II 894-5, 1095 etc. Tai. Āraṇ. 1.2. is very obscure, but it appears that the Sun is here conceived as the perennial source from which proceeds the river of time. The main stream—that of the year—constantly swells and returns not— (*Contd.*)

theory of development through immanent forces, but its explicit denial of free will is more directly reminiscent of Gosāla.[146] But, then, could they have been called Kriyāvādins?[147] That term seems to have meant usually a belief in the possibility of individual initiative;[148] Svabhāvavāda on the other hand declares "Svabhāvāt sampravartante nivartante tathaiva ca/ Sarve bhāvāstathābhāvāḥ puruṣārtho na vidyate//"[149]

We have here, it appears, a confusion or an error.

Niyativada.—Niyati or Necessity, it seems, may mean either a natural (causal), or a supernatural (Fatal, or Divine), a moral (Karmic) or a logical necessity. The Niyativādins could hardly have had the last meaning in mind, and since they denied responsibility[150] they could not have meant moral necessity either. Śīlāṅka explicitly tells us that causal necessity was intended,[151] but he could easily have read later views into earlier texts. The belief in a natural Niyati and the belief in a supernatural Niyati, it must be noted, arise from two diametrically opposite sources. The former is the result of reflection over the regularity of phenomena; the latter of reflection over their accidentality, especially in

Nadīva prabhavāt kācid akṣayyāt syandate yathā | Tāṃ nadyó bhisamāyanti / soruḥ satī na nivartate | Evaṃ nānāsamutthānāḥ | Kālāḥ saṃvatsaraṃ śritāḥ | aṇuśaśca mahaśaśca | sarve samavayantritam || Sa taiḥ sarvaiḥ samāviṣṭa | ūruḥ sanna nivartate | (Ib.).

Śvetāśvat. up. 6.5 distinguishes between time and eternity ("Parastrikālādakalopi dṛṣṭaḥ"). Mait. up. 6.14 says "Dve vāva brahmaṇo rūpe kālaścākālaśca.....yaḥ prāgādityātsó kālaḥ......."

146 Schrader pp. 31-32.
147 Cf. Ib. p. 31.
148 See below.
149 Mbh. XII 222. 14. Also cf. Bhagavad Gītā XIII, 27.
150 Schrader p. 33.
151 Op. cit. pp. 32-33.

the sphere of human matters. Since the accidental is merely that the cause of which is unknown, in earlier times when curiosity ran very much ahead of knowledge, the idea of a supernatural Necessity is likely to have impressed the minds of men forcibly. In accordance with probability, therefore, Niyativāda should, in general, be taken to have reference to this type of Necessity.

Yadrcchavada.—"Yadṛcchāvāda", if we are to believe Malayagiri, was a remarkably Humian denial of the principle of causality. It was, however, more probably the same as "Adhiccasamuppāda", and Schrader appears to be correct in saying that "Vielleicht bezieht sich diese Behauptung nur aus den ersten Anfang, ebenso wie Ed. v. Hartmann die Welt für das, absolute Zufällige erklärt, ohne doch die Naturnotwendigkeit zu bestreiten."[152]

The cause of the thought ferment–a hypothesis.—It is clear that Kālavāda, Svabhāva°, Niyati°, Yadṛcchā° and Īśvara°,[153] as reported in Jaina works, are not complete philosophical systems, but different answers given to a specific problem—that of the "World-process" esp. its first origin. More significant is it that all these views have a common and striking implication with reference to the problem of the path to salvation, viz. a denial of the power of man to overcome "Saṃsāra" through his own efforts. The tendency of these views, again, to have a subversive repercussion on the principle of moral responsibility is clearly palpable. It is probable that it

---

[152] Op. cit. p. 38 fn.

[153] The view is mentioned at several places in the Sk. I. 1.3, 5-10; 1-i.9; II. 1., The second reference "Jahā ya Paṭhavīthūbhe ege nānāhi dīsai | Evam bho kasiṇe loe vinnū nāṇāhī dīsai // apparently alludes to Upaniṣadic Pan-Ātmanism. Śīlāṅka quotes "Puruṣa evedaṃ sarvam etc." cf. the well known but a little enigmatic verses from the Śvetā up. 1-2 which speak of Kāla, Svabhāva, Niyati Yadṛcchā, Bhūtāni and Puruṣa.

was the investigation into the connected practical and ethical problems of salvation and responsibility that led to the forementioned metaphysical formulations. It appears that whereas the doctrine of perennial Rebirth was generally accepted, there was as yet no unanimity about its cause i.e. Karman.[154] It appears that the contemporary thought-world had become aware of a doctrine of such momentous import that the intellect felt it imperative to try all other alternatives before accepting it finally. It is a noticeable logical recklessness, Ekāntagrāhitā of the Dṛṣṭis with which so obviously partial explanations are pushed well-nigh to the extreme of a reductio ad absurdum.

Akriyavada.—The Jainas considered Akriyāvāda one of the most important features of heresy.[155] The Ṭhāṇaṅga enumerates eight types of Akriyā, Schrader has explained the terms almost wholly on the basis of the commentary of Abhayadeva,[156] whose lateness, however, needs to be taken into account. It is thus, doubt-

[154] According to the MN II 222 some regarded present experience due to "Pubbakata", some to "Issaranimmāna", some to "Saṅgatibhāva", some to "Abhijāti", and some to "Diṭṭhadhammupakkama".

[155] The commentarial Jinist works give us a scheme of 363 philosophies divided under the four general heads of Kriyāvāda, Akriyāvada, Ajñānavāda and Vinayavāda (cf. Schrader p. 3). The detailed classification, it may be supposed, is largely speculative and formal. The general fourfold division is, however, mentioned in the Sk. I. 12. The Akiriyasamosaraṇa is supposed to have believed "Nāïcco udeï na atthameï—salilā na sandanti ....Vañjho niyao kasiṇo hi loe//"

The statement is paradoxical to the extent of unintelligibility; the doctrines attributed to Pakudhakaccāyana may however be compared. Also cf. "Na vātā vāyanti na najjo sandanti na gabbhiniyo vijāyanti na candimasūriyā udenti vā apenti vā esikaṭṭhāyiṭṭhitāti." (SN. III 202).

[156] Op. cit. pp. 54-57.

ful if Sāmānya-vāda can really be regarded a doctrine so early as the sixth cent. B.C. The term Samucchedavāda raises a difficult problem: is the reference to the Buddhists[157] or to those whom the Buddhists addressed as Ucchedavādins?

Makkhali Gosala.—The views of Makkhali Gosāla provide a striking illustration of the acceptance of the trammels of Saṃsāra and the rejection of individual initiative in the process of liberation from them. Buddhist references to Gosāla's doctrines are at places confused, e.g. in Aṅgutara N.III.383 his classifications are attributed to Pūraṇa and in MN.I. 513, part of his doctrines is combined with those of Pakudha.[158] But a comparison of the Buddhist references with those found in the Jinist sources enables one to form a tolerably clear picture of the fundamentals of Gosalian dogmatics.[159]

Samsaravisuddhi.—Ajātasattu is supposed to have characterised the philosophy of Makkhali Gosāla as a

---

[157] Such is the implied view in the commentary, although "die Buddhisten werden nicht erwähnt" Ib. p. 56 fn.

[158] Vide Thomas—Life p. 130. Cf. IC. 1947, pp. 107 ff. Cf. A. L. Basham: History and Doctrines of the Ājīvakas: A Vanished Religion (London, 1951), who concludes that Pūraṇa and Pakudha as well as Gośāla had an important part in forming Ājīvaka doctrines (see the just criticism of this particular point in the review of the book in IHQ by Dr. N. Dutt).

[159] Dr. Barua has exhaustively listed the sources in JDL II. p. 23. These are—

(i) Jaina—(a) Sk. I. 1. 2. 1—14; I—1. 4. 7—9; II. 1 2, 9; II. 6. (b) Bhagavatī Saya XV. udd. I. (c) Leumann—Das Aupapātika Sūtra secs. 118 and 120.

(ii) Buddhist—(a) Sāmññaphalasutta (b) SN. III. p. 69; (c) A. N. I. p. 208; (d) A. N. IV pp. 383-384; (e) M.N.I. p. 231 ff. Cf. also Ib. I. p. 36 (f). The Chinese and Tibetan versions of the Sāmaññaphalasutta translated by Rockhill, but hopelessly confused; (g) Milindapañho (ed. Trenckner) p. 5, (h) Mahābodhi-jātaka, no. 528. For a new treatment, see Muni Nagraj, Āgama Aur Tripiṭaka Eka Anuśīlana, Vol. I, p. 20 ff.

doctrine of "Saṃsāravisuddhi"[160] and it appears that the characterization is eminently just, for the central tenet of Makkhali may be stated thus—the process of Saṃsāra is like the unalterable working out of a coiled up necessity.[161] In as much as the process of Saṃsāra is moving towards Visuddhi or the end of misery,[162] it may be considered an evolutionary process. As to the nature of the forces behind it we have the statement "sabbe ......niyatisaṅgatibhāvapariṇatā..... Sukhadukkhaṃ patisaṃvedenti."[163] According to Buddhaghosa's explanation we have here three co-ordinate determinants of experience, the first being destiny.[164] His own explanation, however, of the second[165] suggests that it should be considered subordinate to the first.[166] The third was, in all probability, regarded as at least the cause of the differential manifestation of Niyati. But if it was not the sole determinant of Niyati, it is clear that part of the Niyati-as-operative must proceed from a source outside Bhāva or the nature of things. Thus partly at least the governing necessity of Saṃsāra appears

---

160 "Saṃsāravisuddhiṃ vyākāsi" (see Uvāsagadasao—ed. P. L. Vaidya—p. 201).

161 Cf. "Seyyathāpi nāma suttaguḷo khitte nibbeṭhiyamānameva phaleti......" (Ib).

162 "Saṃsaritvā dukkhassantaṃ Karissanti" (Ib., p. 200) "sijjhaṃti bujjhaṃti muccaṃti savvadukkhānamantaṃ...." (Ib. p. 160).

163 Ib. p. 197.

164 "Evam niyatiyā ca saṅgatiyā ca bhāvena ca." (Ib.)

165 "Saṅgatīti channam abhijatīnaṃ tattha tattha gamanam." (Ib.)

166 Since Niyati would probably be the cause of this determination of Abhijāti. In fact Sk. I. ii. 3 refers to a doctrine which denied that one's experiences (Vedanā) were due to one's own previous acts or to those of another; they were held to result from "Saṅgati". Śīlāṅka comments: "Saṅgaiyam sāṅgatikaṃ samyak svaparināmeṇa gatiḥ, yasya yadā yatsukhaduhkhānubhavanaṃ *sā saṅgatirniyatiḥ*".

to have a transcendental spring-board. The vehement denial of the freedom of will[167] and the non-mention of any divine agency suggest that "Niyati" itself was considered an ultimate principle. The denial of any reason or cause behind the "Saṃkilesa" or "Visuddhi" of men[168] shows that destiny was considered "blind" i.e., as equivalent to a causeless necessity.

Makkhali's views on 'Kaṃma' appear to have been peculiar. The classifications found in the Sāmaññaphala passage are obscure and Buddhaghosa sheds little light. We have, however, the highly interesting statement "Tattha natthi....aparipakkam vā kammaṃ paripācessāmi, paripakkaṃ vā kammaṃ phussa phussa vyantikarissāmīti. Hevaṃ natthi Doṇamite sukhadukkhe...."[169]

From this it appears that once earned, the inheritance of Kaṃma was held to be independent of individual will and supposed to work its way out along its own logic. As a matter of fact, as noticed, will itself was denied.

From the statement just quoted[170] it appears that Kaṃma was considered to be in some way causally connected with Sukha-dukkha. How, then, was it supposed to be related to the triad of Niyatisaṅgatibhāva? Since individual initiative is denied, Niyati probably was considered to be the cause of Kaṃma.

It was considered necessary to exhaust the numerous

---

[167] Often asserted, e.g., Uvāsaga—p. 197; Ib., p. 51. "Natthi uṭṭhāṇe vā jāva parakkame i vā, niyayā savvabhāvā".

[168] Uvāsaga—pp. 196-197.

[169] Ib., 200-201.

To "Sukha" and "dukkha" are, at another place, added "lābha", "alābha", "Jīviya", and "Maraṇa" (B. XV.).

[170] i.e., from the way in which the unalterability of Kaṃma and of Sukha-dukkha are asserted together.

but enumerated types of Kaṃma[171] prior to the attainment of liberation.

Gosāla, in short, considered man bound to the cycle of rebirth by a force—Kaṃma, or Niyati—over which he had no voluntary control.[172]

Ajivaka morality.—On the history of the Ājīvakas and their relations to the Nigaṇṭhas much work has been done by Profs. Hoernle and Barua.[173] The former, after an examination of the evidence, is inclined to agree with the Jinist condemnation of the Ājīvakas and accuses Gosāla of hypocrisy and incontinence.[174] Dr. Barua, on

---

[171] The list in the Sāmaññaphala is not the same as given in the Bhagavatī; for the latter see Uvāsaga—p. 160.

[172] Some of the details of Gosāla's system have already been explained (by Hoernle & Barua) but many remain obscure as, e.g., the enumerations of Kaṃma. The very curious doctrines of the "Trairāśikas", a class of Gosāla's followers, may be noted. According to them the soul (ātman) is dragged down by "krīḍā" and "Pradveṣa" from a state of release (Mokṣa) to a long stretch of Saṃsāra, passes out of it into Release and repeats this cycle endlessly. The released soul is passionless (Suddha) and actionless (Akarmaka) and yet gradually degenerates through the enjoyment of its own position in the same way as an immaculate cloth is soiled through use (vide Śīlāṅka on Sk. 1. 1. 3. 11-12) cf. Syādvādamañjarī, p. 4.

On Ājīvaka Akiriyavāda cf. M. N. I., p. 483. Also cf. "Mā kṛta karmāṇi mā kṛta karmāṇi śāntirvaḥ śreyasītyāhāto maskarī parivrājakaḥ". " (Patañjali, Mahābhāṣya III. 96. ed. Kielhorn). Those mendicants who advocated Kaṃmavāda Kiriyāvāda are placed in the "Nīlābhijāti" (AN. III. 383). The classification is attributed by Ānanda to Pūraṇa kassapa, but that appears a confusion.

[173] ERE I; Pre-Buddhistic Indian Philosophy; JDL II. On the nature of the "Paüṭṭaparihāravāda", while Hoernle agrees with the Jinist ridicule of it (ERE I, p. 263), Barua discovers in it a far reaching theory of evolution (Pre-Buddhistic Indian Philosophy). From the explanation which Abhayadeva gives of the doctrine it does not seem possible to see any profundity in the view nor does it seem possible to turn it into one of the basic doctrines of Gosāla by identifying it with the "Pariṇāmavāda" referred to in the Sāmaññaphalasutta.

[174] ERE I, p. 263; 265.

the other hand, considers these strictures merely sectarian and it appears that he is at least partially right, since he has revealed some discrepancies within the Jinist account.[175]

Determinism and amoralism.—The Buddhists and the Jinists, it appears, regarded the Ājīvakas as amoralists and proceeded to condemn them as immoral in practice. It appears imaginable, however, that one might,—rightly or wrongly—distinguish between the denial of moral responsibility and the denial of morality. One may thus hold, for instance, that although a distinction in fact exists between right and wrong actions, yet one cannot help the actual course of one's own actions. Considerable variety of belief is in this respect possible. We know that the Calvinists and many of the 19th century materialists, though denying the freedom of will in man, did not repudiate the distinction between right and wrong. Of course a conscious or unconscious acceptance of the Kantian dictum that what we ought to do must lie within the sphere of what we can makes a logical transition inevitable from the denial of responsibility to the denial of moral distinctions. But there is no reason to suppose that such an acceptance formed part of the Ājīvaka premisses.

Determinism and immorality.—To justify one's wrong actions, however, it is not necessary to go to the length of denying the objective validity of the distinction between right and wrong. One might simply repudiate free will and responsibility, and the Jinists would suggest that this "rationalization" was in fact the origin of the Ājīvaka-determinism. It is quite impossible to prove or disprove the correctness of the suggestion.

[175] Cf. JDL. II, pp. 12-13.

Ajivaka doctrine Vis-a-vis the Niganthas.—Apart from those relating to practice,[176] the chief differences between the Ājīvakas and the Nigaṇṭhas concerned the nature of will and of the soul. As to the latter, Buddhaghosa informs us that while Gosāla held the soul to be Rūpī, Mahāvīra considered it Arūpi.[177] The precise import of the distinction is not clear.

Among the striking similarities between the two doctrines one may mention the common expression "Sabbe sattā sabbe pāṇā . . . . bhūtā . . . . Jīvā", the division of animals into Ekendriya, Dvīndriya, etc., and the correspondence between the "leśyās" and the "Abhijātis".[178] Belief in the omniscience of the released was also common.[179]

Another variety of Akiriyavada. Purana Kassapa: denial primarily, not of freedom in action, but of action in soul.—The doctrine of Pūraṇa Kassapa was, according to its Buddhist description,[180] amoralist: one might do whatever one pleases without becoming sinful or virtuous. On the other hand, we are told that the doctrine of Pūraṇa was one of "Akiriyā" i.e. one never really acted.

Purana Kassapa, Sankhya, and causality.—The view of this thinker thus appears to have been that ethical distinctions between actions were unreal simply because action itself was unreal. Now the Sk.[181] mentions a somewhat similar view which Śīlāṅka calls Akārakavāda and which he implicitly identifies with the Sāṅkhya

[176] Summarized by Hoernle ERE I, pp. 265-266.
[177] Ib., p. 261.
[178] SBE 45, pp. xxx-xxxi.
[179] Cf. MN. I. 171; B. XV.
[180] Sāmaññaphalasutta.
[181] Sk. I. 1. 13.

view. The identity between the view of Pūraṇa Kassapa and this "Akārakavāda" is probable though not certain.[182] There is little reason to suppose that Puraṇa Kassapa held the doctrine of "Adhicca-samuppāda". In fact, if the Jinist account really refers to the views of Kassapa, and Śīlāṅka is correct in explaining it, it follows that the assumption of Dr. Barua about Adhiccasamuppāda is false, since the Sāṅkhya thinkers were not disbelievers in causality. Dr. Dutt,[183] who agrees with Dr. Barua in this conjecture, shows no grounds for doing so. Events may "have nothing to do with 'soul'" and yet may not be fortuitous in origin.

Still another variety of Akiriyavada—Pakudha Kaccayana—no "interaction" possible.—According to the Buddhist version,[184] Pakudha Kaccāyana believed in seven ultimate substances (Kāyā) existing immutably in emptiness (Vivara). Thus interaction between the four types of matter, sukha, dukkha and Jīva, was impossible, and hence such action as involved interaction, for instance, killing another, was also impossible. The concept of Vivara, it seems, is used in order to explain apparent motion. Since the admission of "Vivara" as a substance will conflict with the initial statement of the doctrine, it appears that "Vivara" is to be understood as merely "non-resistance" hypostatized. However, from Jinist sources[185] we know of what Śīlāṅka calls "Ātmaṣaṣṭhavāda", which resembles the doctrines of Pakudha but in which the existence of Ākāśa is distinctly recognised. Moreover this version omits "Sukha" and "Duk-

---

[182] Cf. Pre-Buddhistic Ind. Phil.—pp. 278-279.
[183] Early Monastic Buddhism I, pp. 35-6.
[184] Samaññaphalasutta.
[185] Sk. I. I. 15. 16; II. 1.

kha" as independent principles, thus having in all only six immutables.

Sankhya or Vaisesika.—Śīlāṅka partly calls attention to the similarity of the view with some parts of the Sāṅkhya system and also refers to some passages of the Bhagavadgītā having a similar import. This "Sattakāyavāda", it may be noted, furnishes an instance of what the Buddhists called "Sassatavāda". Its plurality of substances recalls Vaiśeṣika;[186] its denial of interaction between soul and matter as also the aloofness of soul from sukha and dukkha recall Sāṅkhya.

Kassapa, Kaccayana and the thought-ferment.— Both Kassapa and Kaccāyana, it may be assumed, denied not the appearance but the reality of action. In particular, they asserted that the 'soul' was really untouched by change and hence was superior to good and evil.[187] It is perhaps not too much to imagine that this doctrine was formulated in opposition to that doctrine of "Saṃsāra" which supposed that the soul suffered and was itself responsible for its sufferings. Were not the malady and its imagined causes, both unreal and illusory? Of the later theory of "Paramārtha" and 'Vyavahāra' which reconciled these two views, there was hardly as yet any question, at least there is little evidence for regarding our two philosophers acquainted with it.

We may thus state that whereas Gosāla, or perhaps one ought to say the Ājīvaka school, accepted the process of Saṃsāra but gave of it a new explanation, Kassapa and Kaccāyana, apparently Brāhmaṇas and

---

186 Cf. "This seems to have been a primitive or a popular form of the philosophy which we now know under the name of Vaiśeṣika". (Jacobi—Jaina sūtras—Part II, p. XXIV).

187 This doctrine is clearly found in the Upaniṣads, and is as much Vedāntic as Sāṅkhyan.

hence probably acquainted with Upaniṣadic speculation, were still more radical and proceeded to deny the real existence of the problem itself.

Agnosticism—probably not "evasionist" (cf. "Vikkhepaṃ byākāsi" DN. S. 2).—Another line of thinking current on the subject was agnostic. Sañjaya Belaṭṭhiputta[188] thought that the other world, the "Opapātika" beings, the law of Kaṃma, and the future life of the "released" were matters on which no certain knowledge was to be had.[189] From the Buddhist version it would appear that his agnosticism had no surer ground than that of ignorance. Because the answer was in fact not discovered, therefore it was assumed to be undiscoverable. The ancient Jinist texts too, which refer to similar "Annāṇa" vāda, call at one place a thinker possessing such a view as merely "Annāṇabhayasaṃviggo."[190] Śīlāṅka, however, in his comment on Sk. I. ii. 16 tells us "Tatra ko vettītyasyārtho na kasyacidviśiṣṭaṃ jñānamasti yo tīndriyān jīvādīnavabhotsyate/ na ca tairjñātaiḥ kiñcitphalamasti//" This information would, if authentic, give a different picture of the situation. Ajñānavādins would be, not ignorant and insincere, but convinced agnostics basing their conclusions on critical considerations.[191]

Materialism.—Among some thinkers materialist nihilism (ucchedavāda) held sway.[192] Ajitakesakambalī

---

[188] Jacobi supposes that Mahāvagga I. 23 and 24 refer to the "agnostic" Sañjaya (SBE 45, p. xxix). This is not impossible but that is all one can say.

[189] Sāmaññaphalasutta.

[190] Sk. I. ii. 7.

[191] Cf. the Scepticism of Dīghanakha who said 'Sabbaṃ me na khamatīti" (MN. I 497).

[192] There is mention of "Lokāyatika" views at a few places in the Buddhist canon, though it is not easy to relate them with

was one of them. The similarity between the report of the Sāmaññaphalasutta and Sk. II-1 has already been noted.[193] Pāyāsi-Paësi was another materialist.[194] In the Rāyā Paseṇiya he finds it difficult to abandon his "Bahupurisaparamparāgayaṃ kulanissayaṃ diṭṭhiṃ,"[195] which incidentally reveals his family to have been quite a stronghold of heresy. Both from this Jinist report and the parallel Buddhist version in the DN it is clear that Paësi's disbelief in the 'soul' was on account of its supersensibility which made its detection along ordinary means of observation impossible. In common with Ajita, Paësi denied that anything real could correspond to the "current transcendental ideas."[196] The very vigour of the Agnostic and Materialist views appears to show the abundance with which "transcendental ideas" seem to have cropped up in that age.[197] Buddha's "silences" also presume such a situation.

---

the conception associated with the expression in later ages cf. SN. II. 77; Rockhill p. 44.

"Lokāyata" is one of the three branches of Ānvīkṣikī mentioned by Kauṭalya (I. p. 27).

193 Jacobi op. cit.

194 The chronological position of this thinker is however uncertain.

195 p. 140 (Sūtra 75) (The edition of the Agamodaya Samiti).

196 Cf. Jacobi–loc. cit., cf. the sceptical Prince Jayasena in M. N. III 129.

197 The Āyāraṅga, it may be noted, refers to many problems and answers as futile. Such are "Atthi loe natthi loe, dhuve loe, adhuve...., sāsaye....sapajjavāsiye...., sukaḍetti dukkaḍetti vā, kallāṇetti vā, Pivaettivā, sāhutti vā......siddhitti vā...... nirayetti vā.... (As. I. 8.1.).

This is important not so much for the views mentioned as for the psychological attitude of our author. We seem to contact a mind weary of interminable speculative wrangling. This ought to be remembered in considering Buddha's "silence". A similar situation contributed in the history of Greek philosophy to the Sophist movement, see Zeller (Outlines of the History of Greek Philosophy p. 75).

The Brahmajalasutta.—Many of these views find mention in the Brahmajālasutta though with a difference in form, e.g. the views of Sañjaya appear to be subsumed under those of the "Amarāvikkhepikas". It has been usually supposed that the dogmas mentioned in this text were taken over from contemporary non-Buddhist belief. Dr. N. Dutt combats this opinion saying "The so called sixty-two views are really a systematic exposition of the experiences of a Buddhist monk and have very little to do with the then existing non-Buddhistic opinion".[198] It is of course unquestionable that the sutta under consideration owes much to Buddhist systematization yet the acceptance of Dr. Dutt's view must be qualified by the following facts: (*a*) some of the views mentioned in the Brahmajālasutta can be shown to have been actually held by Non-Buddhist thinkers;[199] (*b*) some views were, according to the sutta itself, believed in because of reason (Takka), not special mystic experience; (*c*) and, finally, a good deal of the "experiences of a Buddhist monk" were the same as of some or the other of non-Buddhist thinkers.

The contents of the Sutta are already well known though it may be remarked that the greater part of the dogmas mentioned relate to the past and the future of the soul and the world. They could hardly have arisen except in an age when the doctrine of Saṃsāra was not as yet clearly and universally established down to its details. Such are many of the Amarāvikkhapika and Uddhamāghātanika views.[200]

---

[198] Op. cit. p. 42 fn. 4.

[199] Cf. the views of Sakuludāyin mentioned M. N. II—32-33; or those in Sk. i. 1.4.6.

[200] Suttas detailing heretical views like those in the Brahmajāla are the Mahānidāna, the Pañcattaya, the Poṭṭhapāda.

The Niganthas.—The Nigaṇṭhas or the Jainas were an already well established sect in the age of Buddha. They claim a hoary antiquity for themselves which seems quite plausible.[201] There is no doubt that they were wholly independent of the Buddhists,[202] and Pārśva at least of their Tīrthaṅkaras is now generally accepted to have been a historical person.[203] They appear to have belonged to the non-Vedic Munis and Śramaṇas who may have been ultimately connected with pre-Vedic civilisation.[204]

Syadvada—a later development.—Although the Jainas have been remarkably conservative, it seems clear that with the passage of time their beliefs changed, tending towards increased complexity and subtlety. To picture their earliest beliefs we must rely on the earliest available texts,[205] and when we find that these are silent about the Saptabhaṅgī Dialectics, for instance, it will perhaps not be unreasonable to infer that this remarkably complex and subtle theory was a later development. It is true that the Bhagavatī and the Pannavaṇā refer to the sevenfold Naya[206] but these texts contain a good deal of later material. There does not seem sufficient reason to see in Sk. Niryukti-Skandha 1, Adhyāya 12, a reference to the Syādvāda, as assumed by Dr. Vidyabhusana.[207] And in any case,

[201] On the "primitive" character of Jaina doctrines, cf. Jacobi's Int. to SBE 45.

[202] SBE 22. INT; SBE 45. Int; IA. 1880, p. 161; cf. CHI. I, p. 152.

[203] CHI. I, p. 153; Uttarādhyayana (Charpentier's Int., p. 21).

[204] See above.

[205] See Appendix.

[206] S. C. Vidyabhusana: A Hist. of Ind. Log., p. 161 fn. 4.

[207] Ib., p. 167. Dr. P. L. Vaidya's edition of the Sk. has "annāṇiya" for "abhāṇiya" (Sk., p. 145).

Bhadrabāhu lived a good deal later than the period we are considering. Dr. Jacobi, assuming without question that Mahāvīra established the Syādvāda, explains this as having been done in opposition to the Agnosticism of Sañjaya[208] but the basic assumption itself is unproved. In fact, Jacobi has himself stated elsewhere that the Jinists do not associate any doctrinal innovation with Mahāvīra. Sañjaya was simply agnostic about transcendental entities, Syādvāda bases itself not only on a dialectical conception of reason, but on a dialectical conception of reality also.[209] The philosophical gulf between the two is wide enough to allow a considerable time interval. In fact, even in so late a work as the Tattvārthādhigama, dialectics is hardly noticeable. It should, however, be remarked that even the earliest Jaina works show a striking love of paradox.[210]

Similarly the simplicity of the earliest texts on cosmology and the atomic theory would seem to show that the extravagant elaboration of these as found, for instance at places in the Bhagavatī, ought to be regarded as a comparatively later development. Similarly, as will come out in the following survey, the earliest state of the doctrine of Karman was much less systematized and clear than that revealed in the later Karmagranthas.[211]

The evolution of Jainism mainly linear.—The conservativeness of Jainism should only be taken to mean that its evolution was much more in a straight line, and,

---

[208] SBE—45, pp. xxvii-xxviii.

[209] See below.

[210] e.g., As. I. 4.2.1: "je assavā te parissayā". On Mahāvīra's love for dilemma see Majjhima Nikāya, I. Abhayarājakumāra sutta; Saṃyutta Nikāya, IV, pp. 323-325; Bhagavatī, 9.6. (sutta) 387.

[211] See below.

where the basic principles were concerned, it was shorter than was the case with its two chief rivals in India. Whatever development there took place was along the multiplication and systematisation of details. On the fundamentals there were few internal dissensions. The followers of Pārśva and of Mahāvīra,[212] the Śvetāmbaras and the Digambaras[213] differed chiefly on practical issues. Whether the Ājīvakas ever really formed a part of the Nigaṇṭhas, as supposed by Hoernle,[214] is doubtful, and the Jinist tradition about Rohagutta's metaphysical originality is justly criticized by Jacobi.[215] That wealth of schism which enriched Buddhism philosophically, the Jainas never appear to have experienced. On the whole, it may be stated that their earliest thought was dominantly practical and ethical, while, much later, they developed a systematic logic and a great predilection for dialectic.

The early Jaina faith in outline.—Mahāvīra's sermons are at one place described to have been about how souls get bound, freed and suffer.[216] At another place the Jinist view is defined as "Kiriyavāda", knowledge of "Attā" and "loga", 'gati' and 'agati', permanence and impermanence, "āsava" and "Saṃvara".[217] The insistence of the Nigaṇṭhas on "Kiriyavāda" comes out from many Buddhist references also, whence their central belief may be thus summarised: through the expulsion (Nijjarā) of Kamma by ascetic practices, one attains to freedom from Dukkha and to omniscience. Ascetic

---

212 See U. XXI.

213 See ERE—IV. 704.

214 Article on the Ājīvakas in ERE.

215 Op. cit. pp. xxxvii-xxxviii.

216 "Jahā jīvā bajjhaṃti muccaṃti jahā ya kilissaṃti"—Nyāyā, sūtra 22. (ed. Āgamodaya samiti.)

217 Sk. I. 12.20-21.

immoderation and an everpresent omniscience—both are ridiculed by the Buddhists.[218]

The Jaina conception of the soul as essentially a transcendent noetic principle.—The difference on the subject of the soul between the later systematic works and the earliest available texts is not fundamental, but merely one of refinement and detail. The soul in its essential nature transcends all possible sensible experience;[219] more, it is not accessible to discursive knowledge either.[220] Any analogical description of it is equally impossible.[221] Thus the soul *'an sich'* cannot be the object of perception, conception, or imagination. This, however, never meant for the Jinists an agnostic position, since from the first they asserted the essential nature of the soul to be knowledge[222] which was, with the growth of philosophical controversy, explicitly declared to be self-luminous.[223] Since the noetic character of Kaivalya was apparently never questioned by the Jainas, it might be safely assumed that this later view was really implicit in the earlier teaching.

That in its pure state a soul possesses infinite know-

---

[218] See below.

[219] "Se na dīhe na hasse—na kiṇhe na nīle....arūvī sattā.. ..se na sadde na rūve na gandhe na rase na phāse...." (As. I. 5.6). According to Buddhaghosa, the Nigaṇṭhas regarded the soul as Arūpī—(Sumaṅgalavilāsinī I. p. 119).

[220] "Takkā jattha na vijjaī maī tattha na gāhiā" (As. loc. cit.). Umāsvāti's own comment on Tattvārthādhigama s. 1.31. "Atha kevalajñānasya pūrvairmatijñānādibhiḥ kiṃ sahabhāvo bhavati netyucyate......" (p. 27 ed. As. Soc. of Bengal). See below.

[221] "Parinne sanne uvamā na vijjaī" (As. loc. cit.); cf. Chap. on Nirvāṇa—on Saññā.

[222] "Je āyā se vinnāyā je vinnāyā se āyā. Jeṇa vijāṇāi se āyā Tam paḍucca paḍisaṅkhāē esa āyāvāī" (As. I. 5.5).

[223] Syādvādamañjarī p. 147.

ledge[224] formed one of the leading dogmas. The "pure" knowledge (Kavalajñāna) of the soul, it was supposed, mirrored the entire universe within itself[225] and later exposition tells us that this omniscience should be considered simultaneous and direct.[226] In it all knowable forms belonging to all time become, as it were, revealed in a single flash, which is, however, not to say that it was a mere momentary knowledge.[227]

Omniscience is accompanied by infinite happiness[228] or perhaps it would be more accurate to speak of an absolute knowledge which is beatific.[229] But this refinement was perhaps not present to the earlier authors.

Later on at least it was held that when freed from the dross of Karman-matter the soul enjoys unhindered power of action.[230] Even in the state of bondage this power is not wholly lost, though its exercise in the absence of true knowledge only leads to Saṃsāra.[231] It

[224] Knowledge here stands for both "Jñāna" and "Darśana". According to later explanation the latter emphasized the general, the former the particular aspects of the object (see Śīlāṅka on Bhagavatī Sūtra 17. ed Āgamodaya Samiti; Syādvādamañjarī. loc. cit. etc.). In some of the earlier Buddhist texts also Ñāṇa and Dassana occur together. What exactly was the most ancient distinction is difficult to determine.

[225] As. I. 8.4; I. 3.4. (with which cp. Pravacanasāra 1.48-49); Ib. I. 1.7.6.

[226] Pravacanasāra pp. 30 ff. esp. p. 50. cp. Bhagavatī sūtra 185, 198.

[227] On the Buddhist ridicule of the Jinist conception of omniscience see AN. I pp. 220-21, MN. II 31, I 482.

[228] Vide e.g. "Arūviṇo jīvaghaṇā nāṇadaṃsaṇasanniyā |
Aülam suhaṃ samvaṇṇā uvamā jassa natthi u. ||

Pravacanasāra pp. 15.26, 76, 86, 87 etc. (Uttarajjhayaṇa xxxvi 67).

[229] See Prav. sā p. 77.

[230] See Prav. sā.

[231] Cf. Prav. Sā "Sā (kriyā)....mohasaṃvalitasya saphalaiva. Saiva mohasaṃvalanavilaye paramadravyasvabhāvabhūtatayā paramadharmākhyā bhavatyaphalaiva." (pp. 164-5). On the

was a cardinal principle with the early Jainas that although man's own actions must be held responsible for his troubles[232] he is yet capable of working out his own salvation unaided.[233] This is what was meant by their calling themselves Karmavādins and Kriyāvādins.[234]

The soul is naturally light and when freed from the downward drag of Karman dwells on the top of the world.[235] According to later exposition its movement upward is instantaneous and rectilinear.[236]

The souls are ultimately many and in various stages of evolution.[237] Their classification and gradation appear to have been important from the beginning. Some souls have become perfect (Siddha) while others are still in the process of Saṃsāra.[238] These latter are

---

other hand B. sūtra 21 states "Vītarāgasaṃjayā akiriyā" cf. Sk. I 8-9.

232 "Attakaḍe dukkhe no parakaḍe no ubhayå" (B. Sūtra 602) whether dukkha is caused by self, or another, or both or none, appears to have been a familiar controversy in the 6th cent. B.C. The Buddhist texts often allude to it e.g. the dialogue with Timbaruka in the Nidana Samyutta.

233 e.g. "Purisā tumameva tumaṃ mittaṃ kiṃ bahiā mittamicchasi" (As. I. 3.3).

Cf. Prav. sā. p. 21 "Svayameva ṣaṭkārakīrūpeṇa upajāyamānaḥ (Ātmā).

234 "Se āyāvāī logāvāī kammāvāī kiriyāvāī ya" (As. I. 1.1).

235 "Aloë paḍihayā siddhā loyagge ya païṭṭhiā |
Ihaṃ bondiṃ caïttāṇaṃ tattha gantūṇa sijjhai ||;
(U. xxxvi-57) also U. xxxiii 83.

236 Tattvārtharājavārtika. pp. 96-7 (ed. Sanātana Jaina Granthamālā).

237 Cf. Śīlāṅka on Sk. II. 2. about the gradation of Ajīvas, Asañjñins, Sañjñins and Siddhas. The beings in the first class neither know (Vidanti) nor feel (Anubhavanti), in the second they feel only, in the third they know and feel, while in the fourth they know only. Evolution is thus, from insentience to pure knowledge.

238 U. xxxvi. 49; B. sūtra 16; cf. Tattvārthādhigama sūtra II—10.

....

grouped in various ways in the earlier texts,[239] but some general features emerge out as common. The four material elements were supposed to be endowed with soul just as much as the plants and the animals. These souls differ according to their powers of motion, sensation and understanding. Thus some are 'Thāvaras', others "Trasas". The division according to the number of senses and that into Pāṇā, bhūyā, jīvā and sattā, are supposed to have been originally Ājīvaka tenets.[240] It is perhaps not insignificant that the As. I.—probably the earliest extant Jinist text—lays the greatest emphasis on "elemental" souls.[241] Perhaps the earliest classification of souls was into the Chajjīvanikāyas.[242]

The Theory of Kamma—The principle differentiating the conditions of the souls is Kaṃma.[243] It is this which forms the leading refrain of the earliest texts and probably represents the most ancient as well as the most original feature of Jinist thought.

How far the later exposition of the doctrine found in the systematic karman works may be considered "early" is a point difficult to decide. According to Jacobi "this karman-theory, if not in all details, certainly in the main outlines, is acknowledged in the oldest parts of the canon and presupposed by expressions and technical terms occurring in them."[244] According to Glasenapp

---

239 See As. I. 1.4; I. 9.1; I. 4.1; U. X 5-15; B. XII. Ud. 10; Sk. II 3; Ib. 1.7.1-2.

240 See Barua, Pre-Buddhistic Indian Philosophy.

241 This links the Jaina soul theory to primitive Animism.

242 Sk. I. 4.4.5.

243 "Adu thāvarā ya tasattāë tasajīvā ya thāvarattāë | Adu savvajoṇiyā *sattā kaṃmuṇā kappiyā puḍho bālè* ||" (As. I 9.1.14) The Uvahāṇasuya in which this verse occurs is admittedly very ancient; "....Kammā nānāvihā kaṭṭu *puḍho* vissambhiyā payā" (U. III 2 ff).

244 ERE VII p. 472.

a final judgment on the problem would be possible only after a comparison of the ideas developed in the Karman works with those of the entire canon. Nevertheless he regards the most important karman doctrines as actually contained in the Siddhānta, "of which any one can easily convince himself, if he but superficially consults the Sthānāṅga Sūtra, Bhagavatī Sūtra, Aupapātika Sutra, Uttarādhyayana Sūtra."[245] Further the Karmagranthas claim to have been based on the Diṭṭhivāya tradition referred to elsewhere also.[246]

An earlier stage than in the Karmagranthas likely.-- It should however be noted that such technical terms and descriptions as imply a developed theory of Karman are generally confined to the later parts of the canon. Thus U.XXXIII describes the eight varieties of Kaṃma, and calls it "Paësagga". The Bhagavatī gives much technical information at various places, e.g., VIII.40.8 describes the relation between the eight varieties of Kaṃma and the twenty-two Parīsahas, VIII. ud. 10 considers the interrelations of the Kaṃma-classes, 1.1.12 quotes a gāthā[247] containing a number of technical expressions relating to Kaṃma-processes.[248] On the other hand As.I, Sk. I and the earlier portions of the U give a very general and much simpler picture. Such occasional references as for example to "Daṃsaṇāvaraṇa" in Sk. I. 15 1. do not prove much.[249] But there is a dialogue in the Nāyā sūtra 62 according to which the Jīvas

[245] The Doctrine of Karman in Jaina Philosophy. Eng. tr. p. XV.

[246] op. cit. pp. XIV-XV.

[247] cf. B. sūtra 14. Similarly Ib. sūtra 7, 21.

[248] B. Sūtra 34 states that "Joga" leads to "Pamāya" and that to "Kaṇkhāmohaṇijja".

[249] So U. IV. i......"*Uvasantamohaṇijjo* sarai porāṇiyaṃ jāïṃ"; Ib. xxxii 108.

heavy with the eightfold Kaṃma descend into the world, and the dialogue looks otherwise ancient. More intensive search will perhaps reveal a few other ancient fragments of a similar character. The problem is thus not finally soluble, although general probability as well as the weight of available evidence is towards assuming an earlier stratum of the theory of Karman, simpler and less systematic than in the later Karmagranthas.

Its simplicity.—This earlier stage of the theory seems to have consisted of a few simple ideas repeated often and in picturesque ways. The soul, ignorant[250] and sticky with the passions,[251] engages in selfish activity, causing injury to other living beings[252] and contacting matter of which there takes place an influx into the soul.[253] It is this matter that has entered into a sort of

---

[250] "Kiriyā Kajjai Pamāyapaccayā joganimittaṃ ca" (B. III. 152).

[251] Termed usually Kaṣāyas. U. XXIII 36, 38, 53 speak of five kaṣāyas Ib. 48 speaks of "Bhavataṇhā" which is more familiar in connection with Buddhism.

According to Tattvārthādhigama Sūtra VIII-2 "Sakaṣāyattvājjīvaḥ karmaṇo yogyān pudgalānādatte". In substance the idea is found in the oldest texts—Thus As. I. 4 speaks of Āyāṇasoyagaṭhiye bāle"; Ib. 2.6.1 which mentions "Āyāṇiya" (with "Āyāṇa" may be compared Buddhist "upādāna"). The cause of "grasping" or attachment is declared to be "Rasa" (U XVIII 3. Ib. xx 39), or "Rūva" or "Chaṇa" (As. I. 5-3), or "Guṇa" (As. I. 1.5., Ib. I. 2.1.; U. IX 36. The relation of this "Guṇa" to the "Guṇas" of Sāṅkhya needs investigation), or Kāma and Chanda (As. I. 6. 1. Ib. I. 6. 4. etc.). As. I. 3. 2. 3, says: "Nivvinda Nandiṃ. . . ." which is remarkably "Buddhist" in expression.

[252] Violence was considered so intrinsic to action that Kamma and Daṇḍa were almost interchangeable terms. See MN. sutta 56. (also SBE 45, p. XVII) Cf. As. I. 1. 4.; I. 4, 3, 1, I. 5. 3. 3.; Sk. I. i, 2. 3.

[253] Samavāyaṅga sutta 5 enumerates five Āsavadāras—Micchatta, Aviraï, Pamāyā, Kasāyā, and Jogā. Thāṇaṃga-sūtra 419 agrees with this. Tattvārthādhigama sūtra VIII—1—calls these five "Bandhahetus". It defines Āsrava as "Kāyavāṅmanaḥkarmayogaḥ"— (VI—1—2). *(Contd.)*

union with the soul as a result of the latter's ignorant and impulsive activity which is termed "Kaṃma". It drags down the soul, obscures its faculties and is the cause of the varied experience of misery in the world.[254]

Whatever is experienced within "Saṃsāra" is in the final analysis painful. It was asserted that "Kiccaṃ Dukkhaṃ phussaṃ dukkhaṃ kajjamāṇa kaḍam dukkhaṃ kaṭṭu kaṭṭu pāṇā bhūyā jīvā sattā veyaṇam veyaṃti."[255] In this connection the occurrence of the term "Uvahī" may be noted. Under the form "Upadhi" it is found in early Buddhist literature also.[256] According to As. I 9-1-15 "Sovahie hu luppāī bāle". As. I.3.1. tells us "Kaṃmuṇā uvahī jāyāī B.XVIII.7.633 is more precise and speaks of three kinds of "Uvahī", viz. Kaṃma°, sarīra°, and Bahirabhaṇḍabhattovagaraṇa°. The term seems to have referred in a general way to the various limitations under which the soul acts and lives in the world.

Although the term Kaṃma is sometimes used loosely so as to comprehend the causal activity of the soul also,[257]

Paṇhavāgaraṇa distinguishes between Āsrava and Āsravadvāra regarding the latter alone as fivefold. . It also uses the term Aṇhaya.

[254] The early theory of Kaṃma is thus summarized simply in U. XXXII 7. "Rāgo ya doso vi ya kaṃmabījam,
Kaṃmaṃ ca mohappabhavaṃ-vayanti |
Kammaṃ ca jāīmaraṇassa mūlam,
Dukkhaṃ ca jāīmaraṇaṃ vayanti ||"

[255] Thāṇaṃga sūtra 166-7.

[256] See Chap. on Nirvāṇa.

[257] At some places in the canon we are given classifications and enumerations of "Viriya"—B. III 150; Sk. II. 2.

Since all "action" (Kiriyā) in the state of ignorance, whether intentional or otherwise, must lead to the accumulation of Kamma, an "action" was held sinful by the Jinists even in the absence of a corresponding motive behind it. This distinctive doctrine was ridiculed by the Buddhists. cf. Sk. II. 4.

yet it is more frequently applied to the resultant substantial product in which matter enters from outside the soul. Thus Kaṃma is often compared to or just called "Raja".[258] This realistic conception has sometimes been called particularly primitive. It may be noted that sin and guilt were for the Orphic "as for the Greek generally, conceived as material and physical".[259] Hence Orphic asceticism included physical purifications and restraints.

The later elaborate theory of Kaṃma which describes it in detail according to Prakṛti, Sthiti, Anubhāga and Pradeśa has already been clearly and concisely summarised in the forementioned work of Glasenapp and hence does not need to be treated here.

Thus bound by Kaṃma the soul wanders in Saṃsāra.[260] It might lead a sub-human or a human life. Very good actions might cause it to be born in heaven while evil ones might lead it to hell. On hell, especially the early Jaina texts, are fond of dwelling.[261]

Gati.—Thāṇaṃga sūtra—462 has a curious theory of which the age is difficult to determine. According to it "Pañcavihe Jīvassa ṇijjāṇamagge—pāehiṃ urūhiṃ uṛeṇaṃ sireṇaṃ savvaṅgehiṃ." These make the soul

258 U. VII. 8; Sk. I. 2.1.15. cf. As. I. 5.3; U. III. 11, 20; Sk. I 2.2.1; The association of Rajas with Rāga and Karman is also found in Sāṅkhya. Between this meaning of Rajas and that common in Vedic literature a bridge still remains to be built.

259 Mclure—The Early Philosophers of Greece, p. 35.

260 The nature of the soul in bondage is thus described in the Pravacanasāra (p. 175) "Tamhā Ṇāṇam Kaṃmaṃ phalaṃ ca ādā muṇeyavvo". And these are "Ṇāṇaṃ atthaviyappo kaṃmaṃ jīveṇa jaṃ samāraddham | Tamanegavidhaṃ bhaṇidam phalatti sokkham va dokkham va ||" (Ib., p. 173). The soul in bondage is thus simply the soul with its faculties partly obscured by Kamma.

261 U. VII 10. (cf. the form of expression with that in Īśopaniṣad—3); Sk. I. 5 (Ib. I. 5.2.5 perhaps only a variant of Ib. I. 5. I).

respectively Nirayagāmin, Tiriyagāmin, Maṇuya°, Deva°" and Siddhigatipajjavasāṇo. The question, it may be remembered, interested the Upaniṣadic seers also.[262]

The way out: Samvara or discipline.—To cross the misery of Saṃsāra it is necessary for the soul to stop the further influx of Kaṃma and expel its past accumulation. The former process is called "Saṃvara" and implies in practice principally the five great vows.[263] Before Mahāvīra, however, it was, in expression at least, fourfold.[264]

Non-technically, Saṃvara is simply self-restraint,[265] and in this more general form too it is frequently advocated in the earliest texts. Thus Ātmābhinigraha is admired (As. I.3.4.) while Āśā and Chaṇda are condemned (Ib-4). In what is possibly a genuine quotation, Mahāvīra is supposed to have taught constant alertness.[266] The precept may be compared with the "last advice" of the Buddha. Celibacy,[267] non-violence[268] and detachment in general[269] are other ingredients of self-discipline.[270]

---

[262] Kaṭha 6. 16; Praśna 3. 7. [263] Sk. I. 1. 4.13; U XII, 42.

[264] "Cātuyyāmasamvara" is spoken of in the celebrated passage of the Sāmaññaphala (Dīgh N.); "cāujjāma" is stated to have been held by the followers of Pārśva on whose doctrines see U. XXIII; B. sūtra 76; Sk. II 7. cf. Hoernle in ERE—Ājīvakas"; As. I. 8. 1. speaks of three Yāmas only.

[265] According to U. I. 16 the way out consists of "Saṃyama" and "Tapas".

[266] As. I. 2. 4. 3. "Uyāhu vīre 'Appamāo mahāmohe'."

[267] U. XV describes ten Bambhacerasamāhiṭṭhānas; cf. Samavāyāṅga 15; As. I. 5-4 considers woman as Temptress; so Sk. I. 4. ff.

[268] As. I. 4.1. Ib. I. 8.1; Sk. I. 11.9; Ib. 1.9.11 ff. etc.; cf. Jaina—Outlines of Jainism, p. XL.

[269] As. I. 3. 1; Ib. 5; U XIV 18, etc.

[270] The regulations relating to Samiti, Gupti and Parīṣaha, etc. are generally considered parts of Saṃvara (See Tattvārthā-

The way out: Nijjara or self mortification.—But this is only preliminary to "Nijjarā" which implies in practice self-mortification.[271] The extreme character of Jinist asceticism is well known. Winternitz observes that there is a remarkable contradiction between "this exaggerated love of death on the part of the Jaina saint, and on the other hand the equally exaggerated fear of killing any living thing.....[272] Perhaps it is true that "we must recognize a distinctly psychopathological element in much of the self-torture and self-abnegation that goes by the name of asceticism".[273] Yet, and in spite of Winternitz, it must be admitted that the Jinist practice in this respect is at least consistent with Jinist theory. What is outwardly the death of the saint is really the last stage in his attainment of freedom. If body is regarded as a principle of limitation, some form of "Suicide" must be regarded as ultimately desirable.[274]

It may be mentioned that under special circumstances even in Brahmanic thought, suicide was permitted to the Vānaprastha.[275] But "Tapas" in Jainism is to

---

dhigama sūtra—IX 1.2); vide U. XXIV on Samitis and Guptis; B. XXV. 7. 800 on sāmāyārī, so U. XXXI, Ib XXII on the Parīṣahas, Ib II on twenty-two Parīṣahas. Cf. Samavāyāṅga—16 on ten samaṇadhammas.

271 On Nijjarā cf. AN. I. pp. 220-1; MN. Devadahasutta cf. U. xxviii—35.

272 Hist. of Ind. Lit. II p. 452.

273 ERE. II. p. 63.

274 On suicide see As. I. 8.4, 5, 6; I. 8.8. It is permitted to a monk if he deems himself unable to live up to the discipline. If he is unable to conquer the senses he may take poison; if sickness is overpowering, he may leave off food, or commit suicide through "Ittiriya". cf. Dr. Upendra Thakur, The History of Suicide in India.

275 See Manu VI 31; Yāj. III 55. One may mention in this connection the practice of suicide at certain specially holy spots. which appears to be very ancient—vide Mbh. Śalyaparvan, 39. 33.4.

be sharply distinguished from "Tapas" in the Vedic literature. The latter has little to do with mortification. It seems to have meant some sort of spiritual "energizing" which gave one "creative power".[276]

Mahavira's asceticism.—The Jaina monk engaged in austerities imposed severe restictions on his food,[277] drink, clothes, sleep and society. Mahāvīra himself renounced cold water for more than two years.[278] And, we are told, he left off the use of clothes in the second year of his asceticism. Wandering in Lāḍha, Vajja and Subbha for over thirteen years he had no fixed abode.

He also renounced bathing, cleaning the teeth etc. and took on special penances like silence, walking and meditating with eys fixed on a limited extent of space, cultivation of utter solitude, sleeplessness, constant meditation, forbearance etc.[279]

Ascetic practices.—U.XXX divides 'Tava' into external and internal, explaining each as sixfold. The former consists of Aṇasaṇa, Avamoyariya, Bhikkhāyariyā, Rasapariccāo, Kāyakileso, and Saṃtīṇayā; the latter consisted of Pāyacchitta, Viṇao, Veyāvacca, Sajjhāo, Jhāṇa, and Viosagga. This classification is practically the same as in the later systematic treatise Tattvārthā-

[276] See K. Chaṭṭopādhyāya—Presidential Address to Sect. 1. All India Oriental conference Ninth session. pp. 40-1— (Separate reprint); later, the meaning changed. "Tapas" as clearly cathartic in the Yogadarśana (see Vyāsa ad YS. II. 1, 32, 43). Śaṅkara in his commentary on the Vedanta sūtra (III. 4.20) takes it to mean primarily self-mortification (Kāyakleśa) "Tapaścāsādhāraṇadharmo vānaprasthānāṃ Kāyakleśapradhānatvāt tapaḥśabdasya tatra rūḍheḥ. Bhiksorhi dharma indriyarsaṃyamādilakṣan naiva tapaḥśabdenābhilakṣyate" (l. c.).

[277] Cf. "The outstanding feature of early Orphic asceticism was the prohibition of animal food" (ERE II 8.80).

[278] As I. 9.1. Cf. U II. 4. Nor was fire to be lighted (Sk. I. 7-6) cf. MN. I. 376.

[279] As I 9.

dhigamasūtra—9.19.20. Thus although as such it cannot be taken to be very early yet in substance most of these practices are referred to in older texts.[280]

The conclusion.—The three planks of the early Jaina world-view, thus, are the conception of an immaculate spiritual substance, of a material principle of defilement, and of an ascetic process of purification. All the three are interwoven in the close synthesis of a theory of Saṃsāra.

A Note on some later development.—In this early stage of the Jinist teachings there is as yet little evidence to suppose the existence of some of those metaphysical doctrines which became important later. Such are—the doctrine of several kinds of bodies,[281] of the systematic division into ontological categories,[282] and the complex "atomic" theory.[283] Of the antiquity of the fivefold division of knowledge it is difficult to be certain. In U.XXIII.3. Kesi is said to have been "Ohināṇasuë". The term "Manaḥparyāyajñāna" finds expression in early Buddhist literature also. The term "Kevalajñāna" is perhaps as old as Jinism itself. Owing to the importance of tradition "Śruta" was probably early recognised as a distinct source of Knowledge. There is therefore nothing against supposing the fivefold division to be very old. U. XXVIII is fully acquainted with it. So is Thāṇaṃga-sūtra 463.

The theory of the Leśyās is, as generally supposed, probably derived from the corresponding theory of the

---

280 See As. I. 5. 4; Sk. I. 15. 6; U. I. 10; Ib. XXIX; Ib. I. 6. 16; Sk. I. 8. 26.

281 Cf. B.' I. 45; VII. Ud. 9.

282 Cf. B. II 118-25 (on the Atthikāyas); Ib. XIII. 4.481; U. XXXVI, Ib. XXXVIII; B. X. Ud. 1.

283 Cf. B. VIII Ud. 1; XII. Ud. 3-4; XX. 4.667; XI Ud. 10.

Ājīvakas.[284] The early Buddhist conception of the four-fold Kaṃma,[285] which is found also in the Yogabhāṣya,[286] may be compared.

[284] Vide U. XXXIV.
[285] AN. II 232-3.
[286] On YS. IV. 7.

CHAPTER X

THE LIFE OF BUDDHA

Sources.—A complete biography of Buddha is not to be had in the Pali canon. Four suttas in the Majjhima, however, describe the days of his wandering in search of Truth.[1] In several more suttas spread over the four Nikāyas and the Mahāvagga there are references to Buddha's Enlightenment.[2] The Mahāvagga further attempts to narrate the history of the days following the sambodhi, just as the Mahāparinibbāna sutta pieces together fragments relating to Buddha's last days and tries to build a continuous narrative.[3] In the Mahāpadāna sutta one finds that the attempt to schematize Buddha's life theologically is already far advanced.[4] Besides, there are other incidental references in the Nikāyas which shed some light on Buddha's personality.

Much later is the sketch presented in the Nidāna Kathā. Still later, and of only hagiological importance, is the Pali poem Jinacarita, while Mālālaṅkāra vatthu is a quite modern work of uncertain date.[5]

An early form of the Sanskrit tradition is visible in the collection of legends in the Tibetan scriptures, especially the Vinaya. The most important have been translated into English by Rockhill as Life of the Buddha. Mahāvastu, belonging to the Vinaya of the Lokottaravādins, contains much legendary material for Buddha's

---

[1] Suttas 26, 36, 85, and 100.

[2] See below.

[3] For the composition of this sutta, see above, Ch. on DN.

[4] See above, Ch. on DN.

[4a] Cf. Frauwallner's view that the core of the Vinaya was "enclosed by a biography of the Buddha" (The Earliest Vinaya and the Beginnings of Buddhist Literature, p. 52). On this see my comments in Bauddha Dharma Ke Vikas Ka Itihas.

[5] Translated by Bigandet under the title, The Life or Legend of Gautama —See Rhys Davids, American Lectures p. 87.

biography.[6] Lalitavistara, in its present form a Mahāyāna sūtra but containing some clearly old passages, gives a continuous narrative of Buddha's life.[7] The Abhiniṣkramaṇa sūtra, existing only in a Chinese translation, has been published in an abridged translation in English by Beal as The Romantic Legend of Sakya Buddha. It agrees in the main with the Mahāvastu.[8] Finally, the Sanskrit epic-Buddhacarita of Aśvaghoṣa—may be mentioned.

The Point of View.—It seems that the earlier disciples of Buddha paid much less attention to his life than to his teachings, and were inclined to regard him as essentially a human being, a Śākya, a Gautama, who, through his own efforts, became Awakened, and finally, at his death, entered a mysterious state beyond common comprehension. He was remembered as a Great Ascetic, a Great Sage; his Dhamma was what remained on earth after his death as the source of inspiration for his followers. The recollection of Buddha's life played a small part in the practice of Dhamma, and hence little attention was devoted to the compilation of his historical biography. Within a century, however, the situation began to change through the gradual apotheosis of Buddha (see below), and accounts of his life were embellished and systematised in accordance with the requirements of Buddhological theories. Modern historical enquiry has resuscitated the earlier human point of view.

Certain evidence for Buddha's life is small. Only the leading events and features can be historically deli-

[6] Cf. Winternitz—Ind. Lit. II p. 240. The nucleus of the work is placed in the 2nd cent. B.C. (Ib. p. 247).

[7] Cf. Ib. 248.

[8] Thomas, Life p. XX.

neated. The task has already been attempted by several scholars.[9] In the present study, however, a special standpoint has been adopted, viz., that of considering the leading events of Buddha's life in the light of the psychology of saints and prophets and of trying to determine the influence of his life on his doctrines.

Birth.—The date of Buddha's birth is now usually fixed at 563 B.C.[10] The place of his birth would have been the chief city of the Sakyas, Kapilavatthu,[11] the ancient site of which was probably near the place where the Lumbini P.E. of Aśoka has been found.

The Sakyas.—The Sakyas are described as proud Khattiyas of pure descent,[12] though at the same time the Brāhmaṇa gotra of Gotama is ascribed to them.[13] On the other hand, the tradition of close inter-marriage associated with them suggests some non-Aryan affinities.[14]

The Sakya territory was spread over the lower slopes of the Himālayas, and included, beside Kapilavatthu, the towns of Cātumā, Sāmagāma, Khomadussa, Silāvatī, Meḍalumpa, Nagaraka, Ulumpa, Devadaha and Sakkara.[15] Devadaha was the town next in importance to Kapilavatthu.[16] Politically, the Sakyas were practically independent till Viḍūḍabha invaded them.[17] The administrative and the more important judicial business of

---

9 Thomas, op. cit.; Rhys Davids, op. cit., Lecture III; Oldenberg—Buddha.

10 Thomas, op. cit., p. 27, fn. 1; Winternitz, op. cit., p. 597

11 Rhys Davids, op. cit., p. 90.

12 D. I. Ambaṭṭhasutta, Jāt. I. 88 "Sākiyā nāma mānajātikā mānatthaddhā".

13 Thomas, op. cit., pp. 22-23, where a possible explanation is discussed.

14 Ib. cf. Rhys Davids, op. cit., p. 91.

15 C.H.I., p. 175.

16 N. Dutt, Early Monastic Buddhism I, p. 174.

17 C.H.I. I, pp. 181-182.

the clan was carried out in public assembly, at which young and old were alike present.[18] The headship of the state was vested periodically in an elected chief entitled Rājan.[19]

Economic life was simple, and rested on villages surrounded by rice fields, pastures and forests.[20] Large cities like Bārāṇasī, Sāvatthī and Vesālī were apparently not included in Sakyan territories.[21] In this background the story of Buddha's having had in his early life three different palaces for the three seasons does not appear very plausible.[22] This may represent a beginning of the later tradition which makes Buddha the son of a King.[23] The growth of the ideal of the King of Righteousness might also have contributed to this development.[24]

Family.—The detailed and conflicting genealogies of Buddha with which later works present us[25] are quite unknown to the Nikāyas.[26] There is no means of testing their truth. From the Mahāvagga narrative, however, the name of Buddha's father appears to have been Suddhodana. Mahāpajāpati Gotamī is mentioned at several places in the Vin. and the Nikāyas,[27] but her relationship with Buddha is not explicitly specified in the latter. Similar is the case with Daṇḍapāṇi.

---

[18] Ib., p. 176. [19] Ib., p. 177.
[20] Ib. 200ff; Rhys Davids, Buddhist. Ind., 44f.
[21] Buddh. Ind., p. 34f.
[22] AN. I. 145ff; MN. sutta 75.
[23] Cf. Rhys Davids, op. cit., pp. 91-92.
[24] See Rhys Davids, Hibbert Lectures, pp. 129-140.
[25] Thomas—op. cit., 24-26.
[26] For the Nikāyas, see Brewster—The life of Gotama the Buddha, pp. 103-104. Also Sn. Nāḷakasutta, verse 7; DN. pt. II, p. 7 (Nāg. ed.), where the name of the mother is given as Māyā.
[27] Vin. II 253ff; AN. IV 274ff; Ib. I. 25; MN. III. 253ff. See Malalasekara, D.P.P.N. II 522ff.

Early life.—The miracles attending Buddha's birth and listed in the Acchariyabbhutadhammas have importance only for the history of Buddhology.[28] The story of the prophecy of Asita has little claim to be regarded authentic.[29] On Buddha's education the earliest records are just as silent as they are on the name of his wife or wives, a point regarding which later traditions contradict each other exceedingly.[30] Rāhula figures as a monk at several places in the Nikāyas,[31] but is not called Buddha's son. Only in Mahāvagga is a person of that name so described and his mother is spoken of without being named.[32]

Abhiniskramana.—At the age of twenty-nine Buddha "went forth" into the homeless state.[33] Later traditions assert that the crisis came on suddenly and was caused by the first sight of old age, sickness, death and an ascetic.[34] Sudden conversions are doubtless not unknown in religious history[35] but the evidence for

---

28 Thomas, op. cit., 29ff.

29 Ib. 38ff. where the different versions are compared.

30 Thomas, op. cit., pp. 48-50. The Tibetan Vin. speaks of three wives—Yaśodharā, Gopā and Mṛgajā (Rockhill, op. cit., 20-24). Gopā is mentioned as the wife of the Bodhisattva in Lalita Vistara (I. 157).

31 See Malalasekara DPPN. II, pp. 737 ff.

32 Brewster—Loc. cit.; cf. Jāt. I, p. 58.

33 Thomas, op. cit., p. 60 fn. 1; Rhys Davids, op. cit., p. 96; cf. Brewster, op. cit., p. 45.

34 Nidāna Kathā, Jāt. I, p. 59; LV I, p. 187ff (ed. Lefmann) Budd. carita. III. 27, 40, 54, V. 16; Rockhill, op. cit., 22, Catena, p. 132; Brewster, op. cit., pp. 15-18.

Wassiljew sees political intrigue behind Buddha's abandoning home-life! (Der Buddhismus, vol. I, p. 12).

35 W. James—The Varieties of Religious Experience—pp. 217ff where conversion would include not only Abhiniṣkramaṇa but also Sambodhi. Abhiniṣkramaṇa was only a step towards full "conversion" (cf. Ib., p. 171 fn. 1). See also Pratt—The Religious Consciousness, p. 128 fn. 6. Theologically, to be converted "is to receive grace......to gain an assurance" (James,

believing Buddha's "renunciation" to have been an instance of this kind is not convincing. The contradictions and miraculous elements which the later accounts contain may not be essential to them,[36] but it seems difficult to believe that the "Bodhisattva" could have lived for twenty-eight years without encountering sickness, old age, death and asceticism. The silence of the Nikāyas over the story deepens our doubt. Further, the earliest accounts of the "renunciation" show clearly that their authors were ignorant of the episode of the Four Signs as narrated in later writings. The Sn. simply says "Cramped is this household life, the home of dust. Free as air is going forth. Thus seeing he went forth."[37] This description, however, is quite conventional and has little biographical significance. The Ariyapariyesanā sutta in the MN. claims to record as a reminiscence of Buddha that before he was fully enlightened, himself "subject to birth, old age, disease, death, sorrow and corruption", he sought "what was subject to birth, old age, disease, death, sorrow and corruption".[38] Then perceiving the wretchedness of these states, it occurred to him "to seek the incomparable security of a Nibbāna free from birth, old age, disease, death, sorrow and corruption?"[38] Afterwards, "while yet of tender age, with the black hair of a lad in the fulness of youth, just entering manhood, against the wishes of weeping parents,"[38] he had his hair and head shaved off, put on the yellow robes and went forth from the home to the homeless

p. 189) and this would correspond to "Niyāmappatti" which occurs when one attains to the stage of the "Stream-Winner" (Sotāpanna) cf. Points of Controversy–App. on Niyāma.

[36] See Thomas, op. cit., pp. 57-58.

[37] Brewster, op. cit., p. 43.

[38] Brewster, op. cit., pp. 23-24.

state. Thus he became "a recluse, searching for what is good, seeking the peerless way of desirable peace. . . ."[38] A sutta in the AN. tells us how Buddha at first dwelt in luxury and how through reflection over the subjects of old age, sickness and death he lost all pride of youth, health and life.[39]

It is quite intelligible that meditation on the fact of old age, illness and death should have induced Buddha to renounce secular life. This simple tradition appears to have become transformed into the picturesque story of later times.[40] A factor that aided the transformation may be found in the popular usage which called old age etc., "divine messengers" (Devadūtas).[41] It was now supposed that the gods actually arranged for Buddha the sights of an old man etc. so that he might reflect on the ills of life. This was for the later story a necessary deus ex machina. The apprehensive parents of Buddha are made to place him in such secluded luxury that he could get out of it only through divine intervention. The exaggerated description of the Bodhisatta's seclusion and luxury at home served the purpose of supplying a striking background for his later life. Literary effect rather than historical fidelity dominates the whole treatment.

Even as a boy Buddha seems to have been of a serious, meditative temper.[42] He must have early seen wandering mendicants in his home town, "the place of the tawny-clad" (Kapilavatthu)[43] and had probably

---

39 Ib. pp. 5-6, cf. Buddhacarita V. 14.

40 Thomas, op. cit. pp. 50-51, 58.

41 AN. I. 138, 142, MN. II. 75, III. 179.

42 MN. I. 247; Lalita Vistara I, p. 263; LV. I 128ff seems to be a later invention based on the traditions just referred to. Cf. Chap. on the Way.

43 See chap. on Vedic Background.

heard about their disparagement of the world. A definite problem seems to have gradually shaped itself before him. "Alas! this world has fallen upon trouble. There is getting born and growing old and dying and falling and arising, but there is not the knowing of an escape from Suffering, from decay and death."[44] Buddha's quest thus had two closely associated aspects: on the one hand, he sought the extinction of the passions and desires for this impermanent, unsatisfactory world; on the other, he wanted to attain to eternal peace. He sought the way to "detachment, to absence of passion, to cessation, to abatement, to higher knowledge, to full enlightenment, to Nibbāna."[45] His quest was for "what is good—the peerless way of desirable peace" (Kiṃkusalagavesī anuttaraṃ santivarapadaṃ pariyesamāno).[46]

It was thus under the stress of a definite seeking that Buddha "went forth" into the homeless state.[47] The precise circumstances under which the actual Abhiniṣkramaṇa took place are no longer ascertainable. The decisive change was precipitated much later than adolescence, but there is no reason to believe that it was a sudden revolution. Intellect and will appear to have played a much larger part in Buddha's conversion than emotion.[48] It was not the weak man's sudden flight from the

[44] Brewster, op. cit., p. 40.

[45] Ib., p. 25.

[46] MN. I. 163; cf. Rockhill—op. cit., p. 24.

[47] According to Mrs. Rhys Davids Buddha never became a monk. The Paribbājakas were merely wandering students, like those of mediaeval Europe (Sakya p. 121).

[48] Cf. Pratt. op. cit. p. 151ff. Herzberg sees in the Buddha legend an illustration of his theory that the leading factor in the lives of great philosophic thinkers is the frustration of basic impulses as far as their satisfaction in normal ways is concerned. (The Psychology of Philosophers pp. 203-4) Cf. Mrs. Rhys Davids on Gotama as a man of will. Original Gospel, p. 14. Also Oldenberg—Buddha, p. 132 fn.

world caused by an emotional crisis, but the quest of something higher by one who had tasted all the joys which life could offer and found them wanting. Buddhist theology, in the spirit of modern psychology, interprets it to have been the final upshot of a long period of anterior preparation.[49]

The Noble Quest (Ariyapariyesana).—Then followed several years of restless wandering and seeking. The names of only two teachers under whom Buddha sought spiritual instruction are mentioned in the Nikāyas. They are Āḷāra Kālāma and Uddaka Rāmaputta.[50]

---

[49] See Ab. K. IV avant—propos iv. ff. the Nidānakathā tells us that the great being who ultimately became Gotama Buddha took the resolve to become a Buddha during the time of Dīpaṅkara Buddha (Jāt. I. 13). He was advised to cultivate the Buddhakārakadhammā or the ten Pāramīs (Ib. 20-4), in the practice of which were passed more than a hundred thousand cycles (Kappas)—Ib. 44; M. S. A. IX 1.2.

[50] M. N. Ariya pariyesanā & Bodhirājakumāra-sutta. Āḷāra Kālāma is obviously different from Bharaṇḍu Kālāma who is at one place spoken of as an old fellow-student (Sabrahmacārin) of Gotama (see chap. on AN) Aśvaghoṣa ascribes to Āḷāra doctrines which partly resemble the Sāṅkhya (Budd. Carita—canto XII); we are, however, quite in the dark about the source he relies upon.

A Rāmaputta is spoken of as a Titthakara in AN. II. 180. According to DN. III. 126-7 a Rāmaputta interpreted "Passaṃ na passatīti" to mean "Khurassa....talam passati-na dhāram". This is condemned. The point controverted is not clear. SN. IV. 83-84 quotes a saying of Uddaka Rāmaputta: "Idaṃjātu Vedagū Idaṃ jātu sabbaji Idaṃ jātu palikhitaṃ Gaṇḍamūlaṃ palikhaṇīti". It is declared, however, that he was not justified in making the statement.

The Lalita Vistara speaks of Arāḍa Kālāpa and places him at Vaiśālī (I. 238-9). The other teacher of the Bodhisattva is named Rudraka Rāmaputra and placed at Rājagṛha (Ib. 243). It also tells us that before meeting Ārāḍa the Bodhisatta had stopped at the hermitage of the Brāhmaṇī Padmā and the Brahmarṣi Revata (Ib. 238). At Rājagaha Buddha is supposed to have met Bimbisāra, Rockhill op. cit. p. 27; Sn. pabbajja°, vv. 4ff; Lalita Vistara I. 240ff, where the meeting is placed after that with Ārāḍa (In Rockhill it is placed earlier).

Under them Buddha learned to attain to the third and fourth "immaterial trances" (Arūpa Samāpattis) respectively. The trances were, however, considered unsatisfactory by him since they did not lead to the quiescence of passions, and "higher knowledge" (Abhiññā), and thus failed to answer his quest. The 'immaterial trances' are obtained by the withdrawal of the mind from the world of objects, till it rests in emptiness. This is the state of 'Nothingness' or Ākiñcanya. When consciousness becomes so subtle that although its existence continues, it cannot yet be discerned, the further state of 'Neither-consciousness-nor-unconsciousness' (Naivasañjnānāsañjñāyatana) is reached. Āḷāra Kālāma taught the earlier stage, Uddaka Rāmaputta the later one. In themselves, these trance states only create a temporary cessation of mental functioning; so that sooner or later one must emerge out of them. Unless the light of supreme Prajñā has dawned, the mere practice of mental quiescence cannot lead to lasting freedom from suffering.[51]

Padhana.—Passing through the land of Magadha, Buddha approached the town of Uruvelā. Here he "saw a well placed plot of ground a serene dense grove, a clear flowing stream, suitable for bathing, refreshing, all about were villages in which to go for alms."[52] Here it struck him that no amount of spiritual striving could kindle knowledge in a mind wet with desires and pas-

[51] See Yogasūtras I. 19-20 and the comments thereon by Vyāsa, Vācaspati, and Vijñānabhikṣu. Very illuminating are the comments of Hariharānanda on these sūtras in his Bengali Comy. Pātañjala Yogadarśana, pp. 47ff. (Published Calcutta University 1949). See also Ab. K. VIII. 5ff, which distinguishes the 'anāsrava' states of meditation from the other varieties.

[52] Brewster—op. cit. p. 26; cf. LV. I. p. 261.

sions.[53] He thereafter set to practice effort (Padhāna). At first he sought to control the mind by a frontal assault. He is described to have gritted his teeth and pressed his tongue to his palate. He found, however, that the procedure resulted in excessive heat in the body and much unrest. After this he tried concentration with held breath, but discovered that "violent winds", sharp pains, and burning created disturbance.[54] Finally he tried fasting and found out that it led to weakness.[55]

Enlightenment.—Thus having convinced himself that he had as much of austerities as anyone else and yet had not attained to the goal, Buddha abandoned the ascetic path.[56] He recalled to himself his early experience in Jhānic concentration[57] and shed his fear that

---

[53] This is the meaning underlying the three "similes" (Upamās) which occur in the Nikāyas (MN: Bodhirājakumāra°; SN. II. Nid. Sam (see Chap. on SN.) MN. sūtra, 36 as well as Lalita Vistara (I. 246ff). The text of the latter is here clearly a "Sanskritization" of some Prākṛta original. See the comy. of Vyāsa on YS. II. 1. on the rôle of Tapas in Yoga.

[54] At one place at least it is reported that Buddha suffered in later life from "Vāta" (SN. I. 174). According to Buddhaghoṣa it was due to his austerities (Comy. on DN. III. Saṅgītisutta).

[55] Brewster, op. cit., p. 32; Jāt. I, pp. 66. 7; Lal. Vist. I, pp. 250 ff. The term "Āsphānaka" used in the last appears to have resulted through the "Mis-sanskritization" of some Prākṛta original corresponding in fact to Sanskrit "Aprāṇaka". The resemblance with Pali is in these sections of the LV again very close although the incident about Māyā (LV. I 252-53) is peculiar to the latter.

[56] Cf. "Then he realised the truth of the medium course, that like the man, who would discourse sweet music, must tune the strings of his instrument to the medium point of tension. . . . ." (Beal, Catena, p. 133). On asceticism and mortification, and on the "lute simile", see Chap. on the Way.

[57] "Tassa mayham—etadahosi Abhijānāmi kho panāhaṃ pitu Sakkassa Kammante sītāya jambucchāyāya nisinno vivicceva kāmehi—pe—paṭhamajjhānaṃ upasampajja viharatā, siyā nu kho eso maggo bodhāyāti, Tassa mayham—satānusāri viññāṇaṃ ahosi Eso'va maggo bodhāyāti." (MN. I. 247)

all happiness including pure or non-sensuous happiness was bad.[58] To strengthen himself, he resumed the taking of food, at which his companions left him in disgust.[59]

Through the practice of Jhāna Buddha obtained Enlightenment which consisted in the intuitive knowledge of Reality in its twofold aspect and spent several weeks enjoying the bliss of emancipation.[60] It has been suggested, though unconvincingly, that the tradition of Buddha's having attained Enlightenment under the "Bodhi tree" is just a piece of popular legend or myth.[61]

Cf. Lalita Vistara I, p. 263—"Tasya me—etadabhavat. Yadāhaṃ Piturudyāne jambucchāyāyāṃ niṣaṇṇo Kāmairviviktaṃ....prathamaṃ dhyānamupasampadya vyāhārṣam Yāvaccaturthadhyānamupasampadya vyāhārṣam. Syātsa mārgo bodhes ....tadanusāri ca me vijñānamabhūt. So mārgo bodheriti". This furnishes a particularly striking instance of the almost literal agreement of the two sources at places. It may, however, be noted that while the MN. speaks of only the first Jhāna, Lalita Vistara speaks of all the four Dhyānas. Cf. Buddha carita, V. 7ff., where also only the first Dhyāna is mentioned. Cf. Diwakar, R. R. Mahāyogi, pp. 126-7, where parallels are adduced from the lives of other mystics.

[58] "Kiṃ nu ahaṃ tassa sukhassa bhāyāmi, yaṃ taṃ sukhaṃ aññatreva kāmehi aññatra akusalehi dhammehi." (MN. Loc. Cit.). This clearly refers to Jhāna-sukha and suggests that in Buddha's memory jhāna and sukha were closely associated. It further suggests that his early Jhāna experience did not extend to the fourth Jhāna as Lalita Vistara would tell us, since in the last two Jhānas "Sukha" is transcended and yields place to hedonic neutrality—upekkhā. The mistake of Lalita Vistara could have easily originated in the practice of repeating mechanically a formula in full where part of it occurs.

[59] These were the Pañcavaggīya Bhikkhus—MN. Pt. II, p. 289 (Nāg. ed.); LV. I, p. 264 which speaks of "Pañcānāṃ bhadravargīyāṇāṃ." But cf. Thomas, op. cit., p. 80.

[60] On the stages and nature of the experience of Sambodhi see chap. on Nirvāṇa. On the Five Dreams of the Bodhisatta prior to Enlightenment see AN. III. 240-2.

[61] See Thomas, op. cit., p. 68 fn. 1 who points out in this connection the silence of the Majjh. narrative over the tree, which is mentioned in Mahāpadānå (DN. II) as Assattha. The

Contest with Mara.—According to Thomas "the whole story of the contest with Māra is a mythological development......It is not found in the pali canon except that phrases in some of the later parts, such as Māra's army (Mārasenā), Māra's assembly (Māraparisā), victor of Māra (Mārābhibhū), imply that the legend was then known."[62] Oldenberg has already combated a similar opinion expressed by Senart.[63] Rhys Davids has attempted to see in the Māra—story "a subjective experience under the form of objective reality". The struggle with Māra was really a psychological struggle with secular temptations.[64]

Māra is at places identified with Death (Maccu)[65] and this agrees with the etymology of the word. This meaning is also implicit in those texts where Māra waits to receive the dying Arahant.[66] His fetters (Pāsa) are spoken of.[67] Māra has thus some features likening him to Yama.

On the other hand, in the Māra Saṃyutta of the

---

tradition, however, must be much earlier than this sutta where "enlightenment under a tree" has already become a "dhammatā".

[62] Op. cit., p. 74 for a comparative analysis of the various versions of the 'Padhānasutta" of the Sn. see Ib., pp. 71-73.

[63] Buddha—pp. 101, 107.

[64] Cf. Thomas., op. cit., p. 230.

The following were the tempting visions according to Tibetan tradition: Devadatta subduing Kapilavastu, seizing the Palace, and crushing the Śākyas; apparitions of Yaśodharā, Mṛgajā, Gopā, Devadatta and the Śākyas; Enlightenment as impossible; Māra's three daughters—Desire, Pleasure and Delight—(Rockhill—op. cit., p. 31). In the light of Rhys Davids' hypothesis these would be very well explained as the final resurrection of former fears and attachments.

[65] SN. I. 156, Sn. Verses 357, 581, 587, etc.

[66] See the narrative in SN. I. 4. 3. 3.

[67] Maccupāsa—Sn. 166; Mārabandhana—Dhp., 37, 276, 350.

SN, he figures mainly as the Tempter. Here he is similar to the latter-day conception of "Kāma".[68]

These two meanings are closely connected in Buddhist thought, for it is the forces of worldly desire which confine man to the realm of the mortal. To attain Enlightenment it is necessary to vanquish these forces or Māra. Rhys Davids' psychological explanation has, thus, a strong plausibility. It was probably around this nucleus that legends and myths clustered to evolve into various Māra-stories.[69] If, however, this is correct, a satisfactory explanation of the Majj. narratives over Māra would need to be offered. Perhaps it is a mistake to assume that these narratives were intended to be full.[70]

First words of the Buddha.—The earliest version of the first words uttered by the Enlightened is to be found in the Udānas beginning with "Yadā have pātubhavanti dhammā etc." reported in the Mahāvagga and the Udāna. The Dīghabhāṇakas, and Buddhaghosa, however, call the Dhammapada-verses beginning "Anekajātisaṃsāraṃ" etc., the "first words".[71] Lalitavistara gives two quite different versions of the "first Udāna".[72] Still another is presented by the Tibetan Vinaya.[73] These conflicts in the evidence would be curious if a definite memory

[68] Cf. History of Philosophy, Eastern & Western I, p. 189, Note 52.

[69] Cf. Oldenberg—Buddha—p. 106 fn. 1. On the combination of Death and the Tempter in the Yama of the Kaṭhopaniṣad, see Ib., p. 100; Söderblom—The Living God, p. 95.

[70] See chap. on the stratification of the MN. where these suttas are discussed. Cf. Jāt. I. 11 ff. for a late though detailed version of the Mara conflict.

[71] Thomas, op. cit., p. 75.

[72] LV, p. 351, 355; 356. The former of these occurs in the Mahāvastu which, however, has also another quite different Udāna (Thomas, op. cit., pp. 76-78).

[73] Rockhill, op. cit., p. 33.

of the "first words" of the "Buddha" had actually existed in a generally known manner in pre-sectarian Buddhism.

Events after Sambodhi.—According to Vinaya, Buddha remained four weeks at the Bodhi-tree after obtaining Enlightenment. Later authorities make the period one of seven weeks, while there are indications in the Lal. Vist. and the Tibetan Vinaya to the effect that the period was of one week only.[74] After this comes in the Mahāvagga narrative the acceptance of Tapussa and Bhallika as lay disciples, which is followed by the description of Buddha's hesitation to preach and the final decision to engage in preaching at the entreaty of Brahmā.

In the Majjhima narratives, on the other hand, there is no reference to either the several weeks spent after Enlightenment in the enjoyment of the bliss of emancipation (Vimuttisukha) nor to the conversion of Tapussa and Bhallika. There hesitation and Brahmāyācana[75] follow Sambodhi immediately.

Entreaty by Brahma.—This episode regarding Buddha's doubts about the capacity of men to understand his doctrine and his being reassured by Brahmā is in striking contradiction to Buddha's supposed attainment of omniscience.[76] Mrs. Rhys Davids suggests that the narrative is a later confused version of an earlier tradition about Buddha's having received an inspired mandate from a deity to preach the Dhamma according to which each man was, like the lotuses in the pool, at a different stage of growth towards full efflorescence but

[74] Thomas, op. cit., p. 85.

[75] These two events (hesitation and entreaty by Brahmā) are also described in the Mahāpadāna sutta (DN) and the Brahmasaṃyutta (SN).

[76] A point on which the Buddhist tradition is unanimous.

would so "become" as to "come to know".[77] This interpretation, however, departs so far from the text—in which little confusion is noticeable—as to appear quite arbitrary

Dr. N. Dutt remarks that "it is not probable that Buddha who became a sarvajña (Omniscient) could have required Brāhmā's intervention for ascertaining that there were some suitable hearers."[78] Buddha's vision was beyond concept and hence incommunicable in words. "He determined that he would speak about the path only and not about what is Nirvāṇa or the highest Truth."[78] The explanation is plausible, but it seems to us that the real significance of this episode is in relation to the spiritual as distinct from the historical birth of Mahāyāna. As the 'Sun of Knowledge' dawns, the 'Lotus of Compassion' blooms and with that is dispelled the temptation of soteriological egoism, of retiring from the world without setting in motion the wheel of Right.[79] As Plato pointed out, the education of the human race will remain incomplete unless the process of spiritual ascent is followed by a deliberate Descent (Katabasis) of 'those who have seen the light' into the dark world of common humanity.[80] Buddha's hesitation and Brahmā's entreaty represent a symbolic and dramatized version of Buddha's temptation to be content with his own salvation. His "hesitation" reflects the birth throes of the Bodhisattva-ideal. The urge to enter Parinirvāṇa is at many places in the Nikāyas explicitly called a temptation due to Māra.[81]

---

[77] What was the Original Gospel—pp. 16ff.

[78] Op. cit., p. 100. [79] Cf. Söderblom—op. cit.

[80] Republic 520 C. 1. cf. Sri Aurobindo's Life Divine II (2) pp. 1151-2.

[81] As e.g., in the Mahāparinibbānasutta (DN. II). According to one tradition, Buddha hesitated fearing the power of evil

At Banaras.—According to the Majjhima narrative, having decided to preach, Buddha thought of the proper recipients of his message. His former teachers Āḷāra and Uddaka had died recently, but the Five Bhikkhus were still alive and at Banaras. All this information was received by Buddha apparently in a psychic manner. On his way to Banaras the Pañcavaggiyas were at first hostile but were converted.

The silence of this narrative over the "first sermon" is hardly sufficient to regard the latter as wholly legendary.[82] The scepticism of Mrs. Rhys Davids over the authenticity of the "first" and "second" sermons in their present form appears more reasonable.[83] The "second sermon" as in Pali, it may be remembered, is not to be found in the Lalitavistara.[84]

After this point there is no continuous narrative of Buddha's activities in the Nikāyas till the last days of his life which form the subject of DN., Sutta 16.

Narrative in the Vinaya.—The narrative in the Vinaya, however, goes further and describes the conversion of Yasa and his friends, the sending forth of the first missionaries, the conversion of Kassapa—the leader of the Jaṭilas, the delivery of the Fire sermon, the conversion of King Bimbisāra and the conversion of Sāri-

would prevent many from embracing the truth of his doctrine. " (Beal-Catena. p. 134). The idea seems to be the same as in "Rāgarattā na dakkhanti tamokhandhena āvaṭā". cf. Lalita Vistara 1.397.

[82] Cf. Thomas op. cit. p. 86; cf. Kern "Buddha" I. p. 247ff. (French Tr.). See also above, Chap. on SN.

[83] The Birth of Ind. Psy. pp. 196-7. See also Chap. on the stratification of SN. The Tibetan canon contains at least six versions of the First Sermon (Rockhill op. cit. p. 37).

[84] For the absence of the Anattasutta in the Lalita Vistara cf. Dutt. op. cit. p. 103.

putta and Moggalāna—the former disciples of Sañjaya.[185] In the conversion of the Jaṭilas the miraculous is prominent. This is hardly the usual method of Buddha as revealed in the Nikāyas.[86]

Spread of Buddha's Doctrine.—A systematic description of the traditional account of the days of Buddha's ministry has been given by Kern and Thomas and Dr. N. Dutt.[87] The tradition, however, is for the greater part post-canonical. Though in some cases the inventions of the Commentators can be detected,[88] the authenticity of much of the information supplied by them must remain uncertain in the absence of earlier evidence. Some information about the spread of Buddha's doctrines during this period may, however, be gleaned from the Nikāyas and the Vinaya.

Kasi.—The first scene of Buddha's activities was Isipatana, near Bārāṇasī. If the account of the Vinaya is trusted it was the rich Seṭṭhi class of the place which was foremost in espousing Buddha's doctrines. According to tradition Buddha passed the first Vassā at Isipatana and passed through it after the twelfth on his way from Verañjā to Vesālī.[89]

Magadha.—Magadha was among the leading Kingdoms of the age. At Uruvelā Buddha is supposed to have converted a band of matted-hair ascetics (Jaṭilas)

---

[85] See Brewster—op. cit. p. 67ff. whether this Sañjaya is to be identified with the agnostic of that name is impossible to decide.

[86] Cf. Thomas op. cit. p. 91.

[87] Manual of Ind. Buddh. pp. 23ff; Life—Chaps. VIII & IX: N. Dutt, EMB. I. Ch. XI.

[88] Thus see Thomas (op. cit. pp. 102-104) on the story of the conversion of Upāli, Bhaddiya, Anuruddha, Ānanda and Devadatta. Brewster op. cit. 142ff.

[88a] Dr. Wagle has exhaustively listed the people addressed in the Nikāyas and their social affiliation, op. cit. pp. 192 ff.

[89] Dutt. op. cit. p. 138.

dwelling in forests and devoted to fire-worship.[90] To them was delivered at Gayā the Ādittapariyāya.[91] Senses, sense-objects, sense-contacts, and sense-perceptions are all blazing under the three fires of Rāga, Dosa and Moha. There is a quaint irony in this Fire sermon being delivered to Fire worshippers.

Rajagaha.—At Rājagaha is supposed to have taken place the conversion of Bimbisāra, the king of Magadha, who is reported to have presented Buddha with the Bamboo-park (veḷuvana).[92] Ajātasattu does not appear to have been favourably disposed towards Buddha at first.[93] Towards the end of Buddha's life, however, he is supposed to have experienced a change of heart as a result of listening to the Sāmaññaphala-sermon, although the force of the sin of parricide prevented him from obtaining the spotless eye of Righteousness.[94]

Other places in Magadha.—Nālandā appears to have been a small but prosperous village near Rājagaha. It was apparently a Nigaṇṭha stronghold.[95] Pāṭaligāma was only a village, although it was being fortified towards the last days of Buddha.[96] In the village of Ekanālā is placed the conversion of Kasibhāradvāja.[97] The distinguished female lay-devotee Nandamātā also lived here.[98]

---

[90] Brewster op. cit. p. 79ff.

[91] Ib. 87 ff.

[92] Ib. 89. Dutt op. cit. p. 150 fn. 1.

According to Ṭhāṇaṅga (Sūtra 693) King Seṇiya Bhimbhisāra was destined to be born in hell; later, however, he was to be born as King Mahāpaüma and follow the Jaina faith.

[93] This is implicit in SN. I. Kosala Saṃ; Brewster op. cit. pp. 147ff; Dutt. op. cit. p. 142 fn. 2.

[94] DN. sutta 2.

[95] Malalasekara, DPPN. II. p. 57.

[96] DN. 16.

[97] SN. I. pp. 172-3, which occur in the SN. also.

[98] Dutt. op. cit. p. 154.

Among the Brāhmaṇas of Magadha Buddha does not seem to have been very successful.[99] Among the heretical Paribbājakas of Magadha he is stated to have come into contact with many.[100] The lay devotees of Magadha included Gāmaṇīs, Seṭṭhis and Gahapatis, princes and princesses.[101]

Kosala.—King Pasenadi of Kosala appears in the Nikāyas as an admirer of Buddha[102] to whom Queen Mallikā was also devoted.[103] Princesses Somā, Sakulā and Sumanā too figure as interested in Buddhist doctrines.[104]

From the Seṭṭhi class of Kosala the two most important names are those of Anāthapiṇḍika and Visākhā—the daughter-in-law of Migāra (though called Migāramātā). The former is reported to have made the gift of the Jetavana vihāra, the latter of the Pubārāma Migāramātupāsāda.[105]

Among the rich and influential Brāhmaṇas of Kosala who gave their adherence to the new faith the names may be mentioned of Jānussoṇi, Aggika Bhāradvāja, Dhānañjani, Pokkharasādi, Lohicca, and Caṅki.[106]

Sāvatthi was a favourite resort of the Paribbājakas esp., the Ājīvakas. Queen Mallikā had provided them with an Ārāma. The most notable converts from among them were Vekhanassa and Poṭṭhapāda.

---

[99] Ib. pp. 140-141.

[100] See Ib. p. 144; Malalasekara, DPPN. on Nigrodha, Dīghanakha, Anugāra, etc.

[101] See the list compiled by Dr. Dutt op. cit. p. 147.

[102] SN. I. Kosala Saṃ; MN. II. 123; cf. AN. V. 65ff.

[103] SN. (Loc. cit.); MN. II. 106ff; cf.. A. II. p. 202.

[104] MN. Kaṇṇakatthala sutta.

[105] Malalasekara—Dict. of Pali proper Names II. 628; I. 963f.

[106] Dutt op. cit. pp. 161-2; Malalasekara, DPPN. passim.

Evidence has been brought forth to show that the Śākyas were not at first favourably disposed towards Buddha.[107] The ordination of Rāhula is, however mentioned in the Vinaya.[108] The tradition relating to the conversion of Suddhodana and the mother of Rāhula is of later date.[109]

Licchavis.—Just as Sāvatthi was the head-quarter of the Ājīvakas so was Vesāli of the Niganṭhas who were consequently the chief opponents of Buddha's work among the Licchavis.[110]

Other Clans.—The most notable success of Buddha here was the conversion of the Niganṭha upāsaka Sīha—a Licchavi general.[111] From among the Bhaggas of Suṁsumāragiri came the three distinguished lay adherents—the parents of Nakula[112] and Bodhirājakumāra.[113] Suppāvāsā Koliyadhitā has been praised as the best of the "Bestowers of excellent food" (Paṇītadāyikā).[114] The two most well-known converts from among the

---

107 Dutt op. cit. pp. 170-1; cf. Jāt. I. p. 88 where it is reported that the proud Sākiyas would not bow to Buddha thinking "Siddhatthakumāro amhehi daharataro amhākaṃ kaniṭṭho bhāgineyyo putto nattāti". And Buddha is forced to bend them by a miracle.

108 Brewster op. cit. pp. 103-4; Jāt. I. pp. 91-2.

109 Thomas op. cit. pp. 97ff.

110 Cf. Rockhill—op. cit. pp. 65-67.

111 Vin. I. 1.223f; AN. IV. 179f; cf. A. IV 79ff; Ib. III. 38f. Buddha's admiration for the Vajjis is mentioned in the Mahāparinibbāna sutta. He is reported to have given them sound political advice—Ib. A. IV. 16. Some have seen in the Vesālian constitution the proto-type of that of the Saṅgha. Jayaswal—Hindu policy I. 45-8; cf. R. C. Majumdar—Corporate Life in Anct. Ind. pp. 226-7. Cf. Gokuldas De, Democracy in the Buddhist Sangha, Pande, Bauddha Dharma Ke Vikas Ka Itihas, pp. 136 ff.

112 AN. II. 61; III.295; IV. 85, 268, SN. IV. 116. Dutt. op. cit. p. 181.

113 MN. II.91; Malalasekara op. cit. II p. 316; Vin. II. 127 f.

114 AN. I.26. II 62; Malalasekara—op. cit. II. 1222.
On Kakudha Koliyaputta see AN. III. p. 122.

Mallas were Dabba Mallaputta and Cunda Kammāraputta.[115] In Aṅga Buddha is reported to have disputed with the Brāhmaṇa teacher Soṇadaṇḍa of Campā.[116] Some discourses of Buddha have been placed at Kosambī,[117] Verañjā[118] and the Kuru villages Kammāsadhamma[119] and Thullakoṭṭhita.

Buddhism and the various social classes.—It appears thus that geographically the sphere of Buddha's activities embraced principally the kingdoms of Kosala and Magadha. Among the lay disciples an important part was played by the moneyed and ruling classes. Women too figured prominently, as nuns and as lay-devotees.[120] The religious pretensions of the Brāhmaṇas were attacked;[121] but the opposition was ideological and sec-

---

[115] Malalasekara DPPN. I. 879, 1059f.

[116] DN. I. sutta, 4.

[117] DN. I.159; MN. I. 320, III. 152 Ghoṣitārāma has been discovered by the A. U. Archaeological Expedition to Kauśāmbī, directed by Sri G. R. Sharma.

[118] AN. IV. 172, 197 ff.

[119] DN. II. 55; SN. II. 92; DN. II. 290; MN. I. 55; MN. II. 26, etc.

[120] On the story of the entry of Women into the Saṁgha—see Thomas—op. cit. pp. 108-10. He is not correct in stating that "there is not the slightest historical evidence" for the existence of non-Buddhist female ascetics in the time of Buddha. The earliest Jaina works speak of Nigganthīs (Kalpasūtra) and there is a Buddhist reference to Ājīvakinīs in the Aṅguttaranikāya. Besides, there are no obvious reasons for considering the story of the Sundarī paribbājikā very late (see Malalasekara op. cit. II. p. 1216).

[121] Ambaṭṭha Sutta, Soṇadaṇḍa°; Tevijja°; Madhura°; Assalāyana°; Esukāri°; AN. III. 221 ff: DN. III. 81-3, AN. II. 42-43; Vin. I. 36; AN. Tikaṇṇa° and Jānussoṇi°. The protestant strain is clear in these discourses. The protest was against caste distinctions based on birth, sacrifice, and similar merely external rituals like bathing, bowing to the sun etc. Everywhere the emphasised contrast is of character and "internal worth" in a forceful way. SN. I. 183 advocates a dip in dhamma as against Purity through Water (Udakasuddhi). With this may be com-

tarian, not social. In fact, an attempt was made to re-interpret the word "Brāhmaṇa" in a spiritual manner.[122] Many Brāhmaṇas joined the new order, and there were followers from the lower classes too. Primarily the founder of an ascetic and monastic order, Buddha had a message for the laity too. The Saṁgha or Order of Monks was indifferent to caste and all could join it on a footing of equality, except for government servants, debtors, slaves, certain kinds of proclaimed criminal offenders and those suffering from certain incurable physical defects. These could not become Buddhist monks.

Buddha's personality.—A few individual traits of Buddha's personality stand out unmistakably. He was of a meditative turn of mind-Jhāyin, Jhānasīlin.[123] His love of silence was most noticeable. The Paribbājakas are often made to refer to him as "Appasaddakāmo.[124] His assemblies were notably free from noise.[125] He recommended to his disciples the Noble Silence

---

pared the admonition addressed to Sundarikabhāradvāja in the MN. These ideas become significant when placed by the side of such Vedic texts as Tai. Saṃ 1.1.1. "Apośnātyantarata eva medhyo bhavati". SN. IV. 117-8 contrasts ancient and contemporary Brāhmaṇas, mainly on the score of character (This sutta is perhaps late since it is supposed to have been delivered by Mahākaccāna in the Avantis). Dr. Keith's opinion on the subject is quite unconvincing (B. P. p. 121) cf. Lalita Vistara I. p. 138, 318.

[122] Apart from the texts just cited—SN. I. 168; Sn. Vāseṭṭha°; Dhp-Brāhmaṇavaggo; with SN. I. 168 "Mājātiṃ puccha caraṇaṃ puccha"—cf. "Kim Brāhmaṇasya pitaraṃ kimu pṛcchasi mātaraṃ śrutaṃcedasmin vedyaṃ sa pitā sa pitāmahaḥ" (Kāṭh. Saṃ. p. 307).

[123] See Chap. on "Way".

[124] e.g. DN. Pt. I. p. 208 (Nāg. ed.) Malalasekara op. cit. I. p. 806.

[125] MN. Sutta 77; DN. Pt. I. p. 60 (Nāg. Ed.).

(Ariyo Tuṇhībhāvo).[126] Once he was so displeased with the Bhikkhus at Cātumā on account of their noisiness that he asked them to leave the place.[127]. As a matter of fact, the love of silence is merely a corollary of the love of Jhāna.

Associated with Buddha's love of Jhāna and silence, is his love of Solitude.[128] Some of his adverse critics went so far as to state "Suññāgārahatā Samaṇassa Gotamassa Paññā, aparisāvacaro Samaṇo Gotamo, nālaṃ, sallāpāya, so antamantāneva sevati."[129]

The compassionate nature of Buddha has been famed down the ages, and it seems inconceivable that it should have been without a very real foundation in history.[130]

The independence of Buddha's character is another noticeable feature. It is reflected in his abandonment of asceticism, critical attitude towards belief on faith alone,[131] exhortation to self-reliance,[132] emphasis on the the realization of truth by one's own self[133] and the admiration of democratic constitutions.[134]

---

[126] MN. I. 161. cf. SN. II. 184 and Mrs. Rhys Davids, Sakya p. 185.

[127] MN. I. 456.

[128] Cf. Sakya. p. 163.

[120] Kimura's translation of "Suññāgarahatā Paññā" as "Perception in the wisdom of Emptiness" is ludicrous. (Origin of Mahayana Buddh. p. 99).

[130] Cf. MN. Suttas 4, 12, 58. In the last occurs "atṭhi Rājakumāra Tathāgatassa sattesu anukampāti". See also the Chap. on the Way to Nirvāṇa.

[131] Mm. Vidhushekhar Bhattacharya—Basic Conception. pp. 9-12. Also, Chap. on "Way"; cf. Keith B. P. pp. 13-14.

[132] "Attadīpā Viharatha...." SN. III. 42, V. 154, 163, DN. Pt. II. p. 83 (Nāg. Ed.); DN. Sutta 26, §1.

[133] The Dhamma is "Paccattaṃ Veditabbo Viññūhi....." (e.g. D. II. 224).

[134] This is implicit in the admiration for the Vesālian constitution (DN. Sutta 16) and the fundamental character of the

Buddha was opposed to dogmatism which he sought to replace by a profoundly based critical attitude. He recognised certain problems to be logically indeterminate and on these preserved silence.[135] Buddha was very practical. He wanted action and not mere speculations which can in no way lead one to the goal.[136]

The greatness of Buddha's personality is manifest from the fact that no other individual has left as strong an impress on the history of Indian culture as he. He has been regarded as the very embodiment of knowledge (Bodhi) and Love (Karuṇā).

Life and Teachings.—The survey of Buddha's life throws considerable light on his teachings. The starting point of his thought was a definite problem which he enunciated clearly for the first time in Indian philosophy: "Life" is subject to various limitations typified by disease. old age and death. Being full of misery (dukkha), it cannot satisfy the quest (Pariyesanā) for supernal peace (Anuttaraṃ santivarapadaṃ). How is that Peace (Nirvāṇa)[137] to be obtained?

The starting point is thus dukkha. That gives to the Buddhist quest, from the narrow worldly standpoint, a certain negative character. What is sought after is

---

organisation of the Buddhist Saṁgha, which was held together not by the force of individual authority, but by that of the Dhamma (see MN. III, pp. 9-10).

[135] On his method of preaching—See Dutt, op. cit., Chap. X.

[136] Mm. Vidhushekhara Bhattacharya, op. cit., p. 12; Dutt, op. cit., p. 100.

[137] Sogen draws attention to the fact that Śāntaṃ Nirvāṇaṃ not only means the pacification of dukkha but also the transcendence of words (Systems of Buddh. Thought—pp. 28ff). Śānti in fact should be equated to "Prapañcopaśama", Prapañca being the same as "Nāmarūpa", whether these be taken to mean simple "Name and-form" as in the Upaniṣads and a few early Buddhist texts or "Mind and Matter" as in later Buddhist explanations.

conceived primarily in terms of "Peace" (Śānti) rather than bliss (Ānanda). This is in contrast to the usual Vedic and Upaniṣadic formulations of the Goal.

Buddha attained to the end of his quest through knowledge (Sambodhi) born of the practice of Jhāna. It is logical to infer that it must have been a similar Path he taught to others. It was the force of Compassion (Karuṇā) which laid on him the mission to preach the Dhamma which stood for transcendent as well as empirical truth, and for the moral and religious life appropriate to its realization.[138]

On the metaphysical nature of the Goal or Nirvāṇa, Buddha preferred to keep silent, since he found it incommunicable. But he emphasized the non-ultimacy of mind and matter and taught the way to their transcendence. In brief, Buddha taught that Saṃsāra is dukkha, Nirvāṇa is peace ineffable, the Mārga is primarily Jhānic practice. To this one might object—But that is making Buddha "monkish". Did he not preach a world-Gospel, a course of better life for Everyman? Kern had already said of Buddha that "son action révolutionnaire..... consista.....dans une proclamation populaire de métaphysique et de morale qui avaient cours dans les écoles."[139]

However, the popular element in the earliest Buddhist teachings appears to have been slight. No doubt Buddha is supposed to have lectured to householders on Dānakathā, Sīlakathā, Saggakathā, etc. but all that was only meant as preparation. It was the apotheosis of Buddha which alone made Buddhism popular. and that came later.

---

[138] See below.

[139] Histoire du Bouddhisme dans l' Inde—Vol. I, p. 3; cf. Burnouf—Introduction—pp. 137-8.

PART III

STUDIES IN EARLY BUDDHIST DOCTRINES

CHAPTER XI

SUFFERING AND ITS ORIGIN

Ariyasaccani.+—The scheme of the Four Truths, it appears, has an apt application to the teachings of Buddha, even though he may not have actually propounded it. Stcherbatsky has pointed out that there is nothing distinctive in the Four Truths, the meanings of which change according to the content poured into them.[1] It is true that the formula occurs in non-Buddhist systems also;[2] still, it must be remembered that nowhere else has such an importance been attached to it as within the Buddhist circle of thought.[3] It appears thus that the scheme arose originally within Buddhism and only later became current philosophical *Kôine*.

Modern scholars have generally held that the Four Truths belong to the most ancient state of the Buddhist doctrine.[4] Mrs. Rhys Davids has, however, shown some

+ Words like Duḥkha, Pratītyasamutpāda and Nirvāṇa are given in their Pali or Sanskrit forms according to context.

[1] Stcherbatsky—the Conception of Buddhist Nirvāṇa p. 55. fn. 1. He quotes from the Nyāyavārtika (ed. B. I. p. 13): "Etāni catvāryarthapadāni sarvāsvadhyātmavidyāsu sarvācāryairvarṇyanta iti".

[2] Thus in the Yogabhāṣya on YS. ii-15; Nyāyabhāṣya on Nyāyasūtras 1.1.1; Sāṅkhyapravacanabhāṣya—p. 6 (Chowkh. ed).

[3] Even so late and independent an author as Dharmakīrti says "Tāyo vā catuḥsatyaprakāśanaṃ" (Pramāṇavātika: 1.148 ed. with Manorathanandin's comy. in JBORS. 1938) cf. "Though the Hīnyānists and the Mahāyānists did not agree regarding the conception of Śūnyatā, there was no disagreement among them in regard to the fact that Buddha preached the Four Truths (Āryasatyas) and the Causal Law (Pratītyasamutpāda)." (N. Dutt. Aspects of Mahāyāna Buddhism, p. 49).

[4] Thus Thomas—Thought—p. 42; Franke—ZDMG. 1915, pp. 470-71; Winternitz II. p. 2; cf. Beal—Catena p. 55.

cause for doubting it.[5] As *titular items,* the Four Truths do not appear in the Fourth Nipāta of the AN, or the Saṅgīti Sutta of the DN.[6] It may be noted that they do not form part of the list of the thirty-seven Bodhipakkhiya Dhammas which are supposed to have been the dying charge of the Master.[7] They doubtless occur in the present form of the first sermon, but it is possible that this form of the first sermon is the result of patchwork.[8] When this possibility as well as the omissions mentioned above—which have as yet not been satisfactorily explained[9]—are taken into account, it seems difficult to be certain that the scheme of the Four Truths, made popular by Buddhism, belonged to its earliest stage.

Their connection with the medical science.—It has been suggested that the fourfold formula in question was taken over by the Buddhists from the medical science.[10] Buddha has been called the Vaidyarāja,[11] and a "Vyādhisūtra[12] existed which explicitly compared the four truths to the medical fourfold of disease, diag-

[5] JRAS. 1935 p. 723; cf. also What Was The Original Gospel? App., in answer to Winternitz—Visva Bharati Quart. (NS) II. 1. p. 47.

[6] Original Gospel p. 139.

[7] DN. sutta 16, 3.50.

[8] See Mrs. Rhys Davids in JPTS. 1924-7. p. 244; Deussen (quoted, loc. cit.); contra, Oldenberg (quoted loc. cit.). See above Chap. on SN.

[9] See Mrs. Rhys Davids Int. to AN. VI. (Index); "Original Gospel"; App; Winternitz loc. cit.; see below, Chapter on "The Way to Nirvāṇa".

[10] Kern—Manual p. 47; La Vallée Poussin, JRAS. 1903 pp. 578-580.

[11] Lalitavistara pp. 4; 107; 275; 351; 448; 458; "Bhisakko" is among the eight "adhivacanas" of Tathāgata. AN. 8.9.35 (=IV p. 340). Itv. sutta 100 has "anuttaro bhisakko".

[12] Yaśomitra quoted, La Vallée Poussin—loc. cit., also cf. Ab. K. Vol. IV. p. 121 fn. 4.

nosis, cure and medicine. The term "Dhātu" too is supposed to have been borrowed from medicine.[13] It may be mentioned that the tenfold path has been called "ariyavirecana" and "°vamana".[14] It appears probable, therefore, that the archetype of the "Ariyasaccāni" originally existed in the medical science.[15]

Their contents according to Abhidharma.—The contents of the Four Truths were differently specified by the different sects. According to the Vibhāṣā,[16] the "masters of Abhidharma" declared the first truth to comprise the five "Upādānaskandhas", the second all "sāsravahetus", the third "Pratisaṅkhyānirodha" and the fourth the "Śaikṣa" and "Aśaikṣa" dharmas, which lead to sanctification. The Dārṣṭāntikas thus explained the four truths—1. Nāmarūpa; 2. Karman and Kleśa; 3. The destruction (Kṣaya) of these; 4. Śamatha and Vipaśyanā. The Vibhajyavādins explained 1. that the Sāsravadharmas, apart from those which have the eight characteristics of Duḥkha,[17] are Duḥkha but not Duḥkhasatya; 2. that the Tṛṣṇā which produces "existence ultérieure" is Samudaya, all the other Tṛṣṇās being merely "Sāsravahetu" not Samudaya; 3. that the destruction of this Tṛṣṇā is Nirodhasatya, that of the others being merely Nirodha; 4. that the Eightfold Path is the

[13] Stcherbatsky—Central Conception, p. 9. Dhātu is already used in Kaṭh. 1.2.20 (Śvet. 3. 20) or is it Dhātuḥ (gen. of Dhātṛ)? "Nidāna" is another word with medical association.

[14] AN. 10. 11. 8. & 9.

[15] Cf. Vijñānabhikṣu—loc. cit.

[16] Quoted by La Vallée Poussin—Ab. k. Vol. IV, p. 122 fn. 3.

[17] Cf. Beal, Catena, pp. 160-172, where on the basis of the Mahāparinibbāna° the following eight marks are mentioned:

(i) birth; (ii) old age; (iii) disease; (iv) death; (v) removal of the loved; (vi) presence of the disliked; (vii) inability to obtain the sought; (viii) the five skandhas.

Mārgasatya, other Śaikṣa Dharmas and all the Aśaikṣa Dharmas being merely Mārga.

These explanations and distinctions breathe the atmosphere of later dogmatics, but the simplicity of the "Dārṣṭāntika" view may be noted.

Whether original or otherwise, the scheme of the Four Truths certainly provides convenient divisions under which to consider early Buddhism. It contains less chances of overlap and distortion than would be entailed by the utilization of other possible schemes as, for example, those used in later Abhidharma works, or by the introduction of modern rubrics.

Duhkha, and its place in Buddha's teachings.—From what we know of Buddha's life[18] and of the tendencies of the later Brāhmaṇic[19] as well as Śramaṇic thought[20] which formed its intellectual environment, it appears natural that the concept of Duḥkha should have played a leading rôle in the teachings of Buddha. There seems no reason to doubt the unanimous Buddhist tradition that it supplied the new gospel with its starting point.

Mrs. Rhys Davids' scepticism.—Mrs. Rhys Davids' contrary view seems to be based on *a priori* considerations, and is, besides, difficult to reconcile with the weight of evidence. She starts with a hypothesis—"Man, say the great religions, imperfect, minor, infant, as, in his earth-stages, he more or less always is, has it in his nature to become utterly well."[21] Consequently Buddha could not have taught the end of the spiritual journey

---

[18] See the Chap. on the Life of Buddha.

[19] See the Chap. on Review of the Vedic Background.

[20] See the Chap. on Religious Conditions in the Age of Buddha.

[21] Sakya, pp. 16-7.

to be merely the cessation of ill, and hence the starting point of his teaching could not have been merely the negative one of avoiding ill. The negativist version of Buddha's gospel should therefore be attributed to monkish "more-wording".[22]

Not sufficiently grounded.—One may begin by observing that the number of great religions minus Buddhism is too small to permit any convincing induction of the major premiss basic to the above reasoning. Further, whether the riddance of Ill is or is not the same as the attainment of Good, is an issue which cannot be uniquely decided without assuming one or another of several possible philosophic positions. Thus the view of the Naiyāyikas would run directly counter to that implicit in Mrs. Rhys Davids's argument. Finally, although the fact of negativist monkish "more-wording" seems undeniable, it is perhaps not unreasonable to suggest that this process had its distant roots in the character of the original mandate itself. The development appears to have been more a one-sided accentuation than a radical inversion.[23] There is little reason to suppose that Buddha addressed himself to Everyman and not to the monk. As a matter of fact, the Buddhists appear to have been from the beginning primarily a community of monks.[24] From the founder of such a community it is only natural to expect that he should start his discourse with the ills of the world.

[22] Cf. What Was the Original Gospel? pp. 52-58.

[23] Cf. Rosenberg—Die Probleme p. viii. according to whom an identical Buddhist Weltanschauung runs through all the changes in its philosophy.

[24] On Mahāyāna cf. La Vallée Poussin "It cannot be denied that from the beginning it had a tendency to place the lay-supporters on the side of, if not above, the monks" (Foreword to N. Dutt's Aspects—p. vii).

Dukkha in the Nikayas.—And the texts seem to support this view. The famous Gayā sermon has its refrain in Dukkha.[25] Its leading idea—the comparison of the world of desire with a world on fire—occurs so often that it would not be surprizing if it went back in some form to Buddha himself.[26] Further Dukkha enters integrally in some very commonly occurring formulae viz. those of the Paṭiccasamuppāda, the Three Lakkhaṇas and the three Dukkhatās.[27] Finally, ascetic sermons regarding Ill are too numerous to be dismissed as just later additions, and sometimes they occur in recognizedly early sections of the Nikāyas e.g. in the Sagāthavagga of the SN or the Aṭṭhakavg. of the Sn.[28]

The nature of Dukkha.—According to Mrs. Rhys Davids "it is possible that the word dukkha was never used for any ills beyond those of mind and body, especially body."[29] Thus the First Utterance describes dukkha as birth, disease, old age and death, and then

---

[25] Vin. I. pp. 34-5.

[26] Consider the Aggikhandhopama sutta=AN. 7.7.58; AN. 3, 6.52; the expression "Aṅgārakāsūpamā kāmā" which recurs e.g. AN. 8.3.8; AN. 8.8.4; the three fires of Rāga etc. e.g. Itv. 3.5. 4; the implication of the "extinction similes" and such expressions as "Sītibhūto" e.g. SN. I. 141; the root meaning of Nirvāṇa itself.

It should be noted that when Buddha called the world a fire, he did not, like Herakleitos, refer to its changeful, but only to its painful, character (Contra—Radhakrishnan I. P. I. p. 368; on Herakleitos and Fire see Burnet—Early Greek Philosophy p. 161—2nd ed.)

[27] On the "Dukkhatās" see SN. IV. 216; V. 56; IV. 207, 396; DN. III. 216. "Dukkhatā" is probably an ancient word—see chap. on The Stratification of the Nikāyas: Problems and Methods.

[28] See chaps. III and VI.

[29] The Original Gospel p. 56. On the 3 "Devadūtas" see AN. 3.45; On the 5 "Devadūtas", MN. Sutta 130. On the significance of the Devadūtas for Buddha's life and problem, see chap. on The Life of Buddha.

mentions the "mainly mental woe of union with the undesired, absence from the desired". "The only ones 'harped upon' ad nauseam are a trinity of old age and dying, with birth and disease as alternative third." Mrs. Rhys Davids concludes that a religion which derives its dynamics from the idea of the riddance of bodily and mental ills "is good gospel for the work of doctor or social reformer, but as religion, as most of us understand religion, namely, the quest of an ultimate goal beyond the worlds, it has no fit basis."[30] This conception of dukkha which contains little "that can be called distinctively spiritual ill" is due, according to her, to "monk-aftermen".

Such expressions as define dukkha in terms of birth, disease, old age and death should, it appears to us, be understood symbolically, not literally. When the Buddhist, contemplating life, was sorely distressed to see its limitation and uncertainties, he was surely feeling what may be called spiritual discontent. When he came to summarize his view in formular terminology and declared "Saṅkhittena pañcupādānakkhandhā dukkhā", he did not mean merely to speak of a discontent of body and mind, but rather of discontent *with* body and mind, and this latter is the form of all spiritual discontent. One seeks what is beyond body and mind when one is dissatisfied with them. This dissatisfaction may, of course, originate in the perception of an actual or potential failure to satisfy the impulses of the body or the mind or both. But it comes to acquire spiritual significance only when it perceives its cause 'sub specie aeternitatis', as it were.[31]

---

[30] Ib., p. 57.

[31] Cf. Aurobindo, Savitri II. 6. 2. "The Way of Fate and the Problem of Pain", where it is shown that suffering is at once the sign of limitation and the motive for its transcendence.

Some scholars, following ancient precedent,[32] have proposed to equate dukkha to commotion or unrest.[33] Dukkha thus becomes from a psycho-ethical a physico-metaphysical category. Instead of being a certain tone of experience, it becomes a quality of the experienced. This would assimilate the Buddhist position to that of Sāṅkhya.[34] In its psychological aspect the view implies that dukkha instead of being an effect of the awareness of changefulness is basically the changefulness of awareness itself.[35]

This, however, seems to confuse dukkha with one of its necessary conditions. Far from being in itself dukkha, the perpetual flux of elements does not even enter directly into the causation of dukkha. It causes dukkha only in as much as its ignorance begets expectations which are frustrated. Even the necessary unrest of empirical consciousness is felt as painful only because Ignorance endows it with 'selfhood'. The saint, free from ignorance, lives, so long at least as he retains his body, in the constant vision of flux, yet wholly untouched by dukkha.

It may be noted that Stcherbatsky's view of dukkha is closely bound up with his view of Nirvāṇa. If Dukkha is the "commotion" of "elements", it is something "objective", a real pervasive feature of the universe, and escape from it can come, consistently with the denial of

---

[32] See below.

[33] Stcherbatsky, Central Conception, p. 48. cf. J. G. R. I. II, pt. 4, Aug. 1945, pp. 357-368; where the view is somewhat different and more plausible.

[34] Cf. Dasgupta–Hist. of Indian Philosophy I, pp. 242-3.

[35] Some texts seem to favour this view, e.g., SN. i. i. 2. 1, implies Dukkha as the disquiet (avūpasama) of the saṅkhāras. But here too much depends on the interpretation of "Saṅkhāra"

"uccheda", only through non-experience. Nirvāṇa becomes akin to endless sleep!

Dukkha in the Nikāyas seems to mean primarily pain or disagreeable feeling,[36] actual or potential, and secondarily, through the extension of meaning, what may be proximately or remotely causal to such feeling.[37]

This ambiguity of usage, however, caused confusion. On the one hand, some texts asserted that Dukkha was only one of the three possible classes of feelings,[38] that the "assāda" aspect[39] of experience was quite as real as the "ādinava" aspect; on the other hand, some texts declared all things to be dukkha in an unqualified manner.[40] Some schools such as the Kukkula-vādins took the latter class of texts quite literally and denied that there was any pleasure in the world.[41] The Theravādins[42] and the Sarvāstivādins,[43] however, held to what

---

[36] With AN. II. 415 "Yo kho panāvuso ābādho dukkhaṃ etaṃ vuttaṃ bhagavatā," cf. "Na ca mukhyameva duḥkhaṃ bādhanāsvabhāvamavamṛśyate kintu tatsādhanaṃ tadanuṣaktaṃ ca sarvameva" (Nyāyamañjarī, Vizianagaram ed. p. 507). Cf. Stcherbatsky, Nirvāṇa pp. 55-56. Cf. "Vibhāṣā 77.12 Pārśva dit que Pīḍana est le caractère du dukkha; Vasumitra dit que pravṛtti (ou saṃsāra, saṃcāra—) est le caractère du dukkha. . . ." (Ab. K. Vol. iv. p. 130 fn. 2). Vasumitra would appear to approach Stcherbatsky closely, esp. if "Saṃcāra" was the word used.

[37] Cf. Vm. (Nāgarī ed.) p. 349 "Ṭhapetvā dukkhasaccaṃ sesaṃ dukkhasaccavibhaṅge āgatam jāti ādi sabbam pi tassa tassa dukkhassa vatthubhāvato pariyāyadukkhaṃ Dukkhadukkhaṃ pana nippariyāyadukkhanti vuccati". Cf. Nyāyavārtika p. 2 (Chowkhamba ed.) where duḥkha is called "Ekaviṃśatiprabhedabhinna". [38] e.g. Nid. Saṃ. sutta 62.

[39] SN. III. 69-70. cf. MN. III. 207.

[40] See the controversy in Kv. I. 208ff. where both the parties quote Nikāya texts in their support.

[41] Kv. loc. cit.; Ab. K. Vol. iv. p. 127—fn. 3; Ib. 129—fn. 1.

[42] Kv. loc. cit.; Vm. loc. cit.

[43] Thus Ab. K. Vol. iv. p. 131 "Si cette sensation etait indesirable ensoi qui pourrait jamais s'y attacher?" Cf. Vyāsabhāṣya on YS II. 16, which points out that the painfulness of all things is apparent only to the sensitive soul of the Yogin.

must appear to common sense to be the more reasonable view—unless there were pleasure, how could attachment arise? The difficulty was noted in the Nikāyas themselves,[44] and the theory of the threefold "Dukkhatā" was possibly advanced to effect a reconciliation of the conflicting statements about dukkha.[45]

The Origin of Dukkha.—It is not only intelligible but appears necessary that Buddha, like other thinkers of his age, should have advanced some explanation of Dukkha. In his own life he had sought freedom from Suffering and had obtained it through the realisation of the principle underlying its origin and forming the content of the Second Noble Truth. The formula of Paṭiccasamuppāda is commonly supposed to represent Buddha's explanation of suffering. The obscurity of this formula is, however, well known, and it has long been a puzzle to scholars. Thus Schrader speaks of it as ". . . . . Buddhisten und Nichtbuddhisten gleich rätselhaften Formel . . . . Dem ältesten Evangelium fremde nicht sehr glückliche Nachbildung gewisser Evolutions-reihen der heterodoxen Philosophie."[46] Franke calls it "ein Surrogat für die zweite Wahrheit," "ein wirrer Knäuel" and thinks that this "Sammelsurium" was certainly not original but was perhaps built up from the use of the word 'Paṭiccasamuppanna' which was earlier probably equal to "durch Durst . . . . . oder durch Vorstellung (Saṅkhāra) bedingt."[47] Mrs. Rhys Davids refers to the formula as a "mysterious old rune" (BPE XXIV). Oldenberg calls

[44] Thus SN. IV. 216.

[45] See Ab. K. Vol. iv. p. 125 and the sūtras quoted there in addition to those already cited. SN. IV. 207 seems to suggest a state of transition in the formulation of this theory.

[46] Schrader, op. cit. p. 6.

[47] ZDMG. 1915. pp. 470-71.

it "......an Dunkelheiten reichen Antwort auf die kühne Frage."[48] On the other hand, in the light of later Abhidharma, the formula becomes clear enough. Thus Rosenberg exclaims, "Die Kenner der Dogmatik der alten Schule würden sich sehr wundern, wenn sie erführen, dasz die 12–gliedrig Formel etwas Unverständliches oder Unklares enthält."[49]

The Interpretations of Paticcasamuppada.—Passing over some of the earlier interpretations,[50] we may notice Jacobi's suggestion[51] that the formula of Paṭiccasamuppāda ought to be derived from the Sāṅkhya scheme of evolution. Schrader endorced the idea, and Senart posited the influence of Yoga (Oldenberg, loc. cit. fn. 1). In spite of Keith (BP. p. 106), and Belvalkar and Ranade (Op. cit. p. 416) the comparison between the Sāṅkhya scheme of the Tattvas and Pratītyasamutpāda appears forced. Keith equates Buddhi to Vijñāna, Ahaṅkāra to Nāmarupa, and Upādāna to Dharmādharmau. Jacobi in effect adduces the following Sāṅkhya sequence about the origin of Dukkha as a complete parallel to Paṭiccasamuppāda.— Avidyā — Saṃskāra — Buddhi — Ahaṅkāra —Indriyāṇi and Tanmātras — Indriyārthasannikarṣa-Abhiniveśa — Dharmādharmau — Saṃsāra (ZDMG 52 12—15). He further states that the Sāṅkhya scheme of evolution has primarily a psychological, not cosmogonic, standpoint (Ib.p.6).

In the first place, it must be pointed out that the Buddhist sequence is an illustration of the principle

[48] Buddha, (9th ed.) p. 255.

[49] Die Probleme, p. 210.

[50] On the older interpretations, see Kern, L'Histoire, 1.246f; 355-62; Burnouf, p. 432; Keith, BP. 106f, Rhys Davids, Dialogues, II. p. 42f.

[51] ZDMG. 52.1f.

of Pratītyasamutpāda, while the Sāṅkhya illustrates Pariṇāmavāda; and the two are very different. Thus the logical relation between the Nidānas and those between the Tattvas are disparate.

Avidyā may be common to both but then Avidyā is in a way common to almost all systems of Indian thought. The meaning of Saṃskāra is widely different in the two systems. Empirical Vijñāna cannot exist independently of Nāmarūpa, while Buddhi has no such dependence on Ahaṅkāra. Transcendental Vijñāna is nearer to Puruṣa than to Buddhi. Nāmarūpa are the concrete individual or sometimes the concrete bases of individuality; while Ahaṅkāra is only the bare sense of individuality.

It is of course true that the Sāṅkhya, like Buddhism, sees the origin of Duḥkha in desire-prompted actions, and the origin of desire in some sort of "ignorance". But this general idea belongs to Śramaṇa-culture as a whole. Buddha need not have borrowed it from Sāṅkhya.[52] On the origin of the formula, Franke[53] seems to be perfectly correct in suggesting that its present form has been built upon simpler earlier statements relating to Dukkha-samudaya, but he seems to miss the significance of the distinction between the general and the applied formulations of the law of Paṭiccasamuppāda. Mrs. Rhys Davids regards the title Paṭiccasam° as "almost certainly a name given by the compilers of the Sutta-Piṭaka at a later date" to what Gotama called "the doctrine by the middle".[54] She ascribes the actual authorship of the cause gospel to Kappina—rather than to Buddha.[55]

---

52 See below, Chap. XIV.

53 Loc. cit.

54 KS. II. p. v.

55 Sakya pp. 138-48

On the origin and significance of the formula of Paṭiccasamuppāda, modern opinion has varied. Dr. Keith thought that the chain aimed at explaining the origin of evil, and that the interest in causation was wholly subordinte.[56] On the other hand, Dr. Rhys Davids considered the formula as the first clear enunciation in history of the principle of natural causality in all phenomena.[57] The chain of twelve links was only a particular application of the causal law to the psychological region, where suffering originates. It expressed the course of normal human life.[58]

The idea of Prof. Rhys Davids has met with wide acceptance.[59] But it seems to us to make Buddha a forerunner of Comte, or of modern psychology. To apply the causal law to man's mental and moral life would only lead to a variety of naturalist positivism, unless it were combined with some other more fundamental idea. If Buddha remains a great figure in the religious history of mankind, he could not have been merely an advocate of the method of modern science.[60] As Kant saw so clearly, the great distinction of religion from science lies in the fact that whereas the latter recognises nothing except the heteronomous world of cause and effect (Paratantralakṣaṇa), the former seeks to transcend it and secure freedom for man.

---

[56] Keith, BP. pp. 106 ff.

[57] Rhys Davids, Dialogues, II. pp. 42 ff.

[58] Cf. Mrs. Rhys Davids, KS. II. p. vi. fn. i; Buddhism (HUL) p. 96; Sakya p. 152. Rhys Davids, American Lectures (published Susil Gupta, Calcutta) pp. 85 ff, which is an excellent exposition (within the limitation of the standpoint).

[59] e.g., History of Philosophy, Eastern and Western I (ed. S. Radhakrishnan) pp. 159-60.

[60] Cf. Keith, BP. III.—If there is no divine intervention and the individual is only a transient aggregate, how will the beginningless process of Avidyā be brought to an end?

Several attempts have been made to give a spiritual significance to this application of the causal law by Buddha to man's psycho-ethical life. Mrs. Rhys Davids thought that Buddha utilised the causal idea in favour of his gospel of the way as a becoming better through the exercise of will, since perception of causal uniformities can become an aid in changing ourselves and realising our ideals.[61] This, however, does not appear to be much different from a programme of moral reform such as any sensible psychologist would suggest today. It is curious, indeed, that Buddha should need the cosmic consciousness of the Enlightenment in order to discover a principle which naturalist philosophers have speculatively discovered in all ages, and which is a commonplace of modern thought. Besides, action or the exercise of the will in accordance with Law (Dammacchando) may make man better; it will never lead to ultimate spiritual freedom (Cetovimutti, Paññāvimutti). Even the most virtuous life is involved in impermanence and suffering.[62] Nirvāṇa lies beyond the opposites of good anl evil,[63] and even Dharma has to be left behind, like the raft, as one reaches the other shore.[64] Karma is inadequate to the attainment of the final Peace, which can come only through perfect Awakening (Sambodhi). The Goal is attained not merely by the transformation of body and mind, themselves necessarily involved in transformations, but by the Intuition which dispels Ignorance and reveals the Eternal (Amatapadaṃ).[65]

---

[61] Sakya, pp. 148-62.

[62] See above.

[63] See below, next chapter.

[64] The Parable of the Raft, MN. I. 134-5.

[65] See below.

Oldenberg considered the general significance of Paṭiccasamuppāda to consist in the view that within the phenomenal realm, becoming, not being, is the final category.[66] This interpretation suffers from obvious Ativyāpti, and fails to characterise the idea of Buddha in its distinctive aspects.

Coomarswamy brings a deeper insight to the solution of the problem. "It is the grasp of the very fact that we are mechanisms, causally determind......that points out the way of escape."[67] Our bondage is the result of ignorantly seeing the self in what is not our self (anattani attānaṃ), but only a process. Coomarswamy here uses the well known principle of Sāṅkhya and Vedānta that the attainment of freedom consists in the discrimination of the Sprit from the heteronomous world of Nature, to which man's mental and moral life belong. The idea has an undoubted appeal, but it is very curious if, having explained the origin of Suffering in terms of the involvement of the spirit in the contingent life of Nature; Buddha should place all the emphasis on her contingency and so little on the spirit and its freedom that his followers soon denied their very existence!

Many scholars have sought to explain the principle of Paṭiccasamuppāda in terms of the Abhidharmas of Theravāda[68] or Sarvāstivāda,[69] but as will be seen below, the traditional views represent later and partial developments of the original teaching. They are highly valuable but cannot be equated with Buddha's own idea which was so comprehensive and so non-technically

---

[66] Buddha, pp. 286, 289.

[67] Hinduism and Buddhism. p. 80, note 225.

[68] e.g., N. Dutta, EMB I. 266 ff.

[69] e.g., Rosenberg, loc. cit., Stcerbatsky, Central Conception. pp. 28-9.

phrased that it became the source of diverse later interpretations. Buddha saw Truth intuitively as a whole and did not care for definitions and formulae. Philosophers and schoolmen tried to define his synoptic vision, and succeeded in elaborating fragments, creating 'views'.

Authenticity of Paticcasamuppda.—All schools of Buddhism are agreed on the central importance of Paṭiccasamuppāda which has been identified with Dhamma and Buddha in ancient sayings as well as later texts,[70] Hīnayāna and Mahāyāna. The universally recognized importance of the idea, its equal obscurity, and its occurrence in some of the most ancient passages of the Nikāyas testify to its authenticity. The authenticity of the general idea of Paṭiccasamuppāda does not, however, imply the authenticity of the term itself, or of the meanings read into it later, nor of that puzzling formula of Twelve Links.[71] We can only say that the principle is generally termed Paṭiccasamuppāda, though it is also called Idappaçcayatā and Majjhena Dhammo.[72]

The Two Aspects Of Paticcasamuppada.—We have seen that there is a duality in the meaning of Dukkha.[73] It some times stands for suffering and has a psychological meaning; at others, for phenomenal unrest. The more extended meaning is connected with the narrower one as ground with consequent. Corresponding to these two meanings of Dukkha, Paṭiccasamuppāda too has a double aspect—a primary and general one indicating the fundamental ground of Dukkha, and an applied and secondary aspect which indicates the proximate

[70] N. Dutt. Aspects of Mahayana, p. 51, which collects most of the important references.
[71] See below. Cf. Mrs. Rhys David's view referred to above.
[72] See below.
[73] See above.

cause of Dukkha in psychological terms. Just as seeking to explain growing unemployment, for example, we may indicate its cause in terms of falling prices and similar proximate causes, or we may go deeper and point out its ultimate ground in the capitalist system, so Buddha sometimes explained Dukkha in terms of psychological causes, at others, in terms of its metaphysical ground.

The knowledge of the primary principle of Paṭiccasamuppāda, being the revelation of the ultimate ground of Dukkha, negates Avidyā or spiritual blindness. The secondary applications of the law trace the evolution of suffering from Thirst and striving within the life of Ignorance.[74] One is reminded here of the Vedantic distinction between primary and secondary Avidyā.

The general principle of Paticcasamuppada: its discovery and significance.—Buddha is stated to have discovered the principle of Paṭiccasam° during his Enlightenment,[75] and finding it too difficult for ordinary comprehension, to have hesitated in preaching it. The small space given to it in the Nikāyas seems to indicate

[74] Cf. Rosenberg on the "Gegenstand der Untersuchung" in Buddhist philosophy, op. cit. pp. 69-70; Ib. 95. On two aspects of Paṭiccasam°, cf. Ab. K. Vol. II. p. 67.

[75] DN. II. Mahāpadāna sutta; SN. I. 6.1.1; Ib. II. 1. sutta 65; with the last compare the Nidānasūtra as found in Sanskrit in Touen Houeng by the Pelliot Mission (ed Lévi—in J. A. 1910—Nov.-Dec.). The sūtra occurs twice in the Āgamas, Saṃ-Ā (Nidānasaṃyukta—Guṇabhadra's tr) and Ekottarāgama (Dharmanandin's tr) where it is placed in the "Ṣaṭkanipāta". In the last independent Chinese translation of the sūtra, it is named "Sūtra de la parabole de la vieille ville" (op. cit. pp. 435-436). Was the original title "Purāṇanagaropamasūtra"? cf. also the Gopalpur Brick Ins. which closely resembles SN. ii. 1. and belongs to c. 500 A.D. (JRAS. 1938—547ff. Johnston). So Mahāvagga (Brewster op. cit. pp. 49-50); Udāna-suttas 1—3.

that his fears were not groundless.[76] The discovery of Paṭiccasam° has been likened to that of an ancient city.[77] The comparison indicates that it was regarded as an objective and impersonal feature of phenomena.

In the classical passage within the re-current Brahmāyācana context, Buddha dichotomises his Dhamma into Paṭiccasam° and Nibbāna.[78] Such a division of Truth into a fundamental two is not unknown in several other philosophies. Since Nibbāna is apparently the final principle or experience, Paṭiccasam° may be designated as the principle of non-ultimate experience and what corresponds to it; in short, as the principle of phenomenality, of the nature of things transcended in Nibbāna. The relation between the two appears to us parallel to the relation between Brahman and Māyā in the philosophy of Śaṅkarācārya.[79]

We can notice, however, a tendency early in Buddhist thought to the dialectical annulment of the distinction between the phenomenal and the transcendent. Paṭiccasam came to be identified with Dhamma, Buddha, and Dhammatā.[80] A text occuring in the SN (II. 25) as well as SĀ (see Ab.K.II.77fn. 1) describes it as independent, self-subsistent, and eternal reality (Dhammadhātu, Dharmāṇāṃ dharmatā). The Mahiṃsāsakas and Pubbaseliyas declared it "Asaṅkhata"[81] and the Mādhyamikas made it indifferently not only the principle of

[76] Cf. Mrs. Rhys Davids, KS. II. p. ix; Sakya p. 152.

[77] Cf. Barua Mahabodhi, 1914 March-April p. 60.

[78] SN. II. pp. 105-6.

[79] For further discussion of the relation between Paṭiccasam° and Nibbāna, see below chap. XII.

[80] MN. I. 191; MKV. pp. 2, 50; Vigrahavyāvartanī, sub. verse 55.

[81] Kv; VI. 2; see also Ab. K. Vol. II. p. 77. fn. 1.

phenomenal unreality but also of transcendent reality.[82] On the other hand, in contrast to them, the Theravādins and Sarvāstivādins identified Pratīyasamutpāda with the Saṃskṛtadharmas, taking them to be, at the same time, real rather than phenomenal.[83] These views thus depart from the original standpoint in various ways.

Mystical aspect of Paticcasamuppada.—The mystery of Paṭiccasamuppāda has been alluded to above. An ancient text describes it as "deep, difficult to see, difficult to awake to", beyond the realm of thought (atakkāvacaro)."[84] Its difficulty arose from the fact that it was a principle apprehended in mystical intuition, and although it solved for Buddha the manifold antinomies of thought, the solution was incapable of being positively conceptualised. The only way to communicate it lay through negations.

---

82 See below.

83 See below.

84 "Adhigato kho me ayaṃ dhammo gambhīro duddaso duranubodho santo paṇīto *atakkāvacaro*—ālayarāmāya kho pana pajāya....duddasaṃ idaṃ ṭhānaṃ yadidaṃ idappacayatā paṭiccasamuppādo...." (DN. II. p. 36; SN. I. p. 136; MN. Suttas 26 and 85. Cf. Lalitavistara I. 390, 395-7).

Buddhaghosa explains the profundity to be fourfold (Vm. pp. 412-13. Nāg. ed.) Cf. SN. II. 92; DN. II. 55 (where also the expression "idappaccaya" occurs).

Corresponding to the text just quoted, the Lalitavistara has two versions. The shorter one closely approximates to the Pali text (See LV. I. pp. 395-6). The most important respect in which it differs from the latter are: (i) it does not introduce the distinction between Pratītyasamutpāda and Nirvāṇa, which the Pali version contains; in fact it is quite silent over Pratīyasamutpāda and speaks only of Nirvāṇa. (ii) It introduces the phrases "śūnyatānupalambhaḥ" as an adjective of Nirvāṇa.

The second and longer version in LV (I. p. 392) appears to be an elaboration of the shorter one. It stresses the transcendentality of Nirvāṇa strongly.

Paticcasamuppada as the Negation of Finite Self-subsistence.—All Buddhist schools, Hīnayāna as well as Mahāyāna, are agreed over the authenticity of that well known formulation of the abstract principle of Paṭicca-samuppāda,[85] which even Mrs. Rhys Davids is prepared to grant as possibly the Founder's own.[86] It runs thus: Imasmiṃ sati idaṃ hoti; imassa uppādā idaṃ uppajjati; imasamiṃ asati idaṃ na hoti; imassa nirodhā idaṃ nirujjhati.[87] Another formulation of the same idea occurs in the well known Gāthā "Ye dhammā hetup-pabhavā" etc., which is common to all the schools.[88]

These formulations, it seems to us, ought not to be taken literally, as if they were careful scholastic products.[89] On the contrary, they appear to be merely mnemonic and summary indications[90] of Buddha's negation of the independence or self-subsistence of finite objects, in particular, of the empirical "self" which is really equivalent to causally conditioned psycho-physical states.[91] Common sense is apt to regard its world as an anarchy of substances, where each individual person and thing enjoys the independence of its nature. We take a great step away from this conception as soon as we realise that the denizens of our finite world do not enjoy

85 On the various interpretations of the term Paṭiccasamup-pāda, see Vm. 362-65; Ab. K. Vol. II. pp. 78-80; MK. V. I. pp. 5-10. ....

86 Buddhism (HUL) p. 92.

87 MN. I. 262, II. 32; III. 63; SN. II. 65, 95, 96; Ud. suttas 1-2; Ab. K. Vol. II. pp. 81-83. (which discusses the significance of saying separately "Asmiṃ sati...." and "Imassa uppādā.... .."); MKV. I. p. 55.

88 See Vinaya I. 40; Beal, Catena, p. 155.

89 Which is, however, the attitude that Abhidharma naturally adopted—e.g., see Ab. K. II. pp. 81ff.

90 Cf. KS. II. p. vi, fn. 1.

91 See e.g., S. 2.1.2. sutta 15. section 6; Ib. 2.1.4. sutta 37.

any absolute and sovereign right of existence, but derive it in their brief tenure from their dependence on others. As parts of an ordered world of relations, they possess only a conditional reality.

Buddhaghosa points out that the emphasis in this formula is not on origination (Uppādo) but on conditions and relations.[92] He declares that "Paṭiccasamuppādo ti paccayadhammā veditabbā."[93] Vasubandhu identifies Pratītyasamutpāda with all "Saṃskṛtadharmas".[94] The Mādhyamikas go beyond the Theravādins and the Sarvāstivādins and argue that the formula not only points out the causally conditioned character of individual objects, but goes deeper and hints at their logical instability.[95] The Mādhyamika view is a dialectical development out of the earlier views which, emphasizing causality, could limit only the actuality rather than the ideality of things. They robbed individual things of independent existence but not of independent conceivability, leaving them quasi-substances. Buddhist logic and dialectic have evolved through the attempt to define the exact nature of that dependence of things which the principle of Paṭiccasamuppāda implies.

Stcherbatsky has very happily suggested that this fundamental relatedness of things is much more intelligible in terms of mathematical "functionelle Abhängigkeit"[96] than in terms of the conventional idea of causality.

---

[92] Vm. pp. 363-64.

[93] Ib. p. 364.

[94] Ab. K. II. p. 73.

[95] MK. V. I. p. 10. "Asmin satīdam bhavati hrasve dīrghaṃ yathā satīti....hrasvampratītya hrasvamprāpya hrasvamapekṣya dīrghaṃ bhavatīti...." The Mādhyamika interpretation was altogether an innovation. Cf. SN. II. 150; also AN. I. 258.

[96] Nirvāṇa p. 41; Buddhist Logic I pp. 119-24; II. 126 fn. 5.

The general principle of Paṭiccasam° thus becomes nothing more than the enunciation of a certain functional relationship. It will, however, be a mistake to see here the statement of the functional relation as such, since the latter "contains nothing more than the notion of determinate correspondence in its abstract form."[97] To specify a functional relation between x and y, one only needs to say that "to some values of x at any rate correspond values of y."[98] The formula of Paṭiccasam°, on the other hand, asserts, in effect, that if x assumes any of the two values "ϵ, $\sim\epsilon$", y also assumes the same and that "ϵ, $\sim\epsilon$" must be interpreted as "existent, non-existent". That is to say, it not only refers to what is but a special type of Function, it also lays down an ontological interpretation of the domain of the function. The idea of Paṭiccasam°, thus, though less general than the idea of Function, is yet more general than the idea of cause which is usually associated with such ideas as those of "action" "force, production out of something."[99]

Paṭiccasam° is the abstract law of contingency applied to "things" (dhammā).[100] It asserts that given anything, there is also given something else which is its necessary and sufficient condition.[101] The essential intention of Paṭiccasam° was the purely negative one of

---

[97] Hobson—The Theory of Functions of a Real Variable Vol. I. p. 257. 2nd ed.

[98] Hardy—Pure Mathematics p. 41. 7th ed.

[99] See below.

[100] Cf. "Traiyadhvikāḥ Pratītyasamutpādaḥ; ta eva ca Pratītyasamutpannāḥ" (Ab. K. Vol. II. p. 73, fn. 1).

[101] Cf. "Tattha tabbhāvabhāvibhāvākārmattopalakkhito Paṭiccasamuppādanayo" (Abhidhammatthasaṅgaho—p. 140). See also Compendium, p. 187, 188 fn. 1.

denying the independent existence or reality of finite things.[102]

Paticcasamuppada as the Middle Way.—It is however, not nihilistic, and emphatically denied the total unreality of things. This comes out clearly in a few suttas of SN[103] where it is called the Middle Doctrine (Majjhena Dhammo).

In SN 2.1.15 (SN. II. p. 17) Buddha explains to Kaccāyana that the Middle Way avoids the extremes of Being (Atthitā) and Non-Being (Natthitā) to which the world is attached. Further explanation of the Middle Doctrine is given in terms of a set formula which ought to be regarded as a late misfilling of the original answer.[104] This sutta is apparently quoted in Khandha Saṃyutta, Sutta 90. Nāgārjuna quotes it by name (Kātyāyanāvavāda) and content, and it seems to have formed, in fact, the ancient source of his theory of Śūnyatā.[105] Candrakīrti declares that this sūtra is common to all the sects, but the form in which he quotes it shows partial divergence from the Pali version and appears to contain a Mahāyānic misfilling.[106]

In SN 2.1.17 (SN. II p.20) Buddha explains to Acela Kassapa that Dukkha is neither "Sayaṃkata" nor "Paraṃ-

---

102 Cf. "Yaḥ Pratītyasamutpādādbhūtārthamavalokate Sa jānāti jagacchūnyamādimadhyāntavarjitaṃ (Mahāyānaviṃśaka —Nāgārjuna verse, 15 ed. Mm. V. Bhattacharya).

It is of the essence of the Mādhyamika position that all individual existents, lacking independence, lack ultimate reality.

103 The question of their antiquity has been discussed above. They represent a mosaic of early and late elements.

104 Mrs. Rhys Davids, Sakya pp. 91-3; Intr. to KS. II.

105 MK. XV. 7.

106 MKV. (on XV. 7): "Idañca sūtraṃ sarvanikāyeṣu paṭhyate...... Tathāstīti Kāśyapa...... Dvayorantayormadhyaṃ tadarucyamanidarśanamapratiṣṭhamanābhāsamaniketanamavijñaptikamidamucyate Kāśyapa madhyamā pratipadā. ......"

kata" nor addhiccasamuppanna" but that in order to avoid the opposites of 'Sassata' and 'Uccheda' he teaches the Middle Way, which is Paṭiccasamuppāda.

The next Sutta (SN. II. p. 23) has a similar idea. Timbaruka Paribbājaka is told that the feelings of pleasure and pain can neither be identified with nor distinguished from the experiencing subject, for the former would represent them as "caused-by-self" (and hence as necessary and inalienable), whereas the latter would make them "caused-by-another" (and hence capricious, beside violating our sense of moral responsibility). Paṭiccasamuppāda avoids making the experience of pleasure and pain "autonomous" or "heteronomous".

Sutta 35 (SN. II. p. 61) seems to contain a fragment in the midst of later material when it declares that Buddha's Dhamma avoided the two extremes of "Taṃ jīvaṃ taṃ sarīraṃ" and its opposite. This very idea seems to be contained in Sutta 37 which has "Nāyaṃ......kāyo tumhākaṃ nāpi aññesaṃ". Sutta 46 (Ib. p. 76) seeks to avoid identifying or separating the agent of an action and the experiencer of its consequence. Sutta 47 seeks the 'middle way' between "Everything is" and "Everything is not". Sutta 48 adds to the antinomy of Sutta 46 a new one, viz., "It is all unity", "It is all plurality". These dead-ends are to be avoided.

Mrs. Rhys Davids interprets the Middle Dortrine as the doctrine of Becoming which is supposed to resolve the antithesis of being and non-being.[107] This naturally reminds one of Herakleitos[108] and Hegel.[109] It seems to

[107] Buddhism (HUL) pp. 94ff. Radhakrishnan, IP I pp. 368-9

[108] See Burnet, Early Greek Philosophy (4th edition pp. 145f; Cornford, op. cit. 189-91; Hegel, History of Philosophy I. pp. 282 ff (Tr. E. S. Haldane).

[109] See Hegel's Logic (Tr. Wallace) pp. 158-68.

us, however, that Buddha's Madhymā Pratipad sought to resolve the opposition of being and non-being, not by synthesizing the two categories, but by transcending them both. The *fact of Becoming* shows the inadequacy of the *ideas* of pure Being and pure Non-being as categories for determining the nature of reality, but the *idea of Becoming* does not offer a finally satisfactory and adequate category in its turn.

The Upaniṣads rejected 'Asadvāda' in favour of 'Sadvāda'[110] and, at times, they saw that it should lead them logically to deny the reality of becoming and of particular and determinate existence, to Vivarta-vāda, in short.[111] The Sāṅkhya, advocating Sadvāda and Śāśvatavāda,[112] and at the same time holding to the reality of change, lands itself in the illogical position of Pariṇāmavāda, which has to explain causation as manifestation[113] and yet has no place for the ultimate and

---

[110] Ch. Up. VI. 2.1.2. Cf. Ib. III, 19, 1. The theory of Asat to which Āruṇi (Ch. Up. 6) refers seems to have had a purely cosmological intention whereas his own theory of Sat has a metaphysical springboard. Besides, he uses Sat for a positive principle not only free from particularity (Nirviśeṣa) but also sentient. Thus his refutation of Asadvāda was interpreted later not only as the rejection of cosmological nihilism, but also of metaphysical nihilism (which was attributed, though mistakenly, to the Buddhists—vide STK; Vedāntasāra) and of the Sāṅkhyan Pradhānavāda.

[111] Ib. VI. 1. 4; Bṛ. IV. 5.15; Ch. VII. 24, 1; TĀ, III, 12, 7; Kaṭh. 2.4. 10-11.

[112] For the Sāṅkhya, Sadvāda implies the reality of change, Śāśvatavāda, the changeless eternity of the spirit. Cf. "Sataḥ Sajjāyate" (STK. on SK. 8); Cf. "Hātuḥ svarūpamupādeyaṃ heyaṃ vā na bhavati. Hāne tasyocchedavādaprasaṅga upādāne ca hetuvāda ubhayapratyākhyāne ca Śāśvatavāda iti." (Vyāsa on YS. II. 15). Here Ucchedavāda stands for materialism, Śāśvatavāda for Sāṅkhya. Hetuvāda seems to be Buddhism.

[113] Mm. G. Kaviraja in Saraswati Bhavana Studies I. (pt. I), p. 39; Vācaspati Miśra on SK. 9—"Kāraṇāccāsya satobhivyaktirevāvaśiṣyate."

distinct reality of Time. The position of Brahmaprakṛtivāda, which seems to be the usual one in the Upaniṣads and is upheld as such by Bādarāyaṇa,[114] suffers from a similar defect. In fact, by trying to combine the immutable purity of the Spirit with causal function conceived on the lines of Pariṇāmavāda, the view creates for itself dialectical difficulties which come out in the Vilakṣaṇatvādhikaraṇa of Bādarāyaṇa referred to above.

Saṭ and Asat, Śāśvata and Uccheda are dialectically connected.[115] The attempt to hold the first leads to the dead-end of the second. If one asserts that pure, eternal being is the only reality, one condemns the life of change and, with it, moral and spiritual effort to the realm of pure illusion. On the other hand, to assert the perfect and full reality of the finite world involved in impermanence and rigidly determined *by causal* laws, leads to a positivist and materialist point of view which denies spiritual freedom and the possibility of eternal life. From both sides, Śāśvata leads to Uccheda, Sat to Asat.

Paticcasamuppāda as the "Middle Doctrine" seeks to avoid both these dead-ends,[116] and thus to preserve the

---

[114] See BS. I. 4. 23-27 (Prakṛtyadhikaraṇa; mark especially Ib. I. 4. 26) Ib. II. I. 4-12 (Vilakṣaṇatvādhikaraṇa). The relevant Upaniṣadic texts are quoted by Śaṅkara in his comy. on the Sūtras. His own position of Vivarta is, of course, very different; mark his comments on Ib. II. 1. 9. where he reveals his real position in what would be from Bādarāyaṇa's point of view a "prauḍhivāda".

[115] In Buddhist discussion the theories of Being and of Permanence seem to be identical, just as the theories of Non-being and Annihilation seem to be so.

[116] This tendency can be seen earlier also. RS. X. 129 declares that the distinction between Sat and Asat did not touch the Primal One. In this strain Śvet. Up. IV. 18 states "Na Sancāsañchiva eva kevalaḥ" (cf. Bhagavadītā XIII. 12). This reminds one of Nāgārjuna who describes Pratītyasamutpāda as "Prapañcopaśama" and "Śiva" (MK.) Cf. Mm. Vidhushekhar

reality of present action as well as of its ultimate transcendence. If things were real, they would not cease to be; if they were unreal, they would not come to be.[117] In a similar spirit Advaita Vedānta refuses to describe Māyā as existent or non-existent.[118] Paṭiccasam° is essentially the principle of transcendental dialectic. It can only be understood through a series of negations. It denies that things just are, pure and immutable, or that they are a nihil. It denies that they just happen without an intelligible law, as a matter of chance, or fiat, or natural freak. And it denies that one thing actively produces another, or that one thing comes out of another. It denies Eternalism (Sassatavāda) Nihilism (Ucchedavāda), Fortuitionism (Adhicoasamuppāda), and anthropomorphic, or dynamic causality.[119]

Bhattacharya, Jha Comm. Vol.; Āgama Śāstra, pp. 102-4. Cf. Mbh. Ś. p. 219.6. "Ucchedaniṣṭhā nehāsti bhāvaniṣtha na vidyate" (Nīlakaṇṭha: Ucchedaniṣṭhā nāśe paryavasānam...bhāvaniṣṭhā viśeṣe paryavasānam); Ib. 41 "evam sati ka ucchedaḥ śāśvato vā kathaṃ bhavet. Svabhāvād vartamāneṣu sarvabhūteṣu hetutaḥ."

[117] SN. II. 17. Cf. BG. II. 16. Buddha implies that from the changeability of the (empirical) self, it could neither be called real nor unreal. The Gītā says, since the Self is undoubtedly real, it must be unchangeable. Śaṅkara was to conclude, since the world of particular things is changeable, it must be unreal.

[118] The Vedantic use of Sat and Asat shows ambiguity. Ultimate reality as changeless pure being (Nityanirviśeṣasat) is described as beyond Sat and Asat. When Māyā is judged indescribable in terms of Sat and Asat, these terms stand for the bare notions of being and non-being without further qualification. The Buddhists generally use these terms only in their empirical signification.

[119] On the inadequacy of speculative views to express truth, see the parable of the elephant and the blind, Udāna, Sutta 54; The Kiṃsuka parable, SN. (Saḷāyatana saṃyutta, Sutta 204) Cf. Vm. p. 365: "Purimena sassatādīnamabhāvo, pacchimena tu padena ucchedādivighāto, dvayena paridīpito ñāyo"; Candra-

Paticcasam° and Flux.—Phenomenal things are undoubtedly impermanent and subject to becoming.[120] Paṭiccasam° appears now as a law relating to events which do not happen in isolation. It thus resolves the world into a procession,[121] and sees a necessary order in its sequence. The simultaneities and successions of events have abiding uniformities. An impersonal norm[122] underlies the beginningless phenomenal flux. Of incessant and instantaneous change there is as yet no

---

kīrti, MKV.—Tadevaṃ hetuprayayāpekṣam bhāvānāmutpādam paridīpayatā bhagavatā ahetvekahetuviṣamahetusambhūtatvam svaparobhayakṛtatvaṃ ca bhāvānām niṣiddham bhavati". I.p. 10. Cf. STK. (on SK. 8) which describes the Buddhist view of causality as "asataḥ sajjāyate". This representation is based on regarding causation as "production out of something", and fails to think of it as merely a correlation of necessarily successive functions.

[120] MN. I. 228, 260, 236, II. 261, III. 25; SN. II. 28, III. 22, 37, 142-3. Ib. V. 181; AN. 4.9.19; Ib. V. 59ff, etc. Cf. "Uktaṃ hi Bhagavatā Trīṇīmāni bhikṣavaḥ Saṃskṛtasya saṃskṛtalakṣaṇāni Saṃskṛtasya bhikṣava utpādo pi prajñāyate, vyayopi sthityanyathātvamapi...." (MKV p. 44. Calcutta ed.).

Mind (Citta) is regarded in some ancient texts as more variable than matter—AN. I. 10, SN. II. 95, According to later Theravāda, the former flowed seventeen times faster than the latter (Abhidhammatthasaṅgaho. p. 68). The Andhakas believed in diurnal duration for the Citta (Kv. I. 204ff). The Theravādins, seeing that a complete act of perception required more than one "Moment", reconciled the momentariness of objects with the possibility of their direct perception through constructing a double set of "Moments" (rūpakkhaṇa and cittakkhaṇa). The Sautrāntikas, it may be remembered, abandoned the directness of perception.

The Andhakas apparently base their curious theory on the misunderstanding of some scriptural sayings. Perhaps the observation of the fact that there is an apparent break of mental life in sleep was a consideration with them.

[121] Oldenberg—Buddha p. 289, 9th ed; cf. ERE IX. p. 805.

[122] On Paṭiccasam° and the Norm, see above; also chapter XII. cf. Bhāmatī ed. BS. II. 2.32.

speech.[123] And the gospel of universal impermanence is, in a general way at least, probably pre-Buddhistic.[124] Still, the originality of Buddha is striking if we just consider the Upaniṣadic ideas.

Paticcasam° and the Brahmano-upanisadic Background.—The Brāhmaṇa texts are doubtless familiar with the inevitability that belongs to the efficacy of certain types of actions—sacrificial, magical, divine—yet caprice looms so large in their narratives that it may be safely concluded that their authors had not as yet attained to the causal conception of the universe.[125] The advance of cosmogonic enquiry and the rise of "natural philosophers", reminiscent of the Milesian thinkers, brought in their wake the conception of an arché or First Cause[126] which is sometimes regarded as personal, at others impersonal.[127] Sometimes the cosmos is made to arise from an original "nihil" (Asat).[128] More usually the process of cosmogenesis is conceived as a series of emanations.[129] Sometimes the personal creator is also regarded as the immanent ground[130] and regulator of the universe.[131] At a few places this immanence is emphasised to the point of declaring all phenomena illusory. In these cases we have a veritable Parmenidean philosophy of Being.[132] Everywhere the world has a first begining, and nowhere is the idea of an imper-

---

[123] The Nikāyas are unaware of it. In the Kv. (XXII. 8) the Pubbaseliyas and the Aparaseliyas are found to declare "ekacittakkhaṇikā sabbe dhammāti".

[124] See AN. Nip. 7. sutta 70; also chapter VIII above.

[125] Cf. Oldenberg, WB. p. 127.

[126] See above Chapter VIII.

[127] See above Chapter VIII.

[128] Ib. [129] Ib.

[130] Praśna 6; Tait. 3; Ch. Up.—6.3.

[131] Bṛ. 3.7.; Śvet. 1.10, 12. [132] Ch. up. VI; Kaṭh II. 4.

sonal cosmic norm very important, although it is faintly adumbrated in some texts.[133]

Buddha's originality.—For Buddha, becoming is an undeniable and extremely significant fact about the world of finites. Causality has become universalized and impersonalized. A first Beginning and a personal creator are consequently excluded.[134] Further, causality is conceived not as a relation between substances based on the expression of personal or material energy, but as an invariance of order between events and their conditions[135] (cf. Ab. K. vol. II. p. 77). And, finally, realising

---

[133] e.g. "Ṛtameva Parameṣṭhi | Ṛtaṃ nātyeti kiñcana | Ṛte samudra Āditaḥ | Ṛte bhūmiriyaṃ śritā...." (TB. p. 256—cf. Ib. u. 389 Ānandāśrama).

On the affinity of Ṛta to Chinese Tao, Persian Asha and Greek Dike, cf. Cornford: From Religion to Philosophy...... pp. 172 ff.

Apart from Ṛta, "Dharma" also is at one place in the Upaniṣads used in the sense of the norm "Yataścodeti sūryo'staṃ yatra ca gacchati | Tandevāścakrire dharmaṃ sa evādya sa u śvaḥ". (Bṛ. Up. 1.5.23).

[134] In the Brahamajāla° "opinions" (diṭṭhis) about Pubbanta and Aparanta are rejected; instead, a form of Paṭṭiccasmuppāda is preached. So in Majjhima, sutta 79. "Api ca Udāyi tiṭṭhatu pubbanto, tiṭṭhatu aparanto Dhammaṃte desessāmi imasmiṃ sati....". The wheel of the cosmic order goes on "without maker, without known beginning, continuously to exist by nature of concatenation of cause and effect" (Vm. XVII. quoted Radhakrishnan op. cit. p. 374) Cf. MK. XI. 1. Also, Cf. Ab. K. Vol. II. p. 67 fn. 2-3. With respect to the impersonality of Paṭiccasam°, cf. Bhāmatī on Brahmasūtra, II. 2. 19 "idampratītya prāpyedamutpadyata ityetāvanmātrasya—dṛṣṭatvāccetanādhiṣṭhānasyānupalabdheḥ." The information of Vācaspati Miśra seems to have been derived from the Āryaśālistambasūtra (compare Vācaspati's explanation of Pratītyasam° given under B. S. II. 2.19 and the long quotation from the Āryaśāli° found in Candrakīrti's comy. on MK. XXVI. 12).

[135] The general formula of Paṭiccasam° states, not 'idaṃ uppannaṃ idaṃ uppādeti" or "amhā idaṃ uppajjati" but merely "imassa uppādā idaṃ uppajjati". The probably implicit spirit of this formulation may be contrasted with that underly-

the antinomies inherent in the question, it refuses to categorise the metaphysical status of things involved in becoming.

The Development of the Idea of Paticcasam°.—The general idea of Paṭiccasam° developed along different lines in the Hīnayāna and the Mahāyāna. The former in its Abhidharmas of Theravāda and Sarvāstivāda elaborated realistic theories of causation;[136] the latter, in pursuance of transcendentalist and idealistic metaphysics, showed the limited significance and ultimate unreality of Paṭiccasam° if understood merely in causal terms. Thus Candrakīrti says "Yastu viparyāsānugamānmṛāṣātvaṃ dharmāṇāṃ nāvagacchati pratītya bhāvānāṃ svabhāvamabhiniviśate sa...... saṃsārepi saṃsarati ......" (MKV. I. p. 45); "Yatra yatra ete pratītyasamutpādādaya uktā na te vigatāvidyātimirānāsravaviṣayasvabhāvāpekṣayā" (ib. p. 41). Nāgārjuna identified Pratītyasamutpāda and the Madhyamā Pratipad with Śūnyatā. Thus MK XXIV 18 declares "Yaḥ pratītyasamutpādaḥ śūnyatāṃ tāṃ pracakṣmahe Sā prajñaptirupādaya pratipatsaiva madhyamā." The two Antas are "Asti yaddhi svabhāvena na tannāstīti śāśvatam Nāstīdanīmabhūtpūrvamityucchedaḥ pravartate.//" (MK XV. 11) The middle way is Śūnyatā and Śūnyatā is "svabhāvānutpattilakṣaṇā" (Candrakīrti ad MK XXIV 18). Gauḍapāda explains the idea very clearly thus "Yathā māyāmayādbījājjāyate tanmayoṅkuraḥ/ Nāsau

ing such statements as "Sa aikṣata bahu syām prajāyeyeti" and "Ātmano vā ākāśaḥ sambhūtaḥ". Much later, this departure became explicity formulated. (see Stcherbatsky. BL. I. p. 121) Things neither produce nor are produced out of one another, but some function as the condition of the uprise of others, and the order between them is invariant.

[136] See note at the end of this Chapter.

nityo na cocchedī tadvaddharmeṣu yojanā// Nājeṣu sarvadharmeṣu śāśvatāśāśvatābhidhā/ Yatra varṇā na vartante vivekastatra nocyate//" (ĀŚ IV. 59-60). Śūnyatā was misunderstood by its opponents as Nihil. The Yogācāras similarly criticised the reality of the causal law and the world governed by it.[137]

Paticcasamuppada—the applied form.—We find in the Nikāyas a number of short, though significant, utterances relating to the origin of Dukkha. These are generally similar, though varying in terms, emphasis, complexity and profundity.

Sometimes a number of them are grouped together to form a sequence of cause and effect. Through the gradual fusion of more than one such sequence appears to have arisen the law of Paṭiccasam° with twelve "links". It is in a way a "hyper-series", and this accounts for much of its apparent inconsistency.

Kamma and Dukkha.—It has already been seen how Buddha's contemporaries held a variety of views on the subject of the origin of Dukkha.[138] The most important of these was the theory of karman advocated in different ways by some Upaniṣadic thinkers, the Jinists and some other Śramaṇa sects. The Nikāyas often show us Buddha preaching this very doctrine.[139] In a forceful recurrent line we are told "Kammassakā sattā kaṃma-

[137] See N. Dutt, Aspects, pp. 230-31; Stcherbatsky, BL. I. pp. 140-41.

[138] Religious Condition in the Age of Buddha.

[139] MN. III. 203ff. (Kammaṃ) Satte vibhajati;Kāyakaṃma, mano°, vacī (Ib. II. 206, 222, 224, 415ff) ; Kāya°, vacī°—(Ib. II. 26ff; III. 289) ; Ib. I. 389 (K°: fourfold) Kasala K° Ib. II. 104; Pāpa—K° SN. I. 93, 372; II. 121; III. 164, 181, 186, 210; Ib. I. 70, 390, Ib. III. 203ff; Ib. III. 357; I. 8. II. 80; I. 287ff; AN. III. 186, IV. 382, II, 230ff, I. 32, V. 292; SN. II. 92, 255, 65, 122, 123, V. 266, 304; IV. 320, 132, 348; Sn. Vāseṭṭha° Verse 60.

dāyādā kaṃmayonī kaṃmabandhū kaṃmappaṭisaraṇā."[140]

It may well be an ancient quotation. Kaṃma is declared to be the principle differentiating men's experiences.[141] Its effects must inevitably be gone through,[142] although some texts, strangely enough, do not seem to regard it as the sole cause of all the misery of man.[143] It is divided into four classes—a division which on account of its colour-terminology is reminiscent of Jinist Leśyās and Ājīvaka Abhijātis.[144] The classification is found identically in the Yogasūtras.[145]

---

[140] MN. III. 203; AN. V. 288; Ib. III. 186.

[141] "Kaṃmaṃ satte vibhajati yadidaṃ hīnappaṇītatāyāti (MN. III. 203).

[142] "Nāhaṃ sañcetanikānaṃ kammānaṃ katānaṃ upacitānaṃ appaṭisaṃviditvā byantibhāvaṃ vadāmi...dukkhassantakiriyaṃ vadāmi" (AN. V. 292. Cf. MN. III. 209) (*i.e. all willed acts past and present, have a consequent affective reaction (Paṭisaṃvedana). This is in a way the "law of Kaṃma"*. On the basis of this text the Mahāsaṅghikas concluded "Sabbaṃ kaṃmam savipākaṃ ti" i.e., there are no vipākābyākatā and kīriyābyakatā cetanās (Kv. XII. 2). It may also be noted that the Theravādins distinguished between kammavipāka and °phala (Kv. Vol. II. p. 313) AN. IV. 382 effects a distinction between "Diṭṭhadhammavedaniya" and "Samparāya"—Kaṃma.

[143] AN. III. 186; SN. IV. 132-133, 230-231, "Buddha" here recognizes kaṃma to be only one of the eight possible causes of pain and pleasure. There are Pitta, Semha, Vāta, Sannipāta, utu, visama. upakkama, kaṃmavipāka. Those who hold kamma to be the sole cause are criticized as going against reason and common experience. Bodily troubles are sometimes due to purely external and (from the standpoint of the individual) accidental circumstances. This is not a view which is often mentioned in the expositions of the Karman doctrine, but, it may be noted, the Milindapañho attaches considerable importance to it (pp. 134-8 ed. Trenckner).

[144] MN. I. 389; DN. III. 230; AN. II. 232-233 "Atthi kammaṃ kaṇhaṃ ...... sukkaṃ ...... kaṇhasukkaṃ .... akaṇhāsukkaṃ......" The Abhidharma, it may be remembered, usually speaks of only three classes—Kusala°, Akusala° and Abyākata. Cf. Dhammapada verse 87 which speaks of Kaṇha and Sukka kamma only.

[145] IV. 7.

Kamma functional, not substantial.—The essence of kamma is will,[146] and the most important type of kamma is, therefore, the voluntary mental act[147]—through association with which alone do speech and physical action become kamma. Both these ideas distinguish the Buddhist view of kamma sharply from that of the Jinists who regarded Kamma as a substance rather than as a function.[148] The division of kamma into mental. "vocal", and physical, it may be noted, is already found in pre-Buddhist Brāhmaṇic literature.[149]

Although a function of the mind, kamma is, yet, in its sequence, to be viewed impersonally. It is not proper to say "Because I, or someone other than myself, did so and so, therefore, I am today having such and such an experience;" one should rather say "Because such and such an act came to pass, therefore such and such is now coming to pass." To bring in terms ex-

---

[146] "Cetānāhaṃ bhikkhave kaṃmaṃ vadāmi; cetayitvā kaṃmaṃ karoti kāyena, vācāya manasā......"

SN. II. 39. 40; AN. II. 157-158 On the meaning of "cetanā" see Mrs. Rhys Davids' note in "Compendium of Philosophy" p. 236, fn. 2. cf. AN. II. 179—where the conative aspect of "cetanā" is apparent. "Will" is here not so much the fusion of "reason" and "impulse" as impulse risen to consciousness (cf. Aung's note—Op. cit. pp. 235-236) Cf. also Ab K. iv. i. which defines kamma as cetanā and "cetayitvā karaṇam". (Stcherbatsky—Central conception—p. 32). Cf. Nāgārjuna "Cetanā cetayitvā ca karmoktaṃ paramarṣinā. Tasyānekavidho bhedaḥ karmaṇaḥ parikīrtitaḥ. Tatra yaccetanetyuktaṃ karma tanmānasaṃsmṛtam. Cetayitvā ca yattūktaṃ tattu kāyikavācikaṃ....... (MK. XVII. 2-3).

Kamma thus originates in will; it is destroyed too through will "yam idaṃ kaṃmaṃ......tassa pahānāya yā cetanā" (AN. II. 232). The process of freedom from Kamma thus implies a struggle between the forces of past and present volition.

[147] M. III. 207.

[148] See above, Chap. "Religious Condition in the Age of Buddha."

[149] See above, Chap. "Review of the Vedic Background."

pressive of an agent (Kārako) and an experiencer (Paṭisaṃvedetā) is to raise the problem of their mutual relation. Are they identical, or are they different? The former answer assuming an unchanging self, denies moral progress, the latter with the opposite assumption, denies moral responsibility. We have thus an impasse. Buddha sought to steer clear of both these extremes.[150] His view seems to have been that change is not to be regarded as the superimposition of a series of varying modifications on an underlying identical substance; rather, we must think here of a sequence of events in necessary order. The ideas of identity and unity, in short, are to be replaced by the ideas of continuity and uniformity.[151] The explicit formulation of this view doubtless belongs to the days of later systematic philosophy,[152] but it seems to be implicit in the ancient fragments on the Middle doctrine. Their emphasis is mainly negative: extremist views of identity and difference, as of sassata and uccheda, are to be avoided through the comprehension of Paṭiccasam°. The consistent logical expansion of this theory on its original positive side would lead to the traditional interpretation sketched above.[153]

---

[150] See above.

[151] The unity belonging to the empirical self thus becomes merely the unity of a complex continuum. The idea is strikingly "heterodox" and was early criticised. See Mbh. Ś. P. 218. 34ff.

[152] Cf. "Tassā tassā paccayasāmaggiyā santatiṃ avicchinditvā tesaṃ tesaṃ dhammānaṃ sambhavato majjhimā paṭipadā." (Vm., p. 365).

[153] Consider the following Nikāya texts: Anattakatāni Kammāni S. II, pp. 64-5; SN. III. 103-4: "Nāyaṃ kāyo tumhākaṃ na pi aññesaṃ. Purāṇamidaṃ.....kammam abhisaṅkhataṃ abhisañcetayitaṃ vedaniyaṃ daṭṭhabbaṃ. Tatra.......... ariyasāvako paṭiccasamuppādaññeva.....sādhukaṃ manasikaroti. Iti imasmiṃ sati idaṃ hoti etc."; Ib. 64 "Taṃjīvaṃ taṃ sarīramiti vā.......diṭṭhiyā sati brahmacariyavāso na hoti.

Popular version of the Kamma theory.—Alongside this refined presentation of the karma-theory, the Nikāyas also show at a few places a more popular version of it.[154] The latter gives expression to the principle of moral retribution operative beyond this life. It employs for this purpose exaggeration and vivid imagery. The difference between these two versions was probably caused primarily through a difference in the respective classes of addressees.

The genesis of Samsara.—Radically, kamma is striving—cetanā, saṅkhāra.[155] But striving itself is not an uncaused ultimate fact. If action leads to the experience of pleasure and pain, the latter in turn through evoking desire and aversion lead to action. This indeed is the closed cycle of life proceeding from beginningless time.[156] It does not however form an unbreakable vicious circle, since both its "synapses" function effectively only if a

Aññaṃ jīvaṃ........"; Ib. 61; Ib. 41-2; Buddha repudiates the views which regard dukkha as sayaṃkata, Paraṃkata or Adhiccasamuppanna, and says, "Paṭiccasamuppannaṃ.......dukkhaṃ vuttaṃ mayā"; Ib. 38-9 which has sukhadukkha for dukkha; Ib. 35-6; Ib. 19-23; Cf. Ib. I, p. 134. "Nayidaṃ attakataṃ bimbaṃ nayidaṃ parakataṃ aghaṃ Hetuṃ paṭicca sambhūtaṃ hetubhaṅgā nirujjhare."

Also cf. Mrs. Rhys Davids—Intr. to K. S. II.

For the clear formulation of the doctrine in later literature, see, e.g., Milindapañho......pp. 46-8 (Trenckner); MK. XVII. 28. cf. La Vallée Poussin. JA. 1902. XX. 237ff.

154 MN. Suttas 129-30, 135-6; SN. I, pp. 37, 72, 93, 95, 97, 227. cf. Winternitz, op. cit., p. 53.

155 On Saṅkhāra see below.

156 See the Anamataggasaṃ° with the forceful refrain "Anamataggāyaṃ bhikkhave Saṃsāro pubbā koti na paññāyati avijjānīvaraṇānaṃ sattānaṃ taṇhāsaṃyojanānaṃ sandhāvataṃ saṃsarataṃ" (SN. II, pp. 178-93).

Cf. Candrakīrti ad Mk. XVII. 28 "Yathoktaṃ sūtre avidyānivṛtāḥ sattvāstṛṣṇāsaṃyojanāḥ." Nāgārjuna quoted the Anamatagga refrain in the following lines "Pūrvā prajñāyate koṭirnetyuvāca mahāmuniḥ. Saṃsāronavarāgro hi nāsyādirnāpi paścimam." (MK. XI. 1).

background of ignorance exists.[157] So soon as it is realized that all the objects of craving—whether mental or physical—are necessarily impermanent, that whatever is impermanent must ultimately turn out to be inadequate to man's longing for lasting satisfaction, and that, consequently, it is, to say the least, unwise to hold on to these impermanent objects as oneself or one's own—so soon as this is realized—the desire for them wanes. Ignorance has, however, settled over man's mind as a hardened film and needs a prolonged and special discipline for its removal.

Paticcasam°, the growth of formula.—In short, in a field of ignorance primitive impulses and affective experience mutually condition and further each other. This is the process of life or Saṃsāra. It was probably some such idea which Buddha in various ways gave utterance to. Apparently he did not put it into a fixed formula, but very soon the tendency to weave the content of his sayings into formulae made its debut, and after a period of fluctuation gave us the celebrated twelve—linked Paṭiccasamuppādanayo..

The Three stages.—Preceding its final stage, at least two other stages may be distinguished in the history of this formula. To the first stage belong the more or less simple statements about the origin of dukkha, claiming to find it in Taṇhā or Chanda or Upadhi or Upādāna.[158] To the second belong those texts which

---

[157] SN. III. 96 cf. Ab. K. Vol. II. p. 71 fn. 4. Ib. p. 72. "*Sāvidyasparśapratyayā vedanā| Sāvidyavedanāpratyayā tṛṣṇā.*"

[158] Perhaps the most ancient picture of this state of the doctrine is to be had in the Aṭṭhakavagga of the Sn. See esp. the Guhaṭṭhaka sutta verses 1-3, 5. 7. Icchā, sāta, kāma, taṇhā, mamāyita, chanda, phassa and saññā—these are the terms which here serve to describe the cause or causes of dukkha.

reveal the formula of Paṭiccasam° in an as yet incomplete

Tanha.—In the fixed wording for the second truth, Taṇhā is described as "Yāyaṃ taṇhā ponobhavikā nandirāgasahagatā tatratatrābhinandinī seyyathīdaṃ kāmataṇhā, bhava°, vibhava°." This formula for the "origin of dukkha" (Dukkhasamudaya) occurs identically in a Sanskrit version also. It is so quoted by Manorathanandin in his comy. on Pramāṇavārtika p. 74 (ed. JBORS 1938).

Taṇhā is the thirst or craving for pleasure. It originates in "piyarūpaṃ", "sātarūpaṃ" (DN. II. p. 308). According to Itv. suttas 14-15, man (puriso) is not able to cross the faring on of the changeful world (itthabhāvaññathābhāvaṃ saṃsāraṃ nātivattati) because he is fettered with craving (taṇhāsaṃyojana) and covered with ignorance (Avijjā=moha=tamokkhandha= Nīvaraṇa). This is in essence not very different from Bṛ. up. IV. 4. 5-6 where men are divided into "Kāmayamāna" and "Akāmayamāna". The former alone wander through the worlds (lokas). "Atho khalvāhuḥ kāmamaya evāyam puruṣa iti sa yathā-kāmo bhavati yatkraturbhavati tatkarma kurute yatkarma kurute tadabhisampadyate." Taṇhā seems to have stepped in the place of karma.

On Taṇhā see SN. I. 1. 6. 5; SN. I. 8, 12; MN. I. 6, II. 256; AN. IV. 400, III. 416; Sn. p. 36 (Nāg. ed); Itv. suttas 30, 50, 58 and 105; Ud. p. 34. (Nāg. ed).

Tanha and Avijja.—The relation of Taṇhā and Avijjā in the causation of dukkha presents a problem. Some doctors of Abhidharma considered the former alone as dukkhasamudaya, see Ledi Sadaw JPTS, 1914, 135. On the other hand, Buddhaghosa says "Bhagavā hi vaṭṭakathaṃ kathento dve dhamme sīsaṃ katvā katheti avijjaṃ vā, yathāha...... (DN. V. 113)......bhavataṇhaṃ vā, yathāha...... (AN. V. 116)......" (Vm. p. 368). Of neither is there a first beginning, although both originate contingently. He further points out that some texts emphasize the one (e.g. SN. II. II. 31), some the other (e.g. SN. II. 84) and some both (e.g. SN. II. 23-4) (Ib). This depicts the position of the Nikāyas soundly. It is the concurrence of Taṇhā and Avijjā that causes dukkha. See supra. This is clearly the position in SN. II. 178f. Cf. the gāthā from the Saṃyukta quoted in Ab. K. IV. p. 136. fn. 2. which sees the origin of dukkha in Karman, Tṛṣṇā and Avidyā. AN. V. 113 calls Avijjā beginningless but "dependent" on the 5 Nīvaraṇas......

Chanda as the root of dukkha—SN. I.22, III. 232-4, IV. 328-30, V. 272-3; MN. III. 16; the parable of the bullocks and the yoke with reference to Chandarāga (SN. IV. cittavagga; Sal. sam. sutta 205 §§ 4-5; it is quoted in its Sanskrit version by Candrakīrti in his comy. on the Catuḥśatikā, see Mem. A. S. B. III. p. 474).

form.[159] An important factor in its growth appears to have been the fusion of at least two distinct approaches to the problem of Saṃsāra. On the one hand it was sought to be explained (*a*) in terms of "clinging" or

---

"Upadhi" as the cause of dukkha–Itv. p. 55; Sn. pp. 3-4, 86, 112; Ud. sutta 14, "Upādāna" as the basic evil–AN. I. 142 III. 311. "Phassa" as samudaya–AN. IV. 339, V. 107; SN. II. 33. Misery as "Piyajātika"–MN. II. 106.

In this first form the "formula" is already adumbrated in the Upaniṣads–See Bṛ. up. loc. cit; cf. Śaṅkara on Ch. up. VII. 23. I. It is this state that is reflected in the description of the Buddhist view in Mbh. Ś. P. 218. 32-4: "Avidyākarmaceṣṭānāṃ Kecidāhuḥ punarbhave Kāraṇaṃ lobhamohau tu Doṣāṇāṃ tu niṣevaṇam|| Avidyāṃ kṣetramāhurhi Karma bījam tathā kṛtam. Tṛṣṇā sañjananaṃ sneha eṣa teṣāṃ Punarbhavaḥ|| etc."

159 This stage is reflected in *many suttas of the Nidānasam°* (see the Chap. on the stratification of SN.), SN. IV. 87; DN. Mahānidānasutta; MN. 1. 266 (cf. Vm. p. 367); AN. IV. 400 Ib. v. 113-6; DN. sutta 1 (cf. Sumaṅgalavilāsinī I. p. 125 PTS ed.).

This falsifies the opinion expressed in the Pali Dictionary (PTS) that the earliest version of Paṭiccasam° contained ten Nidānas.

The Sakkapañha sutta (DN. II.) and Sn. pp. 77-8, 94-5 also probably belong to this stage, since, in spite of the opportunity, they do not give us the usual formula of Paṭiccasam° (Cf. Keith–B. P. pp. 97-9; Sakya–p. 187).

The irregularity in the versions of Paṭiccasam° is indeed so marked that it was noted by later Buddhist and even Non-Buddhist writers See Ab. K. II. 60-1 (fn. 1) where it is stated that the sūtras sometimes speak of 12 Bhavaṅgas, sometimes 11, sometimes 10, sometimes 9 and sometimes 8. Saṅghabhadra utilized this evidence to establish that "Le Pratītyasamutpāda n'est donc pas seulement de douze Aṅgas" (Ib). *This is perfectly correct.* Buddhaghosa, on the other hand, faced with the same fact says "Kasmā panevaṃ desetīti? Paṭiccasamuppādassa samantabhaddakattā, sayañca desanāvilasappattattā" (Vm. pp. 366-7).

As to Non-Buddhist writers Śaṅkara seems to have noted it. See his comy. ad. BS. 2. 2. 19. "Te cāvidyādayaḥ......Kvacit Saṅkṣiptā nirdiṣṭāḥ kvacit prapañcitāḥ."

Cf. P. Masson Oursel. Esquisse d'une Histoire de la Philosophie Indienne–p. 87 f.

The general idea of Paṭiccasam° was applied to form other causal sequences also than the one of the Twelve Nidānas. See AN. IV. 99; III. 19-20, 81, 191; I. 258; SN. II. 30-1, 150 (the last may be aptly called Paṭiccapaññāpana).

"craving" resulting from "contact" and "feeling";[160] on the other (*b*) in terms of the entanglement of Viññāṇa in Nāmarūpa.[161] The former approach was more psychological; the latter more metaphysical. Finally the two fused.

The meaning of the Paccaya-relation.—It has been observed that the relation between the Nidānas is not uniform.[162] Thus the relation between Avijjā and Saṅkhāra is not identical with that between Jāti and Jarāmaraṇa. And neither is identical with that between Viññāṇa and Nāmarūpa. But one can still say that in every case the antecedent in the sequence of Paṭiccasam° is a condition necessary and sufficient to the subsequent. This is the implication of the method of specifying the relation between the terms in the Anuloma and Viloma orders. The former order shows that the "Paccaya" is sufficient to the "Paccayuppanna"; the latter that it is necessary. The attempt to specify exactly the nature of Paccaya in each case probably led to the development of the Abhidharma theory of the Paccayas.[163]

---

[160] Thus in SN. II. Nidāna vagga sutta 32, 43, 52-3, 55-60; DN. sutta 1.

[161] Thus in the Nidānavagga—suttas 38-40, 64; SN. III. pp. 9, 53; Ib. V. 184. See also the Chap. on Nirvāṇa.

[162] Keith—B. P. p. 96; Rhys Davids—American Lectures p. 160; N. Dutt—Early Monastic Buddhism—Vol. I. pp. 266-7 "......any two links are related to each other in one or more of the twenty-four ways (Paccayas), for which the general expression is "imasmiṃ sati idaṃ hoti........" Thus viññāṇa is related to Nāmarūpa as aññamañña, Jāti is related to Jarāmaraṇa as pure-jāta and upanissaya, and so forth." Cf. Kv. XV. 1-2.

[163] Cf. "Tattha tabbhāvabhāvibhāvākāramattopalakkhito Paṭiccasamuppādanayo Paṭṭhānanayo pana āhacca Paccayaṭṭhitimārabbha pavuccati. Ubhayam pana vomissitvā papañcenti Ācariyā" (Abhidhammatthasaṅgaho p. 140). The reference is to Buddhaghosa (Ib. 141). In the Ab. K. also the general theory of Hetus and Pratyayas is treated separately from Pratīya-

The various Nidanas: Avijja.—Avijjā is usually defined as the ignorance of the Four Truths,[164] but the texts in which this definition occurs can hardly be considered very early.[165] In one ancient text already quoted it is called Moha and Tamokhandha.[166] Perhaps originally it did not mean merely error or ignorance (taken literally).[167] The entire system of subliminal impressions and habits predisposing man to erroneous belief and speculation was also, perhaps, intended to be understood by the expression Avijjā. Thus would Avijjā be a Nīvaraṇa and require a strenuous discipline to unsettle it.

Sankhara: Saṅkhāra is used variously in the Nikāyas,[168] but seems to signify in the sequence of Paṭiccasam°, the conative factors making for rebirth and persisting

---

sam°. Cf. "Compendium"—pp. 187-8. Nāgārjuna too treats the theory of Pratyaya in independence of that of the 12 Aṅgas, the first occupying the opening chapter of MK. the second the 26th.

164 Nidāna sam. vg. I. sutta 2. (Vibhaṅga); MN. Sammādiṭṭhi°°; See also the ref. in Ab. K. vol. II. p. 75 fn. 2. On the meaning of this ignorance cf. Ab. K. Vol. II. p. 92.

165 See Chaps on the stratification of SN. & MN.

166 Cf. the quotation in Ab. K. vol. II. p. 71 fn. 2; Also Sogen-System—p. 131. Candrakīrti says "Tatrāvidyātamaḥ sammoha iti paryāyāḥ" (ad MK. XVII. 28 which seems to have an implicit reference to some such scriptural text as the refrain of the Anamataggasaṃ°).

167 Cf. Ib. p. 88 Among others it is established that "Lávidyā n'est pas, de se nature, prajñā" (Ib. p. 91). It is as different from the latter as rāga is from thought. (Ib. fn. 2).

Also cf. "Bhadantaśrīlābha evam manyate avidyeti sarvakleśānāmiyaṃ sāmānyasañjñā na rāgādikleśavyatiriktāvidyā nāmāstīti". (Ab. K. Vyākhyā fol. 150. quoted in Minayeff op. cit. p. 226).

168 AN. IV. 100, 311, 313; Ib, III. 441f; AN. II. 94; AN. I. 26f. Ib. III. 443, Ib. VIII; Ib. I. 286; SN. I. 6, 200 Ib. II. 191-193, Ib. III. 132-134. Ib. I. 188, 135 Ib. II. 82. The significance her is generally vague.

into another life.[169] It is practically equivalent to Kamma.[170]

Vinnana and Namarupa.—It is well known that some major versions of Paṭiccasam° stop with viññāṇa, contenting themselves with declaring viññāṇa, and nāma-rūpa interdependent.[171] In some texts viññāṇa seems practically to play the part of "soul" or "spirit".[172] Similarly in some texts "Nāmarūpa" seems to have a more general signification than that of the Five Khandhas.[173] It was probably later that viññāṇa came to be restricted to the cognitive factor in the mental complex.[174] It thus appears that there is no breach of continuity in the development of the ideas of Viññāṇa and Nāmarūpa from the Upaniṣads to later Buddhism.

---

169 See MN. Saṃmādiṭṭhi sutta; Saṅkhāruppatti°; Nidānavagga—2 (2)—consider SN. II. 66, 101 SN. II. 4, 39-40, IV. 293; AN. V. III; I. 122, II. 158, 231, II. 41.

170 See "Compendium" p. 274; Keith—BP. p. 100 Cf. "Punarbhavāya saṃskārānavidyānivṛtastathā. Abhisaṃskurute yāṃstairgatiṃ gacchati karmabhiḥ." (MK. XXVI. 1).

171 Mahāpadāna° (DN.), Mahānidāna° (DN.); SN. II. Nid. Saṃ s. 65; Ib. s. 67.

172 DN. Sutta 15 describes Viññāṇa as descending into the mother's womb and receiving a platform (Patiṭṭhā) in Nāmarūpa. Similar is the import in the Nidāna saṃ suttas 38-40 and 64 (See comments in Chap. on SN. above); with these should be correlated the texts referring to "Gandharva" (MN. pt. II. 367-8 Nāg. ed). See Poussin, "Dogme" p. 14; Mrs. Rhys Davids, Sakya pp. 158-159.

173 DN. Pt. II. p. 49 (Nāg. ed); SN. II. 66, 90, 101f (the Khandha theory is probably not assumed here) SN. I. 13, 15, 35, 60, 165; SN. I. 1. 7. 1. MN. III. 17; Cf. SN. II. p. 3 (Nāma is here analysed into Vedanā, Saññā Cetanā, Phasso, and Manasikāro); cf. Sn. pp. 36, 55, 82, 102, 110, 115, 118; Itv. p. 31; Dhp. verse 221, 367; AN. IV. 385 (Nāmarūpārammaṇā uppajjanti saṅkappavitakkā). The meaning of Nāmarūpa does not seem to remain the same in these texts. In some cases it appears to be nearer the Upaniṣadic than the Abhidhammic usage.

174 See Chap. on Nirvāṇa.

Ayatanas.—The six Āyatanas doubtless refer to the six spheres of cognitive consciousness viz., of the five senses and the mind regarded as the sixth sense.[175] "Sense" and "Sense-object" are here taken together.[176]

Phassa.—Although there can hardly be a doubt about the general meaning of "Phassa" being sense contact, its precise status and function are not uniformly described in the Nikāyas.[177]

Vedana and Tanha.—The same is the case with Vedanā.[178] Taṇhā in spite of its great importance, is

---

[175] MN. I. 52, II. 237 etc. cf. MN. II. 233.

[176] Cf. MN. I. 61, III. 32, 63, 216, 280f.

It is curious that the Mahānidāna° not only omits "Avijjā" and "Saṅkhāra" but also Ṣaḍāyatana! It says "Nāmarūpapaccayā phasso ti", dividing "Phassa" into "Adhivacanasamphassa" and "Paṭigha°" and declaring both these interdependent.

[177] See Chap. on the stratification of SN. Phassa as conditioning Vedanā—SN. II. 6, III. 101, IV. 32 f. etc; as conditioning **Saññā** and Saṅkhāra—Ib. III. 101-2; as the condition for the 'Paññāpanā' of Vedanā, Saññā and Saṅkhāra—MN. III. 17; as a factor of Nāmarūpa—SN. II. 3 (So the Sammadiṭṭhi s. in the MN.); as one of the four Āhāras—SN. II. 11, 13, 98f etc.

[178] It is sometimes divided into two—pleasure and pain; sometimes, through the addition of a neutral feeling, into three —see MN. I. 386, SN. IV. IV. 223; MN. I. 302f, 376f, 475f, 500, II. 236, III. 208, 285 etc. In SN. IV. 223—Pañcaṅgika Thapati says to Udāyin "Na kho tisso vedanā vuttā bhagavatā. . . .yāyaṃ adukkhasukhā vedanā santasmiṃ esā paṇite sukhe vuttā. . . ."

At one place in the MN. there is talk of a "sukha" which is not a Vedanā. SN. IV. 231 speaks of the following classifications of Vedanā: into 2 (kāyikā ca cetasikā ca—this is different from SN. IV. 223); into the usual three; into 5 (Sukhindriyaṃ, dukkhi°, somanass°, domanass° and upekh°); into 6 (cakkhusamphassajā. . . .mano°); into 18 (the three sixes of somanassupavicārā, domanss°, upekh°); into 36 (each of the sixes just mentioned divided into geddhasita° and nekkhama°); into 108 by considering each of the 36 with reference to past, present and future. Cf. MN. I. 396; 6 Vedanākāyas—in SN. III. 59-60; Cf. the divisions of veyaṇā into sīyā, usiṇā, sīyusaṇā in Bhagavatī X. Ud. 2.

sometimes incorrectly rendered "desire".[179] With it seem to have been associated the ideas of sensuous pleasure-seeking and insatiability.[180]

Upadana.—Upādāna[181] is the clinging to an object thirsted after, and is hence "conditioned" by taṇhā.

Bhava.—The exact and full import of Bhava in the Nikāyas (i.e. not counting the later parts of the Khuddaka) is not clear. It has been classified into kāma°, rūpa° and arūpa°[182] Mrs. Rhys Davids' arguments to prove that "Bhava" was once not a depreciated term are unconvincing.[183]

Conclusion about the 12 Nidanas.—This treatment of Paṭiccasam° (i.e. the 12 membered formula) repudiates the assumption that it was the result of deliberate

---

[179] Mrs. Rhys Davids puts the point forcefully. "We cannot afford to impoverish our ethical (and aesthetical) concepts by squandering this term (Desire) outright on taṇhā, and thereby, so to speak, making the devil a present of all desire.... craving (or unregenerate desire, Begierde) serves admirably for taṇhā. Desire belongs to our psychology of feeling plus will as a term of unmoral import as such. Hence (it ought to be retained) for chanda, which....is, as a cetasika, unmoral. Dhammachanda is moral, and is only immoral as Kāmachanda, or when substituted for taṇhā." ("Compendium" p. 215 fn.). It may be noted that the Pubbaseliyas maintained that "Dhammataṇhā abyākatā" and that "Dhammataṇhā na dukkhasamudayo" (Kvu. xiii. 9-10). Cf. MN. I. 352—Dhammarāgo, °nandī. Nāgārjuna condemned Dharmacchanda also.

[180] Taṇhā is sometimes described as 3 fold: kāma°, bhava°, vibhava°, e.g. SN. II. 100, III. 26 AN. III. 445; sometimes as 2 fold e.g. Ud. p. 34 (bhava°, vibhava°). Sometimes as 6 fold (with ref. to the senses) e.g. DN. sutta 15, SN. II. 3. on Taṇhāvicaritas see AN. II. 212f. Taṇhā was considered to belong to the same class as Rāga, Chanda, Pema, Pipāsā, and Pariḷāha (AN. II. 174) cf. Taṇhāvagga in Dhp. The simile of the Māluvā creeper is found also in MN. sutta 45.

[181] It is described as 4 fold (kāma° diṭṭhi, sīlabbata°, and Attavāda) in DN. Sutta 15, and Nidāna saṃ° sutta 2 (2).

[182] Loc. cit.

[183] Cf. however, Dhp. verse 282.

thought on the part of any one individual, and consequently it is futile to attempt to uniquely determine the meaning of its terms and their relations. They are amenable only to a historical treatment. Apart from the central idea—in its generality and in its application to dukkha-samudaya—the formula has grown through accretions, fusions and analyses. In its full grown form, consequently, it has about it an aura of vagueness, and in the details, even of inconsistency. To appreciate the oddities sometimes resulting from a long process of meandering growth is perhaps more the historical student's task than to seek to reduce these to systematic uniformity.[184]

---

[184] (a) *The interpretation of Paṭiccasam° in later Theravāda*: Paṭiccasam° is an extended statement of the fundamental principle that the Kammabhava of one life determines the Upapattibhava of another. Avijjā, taṇhā, upādāna, saṅkhāra and kamma constitute the Kammabhava, while Viññāṇa, Nāmarūpa, Saḷāyatana, Phassa and Vedanā, constitute the Upapattibhava. The formula mentions only two elements of the kammabhava of the past life (the rest being implied in them), all the five elements of the present kammabhava (the rest being implicit), while it merely indicates the future upapattibhava by mentioning Jāti and Jarāmaraṇa. (Aung's note in "Compendium" pp. 262-264). On the explanation of the separate terms and relations see Vm. p. 369f. Avijjā is an obstruction to true vision, Saṅkhāra essentially conation—cetanā, viññāṇa—the 6 fold **"resultant"** consciousness and Nāmarūpa the remaining four khandhas. Bhava is two-fold-kamma° and upapatti°.

(b) *In Sarvāstivāda*: Vijñāna is the first moment of a new life arising out of pre-natal forces (Avidyā and Saṃskāra). The next seven members mark the development of the embryo into a child, youth and grown-up man. The stage of tṛṣṇā corresponds to that of sexual maturity. The last two members refer to the future life. All the elements are present throughout, the difference being only that of relative prominence.

(Stcherbatsky-Conception pp. 28-29). This interpretation, it may be observed, receives in some measure the striking though solitary support of *MN. I.* 265-270.

Rosenberg distinguishes between a popular and a philosophical interpretation of the formula. The former sees in it "eine *Lebensbeschreibung des bewuszten Wesens* wobei diese

Beschreibung drei aufeinanderfolgende Leben umfaszt" (Die Probleme—p. 211). Here the following term in the sequence is not derived from the preceding in any logical or dynamical sense, but it is determined by the latter in the sense "dasz er in der Folge des ersten in die Erscheinung tritt" (Ib. p. 215).

The task of philosophical interpretation is to explain the twelve-linked formula from the standpoint of the "Dharmatheorie" (Ib). From this standpoint there is *"eine endlose Transformation des Dharmakomplexes,* es erfolgt *eine Umgruppierung der Substratelemente*....die aber doch individual verschieden sind and sich niemals wiederholen (Ib. p. 216)." In the Ab. K., Avidyā is defined as Pūrvakleśadaśā and Saṃskāra as old Karman (Vol. II. p. 62 fn. 1) Bhava is explained as "Bhavatyanena" (Ib. p. 64). That is, Bhava is equated to Kammabhava.

Pratītyasam° is considered to be fourfold—Kṣaṇika, Prākarṣika, Sāmbandhika and Āvasthika (Ib. p. 65f). The first indicates that in any act of passion twelve factors are realized—Moha (Avidā) cetanā (Saṃskāra), a certain vijñāna, concomitant skandhas (four or three), the senses, the application of these, feeling, rāga (taṇhā), the Paryavasthānas (like ahrī etc. —upādāna), action (Bhava) the production of all these dharmas (Jāti), their Paripāka (Jarā) and Bhaṅga (maraṇa). This emphasizes the immanence of Pratītyasam° in all life of passion (Kleśa). It is, further, Prākarṣika, being "Prabandhayukta" and Sāmbandhika, being "Hetuphalasambandhayukta" (Ib. fn. 1). It is Āvasthika since it consists of a succession of the states of the five skandhas. According to Saṅghabhadra, the Masters of Abhidharma held that Buddha taught Pratītyasam° in this last aspect (Ib. 66 fn. 5).

CHAPTER XII

NIRVĀṆA

Controversies regarding Nirvana, and the historical perspective.—From ancient times there has been a great diversity of interpretations concerning the nature of Nirvāṇa as taught by Buddha. Partly at least it has been due to the fact that in the light of the later developed philosophic thought the original texts appeared to be deficient in precision. The interpreter therefore concerned himself with determining the unexpressed implications of his texts, and in this he naturally took the assistance of his own philosophy about things. Since different interpreters had different philosophies, a diversity of interpretations was the inevitable consequence. Further, in accordance with their philosophic predilections, different interpreters emphasized different texts, even to the extent of composing new ones and suppressing some of the more disagreeable ones.[1] Still it must be said that some at least of these later philosophic theories do have some basis in the original or Nikāyan texts. And but for the wealth of these later ideas, indeed, the catholicity and profound suggestiveness of some of the Nikāya texts would have been partly lost. We have here a historical relation which has some parallels to that between the Upaniṣads and the later schools of Vedānta. One is inclined to say that Nāgārjuna is to

[1] Thus the greater part of the Mahāyāna sūtras, which claim to be authentic, is recognized to be "late". Even before Mahāyāna, the sects occasionally quarrelled about the authenticity of particular sūtras—See Ab. K. Vol. V. p. 251.

"Buddhavacana" what Śaṅkara is to the Upaniṣads. The demonstration of this opinion, it is hoped, will emerge from the following pages as a whole.

The interpretations of Nirvana: (*i*) Ancient (*a*) Theravadin.—Commentarial tradition identifies the "Asaṅkhatadhātu" of the Dhs with Nirvāṇa but according to Mrs. R. Davids this represents a later development.[2] The Asaṅkhata-dhātu is described in the Dhs as ethically "abyākata", "void of the working of conception or thought discursive", infinite (appamāṇa), not a cause nor associated with one, invisible and non-impinging, without material form, supramundane, not of the intellect, not derived, not joyous, unaccompanied by joy, ease or disinterestedness, and something having no Beyond.[3] It is contrasted with all Form (Sabbaṃ rūpam)[4] and distinguished from Arahatta by "neither pertaining nor not pertaining to studentship....."[5]

The word "Nibbāna", on the other hand, occurs but once in the Dhs and that too in its closing sentences where Nibbāna is called one of the two kinds of Vimutti.[6]

May it not be suggested that the Asaṅkhata and Nibbāna of Dhs are the same thing viewed in two ways: metaphysically or "an sich", and as the ultimate goal of spiritual efforts?

Kathavatthu.—In the age of Kv. (or rather, in one of the periods represented by Kv) the Theravādins ri-

[2] B. P. E. p. 166—fn. 1; 367.
[3] Ib. pp. 368-369.
[4] Ib. p. 166—fn. 1.
[5] Ib. pp. 264-265.
[6] Ib. p. 259 & fn. 2. Cf. "Tattha aṭṭha samāpattiyo sayaṃ vikkhambhitakilesehi vimuttattā vimuttīti vuttā, nibbānaṃ pana sabbakilesehi accantavimuttattā vimuttīti" (Aṭṭhasālinī—p. 322 ed. Bapat & Vadekar).

gorously insisted on the oneness of Nibbāna[7] which was conceived as "Dhuvaṃ sassataṃ aviparināmadhammaṃ"[8] anārammaṇa,[9] cittavippayutta.[10]

In the Milindapañho Nibbāna is considered to be something positive,[11] non-temporally eternal[12] and supremely beatific.[13] It can be experienced[14] though not described.[15]

Buddhaghosa.—Buddhaghosa describes Nibbāna as "Santilakkhaṇaṃ, accutirasaṃ assāsakaraṇarasaṃ vā, animittapaccupaṭṭhānaṃ nippapañcapaccupaṭṭhānaṃ vā."[16] He vigorously combats the view that Nibbāna is a non-Ens, or a mere absence or annihilation of the passions etc.[17] The terms sa-upādisesa and anupādisesa are only upādāyapaññattis of Nibbāna, the essence of which is indescribable (though experienceable).[18]

Anuruddhacariya.—The view of Anuruddhācariya is basically the same, though more clearly and briefly expressed. Nibbāna is, for him, eternal, transcendental, supreme, "realizable"[19] and unique. It is the "ārammaṇa" of the "maggaphalas".[20]

Theravāda, thus, throughout its long history, consistently held Nibbāna to be positive, experienceable, indescribable and supreme—the most worthwhile.

---

[7] Points of Controversy p. 137—fn. 4.
[8] Kv. 1.6.
[9] Ib. 9.5.
[10] Ib. 14.6.
[11] MP. (Nāgarī ed.) p. 265.
[12] Ib. p. 316; 264.
[13] Ib. p. 317, 72, 306 (It is called paramaṃ sukham, ekantasukham).
[14] Ib. p. 263, 265.
[15] Ib. p. 309-310.
[16] Vm. p. 355.
[17] Ib.
[18] Ib. 356 cf. Dutt, Aspects pp. 170-71.
[19] Sacchikātabba.
[20] Abhidhammatthasaṅgaho pp. 124-125 (ed. Kosambi).

The three Nirodhas: (*b*) **Vaibhasikas.**—According to the Vibhāṣā there are three kinds of Nirodhas—Pratisaṅkhyā°, a°°, anityatā°.[21] The first two are asaṃskṛta while the third is saṃskṛta. The Jñānaprasthāna explains the first as "tout Nirodha qui est disjonction (viṣaṃyoga)."[22] This Viṣaṃyoga is not produced; there is only a "prāpti" of it through pratisaṅkhyā.[23] Apratisaṅkhyā° is defined as "tout Nirodha qui n'est pas disjonction."[24] Anityatānirodha is "la dispersion, la brisure, la cessation, la chute, la mort, la perte des saṃskāras." By this one only wants to indicate that the activity of the Saṃskāras comes to an end. Their "svabhāva" is, however, not destroyed.

Nirvana.—The first Nirodha is termed Nirvāṇa which is Asādhāraṇa in the sense that all do not acquire it simultaneously and asabhāga in the sense that it has no sabhāga-hetu. It is Kuśala and Nitya.[25] It is neither a Skandha, nor merely the absence of the Skandhas, but "c'est seulement relativement aux skandhas impurs (Sāsrava) qu'il obtient son existence propre."[26] One of the explanations offered for its being called Avarṇa is that it is realized by the Aryas "dans une conaissance immédiate" (Pratyakṣa).[27] It is Parama, Prativedha, Paṇḍitapremaṇīya, Praṇīta and Nissaraṇa; when it is "Nirupādhi" there remains nothing but Dharmatā.[28]

---

[21] La Vallée Poussin B. L'Ec. Fr. 1930 p. 1.

[22] Ib. p. 2.

[23] Ab. K. Vol. I. pp. 8-9. Pratisaṅkhyā is unique as a class (Ib); La Vallée Poussin op. cit. p. 6.

[24] Loc. cit. cf. Ab. K. I. p. 10: Sogen, Systems—pp. 164-165.

[25] La Vallée Poussin op. cit. pp. 8-9.

[26] Ib. p. 10.

[27] Ib. p. 16. Pratisaṅkhyā or Prajñā is non-discursive (Atīraṇa) and intuitive—Ab. K. I. p. 81.

[28] Ib. p. 27, cf. Ab. K. I. pp. 70-71.

Nirvana as "noumenal".—Nirvāṇa is thus conceived as real and eternal. It is the Dharmasvabhāva which alone remains on the cessation of Dharmalakṣaṇa. Stcherbatsky aptly compares it to the Prakṛti of the Sāṅkhyas.[29] It is impersonal and inexplicable. "La nature des choses est profonde; certainement, elle ne peus pas être établie par le raisonnement."[30] It is, in short, the non-temporal nature of the elements which we experience as active in time.[31]

(*c*) **Sautrantikas.**—They believed generally in the purely negative character of 'Nirvāṇa';[32] although they at the same time believed in the "survival of a subtle consciousness merged in the plane of complete quiescence." But some denied this (Obermiller, op. cit. pp. 235—37; Stcherbatsky, op. cit. pp. 29—31; Dutt, op. cit. pp. 177—82).

(*d*) **Vijnanavadins or the Yogacaras.**—According to Yogācāra, the Bodhisattva acquires Mahāparinirvāṇa through the manifestation of Parāvṛtti. Nirvāṇa is in its nature essentially pure but like the moon covered with clouds it becomes visible only when the wind of the Way dissipates its adventitious veils. This manifesta-

---

[29] Nirvāṇa—pp. 27-28. Some Vaibhāṣikas, however, believed in the "survival" of a pure spiritual principle—See Obermiller—I. H. Q. X. p. 235.

[30] Ab. K. IV. p. 65.

[31] Prof. Dutt says that the interpretation of Stcherbatsky is "unsupported by the canonical as well as the non-canonical texts" (op. cit. p. 163) i.e. there are no reasons to identify the Asaṃskṛta dhātu called Nibbāna with the Dharmasvabhāva of the saṃskṛta elements. Prof. Dutt would find an analogue of Nirvāṇa in the Puruṣa of Sāṅkhya in case the innumerable Puruṣas formed one Asaṃskṛta Dhātu (Ib. p. 164).

[32] It is apparently this view that Śaṅkara criticizes in his comy. ad. BS. 2.2.24: "Avastu nityaṃ ceti vipratiṣiddhaṃ Na hyavastuno nityatvamanityatvaṃ vā saṁbhavati, vāstavāśrayatvāddharmadharmivyavahārasya."

tion is called the attainment of Nirvāṇa. Four kinds of Nirvāṇa are distinguished in the Vijñaptimātratāsiddhi. (of Hiuan Tsang, tr. La Vallée Poussin, Vol. II. pp. 670 ff.).

(1) *Anādikālika-prakṛti—śuddha-nirvāṇa.*—It is pure in itself; provided with numberless and measureless excellent qualities; free from production and destruction, like space; equal (sama) and common (sādhāraṇa) for all beings (cf. Saddharmapuṇḍarīka V. 83); neither identical nor different from the Dharmas (being Dharmatā itself); free from all 'nimitta' and 'vikalpa'; beyond 'vitarka-vicāra'; beyond words; realised within. It is the eternally quiescent (prakṛtiśānta) Tathatā.

(2) *Sopadhiśeṣa-nirvāṇa.*—It is equivalent to Tathatā freed from the veil of Kleśas (Kleśāvaraṇa-parimukta). Upadhi, however, remains, i.e., "des Dharmas de rétribution, qui sont le support d'une douleure subtile, n'ont pas encore pris fin."

(3) *Nirupadhiśeṣa-nirvāṇa.*—This is Tathatā freed from the suffering of Saṃsāra; not only are Kleśas exhausted but also all Upadhi which is 'sāsravaduḥkhaphalāśraya'.

(4) *Apratiṣthita-nirvāṇa.*—Which is Tathatā freed from Jñeyāvaraṇa, and hence ever-assisted by Mahākaruṇā and Mahāprajñā. By virtue of the latter, it is not fixed (pratiṣṭhita) in Saṃsāra, and Karuṇā prevents it from becoming 'pratiṣṭhita' in 'nirvāṇa'. It is 'aparāntakoṭiniṣṭha', although ever quiescent. Of these the last three are the successive manifestations in spiritual experience of the first, which is Nirvāṇa in its eternity. (Vide Siddhi II. 679).

Nirvāṇa is, thus, the ultimate essential reality (paramārtha, pariniṣpannalakṣaṇa). It is Nirāvaraṇa-Tathatā, Suviśuddha-Dharmadhātu (Siddhi. loc. cit.). It is a monistic spiritual principle i.e., there is no ultimate difference between Nirvāṇa and Saṃsāra. "In their imputed aspect......the causally dependent elements constitute phenomenal life......in their absolute aspect......the same elements represent Nirvāṇa. The transition from Saṃsāra to Nirvāṇa consists in the change of the main point of view."[33] Concentrating on the absolute essence the Yogin is fully absorbed in it. This process does not destroy the phenomenal elements but "only conveys....their perfect transformation (āśraya-parāvṛtti) into component elements constituting the personality of the Buddha."[34] This is the Dharmakāya which is equivalent to Prapañcopaśama, is eternally quiescent (ādiśānta) beyond the forms of the quadrilemma (catuṣkoṭi-vinirmukta), the unique essence of the elements (Paramātman).[35]

(*e*) **Madhyamikas.**—The correct interpretation of their views has been only a little less subject to controversy than that of the views of Buddha himself. The Brāhmaṇic philosophical tradition and many European scholars have represented them as utter nihilists. The consensus of Japanese scholars is, on the other hand, definitely opposed to such an interpretation, and Prof. Stcherbatsky, who has examined the question at length, supports them.[36] He thinks that Śūnyatā meant only

[33] Obermiller op. cit. p. 241.

[34] Ib. p. 242. See Laṅkāvatāra Sūtra, 98; Siddhi II. pp. 610-11; 661ff.

[35] Ib. pp. 256-257 cf. Stcherbatsky—op. cit. pp. 31-34; Suzuki —Outlines,—Chap. XIII, esp. pp. 345-346 and pp. 349-352 on the important conception of Apratiṣṭhita Nirvāṇa, on which also cf. Stcherbatsky op. cit. p. 185, fn. 3 and Obermiller—op. cit. pp. 254-255, and Suzuki—Studies in the Laṅkāvatāra—pp. 127f. Laṅkāvatāra Sūtra 184-5. Cf. Buddhist Texts pp. 206-7 (ed. Conze).

[36] Op. cit. p. 35f.

the relativity of individual things and ideas. The Mādhyamikas showed the dialectical and discrepant character of all our ideas about reality only with the intention of showing that although the picture of the world as constructed by the senses and intellect is valid for practical purposes, it is not ultimately satisfactory. Thus it is that one is constrained to say that absolute or independent reality cannot belong to individual or finite objects i.e. all dharmas are svabhāvaśūnya. Of absolute reality itself it is impossible to say anything, for to speak about it will be to determine it, to make the absolute relational.[37]

Nāgārjuna in his treatment of Nirvāṇa seems to offer a consistent philosophical explanation of the traditional silence of Buddha when asked to define transcendental objects like the Tathāgata beyond death and the Attā in terms of existence, non-existence etc. Buddha kept silent because the asked for determinations were inapplicable. Thus Nirvāṇa cannot be non-existence, else it will cease to be uncaused and unconditioned.[38] It cannot be existence for the same reason.[39] It cannot be both, for both are conditioned (Saṃskṛta) while Nirvāṇa is unconditioned (a°).[40] To call Nirvāṇa "neither existence nor non-existence" will be tantamount to speaking the unspeakable.[41] It is just the

[37] See below....where other explanations of the "silence" are also discussed.

[38] See e.g. M. K. XXV 8. On the supposition of an absolute non-existence (anupādāya abhāvaḥ) Candrākīrti says "Vandhyāputra iti śabdamātramevaitannāsvārtha upalabhyate" (Ib. p. 196. Cal. ed).

[39] Ib. Kārikās 4-7.

[40] Ib. Kārikā—13. Candrakīrti says "svahetupratyayasāmagrīsambhūtatvāt saṃskṛtaḥ...."

[41] See Stcherbatsky—op. cit. p. 210 fn. 2; and Candrakīrti's Comment on MK. XXV. 16.

eternal quiescence of all phenomena (Prapañcopaśamaḥ) the utterly well (śivaḥ).[42]

The Buddhist conception of Nirvana: "Santa" and "Asamskrta".—This survey shows that hardly ever did the Buddhists regard Nirvāṇa as just the blank of annihilation. Even the Sautrāntikas generally admitted the survival of a subtle spiritual consciousness. Further, there is a complete unanimity among the schools about the Asaṃskṛtahood of Nirvāṇa. Nirvāṇa is eternally beyond the pale of causes and conditions. The schools, further, agree that since Nirvāṇa presents no particularizing traits, it is impossible to properly express it in speech; it can only be intuited. Finally, it is the ultimate Good, the end of all restlessness and striving. We may generalize and say that the Buddhist conception of Nirvāṇa always includes that of eternal and ineffable peace.[43]

(II) Modern: *Wassiljew.*—Wassiljew says "Der ursprüngliche Begriff des Nirvāṇa oder desjenigen Zustandes. . . . ist nichts anders als der Begriff der vollständigen Vernichtung oder des Austritts aus der Reihe der

[42] M. K. XXV. 24 & Candrakīrti's comm. upon it. Cf. Śvet. Up. 4.18. Stcherbatsky says that Nāgārjuna has in effect three Nirvāṇas "The first represents the world sub specie aeternitatis. . . The second is the condition of the Mahāyānistic saint. . . . The third corresponds to his disappearance in final Nirvāṇa. The first alone is ultimately real, the two others are immanent in it, they are not separately (svabhāvataḥ) real" (op. cit. p. 185 fn. 2).

Cf. Suzuki—Studies in the Laṅkāvatāra—p. 129—"True Nirvāṇa is that which is realized in the oneness of Nirvāṇa and Saṃsāra, absolute or Śūnya in its nature, and above the relativity of eternalism and nihilism."

[43] Sogen calls "Nirvāṇaṃ śāntam" one of the three cardinal principles of all Buddhism—op. cit. p. 7, 28f; Rhys Davids compares Nirvāṇa to the advent of the kingdom of Heaven within a man, "the peace that passeth understanding". (American Lectures—p. 164); Dutt op. cit. pp. 46-47.

Existenzen."[44] The cessation of Saṃsāra, however, is not the same as "complete annihilation".

Kern.—Kern distinguishes a cosmological and a philosophical meaning of Nirvāṇa.[45] The former is threefold, the divisions corresponding to Nirvāṇa, Parinirvāṇa and Mahāparinirvāṇa. The latter is not a specifically Buddhist concept, and in spite of the divergences between the schools, according to the orthodox opinion 'chez les philosophes bouddhiques aussi bien que chez les autre, la délivrance, quel que soit le mot qui la désigne, se ramène à un état d'inconscience absolue."[46]

La Vallee Poussin.—in his "Way to Nirvāṇa" Poussin stated that Nirvāṇa could be regarded as immortality, as annihilation, or as the cessation of pain, without further qualifications.

The first he considered impossible, the second as following logically from the doctrine of Anatta and the third as the actual attitude of Buddha. The opinion of Rhys Davids as expressed in his American Lectures seems to resemble this.[47] At another place Poussin stated "Je crois l'interprétation des Mādhyamikas conforme à l'esprit des textes palis......"[48] Finally, however, Poussin came to believe "Je suis actuellement très certain que le Nirvāṇa est une "chose en soi" un Absolu eschatologique, le refuge éternel."[49] The idea of Nirvāṇa was derived from Yogic ecstasy. In the Saññāvedayitanirodha "l'élément immortal se manifeste", this

[44] Der Buddhismus I. p. 101.

[45] L'histoire du Bouddhisme (French tr.) I. pp. 384-385.

[46] Ib. pp. 385-387.

[47] p. 164.

[48] J.A. 1902. t. XX. p. 247 fn.

[49] L'Inde Jusqu'en 300 avant J. C. 312 fn; cf. also Opinions ....p. 75.

being the foretaste of the final beatitude.[50] Yet, Poussin thought that for the European, Nirvāṇa must remain utter annihilation since "nous ne pouvons, en occident, concevoir l'existence indépendamment des choses corporelles ou mentales; car nous ne pouvons concevoir une béatitude, sukha, qui ne soit pas concience de la béatitude, sukhasaṃvedana."[51] The remark is significant and deserves to be noted as the probable explanation of why many European writers have called Nirvāṇa purely "negative".

Stcherbatsky.—Stcherbatsky in his "Nirvāṇa" criticizes Poussin severely, but himself adopts the very unhistorical procedure of attributing to Buddha the views of the Vaibhāṣikas without further ado. He has been criticized by Prof. N. Dutt.[52]

N. Dutt.—Prof. Dutt concludes that the conception of Nirvāṇa in the Nikāyas is threefold—ethical, psychical and metaphysical. In the first aspect it implied the destruction of evil propensities etc. and the attainment of the highest bliss. In the second aspect it is the same as the Saññāvedayitanirodha "provided that the adept complied with the other necessary conditions of Arhathood." In its third aspect it appears to be something positive although infinite and indescribable like Ākāśa.[53] This only amounts to pointing out the obvious attributes of Nibbāna Vimutti, Nirodha and Asaṅkhata. Besides, the identification of 'saññāvedayitanirodha' with Nibbāna is not correct.

Keith.—Although Dr. Keith admits that a section of the early disciples probably did accept the existence of an absolute reality as the basis of their depreciation of the world,[54] he thinks that there are no reasons whatever to regard Buddha himself as anything but an agnos-

[50] Dogme p. 46-47.

[51] Ib. p. 51.

[52] See Aspects p. 154 ff.

[53] Op. cit. pp. 167-169.

tic in the sense of one who studied the various prevalent systems of ideas "without deriving any greater satisfaction from them than any of us to-day do from the study of modern systems."[55] This opinion appears to be the product of prejudice coupled with a failure to appreciate the really "deep sayings of the Tathāgata".[56]

Oldenberg.—Oldenberg seems to think that although logically the Nirvāṇa beyond death ought to have signified just Nothing[57] and although the official position on the subject was to refuse to answer the question,[58] there are some texts which would interpret the silence of Buddha to have been really due to the indescribable character of Nirvāṇa. Thus "Das Verlangen des nach Ewigem trachenden Herzens hat nicht Nichts, und doch hat das Denken kein Etwas, das es festzuhalten vermochte."[59]

Mrs. Rhys Davids.—Mrs. Rhys Davids suggests that the first Buddhists worded the Goal as "Attha", not Nirvāṇa. The latter indeed is "an end without the man in it; it is negative; it prejudges the as yet inconceivable." These are precisely the features which ought to have been avoided by a message meant, "not for the monk as such, not for the academic sophist" but for the "manyfolk (Bahu-jana)."[60] She has, however, only succeeded in showing that Attha was also one of the many earlier words for the Goal, that an exclusively "negativist" interpretation of the goal as conceived in early Buddhism

---

55 Ib. p. 63.

56 The sayings are discussed below. For an eloquent refutation of Dr. Keith see Radhakrishnan I. P. I. p. 679f; Schrader JPTS—1904-5. pp. 157-158.

57 Buddha (9th German ed.) p. 312.

58 Ib. p. 315.

59 Ib. p. 328.

60 What was the Original Gospel—I. pp. 79-84; Sakya—112-114.

does not do justice to all the evidence, and that the message of Buddha must not be interpreted entirely from the standpoint of the monk as understood in mediaeval Ceylon. These are, of course, valuable contributions.

Radhakrishnan.—Prof. Radhakrishnan points out that if Buddha believed in an absolute reality not subject to the changes of this world, then Nirvāṇa is its attainment and the "Enlightened One" the permanent Self. If, however, Buddha did not believe in an absolute reality, then Nirvāṇa is nothingness and a permanent self apart from the changing aggregates an illusion.[61] Like Mrs. Rhys Davids, Prof. Radhakrishnan and Schrader appeal to forcible *a priori* considerations against regarding Buddha an agnostic or a "nihilist".[62] How could so profound a thinker as Buddha see nothing "behind or above or beside this transitory world we conceive by our senses and supply by our fancy?"

Schrader.—Prof. Schrader further argues that since the theory of Anatta applies only to the five khandhas and the three Avacaras it fails to touch the Absolute. Hence it cannot be claimed as an argument against the positive alternative of the problem of Nirvāṇa.[63] The usual formula of Anatta—Netaṃ mama etc. was meant only "to reduce to cause (Pratyaya) everything in nature, and thereby to prove that our real entity must not be looked for in, but beyond the world."[64] The Absolute has a cosmic and an acosmic aspect. The former found

---

61 Op. cit. pp. 676-677.

62 Ib. p. 679; 690-691; JPTS 1904-'5—p. 159. Prof. Radhakrishnan's ref. to Burnet—Greek Philosophy pp. 1-2—on the place of faith in the interpretation of philosophies of an earlier age is extremely just.

63 Op. cit. pp. 160-161.

64 Ib. p. 164.

its classical expression in the Upaniṣadic "Tattvamasi", the latter in "Neti Neti" and reached its climax in Buddha,[65] who for the first time saw clearly that "only ignorance can devise any relation at all between nature and the supernatural one."[66]

Barua.—Prof. Barua's views are considered below but he clearly repudiates the "negativist" version of Nirvāṇa.[67]

Conclusion.—It appears thus that the weight of recent scholarly opinion also is against regarding Buddha an agnostic or a "nihilist".

The problem of Nirvana.—With respect to Nirvāṇa the following questions must be answered if its nature is to be understood:—(*a*) How is Nirvāṇa realised? This involves the analysis of Sambodhi and its content. (*b*) How is Nirvāṇa related to being and experience? Can it be adequately described as non-being or non-experience? If it is an infinite principle, what is its relation to finite life and existence? This involves an analysis of the relation of Nirvāṇa to Dharma and Pratītyasamutpāda. (*c*) Who realises Nirvāṇa? Or, is such a question impermissible? This involves an analysis of the vexed question of Attā and of Buddha's "silence".

Sopadhi and Nirupadhi.—From the standpoint of the Nikāyas the distinction between Sopadhisesa Nibbāna and Nirupadhi° does not appear to be very early. At one stage of its history upadhi had no reference to the khandhas.[68] Even while living one could be Niru-

[65] Ib. pp. 161-162.

[66] Ib. p. 163.

[67] The Mahābodhi—1944—March-April. p. 61f.

[68] MN I. 262 contrasts upadhi with Nibbāna equating the former to wife and children, slaves....wealth (cf. Ib. p. 106)· SN. I. 6, 107-8; Sn Dhaniyasutta—verses 16-17.

padhi°,[69] and there could be no Nibbāna unless one "abandoned" the upadhis.[70] After the realization of Nibbāna the Worthy could undergo only an external transformation. For him, death was quite inconsequential.[71]

Buddha and Arahant.—It is improbable that there was originally any distinction between the Buddha and the Arahant.[72] Having become enlightened Gotama preached to others the way to attain to the same status as he himself had done and become a Buddha, an Arahant. Later on a distinction came to be effected between Arahatta and Buddhahood, the latter being considered unnecessary to the attainment of Nirvāṇa. The Mahāyānists appear to have rightly protested against this view.[73] Only the Buddha can be said to

[69] This seems to be implicit in the Dhaniya sutta where home life is contrasted to homelessness, not a state to be attained after death. Cf. Itv. sutta 44 where the prose might really contain a different view than the verse.

In AN. IV. 75 Bhikkhunīs, indicated as these (Etā) are called some Vimuttā and some anupādisesā suvimuttā: obviously these latter also were living.

[70] SN. I. 117, 118, 136, 124, 134, II. 107, 108-9, III. 132. Ib V. 226; MN. I. 136f, 167, 436, 453, III. 245.

[71] Cf. Candrakīrti on MK. XXV 1f.

One can argue that if the destruction of upadhi in the sense of the Khandhas were essential to it, Nirvāṇa would cease to remain uncaused. If the said destruction were essential only to the knowledge of Nirvāṇa, it would follow that even in the moment of perfect Awakening Buddha did not know Nirvāṇa properly. As a matter of fact the Arahant is described in a recurrent formula as "anuppattasadattho".

After Enlightenment, death must be regarded as really irrelevant from the standpoint of spiritual progress. *As conceived in later scholasticism* the distinction between Sopadhisesa and Nirupadhisesa is relevant neither to the nature nor "realization" of Nirvāṇa. It is relevant only to the biography of particular Arhants.

[72] Dialogues II intr. to the Pāṭika sutta.

[73] A similar feeling would appear to underlie Mrs. Rhys Davids' distrust of the "narrow-minded monk-aftermen" as adequate guides to Buddha's thought.

realize Nirvāṇa, and Buddhahood is potentially open to all. At any rate, since we are only concerned with Buddha's conception of Nirvāṇa, let us not judge it wholly with reference to the experience of those Hīnayānist Arahants who themselves admitted that they had not become Buddhas.[74]

Sammāsambodhi and Nibbāna should, in short, be considered to be essentially associated.[75]

Bodhi.—In the Bhayabherava sutta, the Saṅgārava sutta and the Mahāsaccaka sutta of the MN, we are told that during his Enlightenment Buddha, having reached the fourth Jhāna, attained the three Vijjās in the three successive watches of the night. In the Tevijjavacchagottasutta of the MN, Buddha denies the possession of omniscience in any sense other than that of possessing the three Vijjās.[76] The Sāmaññaphala sutta of the DN implies that the attainment of the three Vijjās is the final fruit of Śramaṇaship, and a large number of suttas in the DN, as well as the MN echo the opinion. In the SN[77] Susīma, a recent convert, hearing that some monks

[74] Cf Dutt. op. cit. p. 135, 198-210. In spite of their lateness, the Mahāyānist interpretations would appear to be in some cases nearer Buddha than the corresponding Hīnayānist ones. Cf. "Religious faith often seems able to break through the barriers of space and time, and so to apprehend its object directly". (Burnet-Greek Philosophy—1943—p. 1).

[75] Cf. "Religion means both experience and its expression in thought and action....It is essential to correlate the expression with the experience to which it testifies." J. Wach in Twentieth Century Sociology—p. 425. (ed. G. Gurvitch & W. E. Moore).

[76] II. 121. f.

[77] At another place, however, he denies only simultaneous omniscience (sakideva sabbaṃ ñassati—MN. II. 127). The view refuted here was the one that was later held by the Mahāsāṅghikas and the Vātsīputrīyas—see Ab. K. V. pp. 254-5. The Jainas also held a similar view, but their very claim to omniscience, let alone simultaneous omniscience, was ridiculed (see

had declared their attainment of Aññā,[78] questions them, among other things, about the three Vijjās.

The Vijjas.—We may conclude that there existed a tradition which identified Sambodhi as well as the last stages of the march to Arhatship with the attainment of the three Vijjās.[79] The story of Susīma further shows how many non-Buddhist Paribbājakas unacquainted with what were probably more recent developments[80] still continued to entertain this opinion about the Buddhist belief on the subject.

Vimutti.—The culmination of the three Vijjās[81] is reached in the self-conscious freedom of the Citta resting in the satisfaction of having attained the end. The recurrent formula thus states "Cittaṃ vimuccati, vimut-

---

MN. I. Sandaka Sutta). The Sarvāstivādins thought Buddha omniscient in the sense that he could know immediately whatever he wanted to (Ab. K. l. c.).

[78] *Aññā.*—Aññā appears to be on the whole, the knowledge that leads on to the Highest. The Sambuddhas are Sammadaññas (SN. I. 4); through Sammadaññā the Ariyas enter Parinibbāna (SN. IV. 128). Aññā follows khayañāṇa, but precedes Aññāvimuttassa (vimutti-) ñāṇa (Itv. Sutta 62. cf. SN. V. 204, DN. III. 219). Emancipation—through Aññā (Aññāvimokkha) destroys Ignorance (Avijjā)—AN. I. 134. See also SN. I. 24; SN. V. 129; AN. III. 82, 143, V. 108 (where "ditṭheva dhamme aññā" is contrasted with "upādisesa anāgāmitā"); SN. II. 267, AN. III. 437 cf. Mrs. Rhys Davids. "The Birth of Indian Psych." p. 264.

[79] Lalitavistara also describes the Sambodhi as attained through the Four Dhyānas followed by the Three Vidyās (I. pp. 343-50). The three Vidyās are described as "Sattvānāpaśyati sma cyavamānānupapadyamānān....", Pūrvanivāsānusmṛtijñānadarśana and Āśraya (sic.)—kṣayajñānadarśana. The last is attained through the knowledge of Pratītyasam°. The description of Āśravakṣaya is much "expanded" (cf. N. Dutt. E. M. B. I. p. 97).

[80] On the distinction between the Paññāvimutta and the Ubhatobhāga° cf. Dutt. op. cit. pp. 250-251. 279.

[81] For an exceedingly able, though brief and general, description of the Vijjās see Barua—op. cit. pp. 64-65.

tasmiṃ vimuttaṃ ti ñāṇaṃ hoti, khīṇā jāti vusitaṃ Brahmacariyaṃ Kataṃ karaṇīyaṃ nāparaṃ itthattāyāti pajānāti."[82] This freedom is called Cetovimutti and Paññāvimutti.[83] It is the emancipation of the cita *from the Āsavas* and *through Paññā.*[84]

Sambodhi and intuitive knowledge.—In the context of Sambodhi sometimes Ñāṇa,[85] Vijjā and Paññā have the same meaning. Thus we are told "Pubbe ananussutesu dhammesu cakkhumudapādi ñāṇamudapādi paññā udapādi vijjā udapādi āloko udapādi."[86] The talk here is of knowledge in its intuitive level.[87] It is repeatedly stated how the following are to be directly realized (sacchikātabbo)—sāmaññattho brahmaññattho,[88]

[82] Cf. MN. Sutta 76 where it is stated "Tassa carato ceva tiṭṭhato ca suttassa ca jāgarassa ca satataṃ samitaṃ ñāṇadassanaṃ paccupaṭṭhitaṃ hoti-khīṇā me āsavāti". The knowledge of freedom is a constant possession.

[83] Cf. the expression Vijjāvimutti—SN. V. 28, 73, 329, 333-5, 340.

[84] MN. Sutta 71, sutta 6; cf. Ab. K. 6, 76; AN. II. 214; Pali Dictionary (P.T.S.); cf.—Vyāsabhāṣya ad. Y. S. II. 27. The fourfold Vimukti has contents corresponding to those of the fourfold insight into Dukkha and Āsava referred to in the Buddhist formula for Āsavakhaya. According to MN. Sutta 80 "Evaṃ kira sammābandhanā vippamokkho hoti yadidaṃ avijjābandhanā".

[85] MN. Sutta 102. speaks of "Paccattaṃ yeva ñāṇaṃ parisuddhaṃ pariyodātaṃ" (II. 234). *The expression ñāṇabhūto* (MN. I. 111, III. 195, 224) *suggests an experience where thought and being meet.* As in the early Jinist so in the early Buddhist works also Ñāna often occurs in conjunction with Dassana. In the Sn., esp. in the Aṭṭhakavagga, it is important to note, Ñāṇa is apparently often taken in the sense of discursive knowledge and deprecated. The Mādhyamikas, on the other hand, gave this meaning to Vijñāna, reserving for Jñāna the meaning of transcendental knowledge. (cf. Stcherbatsky—Nirvāṇa p. 202 fn. 3).

[86] SN. II. 105, DN. II. 33 etc.

[87] Cf. Barua—op. cit. 65-66 where the reference to W. James is apposite.

[88] SN. II. 15, 44, 129, III. 50, 192, V. 195, 433.

brahmacariyapariyosānaṃ,[89] paramassāso,[90] tisso vijjā,[91] alamariyañāṇadassanaviseso,[92] saccāni,[93] arahattaphalaṃ,[94] vijjāvimuttiphalaṃ,[95] cetovimutti, paññā°,[96] anuttarā vimutti,[97] amataṃ,[98] Nibbāna.[99] This is in line with the distrust of discursive rational knowledge which is often expressed in the older texts.[100]

Panna.—Paññā is described as noble—Ariyā.[101] It is the "eye" that is superior to the eye of flesh or of the Gods.[102] Ordinarily in a turbid state, it is the intuitive faculty which must be cultivated.[103] Guiding man in his spiritual journey,[104] it finally enables him to see

[89] Ib. II. 278.85.

[90] Ib. IV. 254-'5.

[91] Ib. IV. 63.

[92] Ib. IV. 337-'9; cf. MN. II. 203.

[93] Ib. V. 10-11, 49, 141, 167, 185, 206, 422 ff.

[94] Ib. IV. 252, V. 202.

[95] Ib. V. 93, 95, 126; Cf. MN. III. 290.

[96] Ib. II. 214, V. 203, 257, 266, 356.

[97] Ib. I. 105.

[98] Ib. V. 181-'2.

[99] Ib. 251-'2.

[100] Thus Sn. Āmagandhasutta, verse 12, Ib. Sabhiyasutta v. 29, the four "aṭṭhaka" suttas, Māgandiya sutta, Cūḷaviyūha sutta. Cf. Itv. p. 25 (Nāg. ed. Sarnath) where the expression "Phuṭṭhuṃ sambodhimuttamaṃ" is suggestive.

[101] MN. III. 245; Ib. I. 144, II. 260 (where it is said to have "Satthaṃti Adhivacanaṃ") MN. III. 29, 245; Ib. I. 81.

[102] Itv. Suttas 61, 62, cf. M. I. 293.

[103] MN. II. 12, III. 72; I. 293, II. 180; AN. II. 187, 189.

[104] "Saddhā dutiyā purisassa hoti paññā cenam pasāsati" SN. I. 38. This reminds one of the function of "Buddhi" in the Kaṭhopaniṣad (see the paper on "The status and role of Buddhi in Kaṭhopaniṣad and Bhagavadgītā" by Mr. Jaidev Singh read at the Ind. Phil. Cong. held at Madras in Dec. 1940) (In the Chāgaleyopaniṣad the Prājña Ātman is given the function of the charioteer which is here conceived differently. See Four Unpublished Upaniṣads by S. K. Belvalkar pp. 11-12. In SN. V. 6 Paññā is along with Saddhā yoked to the Dhammayāna).

directly into reality (Yathābhūtaṃ),[105] abandon the Āsavas[106] and attain to Aññā[107] and Bodhi.[108]

Paticcasam° and Sambodhi.—The week following Enlightenment (Abhisambodhi) is said to have been spent by Buddha in experiencing the bliss of emancipation (Vimuttisukhapaṭisaṃvedī).[109] After this he reflected over Paṭiccasam° in three ways during the three watches of the night. This is curious. Were there two different traditions such that according to one the night of Enlightenment was spent in learning the three Vijjās while according to the other it was spent in learning Paṭiccasaṃ°? Or was the sequence of events thus: the night of Enlightenment (Abhisambodhi) when

---

105 Paññāya abhisamayo—SN. II. 5-9, 104; Paññāya suphussitaṃ. Ib. I. 128, °suppaṭividdho Ib. II. 68, III. 6, °ativijjhati—Ib. V. 226-'7, 278, 378-'9; Nibbedhikā (Paññā) Ib. V. 392, 395, 402 cf. AN. II. 178 Mrs. Rhys Davids treatment of Paññā (The Birth of Indian Psychology etc. pp. 265-'70) is able, although her interpretation of "Yathābhūtaṃ" does not carry conviction. On Paññā and "Yathābhūtaṃ" see, e.g. SN. III. 45: "Evaṃ etaṃ yathābhūtaṃ sammappaññāya daṭṭhabbaṃ" cf. "Tato'sya Prajñā Yathābhūtaṃ prajānāti" (Vyāsa on YS. II. 45); on Abhisamaya see Ledi Sadaw quoted in Points of Controversy p. 382. Cf. Vyāsa ad Y. S. I. 49 where also Prajñā is called "Viśeṣārthā".

106 MN. I. 479, III. 28; SN. III. 45 "Evaṃ etṃ sammapaññāya passato cittaṃ virajjati vimuccati anupādāya āsavehi".

107 SN. V. 223.

108 **Bodhi.**—Ib. V. 231, 237. According to the Vibhāṣā, Bodhi appears to be "la science necessaire au Nirvāṇa et la certitude du Nirvāṇa—mais lui (Buddha) manque l'omniscience, la pitié" etc. La Vallée Poussin—Dogme—p. 169). According to Ab. K. Bodhi is the knowledge (Jñāna) of Āsravakṣaya and Anutpāda. (Ab. K. 6.67). Anutpādajñāna, it may be remembered, has a different meaning in Mahāyāna (see Suzuki—Studies in the Laṅkāvatāra—pp. 122-7). According to the Mahāyānasūtrālaṅkāra (chap. IX) Bodhi is omniscience (Sarvākārajñatā) and "Suchness" (Tathatā). According to Buddhaghosa "Bodhi vuccati catusu maggesu ñāṇaṃ" Vimutti is apparently its result. (Samantapāsādikā V. pp. 952-4. P. T. S. ed). Cf. MN. sutta 44 where Vimutti is called the Paṭibhāga of Vijjā.

109 Mvg. (Vin. I. pp. 1-2), Ud. the first three suttas; cf. Rockhill, Op. cit. p. 33; Lalita Vistara I. 369.

the 3 Vijjās were learnt; a week of experiencing the bliss of emancipation (vimutti) resulting from Enlightenment; a night over Paṭiccasam°? But this would imply that the knowledge of Paṭiccasam° was not necessary to Abhisambodhi. This is contradicted by SN. II. 105 and is against the general presumption.[110] The destruction of avijjā—one of the three cardinal āsavas—or Paññāvimutti is hardly conceivable apart from the knowledge of Paṭiccasam°. It would thus seem advisable to suppose that the texts from Mvg. and Ud. just referred to have in mind only a reflective revision of the principle of Paṭiccasam°. The words "Sādhukaṃ manasākāsi" also suggest that we have here not a novel intuition but the retrospective conceptualization of a previous intuitive experience.[111] For the first direct experience of Paṭiccasam° the expression has a quite different tone "yoniso manasikārā ahu paññāya abhisamayo."[112] The knowledge that resulted is likened to the dawn of light.[113]

Sambodhi.—In successive watches of the night of *Sambodhi,* Buddha realized Pubbenivāsañāṇa, Dibbacakkhu, Paṭiccasam°, and, finally, at dawn, Omniscience (LV, l.c; Nidāna Kathā). He then surveyed[114] suffering

---

[110] In Lalita Vistara the knowledge of Pratītyasam° definitely and explicitly precedes Āsravakṣayajñānadarśana (loc. cit).

[111] Retrospection (Paccavekkhaṇa) over jhānic experience was an essential part of Jhānic practice—see Vm. p. 93.

[112] SN. loc. cit.; DN. II. p. 35.

[113] Ib.

[114] "Sele yathā pabbatamuddhaniṭṭhito yathā pi passe janataṃ samantato Tathūpamaṃ dhammamayaṃ sumedha pāsādamāruyha samantacakkhu Sokāvatiṇṇam janataṃ apetasoko avekkhassu jātijarābhibhūtaṃ (MN. Ariyapariyesana sutta. Bodhirājakumāra°; DN. Mahāpadāna°; SN. I. p. 136ff; Mvg. (Vin); Itv. sutta 38). The balladic form of the group of verses among which these lines occur may be noted cf. "Paññāpāsādamāruyha asoko sokinim pajaṃ Pabbataṭṭho va bhūmmaṭṭho dhīro bāle avekkhati". (Dhp. verse 28).

humanity (sokāvatiṇṇaṃ janataṃ) with great compassion[115] (Kāruññataṃ Paṭicca Buddhacakkhunā[116].... volokesi). Knowledge, freedom, bliss and compassion—these then are the aspects of Buddha's supreme experience (Sammā Sambodhi). *The knowledge (Paññā) is intuitive and synoptic, involving an insight into phenomenal contingency (Paṭiccasamuppāda).*[117] *As a result*

[115] Through developing his as yet imperfect knowledge and compassion the Bodhisattva in time attains to the supreme knowledge and compassion of Buddha. Thus both Prajñā and Karuṇā have a twofold aspect. In the Hīnayāna the emphasis is mainly put on these as means or faculties. But it is clear that the Mahāyāna doctrine is present in a germinal form even in the oldest texts.

[116] "Buddhacakkhunāti indriyaparopariyattiñāṇena ca āsayānusayañāṇena ca. Imesaṃ hi dvinnaṃ ñāṇānaṃ Buddhacakkhūti nāmaṃ...." (Samantapāsādikā loc. cit. below).

[117] **Panna and Dhammapatubhava.**—On the verse just quoted Buddhaghosa comments thus "sumedha sundarapañña sabbaññutañāṇena samantacakkhu bhagavā dhammamayaṃ paññāmayaṃ pāsādaṃ...." (Samantapāsādikā vol. v. pp. 961-63) with this may be compared the verse quoted in Vyāsa-bhāṣya ad. Y. S. II. 47 "Prajnāprāsādamāruhya aśocyaḥ śocato janān Bhūmiṣṭhāniva śailasthaḥ sarvān prājñonupaśyati". The verse is practically identical with Dhp. (loc. cit.), and is attributed in the Tattvavaiśāradī and the Vārtika to "Paramarṣi". The gāthā, as it has been called, is doubtless very old. With reference to this "Prajñā" Vyāsa says "Bhūtārthaviṣayaḥ kramānanurodhī sphuṭaprajñālokaḥ". This reminds one of the common enough phrase in the context of "Saccābhisamaya"—Yathābhūtaṃ pajānāti & of "Paññā udapādi....āloko udapādi....". The comparison with light indicates the intuitive or immediate character of Prajñā just as the term "Kramānanurodhī", the comparison with vision from the mountain top, and the expression "samantacakkhu" point out its synoptic and simultaneous character [Cf. "Sarvaṃ tadekacittekṣaṇasamāyuktayā prajñayānuttaraṃ samyaksambodhimabhisambudhya traividyādhigatā" (Lalita Vistara I.p. 350. N. Dutt has "Ekacittakṣaṇa" E.M.B. I. p. 98)]. Consciousness is here non-temporal and all-embracing. Cf. Vm. pp. 490-491 (Nāg. ed.); Oldenberg—Buddha p. 132, fn. where the "Weltganzen überschauenden Intuition" of Buddha is compared to what W. James calls "Cosmic consciousness".

In this experience are revealed all phenomena in their contingency—"Yadā have pātubhavanti dhammā ātāpino jhāyato

there is an emancipation (Vimutti) from ill (dukkha) and its sources (āsavas). This freedom is beatific (sukha), though its bliss is not inconsonant with compassion towards the still suffering.

Nirvana and experience.—As to the relation of Nirvāṇa to experience one may now conclude thus: there is a certain supreme noetic and beatific experience which alone makes the attainment of Nirvāṇa possible. On the basis of the ancient texts further precision is impossible. Later schools offer varying interpretations. At one pole the Theravādins regard Nirvāṇa as only the object of experience, while, at the other, the Yogācāras would annul the distinction between the two. The question would have been soluble for the ancient texts only if they had indicated their epistemological position clearly.

The problem of Dhamma and its significance.—Now in Sambodhi Buddha is said to have 'obtained' Dhamma profound, quiescent and beyond intellect.[118] Paṭiccasam°, and Nibbāna are the two sides or aspects of this Dhamma. The meaning we put on Dhamma will con-

---

brāhmaṇassa yato pajānāti sahetudhammaṃ (Ud. s. 1; Vin I. 2). Buddhaghosa says "Athavā pātubhavantīti pakāsenti abhisamayavasena byattā pākaṭā honti dhammāti caturāriyasaccadhammā ...." (Samantapāsādikā V. pp. 952-954). "Dhammapātubhāva" is at least a major aspect of the final Paññā cf. S. IV. p. 79. "Samāhite citte dhammā pātubhavanti" i.e., truths are revealed. Cf. W. James "They are states of insight into depths of truth unplumbed by the discursive intellect" (Varieties of Rel. p. 380 cf. Barua op. cit. pp. 65-66).

118 "Adhigato kho me *ayaṃ dhammo* gambhīro duddaso duranubodha santo paṇīto atakkāvacaro nipuṇo paṇḍitavedanīyo...."; "Kicchena me adhigataṃ halaṃ dāni pakāsituṃ, rāgadosaparetehi *nāyaṃ dhammo* susambuddho" (DN. Mahāpadāna sutta; MN. suttas 26 and 85; S. I. Brahmasaṃ° sutta 1. Mvg. loc. cit.; cf. M. I. 487). With the second quotation, cf. Lal. Vist. I. p. 397; with the first cf. Ib. p. 392, 395-6.

dition, not necessarily determine, our attitude to the problem of the relation of Nibbāna to experience,— whether Nibbāna is a sentient or an insentient, a personal or an impersonal, a concretely existing or a merely abstractly "subsistent" principle.

Interpretations of Dhamma—Rosenberg.—According to Prof. Rosenberg the concept of Dharma is to Buddhist philosophy what that of "idea" is to the philosophy of Plato.[119] It is found to be used in the following senses in Buddhist literature. "Eigenschaft, Attribut, Prädikat. 2. Substantieller Träger, transzendentes Substrat des einzelnen Elementes bewuszten Lebens. 3. Element, d.h. Bestandteil des bewuszten Lebens. 4. Nirvāṇa, d.h. <<dharma>> par excellence, dasz Object der Lehre Buddhas. 5. Das Absolute; das wahrhaft Reale u.s.w. 6. Die Lehre, die Religion Buddhas. 7. Sache, Gegenstand, Object, Erscheinung."[120] Of these the second meaning—"transzendenter Träger"—is the most important and usual.[121] Underlying the apparently stable entities of experience are sequences of momentary elements. These are irreducibly simple though mutually conditioned.[122] Even these are, however, only the phenomenal appearances of noumenal substrata; they are dharmalakṣaṇas as distinguished from the dharmas. The relation envisaged here is different from that between substance and quality, since in a substance a number of qualities inhere whereas each dharma bears only its specific mark. So far, we are told, the Buddhist

[119] Die Probleme der buddhistischen Philosophie—p. XIII.

[120] Ib. p. 83. See the Pali Dictionary on the meanings given by Buddhaghosa.

[121] Ib.

[122] They are "Pṛthak" though "Sapratyaya"—see Glasenapp ZDMG. 1938 pp. 392-393.

schools agree but they differ when it comes to defining the nature of the transcendental dharma or dharmas. The Vaibhāṣikas hold them to be many and ever-present. The Sautrāntikas make them immanent in the phenomena. The Śūnyavādins insist on impredicability while the Vijñānavādins posit behind every world of individual experience a single Ālayavijñāna.[123]

Phenomenal unrest has no absolute first beginning, yet is itself merely an appearance due to Ignorance, although subject to the force of karman and "causal" relationships. Underlying it is dharma in its timeless nature or the Absolute (if the Dharmas be many, the Absolute becomes a sort of system)[124]—the eternal rest that is Nirvāṇa. *"Dann hört die gegebene Persönlichkeit auf, empirisch zu sein*, dann wird schon kein dharma mehr geboren. Ein Teil des Lebensmeeres hört auf zu tosen und versenkt sich in ewige Ruhe, ins wahre Sein, auf welches man die Ausdrücke des empirischen Seins nicht anwenden kann, aber welches dessenungeachtet für den kontemplativen Mystiker die höchste Glückseligkeit bedeutet."[125]

The whole theory may be thus summarized: Nirvāṇa is the eternally restful state of reality as distinguished from appearance. It depends on attributing to Dharma the basic meaning of "non-empirical ground of temporal appearances." The data consist of the Abhidharma literature of Sarvāstivāda and Vijñāṇavāda.

---

[123] Ib. Chapters V, VI & XVIII esp. pp. 72; 101: "dharma heiszen die wahrhaft-realen, transzendenten, unerkennbaren Träger oder Substrate derjenigen Elemente, in welche der Bewusztseinsstrom mit seinem Inhalt zerlegt wird". This definition clearly implies the principles of Vijñaptimātratā and the three Lakṣaṇas; pp. 231-235.

[124] Cf. Ib. p. 239.

[125] Ib. pp. 241-242.

In essentials Prof. Stcherbatsky agrees with this view.[126]

Whatever might be its validity with respect to the Abhidharma stage of Buddhism, it clearly remains a merely interpretative hypothesis as far as the earlier Nikāya period is concerned. In fact, the 'Dharma-theory' in this sense seems to have been a product of the growing vogue of metapsychological analysis in the Post-Nikāya period.*

Keith and Schayer.—Dr. Keith espouses Prof. Schayer's view that in "pre-canonical" Buddhism the elements of Rūpa alone were considered impermanent.[127] In contrast to Rūpadhātu, Dharmadhātu represented the eternal supersensuous reality which formed the object of the Dharmacakṣus of the Omniscient Buddha alone.[128] Salvation is conceived as the passage from the perishable Rūpadhātu to the imperishable Arūpadhātu (of eternal Dharma).[129]

Here again, as in the previous view, Dharma tends to approach in meaning the Mahāyānic dharmadhātu. In fact, Schayer considers Mahāyāna directly connected with Primitive Buddhism. Such a supposition needs more extensive substantiation. It is true, however, that the expression "dhammacakkhu" seems to mean in the Nikāyas supernormal insight of a religiously saving character.[130]

---

[126] See his Central Conception of Buddhism.

* See below.

[127] I. H. Q. Vol. XII—1936.

[128] Cf. the views of the Prājñika Svābhāvikas referred to in Schrader—Über den Stand der indischen Philosophie etc. pp. 31-32.

[129] See Mlle Marcelle Lalou in IHQ. 1949.

[130] DN. I. 86, 110; SN. IV. 47; AN. IV. 186 etc. See Pali Dictionary (PTS). In AN. I. 242 the attainment of Dhammacakkhu is compared to the breaking forth of the autumnal sun.

Geiger.—Geiger assimilates Dhamma to Upaniṣadic Brahman.[131] The arguments may be thus summarized: a verse[132] speaks of Brahmapatha, which is probably equivalent to Amatapatha; this taken with the recurrent expression "Brahmabhūtena Attanā" implies that Nirvāṇa must be similar to merging in Brahman.[133] Dhamma and Brahman are apparently interchangeable in a number of expressions. These are: Dhammacakka-Brahma°, Dhammayāna-Brahma°, Dhammajāla-Brahma°, Dhammakāya-Brahma°, Dhammabhūta-Brahma°, Dhammaja-Brahmaja. Dhammanimmita-Brahma°, Dhammadāyāda-Brahma.[134] It is concluded that Dhamma stepped in the place of Brahman and necessarily turned into the highest "übersinnlichen Begriff", the "rein geistigen kosmischen und sittlichen Potenz", the highest impersonal Being.[135] It is clear that in certain

[131] Dhamma und Brahman.

[132] Thag. 689, AN. III. p. 346.

[133] Op. cit. p. 5.

[134] Ib. pp. 6-8.

[135] **Brahman.**—Ib. There is no definite evidence to suppose that the Nikāyas show acquaintance with the monistic conception of Brahman. The expression "Brahmabhūto" sometimes used for Buddha (DN. III. 84; AN. V. 226; SN. IV. 94,, AN. II. 206, V. 256; MN. III. 224) is, however, suggestive. The meaning of Brahma in Brahmapatti (SN. I. 169, 181; IV. 118) and Brahmayāna (SN. V. 4-6) is also not perfectly clear.

The Upaniṣadic word "Brahmaloka" occurs many times (e.g. DN. II. 241, SN. 141, 155, V. 265, 282) but is supposed to mean something lower than Nirvāṇa (This is very clear in SN. V. 410. Cf. DN. pt. II. pp. 186-7. Nāg. ed.). The Brāhmaṇas are declared to be "Brahmalokādhimutta" (MN. p. 402—Nāg. ed.).

Brahmā is described as the highest of gods, but not the Highest (AN. III. 202, IV. 105). The way to "Brahmasahavyatā" is stated to have been preached by teachers of old like Sunetta, Mūgapakkha, Aranemi, Kuddāla, Hatthipāla, Jotipāla, and Araka. Buddha himself taught it in the shape of the "Four Brahmavihāras" (DN. I. Tevijjasutta).

Between the ideas associated with Brahman in the Upaniṣads and the Nikāyas the differences are of a character as to sug-

contexts the Nikāyic use of Dhamma is parallel to the Upaniṣadic use of Brahman, both the words referring to the Highest Reality. But this generic similarity of literal usage does not entitle us to conclude that the Upaniṣadic conception of the 'highest reality' agreed with its Nīkāyic conception. The use of the same word in the same dictionary-meaning does not imply the identity of technical signification.

Mrs. Rhys Davids.—Mrs. Rhys Davids advocates a similar opinion. She thinks that in Sakyan teaching Brahman did figure, although the emphasis was now placed on dhamma which meant the Deity conceived "as not only immanent, but as moving, urgent, ideal, as 'conscience' as 'duty' as 'the ought and ought not.' "[136]

Two meanings of Dhamma.—It appears that the Nikāya usage of Dhamma fluctuates between at least two major classes of meanings which may be called the empirical and the transcendental. Thus when we are told "Sabbe dhammā nālaṃ abhinivesāya"[137] or when there is speech of 'dhammānaṃ uppādo vayo",[138] the former meaning is the one clearly intended. On the other hand,

---

gest a certain gap of time and a change of scene. In the Nikāyas the neuter Brahman is a shadowy figure occurring only in some compounds. Brahmaloka is one among many heavenly worlds, and part of the phenomenal flux. The mythological figure of Brahmā, pompous and at times even resorting to lying, (see DN. I. Kevaḍḍha Sutta) is prominent.

[136] Ind. Psy. p. 229f; What was the Original Gospel: Chap. 4. According to MM. V. Bhattacharya the Buddhist "theory of dharma seems to be exactly the same as that of the tattva of the Sāṅkhyas" (Āś pp. 90-1). The "sameness" consists in the fact that both the schools of thought deny all distinction between substance and attribute, and divide the universe into Tattvas or Dharmas.

[137] SN. IV. 50.

[138] Ib. III. 37-38.

when dhamma is called atakkāvacaro[139] or such expressions as "dhammābhisamaya",[140] "dhammaniyāmatā"[141] or "dhammabhūta"[142] are used there can hardly be a doubt that dhamma is here used in a very different sense.[143] In the context of Sambodhi this latter meaning alone will fit. What Buddha "awoke to" was the real as distinct from the apparent nature of things. This does not indeed solve all the various epistemological and ontological problems with which we started, but it certainly runs counter to the assumption sometimes made that Buddhism does not recognize any reality which may be a More than the world of appearance. This, however, does not of necessity mean any ultimate dualism

---

[139] Ib. I. 136. With the description of Dharma as atakkāvacaro & aṇu (SN. I. 136) comp. Kaṭh–up. 1.2.13. "Dharmyamaṇumetamāpya"; Ib. 1.2.8 "Atarkyamaṇupramāṇāt".

The epithet "Aṇu" is frequent in the Upaniṣads. Kaṭh. up. 2.4.14 "Evaṃ dharmān pṛthak paśyan" is intriguing. The verse is far from being clearly intelligible. See Stcherbatsky (Central Conception. p. 68) for a possible interpretation. Usually, however, Dharma means in the Upaniṣads "righteousness" see Ch. up. 2.1.4, 2.23, 1, 7.2.1; Bṛ. up. 1.4.14, 4.4.5; Tait. up. 1.11.1. But cf. Bṛ. up. 1.5.23.

[140] Ib. II. 134 "Dhammābhisamaya" is here identified with "Dhaṃmacakkhupaṭilābho".

[141] Ib. 25. So "Dhammaṭṭhitatā" cf. Barua op. cit. p. 61. The abstractness of the terms Dhaṃmatā, Dhammaniyāmatā, Dhaṃmaṭṭhitatā does not necessarily bespeak their lateness. The Bṛ. up. already uses prajñatā, satyatā, anantatā, ānandatā and sthititā.... (II. pp. 1482-1484. ed. Accyutagranthamālā); Barua op. cit. p. 61. fn. 11.

[142] See Geiger loc. cit. This implies a clear and definite epistemological position; but the expression is isolated and may not have been rigorously meant.

[143] Other expressions of similar import are "Yo Paṭiccasamuppādaṃ passati so dhammaṃ passati yo dhammaṃ passati so paṭiccasamuppādaṃ passati" (MN. I. 191); "Yo dhaṃmaṃ passati so maṃ passati yo maṃ passati so dhaṃmam passati" (SN. III. 120; see Sakya–p. 305); Dhaṃmasākacchā–AN. II. 140, IV. 361. Cf. Dhp. verses 114-5 where "amataṃ padaṃ" and "dhaṃmamuttamaṃ" are apparently interchangeable.

beween "appearance" and "reality", for the difference between them may be conceived to reflect only a difference of insight. Such for instance was the Mādhyamika view.[144]

Sambodhi and Dhamma.—The content of Sambodhi, thus, was Dhamma in the sense of ultimate reality and as such identical with Nirvāṇa. The word was, however, also used for the innumerable appearances which are every moment temptingly before our senses but must not be indulged in (nālam abhinivesāya); and the word Dhamma also signified the way which led from Appearance to Reality, i.e., the doctrine.[145]

Nibbana and Paticcasam°.—Reality revealed itself to Buddha in two aspects—as Paṭiccasam° and as Nibbāna. What did he conceive the relation between them to be?

To perceive Paṭiccasam° is to perceive the world of becoming in its limitation and orderedness.[146] It is, in other words, to have an insight[147] into the deepest formal aspect[148] of reality as in time.[149] What is impermanent is contingent.[150] The temporal is necessarily relative.

---

[144] See MK. XXV. 9.

[145] Cf. "Dharmaśabdóyaṃ pravacane tridhā vyavasthitaḥ svalakṣaṇadhāraṇārthena kugatigamanavidhāraṇārthena pañcagatikasaṃsāragamanavidhāraṇārthena. Tatra.. ... Pāñcagatikasaṃsārāgamanavidhāraṇārthena Nirvāṇamucyate...." (MK. V. p. 109 Cal. ed.)

[146] Niyāmatā cf. "Dhaṃmā anupadavavatthitā" MN. III. 25.

[147] Abhisamaya, Paṭivedha.

[148] Lakkhaṇa.

[149] The distinction between temporal and timeless reality is clearly made out in the Upaniṣads; Bṛ. up. 7.2.20; Śvet. 6.5; Māṇḍ. and Maitr. are clearer though of indefinite date. The temporal is, in Buddhist language, Jarāmarṇalakkhaṇa cf. ŚB. I. 189. For the contrast between the permanent and the impermanent—Kaṭh.—1.2.10, 2.4.2; Ch. up. 7.4.3; Bṛ. up. 1.5.14-15; Śvet. 2.15.

[150] One may put it in Pāli "Yaṃ samuppajjati nirujjhati ca taṃ sabbaṃ paṭicc'eva; sapaccayā aniccalakkhaṇassa pavatti."

In short "Aniccatta" and "Saṅkhatatta" are co-extensive. To grasp Paṭiccasam° is to grasp phenomenality [151]—impermanence and contingency, the very principle of limitation.

That Nibbāna should be interpreted as the logical counterpart of this notion is only natural to suggest. That is to say, it should be interpreted as the Absolute—the eternal and infinite principle. *Paṭiccasam° relates to the conditioned;*[152] *Nibbāna is the Unconditioned.*[153]

The Nature of Nibbana: Nibbana as transcendent reality.—Thus we are told "atthi ajātaṃ abhūtaṃ asaṅkhataṃ tasmā jātassa bhūtassa saṅkhatassa nissaraṇaṃ paññāyati."[154] On the one hand, there is the "Jātaṃ bhūtaṃ samuppannam kataṃ saṅkhatamaddhuvaṃ", on the other "tassa nissaraṇaṃ santaṃ atakkāvacaraṃ dhuvam ajātam asamuppannaṃ asokaṃ virajaṃ padaṃ"[155] Not only is Nibbāna timeless, it is the ultimate reality[156] and the truly real is eternal.[157]

---

[151] Dhammatā—Cf. SN. II. 25.

[152] Saṅkhatalakkhaṇa.

[153] Asaṅkhatalakkhaṇa. Some later schools recognized several Asaṃskṛtas.

[154] Ud. Sutta 73; Itv. sutta 43. cf. SN. IV. 359 "Asaṅkhatañca desissāmi°gamiñca maggaṃ...." Cf. DN. III. 247; M. III. 63, SN. Asankhatasaṃyutta.

[155] Itv. Sutta 43 cf. "virajaḥ para ākāśāt aja ātmā mahān dhruvaḥ |" (Bṛ. Up. 7.2.23).

[156] Paramaṃ saccaṃ—MN. II. 173; cf. MN. III. 70; Ib. I. 180. Cf. "Sabbaṃ vitathamidaṃti ñatvā loke...." (Sn. p. 9); 'Yo nājjhagamā bhavesu sāraṃ...." (Ib. p. 5) on the other hand the khīṇāsava is "Sāre patiṭṭhita" (Ud. p. 4).

[157] "Taṃ hi—musā yaṃ mosadhaṃmaṃ taṃ saccaṃ yaṃ amosadhaṃmaṃ nībbānaṃ...." (MN. III. 245); Sn. p. 82; cf. MK. XIII. 1. "Tanmṛṣā moṣadharmā yadbhagavānityabhāṣata Sarve ca moṣadharmāṇaḥ saṃskārāstena te mṛṣā." Candrakīrti quotes—Etaddhi khalu bhikṣavaḥ paramaṃ satyaṃ yadidamamoṣadharma nirvāṇaṃ sarvasaṃskārāśca mṛṣā. moṣadharmāṇa iti. This agrees with Śaṅkarācārya's point of view that the real must be changeless, vide his comy. on BS. II. 1.11 and BG. II. 16

Nibbāna is the changeless,[158] the immortal.[159] It is transphenomenal,[160] beyond thought[161] and does not

[158] Anaññathābhāvi (Vin. I. 36); Ajātaṃ, ajaraṃ, amataṃ (MN. I. 163); Accutaṃ (SN. III. 143; cf. Sn. 1086; Dhp. 225).

[159] Amata—so well known from Brāhmaṇic literature Amataṃ padaṃ SN. I. 212; Ib. II. 280; °Dvāraṃ Ib. I. 137, II. 43, 45, 58, 80 MN. I. 227; AN. V. 346; °dundubhī—MN. III. 67; °dhātu—AN. III. 356, °gāmī maggo—SN. I. 123; AN. III. 329; SN. IV. 370, V. 8. cf. SN. 3. 1. 32 where Nirodha is described as apabhaṅgu. Amataphalo SN. I. 173; Buddha is called in a frequent formula as Amatassa dātā SN. IV. 94 AN. V. 226, 256. Amata is the Ogādha, Parāyaṇa, Pariyosāna—SN. V. 41, 54, 181, 184, 220, 232; AN. III. 79, 304. IV. 46ff, 317, 387, Ib. V. 105.

[160] **Transcendence.**—Appapañca—AN. II. 161f; Ib. IV. 174. Papañcanirodha—Ib. II. 162ff; IV. 235; Papañcavūpasama—Ib. II. 162. Nippapañca—Ib. AN. III. 431f, 294f; IV. 229, 233, 235. Cf. MN. I. 109, 112, 271, 283; III. 118; MN. I. 65. SN. IV. 71.3, cf. Udāna p. 80; cf. SN. IV. p. 71. The word prapañca occurs in Śvet. up. 6.6; Māṇḍ. 7, 12.

On the meaning of Prapañca in later Buddhist thought, see Candrakīrti "Te ca vikalpā anādimatsaṃsārābhyāsājjñānajñeyavācyavācakakartṛkarma — kriyāghaṭapaṭamukuṭaratharūpavedanāstrīpuruṣa— lābhālābhasukhaduḥkhayaśóyaśonindāpraśaṃsādilakṣaṇādvicitrātprapañcādupajāyante" "Prapañco hi vāk prapañcayatyarthāniti kṛtvā" (quoted in Āś. p. 8). Prapañcopaśama characterises the Nirvāṇa of the Mādhyamikas as well as the Mokṣa of the Vedāntists belonging to the school of Gauḍapāda and Śaṅkara (see Āś. pp. 43-4). Cf. the "lokuttara dhaṃma" of MN. II. 181. The Mahāyānists distinguished a "lokottaratama" —Suzuki, Studies. p. 139 . One is reminded of the expression Turīyātīta.

Cf. Nibbāna as the end of the Loka—AN. IV. 430—432; cf MN. III. 115. The state of the Khīṇāsava is neither higher, nor lower nor equal to any worldy state—AN. III. 359. Nibbāna is Akaṇha, Asukka—AN. III. 384, Cf. "Sabbaṃ accagamā imaṃ papañcaṃ"—Sn. p. 1. cf. Ib. 95, 99. "Saṃsāramaticca Kevalī" Ib. 54. Cf. "Anuvicca papañcanāmarūpam ajjhattaṃ bahiddhā ca rogamūlaṃ"—Ib. 55.

Papañca is thus equivalent to Nāmarūpa to end which is to reach the highest attainment (patti) Ib. p. 56. Cf. "Nippapañcā Tathāgatā" Dhp. 225.

The utterly transcendental character of Nibbāna is powerfully expressed thus :

"Yattha āpo ca paṭhavī tejo vāyo na gādhati,
Na tattha sukkā jotanti ādicco na ppakāsati,
Na tattha candimā bhāti tamo tattha na vijjati,
Yadāca attanā vedi muni so tena brāhmaṇo,

rest *on any other.*[162] *It is without limits or measure, infinite.*[163]

One would, therefore, seem to be justified in concluding that whereas Paṭiccasam° is the deepest form exhibited by the world in time, Nibbāna is the timeless Absolute. Buddha came to be "enlightened" about the essence of phenomena and what lies "beyond" them. "Tathāgata, the great Śramaṇa, spoke of the cause of

---

Atha rūpā arūpā ca sukhadukkhā pamuccati."
(Ud. Sutta 10)

With this Cf. Kaṭh. Up. 2.5.15 "Na tatra sūryo bhāti na candratārakaṃ nemā vidyuto bhānti kuto'yamagniḥ". So Muṇḍ 2.2.10.

Ud. Sutta 71 is equally expressive: "Atthi bhikkhave tadāyatanaṃ, yattha neva paṭhavī na āpo na tejo na vāyo na akāsānañcāyatanaṃ na viññāṇā° na ākiñcaññāyatanaṃ na nevasaññā-nāsaññāyatanaṃ nāyaṃ loko paraloko ubho candimasūriyā, tadāhaṃ bhikkhave neva āgatiṃ vadāmi na gatiṃ na thitiṃ na cutiṃ na upapattiṃ appatiṭṭham apāvattam anārammaṇaṃ taṃ esevanto dukkhassāti."

Cf. Lalita Vistara I. 392 where the content of Buddha's Sambodhi is described to be the utterly transcendental, ineffable Nirvāṇa ("Ṣaḍviṣayasamatikrāntaḥ akalposvikalpo nābhilāpyaḥ")

161 Acinteyya–AN. II. p. 80 (Buddhānaṃ buddhavisayo) on the Acinteyyas see Ledi Saydaw, Expositions p. 25f ed. Mrs. Rhys Davids Cf. SN. III. 71-73 according to which only the past, present and future are "niruttipathā, adhivacana°, paññatti°".

Cf. DN. Mahānidānasutta (DN. II. 63, 68). MN. I. 487: Atakkāvacaro. cf. Sn. Upasīva māṇava°–"Takkaṃ pahāya na upeti saṅkhaṃ".

162 SN. 1. 1. 1. 1. describes the Parinibbuta as "Appatiṭṭha". The Upaniṣadic meaning of Pratiṣhita is "grounded", see Ait. Up. 5.3. Ch. Up. 7.5.2. Bṛ. 4.1.7. Praśna–2.6. Ch. Up. 7.24. "Yo vai bhūmā tadamṛtam yadalpaṃ tanmartyaṃ sa bhagavaḥ kasmin pratiṣṭhita iti sve mahimnīti yadi vā na mahimnīti".

Independence and self-dependence are thus identical.

163 Accanta AN. I. 291. V. 326ff; Appamāṇa SN. IV. 158. The Chāndogya conception of Bhūman approaches that of Hegel's true as distinguished from "spurious infinity". The Nikāya conception is apparently not so philosophical. Rāga, dosa, and Moha create limitation (Pamāṇakaraṇa) MN. I. 298. cf. MN. III. 4: "Accantaniṭṭham nibbānaṃ ārādhenti".

things born of cause, and of their transcendence."[164] It is well known how human thought has in its highest reaches more than once envisaged the possibility of such a two-fold realization, at once cosmic and acosmic.

Dr. Barua on the relation of Paticcasam° and Nibbana.—Dr. Barua would apply Paṭiccasam° to Nibbāna also, arguing that in order to be real it must be all-inclusive.[165] Thus Nibbāna too becomes a causal sequence. Its distinctive feature lies in the fact that within it change takes place "in a progressive order between two counterparts or complements, or between two things of the same genus the succeeding factor augmenting the effect of the previous one." Here there is a "procession from good to greater good, from the wholesome to the more wholesome." The rotatory play or strife between the opposites is limited to the Kāma or non-Jhānic sphere of consciousness. In the sphere of Jhāna and religious experience there is an infinite and continuously progressive gradation. Nirvāṇa is called the final only in order to avoid an infinite regress in thought.

The view is based on considerations of philosophic consistency, the exposition by Dhammadinnā in the MN, and some implicit Mahāyānic influences.

There is no doubt this much of truth in this theory that whereas Saṃsāra is cyclic, it is of the essence of the way (Maggo) to lead one out of it and continuously on towards Nibbāna. And Dhammadinnā—her histori-

[164] On the justification of translating Nirodha as transcendence, see the lines quoted above from Ud. Suttas 10 and 71, and compare them with the corresponding lines in DN. I. 223, from which it will emerge that the idea of Nirodha is not that of annihilation but of transcendence. For further discussion of the meaning of Nirodha, see below.

[165] Op. cit. p. 62ff.

city as well as the age of the text ascribed to her are both indefinite—probably meant no more. Nibbāna was far from being regarded as a merely 'limiting' conception; it was considered actually realizable.[166] As to Nibbāna being a process, all the ancient evidence is against taking such a view. It was not a More, but the Most.[167]

Nibbana and Samsara.—On the metaphysical relation of Nibbāna to Saṃsāra there is little precise evidence in the earlier texts. Certainly the one was not regarded as the cause or ground of the other. This distinguishes the doctrine from the prevailing Upaniṣadic view on the relation between absolute and relative reality. The world existed from beginningless time,[168] and Buddha frowned on views postulating a first beginning or a final end of the universe. This point of view is logically implied by the doctrine of karma which cannot postulate a first beginning without shifting the responsibility of human suffering from man to God or Chance. Creationism, in order to be logical, has either to make of suffering a blessing in disguise, or has to acquiesce in the idea of a Limited God.

N. as the Goal.—A practical answer to the question about the relation of Nibbāna to Saṃsāra is, however, clearly to be discerned in the discourses. Nibbāna is the ultimately sought for end, the most worthwhile.[169]

---

[166] Pattabba—AN. IV. 455; AN. I. 162 (adhigacchati) SN. I. 214. Sacchikātabba—MN. I. 56, 63, 340; II. 242; III. 236; AN. I. 8; III. 423; V. 194.

[167] Anuttara—MN. sutta 52; uttama; parama (see below). Cf. What was the original Gospel....? p. 83 cf SN. III. 189; Ib. V. 218.

[168] Thus SN. II. Anamatagga Sam.

[169] **Attho.**—See SN. p. 4, 18, 33; Itv. p. 15. AN. V. 16. Nipuṇattha Sn. p. 17; Paramattho—See Ib. p. 6, 21, Itv. p. 83; Uttamattha—Dhp. verse 386.

It is the goal of the spiritual pilgrimage,[170] that where one finally goes beyond all sorrows.[171] It is the safe "other bank".[172] Here there is no more dissatisfaction but instead eternal peace.[173]

The Upaniṣads use "Artha" in at least three senses (a) for things in general. Thus Īśa–8 "Arthān vyadadhācchāśvatībhyaḥ samābhyaḥ". (b) For sense objects–Thus Kaṭh 3.10 "Indriyebhyaḥ parāhyarthā arthebhyaśca paraṃ manaḥ" Praśna: Śrutamevārthamanuśṛṇoti...." Mait. 4.2 "Śabdasparśādayo hyarthāḥ......"; Ib. 6. 28–"bhūtendriyārthānatikramya". (c) For summum bonum or śreyas (Niḥśreyasa). Thus Kaṭh–2.1. "Hīyaterthādyaü preyovṛṇīte" Śvet. 2.14. "Kṛtārtho bhavate vītaśokaḥ". It may be noted that the Nikāyas sometimes use the expression Atthacariyā–AN. II. 32, 248; IV. 219, 364 (cf. Brahmacariya). Cf. MN. I. 163–"Yogakkhemaṃ Nibbānaṃ pariyesati". "Anuttaraṃ yogakkhemaṃ"–Ib. I. 167; Sn. p. 8. Itv. pp. 8-9; Dhp. verse 23; Sotthi: Sn. 235; Khemaṃ: AN. I. 142; AN. III. 311–"khemappattā sukhino". Cf. Kv. XIX. 6 where the Andhakas regard N. as Kusala. Cf. "Patto ca sambodhimanuttaraṃ sivaṃ" (Sn. p. 48).

[170] Amatogādhā sabbe dhammā" AN. V. 107; "Nibbānogādhaṃ brahmacariyaṃ" MN. I. 304; "Yaṃ kho pana kiñci bhūtaṃ saṅkhataṃ paṭiccasamuppannaṃ nirodho tassa nissaraṇaṃ" Itv. Sutta 72. This bears directly on the relation between Paṭiccasaṃ° and Nibbāna. The way leads to "Samaṃ bhūmibhāgaṃ ramaṇīyaṃ" (N)–SN. III. 108–9. The way simile is itself significant; cf. Kaṭh. 3.9. "(A) dhvanaḥ paraṃ".

[171] "Gacchati anivattantaṃ yattha gantvā na socati" (Sn. p. 8).

[172] AN. IV. 160; "Tiṇṇo pāraṅgato thale tiṭṭhati Brāhmaṇo" Itv. Sutta 69, AN. IV. 13; AN. II. 24 (Akutobhayaṃ); Pārimaṃ Tīram. SN. IV. 175, (So SN. I. 192). The figure of the "other bank" is of frequent occurrence in the Upaniṣads–Ch. 7. 13–"Śokasya Pāraṃ....". 26.2: "Tamasaḥ pāraṃ" Kaṭh. 2.11. "Abhayasya Pāraṃ"; Ib. 32. "Abhayaṃ titīrṣatāṃ pāraṃ"; Muṇd. 2.2.6; Praśna–6.8; Mait. 6.21, 28, 30.

[173] **Samatho**—the pacification of all striving (Stcherbatsky's interpretation is not convincing for the ancient texts at least)–Itv. Sutta 72. SN. I. 136 (this text, as pointed out, occurs in the DN, the MN and the Mvg. also) Santipadaṃ–Sn. 933, Dhp. 286; Anuttarraṃ samtivarapadaṃ –MN I. 165f; Santaṃ AN I. 133; Atthuttarim padaṃ santaṃ–AN. IV. 70, 74; SN I. 2. I. (Saṅkhārā) tesaṃ vūpasamo sukho...." On śānti cf. Kaṭh. I. 1. 17; Ib. 2. 5, 13; Māṇḍ. 7.12; Śvet. 4. 11 Dhp. 369, 38 "padaṃ santaṃ saṅkhārupasamaṃ sukhaṃ". For the equivalent Sanskrit version–see Lévi–

The nature of Quiescence.—But is not the peace, the peace of "death"? For is not Nibbāna described in terms of cessation,[174] disappearance[175] and extinction.[176] This is not plausible, as all these negative terms were only intended to negate the phenomenal (Saṃsāra).[177] This alone will render intelligible the nu-

---

JA 1912 Sept.—Oct. where the Chinese translation is thus rendered "son movement s'arrêtant, il est eternellement calme" (Ib. 275).

[174] N.=Āsavānaṃ Parikkhayo AN IV. 545; Esanānaṃ khayo Itv. Sutta 55; Rāgakkhaya etc. SN. IV. 251 Bhavanirodho nibbānaṃ AN. V. 9; SN. II. 117, III. 14, IV. 86. N=Virāgo—AN. II. 34, 118; III. 164, IV. 423f. etc. Visaṃyoga—AN. III. 156 (cf. the Vaibhāṣika def. of Pratisaṅkhyānirodha); N=Taṇhāyavippahānaṃ SN. I. 39. Nirodho, Itv. Sutta 51, 72, 73; Asesam (nāmañca rūpañca) uparujjhati—SN. I. 13, 15, 35, 60, 165; DN. I. Kevaḍḍha sutta; upadhikkhayo, °saṅkhayo AN. IV. 150 II. 24, III. 382.

According to Dr. Dutt "The 'not—being' (Asat) is termed in Buddhism Nirvāṇa or Buddhatva" (Early Monastic Buddh. I. p. 16), this really represents a misunderstanding—cf. "Asadevedamāsīdityabhāvabrahmavādinaḥ śūnyabhuvamavagāhya sthitāḥ. Mādhyamikā api evameva" (Pratyabhijñāhṛadayam ed. J. C. Chatterji pp. 17-18). Cf. Vedāntasāra p. 8.

[175] Sn. Upasīvamāṇavapucchā.

[176] "Pajjotasseva nibbānaṃ" SN. I. 159; MN. I. Aggivacchagotta Sutta; MN. III. 245.

[177] We see that the items destroyed in Nirvāṇa are—Āsavas, Eṣaṇās, Rāga etc., Saññojanas, Taṇhā, Vaṭṭa, Bhava, Nāma and Rūpa, Saṅkhāras, Upadhi etc. That is, ignorance and the passions, phenomenal existence (Bhavavaṭṭa), craving and impulses, misery; in short, the whole of Papañca (Nāma-rūpa). Nibbāna is thus the pure (Asaṃkiliṭṭha) and the transcendental (Appapañca). It is beyond the elements; words fall back from it:—

"Yattha āpo ca paṭhavī tejo vāyo na gādhati
Ato sarā nivattanti ettha vaṭṭam na vaṭṭati
Ettha nāmañca rūpañca asesamuparujjhati" (SN. I. 15)

Cf. Tait. Up. "Yato vāco nivartante etc." (2.9). The very expression "Ettha" signifies that Nibbāna is not the cessation of "name and form"; it is *that where* "name and form cease."

Nirodha and "Blowing Out".—Cf. Heiler quoted in the Pali Dictionary, (PTS). In Praśna I.10 Nirodha is equivalent to Apunarāvṛtti. According to Ch. 8. 6—what is Nirodha to the fools is "Prapadana" to the wise. Cf. Vijñānabhikṣu—Yogasārasaṅgraha (Chowkhambha ed.) pp. 3-4: "Nirodho na nāśo'

merous utterances about the supreme bliss of Nibbāṇa.[178] It is incorrect to argue that these statements about bliss refer only to Nibbāṇa-in-this-life and not to the Nibbāṇa beyond it,[179] for between the two there is no difference qua Nibbāṇa, and there is no reason to suppose

---

bhāvasāmānyaṃ vā" etc. For the true meaning of the "blowing out" simile see Śvet. 1. 13; Kaṭh 25. 9, Schrader JPTS 1904–'5. Keith B.P. pp. 65–66. "Extinction" is not simple destruction but absorption in the unmanifest source.

Cf. the controversy between Bharadvāja and Bhṛgu on the meaning of extinction in Mbh. Śānti. p. 187–2–6. The former whose standpoint is materialistic says "Naśyatītyeva jānāmi śāntamagnimanindhanam| Gatirasya pramāṇaṃ vā saṃsthānaṃ vā na vidyate||" The latter assures him that it continues to exist but in an imperceptibly subtle form. Cf. Maitrāyaṇīyāraṇ°. 6.34. v. 1." "Yathā nirindhano vahniḥ svayonā upaśāmyati Tathā vṛttikṣayāccittaṃ svayonā upaśāmyati" Cf. YS. I. 2. Yogaścittavṛttinirodhaḥ". Cf. Nirodha beyond the "4 Koṭis"—AN. II. 161.

[178] **Bliss and Peace**—Paramaṃ sukham MN. I. 508; DN. II. 94; Etaṃ kho paramaṃ ñāṇaṃ etaṃ sukhamanuttaraṃ Asokaṃ virajaṃ khemaṃ. . . ." AN. III. 354; AN. III. 442; Sn. p. 33; Acalaṃ sukhaṃ Ud. p. 96, cf. Ib. p. 16; Sn. p. 82; Dhp. verses 202–206; SN. I. 212. Ab. K. IV. 127 fn. 3 "Le sūtra dit: <<par le plaisir (sukha) du chemin, on obtient le plaisir du Nirvāṇa>>" (Vibhāṣā), cf. Sakya pp. 304–5; throughout Mvu Nibbāṇa is conceived as Sukha (Dutt. Aspects—p. 30 fn.)

Śānti in fact is peace, not mere "quiescence". Quiet is here suffused with bliss—upasamasukhaṃ=Sambodhi° AN. IV. 341 (This gives a blend of quiet and Enlightenment); cf. Lalita Vistara I. p. 380; Candrakīrti says "Yadā caivaṃ sarvatyāgena sarvapāṣaṇḍinām nirvāṇamabhimataṃ. . . ayaṃ viśeṣo yattīrthikānāṃ sarvatyāgābhiprāyamātraṃ na tu punaḥ sarvatyāgopakhyānaṃ." (on Catuḥśatikā—Mem. As. SB. III. p. 494), but Candrakīrti at the same time speaks of Nirvāṇa as "Anapāyasukhaikarasaṃ śivam". (Ib. p. 476). This suggests that the negativist emphasis of the Buddhist had a practical purpose in view—that the bliss of Nirvāṇā may not be confused with anything worldly. The statement of Candrakīrti may be compared with S. IV. 15 where also the dhamma is said to be "Sabbappahānāya" "All" is however defined to be equivalent to the senses, the mind and their objects: "cakkhuñca rūpañca. . . .mano ceva dhammā ca idaṃ vuccati sabbaṃ".

[179] As assumed e.g. by La Vallée Poussin—"Nirvāṇa" ERE (IX. p. 378).

that the bliss of Nibbāṇa is merely accidental to it. It is an error in fact to conceive this bliss as a kind of pleasure and then refer it to the life of the Khandhas or Saṃsāra.[180]

Emancipation.—Not only does Saṃsāra cease, there takes place an emancipation from it.[181] This freedom

[180] MN. I. p. 400—"Aññatitthiyā paribbājakā.... 'saññāvedayitanirodhaṃ—gotamo āha tañca sukhasmiṃ paññāpeti, tayidaṃ kiṃsu—kathaṃ su' *Na kho bhagavā sukhaṃ yeva vedanaṃ sandhāya sukhasmiṃ paññāpeti, api ca yattha yattha sukhaṃ upalabbhati yahiṃ yahiṃ....taṃ sukhasmiṃ paññāpeti.*" Cf. Kaṭh. 2.5.14 "Tadetaditi manyante' *nirdeśyaṃ paramaṃ sukhaṃ....*" This bliss is not something determinate or transient. On sukhavedanā vis-à-vis the Arhant—see MN. III. 244–5; SN. IV. 210; MN. II. 227 "Tathāgato..anāsavā sukhā vedanā vedeti".

[181] **Vimutti**—"Sabbaso anupādāya sammā cittaṃ vimuccati .." AN. III. 354; Sabbaganṭhapamocanaṃ SN. I. 210, cf. "Sarvaguhāgranthibhyo vimukto—bhavati" Muṇḍaka Up. 3.2.9; Vin. I. 1. 13, 1; "Na yidaṃ brahmacariyaṃ lābhasakkārasilokānisaṃsaṃ na sīlasampada° na samādhisampadā° na ñāṇadassanā° yā ayaṃ..akuppā cetovimutti etadatthaṃ.." (MN. I. 197) Akuppā vimutti—MN. I. 167, AN. III. 354 SN. II. 239, Cf. the usual formula for Āsavakkhaya; "(Kaṃma) nirodhā vimuttiṃ phusati" SN. IV. 132–133; when not even the Brahma—world binds the citta it becomes emancipated. This is the same as the emancipation from Āsavas—SN. V. 410; Anuttarā Vimutti—SN. I. 105; it is to be directly realized (Sacchikātabbā) Ib. V. 52; MN. III. 290, cf. Ib. III. 297; it is the Paṭibhāga" of vijjā and has its "Paṭibhāga" in Nibbāṇa—MN. I. 304; it is the refuge (Paṭisaraṇa, as the mind of the senses) of Sati and has its refuge in Nibbāṇā—SN. V. 218; apart from the highest emancipation from all Āsava (Akuppā)° there are also "emancipations" at various levels of experience. These are called Vimutti since they lead one away from Rāga etc. Thus we have appamāṇā cetovimutti, ākiñcaññā°, suññata°, and animittā°—MN. I. 297f; SN. IV. 296–'7. The last two may refer to the highest Vimutti.

It is the conception of vimutti which makes intelligible the definition of Amata as Rāgadosamohakkhayo—SN. V. 8. The idea goes back to the Upaniṣads.... "yadā sarve pramucyante kāmā ye sya hṛdisthitāḥ Atha martyo'mṛto bhavatyatra brahma samaśnute" Kaṭh—6. 14. This is the idea of Jīvanmukti and has, in its ethical and practical aspects at least, a close correspondence to that of the Arahā while living. Muṇḍ. 3.2.9. "Guhāgranthibhyo vimukto 'mṛto bhavati" II. p. 1111 (Acyuta-

rests in Nibbāṇa i.e. to be freed from Saṃsāra is to rest in Nibbāṇa.[182]

The problem of Atta.—The question at once arises; whose freedom? The usual answer is in terms of the citta. The problem of the nature of citta is, however, closely bound up with that of the nature of "Anatta".

Modern interpretations: Rhys Davids.—According to Prof. Rhys Davids at the time of Buddha there were prevalent in N. India animistic, polytheistic, pantheistic and dualistic views. The belief in soul was central to all of them. Gotama at one stroke not only ignored it, but held it actually inimical to spiritual progress.[183]

Vidhushekhar Shastri.—The denial of a permanent self has been called the chief claim of Buddhism to intellectual independence.[184] The denial, according to MM. Vidhushekhar Shāstrin, proceeded from the fact that Buddha found in experience nothing that corresponded with the supposed characteristics of the Ātman, viz. independence, permanence and blissfulness.[185] Thus by eradicating the notion of 'I' (Ātman) and 'Mine' (Ātmīya) the Buddha struck at the very root of Kāma 'desire'.[186]

---

granthamālā) "vidyayā tadārohanti yatra kāmāḥ parāgatāḥ" (cf. Vimutti as the Paṭibhāga of Vijjā, supra); Cf. Kv. 1. p. 238f, for the controversy between the Andhakas and the Theravādins; the former identified Vimutti with the destruction of Rāga etc. The latter thought it to be degrading the conception of Nibbāṇa. Compare also the controversy between the Vaibhāṣikas and the Sautrāntikas over the interpretation of "Vimokkho cetaso ahu....". Dn. II. s. 16, which occurs in SN. I. also. See Chap. on DN. In the light of the Upaniṣadic background as reflected in the texts quoted above one is inclined to favour the Vaibhāṣikas.

182 MN. III. 245; MN. I. 167.

183 American Lectures pp. 36-41; Hibbert Lectures p. 29.

184 Thomas—Life—p. 209.

185 Basic Conception p. 64f.

186 Ib. p. 95.

Stcherbatsky.—According to Prof. Stcherbatsky, Buddhism resolved man into a plurality of separate elements without real unity. This was probably a development of the analytical trend shown in some Brāhmaṇic and Upaniṣadic texts.[187]

La Vallee Poussin.—Prof. La Vallée Poussin regards "Nairātmya" and "Karmaphalasambandha" the two most important theses of primitive Buddhism.[188] At another place, however, he is inclined towards the "agnostic" interpretation.[189]

Schrader.—On the other hand, according to Prof. Schrader, from anicca—dukkha—anatta necessarily follows the converse Nicca—Adukkha—Attā. As a matter of fact, Buddha denied the Attā only because that word meant for him "die substantielle individuelle Seele" and not absolute substance. He appeared as a "soul-denier" to his contemporaries only because they conceived of the soul in an extremely anthropomorphic fashion, speak ing of its form, weight, colour etc.[190]

Mrs. Rhys Davids.—Mrs. Rhys Davids has most vigorously advocated the view that Buddha did not preach the 'No-soul' theory at all but that it was a later monkish innovation under the impact of Sāṅkhya "Analysis", the growth of a narrow world-outlook and hostility toward the Brāhmaṇas.[191]

Some other scholars.—The view has been reiterated with modifications by Coomarswamy,[192] and Radha-

---

[187] Central Conception p. 73.

[188] JA. 1903.

[189] ERE—"Nirvāṇa"; opinions—p. 87.

[190] Über den Stand etc. pp. 4-6.

[191] What was the Original Gospel; Sakya; Buddhism (H. U.L.); The Birth of Ind. Psy.

[192] Living Thoughts of Buddha, Int.; Hinduism and Buddhism pp. 57-69; 71-73.

krishnan.[193] According to Sogen[194] and Suzuki[195] Buddhism denies the Ātman in the sense of a finite substantial individual but not in the sense of the absolute unity of the universe.

The Madhyamika standpoint.—The correct standpoint seems to have been indicated by Nāgārjuna who says in MK—XVIII. 6. "Ātmetyapi deśitam prajñapitamanātmetyapi Buddhairātmā na cānātmā Kaściditvapi deśitam." Although some Nikāya texts can be found which appear to assume an Ātman-theory, and others which preach a theory of Ānātman, Buddha's own standpoint appears to have been that ultimate reality belongs neither to the one nor to the other conception. Nāgārjuna believing in the later theory of the "degrees or grades of truth" thought that all the three types of utterances were not really irreconcilable and could be ascribed to Buddha himself without inconsistency. "Sammuti" occurs several times in the Mahāviyūhasutta of the Sn. (Cf. Sammutiñāṇa in DN. III. 226, 277) but the exact degree of metaphysical significance, if any, to be read into it is uncertain. A distinction between the inner realization of the emancipated and "Lokavohāra" is however clearly made out in some texts—M. Sutta 74 'Evaṃ vimuttacitto bhikkhu na kenaci saṃvadati, na kenaci vivadati, yañca loke vuttaṃ tena voharati aparāmasanti' D. Sutta 9—"imā-lokasamaññā lokaniruttiyo lokavohārā °paññattiyo yāhi tathāgato voharati aparāmasaṃti." Such texts probably played a part in the growth of the distinction between Paramārtha—Satya and Saṃvṛti—or Vyavahāra—satya.

---

[193] I. p. I.
[194] Systems of Buddhist Thought.
[195] Outlines of Mahāyāna.

Historical analysis of the Nikaya data: Evidence for the Atman-theory.—Mrs. Rhys Davids has pointed out that had Buddha raised a revolt against the Ātman-theory as accepted in the Upaniṣads it would indeed be remarkable that he should not bring it forward while in controversy with Brāhmaṇas of importance and learning, which is actually the case.[196] From this, however, it does not follow, as Mrs. Rhys Davids would conclude, that Buddha believed in the "Ātman theory" but only that he did not believe in the Anātman theory in an absolute fashion.[197] At least he did not think it helpful for everybody.[198]

Compounds in Atta.—The conclusion that Buddha believed in the Ātman has been sought to be enforced by the argument that there are some compound words which there is some reason to suppose early and yet in which the word Attan seems to be used in a sense different from that of the man as a complex of body and mind only. Such are Ajjhatta, Paccatta, Attabhāva, Pahitatta and Bhāvitatta.[199] In the case of the first compound alone, however, has the argument some

---

[196] Sakya—p. 187 where the suttas implicitly referred to are indicated.

[197] Cf. MK—XVIII. 8 "Sarvaṃ tathyaṃ na vā tathyaṃ tathyaṃ cātathyameva ca Naivātathyaṃ naiva tathyametad-buddhānuśāsanam." Candrakīrti quotes "Loko mayā sārdhaṃ vivadati nāhaṃ lokena sārdhaṃ vivadāmi Yalloke sammataṃ tanmamāpyasti sammatam yalloke nāsti sammataṃ mamāpi-tannāsti sammatamityāgamācca". This would suggest that Buddha did not preach any "theory" in an absolute fashion (The text quoted by Candrakīrti is practically the same as SN. III. 138. "Nāhaṃ bhikkhave lokena saha vivadāmi etc.").

[198] Cf." ......hīnamadhyotkṛṣṭavineyajanāśayanānātvena ātmānātmā tadubhayapratiṣedhena Buddhānāṃ bhagavatāṃ dharmadeśanā pravṛttā...."

(Candrakīrti ad MK. XVIII. 8)

[199] Sakya p. 189f.

weight. Although later Ajjhatta came to be just the inner as opposed to the outer[200] and condemned equally along with it,[201] in some uses, apparently early, it is given a place of value.[202] Man in withdrawing into himself obviously neared something which was prized. This would be difficult to understand were the man no more than an impermanent aggregate.

In Paccatta Attā seems to have the sense of the "individual";[203] in Pahitatta and Bhāvitatta that of the citta, as indeed Buddhaghosa suggests.[204]

Attabhāva is a curious expression. It seems to have meant an individual existence, a particular individual life.[205] It was the result of past kamma and includ-

---

[200] Thus Ajjhattikabāhirāni āyatanāni—MN. III. 63, 272f. In the Āraṇyaka literature the usual contrast is between Adhyātma and Adhideva. Cf. Adhidevañāṇadassana—AN. IV. 304.

[201] e.g. Ajjhattabahiddhā suññataṃ manasi karoti MN. III. 111f.

[202] In such expressions as Ajjhattacintī,° °Rato,° citta; and such utterances as "Ajjhattaṃ sukhaṃ anuyuñjeyya"—MN. III. 230; (Ajjhattaṃ) jalayāmi jotiṃ SN. I. 169. The second of these is peculiarly Upaniṣadic—and it was in conversation with a Brāhmaṇa, in opposition to external sacrifice.

[203] The following passage seems to support Mrs. Rhys Davids' interpretation: "aññātreva....saddhāya....ruciyā.... ākāraparivitakkā...diṭṭhinijjhānakkhanityā atthāyasmato Musīlassa *Paccattameva ñāṇaṃ* bhavanirodho nibbānanti" (SN. II. 117). Cf. the later expression "Pratyātmagati" (Suzuki-Studies in the Laṅkāvatara p. 102f).

[204] Cf. Sakya p. 191 cf. "Pahitatto samāno kāyena ceva paramasaccaṃ sacchikaroti paññāya ca tam ativijjha passati" (MN. II. 173).

[205] AN. I. 134—"Lobha (dosa, moha) samudayaṃ yatthassa attabhāvo nibbattati tattha taṃ kammaṃ vipaccati—— tattha vipākaṃ paṭisaṃvedeti.." Ib. 279—"Oḷārikam attabhāvaṃ abhinimminitvā...." Ib. III. 432—"Yaṃ kho——vediyamāno tajjaṃ tajjaṃ attabhāvamabhinibbatteti puññabhāgiyaṃ vā apuññabhāgiyaṃ vā——ayaṃ vedanānaṃ vipāko.." Ib. IV. 200—' santi mahāsamudde yojanasatikā pi attabhāvā". Attabhāvapaṭilābha: AN. II. 159—"cattāro attabhāvapaṭilābhā...yasmiṃ attasañcetanā kamati no parasañcetanā" etc. Ib. 188—"Tathā.

ed the physical aspect of personality. It could not be permanent, else, naturally, no release from misery would be possible. For those who used the compound, the meaning of Attā taken separately may not have been important.

Atta as the dearest.—Buddha's belief in the Attan is also inferred from the statement in the Mallikā section of the Kosala saṃ° to the effect that the Attā is the dearest in the whole world and that an "Attakāma" should not injure another. The exact interpretation of the text appears to be difficult, but the saying might have been popularly meant.[206] It would then inculcate the same moral as SN. V. 353, and Dhp. 129.

Atta as the sought for and refuge.—The case of "Attānaṃ gaveseyyātha" (Mvg. I. 23) is better, since if we put beside it Dhp. 146. "Andhakāreṇa onaddhā padīpaṃ na gavessatha?" and 'Attadīpā viharatha,"[207] it does not seem too farfetched to imagine that Attā in the Mvg. text is used in a more than merely reflexive sense.[208]

---

bhūto kho ayaṃ lokasannivāso tathābhūto attabhāvapaṭilābho." AN. III. 122—"aññataraṃ manomayaṃ kāyaṃ uppanno tassa evarūpo attabhāvapaṭilābho hoti seyyathāpi dve vā tīṇi vā māgadhikāni gāmakkhettāni.." SN. V. 442—"sukhumattā attabhāvassa" (on purely physical considerations) SN. II. 255-"evarūpopi nāma satto bhavissati——evarūpo pi nāma attabhāvapaṭilābho paṭisaṃvediyatha..". Ib. III. 144—"Ettako Cepi.. attabhāvapaṭilābho abhavissā nicco dhuvo sassato avipariṇāmadhammo nayidaṃ brahmacariyavāso paññāyetha sammā dukkhakhayāya...". MN. II. 32—yāvatakaṃ pi iminā attabhāvena paccanubhūtaṃ.."

[206] Cf. the discussion on the Sutta in the Chapter on the stratification of SN.

[207] SN. III. 42, V. 154, 163; DN. pt. II. p. 83 (Nāg ed.); DN. sutta 26.

[208] See Coomarswamy in JAOS. 1938 pp. 680—681 who, with reference to "Attadīpā viharatha" calls attention to Br. up. IV. 3.6.

The expression "Brahmabhūtena attanā"[209] is more clearly significant. So is "Pahāya vo gamissāmi kataṃ me saraṇamattano".[210]

Atta as conscience.—In a few passages Attā is used in the sense of the "inner monitor" or conscience.[211] This usage is hardly to be met with in the Brāhmaṇas or the Upaniṣads.[211a]

Atta in the Dhp.—Attā plays an important role in the Dhp. It is here an entity very near and dear.[212] Essentially independent or rather "self-dependent", it has great potentialities for evil and for good. It has to be tamed, guarded and educated very carefully. It has a remarkable duality—on the one hand, it is an instrument, a potency in which respect it is the same as "citta" commonly understood; on the other, it is the man behind mind, in a way identical with it, but in another, something more than it—in fact, its own real nature: its innate potentialities for the good struggling from within.

Beside these few and uncertain or more or less popular references to Attā,[213] there are more definite

[209] Geiger loc. cit. Cf. "Amṛtāccāmṛtam prāptaḥ śāntībhūto nirātmavān Brahmabhūtaḥ sa nirdvandvaḥ sukhī śānto nirāmayaḥ". The verse is a great deal Buddhist in appearance. (Mbh. ŚP. 199. 23).

[210] DN. pt. II. p. 96 (Nāg. ed.).

[211] Thus AN. 3.3.10; Ib. 3.4.10; Ib. 2.2.7; Ib. 4.13.121; MN. I. 440f.

[211a] But cf. Manu "Śrutiḥ smṛtiḥ sadācāraḥ / svasya ca priyam ātmanaḥ //"

[112] Dhp. Attavaggo; also verses 103-104, 238, 282 (which truly preaches Mrs. Rhys Davids' Gospel), 315, 323, 379-380. These verses did not escape notice in ancient times. Thus see Candrakīrti ad MK. XVIII.5; with reference to "Attā hi attano nātho etc." it is stated in the Bodhicaryāvatāra "cittamevāsyāṃ gāthāyāmahaṅkāraniśrayatayā ātmaśabdena uktaṃ"; so Abh. k. V. "cittaṃ cāhaṅkārasanniśraya ityātmaśabdenopacaryate" (Cf. La Vallée Poussin JA—1903 p. 274).

[213] There are a few references, however, which it is impossible to fit in with the theory of Anatta as classically understood. These are Ud. Sutta 10 "yadā ca attanā vedi muni monena brāh-

indications to the effect that the beginnings of Pudgalavāda and Vijñānavāda are, in some respects, to be found in the Nikāyas.

Purisa.—In contrast to the Upaniṣads, the word "Purisa" is of rare occurrence in the Nikāyas. Mostly its occurrence too is without much significance, which is more patently the case with "Satta" which is a little more frequent. But in a few cases the usage is hardly in the spirit of the later doctrine of Anatta. **Thus, "Taṇhādutiyo puriso dīghamaddhāna saṃsāraṃ Itthabhāvaññathābhāvaṃ saṃsāraṃ nātivattati.**[214] In the Upaniṣads, puruṣa is sometimes associated with the "heart". There are just a few references to "heart" in the Nikāyas, but they are significant and far from according with the conception of "Hadayavatthu" of later dogma. Thus "Bhikkhu siyā jhāyī vimuttacitto Ākaṅkhe ca *hadayassānuppattiṃ;*"[215] "Atthassa pattiṃ hadayassa santiṃ;"[216] "Ajjhattameva jalayāmi jotiṃ......jihvā sujā *hadayaṃ jotiṭṭhānaṃ*......Attā sudanto purisassa joti":[217] *"Nibbānaṃ hadayasmiṃ opiya......"*[218]

---

maṇo Atha rūpā arūpā ca sukhadukkhā pamuccati"; Sn. Dvayatānupassanasutta verses 33—35; Here the seeing of the self in the non-self or "Name & Form" is condemned (Anattani attamānaṃ passa lokaṃ sadevakaṃ Niviṭṭham nāmarūpasmiṃ idaṃ saccaṃti maññati). And the true self is apparently identified with the eternal Nirvāṇa (Amosadhammaṃ nibbāṇam). Sn. Sundarikabhāradvāja v. 23 is curiously inconsistent—"Yo attanāttānaṃ nānupassati samāhito ujjugato ṭhitatto." Shall ṭhitatto be just Ṭhitacitto?

[214] It....sutta 15; cf. Ib. sutta 58. The expression Purisatthāmo, Purisaparakkamo sometimes occurs, MN. I. 497, 481, 516ff. The relation of will to what is called "self-experience" or the feeling of personality is very close. For men of strong will and introspective understanding not to feel the reality of the "person" is hard to understand. See G. Coster: Yoga & W. Psych. pp. 223—224 (O. U. P. 1934); F. Aveling—Personality and Will. p. 180 (Cambridge U. P. 1931). [215] SN. I. 46—52.

[216] Ib. I. 125. [217] Ib. I. 169. [218] Ib. I. 199.

Purisa-puggala and Puggala.—Midway between the Puruṣa of the Upaniṣads and the Puggala of the Nikāyas is the expression "Purisapuggala". *It signifies the individual acting, believing and experiencing the results of his acts.*[219] Puggala is of frequent occurrence in the Nikāyas.[220] Buddha is himself reported to have delivered sermons dividing Puggalas into various classes.[221] Usually the usage does not indicate any belief in an Ātman, but the well known Bhārahāra sutta[222] is a striking exception. The sutta itself appears to clearly distinguish between the Puggala and the Khandhas. The latter are merely a burden to the former.

Puggalavada.—The Puggalavādins,[223] however,

---

[219] "Micchādiṭṭhikassa—purisapuggalassa—" SN. IV. 307. "evameva rūpattāyaṃ purisapuggalo rūpe patiṭṭhāya puññaṃ vā apuññaṃ vā pasavati.." (MN. I. 230) "Yaṃ kiñcāyaṃ purisapaggalo paṭisaṃvedeti sukhaṃ vā dukkhaṃ vā adukkhamasukhaṃ vā" (Ib. 475; II. 214, 217) So—SN. IV. 230. "catūhi dhammehi samannāgataṃ purisapuggalaṃ paññāpemi sampannakusalaṃ" (MN. II. 24); "sa ce kho natthi paro loko evamayaṃ bhavaṃ purisapuggalo kāyassa bhedā sotthimattānaṃ karissati" MN. I. 403; "Avijjāgato yaṃ bhikkhave purisapuggalo puññañce saṅkhāraṃ abhisankharoti puññūpagaṃ hoti viññāṇaṃ" (SN. II. 82). Cf. "uktaṃ hi Bhagavatā avidyānugato yaṃ bhikṣavaḥ Purusapudgalaḥ puṇyānapi saṃskārānabhisaṃskaroti apuṇyānapi anindyānapi saṃskārānabhisaṃskarotītyādinā." (Candrakīrti's Comy. on MK. p. 57. Calcutta ed.).

[220] On its Buddhist etymologies—See Ab. K. vol. V. pp. 228—229.

[221] MN. I. 314, 411, II. 159 etc.; the AN. devotes the largest attention to such classifications. Cf. Catuḥśatikā—Comy. by Candrakīrti, Mem. As. S. B. Vol. IV. p. 471.

[222] SN. III. 25—26. It is often quoted in later Buddh. lit. (cf. Minayeff. p. 225; Poussin J. A. 1902) Uddyotakara also refers to it. In the light of the Bhārahāra sutta cf. the epithet "Pannabhāra"—MN. I. 139; AN. III. 84; SN. I. 233.

[223] They are called Vātsīputrīyas in the Kośa, and explained as Āryasammatīyas in the Vyākhyā (Ab. K. V. p. 227). Buddhaghosa explains the Puggalavādins as Vajjiputtakas and Sammitīyas. (Debates Commentary—p. 9). According to Stcherbatsky they established their doctrine with the sole aim of supporting a supernatural surviving Buddha (Nirvāṇa—p. 31 fn.). Accord-

adopted a more Buddhistic"[224] position by declaring that the Puggala was neither identical with nor different from the Khandhas. The relation of the Puggala to the Khandhas was held ineffable (Avaktavya).[225] The stock disproof of the Puggala along Anupalabdhi[226] is answered by pointing out that it is known in all perceptions mediately.[227]

The Puggalavādins refused to admit the authenticity of many of the scriptural texts quoted against them. Besides, they argued, what was intended to be preached in such texts as "Sarve dharmā anātmānaḥ" was only that one should not seek the self in what is not the self, not that there is no self whatever.[228]

In support of their own contention the Puggalavādins referred to such texts as the Bhārahārasūtra, the sūtras classifying Pudgalas, and those in which Buddha referred to his past lives.[229] Positive arguments of a phi-

---

ing to Dr. Vaidya they partook of Madhyamika views (Études sur Āryadeva—p. 15). Candrakīrti refers to the following view of the Sammitīyas: "Yasyopādāturdarśanaśravaṇaghrāṇarasanādīni vedanāsparśasaṃskārādīni ca bhavanti sa upādātā pūrvamebhyaḥ astīti sammitīyā vadanti" (Comy on MK. IX. 1.).

[224] Yaśomitra called them Buddhists, Śāntideva Pseudo-Buddhists (Saugatammanya) Ab. K. V. p. 228.

[225] Ab. K. V. p. 232; 237 "ineffable (avaktavya) en ce qui concerne sa relation—avec les elements" The view occurs in a way in the Nikāyas—See SN. III. p. 130 "Na rūpamasmīti vadāmi na pi aññatra rūpā asmīti vadāmi api ca me—pañcasu upadānakkhandhesu asmīti adhigatamayamahamasmīti ca na samanupassāmi". Just as the scent of the flower is of the flower as a whole, not of any of its parts taken separately; so the ego-feeling pervades the whole personality. The simile very nearly implies that to miss the "self" is to miss the wood for the trees.

[226] See Kv. I. 1. f.

[227] Ab. Kv. p. 238f. Cf. Aveling op. cit. p. 183. The relation of Aveling's psychology to that of W. James is reminiscent of the controversy we are just considering.

[228] Ab. Kv. pp. 254—252.

[229] Ib. p. 253, 258, 259, 271.

losophic character were also advanced. But for the Pudgala, Buddha's omniscience as well as all memory would be impossible.[230] And if Buddha disbelieved in the Pudgala why did he not identify the soul (Jīva) with the body (Śarīra)?[231] Why did he not deny the existence of the soul (Jīva) outright?[232] Why did he consider the denial of the Ātman a Dṛṣṭisthāna?[233] If the Pudgala were not there who, indeed, would fare through the "beginningless Saṃsāra?"[234] Finally it must be remembered that the point of the theory of Anātman—that belief in a "self" will cause attachment and bondage[235]—does not really apply to the doctrine of Pudgala. There is bondage only so long as one sees the "self" in what is not the self.[236]

The origins of Puggalavada.—Puggalavāda seems to have originated from the following circumstances: the utter denial of all "self" leads to grave philosophical difficulties, esp. about the nature of Buddha and memory; it is not really necessary to deny "Self" in order to cultivate detachment; it is possible to get over, or at least circumvent, the difficulties which the theory of "Self" usually entails by advocating the conception of a dialectical, impredicable "Puggala"; Buddha himself did not deny the "self" in indubitably clear terms. In a way

---

230 Ib. p. 254f, 273f.

231 Ib. 262 ff.

232 Ib. 264ff.

233 Ib. 270.

234 Ib. 271.

235 Cf. "Yaḥ paśyatyātmānaṃ tatrāsyāhamiti śāśvataḥ snehaḥ snehāt sukheṣu tṛṣyati tṛṣṇā doṣāṃstiraskurute Guṇadarśī paritṛṣyan mameti tatsādhanānyupādatte Tenātmābhiniveśo yāvattāvat sa saṃsāre" (Dharmakīrti—Pramāṇavārtika pp. 86—7. ed with Manorathanandin's comv in JBORS—1938). A similar idea underlies AN. II. 164—5; Ib. 212.

236 Ib. 272—273.

we have here a foreshadowing of the Mādhyamika attitude.[237]

Vinnana as transmigrant.—According to some texts, what survives a man's death is his citta or viññāṇa.[238] The doctrine is almost certainly pre-Buddhist.[239] Buddha seems to have modified rather than rejected it.[240]

---

[237] Cf. Mk. XVIII. 1. "Ātmā skandhā yadi bhaved udayavyayabhāgbhavet Skandhebhyo'nyo yadi bhavedbhavedaskandhalakṣanaḥ." This argument fails to touch the Pudgalavādin's position who himself reasons dialectically.

[238] SN. II. 82; V, pp. 369—70; AN. V. 300; MN. I. 296, SN. III. 143; Dhp. 41, MN. III. 256; on the identity of Citta and Viññāṇa, see Mrs. Rhys Davids—Ind. Psy., p. 237. She is not correct in calling the SN. passage unique, since DN. I. sutta 1. has a passage of similar import (D. pt. I, p. 24, Nāg. ed). There are other passages too of a similar import. Thus AN. I. 170—"Itthaṃ pi te mano iti pi te cittaṃ"; Ab. K. II. 95 fn. 1 quotes a sūtra in Sanskrit which agrees in the main with SN. V. 369 but has (instead of the simple citta of the latter) "Yatpunaridamucyate cittamiti vā mana iti vā vijñānamiti vā—", SN. I. 53. "Niccamutrastamidaṃ cittaṃ Niccamubbiggamidaṃ mano." Traditionally all Buddhist schools appear to use the terms Citta and Vijñāna identically (see ĀŚ. cxxxvii, 68, 153—4). "Mano", however, has in the schools a different meaning than citta—viññāṇa. This is not to say that the three terms did not each have in actual sutta—usage its own distinctive shade of meaning (See Mrs. Rhys Davids, op. cit., p. 237f).

On the relation between "mano" and the senses—MN. I. 295; SN. V. 218; IV. 198; Mano is conceived *as the sixth sense and as the coordinator of the five senses.* With Viññāṇa as transmigrant compare the conception of the Gandhabba (MN. pt. II, pp. 367—'8, Nāg. ed.) who receives an elaborate treatment in the Ab. K. but probably originated in crude animistic beliefs. The idea that the Gandhabba must be present at the time of conception is suggestive.

[239] Cf. Bṛ. Up. "sa eṣajñaḥ savijñāno bhavati" (7.2.3); Ib. 7. 1. 8 "sa vā ayaṃ puruṣah (Vijñānamayaḥ) jāyamānaḥ—mriyamāṇaḥ"; DN. (loc. cit); MN. I. 256f (Sāti's heresy was probably due to extra-Buddhist influences); Mrs. Rhys Davids, What was the Original Gospel in Buddhism—p. 114.

[240] See Pali Dictionary (PTS) on "Viññāṇa". Even in the classical theory of "Vijñānasantāna" there is a persistence or survival beyond death, but the category of identity is replaced by that of continuity. What is transformed is not so much the idea of a surviving Vijñāna as the idea of change (See previous

Viññāṇa doubtless fares on but it must not be regarded an identically permanent entity. It is in fact extremely changeable.[241] Its fate beyond death is determined by the act of the man during his life.[242]

Two aspects of Vinnana as transcendental and as empirical.—It is declared that Viññāṇa must not be taken for the self (Attā), since it is so variable.[243] It has, however, a twofold aspect. In Nirvāṇa its fluctuations cease, it is released from its accidental impurities and rests in its own natural infinity and luminosity.[244]

Chap.) Cf. Bṛ. Up. 6. 9. 33-34 and the implicit answer of the enigma in the light of Sir R. G. Bhandarkar's interpretation of Ib. 6.2. 12-14 "A Peep into Early History of India".

[241] Much more so than the body—SN. II, pp. 94—96; MN. I. 258—259; on the comparison with the ape see Mrs. Rhys Davids—Ind. Psy., p. 240.

[242] This is clearly foreshadowed in the Upaniṣads (see Chap., Vedic Background).

[243] SN. II, pp. 94—96; AN. I. 10; but compare the significant SN. IV. 166. How reconcile it with SN. II. 94?

[244] This is the aspect which is revealed in the following texts:—AN. I. 10 "Pabhassaram idaṃ—cittaṃ—tañca āgantukehi upakkilesehi upakkiliṭṭhaṃ. ." (cf. "Prabhāsvaramidaṃ cittaṃ prakṛtyāgantavo malāḥ Teṣāmapāye sarvārthaṃ tajjyotiravinaś-varaṃ"—quoted with reference to the Yogācāras in the comy. to Śrītantrāloka I, p. 64. The verse has also been quoted in ĀŚ., pp. (XLI, 70); MN. III. 242—3. "Athāparaṃ viññāṇaṃ eva avasissati parisuddhaṃ pariyodātaṃ. ."; MN. I. 329; "viññāṇamanidassanaṃ anantaṃ sabbatopabhaṃ. ." This line recurs along with the following in DN. I, p. 223; "Ettha āpo ca paṭhavī tejo vāyo na gādhati Ettha dīghañca rassañca aṇum thūlaṃ subhāsubhaṃ Ettha nāmañca rūpañca asesamuparujjhati Viññāṇassa nirodhena etthetamuparujjhati." The apparent contradiction created by the last line is explained by Buddhaghosa by saying that the former viññāṇa refers to Nibbāṇa, the latter to "abhisaṅkhāra viññāṇa" (Dutt—Aspects, p. 149 fn. 20; see Mrs. Rhys Davids, Ind. Psy., p. 246 for the more plausible explanation). Cf. "Yattha nāmañca rūpañca asesamuparujjhati viññāṇassa nirodhena etthétam uparujjhati" (Sn. Ajitamāṇavapucchā—v. 6); "Paṇujja viññāṇaṃ bhave na tiṭṭhe" (Ib. Mettagū°—v. 7). The cessation of Viññāṇa in its empirical aspect alone is meant "Saññāvimokkhe parame. . . .Viññāṇaṃ tathāvidhassa Accī yathā vātavegena khitto atthaṃ paleti na

This Viññāṇa resembles the Ātman of some Upaniṣadic texts.

---

upeti saṅkhaṃ Evaṃ munī nāmakāyā vimutto atthaṃ paleti na upeti saṅkhaṃ". (Ib. Upasīva° verses 4. 6). It is not destroyed; it becomes infinite (appamāṇa) Ib. verse 8. It becomes "Appatiṭṭha" SN. I. 122; SN. II. 65–66; SN. III. 53.61; Ib. 124. Cf. SN. III. 45–46 and mark the incongruity between the meanings of the juxtaposed Viññāṇa and Citta. The former here represents the empirical aspect. These texts give the equations–*Appatiṭṭha viññāṇa=vimutta (citta usually in this context*)=the Parinibbuta. Viññāṇa is in this state "Anissita", "Anupādāna"–"Tassa taṃ upekhaṃ anabhinandato anabhivadato anajjhosāya tiṭṭhato na tannissitaṃ hoti viññāṇam na tadupādānam anupādāno Bhikkhu parinibbāyati" (MN. II. 265). "Bahiddhā–viññāṇe avikkhitte avisaṭe sāti ajjhattaṃ asaṇṭhite, anupādāya aparitassato āyatiṃ jātijarāmaraṇadukkhasamudayasambhavo na hoti" (MN. III. 223). (Cf. Ud. S. 74, which most probably has reference to Viññāṇa when it says "Nissitassa ca calitaṃ anissitassa calitaṃ natthi etc."); SN. IV. 102; Itv. sutta 94. SN. IV. 158 ("atthaṅgato so na pamāṇameti, Amohayi maccurājanti brūmi". Of getting the better of Death, Godhika would be an instance). On citta freed and gone beyond limitations (vimariyādikata) see SN. III. 31; cf. the sūtra "des quatre autorités" (Ab. K. V. 246, fn. 2) which says "Jñānaṃ pratisaraṇaṃ na vijñānaṃ" [Leumann considered Jñāna as insight into Reality, and Vijñāna as "das weltliche Erkennen" which agrees with the Mādhyamika view on the subject (see Kirfel in Z. DMG. 3, 1938. pp. 491–498]. The sūtra in question, however, cannot be very early since it distinguishes between "Nītārtha" and "Neyārtha" sūtras (Cf. Poussin's notes–loc. cit.); DN. III. 105 "Purisassa viññāṇasotaṃ pajānāti ubhayato abbocchinnaṃ idha loke patiṭṭhitañca paraloke patiṭṭhitañca..puna ca param..idha loke appatiṭṭhitañca..". Ab. K. IV. p. 137, fn. 1, which quotes a sūtra from the SA. corresponding to SN. III. 54; MN. I. 24–25 "Aṅgaṇa" covers the citta as a Kaṃsapāti; Ib. 36–"saṅkiliṭṭha" citta is like dirty cloth or impure gold; Ib. 91–Lobha, Dosa & Moha are the "upakkilesas" of the citta; MN. III. 83–"cittasaṅkhāra" is quietened, Citta is released; the very famous Dhp. verses 153–154 have a similar import in "Visaṅkhāragataṃ cittaṃ taṇhānaṃ khayamajjhagā". Now cittasaṅkhāra is equivalent to Saññā and Vedanā (MN. I. 301) and it is just these which cease in the Nirodha samāpatti; SN. III. 151–152 and the striking though obscure simile which it contains; SN. IV. 177; Ib. 218–19 (Vedanās accidental= Āgantuka to the citta); SN. V. 92 (The Nīvaraṇas compared to the impurities of gold). This idea of the mind or consciousness (citta, vijñāna) transcending its ordinary empirical

On the other hand, it has a purely phenomenal aspect.[245] This is caused by its getting involved in "Name-and-Form".[246]

Three stages in the Nikaya conception of Vinnana.— It is the second aspect which receives by far the greater attention in the Nikāyas. At first man was simply analysed into body and mind. Città or viññāṇa covered the latter entirely. This is the stage revealed in the expression "Saviññāṇake kāye,"[247] and in the six Dhātu conception.[248] In several texts the Kāya-

---

status and thus becoming infinite occurs already in the Br. up. 5.4.12—16: "vijñānaghana" disappears in the infinite Great Being as salt in water; there is a cessation of consciousness (sañjñā) but of that belonging to the dualistic order only. Empirical consciousness is replaced by "self-consciousness". It is unconsciousness and yet consciousness (Ib. 7. 1. 23f). The same idea is taken up in the Mbh. Śānti Parvan 219.42—3 "Yathārṇavagatā nadyo vyaktīrjahati nāma ca Nadāśca tāni yacchanti tādṛśaḥ sattvasaṅkṣayaḥ Evaṃ sati kutaḥ sañjñā pretyabhāve punarbhavet Jīve ca pratisaṃyukte gṛhyamāṇe ca sarvataḥ".

Some later authors have very clearly stated that the highest reality is nothing but "the mind that has become non-mind". (Cf. MM. V. Bhattacharya—ĀŚ. cxxxv ff; 82).

245 i.e., Viññāṇa as paṭiccasamuppanna, patiṭṭhita, nissita, sa-upādāna. This is the meaning which viññāṇa has when it is the fifth khandha or when it forms part of the chain of paṭiccasam° Cf. Mrs. Rhys Davids, Ind. Psy. p. 245f. This conception of viññāṇa is strikingly expressed in MN. I. 190, 258f. It is the position of the majority of the suttas in the Khandha saṃyutta.

246 SN. II. 65-67; III. 53-61; DN. pt. II. p. 50 (Nāg. ed.). Cf. Br. up. 1.4.7 "nāmarūpābhyāmeva vyākriyate....".

247 AN. I. 132, IV. 53; SN. I. 62 (vyāmamatte kaḷebare saññimhi samanake); SN. II. 252-3; Ib. III. 80, 103, 136, 169-70; Ib. IV. 311. The body was declared to be just "old kaṃma", neither one's own nor of anyone else SN. II. 64-5 (cf. Ib. IV. p. 132).

248 The six dhātus are mentioned in MN. III. 31, 63, 239 (where occurs the expression "chadhāturo ayaṃ puriso"); AN. I. 176; SN. II. 248, III. 231, 234; Mem. As. S. B. III. 481 sūtrānte ṣaḍdhātupāṭhāt......); DN. III. 247; Cf. Tait. up. 1.7 "Āpa oṣadhayo vanaspataya ākāśa ātmetyadhibhūtaṃ"; Caraka—11-

citta distinction is the only one present to the authors.[249]

With the growth of analysis man came to be conceived as a quincunx; viññāṇa then became its centre.[250]

The lateness of the Khandha theory.—Still later, viññāṇa tended to lose its centrality. This is the stage represented by the full-fledged Khandha theory. Mrs. Rhys Davids has powerfully, and it seems in essentials at least convincingly, argued that this theory should be regarded as a comparatively later development.[251] The arguments for this view may be thus summarized: (*i*) There are certain "unorthodox fragments" about Attā and Viññāṇa, which are far from being negligible in quantity or import especially owing to their nearness to the Upaniṣads. (*ii*) The fact that the khandha theory appears as a gloss in several important suttas lends support to it. Such "edited" suttas are, for instance, S. II. 95—96, the First Utterance, the Second Utterance, S.

13-14, 24, 31 (where the sixth dhātu is equated to Ātman) cf. Keith I. H. Q. 1936 p. 5.

[249] MN. II. 17: "Ayaṃ kho me kāyo....idañca pana viññāṇaṃ ettha sitaṃ ettha paṭibaddhaṃ." This forms part of the oft-repeated and ancient Sāmaññaphala text (For the current conception of this viññāṇa see MN. I. 258, Ib. 8; DN. Pt. I. p. 24. Nāg. ed.); SN. II. 94-6; SN. III. 143; "Āyu usmā ca viññāṇaṃ yadā kāyaṃ jahantimaṃ Apaviddho tadā seti parabhattamacetanaṃ" (MN. I. 296 is similar cf. Kauś. up. where prajñāna is identified with Āyus and Prāṇa; cf. Mbh. Ś. P. 219.9: 'Jñānamūṣmā ca vāyuśca trividho vāyusaṅgrahaḥ"); SN. I. 206; SN. IV. 400. Ib. III. 1; Dhp. verses 37, 40, 41; Cf. MN. I. 215 (cf. Mrs. Rhys David's comm—Ind. Psy. p. 199).

[250] The evidence for this intermediate stage is rather small, but see AN. II. 217; SN. IV. 193f; Mrs. Rhys Davids' Gospel pp. 112-113; Sakya—p. 20; SN. III. 9f. where the four khandhas are described as the "Oka" of Viññāṇa; The tendency to consider man as a fivefold reveals itself already in the Brāhmaṇas—Śatapatha Brāhmaṇa, I. 652-3, I. 1084, 1074.

[251] Ind. Psych. pp. 192-203.

III. lf. The examples have been pointed out in the course of the studies on stratification. (*iii*) The silence of several texts about the khandha theory is extremely significant. As Mrs. Rhys Davids says "This comment will be appreciated only by readers who have noticed the untiring way in which the five are paraded in sutta conversations, and further, who know the editorial habit of parading them when the conversation touches on the fact and functions of body and mind" (op. cit. p. 195).

The Khandha theory thus fails to appear in almost the whole of the Dīgha N. till the very end, in the first nine suttas of the Majjhima N., in the first three Saṃyuttas of the Saṃ. N., in the Pañcaka Nip. of the Aṅguttara N., and in the Sutta Nip. (Ib. pp. 200—201). (*iv*) It may be noted that the first four suttas of the khandha—saṃ are delivered not by Buddha but by his disciples Sāriputta and Mahākaccāna.[252]

Thus it is not too much to see in the Nikāyas an early form of Vijñānavāda,[253] which later evolved into a system of monistic idealism having a close resemblance

[252] On the Upaniṣadic origins of Skandhavāda, cf. Stcherbatsky, Central Conception, pp. 72-3.

[253] Cf. N. Dutt—Aspects. p. 169, who summarily calls such passages "interpolated" on the sole argument that they "do not find support in other portions of the same works". The very rarity of such passages, however, marks them as significant. Cf. Mrs. Rhys Davids' rather unkind remarks in Ind. Psy. p. 246. Dr. Keith virtually admits the Nikāya origin of Vijñānavāda—Precanonical Buddhism pp. 6-7 (Reprint from I. H. Q. 1936). The idea of a transcendental aspect of vijñāna, which is found in the Nikāyas, would appear to be in essence the same as the idea of vijñaptimātratā. The latter is thus described:

"Acitto 'nupalambho' sau jñānaṃ lokattarañca tat.
Āśrayasya parāvṛttirdvedhā dauṣṭhulyahānitaḥ.
Sa evānāsravo dhāturacintyaḥ kuśalo dhruvaḥ.
Sukho vimuktikāyo' sau dharmākhyo'yaṃ mahāmuneḥ".

(Triṃśikā—29-30. Hiuan Tsang's Siddhi (tr. Poussin) Vol. II. pp. 606, 693. Cf. MM. Vidhushekara Bhattacharya in I. H. Q. 1934, p. 9. fn. 24). (*Contd.*)

in its basic conception to the "Upaniṣadic" position as interpreted by Gauḍapāda and Śaṅkara.[254]

The theory of Anatta.—Many are the texts which preach the doctrine of Anatta. The doctrine denies that there is in the physical or mental realms anything which may properly be called one's "self" since everywhere within them impermanence and dependence rule.[255] This of itself does not mean the denial of all "self" whatever, but only of the phenomenality of the "Self". What is usually denied is that any of the khandhas may be the Attā, not the existence of the Attā as such. Even in the more positive later literature, the Attā that is denied is often conceived purely phenome-

Sthiramati explains "Tatra grāhakacittābhāvād grāhyārthānupalambhācca acitto' nupalambho' sau—dhruvo nityatvādakṣayatayā sukho nityatvādeva" (loc. cit.). It is clear that we have here to do with knowledge that is eternal, transcends the merely empirical subject-object distinction, and is beatific. It is virtually the same as Brahmajñāna or Brahmabhāva. But vijñānavāda did not *originate* in the Nikāyas; rather, its distant roots are to be traced to the Upaniṣads (see Chap. on Vedic Background. Cf. MM. V. Bhattacharya's article "Evolution of Vijñānavāda IHQ. 1934 p. 1.ff; the same author in ĀŚ. cxxxii).

254 Both the systems distinguish absolute from relative knowledge, and call the former the sole reality. Cf. I. H. Q. 1934—pp. 1-2.

255 Thus the body is not the Attā—SN. IV. 166, nor are the senses. Ib. IV. 28, 49, 146, 148, 56; nor the sense objects—Ib. III. 20-23, 66-67, 77, 82, 187, 178-9, 196-97, IV. 166-67. The khandhas are not the Attā—SN. II. 109f. ad. lib. Sabbe dhammā anattā MN. I. 228 SN. III. 133; similar is the import of AN. I. 27, III. 439 (consider its Pudgalavādin-interpretation already referred to). "Suñño loko (attanā attaniyena vā)." SN. IV. 54 ("Loka", however, is explained as the senses, sense-objects and vedanā). The senses cannot be the Attā because they come to be and pass away—MN. III. 282. The Khandhas are not the self because they are not dependent on oneself i.e. were they the self, the self will not be self-dependent or independent—Vin. I. 13; MN. Sutta 35. Stcherbatsky compares SN. III. 46 to Hume's classical statement (Central Conception, 27).

nally.[256] If it is true that Brāhmaṇical authors have often failed to appreciate the true meaning of śūnyatā, it is equally true that the Buddhists have in general not taken Ātman in that absolutist or idealistic sense which belongs to it in some Upaniṣadic texts, Gauḍapāda, and Śaṅkara. *The differences in this case relate not so much to the conception of ultimate reality as to the correct description of the phenomenal.*[257] It is in actuality more a controversy about the nature than the existence of the "self".[258] Thus in the Poṭṭhapāda sutta

[256] Thus on Candrakīrti's understanding of the Ātman see Mem. As. S. B. III. p. 485. Dharmakīrti says "Ātmani sati parasañjñā svaparavibhāgātparigrahadveṣau Anayoḥ sampratibaddhāḥ sarve doṣāḥ prajāyante (Pramāṇa Vārtika p. 87 ed. with Manorathanandin's comy. in JBORS 1938).

He clearly means by Ātman the individual as excluding other individuals. Cf. Sogen op. cit. p. 17, 24; Dr. N. Dutt points out that the Buddhist notion of Attā corresponds to the notion of Ahaṅkāra as envisaged in Sāṅkhya and Vedānta (op. cit. 142-3).

[257] Cf. Schrader JPTS—1904-5—pp. 160-1. Thus the greatest of the Advaita Vedāntins clearly admitted the basic principle of Buddhism that to imagine the real or ultimate existence of the *individual soul* is the root of all other illusions. Gauḍapāda thus states "Jīvaṃ kalpayate pūrvaṃ" (Āś. II. 16) and Śaṅkara comments "Bāhyādhyātmikānām bhāvānāmitaretaranimittanaimittikatayā kalpanāyāḥ kiṃ mūlamityucyate—jīvaṃ hetuphalātmakam Ahaṃ karomi mama sukhaduḥkha ityevaṃ lakṣaṇam." "*Tatra jīvakalpanā sarvakalpanāmūlamityuktam*" (ad. II. 17). MM. V. Bhattacharya has rightly attempted to show that it is this "Jīvakalpanā" that is called in Buddhism Sakkāyadiṭṭhi or Attavāda (Āś. 26-8).

[258] Cf. Sāṅkhyasūtra 1. 138: "Sāmānyena vivādābhāvāddharmavanna sādhanaṃ." Vijñānabhikṣu says "Ayambhāvaḥ: Yathā prakṛteḥ sāmānyenāpi sādhanamapekṣitaṃ dharmiṇyapi vivādāt, naivaṃ puruṣasya sādhanamapekṣitaṃ; cetanāpalāpe jagadāndhyaprasaṅgato *bhoktaryahampadārthe sāmānyato bauddhānāmapyavivādāt*. . . ." Aniruddha says "Sāmānyena tāvadātmani vivādo nāsti, viśeṣe hi vivādo'neka eko vyāpako'vyāpaka ityādiḥ".

La Vallée Poussin has drawn attention to the significance of these passages on the problem of Nairātmya (JA. 1902. xx. pp. 273-4).

(DN. I.) Buddha does not deny the Attā; he instead asks Poṭhapāda—what is your conception of the Attā? (Kim pana tvaṃ Poṭṭhapāda attānaṃ paccesīti?).[259] The latter advances three conceptions which may be taken to be the current ones. The Attā is either "Rūpī cātummahābhūtiko" or "Manomayo sabbaṅgapaccaṅgī ahīnindriyo" or "Arūpī saññāmayo". Buddha calls these merely the particular individualizations of the Attā (Attapaṭilābhas). They are subject to becoming, *true only for the time being,* and from the ultimate standpoint of the Tathāgata merely empirical and conventional (Lokaniruttiyo lokavohārā lokapaññattiyo).

It will be seen that from the Vedāntist's standpoint the three conceptions of the Attā mentioned above are nearer his idea of the forms of the "body" than his idea of the Ātman.[260] He will be quite as ready to call them "empirical" as the Buddhist. It is significant to note that the Sāmaññaphala text expressly applies the first two of the conceptions mentioned above to the body and asks the Bhikkhu to distinguish his viññāṇa or citta from them.[261] (Buddhaghosa in his comy. on DN. 2 tells us that the conception of soul as Arūpī belonged to the Jinists. For the Buddhist the Arūpa comprised

---

[259] Cf. Bṛ. up. IV. 3. 7. "Katama ātmeti".

[260] Cf. Buddha "porte sur le 'moi contingeant' le méme jugement que les Brāhmanes, mais il ignore délibérement la réalité immanente qu'ils postulent" (La Vallée Poussin, Opinions—p. 74).

[261] Cf. "Mama saṅkappamaññāya satthā loke anuttaro. Manomayena kāyena iddhiyā upasaṅkamì" (Theragāthā V. 901).

It may be remembered that the Rūpī Attā is described as "Manomayo". The description in the verse just quoted is reminiscent of what was later called the "Gurudeha" (Cf. MM. G. N. Kavirāj, Kalyāṇa—Yogāṇka). Cf. Sakya p. 244.

the four well-known trance-states. These are also within the world or Loka).

Similarly in the Mahānidāna° (DN. II.) "Buddha" says that those who explain the Attā explain it as Rūpī or Arūpī. Further they either say "vedanā me attāti", or "Appaṭisaṃvedano me attāti", or "Attā me vediyati vedanādhaṃmo hi me attāti". The first position is untenable since the vedanās are various and variable. The second is impossible since in that case one could not even say "I am" (Asmīti) and if the third were true the Attā will disappear when all Vedanās cease (Sabbaso vedanāya asati). The point of "Buddha" is clear. Attā cannot be anything impermanent. What is denied is that anything within the impermanent world may be the Attā. And, as Schrader and Mrs. Rhys Davids have pointed out, this precisely is the implication of the extremely well-known catechism on the Three Lakkhaṇas if taken apart from the context of later scholastic explanations. The bhikkhu must not grasp the Khandhas, Dhātus and Āyatanas as the Attā since these are impermanent. He should think "Netaṃ mama Nesóhamasmi na méso attāti" (In the Alagaddūpama sutta, for example. Does it not remind one of the famous "Neti Neti" or of the Sāṅkhyan "Nāsmi na me nāhaṃ?"[262] SN. III. 33–34 is still more explicit).

The development of Anatmavada.—With the development of psychological analysis, however, man came to be conceived as just an aggregate of causally connected elements. The analysis of man into Khandhas, Āyatanas and Dhātus is well known. But the Nikāyas do not in general thereby deduce expressly that the "Man is a

---

[262] SK 64; STK. pp. 185–6.

mere name. This drastic step is, as is again well known, taken by Vajirā in the Bhikkhuṇī sam°. Selā, it must be said, comes very near to her. The implication is the same in SN. II. 13. How far the attempt to expel the "ego" could go is seen in S. III. 235f, with which one may contrast the utterance of Musīla in SN. II. 7: "Ahametaṃ jānāmi ahametaṃ passāmi bhavanirodho nibbāṇamiti."

Its difficulties.—A difficulty with this new theory was to explain moral responsibility. It is pointedly noted in the Nikāyas (MN. III. 191, SN. III. 103–4); but hurriedly slurred over (cf. MP. pp. 85ff. Trenckner). The problem of memory is quite unknown to the Nikāyas. Similarly are the Buddhological reasons for circumventing the strictly "No-soul" theory unknown, although it is frequently asked—what happens to the Tathāgata after death?

Its Origins.—The problem may be raised, why was it so strongly insisted upon that the permanent individual who acts, feels etc., is merely an illusion caused by the sequences of associated mental states? Was it only due to the growth of a more scientific psychological analysis? This may be true, but it cannot be gainsaid that there was also probably a practical motive. By denying the reality of the Ego one at once dealt a death blow to the source of the deepest wordly attachment.[263] Dharmakīrti shows the practical aspect of the doctrine

[263] The Upaniṣadic references to the doctrine of Anātman are few and of uncertain date—These are Tait. 2.7 "Etasminnadṛśyé nātmyé nirukte. . . ." (Śaṅkara interprets Anātmye as Aśarīre!); Mait—2.4; Ib. 6. 20—21 (These appear very late, perhaps Post-Buddhist); Kaṭh. "pṛthagdharmān vipaśyati", which is of doubtful import and relevancy (The implied separateness and plurality of the "dharmas", and the verb suggest affinity with Buddhist thought).

clearly when he says that through "Nairātmya darśana" there takes place a destruction of Vāsanā.[264] Similarly Candrakīrti declares that the purpose of Śūnyatā is emancipation from Karma and Kleśa.[256]

The idea of the continuum is as yet practically absent in the Nikāyas.[266]

The middle doctrine beyond Atta and Anatta.— (c) Directly asked, Buddha is reported to have refused to answer the question about the existence of the Ātman either positively or negatively.[267] The same attitude is displayed about the equivalent question on the existence of the Tathāgata after death.[268] The correct interpretation of this "silence" appears to be that Buddha regard-

---

[264] P. V. I. 138–9 (ed. JBORS 1938) MM. V. Bhattacharya says that Buddha strove to extinguish desire (Basic Conception of Buddhism p. 64). Desire requires a subject and an object. Therefore Pudgalanairātmya denied the former, and Dharma° the latter (Ib. p. 74).

Stcherbatsky criticizes the view by saying that for Buddhism desires and desired objects exist without any reference to the subject who, in fact, does not exist. (I. H. Q. 1934–737–9).

Stcherbatsky, however, mistakes the Buddhist position. Desires and desired objects exist in independence of the real existence of the "subject", but not in independence of the imaginary existence of the "subject". It is the false idea of the ultimate reality of the Ego that is the cause of "desire". Thus is it that the realization of Nairātmya or the insubstantiality of the Ego leads to Vāsanākṣaya.

[265] "Atha kim punaḥ śūnyatāyāṃ prayojanaṃ taduktameva...Karmakleśakṣaye mokṣaḥ..." (MK. V. p. 179. Cal. ed).

[266] It is so rare that the present writer could find only one reference in all the Nikāyas (discounting semi-commentarial works included in the fifth Nikāya). The unique reference is DN. III. 105 which speaks of "Viññāṇasota".

[267] SN. IV. 400. The refusal to answer the questions appertaining to the relation between Jīva and Śarīra as well as to that about the relation between Attā and Loka has a similar import.

[268] SN. IV. Abyākata Saṃ. MN. I. Cūḷamāluṅkyaputta. etc.

ed the true state of affairs as falling beyond word and thought. In ultimate reality distinctions disappear; hence predication is impossible with respect to it.

Buddha's silence.—Various interpretations have been proposed about the silence of Buddha.

(*a*) Keith (BP) and Poussin (ERE) think it to have been the result of "Agnosticism", or less politely, of ignorance. The sole argument advanced is that in some texts (MN. Suttas 63 & 72)[269] Buddha refuses to answer merely on the practical plea of the irrelevance of the question to the attainment of Nirvāṇa. If there had been a theoretical reason it would have been put forth. This assumption is, however, quite gratuitous. The metaphysical discussion of Nirvāṇa may really not only be irrelevant but also obstructive (and as much was asserted) to its direct realization. Further, the parable of the Simsapā foliage[270] must also be considered in this context. Between it and the repudiation of the charge of being a close-fisted teacher[271] there is no real contradiction, since Buddha may have communicated all that could be communicated, and yet known much more.

(*b*) There is again the "negativist" interpretation according to which Buddha did not answer the question about the existence of Ātman simply because the latter was to him a meaningless word. This is the interpretation proposed by Rosenberg (op. cit. pp. 155—59) on the basis of the Ab. K. and the Chinese commentators. The theory of the four types of questions (Pañhavyā-

---

269 So in the Poṭṭhapādasutta (DN. pt. I. 219 Nāg. ed.).

270 SN. V. Saccasaṃyutta. sutta 31.

271 Ācariyamuṭṭhi—in a passage in the Mahāparinibbāṇa sutta which occurs elsewhere also (See DN. II. p. 100).

karaṇas) may be really ancient (vide AN. I. 197f; II. 46; DN. III. Saṅgītisutta) but there is no reason to think that the Abyākaraṇīya questions were supposed by Buddha to relate to non-entities.[271a] Nor is there any reason to suppose with Stcherbatsky[272] that it was a custom in Buddha's time to remain silent when one wanted to answer negatively.

(c) The Mādhyamika approach seems to be the only correct one.[273] When Buddha did not speak positively or negatively about the Ātman or the Tathāgata, he indicated his position most precisely, just as precisely as did Bāṣkali to Bādhva (Śaṅkara's Comy. ad. BS. 3. 2. 17).[274] Ātman and Anātman, existence and non-existence do not possess ultimate adequacy.[275] One must

[271a] Jayatilleke's positivistic approach is contradicted by the spiritual intention of early Buddhism, cf. Jayatilleke's Early Buddhist Theory of Knowledge, pp. 288 ff.

[272] La Vallée Poussin's interpretation (JA. XX. 1902. p. 247 fn.) of Sāriputta's dialogue with Yamaka (SN. III. p. 149) seems to be tenable. Sāriputta shows that since the Tathāgata is not to be "got at" even while living, it is meaningless to speak of his existence or non-existence after death. This view is clearly reminiscent of the Mādhyamika argument that non-existence would be a fact only if existence were a fact ! (see MK. XIII. 17 "Yadaśūnyaṃ bhavetkiñcit syācchūnyamiti kiñcana. Na kiñcidastyaśūnyañca kutaḥ śūnyaṃ bhaviṣyati") MK. XXV. 17-18 almost exactly reproduce the central argument of Sāriputta.

[273] See MK. XXV.

[274] Suzuki (Outlines 105 fn. 1) refers to a Chinese Buddhist who after prolonged meditation suddenly realized that "The very instant you say that it is something (or nothing) you miss the mark", cf. also the quotation from the Vimalakīrti sūtra Ib. (p. 106).

Cf. "Na tattha sukkā jotanti. . Yadā ca attanā vedi muni monena brāhmaṇo.

Atha rūpā arūpā ca sukha-dukkhā pamuccati" (Ud. sutta 10).

The "silent self" (monena attanā) may be compared to the "upaśāntó 'yamātmā" of Śaṅkara's quotation. Cf. Gauḍapāda "Nājeṣu sarvadharmeṣu śāśvatāśāśvatābhidhā.

Yatra varṇā na vartante vivekastatra nocyate" (Āś. IV. 60)

[275] Srī Rāmakrishna Paramahaṃsa is reported to have stated that Buddha had reached the state of self-knowledge, a state which is "midway between existence and non-existence".

avoid such "extreme" or categorical characterizations and try to follow the Middle Path in Metaphysics as in Ethics.[276]

There are several arguments in favour of adopting such an interpretation. It does not read into Buddha's silence either ignorance or expediency. Given the silence, it seeks to understand its philosophical implications in the light of Buddha's general attitude towards reality.

Now, beside the texts directly advocating the metaphysical Middle Path, there are others in the most ancient portion of the canon which assert that in reality such distinctions as between Attā[277] and Anattā or between fact and non-fact[278] vanish. Many ancient texts

---

which belong only to Prakṛti and have no reference beyond it. (Kathāmṛta–III. p. 287). Cf. Śrī Aurobindo on Nirvāṇa in Savitri (p. 4. II. & III.) p. 182–"This was self-seeing......no thought arose."

[276] On the two Madhyamā Pratipadās–see MM. Vidhushekhara Shāstrin in Jha Comm. Vol. p. 85f; also Chap. on Suffering and Its Origin.

[277] Sn. Duṭṭhaṭṭhaka V. 8; "Attaṃ nirattaṃ nahi tassa atthi, adhosi so diṭṭhimidheva sabbā"; Ib. Purābheda° V. ii; "Attaṃ vā pi nirattaṃ vā na tasmiṃ upalabbhati" (Is it meant only popularly?); Ib. Tuvaṭṭaka sutta v. 5: "Ajjhattameva upasame, nāññato bhikkhu santimeseyya Ajjhattaṃ upasantassa natthi attaṃ kuto nirattaṃ vā"; Ib. Jatukaṇṇimāṇavapucchā v. 3. "uggahītaṃ vā mā te vijjittha kiñcanaṃ"; Cf. Nairātmyaparipṛcchā according to which the Ātman neither is nor is not; "seyamaparā madhyamā pratipattirdharmāṇāṃ" (JA. 1928 Oct.–Déc. p. 210). Cf. Kāśyapaparivarta: "Ātmeti Kāśyāpa ayameko'ntaḥ Nairātmymiti dvitīyo'ntaḥ Yad ātmanairātmyayormadhyamarūpymanidarśanam°" (quoted in ĀŚ. 103 fn. 5; cf. MK. p. 127 Calcutta Ed.).

[278] Sn. Māgandiya sutta v. 9 "Saccanti so brāhmaṇo kim vadeyya, musāti vā so vivadetha kena"; Ib. Cūlaviyūha° v. 9". Na heva saccāni bahūni nānā aññatra saññāya niccāni loke Takkaṇca diṭṭhīsu pakappayitvā saccaṃ musāti dvayadhammamāhu".

These utterances are right Nāgārjunian. Cf. MK. XVIII. 8. The views "Sassato loko" etc. are only partial truths (Pac-

explain that all discursive thought and belief must be given up for the sake of the highest realization.[279] We have already seen how the utterances about Nirvāṇa make it wholly transphenomenal and ineffable.[280] The Buddha or the Tathāgata too is in many texts conceived transcendentally.[281]

---

cekasaccas)—AN. II. 41; the same is the import of the famous Udāna no. 54. which closes "vivadanti janā ekaṅgadassino ti". These utterances surely shed welcome light over Buddha's "silences".

[279] This may in a sense be described to be the refrain of the ancient Aṭṭhaka—vagga of the Sn. Saññā and Diṭṭhi must be abandoned. The special applicability of Saññā to empirical consciousness comes out in the pronouncement of Yājñavalkya "Na pretya sañjñāstīti" Sn. Paramaṭṭhaka sutta v. 7 connects it with imaginative construction "Pakappitā natthi aṇūpi saññā". In later literature again Sañjñā meant conceptual consciousness (Stcherbatsky: Central Conception p. 18). It was on account of this empirical character of Saññā that it had to be entirely suspended in the highest Jhānic achievement (Nirodha samāpatti). This distrust of Saññā again suggests Nāgārjuna "Nirvikalpamanānārthametattattavasya lakṣaṇam" (MK. XVIII. Kārikā 9). In SN. IV. 71 Papañca and Saññā are seen associated. So in MN. I. 109, 112, 271, 383.

[280] See Supra. cf. R. Kimura, Origin of Mahāyāna Buddhism. p. 95f.

[281] Dhp. 225 "Nippapañcā Tathāgatā"; Itv. p. 50 "Brahmabhūtaṃ Tathāgatam"; so is he called in a frequent formula "Ñāṇabhūto dhammabhūto"; the Tathāgata goes beyond speech (adhivacanapatho, nirutti°; Paññatti°). DN. pt. II. p. 55 (Nāg. ed.); the answer of Khemā to Pasenadi in the Abyākata Saṃ°; as of Gotama to Vacchagotta in MN. Sutta 73; the Buddha is "ananuvejjo"—MN. I. 140—141 (cf. Coomarswamy op. cit. p. 71). Taṃ *Buddhamanantagocaraṃ apadaṃ* kena padena nessatha?" (Dhp. 179 cf. Mbh. Ś. P. 269. 22. "Devāpi mārge muhyanti apadasya padaiṣiṇaḥ") Sn. Sundarikabhāradvāja sutta—v.1; Freed from Saññā and Nāmakāya the Muni neither is nor is not, he is beyond measure and words =Sn. Upasīvamāṇavapucchā vv. 4. 8; Uccheda and Sassata both impossible with respect to the Tathāgata since he is neither identical with nor different from the Khandhas—SN. III. 109f; the object of a Buddha's knowledge is beyond thought=AN. II. 80; Past Buddhas are "Chinnappapañca" (Saḷāyat. Saṃ. sutta 83—Cf. MN. III. 118).

This cumulatively suggests an Absolutist position and supports the Mādhyamika interpretation. And this is hardly surprising, since, already before Buddha, Absolutism is in unmistakable terms expressed in the Upaniṣads. Ultimate reality, we are told, is beyond contraries,[282] contradictions meet here;[283] it is, to be rigorous, beyond thought and words.[284]

There is another consideration. Of Buddha's having been a great Yogin there can hardly be any doubt. And has not a class of mystics proclaimed most loudly that there is a reality which it is impossible to communicate, where contradictions meet?[285]

The correctness of the Mādhyamika interpretation is thus confirmed by the trend of thought about Nirvāṇa in ancient Buddhist literature and by what we know of Buddha's life. Finally, it accords best with the Upaniṣadic atmosphere.

Conclusion.—We have seen that Nirvāṇa is realised through Supreme Knowledge. The realisation confers emancipation from the bondage of past deeds, natural passions and suffering. By destroying the transcendental illusion of the Ego, it takes away the sting of Death and leads to immortality in the sense of the 'Upaśama of the individual in a higher reality',[286] like that of a

---

[282] Kena 3 (neither known nor unknown); Kaṭh.—1.2.14; Praśna 2. 5; Māṇḍ. 7; Śat. Bṛ. II. pp. 1101—1102, 1473.

[283] Īśa—4—5; Taitt. 2. 6.

[284] ŚB II. 1451, 1479; Tait. 2. 9;

[285] It is interesting to note that according to Plotinus the One could neither be called the self nor different from it. In the highest experience all distinctions vanish and yet there is such a world of apparent difference. Select Works of Plotinus. T. Taylor ed. G.R.S. Mead. 1912 p. 320).

[286] For the use of this expression in this context, I am indebted to a suggestion of Principal Jai Dev Singh of Lakhimpur. Cf. La Vallée Poussin's note in Siddhi II. p. 676.

burning flame in its source. The experience of Nirvāṇa is beatific, and provides the beginningless faring on of Saṃsāra with its ultimate goal. Nirvāṇa remains indescribable in terms of finite consciousness, for it is absolutely infinite. One describes it best by preserving "silence", for, to say anything about it would be to make it relational and finite.[287]

On the theoretic side, Buddha appears to have adhered to this position so rigorously that his "silence" has become enigmatic for all ages. For practical guidance, however, he not only indicated that the Absolute alone is eternal and beatific but also suggested a way to its direct realization. This attitude is clearly more "mystical" than "rational".

---

[287] Cf. Sri Aurobindo, "A lonely Absolute negated all:
It effaced the ignorant world from its solitude
And drowned the soul in its everlasting peace." (Savitri—II. 7. 6: Nirvāṇa).

CHAPTER XIII

THE WAY TO NIRVĀṆA

The Way and the Truth.—Setting out to solve the problem of Suffering, Buddha discovered its answer in that transcendental illusion (Avidyā) under the force of which our minds construct for themselves a stable universe of separate individuals and substances, finite "selves" and objects, where life after life is spent in the unavailing pursuit of phantasms. Depending on a beginningless Ignorance, arise Name-and-Form, a world of individual persons and things, and depending on this arises experience by way of contact, and thence pleasure and pain, love and hate. Craving and striving, 'we' lay down the weary burden of one life only to pick up that of another. Thus moves on the impersonal process of Suffering, uncreated, but contingent. It ceases when its basic condition—Avidyā—is removed by Perfect Knowledge (Sambodhi), and Nirvāṇa is thus attained. That knowledge should lead to final deliverance, is in perfect accord with Upaniṣadic ideas.[1] The Way to Nirvāṇa is really the Way to Awakening.[2]

We have seen that the Dharma to which Gotama awoke has a transcendental as well as an immanent aspect.[3] As immanent, it stands for the Law which gives order to phenomena, by which they arise and cease. The Law thus provides a way following which we can obtain knowledge and transcend suffering. The way which leads to the cessation of Duḥkha is naturally the reverse (viloma) of that by which Duḥkha arises. Here we

[1] See supra, Chap. VIII. [2] Cf. Siddhi. II. pp. 676-7.
[3] See supra, Chap. XI.

must begin by placing restraint over actions, passions, and contacts (Sparśa), and by meditating over the insubstantiality of the empirical world—physical and psychical —attain to Prajñā, which would remove the veil of Avidyā.

The Buddhist Way and the Upanisads.—Of this view we can, again, notice an anticipation in the Upaniṣadic thought-world, where at one place, Dharma is declared the Law, following which the sun rises and sets, which is the same to-day as to-morrow (Bṛ. Up. I. 5. 23). In this sense it continues the older conception of Ṛta. But Dharma generally stands in the Upaniṣads for moral and religious observances,[4] and in Bṛ. Up. I. 4. 14, it is interpreted as the principle of Well-being which holds society together, the king of kings, the Truth.[5] In orthodox thought, Dharma came to be used primarily for sacred law governing man's conduct in society.[6] In contrast with the Buddhist usage, which is more metaphysical,[7] the Brahmanical usage of Dharma places greater emphasis on its social and institutional aspect. Besides, the Buddhist usage emphasizes the impersonal and autonomous character of Dharma, while in Vedic usage it is closely connected with the will and ways of gods.[8] Finally, whereas Buddha based his Dharma on personal intuition (Paccattavedaniya), the orthodox Vedic view bases it on faith and revelation (vide Śabara's explanation of Dharma as codanālakṣaṇa).

---

[4] Ch. Up. 7. 2. 1; Ib. 7.7.1; Kaṭh. 1.2.14; Bṛ. 4.4.5; But cf. Kaṭh. 1.2.13; Ib. 1.1.21

[5] Cf. Coomarswamy, The Living Thoughts of Gotama Buddha, p. 23, which gives Buddhist parallels.

[6] Kane, Hist. of the Dh. Ś. I. pp. 2-3.

[7] See above; cf. Bu-ston, I. pp. 18-19.

[8] e.g., RS. X. 21.3; Ib. IV. 53.3; Ib. VI. 7.1; Bṛ.. Up. I. 5.23, where mark "Tan *devāścakrire* dharmaṃ. . . ."

The Ch. Upaniṣad (VI. 14) compares the seeker after spiritual truth with a man who has been led away blind-folded and seeks to reach his destination by gradually discovering and following the way back home. This is akin to the idea of Buddha who claimed to be only the Guide that indicated the ancient highway which leads to Nirvāṇa.[9] Although the Upaniṣads emphasize knowledge as the means to salvation, they point out the need for virtuous action and the restraint of passions for the attainment of spiritual knowledge and freedom.[10] The emphasis on Karma in the sense of ritual is changed into the indispensability of ethical discipline as the first step in spiritual life. This tendency is carried over into Buddhism and accentuated to such a degree that some popular accounts confound Buddhism with simple morality.[11]

The Upaniṣads mention meditation and contemplation as means to knowledge.[12] These Yogic practices come to occupy a central place in the way followed and taught by Buddha. The Awakening which dispels Ignorance arises from the practice of Dhyāna.[13]

Sila-Samadhi-Prajna.—The way to Nirvāṇa thus falls naturally into three stages. Its first stage consists in the practice of virtue and the avoidance of sin. Then comes the practice of Dhyāna or contemplation. And, finally, comes the attainment of knowledge or intuition of Truth.

The ancient Sāmaññaphala text describes a course of the monk's spiritual progress which exhibits well the

---

[9] MN. III. 4-6; SN. IV. 359; SN. III. 108.

[10] Kaṭh. I. 2.23; Ib. I. 3.7-8; Muṇḍ. III. 1.5; Ib. III. 2.4; Śvet. VI. 21. See above.

[11] See below. [12] See above, Chap. VIII.

[13] See above, Chaps. IX, XI, XII, and also below.

threefold division into Sīla, Samādhi and Paññā. It is expressly so divided at many places in the Nikāyas.[14] Sometimes the scheme is made four-stepped through the addition of Vimutti,[15] or it is made a fivefold through the further addition of "vimutti-ñāṇadassana".[16] The threefold division is the basis of Visuddhimaggo, and is found in Sarvāstivāda works also.[17] The fact is that with variations it belongs to the universal repertoire of Mysticism.[18]

It will, however, be a mistake to suppose that Buddha taught the Dharma in neat and precise formulae. Like Jesus, Gotama provided his followers with parables and exhortations. The Dhamma which he left behind was an inspiration, not a detailed handbook. He knew that treading the spiritual path is nothing mechanical and formal. His followers as naturally sought to encompass the Dhamma intellectually and create the Abhidhamma out of it. The very breadth of the founder's vision led them to a variety of different and even conflicting conceptions, for the practical teaching of the Buddha varied according to the need and capacity of the individuals whom he addressed.[19] The Buddha pointed to the moon of Truth; his followers were often content to seize the finger.[20]

---

[14] DN. s. 8; Ib. S. 10. cf. AN. II. 183; AN. III. 14. 15; SN. I. 13. SN. I. 13.

[15] AN. II Suttas 1, 2, 75; Ib. 239. [16] AN. III. 271.

[17] Thomas–Life–p. 44 fn. Cf. Ab. K. IV. p. 142f.

[18] Cf. Pratt, The Religious Consciousness, p. 374.

[19] Cf. "Deśanā lokanāthānāṃ sattvāśayavaśānugāḥ". Quoted from Bodhicittavivaraṇa by Vācaspati Miśra in Bhāmatī on BS II. 2. 18. Śaṅkara too refers the diversity of Buddhist doctrine to Pratipattibheda or Vineyabheda. Cf. MM. G. N. Kaviraj in Sarasvati Bhavana Studies I pt. I. p. 33.

[20] Cf. Siddhi II. p. 669.

What the Way was not.—The negative aspects of the way are more or less clear. External sacrifice and the superstitious worship of Nature-deities were opposed by Buddha.[21] Real sacrifice and worship, he held, were internal and consisted in the practice of virtue.[22] Similarly he opposed the extreme austerities which contemporary Samaṇa sects like the Nigaṇṭhas and the Ājīvakas practised.[23] This, however, must not be taken to mean that he condemned all austerities indiscriminately.[24] He appears to have conceded to asceticism a limited usefulness.[25] Further, in as far as the contemporary "mystic" practices were undertaken to attain to this or that Deva world, Buddha considered them unsatisfactory,[26] although he himself appears to have taught a "Jhānic"

---

[21] DN. Tevijjasutta, Sigālovāda°; Further ref. in Chap. X.

[22] SN. I. 169, 183; DN Kūṭadanta°, Sigālovāda°.

[23] MN. I. 156; SN. I. 103; DN. III. p. 6ff; Vin. I. 159; of AN. III pp. 219–20.

[24] DN. I. 162, 167; under certain circumstances even suicide was not opposed—SN. III. 123. The practice may have been originally affiliated to the Nigaṇṭhas. About Tapa, Gotama's was a Vibhajjavāda, not an ekaṃsavāda. AN. V. 190.

[25] MN. I. s. 45; Ib. II. p. 225.

[26] MN. II. 87; Cf. MN. S. 8. This is opposed to the opinion of Mrs. Rhys Davids who sees in Jhāna, for Buddha, a means for "access" to the Deva-worlds, Sakya, 180. It is hard to agree with this view. Psychic development, including clairaudience and clairvoyance, is certainly claimed in the Nikāyas to be one of the results of Jhānic practice. But there is no reason to suppose that that was the aim for which Buddha engaged in Jhāna. The yogic tradition is opposed to such a utilisation of Jhāna. Further, it sounds not a little strange to hear that the Enlightened One sought enlightenment from converse with the Devas. Moggalāna's instance is of doubtful authenticity here and is isolated. Besides, that he should have felt the need of obtaining "his leader's sanction" is itself significant. AN. II. 184 does not say that one should practise Jhāna for reaching the Devas.

or contemplative way.[27] The precise determination of what Buddha taught positively as spiritual discipline presents difficulties. According to D.s. 16 the dying charge of the Master was what later came to be called the 37 Bodhipakkhiya dhammas.[28] Here the order of the various groups in the list is "just a matter of arithmetical progression, as elsewhere; first the fours, then the fives, the sevenfold, the eightfold."[29] On the other hand, the order of these very groups in SN. V. is more erratic, and what is more, the eightfold Maggo here occupies the first instead of the last place. This suggests that the report in DN. sutta 16 reflects a later stage, when ordering had become more systematic, and when the importance of the eightfold Path had somewhat receded.[30]

Atthangiko Maggo.—It is sometimes believed that the Aṭṭhaṅgiko Maggo represents an original teaching of Buddha.[31] Many passages from the Nikāyas, the most important occurring in the First Sermon, can apparently be quoted in support of this view.[32] On the other hand, Mrs. Rhys Davids is inclined to see in these the working of later systematizing tendency.[33]

Of the originality of the way-figure there can hardly

---

[27] See above, Chap. on "Buddha's life"; & below.

[28] " (there)....in the Piṭakas themselves they occur very rarely as so-called, are never numbered as 37, and never refer to the 37 as a whole, but only to this or that section of them, or to a practice not included in them" (Mrs. Rhys Davids in K. S. V. v—vi).

Cf. MN. II. Mahāsakuludāyi°; SN. IV—360; DN. III. 102 MN. II. 238.

[29] Ib. p. 6.

[30] Cf. Ib. p. 41.

[31] Winternitz—Ind. Lit. II, Visvabharti Quart. May 1936, 44 Thomas—Life; Keith B. P. 119, who points to the lack of system within the eight-fold scheme as evidence.

[32] DN. Pt. I. p. 182 (Nāg. ed.); Ib. p. 103; Ib. Pt. II. pp. 186—187; Ib—p 228, SN. V. Magga saṃ°, in general; MN. I. 16; MN. I. 48, 118, Ib. III. 109; Dhp. 273.

[33] Original Gospel—P. 60; Sakya—89, Cf. JRAS, 1935 p. 723.

be any doubt.[34] The omission of the eightfold scheme as a titular item from the Aṭṭhaka Nip. of the AN. as well as in the Saṅgīti sutta of the DN. is certainly significant and it has not as yet been satisfactorily explained.[35] Perhaps the heaping in of a large number of 'way-suttas' in the Magga-Saṃ° may partly explain the silence of the AN.[36] The fact, however, that in some apparently early passages the Way is spoken of without any reference to its eightfold character is extremely suggestive.[37] Had Buddha himself taught the Aṭṭhaṅgiko Maggo, then, in view of the later fame of the idea, we might have expected that more positive proof of it would have been preserved, and that there would have been less confusion by way of other overlapping and alternative lists.[38] In fact it would not seem wise to attribute *the formula* of the

---

[34] See Mrs. Rhys Davids; Sakya—103; 321. By referring to the Tevijja sutta Mrs. Rhys Davids has indicated that the idea of the way was current in Buddha's contemporary Brāhmaṇa circles too. It may be pointed out that the early Jinists also were familiar with it....See Sk. I. 11.

[35] Cf. Original Gospel—App. Winternitz—Visvabharati Quart. loc. cit.; Chap. on the Stratification of the AN.

[36] See Int. to AN. VI.

[37] MN. s. 107; The poem of Migajāla in the Therag. (See Mrs. Rhys Davids' comm. in Sakya p. 106); SN. V. 6 (the verses do not seem to presuppose the "eightfold" path as the prose implicitly asserts, since the elements they mention do not agree with those of the Aṭṭhaṅgiko Maggo). Sn. Hemavata° v. 24–25 which speak of the Dibba° Ariya-Patha, without giving any hint of its eightfoldness; Ib. Cunda sutta, which is concerned entirely with the Maggo but is silent about the eight "limbs"; *Itv.* Sutta 35 (the verses); MN. I. 63 speaks of the "Ekāyano Maggo" but defines it as the Four Satipaṭṭhānas (Dhp. verses 281—282).

[38] Thus MN. s. 24 explains a seven-stepped Brahmacariya from Sīla to Nibbāna and implicity uses the way-simile too; DN. s. 2 explains the whole course of Sāmañña from Sīla to Āsvakkhaya; MN. s. 107 too has seven steps beginning with Pātimokkhasaṃvara and ending with the Jhānas; the various other sublists comprised in the Bodhipakkhiyas enumerate after

eightfold Path to Buddha himself in the absence of more convincing evidence. It is probable that he spoke only of the middle way between the two extremes of sense-pleasures (Kāmasukha) and austerities (Attakilamatho), while it "crystallized" as eightfold later.[39]

Usually the Nikāyas do not explain the Aṭṭhaṅgiko Maggo beyond bare enumeration.[40] Its lack of system has been referred to. Sammādiṭṭhi apparently preserves a more ancient use of Diṭṭhi than the usual one in the Nikāyas *viz.* as a false view, heresy.[41] The next three Aṅgas are the same as the well known triad of good actions-mental, "vocal", physical.[42] For the explanation of Sammā Ājīva one must go back to D.s.1. Together with the next two, Sammā Vāyāma recurs in the shape of Viriya in Sambojjhaṅgas, Indriyas and Balas.[43] It has been explained in terms of the Sammappadhānas.[44]

---

their own fashion the elements of the Path. And all of these have no essential dependence on the formula of the eightfold Path (Cf. MN. Sutta 39). The formula of the Dasaṅgiko Maggo (see AN. 10. vaggas 13—16) is possibly later still.

[39]See MN. III. pp. 230—231 and mark the difference between the text (Uddesa) and the gloss (Vibhaṅga). The middle way is at one place explained by means of the illuminative lute-simile. Just as in order to obtain sweet notes one should neither tune too high nor too low, similarly should one avoid extremes in action (Mvg.—see Brewster op. cit. p. 105 f; AN. Nip. 6 Sutta 55; the simile occurs in the Sūtra of the Forty-two Sections which was early translated into Chinese (A. O. 1927 pp. 197—237).

[40] But see SN. V. 8—10.

[41] In such expressions as Diṭṭhisaṃyojana, Diṭṭhānusaya, Diṭṭhupādāna, °samudaya, °ogha, °kantāra °jāla etc.

[42] Cf. Ṣaḍviṃśa Brā.—p. 4 ("Trisatyā hi devāḥ") where Sāyaṇa explains "Manovākkāyakarmāṇi Satyāni". Cf. MN. II. 26 which speaks of three Akusalasīlas with reference to Kāyakamma, Vacī° and Ājīva.

[43] The Maggo is described as 'Nicco' in AN. IV. 285, 289, 322. For its relation to the Truths see SN. V. 23-204; for its relation to the Bojjhaṅgas—Ib. 82; with the Sati-Paṭṭhānas—Ib. 179, 294, with the Iddhipādas—Ib. 254, 276. For its relation with the "Sīla-Samādhi-Paññā classification, see: MN. I. Sutta 44.

[44] SN. V. p. 9.

The Importance of Will.—Vāyāma, Viriya, Padhāna, Parakkama, Uṭṭhāna—all these terms entering into the basic vocabulary of the earliest Buddhism emphasize the importance of "will" in spiritual discipline. This emphasis becomes significant if it is remembered that Buddha repudiated the fatalism of teachers like Makkhali Gosāla, as also the independent intervention of a supreme deity. Spiritual progress is neither the "unfolding (Nibbeṭhana) of a predetermined course as the Ājīvakas held, nor is it the result of "grace" as is proclaimed in the Kaṭh. Up. It is the result of man's own exertion put along the right way.[45]

Keith holds this view to be a contradiction to that of universal contingency and Nairātmya.[46] Mrs. Rhys Davids would answer by saying that Buddha did believe in a self which became better or worse in accordance with its exertions. The principle of contingency was proclaimed for the very purpose of freeing man through knowledge. This is in fact her central contention about the gospel of Buddha. For a solution of the philosophical difficulty involved along more orthodox lines the exposition of Rosenberg may be mentioned.[47] Only, it must be remembered that these subtle and speculative

[45] Cf. the vigorous Uṭṭhāṇa sutta of the Sn., with Kaṭh 3. 14 AB. 34. 3; Sk. I. 8. The last clearly shows how "viriya" was regarded as different from "kamma". This distinction, with which may be compared the later Buddhist distinction of Kamma and Kiriyā, has, it will be noticed, far-reaching philosophic implications. It is further noticeable that the Jinist text identifies "Kamma" with "Pamāya" and Viriya with "Appamaya". Now, the Uṭṭhāna sutta also equates Pamāda to "Raja" and advocates Appamāda, the commendation of which is supposed to have been the "Pacchimā vācā" of the Tathāgata (cf. the Appamāda vaggo of the Dhp.).

[46] B.P. p. 116.

[47] Op. Cit. pp. 242–244.

implications were most probably not present to the ancient Buddhist.

Sammappadhana.—The scheme of the Sammapadhānas contains no more than the idea of exertion expressed systematically in the four stages of the Saṃvara and Pahāna of Akusaladhammas and the Bhāvanā and Anurakkhana of Kusaladhammas.[48] Padhāna leads to Nibbāna;[49] depends on Sīla[50] and destroys the Saṃyojanas.[51]

"**Powers and Faculties**".—The five Indriyas and the Five Balas are exactly identical. The old meaning of the two terms was doubtless the same;[52] still, the repetition of an identical list under two titles within the same whole needs explanation.

There is another list of Five Balas, *viz.* Sati, Hiri, Ottappa, Viriya and Paññā.[53] A list of seven Balas combines this with the aforementioned and arranges thus—Saddhā, Viriya, Hiri, Ottappa, Sati, Samādhi and Paññā.[54] In this context another list of Four Balas—Paññā, Viriya, Anavajja, Saṅgha—may also be mentioned.[55]

Five different senses of "Indriya" may be distinguished in the Nikāyas: (a) Physical faculties in general[56] (b) Sense-organs in particular,[57] (c) faculty, mental

---

[48] Cf. AN. II. 16 where the last two Padhānas are explained in a curious manner cf. Ib. 74.

[49] SN. V. 244–'8, IV. 360–364.

[50] Ib. V. 246.

[51] Ib. V. 247–'8.

[52] Cf. Chap. VIII.

[53] AN. III. 10

[54] AN. IV. 3.

[55] Ib. 363.

[56] SN. V. 20f, Ib. II. 2, 42;

[57] *Five.* SN. III. 225–'7, 218–'30, IV. 168–'9; MN. I. 295. Six Ib. IV. 176, V–74, 205, 230.

or moral[58] (d) stages to Arahatta and[59] (e) modes of feeling.[60]

In the third sense, the usual list of five is the same as that of the Balas *viz.* Saddhā, Viriya, Sati, Samādhi and Paññā. One passage omits the last, and has only four.[61] Another has only three—Sati, Samādhi and Paññā. These faculties lead to Upasama and Sambodhi,[62] and to the extinction of the Anusayas and the Saññojanas.[63] These five faculties are mentioned in the Yoga-Darśana, also, where they are supposed to be conducive to Samprajñāta Samādhi.[64]

Their discussion raises at the very outset the problem of Faith in early Buddhism.

Faith.—According to Professors Keith[65] and La Vallée Poussin,[66] faith in the Buddha was essential to the earliest Buddhist belief. An important distinction, however, must be effected. The doctrine as preached by Buddha is not the same thing as understood by his followers later. In Buddha's own realisation faith played but little part. He preached in opposition to established faiths. He criticized believing on faith

---

58 SN. V. 219-20, III. 96, 153, V. 49, 193ff; 277-'9; MN. I. 479.

59 SN. V. 204.

60 SN. V. 207, 209–'11.

61 AN. II. 141.

61a SN. V. 224.

62 SN. V. 202–3, Cf. Ib. V. 223–'24.

63 Ib. V. 236.

64 It is sometimes supposed that Śraddhā, Vīrya, Smṛti, Samādhi and Prajñā represent the natural order in the attainment of knowledge. (MM. Gopinath Kaviraj-Kalyāṇa-Yogāṅka—p. 55).

65 Op. Cit. p. 122.

66 Dogme p. 10, 54.

alone[67] and claimed to teach a doctrine which anybody could directly realize for himself.[68] Faith in a sense implying an authoritarian or traditionist position could obviously have no place in his system.[69]

On the other hand, it is quite clear that "Saddhā" was early considered essential.[70] Saddhā, however, appears to be not simply believing on authority, but has reference also to heartfelt enthusiasm for a cause.

"Mindfulness".—The importance of Sati is apparent from the fact that five out of the seven lists included in the Bodhipakkhiyas stress it, one being devoted entirely to it. Several suttas are concerned with its detailed

---

[67] See DN. I. Tevijja°. MN. II. Canki°. A frequently occurring passage reports Buddha as asserting that belief based on Saddhā, Ruci, Anussava, Ākāraparivitakka and Diṭṭhinijjhānakkhanti is as liable to be erroneous as right (MN. II. 218, 234; AN. I. 189 etc.). Just as Buddha criticized the Brāhmaṇas for accepting on faith and tradition alone, so did he criticize the Nigaṇṭhas—MN. s. 101. In the later sūtra on the Four Pratisaraṇas this very attitude is reflected, as also in the well known quotation from the Ghana sūtra (see Stcherbatsky Buddh. Logic I. pp. 76–77).

[68] In the famous formula for Dhamma—"Sand'ṭṭhiko akāliko ehipassiko opanayiko paccattaṃ veditabbo viññūhi" e.g. DN. II. 222).

[69] MN. I. 320 distinguishes faith based on sight (dassanamūlikā Saddhā) from ordinary—"blind"—faith; cf. the controversy between Citta and Nātaputta in SN. IV. 298.

[70] Thus Saddhā (which, it may be noted, does not form part of the eightfold path) is one of the five Indriyas, is likened to a seed (SN. I. 172), forms a part of the chariot of salvation (Ib. V. 6) and is the great helper (dutiyā) of man (SN. I. 25, 38, IV. 70). It is the best treasure of a man (SN. I. 214), through it one crosses the "flood" (Ib). For those who had faith was the gateway to immortality open (Ib. 138).

This comes out in the usage "Saddhāya vatamhi agārasmā anagāriyaṃ pabbajito" (Ud. p. 36) Cf. Vyāsa ad Yoga sūtra I. 20 "Śraddhā cetasaḥ samprasādaḥ". Tattvaṿaiśāradī says "sa hi cetasaḥ samprasādobhiruciratīcchā śraddhā". The Vāritka explains more clearly "Samprasādaḥ prītiḥ yogo me bhūyādityabhilāṣaḥ." Thus 'faith' is conative, not cognitive.

exposition and it has been called "Ekāyano Maggo". The details of the Kāyagatā Sati,[71] Ānāpāna sati[72] and the four satipaṭṭhānas[73] may represent a later development, but the fundamental idea—the necessity of a constant mindfulness—certainly appears to have been very ancient. From the very start Buddhism appears to have, "in its earnest hopeful system of self-culture, set itself strenuously against a distrait habit of the mind, calling it *tatra-tatrābhinandinī*—'the there-and-there-dalliance'; as it were of the butterfly."[74] It therefore urged the cultivation of Sati-sampajañña—the psychological state of prepared and pre-adjusted sense or voluntary attention.[75]

The function of Sati was conceived as that of a protective censor.[76] It was a faculty higher than mind, and leading to emancipation.[77] It is mentioned in close connection with Samādhi, and reached its perfection in the fourth Jhāna.[78]

---

[71] MN. I. 266 explains Kāyasati as alertness with respect to the senses; Ib. s. 119 describes a number of ways in which it may be practised. Kāyagatā sati appears here equivalent to the Ānāpāna sati as applied to body only and elaborately considered.

[72] MN. III. 82–84; AN. V. III. f.

[73] MN. Satipaṭṭhāna°; DN. Mahāsatipaṭṭhāna°; SN. V. Satipaṭṭhāna Saṃ. Cf. a curious list of Tayo Satipaṭṭhānā in MN. III. 221. The four Satipaṭṭhānas are essentially exercised in introspection-paccavekkhaṇa, on which vide MN. Ambalaṭṭhikārāhulovāda°.

[74] B. P. E. LXIX. [75] Ib. LXVIII.

[76] "Satārakkhena cetasā" AN. V. 30; (Sati) Parivāraṇaṃ SN. I. 33, as Ārakkhasārathi, V. 6, as cetaso ārakkho iv. 27; as Dovāriko 194; Satādhipateyya AN. II. 243–4; Lokasmiṃ jāgaro SN. I. 44.

[77] SN. V. 218.

[78] MN. I. 90, 357. This "Sati-parisuddhi" appears to be quite different from its namesake mentioned in the YS. It may be noted that Smṛti is used in a sense different from that

The Bojjhaṅgas appear to have been meant as an enumeration of the factors tending towards Bodhi. They seem to have been considered especially effective against the Nīvaraṇas,[79] but all of them were not to be cultivated in all states of the Citta. Thus "Viriya" alone is the antidote to "Līnatta", not "Passaddhi".[80] The Sambojjhaṅgas depended for their perfection on the Satipaṭṭhānas and in turn perfected "Vijjāvimutti".[81]

Iddhipadas.—The most natural interpretation of the Iddhipādas would be to regard them as practices tending to bring about "Iddhis" or supernormal powers.[82] So much indeed is at places explicitly asserted.[83] On the other hand, the Iddhipādas are also described as leading to Nibbāna[84] and to be essential to Vimutti.[85] The detailed description of the Four Iddhipādas is not perfectly clear. It is couched in more or less vague and general terms.[86]

---

of just memory in the Ch. Up. (7, 26, 2) and the BG. (18, 73, cf. 2, 63). The close relation existing between "recollection" and "contemplation" is noted in Christian literature too—see—ERE. IV. p. 694; The Practice of the Presence of God (Brother Lawrence) p. 36, (Pub. Samuel Bagster & Sons Ltd.).

79 SN. V. Bojjhaṅgasaṃ°.

80 SN. V. 13-14. Cf. Buddhaghosa's advice on Indriyasamatā. Vm. p. 87.

81 SN. V. 329, 331—'5, 337—'40; MN. III. 82.

82 Buddhaghosa, following Paṭisam°, describes the following types of iddhis: Adhiṭṭhānā, vikubbanā, manomayā, ñāṇavipphārā, samādhivipphārā, ariyā, kammavipākajā, puññāvato, and vijjāmāyā. (Vm. p. 262f Nāg. ed.) With this may be compared YS. IV. 1.

83 SN. V. 276; Ib. 259—60; 264—6, 271—4.

84 Ib. 253, 290.

85 Ib. 257, 276.

86 The four Iddhipādas are Chandasamādhipadhānasaṅkhāra-Samannāgata Iddhipāda, Viriya°, Citta° and Vīmaṃsā°. They are thus described in the Janavasabha° of the DN. The following is the not very enlightening explanation offered in

Mrs. Rhys Davids rightly pleads for a more careful and sympathetic treatment of the whole subject of Iddhi (Sakya. p. 235). The connection of some of the Iddhis with the subject of psychical research is doubtless apparent, although those forming part of the formula for the "iddhividhās" are altogether more "wonderful". Of miracles (Pāṭihāriya) Iddhi is only a part. In DN.-s-11 Buddha is made to distinguish between Iddhipāṭihāriya, ādesana°[87] and anusāsanī°. All these belong to the class of the supernormal (Uttarimanussa Dhammā) Buddha points out that the first two may also be the result of Gandhārī vijjā (magic) or crystal-gazing (maṇikā nāma vijjā). It is the third which alone is truly spiritual, and is consequently advocated. The hostile attitude of Buddha towards 'Iddhi' as commonly understood comes out also in DN. III. (1st sutta).[88]

It appears that in Buddha's times the claim to miraculous powers was common among the samaṇas. Buddha taught a way which incidentally gave to the monk such powers also;[89] but this aspect of the discipline was not encouraged overmuch by Buddha.[90]

---

the SN. (V. 268 f.). "Chandaṃ. . . .nissāya labhati samādhiṃ. . cittassa ekaggatam ayaṃ vuccati chandasamādhi (here the 4 sammapadhānas are described) ime vuccanti padhānasaṅkhārā. iti ayam ca chando ayaṃ ca chandasamādhi ime ca Padhānasaṅkhārā ayaṃ-vuccati chandasamādhipadhānasaṅkhārasamannāgato iddhipādo" and so about the other Iddhipādas. Cf. also SN. V. 263f; 277–8.

Mrs. Rhys Davids concludes "Much insight into the nature of iddhi is neither to be found in, nor expected from the fourfold formula " (Sakya 250). Her interpretation of Chanda as Mantra is interesting but unconvincing.

87 Cf. DN. III. 104.

88 DN. III. 112 which distinguishes between "Ariya" and "No-Ariya" Iddhis.

89 This is apparent from the Sāmaññaphalā.

90 The Suttas just referred to viz. DN. s. 11; DN. III. s. 1.

The Bodhipakkhiya Dhammas: conclusion.—The Bodhipakkhiya dhammas, thus, seem to form a list of lists containing qualities and practices found useful by early Buddhists. Some of these, like good conduct (Sammāsaṅkappo etc.), cultivation through will (Padhāna, Viriya etc.), mindfulness (Sati), and concentration (Samādhi)[91] were already emphasized in the earliest Gospel. It must, however, be remembered that the meaning of those terms, as for instance of Sati, was then probably simpler than in later times. The place and significance in the oldest Gospel of other qualities, like Saddhā, and of practices, like the Iddhipādas, are not so certain.[92]

Moral culture.—The regulation of conduct was thus prescribed in many ways, although it will be a grave error to regard ancient Buddhism as just a simple ethical system—as merely Sīla. Moral formalism (Sīlabbataparāmāsa) was condemned. In spite of the negative form of the list of the Sīlas,[93] the actual spirit of the Suttas regarding the problem of moral discipline is remarkably positive.[94] What is condemned is immoderation and a lazy slavery to sense impressions and impulses.[95] Sīla is essentially moderation (Majjhimā Paṭipadā, Mattañ-

[91] See below. So also for Paññā.

[92] According to SN. V. 108 "other" teachers also claimed to teach the destruction of the Five Nīvaraṇas through the Seven Bojjhaṅgas. These lists were, thus, not supposed to be distinctively Buddhist.

[93] The ten Sīlas as well as the Sikkhāpadas appear to be a development out of the five Sīlas (see Pali Dictionary, PTS). Of the three Sīla texts in DN. s. I, the first which is the shortest, is possibly on that account the earliest.

[94] See Mrs. Rhys Davids in E. R. E. on Buddh. Asceticism; cf. Vm. p. 5.

[95] Cf. MN. Sutta 152 where Buddha criticizes Pārāsariya Brāhmaṇa's way of Indriyabhāvanā.

ñutā), and "the student was not. . . to ignore sense experience, but to break it up into constituent processes and resultants so as to divert the complex impacts of the external world from kindling delusion and passion, and convert them into the cool judgments of the intellect."[96] Into the cultivation of conduct the will necessarily entered by way of "Bhāvanā" and the intellect by way of "Yoniso manasikāra", or, in other words the factors of "Viriya" and "Paññā".

Compassion.—Generally there is not much difference between the particular virtues admired in early Buddhism from those admired in its contemporary non-Buddhist literature.[97] In this respect the most distinctive feature of Buddhism is the emphasis it places on compassion.[98] A Brāhmaṇa is reported to have told Buddha that the following virtues were sufficient for the attainment of the good, *viz.*, truth (sacca), austerities (tapa), celibacy (Brahmacariya), study (ajjhena) and liberality (cāga).[99] The last was asserted to be the most important. Buddha, inter alia, pointed out that liberality was impossible without compassion (anukampā) which would thus be the sixth cardinal virtue.[100] Out of compassion (Kāruññatā) Buddha agreed to preach his gospel.[101] He is called "compassionate to-

96 Mrs. Rhys Davids J. R. A. S. 1902 p. 481.

97 Cf. DN. III. 48—49; Keith B. P. p. 116 who remarks that the main tenets taken over from Brahmanical tradition are expanded and deepened. For illustration vide loc. cit.

98 See Winternitz-Visvabharati Quart. May. 1936 p. 50 f.

99 Cf. Tait up. 1.9. which contains a discussion about the relative merit of the following—Satya, tapas, svādhyāyapravacana.

100 MN. II. 204—'5.

101 SN. I. 138. The form "Kāruñña" occurs in SN. II. 199.

wards all beings"[102] and with the lapse of centuries his followers emphasized this aspect of his teaching more and more.

The Brahmaviharas.—This "compassion" included but was something more than mere non-injury (Ahiṃsā). [103] Even under the direct provocation and harm one must not retaliate.[104] More, the earnest Buddhist must engage in the active cultivation of universal sympathy,[105] friendliness[106] and "Mitfreude". This, of course, does not amount to saying that the practice was an original teaching of Buddha.[107] In fact, in the Bojjhanga Saṃ (No. 46—S. V. 346) the doctrine is described as held in common with the heretics. Makhādeva, king of Mithilā, is made to practise it.[108] So the Brāhmaṇa minister of yore, Mahāgovinda, is supposed to have reached the Brahman-world, through the practice of Karuṇā-vihāra.[109] The Vihāras themselves are called

---

[102] Sabbabhūtānukampī—SN. I. 25; Lokānukampako—Ib. 50—1.

[103] Cf. MN. 61 on the importance of taking into account "Parabyābādhā". On the growth of the idea of compassion in the Brāhmaṇas consider—Ś. B. I. p. 186: "Sarvasya vā ayam brāhmaṇo mitraṃ na vā ayaṃ kañcana hinastīti" *Ib.* 279. "akrodho hyeva dīkṣitaḥ" *Ib.* 380: "Tadyatkrūr-kurvanti yadāsthāpayanti śāntirāpastadadbhiḥśāntyā śamayatastadadbhiḥ sandhattaḥ....". Ib. 384 "Krūrī vā etatkurvanti yat sañjñapayanti" Ib. 433—4: Mitra refuses to strike Vṛtra—soma saying "Sarvasya vā aham mitramasmi" but later agrees to do so out of the fear of expulsion from sacrifice; Ib. 393; "Sarvasya hi.... mitro mitram"; Ib. II. 1195—against anger.

[104] See the famous Kakacūpamovāda of the MN.

[105] Cf. AN. III. 189 which equates Karuṇā to Anukampā and Anudayā. Āmisānukampā and Dhammā° are distinguished in AN. I. 92.

[106] Cf. the Mettāsuttas in the Sn. and the Itv.

[107] According to Mrs. Rhys Davids it was founded by an ex-Brāhmaṇa Paribbājaka—see JRAS 1928, 271f.

[108] MN. II. 76. [109] DN. II.

Brahma-vihāras and are described as the way to Brahma-Sahavyatā and °Patti.[110] The use of the term Vimutti in connection with them is also perhaps not without significance. Finally, the Yoga-sūtras too mention them in fact, though there the practices have shrunk to an individualistic cultivation, and the idea of suffusion (Pharitvā viharati) is lost. All this, however, only suggests that the doctrine of the Four Vihāras originated in an atmosphere full of Brāhmaṇic ideas, and that at one period of its history it became a common possession of many different sects. Its actual origins are obscure, but it appears to have been a feature of original Buddhism, if not an original feature of Buddhism. It must, however, be remembered that apart from the late reference in the Yogasūtras, the Brāhmaṇa and Jinist works are generally quite silent about the doctrine, which finds absolutely no mention in later Vedic literature.[111]

Concentration and Meditation.—Jhāna was the other most important feature of the most ancient Buddhist practice; like Karuṇā, it has retained its chief position in Buddhism.

The Importance of Jhana in Ancient Buddhism.—Having abandoned asceticism, Gotama is said to have fallen back on his childhood experience of Jhāna,[112] and it was that which led him to success. It would be only natural to expect that Jhāna should play a prominent

[110] DN. I. Tevijjasutta.

[111] Quite in contrast to Karuṇā is the position accorded to Pema—AN. II. 213—which is supposed to involve its correlate hatred or dislike (Dosa). But contra SN. I. 6 (with which cf. the famous verse from the Mallikā sec. of the Kosala saṃ). "Pīti"....usually translated "rapture"—was held to be twofold as arising from sense-pleasures (Kāmaguṇa) and as arising in some of the Jhānic levels—MN. II. 204..

[112] M. Bodhirājakumāra°; Nidānakathā,—Jātaka I, 58; Lalita-vistara I. 263, Sakya—p. 162.

part in his teachings. He is more than once described as Jhāyin,[113] as engaged in Paṭisallāna,[114] as earnestly advocating Jhāna.[115] In several descriptions of the Way, Jhāna is accorded the chief place.[116] 'Samādhi' figures

[113] See reference in Sakya p. 178. *Another ref.* A Brāhmaṇa narrates to Ānanda that he had once been to see Gotama and found him sermonising on Jhāna. His memory of Gotama was that "Jhāyī ceva so bhavaṃ Gotamo ahosi jhānasīlī ca", (MN. III. p. 13). With the Magadha Mahāmatta Vassakāra's statement to Ānanda "Jhāyino ceva bhavanto jhānasīlino ca" (loc. cit.) may be compared the malicious observations of Māra "seyyathāpi nāma kotthu ṇadītīre macche magayamāno jhāyati pajjhāyati, nijjhāyati apajjhāyati, evamevime muṇḍakā samaṇakā ibbhā kiṇhā bandhupādāpaccā jhāyino' smā jhāyino' smā ti pattakkhandhā adhomukhā madhurakajātā jhāyanti pajjhāyanti nijjhāyanti apajjhāyanti" (MN. I. p. 334), cf. Sk. I. 11, 27. Jahā ḍhaṅkā ya kaṅkā ya kulalā maggukā sihī. Macchesaṇaṃ jhiyāyanti jhāṇam te kalusādhamaṃ." The reference is probably to the Buddhists see Ib. Vv. 25—6. Sakka (Sakko Devānam Indo) says to Pañcasikha: Durupasaṅkamā kho tāta Pañcasikha Tathāgatā mādisena jhāyī jhānaratā tadanantaraṃ paṭisallīnā" (DN. II. p. 196 Nāg. Ed.). (Is a distinction intended here between jhāna and Paṭisallāna?)

[114] On the identity of Jhāna and Paṭisallāna—MN. loc. cit.; Itv. s. 45; Sn. p. 7; on Buddha and Paṭisallāna—SN. V. 12ff.

[115] In the forceful ending to several suttas "etāni bhikkhave rukkhamūlāni etāni suññāgārāni jhāyatha. Ma pamādattha. Mā pacchā vippaṭisārino ahuvattha. Ayaṃ kho vo amhākam anusāsanīti" (e.g. SN. IV. 359f.).

[116] The Sāmaññaphala° the contents of which are repeated more than once; Gaṇakamoggalāna° (MN); Gopakamoggalāna° (Ib.) where Ānanda explaining the Dhamma to a Brāhmaṇa enquirer shortly after Buddha's death says that the Master did not admire all Jhāna but only some. He condemned a man who overcome with the Nīvaraṇas engaged in brooding "jhāyati pajjhāyāti nijjhāyati apajjhāyati" (cf. the Aṭṭa and Rudda Jhānas mentioned in the Tattvārthādhigama). But Buddha admired the Four Jhānas; the Aṭṭhaṅgiko Maggo itself culminates in Samādhi which is equated to the four Jhānas (SN. V. p. 10; MN. III. 252); Sn. pp. 20, 22, 43; Dhp. vv. 23—27; On the frequency with which Jhāna is mentioned in the Sutta piṭaka see Sakya p. 171 where statistics are given; on the comparative silence of Vin. (Lco. cit.) see below. Sometimes the eightfold path is represented as Samādhi together with seven "Parikkhāras" (AN. IV. 40).

Cf. La Vallée Poussin—Opinions. Avant propos VIII.

importantly in more than one list.[117] Prominent disciples are praised for their ability in Jhāna.[118] An early Jinist text ridicules the upholders of Jhāna, meaning probably the Buddhists.[119]

The Purpose of Jhana.—In some form Jhānic practice was already current in the times of Buddha.[120] It was essentially a method of mental discipline which could be utilized for a diversity of purposes—for attaining to this or that divine world,[121] for the sake of supernormal powers,[122] for the sake of enjoyable experience,[123] for

---

[117] It forms part of the list of Balas, Indriyas and Sambojjhaṅgas. In the first two it is equated to the 4 Jhānas—AN. III. II. 12; SN. V. 196. As a Sambojjhaṅga it is defined "Samathanimittaṃ avyagganimittaṃ" SN. V. 66; "Samādhipamukhā sabbe Dhammā" AN. IV. 339; Ib. V. 107. Buddhaghosa defines Samādhi as Kusalacittekaggatā (Vm. p. 47; the def. occurs without the qualification in the Nikāyas: MN. I. 30). The role of interest in concentration was fully recognized—DN. I. 73. "Sukhino cittaṃ samādhiyati"; so "sukhaṃ samādhattham samādhānisaṃsaṃ" AN. V. 2ff. 311f.

[118] See Sakya loc. cit. [119] SK. Maggajjahayaṇa, verses 25f.

[120] In the Kaṭh, Muṇḍ and Śvet. Upaniṣads there are clear references to "Jhānic" practice. In the Br. Up. the Ātman is called "Nididhyāsitavya". The Jhānas are mentioned in connection with heretic belief and practice in the Brahmajāla° (DN) and Sallekha Sutta (MN).

[121] MN. II. 37; AN. II. 184. It is interesting to note that in this context the word used in MN. s. 16 is "Paṇidhāna" (MN. I. 103—"Aññātaraṃ devanikāyaṃ paṇidhāya brahmacariyaṃ carati"), cf. "Dvividhaṃ dhyānaṃ Bhāvanā praṇidhānañca tatrādyaṃ siddhaṃ kalpitaṃ vā viṣayamadhikṛtya pravartate na vastutattvamavaśyamapekṣate Praṇidhānaṃ Vastutattvaviṣayaṃ......" (Nīlakaṇṭha on Mbh. ŚP. 195-15). Such a distinction between Bhāvanā and Praṇidhāna is not to be found in the Nikāyas.

[122] DN. I. Mahāli.° From Buddhaghosa's treatment of Adhiṭṭhānā Iddhis (Vm. loc. cit.) it is clear that Adhiṭṭhāna (resolve) was effective in this wise only if coupled with Jhāna. In the Y. S. also a class of Iddhis originate in "Saṃyama". Such attainments are clearly the powers of the mind which has been purified through Jhāna. On the power of mind vide Buddha's remark in the Upālis°—(MN) that forests like Daṇḍakāraṇya may be reduced to ashes by the power of the mind.

communion with the true self or the inner reality.[124] In the case of Buddha it served as a footstep to the realization of higher learning (Vijjā) culminating in Bodhi.[125] And this is the sense in which Jhāna is advocated in many Nikāya texts.[126]

Jhāna was valued because it led to Aññā. Normally the citta is covered over with impurities, is distracted and unsteady. Jhāna serves a cathartic function. It renders the citta pure and receptive which sets the stage for the on-come of illumination.[127]

---

[123] Diṭṭhadhammanibbāna (DN. Pt. I. Nāg. ed. p. 44f); Diṭṭhadhamma Sukhavihāra—(MN. I. 40-41).

According to AN. II. 44-45 Samādhibhāvanā may be practised for "diṭṭhadhamma sukhavihāra", "ñāṇadassanapaṭilābha", "sati-sampajañña" and for "Āsavakkhaya"; in the first case alone are the 4 Jhānas spoken of.

[124] This is the purpose in the Upaniṣadic texts. See above.

[125, 126] See the texts quoted and ref. to in connection with Sambodhi in the Chap. on Nirvāṇa.

[127] The Jhānas are described as "Cittasampadā" in DN. pt. I. p. 200ff (Nāg. ed.), as "Cittaparisuddhiyaṅga" in AN. II. 195. cf. AN. III. 93. Their function was to free the mind from its "impurities (Upakkilesas) which are variously described and listed. Sometimes they are the "Nīvaraṇas"—"cittaṃ imehi pañca upakkilesehi vimuttaṃ....mudu ca kamanīyaṃ ca pabhassaraṃ ca na ca pabbhaṅgu sammā samādhiyati āsavānaṃ khayāya...."

(AN. III. pp. 16—17) The simile of the purification of gold is used in this connection (AN. I. 253, 257) Cf. AN. III. 186, "cetaso vivaraṃ cetaso pasādaṃ" Ib. 323 "iti vivaṭena cetasā apariyonaddhena sappabhāsaṃ cittaṃ bhāveti. "SN. V. 92 is similar to AN. I. III. 15—6. On the psychological conditions of the origin of the Nīvaraṇas see AN. I. 3—4—Sometimes a long list of the Upakkilesas is given as in MN. I. 36.

Frequently the basic impurities that have to be destroyed are called the Āsavas. The term occurs in early Jinist literature (in the sense of "flowing in" rather than of "what flows in" which is the Buddhist meaning). This suggests the age of the term, as does also the fact that it is used in early texts in connection with Cetovimuti. At first three, the Āsavas were later increased to four (see Pali Dictionary, PTS). Sometimes the origin of Avijjā was sought in them (see Vm. p. 368;

The Four Jhanas.—If we seek to inquire into the precise content of Jhāna, we find overselves invariably faced with a neat systematic analysis of the progressive simplification of mental processes and content of the Jhāyin, which culminates in a state of entire recollectedness, a state of lucid and one-pointed awareness possessing hedonically a neutral tone.[128] This analysis may

---

cf. MN. I. 55). It was necessary to "cleanse" the mind from them (pariyodapana—MN. pt. I. p. 9. Nāg ed;. Ib. 10. cittaṃ parisodheti). The second sutta of the MN. explains in detail the various ways to be adopted in fighting them. "Bhāvanā" is one of the ways (Bhāvanā is here equivalent to the Sambojjhaṅgas); on the Āsavas cf. Itv. s. 56—57.

[128] "Athāparā upekhā yeva avasissati parisuddhā pariyodātā mudu ca kammaññā ca pabhassarā ca".

(MN. III. 243) cf. "it was a state of attention, more akin to that of the boy Samuel in the Herbrew scriptures; 'speak, lord, for thy servant heareth.' "It was *an attitude for coming to know* (Sakya. p. 37)" "What is stated to be left is sati coupled with emotional indifference (Upekkhā). Now sati was just lucid, introspective awareness, the very state needed by thelistener who is purged of preconceptions, has made his mind a tabula rasa and is waiting to learn" (Ib. 166). On the "simplification" of psychic process and contents cf. Laignel Lavastine. op. cit. pp. 98—99.

In the first Jhāna, the subject is freed from Kāma and the Akusala dhammas though in possession of thought and a pleasant feeling (vivicceva kāmehi vivicca akusalehi dhammehi savitakkaṃ savicāraṃ vivekajaṃ pītisukhaṃ paṭhamajhānaṃ upasampajja viharati").

Vitakka and Vicāra are in later literature at least distinguished as initial and sustained applications of thought. Cf. Vm. p. 95. Buddhaghosa distinguishes five types of Pīti and seeks to indicate the precise relation between Pīti and Sukha—Ib. 96-97.

In the second Jhāna, "Bhikkhu vitakkavicārānaṃ Vūpasamā ajjhattaṃ sampasādanaṃ cetaso ekodibhāvam avitakkam avicāraṃ samādhijjaṃ pītisukhaṃ dutiyajjhānam upasampajja viharati". Sukha is now samādhija not vivekaja (DN. Pt. I. p. 85. Nāg. ed.).

In the third "Bhikkhu pītiyā ca Virāgā ca upekkhako viharati sato ca sampajāno sukhañca kāyena paṭisaṃvedeti yaṃ taṃ ariyā ācikkhanti upekkhako satimā sukhavihārīti tatiyajjhānaṃ upasampajja viharati". Pīti disappears here as "thought" had in the second jhāna.

not be very early, but then we are entirely in the dark about what may have been the ideas relating to Jhāna earlier.[129]

The four Jhānas are apparently referred to in the Mbh. Śānti Parvan[130] and a somewhat similar division is to be discovered in the Yoga sūtras[131] and later Jaina works.[132] In the Abhidhamma-stage the four Jhānas were turned, for the sake of greater system, into a five-fold.[133] A detailed and remarkably clear account of the Jhānas is given by Buddhaghosa in his Visuddhimaggo.[134]

In the fourth "sukhassa ca pahānā dukkhassa ca pahānā pubbéva somanassadomanassānaṃ atthaṅgamā adukkhaṃ asukkhaṃ upekkhāsatiparisuddhiṃ catutthajjhānaṃ upasampajja viharati". Sukha also disappears. According to SN. IV. 225-8 Sukha increases through all the Jhānas and even the Āruppas' Sukha is here apparently used in a peculiar sense. Only lucid mindfulness (Parisuddhā sati) remains; the Bhikkhu is now just pure mind (so imameva kāyaṃ parisuddhena cetasā pariyodātena pharitvā nisinno hoti, nāssa kiñci sabbāvato kāyassa parisuddhena cetasā pariyodātena apphuṭaṃ hoti—op. cit. p. 86). The citta is now concentrated, clear, pure, pliant, efficient and motionless (Evaṃ samāhite citte parisuddhe pariyodāte anangaṇe vigatūpakkilese mudubhūte kammaniye ṭhite āneñjappatte...." Ib. 87, MN. I. 22).

The stillness of the citta (Āneñja) in the 4th Jhāna is referred to more than once—AN. III. 98. 100; MN. III. 111-112; (according to the Vijñānavādins the Asaṃskṛta dharma called "Acala" was attained in the 4th Jhāna—Upādhyāya. op. cit. p. 292). Contra—AN. II. 184 where the attainment of Āneñja is referred to the Nevasaññānāsaññāyatanā; AN. III. 377—8 calls the Khīṇāsava "Āneñjapatta"; MN. 106 describes a whole series of Āṇañjas!

129 Sn. Udayamāṇavapucchā—vv. 2—3 seem to describe the state of the fourth Jhāna but are not identical with the usual formula.

130 Adhy. 195. Here it is promised to describe the "four-fold dhyānayoga" (Dhyānayogaṃ caturvidham) through which the Yogins reach "Nirvāṇa".

131 YS. I. 17: Vitarkavicārānandāsmitārūpānugmāt Samprajñātaḥ".

132 Tattvārthādhigama, IX. 27ff. 133 Dhs. pp. 48—51.

134 Dr. N. Dutt follows it in detail in his Early Monastic Buddhism I. p. 212f.

The Nature of Jhanas.—Jhānic practice, it is apparent, does not aim at producing a state of auto-suggested hypnosis or of coma.[135] Vitality in the sense of mental energy and lucidity is not lowered but enhanced. On the other hand, Jhāna, as has been pointed out, is not "meditation".[136] A suspension of "thought" as of 'feeling' was of its essence.[137] What resulted was not a state akin to sleep or coma, but rather of the mind stilled or hushed before leaping into a far-reaching intuition. The theory was that in the depth of the still and even consciousness reality mirrored itself as in unruffled waters.[138] Transcendental knowledge (Paññā)[139] was not the result of the discursive efforts of the mind; it revealed itself spontaneously.

Jhanas, Aruppas and Nirvana.—Frequently, however, the Jhānas are treated as coordinate to the Ārup-

[135] Rhys Davids, Pali Dictionary (P.T.S.); Thomas—Hist. of Buddh. Thought. p. 74fn.; Cf. JPTS—1906-'7 (Suzuki)—p. 36; Stcherbatsky, Nirvāṇa p. 8f.

[136] Sakya p. 166.

[137] Of Vitakka—Vicāra, Sukha—Dukkha, Somanassa—Domanassa, & Pīti—see the Jhāna formulae. Bhagavadgītā (VI. 24-25) sums up the technique of Yoga which culminates in "not thinking" (Na Kiñcidapi cintayet). On this Śaṅkara says "*Eṣa Yogasya paramo vidhiḥ.*"

[138] SN. IV. 143, 144—"Samādhiṃ bhāvetha. Samāhitassa bhikkhuno yathābhūtamokkhāyatīti; "Ib. 144—5. as above, Paṭisallāna for Samādhi; SN. IV. 79 "Samāhite citte dhammā pātubhavanti"; SN. V. 414—"Samādhiṃ bhāvetha...Samāhito yathābhūtaṃ pajānāti" AN. III. 230—'33: when under the influence of the Nīvaraṇas (the citta is like disturbed water in which nothing can be seen as it is (yathābhūtam); after Āsavakkhaya the Citta is like a clear pool (Sāmaññaphala 82 Nag. ed) Cf. AN. Nip. I. vg. 5; the slightest "dust" must be removed from the Citta as from a mirror (AN. V. 12) cf. the treatment of Vijñāna-vāda origins in the Chap. on Nirvāṇa. The likening of Citta to a mirror which when pure reflects all knowledge is found in other systems of thought also Cf. JPTS. 1906—'7 pp. 40—41.

[139] See chap. on Nirvāṇa; Thomas—Life. p. 186; cf. JPTS 1906—'7 p. 28f.

pas.[140] The four Jhānic levels here belong entirely to the Rūpa-world. "Jhāna" thus ceases to be a way to Nirvāṇa since the latter is beyond both Rūpa and Arūpa.[141] However, some texts would equate Nirvāṇic

---

[140] Which is the usual treatment in the Abhidhamma (vide Sakya pp. 168—'69), in the last Nipātas of the AN., and in many suttas of the MN. The four Jhānas correspond to the Rūpa-worlds, after which come the four Āruppas corresponding to the Arūpa worlds. The latter can only follow the former, and within them each succeeding stage is realizable only in correlation to the preceding. This is the result of increasing abstraction, till at last perception (Saññā) is so subtle as to be unnoticeable.

While the Jhānas are described as Diṭṭhadhammasukha-vihāra, the Āruppas are called Santavihāras (MN. S. 8). At one place it is stated that the Jhānas are Abhicetasika, while "Ye te santā vimokkhā atikkamma rūpe āruppā te kāyena phassitvā (vihareyyanti)" (MN. s. 6). This is curious. The non-material realms should have been the less accessible bodily.

[141] Cf. AN. III. 393-8. While Heiler considers the 4th Jhāna the immediate threshold of full deliverance, Keith and Mrs. Rhys Davids are inclined to disagree (B. P. 126-127; Sakya, 167f). Heiler appears to be right for the earlier stratum of texts, since these show the enlightenment of Buddha as following on the 4th Jhāna. The Sāmaññaphalasutta has a similar implication. It may also be noted that Buddha is in D. s. 16 made to enter the Parinibbāna, not in the Saññāvedayitanirodha, but in the 4th Jhāna. Philosophically too, the 4th Jhāna seems to be nearest the state of mind in which Enlightenment might be expected. Mrs. Rhys Davids herself admits as much indirectly. It may be remembered that according to Zen Buddhism, it is in the "balanced" and "dustless" mind that Mahāprajñāpāramitā is revealed (see Suzuki—JPTS—1906-'7).

On the other hand, Mrs. Rhys Davids has shown that Heiler's opinion is not true in an unqualified manner for a considerable part of the canon, (loc. cit.) esp. the third Piṭaka. What these references show as a matter of fact, is that Jhāna could be about 'worldly' as well as transmundane subjects (lokiya & lokuttara; thus "Tīsu bhūmisu kusalacittekaggatā lokiyo samādhi, ariyamaggasampayuttā ekaggatā lokuttaro samādhi"; Vm. p. 58. The latter is equivalent to the cultivation of Paññā: Paññāya hi bhāvitāya so bhāvito hoti—Ib. p. 60). The practice of Jhāna has in this respect a correspondence to the practice of "Saṃyama" in the Yoga system. Jhāna led to full deliverance only if undertaken with that purpose and ac-

experience to Nirodhasamāpatti[142] for which Jhāna was at least necessary.[143] On the other hand, the description of "Nirodha-samāpatti" comes nearer that of catalepsy than of Sambodhi.[144]

Samatha and Vipassana.—Some texts regard the intellectual consideration of the Four Truths sufficient for their realization, and, by implication, think Jhāna

---

companied with "right knowledge" (Sammādiṭṭhi). The theme of Jhāna had to be religious—e.g., the impermanence of all things—if it was to lead to the realization of religious dogmas. But there could be no realization and deliverance without Jhānic practice of some kind (see Kosambi on Abhidhammatthasaṅgaho p. 22. "Samādhinā asampayuttāni maggaphalāni na santi. So ca samādhi paṭhamajjhāniko vā hoti, dutiyādīnaṃ vā aññatarajjhāniko". This is implicit in Buddhaghosa's treatment in the Vm.). According to Lalita Vistara (I. 348) Gotama attained Enlightenment through "radically considering" (Yoniso manasikāra) the Four Truths after having reached the 4th Jhāna. Jhāna and a proper theme must be associated to attain deliverance.

Nirvāṇic samādhi is described in some texts as threefold—Suññāto, animitto, appaṇihito (AN. I. 299 cf. MN. s. 121).

For explanation see Vm. p. 466 f.

[142] "Saññāvedayitanirodham upasampajja viharati paññāya ca'ssa disvā āsavā parikkhīṇā honti" (MN. I. 160, 175, 204, 209; MN. III. 28). Āsavakkhaya follows Nevasaññānāsaññāyatana when one realizes the impermanence and conditionedness of the Animitto cetosamadhi which succeeds it (MN. III. 107-'8). Nirvāṇa follows the "Nevasaññā°" (MN. III. 244). An Asappurisa can go up to Nevasaññā° but not higher (which would seem to refer to the Nirodha°)—MN. III. 44; cf. DN. 9.

On the other hand, Saññāvedayitanirodha is distinguished from the state of the Khīṇāsava in SN. IV. 217.

[143] Samatha and Vipassanā are both necessary for it (SN. IV. 294; Vm.). It can be realized only *after* the highest Āruppa.

[144] MN. I. 296; SN. IV. 294; Vm. pp. 503-4. Cf. MN. I. 333, where a Bhikkhu in Saññāved° is mistaken for dead. The refs. from MN (supra) show that Saññāved°, was not regarded as incompatible with Paññā. According to SN. IV. 295 knowledge comes when the mind falls back (Vuṭṭhāna) from the Nirodhasam°. This is quite opposed to the MN. refs. DN. 9 (DN. pt. I. p. 214—Nāg. ed.) speaks of "Anupubbābhisaññānirodhasampajānasamāpatti".

inessential.[145] A kind of dualism appears to have sprung up between Samathabhāvanā and Vipassanā. As Buddhist dogmatics grew and Buddhists came to believe in theories and speculation with a zeal paralleled only by the Master's condemnation of them, intellectual understanding came to be regarded as the primary way to the knowledge of truth.[146] To Samatha was now attributed the purely negative function of suppressing (Nirodha) this or that element (Saṅkhāra).[147] This trend, however, did not go unchallenged. The Mādhyamikas relegated all theories to the realm of Samvṛti, stressing the utterly ineffable and non-intellectual nature of

---

145 SN. II. 121ff. cf. Buddhaghosa's ref. to the class of "Sukkhavipassakas" (Vm. 499).

MM. V. Bhattacharya considers the Nirodhasamāpatti at length in ĀŚ. p. 95ff and is inclined to see in it the original contribution of Buddha. He equates it to the Asparśayoga of Gauḍapāda.

One would only like to observe that for Buddha to go beyond his teachers it was not necessary for him to discover a ninth samāpatti (cf. Keith. B. P. pp. 124-5). His originality appears to have consisted in the association of Samādhi and Paññā in order to advance from the Jhānas to the Three Vijjās and Sambodhi.

146 This may explain the slight importance given to Jhāna in the first and third Piṭakas (cf. Sakya pp. 168-171).

147 Cf. Stcherbatsky—Nirvāṇa. p. 8f. The order of suppression (Anupubbasaṅkhāranirodha) is thus described in S. IV. 217.

1st Jhāna	Speech suppressed.
2nd Jhāna	Thought (Vitakka-vicāra)——
3rd Jhāna	"Rapture" (Pīti)
4th Jhāna	Breathing (Assāsa-Pasasāsa)—
Ākāsānañcāyatana	Idea of matter (Rūpasaññā)
Viññāṇa°	The idea of Ākāsā°
Ākiñcañn°	Viññāṇa° saññā..
Nevasaññā°	Ākiñca°
Saññāvedayitanirodha	Saññā & Vedanā——

The state of the Khīṇāsava without Rāga, Dosa and Moha: cf. A. IV. 411 which gives a slightly differing exposition; comp. also the Poṭṭhapādasutta (D).

Reality. This doctrine has been carried into practice in the most extreme fashion by the Zen-school.

Stages of Spiritual Progress.—About the theory of the four spiritual stages, it may be observed that it could not have formed part of the earliest gospel. This is clear from the fact that we find in the Nikāyas an earlier non-technical use of the word "Anāgāmin".[148] Further, had the theory of the Maggas and the corresponding Phalas been early we might have expected some reference to them in the Sāmaññaphala°. Finally, there is little positive evidence in favour of regarding the theory as early.

Dr. Keith suggests that the classification by four stages was possible due to the desire to win over converts who were not altogether enamoured of Nirvāṇa but could be moved by the chance of happier rebirth.[149]

The hypothesis is not really necessary, for in the very nature of the situation an impulse to a more precise development of the theory of salvation is inherent. The difficulties involved in spiritual progress would not rivet attention and there would always be hope so long as Buddha himself was there to guide and help. Further, the earlier disciples, championing a new faith, would be men of spiritual boldness and daring. But the need of assuring men of the spiritual status awaiting this or that degree of effort on their part and of explaining the differences in spiritual attainments would doubtless soon arise. Thus would various stages come to be inserted between the Puthujjana and the Arahant. For reconstructing the history of the theory of the four stages prior

---

148 See Pali Dictionary (PTS).

149 Op. cit. p. 131.

to its being put in formula, the evidence is slight. But it can be noted how the theory is tending to become more complicated in the AN where the division into seven or nine Puggalas occurs several times.[150] The systematic presentation of these elaborations is to be seen in "Abhidhammic" texts like the Paṭisambhidā-mg, (which is only formally part of the Sutta Piṭaka) and the Puggala Paññatti.[151]

---

150 AN. IV. 145-'6, 380-'8.

151 Cf. N. Dutt, Aspects–247ff.

CHAPTER XIV

EARLY BUDDHISM IN RELATION TO ITS RIVALS AND FORERUNNERS

We have already described the beliefs and practices which preceded Buddha and were current in his age. We have also discussed many aspects of the relationship of early Buddhist doctrine to its rivals and forerunners. It remains to sum up and indicate some additional aspects of this relationship.

Buddhism and Jainism: historical contacts.—It has been seen how, when Buddhism arose, Jainism was already an ancient sect[1] with its stronghold about Vesāli which was visited and admired by Buddha, although he frequented Magadha and Kosala more.[2] The Nikāyas contain several references to the Nigaṇṭhas and their doctrines.[3] From the side of Jaina canon there are no direct references to the Buddhists,[4] although indirect references are not totally lacking.[5] For many years Buddha and Mahāvīra were contemporaries,[6] and although there is no report of any personal encounter between them, the Nikāyas would have us believe that the Jaina leader more than once tried to confound his great contemporary by indirectly putting to him embarrassing dilemmas.[7] There can hardly be a doubt that early Buddhists and Nigaṇṭhas were conversant with the doc-

[1] See Chapter—Religious Conditions in the Age of Buddha.
[2] See Chapter—Life of Buddha.
[3] See App. I. IX; Malalasekara, DPPN. II. 60ff.
[4] Cf. C. H. I. i. pp. 160-1.
[5] Sk. I. i. i. 17 clearly refers to the Buddhists; Ib. I. ii. 25ff.
[6] C. H. I. I. p. 160.
[7] MN. I. 392ff; SN. IV. 322ff.

trines of each other. Jainism, being more ancient, might be supposed to have exercised the greater influence at first, which is supported by the fact that whereas the Nigaṇṭhas are a prominent sect in the Nikāyas, the Buddhists do not figure at all in the Jaina canon. Later on, Buddhism became the more influential religion in the country, but, since little historical work has as yet been done on the later history of Jaina thought, it is impossible to estimate the extent of Buddhist influence upon it.

Buddhism and Jainism: Similarities.—Early Buddhist and Jaina writings use a number of common words and expressions, though not always in the same sense. Thus Samavāyaṅga sūtra 10 speaks of the five Kāmaguṇas which are often referred to in the Nikāyas. Sk. 1.14.22 speaks of "Vibhajjavāya". As 1.1.2 uses "Bohī" and "Māra". "Oha" occurs in As. 1.2.3.5. and Sk. 1.11.1, but the meaning is non-technical and corresponds to that of the earlier stages of the history of the word in Buddhist literature.[8] On the other hand AN. V. 215 speaks of ten "Nijjaravatthūni". The term "Āsrava" is common to both literatures though used differently. As. 1.4.1.3. with its "diṭṭhaṃ suyaṃ mayaṃ vinnāyaṃ" is reminiscent of the diṭṭha-suta-muta-viññāta classification of MN. sutta 1. "Nivvāṇa" occurs in Sk. 1.11.21-2, 34.

The idea of past and future **Enlightened Ones** is Buddhist as well Jaina.[9] The case is similar with the idea of the impermanence of worldly pleasures and the futility of pursuing them.[10] Saṃsāra is in both systems

[8] See Pali Dictionary (PTS) on "Ogha".

[9] Cf. As. I. 4.1.

[10] Cf. U. IX. 53; As. 1. 2. 5; Winternitz, II. 425, cf. U. XIV. 13 with the Third Sermon; U. XVIII. 11.

undesirable, without a first beginning and without a personal creator or controller of destiny. Both systems see the roots of Saṃsāra in an ignorance of the true nature of reality, Kāma, and Karman. Both, again, are opposed to Ekāntadṛṣṭi,[11] and stress the importance of Ahiṃsā and Dhyāna.[12] Both regard self-effort as the principal force in spiritual advancement, and advocate "Apramāda".[13]

Most of these resemblances explain themselves through the fact that early Buddhism and Jainism both belonged to a considerable extent to the same Gedankenkreis.[14] Thus the idea of Saṃsāra and an ascetic Weltanschauung belonged to the very Zeitgeist of the sixth century B.C. in India. Disbelief in a creator and controller of the world-process may be called a characteristic trait of Śramaṇa thought.[15] Opposition to Ekāntadṛṣṭi appears to have been the continuation of that "critical" attitude (in the Kantian sense) towards knowledge which Sañjaya seems to have heralded in the history of Indian philosophy.[16] The emphasis on Puruṣakāra",.again, is perhaps to be explained as a reaction to the teachings of thinkers like Gośāla.[17]

Differences.—When, in Hegelian terminology, the "abstract" logic of the Understanding (Verstand) comes in conflict with the commonsense picture of the world.

11 See Nāyādhammakahāo—49; Sk. II. 5; As. I.

12 U. I. 10; ERE VII p. 471; Tattvārthādhigama p. 207; cf. SN. IV. 298.

13 Cf. Nāyā°—60.

14 See Chaps. VIII-IX.

15 Not wholly though; for Buddhism in contradistinction to Jainism appears to have shared in Vedic thought too; see below.

16 On Sañjaya see Chap. IX; on his influence on Buddha see BP. p. 137; Barua—Pre-Buddhistic I. P. pp. 401-3.

17 Cf. Keith loc. cit.; Barua—op. cit. p. 395f.

one may react along one of two possible ways. One may either say that the impasse is due to the inherent defect of ordinary logic which insists on applying to the complexities of real life the strait-jacket of simple identity or difference. One may thus consider the attempt to encompass the true relationship of any A and B in terms of perfect identity or perfect difference as necessarily doomed to failure, and for no fault of A and B. On the other hand, one may make consistency the highest demand of philosophy, and pinning one's faith on rigorous logic, declare the whole world of commonsense illusory. Hegel illustrates the former attitude, Zeno the latter.[18] Classical Jaina dialectic, with its attempt to reconcile the opposing 'Antas', clearly belongs to the "Hegelian" camp. It seeks to avoid the difficulties of dialectical logic by making reality itself dialectical;[19] Syādvāda, thus, comes to be based on Anekāntavāda. Buddhist dialectics, on the other hand, noticing the opposition of the Antas declares all things to be contrary to reason—"Vicārāsahatvaṃ vastūnāṃ tattvam...."[20] Śūnyavāda thus emerges as the basis of Buddhist dialectic.

Here we have a fundamental difference of attitude which goes back in a germinal form to the early days of the two systems. Noticing that the claims of the Ego to remain identical through all changes and to possess an independent existence could not be critically sustained, the early Buddhists felt obliged to declare that the Ego could not possess ultimate reality. Again, with respect to the world (Loka) it was held that one could

[18] Cf. Stcherbatsky—BL. I. p. 424.
[19] Cf. Stcherbatsky, BL. I. p. 415.
[20] Bhāmatī ad. BS. 2.2.31.

neither speak of its eternity nor of its annihilation.[21] The Jainas, on the other hand, did not find the commonsense views of the soul and the world to be wholly incongruous. Jīva and Loga have always been real and will continue to be so, although they are all the while subject to change. They are thus eternal (Sāsaya) as well as non-eternal (Asāsaya).[22] While the Buddhists were logically led to the denial of a substance lurking behind attributes and to the theory of Flux,[23] the Jainas held tenaciously to the theory of Pariṇāminityatā.[24]

The omniscience of the Kevalin has always been an important dogma with the Jainas. The soul freed from all karman is believed to possess a constant and synoptic knowledge of all possible objects.[25] Such an omniscience is held to be innate to the soul, though it is obscured by karman when the soul is in bondage.

At one place in the Nikāyas it is stated that although the Nigaṇṭhas claimed to be omniscient, their behaviour showed plainly that they were not. The Nigaṇṭhas answered by bringing in "Bhavitavyatā". At another place

---

[21] See the famous sermon to Kaccāyana in the Nidāna Saṃyutta (SN. II.).

[22] In a conversation supposed to have taken place between Mahāvīra and Jamāli—B. IX. 6. 387.

[23] Śāntarakṣita thus concludes against the Jainas:
"Tato niranvyayo dhvaṃsaḥ sthiraṃ vā sarvamiṣyatām|
Ekātmani tu naiva sto vyāvṛttyanugamāvimau||
Na copalabhyarūpasya paryāyānugatātmanaḥ|
Dravyasya pratibhāso'sti tannāsti gaganābjavat||
Vividhārthakriyāyogyāstulyādijñānahetavaḥ|
Tathāvidhārthasaṅketaśabdapratyayagocarāḥ||
Udayavyayadharmāṇaḥ paryāyā eva kevalāḥ|
Saṃvedyante tataḥ spaṣṭaṃ nairātmyaṃ cātinirmalaṃ॥
(Tattvasaṅgraha, 321-4)

[24] See Hemacandra on Syādvādamañjarī verse 5. According to MM. V. Bhattacharya the Buddhists also admitted the existence of "eternity" after the Jaina fashion—ĀS. CXL.

[25] See Chap. IX.

Buddha is seen to deny omniscience except in the sense of the Three Vidyās.[26] Elsewhere he repudiates only that one may know all things at the same time (Sakideva sabbaṃ ñassati).[27] The view here repudiated was upheld by the Mahāsaṅghikas and the Vātsīputrīyas.[28] The conception of Bodhi in MSA (IX. 1-2) is akin to it.[29] The Sarvāstivādin view on the point may be supposed to represent an older opinion;[30] only, it must be remembered that one of the earliest descriptions of Bodhi in the Nikāyas contains lines which, when placed by the side of similar lines in the YS, may be justly interpreted to imply some sort of simultaneous and all-embracing knowledge.[31]

Another important difference between early Buddhism and Jainism relates to the nature of Karma. The former regarded it as a psychological function, the latter as a quasi-material substance. Thus Karma is for the former primarily mental, for the latter, primarily physical. In the Upāli sutta of MN we find the difference appearing very clearly.[32] One consequence of this difference is reflected in the conception of Ahiṃsā in the two systems. The Buddhists regarded it as a mental attitude, as Mettā and Karuṇā, and recommended its positive cultivation. The Jainas interpreted it in a wholly negative manner, and in order to avoid violence sought to avoid all action.

---

[26] MN. Pt. II. p. 154 (Nāg. ed.).

[27] MN. Pt. II. p. 331 (Nāg. ed.). [28] Ab. K. V. pp. 254-5.

[29] Tattvasaṅgraha also says: "Ekajñānakṣaṇavyāptaniḥśeṣajñeyamaṇḍalaḥ| Prasādhito hi sarvajñaḥ Kramo nāśrīyate tataḥ|| (3627).

But it mentions other interpretations too—Ib. 3628ff.

[30] Ib. [31] See Chap. XII.

[32] Cf. Sk. II. 6; Mahāvīra is reported to have declared Buddha an Akiriyavāda: AN. IV. 179ff.

Finally, Buddhist asceticism is self-discipline,[33] Jaina asceticism is self-mortification.[34] We know that the difference in this case was due to Buddha's personal innovation. The difference arises, again, from the difference in the conception of karma. Buddhists stress the active aspect of karma as a doing, Jainas stress the mechanical aspect that comes forward in the Karmaphala.

Conclusion.—The similarities between early Buddhism and Jainism are thus to be understood as the product of a common cultural milieu, while their differences are attributable, partly, to the personality of Buddha, and, partly, as will be seen below, to Vedic influence on Buddhist development. There is thus little ground for assuming a direct dependence between early Buddhism and Jainism.

Buddhism and Sankhya: Historical Contacts.—Discussing the origins of Sāṅkhya, we have already suggested that it belonged, together with Yoga, to the Śramaṇa stream of thought. In the Upaniṣads there is an attempt to combine the ideas of Sāṅkhya with theistic ideas. There are no references to the Sāṅkhya system by name in the Nikāyas, although the terms Saṅkhā and Paṭisaṅkhāna are used.[35] The Brahmajālasutta refers to a class of Sassatavādins who held the soul (Attā) and the world (Loka) to be two distinct eternals. This is, so far as it goes, a "Sāṅkhya" tenet, but we are ignorant of the other beliefs of the Sassatavādins. Some of them were apparently Kiriyavādins[36] and could not be believers in Sāṅkhya. Some, however, were Akiriyavādins, as the

[33] ERE. II. p. 70.
[34] See Devadaha sutta in MN.
[35] Cf. Mrs. Rhys Davids, The Birth of Ind. Psych. p. 154 (1936).
[36] See SN. II. p. 20; EMB. I. pp. 50-1.

instance of Pakudha Kaccāyana shows.[37] Pakudha's distinction of the soul from Sukhadukkha is also Sāṅkhyan. The Akiriyavāda of Pūraṇa Kassapa too is reminiscent of Sāṅkhya.[38] According to Aśvaghoṣa, Arāḍa one of the teachers of Buddha—believed in a philosophy which is essentially Sāṅkhyan, although it is strangely silent over the three Guṇas.[39] But we are quite in the dark about the source of Aśvaghoṣa. The Nikāyas only tell us that Ālāra taught the way to Ākiñcaññāyatanasamāpatti.[40]

This is practically all the evidence about Sāṅkhya from the Nikāyas, and, clearly, it is not impressive. It suggests that although in the 6th cent. B.C., a number of Sāṅkhya ideas like the unchangeability, permanence, transcendentality[41] and passivity of the soul were believed in by some thinkers, a completed Sāṅkhya system of philosophy was as yet not to be had. This conclusion is, however, vitiated by two circumstances: in the first place, the "silence" of the Nikāyas about Sāṅkhya is not conclusive, for the Nikāyas are similarly silent about the "Pan-Ātmanism" of the Upaniṣads. In the second place, Upaniṣadic evidence seems to suggest the existence of the Sāṅkhya system prior to Buddhism.[42]

Early Jaina references to Sāṅkhya too are few and indefinite.[43] The Mbh—esp. the BG and the ŚP—clearly presupposes a great development of Sāṅkhya, since we find here repeated attempts made to effect a synthesis

---

[37] Ib. p. 39.
[38] Ib. p. 35.
[39] Buddh. Carita XII. X—16ff.
[40] See Chap. X.
[41] Cf. EMB. I. p. 50.
[42] See Chap. VIII.
[43] See Chap. IX.

between Sāṅkhya and Vedānta.[44] There is however little reason to suppose this mass of epic literature pre-Buddhistic.[45] That it has only a few references to Buddhism[46] proves just as little or as much as the similar silence of early Buddhist literature towards epic Sāṅkhya, Vedānta and Theism.

It appears thus that although Sāṅkhya might have been a developed philosophy prior to Buddhism, the early Buddhists took but slight notice of it. This goes against the validity of the attempts often made to read profound Sāṅkhya influences on Buddhism.

Buddhism and Sankhya: the Doctrines.—Jacobi maintained that Buddhism was "aus den Sāṅkhya-yoga hervorgegangen", being "eine individuelle Umgestaltung des Sāṅkhya".[47] It is argued that Buddha could have been as little free from Sāṅkhya influence as an author in the middle ages from Aristotle. Taking over so much from Yoga, he could not fail to be influenced by Sāṅkhya.[48] Aśvaghoṣa describes the philosophy of Arāḍa as a variety of Sāṅkhya.[49] Both Sāṅkhya and Buddhism set out with the same enquiry and, we are told, the explanation given of the genesis of duḥkha is substantially the same in both.[50] The attempt to derive Paṭiccasam° from the evolution of the Tattvas in Sāṅkhya has already been referred to and discussed above.[50a]

---

[44] See Chap. VIII. Carakasaṃhitā shows an amalgam of Sāṅkhya, Vaiśeṣika and Upaniṣadic views, vide e.g., Ib. 1.1.46-56; Ib. 1.8.3-16.

[45] Contra—Creative Period pp. 462f.

[46] Thus Nīlakaṇṭha appears justified in seeing a reference to Buddhism in Mbh. ŚP. 219. 32ff.

[47] ZDMG. 1898. p. 1.

[48] Cf. below.

[49] Cf. supra.

[50] Cf. Chap. XI.

According to Oldenberg, Sāṅkhya did not influence Buddhism directly,[51] although indirect influence is undeniable.[52] Part of Oldenberg's discussion is, however, vitiated by his failure to distinguish sufficiently between the influences of Sāṅkhya and of "Vedānta". For instance, Nirvāṇa is to be compared, not to the Kaivalya of Sāṅkhya Puruṣa,[53] but to Brahmātmabhāva, since the former does not mean the complete transcendence of individuality.[54] Nor does it seem incontestable that a dualistic system underlies Buddhism, which obtained the apt appellation of Advayavāda.[55]

It has been often pointed out that both Buddhism and Sāṅkhya repudiate the distinction between substance and quality.[56]

Finally, the Sāṅkhya analysis of the Puruṣa as distinct from body and mind has been supposed to influence the growth of Nairātmyavāda.[57] It is certainly undeniable that both Sāṅkhya and Buddhism agree in regarding the psychophysical complex to be changeful and nonself.

On the other hand, the differences between the basic principles of the two systems are prominent. The Sāṅkhya doctrine of Satkāryavāda and its corollary the

---

[50a] See Chap. XI.

[51] LU. p. 294ff.

[52] Ib. p. 296.

[53] Ib. p. 307ff.

[54] Cf. Buddh. Car. XII. 76-7. The state of the freed Puruṣas may be compared with that of the Vijñānakevalas (see e.g., Īśvarapratyabhijñāvimarśinī. II. pp. 223-4). These are distinguished by Āṇava mala.

[55] Cf. Chap. XI.

[56] Stcherbatsky—BL. I. p. 19; ĀŚ. p. 90-2.

[57] Mrs. Rhys Davids in JRAS 1928. p. 283; Keith BP. p. 142; Garbe quoted by Stcherbatsky in IHQ. 1934-0. 754. cf. Oldenberg op. cit. p. 299.

eternal Prakṛti,[58] are clearly opposed to the Buddhist ideas of Pratītyasamutpāda and impermanence.[59] The idea that Sukha, Duḥkha and Moha are the sole constituents of phenomena is quite unacceptable to Buddhism.[60] There is nothing in Buddhism which quite corresponds to the Puruṣa of Sāṅkhya. In Vijñānavāda, whether of the Nikāyas or of later times, it **is** the citta itself which, when purified, becomes the highest principle, not something "utterly distinct" (atyantāsaṅkīrṇa) from citta.[61]

It appears that Sāṅkhya influence on Buddhism has been too lightly assumed. That the world is changeful and full of misery is an idea which was by no means peculiar to Sāṅkhya in the 6th Cent. B.C.

That precise development of the Dharma theory which made the conception of Dharma resemble that of "Guṇa" or Tattva does not belong to earliest Buddhism.[62] The non-selfhood of body and mind belongs to Upaniṣadic Vedānta just as much as to Sāṅkhya.[63]

Conclusion.—It appears thus that, as with Jainism, Sāṅkhya did not exert any direct or distinctive influence on early Buddhism. Sarvāstivāda Abhidharma, however, appears much influenced by Sāṅkhya, but that presents a problem on which historical work still remains a desideratum.[64]

Buddhism and Yoga.—The influence of Yoga on

---

58 SK. 9-10.

59 Cf. Tattvasaṅgraha, 7-45.

60 Cf. SK. 12; Tattvasaṅgraha, 36 ff. Śāntarakṣita's criticism is similar to Śaṅkara's—see Comy. on BS. 2.2-1.

61 YS. Vyāsa's Comy.

62 See Chap. on Nirvāṇa.

63 See Chap. VIII.

64 Cf. below.

Buddhism has been supposed to be patent.[65] An important distinction, however, must be effected between mystical and occult practices in general and systematic yoga strictly so called as found in the YS.[65a] Various "Yogic" practices are mentioned in the Upaniṣads,[65a] and the Nikāyas tell us that Buddha's teachers and many other heretics were proficient in them. Buddha, we are told, learnt from his teachers the attainment of the spheres of 'Nothingness' and 'Neither-consciousness-nor-unconsciousness.[65b] During his Padhāna days he practised concentration with held breath.[66] Systematic practices of abstraction (Arūpadhyāna) and of breath regulation were thus current in Buddha's time and learnt by him. This explains the source of the Āruppas and the Ānāpānasati of the Buddhists. It is probable that the Brahmavihāras also go back to originally non-Buddhist practice.[67]

On the other hand, the antiquity of the system expounded in the YS is difficult to determine. The following are its chief points of contact with the Buddhism of the Nikāyas: The description of the general character of the highest development of Prajñā is similar in both systems.[68] In both, this Prajñā is obtained through the exercise of the same five faculties. Of the four samādhis described in YS 1. 17, the first three correspond to the first three of the five Jhānas described in Abhidhamma.[69] Asamprajñāta Samādhi appears to be

---

[65] e.g., Oldenberg op. cit. 324 ff; Keith—op. cit. 143ff; Jacobi loc. cit.

[65a] See above, Ch. VIII.

[65b] See above, Ch. X.

[66] See Chap. X.

[67] See Chap. XIII.

[68] See Chap. on Nirvāṇa.

[69] See Dhs. pp. 48-51 (Nāgarī ed.).

similar to the eighth samāpatti, since in both the mind is described as Saṃskāraśeṣa and lacking in positive 'ālambana'.[70] The definition of Avidyā in Y.S. 2.5. approximates to the Buddhist notion of it. In both systems is found the conception of three duḥkhatās.[71] Pariṇāma-duḥkhatā is common; the duḥkha° of the Buddhists corresponds to the tāpa° of the YS. But the conception of Saṃskāra° is different in the two. Both use about Ill the same fourfold general analytical scheme.[72] Vyāsa tells us that avoiding Ucchedavāda and Hetuvāda, we must take to Śāśvatavāda, the true doctrine.[73] This reminds one of the Buddhist attempt to steer clear of Śāśvatavāda and Ucchedavāda by means of Pratītyasamutpāda. One may also compare the remark of Vyāsa at another place where in answer to the (later) Buddhist view of *niranvayavināśa* he repudiates Ekāntanityatā as well as Ekāntavināśa.[74] Like the Brahmavihāras of the Buddhists the YS (1. 33) also speaks of the practice of Maitrī, Karuṇā, Muditā and Upekṣā. But it must be noted that while, according to Vyāsa, there is no Bhāvanā and Samādhi with respect to Upekṣā,[75] according to Buddhaghosa, in Upekkhā alone is the fourth Jhāna possible and the other three Bhāvanās culminate in Upekkhā.[76] As a matter of fact, while Upekṣā means for Vyāsa indifference towards sinners, it

---

[70] YS. I. 18, with Vyāsa's comy.; Vm. p. 229. Or, is Asamprajñāta to be compared to the Nirodhasamāpatti? The exact nature, status and role of the latter appear, however, difficult to determine clearly (cf. Chap. XIII).

[71] YS. 2. 15; for the Buddh. refs. see Chap. XI.

[72] Vyāsa on YS. 2.15; on the 4 Truths see Chap. XI.

[73] Vyāsa loc. cit.

[74] ad. YS. 3.13.

[75] ad. YS. 3.23.

[76] Vm. p. 218.

means to Buddhaghosa an evenly balanced state of the mind (majjhattākārappavattilakkhaṇā ca upekkhā).[77]

Various supernormal powers are spoken of at many places in the Nikāyas as well as the YS.[78] In both is found the fourfold division of karman as Kṛṣṇa, Śukla-kṛṣṇa etc.[79] The comment of Vyāsa on YS. 4. 11 contains a formula which bears a generic resemblance to the formula of the Nidānas.[80] The term "Ātmabhāva" of YS. 4. 25 may be compared with the Pali Attabhāva.[81] Commenting on YS. 4. 33 Vyāsa mentions three types of questions—Ekāntavacanīya, Vibhajyavacanīya and Avacanīya. This is similar to the fourfold Buddhist classifications.[82]

Since the antiquity of the Yoga-sūtras has not been determined as yet with any certainty, it is difficult to interpret the evidence adduced above from the standpoint of the historical relation of Buddhism to Yoga as philosophy and system.

Buddhism and the Vedic Tradition.—The Vedic tradition in the 6th century B.C. had two main branches: ritualistic and non-ritualistic. The Nikāyas more than once depict Buddha disputing with representatives of the former.[83] The topics are chiefly caste and sacrifice. Buddhist opposition on these subjects has always been clear. Another point which Buddha is made to criticize is the Brahmanic respect for traditional authority in

---

[77] Loc. cit.

[78] Cf. e.g. the comy. of Vyāsa on YS. 3.45 with DN. Sutta 2§87 (P.T.S. ed.).

[79] See Chap. XI.

[80] Cf. Chap. XI.

[81] Cf. Chap. on Nirvāṇa.

[82] Cf. Rosenberg op. cit. p. 56f.

[83] See Chap. X.

matters of belief.[84] At one place a Brāhmaṇa of great wealth, learning and eminence is sceptical about man attaining to superhuman (uttarimanussa) powers.[85] It may be remembered how even in later times the Mīmāṃsakas (some at least of them) denied that a man may of his own efforts attain to the direct knowledge of supersensuous (atīndriya) objects.[86] Buddha's dialogues with the Brāhmaṇas in the Nikāyas would, in fact, appear to represent the beginnings of the protracted Buddhist-Mīmāṃsaka struggle.

About the "Aupaniṣadas" the Nikāyas are curiously silent. Nowhere is Buddha seen to criticize the Absolutism of the Upaniṣads.[87] Even in later times a Buddhist critique of Vedānta is rare. Rosenberg in fact asserts, "Es ist charakteristisch, das wir nirgends eine buddhistische Polemik mit dem Vedānta finden."[88] Even Śāntarakṣita who devotes a few verses to criticize the Advaitavādin Aupaniṣadas says *"Teṣāmalpāparādhaṃ tu darśanaṃ nityatoktitaḥ"* (Tattvasaṅgraha, 330). Śaṅkara in criticizing Vijñānavāda is silent over Vijñaptimātratā: and, although that might have been due to ignorance, it is undeniable that he was deeply influenced by Buddhism.[89] The Buddhist influence probably reached him via Gauḍapāda whose dependence on Buddhism is beyond question. Now the roots of Śaṅkara's Absolutism go back to the Upaniṣads, while those of Buddhist

---

[84] e.g. DN. Sutta 13; MN. sutta 95.

[85] See Malalasekara, DPPN—II. pp. 246-7.

[86] Cf. Tattvasaṅgraha. Sarvajñaparīkṣā; on Brahman in the Nikāyas, see Chap. on Nirvāṇa.

[87] Keith BP. p. 140.

[88] Op. cit. p. 264.

[89] MM. Gopinath Kaviraj in the Preliminary Essay to Tantravārtika tr. MM. G. Jha (Bib. Ind. 161, Fasc. XIX) p. IX.

Absolutism can be traced to the Nikāyas.[90] If we suppose that the Nikāyas were themselves influenced by the Upaniṣads, it will render clearer the nearness of latter—day Vedānta and Buddhism. This hypothesis is supported by the fact of kinship which exists between the conceptions of Vijñāna in the Upaniṣads and Nikāyas;[91] again, it has been seen, how the attitude of Buddha towards Nirvāṇa is reminiscent of Upaniṣadic absolutism,[92] especially as held by Yājñavalkya.

Thus, although direct evidence is lacking, it appears that early Buddhism was fundamentally influenced by the Upaniṣads which gave to it its early tendencies towards *Idealism and Absolutism.* These tendencies, it may be noted, could not have been derived from the Śramaṇic thought-world.[93] Upaniṣadic Absolutism declares Brahman or Ātman beyond predication, and yet predicates of it Sat, Cit, and Ānanda. Buddha is more consistent and adopts the 'madhyamā pratipad', indicating only the beatific character of the Absolute by speaking of it as 'goal' (Artha) and 'peace' (Nirvāṇa). Vijñāna is the core of Upaniṣadic as well as of Buddhist Idealism, though generally regarded as 'Anitya' and 'Saviśeṣa' in the latter (see Śaṅkara's Commentary on B.S. II. 2.28: "Sākṣiṇovagantuḥ etc.")

Conclusion.—It is clear that Buddha owed much to contemporary Śramaṇa and Brāhmaṇa thought from

[90] Walleser denies that the ĀŚ. is the work of a single teacher named Gauḍapāda. He thinks it to have been the basic work of a Gauḍa school of Vedānta (Der ältere Vedānta-Geschichte, Kritik und Lehre. p. 6ff).
Cf. MM. V. Bhattacharya—ĀŚ. p. LXVIIff.

[91] See Chap. VIII; and the Chap. on Nirvāṇa.

[92] See Chap. on Nirvāṇa.

[93] See Chap. VIII.

which he derived the ideas of Saṃsāra, of the non-selfhood of body and mind, and of the absolute and ineffable nature of the ultimate principle.

Buddha's most original and profound contribution was the abstract formulation of Pratītyasamutpāda.[94]

---

[94] According to Sir R. G. Bhandarkar, "The tide of free speculation culminated in the east into such systems as those of Buddhism and Jainism. In the west, however, a theistic system with a god who had come to dwell among men arose." (Collected Works IV. p. 3). "It appears that the idea of a religion of devotion arose in earlier times, but it received a definite shape when Vāsudeva revealed the Gītā to Arjuna...." (Ib. p. 11). Thus Buddhism and Bhakti became alternative developments of a common basic tendency viz., anti-ritualistic free speculation. We have already commented upon this (supra, Chaps. VIII-IX). It remains to add that neither are the older Nikāyas acquainted with the Bhagavadgītā, nor is the Gītā acquainted with them, whatever the chronological relationship between the two. The theism with which the older portions of the Nikāyas are acquainted is at best the idea of Mahābrahmā as creator. (e.g. DN. I. pp. 20f. Nāgarī edition. Bombay.) They know of gods but not of God, nor of His Incarnation. Cf. K. N. Upadhyaya, Early Buddhism and the Bhagavadgītā.

CHAPTER XV

SOME TRENDS IN THE POST-NIKĀYA DEVELOPMENT OF BUDDHISM

The Origin of Schism.—About the origin of schism within the Saṅgha there are two distinct traditions. The one that is better known represents it to have arisen as the result of the ten un-Vinayic acts of the monks of Vaiśālī.[1] The issue was discussed in a General Council (*mahāsaṅgīti*) and the Ten Points of the Vesālians were condemned. The Ten Points are now found expressed in short and obscure formulae.[2] With respect to some of them there is divergence of interpretation among the different schools.[3]

The second tradition preserved by Vasumitra and followed by Bhavya and Vinītadeva asserts that the first breach in the Saṅgha resulted from the Five Points of Mahādeva.[4] These too are couched in enigmatic formulae, and relate to the Arhant of whom a startling conception is put forth. La Vallée Poussin has shown that these points occur in the Kv. also.[5]

It is not unlikely that the schism began openly with points of discipline, but soon the doctrinal differences

---

[1] The main sources for this tradition are: (a) Cullavagga of the Vin., on which are based the accounts of the Ceylonese chronicles and the Pali commentaries; (b) Vinayakṣudrakavastu —the Tibetan translation of the Mūla-sarvāstivāda Vinaya, on which are based the accounts of Bu-ston and Tārānātha. See Tārānātha—pp. 40ff; Bu-ston II. 91-6.

[2] Cf. Minayeff op. cit. p. 43.

[3] EMB. II. pp. 35-40; Minayeff op. cit. pp. 44-50.

[4] EMB. II. p. 41.

[5] JRAS. 1910—pp. 413ff.

which are discernible in a germinal form in the Nikāyas flowered forth.[6]

The State of Discipline.—The Vesālian Ten Points indicate the existence of demoralization and of the absence of universally admitted and precisely formulated rules of conduct as we now have them in the canon.[7] Further, the accounts of the Second Council reveal the interesting point that the Vinayic division was accompanied with a more or less clear geographical demarcation between the two parties.[8] Mrs. Rhys Davids has suggested that "the real point at issue was the rights of the individual, as well as those of the provincial communities as against the prescriptions of a centralized hierarchy."[9] She says that it could not have been the use of "gold and silver" since there was at that time too much traffic in kind, and besides, the point is put in the tenth place.[10] Dr. N. Dutt also says, apparently supporting the first point of Mrs. Rhys Davids, that the Vajjians imbued with a thorough democratic spirit would have been unlikely to submit to the exclusive powers and privileges which the Arhants claimed for themselves.[10a] It appears

[6] Cf. EMB. II. p. 42.

[7] Minayeff op. cit. p. 51.

[8] The Vesālian protagonists were Easterners (Pācīnakā), and so were Sabbakāmi, Sāḷha, Khujjasobhita and Vāsabhagāmika. Their antagonists were Westerners—Yasa of Kosala, Revata of Soreyya, Sambhūta Sāṇavāsī of Mathurā, and Sumana. There appear to have been three main centres of Buddhism at the time: Vaiśālī, Kauśāmbī and Mathurā. At Vaiśālī and to its south-east, the Mahāsaṅghikas became important; at Kauśāmbī and to its south-west, the Sthaviravādins became important, while at Mathurā and to its north-west the Sarvāstivādins came to be the principal sect. (See Przyluski, quoted by N. Dutt, EMB. II. pp. 29f.)

[9] Sakya p. 355.

[10] Ib. p. 345. It should be noted that the tenth point of the Pali tradition is the seventh of the Mūlasarvāstivāda tradition—see EMB. II. p. 38.

[10a] EMB. II. 43-4.

to us, however, that the mention of 'gold and silver' as a point of dispute is in itself evidence of changing economic circumstances. Besides, the opposition to the authority of Arhants seems to have sprung essentially from the growth of a different conception concerning them. It would be illogical if rules of discipline did not subserve points of doctrine.

And of Doctrine.—An examination of the Points of Mahādeva confirms the judgment of Minayeff about the demoralized state of the Buddhist Saṅgha about the time of the Second Council. Before such points could be discussed it is necessary that bogus Arhants should have become fairly common. The heresy of Ācinṇakappo was clearly dangerous and may have helped the growth of philosophical schism.[11]

The Sects.—Following the first doctrinal schism into the Sthaviravādins and the Mahāsaṅghikas, tradition tells us, eighteen different schools came into existence. Of the genesis of these schools and their relationships there are several different accounts. According to the Kv. A. the Mahāsaṅghikas split up into the Gokulikas and the Ekabbohārikas. From the Gokulikas arose the Paṇṇattivādins and the Bāhulikas or the Bahussutikas out of whom sprang the Cetiyavādins. On the other side, Theravāda split up into the Mahiṃsāsakas and the Vajjiputtakas. From the latter arose the Dhammuttariyas, the Bhadrayānikas and the Sammitīyas. From the Mahiṃsāsakas arose the Sabbatthivādins and the Dhammaguttikas. From the former arose the Kassapikas who in turn gave rise to the Saṅkantikas. Out of these arose the Suttavādins.[12]

---

11 Minayeff op. cit. p. 207.

12 Debates Commentary pp. 2-3. On the origin and doctrines of the sects, see Frauwallner, op. cit., Lamotte, *Histoire du Bouddhisme indien* pp. 138 ff., Bareau, *Les sectes bouddhiques*. On the views of these scholars, see my comments and views in my *Bauddha Dharma Ke Vikas Ka Itihas* pp. 173-91. Dr. S.N. Dube in his *Doctrinal Controversies in Early Buddhism* (under publication) has dealt with the whole subject exhaustively and critically.

According to Vasumitra, the Mahāsaṅghikas split into Ekavyavahārikas, Lokottarvādins and Kaukkuṭikas. Later on the Bahuśrutīyas issued out of the Mahāsaṅghikas, and, still later, the Prajñaptivādins. Towards the close of the second century the discussions of a second Mahādeva gave birth to the schools of Caityaśaila, Aparaśaila and Uttaraśaila. Sthaviravāda divided itself into Sarvāstivāda or Hetuvāda and Mūlasthaviravāda which changed its name into the Haimavata school. Subsequently the Vātsīputrīyas arose from Sarvāstivāda, and themselves gave rise to the Dharmottarīyas, the Bhadrayānīyas, the Sammatīyas and the Channagarika or Ṣaṇṇagarika. Immediately afterwards the Mahīśāsakas arose from the Sarvāstivādins, then the Dharmaguptas out of the Mahīśāsakas, and at the end of the 3rd century, the Kāśyapīyas or the Suvarṣakas out of the Sarvāstivādins. Finally, at the beginning of the 4th century the Sautrāntikas or the Saṅkrāntivādins arose out of the Sarvāstivādins.[13]

The dependence of Bhavya on Vasumitra is as clear as his lack of critical insight.[14] He offers three lists which differ from one another. The first, which is in accordance with Svaguruparamparā, omits the Gokulikas from those springing from the Mahāsaṅghikas, while from the Sthaviras branch off such new names as the Muruntakas, the Avantikas and the Kurukullakas. The second list, according to what *"andere sagen"*, offers the new name of the Tāmraśātīyas, but it differs chiefly in as much as it gives not two but four original sects—Sthavira°, Vātsīputrīya, Vibhajyavādin, and Mahāsāṅ-

[13] Masuda—Origin & Doctrines of Early Indian schools, pp. 15-17.

[14] Walleser—Die Sekten p. 29.

ghika. In the third list the Sthaviras fall apart into three main groups—Sarvāstivādin, Vātsīputrīya and Vibhajyavādin, "zu denen noch die eigentlichen Sthaviras oder Haimavata hinzukommen."[15]

According to the list in the Mahāvyutpatti there were four original sects viz., the Sarvāstivādins, the Sammatīyas, the Mahāsaṅghikas and the Sthaviras. The first broke up into the Mūlasarvāstivādins, the Kāśyapīyas, the Mahīśāsakas, the Dharmaguptas, the Bahuśrutīyas, the Tāmraśātīyas and the Vibhajyavādins. The second split up into the Kaurukullas, the Āvantakas and the Vātsīputrīyas. The third gave rise to the Pūrvaśailas, the Apara°, the Haimavatas, the Lokttaravādins and the Prajñaptivādins. Out of the fourth arose the Mahāvihāravāsins, the Jetavanīyas and the Abhayagirivāsins.[16]

This confusion is lessened if we note the identifications supplied by Tārānātha—(1) Kāśyapīyas=Suvarṣakas (2) Saṅkrāntivādin=Uttarīya=Tāmraśāṭīya (3) Caityaka=Pūrvaśaila=Schools of Mahādeva (4) Lokottaravāda=Kaukkuṭika (5) Ekavyavahārika as a general name for the Mahāsaṅghikas (6) Kaurukullaka, Vātsīputrīya, Dharmottarīya, Bhadrayānīya and Channagarika as doctrinally very similar.[17] Further, neglecting the later schools and sub-branches it appears that the most ancient and the most important sects were the following: Sthaviras, Mahāsaṅghikas, Mahīśāsakas, Sarvāstivādins and the Vātsīputrīyas. With respect to the genesis of these the greatest difference between the lists of the Kv.

---

15 Ib. pp. 22-23.

16 Thomas, Hist. of Buddh. Thought p. 38.

17 See Tārānātha—pp. 270-74. Cf. N. Dutt's comments—EMB. II. pp. 48-50.

A and Vasumitra lies in the fact that the latter derives the Mahīśāsakas from the Sarvāstivādins reversing the procedure of the former. This contradiction is to be explained by the fact that there were two Mahīśāsaka schools, an earlier one agreeing more with the Theravādins and a later one agreeing more with the Sarvāstivādins.[18]

The doctrines of these schools have been studied in detail by a number of scholars—Masuda (in his notes to the work cited), Walleser (op. cit.), Wassiljew and Dr. N. Dutt (op. cit.).[18a] We will therefore confine ourselves to the outlining of the main problems and trends of thought as revealed in the controversies of the earlier and more important parent-schools.

The Main Problems.—The following appear to have been the leading subjects and questions that **exercised** sectarian thought[18b]—1. The transcendentality (lokottaratā) of the Buddha.[19] 2. Whether every word of the Buddha could free the hearer from Saṃsāra?[20] This is partly the consequence of the previous issue 3. Further, when the contradictions in the canon were noted, the question of distinguishing the "Nītārtha" from the "Neyārtha" sūtras came into existence.[21] This, still later, led to the development of the theory of Two Truths in the Satyasiddhi school which was transitional between the Hīnayāna and the Mahāyāna.[22] 4. Simultaneously with the question about the Lokottaratā of the Buddha arose the problems of the manner of His birth and His relations

[18] EMB. II. pp. 111-2

[18a] Bareau (op. cit.) has given the greatest details but his account displays no doctrinal insight—see my *Bauddha Dharma Ke Vikāsa Kā Itihāsa* p. 191; also Dr. Dube's work mentioned above.

[18b] Cf. Bareau, op. cit. pp. 260-89.

[19] Cf. Wassiljew op. cit. I. p. 105.

[20] Cf. Ib.

[21] Cf. Ib.

[22] P. L. Vaidya, Etudes—p. 19; cf. Sogen, System—p. 177

to the Saṅgha.[23] 5. While the conception of Buddha was becoming more sublime, that of the Arhant was declining and this was the most hotly disputed point in the whole range of early sectarian controversy.[24] 6. The problem of the existence of the Pudgala.[25] 7. The problem of Antarābhava. 8. The existence of past and future objects. 9. The nature of Anuśaya or dormant passions. 10. The functioning of Vijñāna. 11. The number of Asaṃskṛtas. 12. The order of Bhāvanā and Abhisamaya.

Lines of Development.—The chief lines of resultant development were: Docetism among the Mahāsaṅghika schools and, later, in Mahāyāna; Pudgalavāda among the Vajjiputtaka schools; Sarvāstivāda; and Dharma theory, mainly in the Abhidharmas of Sarvāstivāda and Sthaviravāda.

The main factors leading to the rise of Buddhist Docetism may be thus summarized.[26] A natural instinct led to the glorification of the Buddha and webs of mythical fancies were woven around his personality.[27] He was invested with superhuman qualities. It was then felt that he could not have been subject to the limitations of ordinary life, since he must be in every respect perfect.[28] Buddhism, it may be remembered, looked upon all life in this world as evil.[29] Buddha, therefore,

---

[23] Cf. Wassiljew op. cit. I. p. 107.

[24] Cf. Ib.

[25] Cf. Ib. p. 110.

[26] Anesaki—ERE. IV. p. 836.

[27] See e.g., DN. suttas 14-16. A perusal of the traditional account of Buddha's life as given by Kern in his Manual will indicate the nature of this mythological growth.

[28] Cf. AN. IV. 36 according to which the Buddha was undefiled by the world (loka).

never really lived as a human being. He *appeared to do so* out of compassion for the ignorant.[30]

At the same time metaphysical speculation about the personality of the Buddha as a Tathāgata pointed in the same direction. If He neither persisted to exist, nor was annihilated at death—if His nature after death was inconceivable and inexpressible—could He, then, be said to have existed during life? Speculation along this line grew clearer in the Prajñā schools[31] and culminated in the Mādhyamika position as represented by Nāgārjuna.

The origin and doctrines of Pudgalavāda have already been considered in a previous chapter.[32]

The leading motive behind the development of Sarvāstivāda is obscure. The canonical grounds indicated by the Sarvāstivādins for their opinions are quite forced.[33] There is, indeed, little in the Nikāyas to suggest even remotely the development of the central Sarvāstivāda thesis. On the other hand, the resemblance with the systems of Sāṅkhya-Yoga is in this respect quite remarkable. The historical relationship of Sāṅkhya—Yoga and Sarvāstivāda, consequently, needs to be investigated before any clear judgment on the genesis of Sarvāstivāda could be formed.

On the Dharma-theory the work of Rosenberg and Stcherbatsky has thrown a flood of light. The main

---

[29] Cf. "(Christian) Docetism was always the consequence of that representation of matter as evil which is the common element of Gnostic schools" ERE. IV. p. 833. It should be remembered that the Mahāsaṅghikas maintained that the ills of the mind (citta) were in reality only accidental to it (EMB. II. p. 103). Here is the germ of the doctrire of Vijñaptimātratā. It goes back to the Nikāyas (see Chap. on Nirvāṇa).

[30] See EMB. II. pp. 62-4; 74ff.

[31] ERE. IV. 837-8.

[32] Chap. on Nirvāṇa.

[33] See EMB. II. pp. 143-4.

contribution of the former towards our understanding of the nature of Dharma has been mentioned in a previous chapter.[34] It may be observed here that the main incentive to the growth of the Dharma-theory or Abhidharma came from the idea of Nairātmya. The soul no longer remaining the centre of philosophical interest, the latter was energetically directed to the analysis of the apparent man—mind and body. As a matter of fact, the very attempt to banish the soul required that the place it occupied in popular imagination should be adequately filled by a better understood picture of the body-mind complex. Essentially, we have here an attempt to replace a rational by an empirical Psychology.

[34] Chap. on Nirvāṇa.

APPENDIX I. EARLY JAINA SOURCES

The Jaina Canon, its History and Authenticity.— Mahāvīra is traditionally supposed to have taught the fourteen Puvvas to the Gaṇadharas. These "original" texts are, however, according to the Digambaras, lost without a trace. According to the Śvetāmbaras, their remnants i.e. the first ten Puvvas, which Bhadrabāhu permitted Sthūlabhadra to reveal to others,[1] were, in the Council at Pāṭaliputra, combined to form the twelfth Aṅga, the Diṭṭhivāya. But in the centuries that followed the council this twelfth Aṅga also got lost. Some little information about its contents is apparently preserved in the Samavāyaṅga, the Nandī and the Chedasūtras. From these it appears that of the five divisions of the Diṭṭhivāya only the third dealt with the Puvvas proper. Obviously the Diṭṭhivāya was more than a mere summary of the Puvvas. In any case, we can hardly be certain that any authentic information about the fourteen Puvvas has survived in these references to the contents of the Diṭṭhivāya.[2]

But the Digambaras go further: even in the Council of Pāṭaliputra they had refused to acknowledge the authenticity of the then compiled eleven Aṅgas. And the Śvetāmbaras tell us that even within this compilation disorder crept in and it had to be centrally re-edited in the Council at Valabhī; and our present Aṅgas represent the text as fixed in this second council which took place a

[1] Cf. Charpentier—Uttarādhy. pp. 14-15 who rejects this tradition.

[2] Charpentier does not regard the recovery of the Dṛṣṭivāda as impossible!

little less than a thousand years after the death of Mahāvīra. All these texts should, therefore, be considered late, except such as can on internal grounds prove their earliness in whole or in part.[3] That in spite of having sprawled over a millennium of literary activity the Jaina canon should still preserve many genuinely early fragments is in itself a marvellous tribute to the conservatism of the Jainas, which, however, must not be strained too far, as Jacobi, for instance, does when he observes that "Der Grund für die Conservirung der alten Lehre scheint mir der zu sein, dass ihre Ideen und Termini mit denen der späteren Philosophie incommensurabel waren, also von letzterer nicht beeinflüst werden konnten. Sie waren gewisser-massen versteinert und wurden in den Zustand von Generation zu Generation unverändert überliefert."[4] The danger in holding such a view too rigidly is that we might consider as early many doctrines which really represent later developments.

A brief consideration of the present Śvetāmbara-siddhānta reveals that only a few works can be regarded with some certainty as "ancient" i.e., going back, in substance at least, to the age of Mahāvīra.

The Painnas.—The Paiṇṇas, as their title indicates, are miscellaneous pieces and their list is in reality "quite indefinite".[5] Of the Cheya suttas, according to Winternitz, only the Kappa, with its supplement—the Vavhāra—and the Āyāradasāo can be considered "early".[6] The

[3] Charpentier concludes "I do not doubt that the principal sacred scriptures represent even in their present shape the actual canon fixed at the Council of Pāṭaliputra". (op. cit. p. 31). He seems to proceed throughout on the assumption that a text, if not proved to be late, should be considered early. In view of the history of the Jaina canon, this rule ought to be reversed.

[4] ZDMG. 38 p. 18.

[5] Winternitz, II. p. 461.

[6] Ib. p. 462; 464-465.

Kalpasūtra of Bhadrabāhu, which forms the eighth section of the Āyāradasāo, is, however, a composite work, and one of its most interesting sections—that dealing with Mahāvīra's biography—cannot be regarded very early because of its style.[7] Of the twelve Uvaṅgas only the first two perhaps contain some early material, the rest being "systematic" and exaggerated dogmatic, "scientific" and mythological treatises. Of the first two Uvaṅgas the Rāyapaseṇaïjja, in particular, seems to be based on an old tradition, since the Pāyāsi sutta in the DN is either an adaptation of it or draws on the same source.

The Angas.—The Aṅgas have in their present shape a mosaic appearance, so that a unity of authorship or that of the age of composition can hardly be predicated of any one of them in its entirety. Some of them are almost wholly of a mythological and legendary content. Such are the Nāyādhaṃmakahāo, the Aṃtagaḍadasāo, the Aṇuttarovavāïyadasāo and the Vivāgasuyaṃ. Any absolute or relative chronological specifications about these are possible only on criteria and evidence drawn from literary and mythological history rather than from the history of philosophic religious thought which alone is of paramount interest in the present inquiry. It may be noticed, however, that of the Aṃtagaḍadasāo and the Aṇuttarovavāïya "the original contents were totally different from the present contents."[8] The tenth Aṅga also appears to be a "later work" which "took the place of the old Aṅga which had got lost."[9] Nor is it possible

[7] Ib. pp. 462-463. The fact that it describes the "transfer of the embryo", which is disbelieved by the Digambaras, shows that it cannot antedate the schism between the two schools by much.

[8] Winternitz, II. p. 450.

[9] Ib. p. 452. Cf. Charpentier, Uttarādhy Intr. pp. 26-27.

to regard the fourth Aṅga as early since it enumerates the eighteen varieties of the Brāhmī and the thirty-six chapters of the Uttarādhyayana,[10] it even refers to the Nandī.[11] The fifth Aṅga too in its present shape cannot be much earlier since some parts of it assume a very developed and exhaustively "systematic" doctrine[12] and the text refers at many places to such works as the Pannavaṇā, the Jīvābhigama and the Nandī. It is possible, however, that many of its dialogues and narratives, which at places approach the Nikāyas in style belong to the very earliest parts of the canon.[13] The third Aṅga resembles the Aṅguttara in form, but is much more schematized. The sprinkling of genuine-looking dialogues is slight and a precise and developed doctrine is assumed. At one place a list of official titles occurs which seems to indicate an administrative system which is, to say the least, post-Mauryan.[14]

The Earliest Texts.—The works that are, then, left over as early are the Āyāraṃga, where the second book appears to consist of appendices and is late;[15] the Sūyagaḍaṃga, where too the second book is comparatively late,[16] parts of the Uvāsagadasāo, such as Chapter VII[17] and the Uttarajjhayaṇa, where the first twenty-three chapters appear to contain, in general, an earlier stratum

---

[10] Cf. Charpentier op. cit. p. 41.

[11] Winternitz, II. p. 442.

[12] This stage of complexity in idea and expression may be compared to that in the Abhidharma.

[13] Cf. Winternitz, II. p. 443-444.

[14] Sūtra 693.

[15] See Winternitz, II. p. 437.

[16] Winternitz, II. p. 438.

[17] Ib. p. 449.

than the chapters which follow.[18] Linguistic investigation points to a similar conclusion about these texts. According to Pischel "Der sprachlich für die Prosa weitaus wichtigste Text ist das erste Aṅga, das Āyāraṅgasutta, das unter allen die altertümlichste Sprache hat. Nach ihm kommt besonders das zweite Aṅga in Betracht, das Suyagaḍaṅgasutta, dessen erstes, vorwiegend metrisches Buch für die poetiche Sprache ist, was das Āyār, für die Prosa........Uttarajjhayaṇasutta, das eine Fülle altertümlicher und eigenartiger Formen enthält ...."[19] Ideological simplicity is a further factor which unifies these texts. As Charpentier observes "The really old texts of the Jaina canon, e.g., the Ācārāṅga, the Sūtrakṛtāṅga, and our text*—seldom give real theological or philosophical explanations in the style of the later—mostly prose—parts of the canon."[20]

References in the Nikayas and their Value.—The Nikāyan references to the early Nigaṇṭhas serve the invaluable function of providing independent evidence about early Jaina belief and practice. Since the composition of the greater part of the Nikāyas was, in all probability, completed by the time of Aśoka, this evidence too should be, in general, supposed to yield a picture comparable to that given by the earliest stratum of texts in the extant Jinist canon.

The Texts.—Jacobi has already discussed[21] the information supplied about the Nigaṇṭhas by the following Buddhist texts: Mahāvagga VI. 31; MN.—the Upāli Sutta; AN. III. 70; and DN.—the Sāmaññaphala Sutta.

[18] Charpentier—Uttarādhy. Intr., p. 39.

[19] Grammatik, p. 18.

[20] Op. cit., p. 37; cf. also the opinion of P. L. Vaidya on the antiquity of the Āyāraṅga and the Ovavāiya. (Uvāsagadasāo, p. X).

[21] SBE. 45, pp. XV-XX. Cf. Muni Nagraj, op. cit. *Uttarādhyayana°.

To these a few more references may be added: MN.—the Kandaraka Sutta which classes the Nigaṇṭhas among the Attantapa Puggalas; the Cūladukkhakkhandha—and the Deva-daha-suttas which present a summary and a critique of some leading Nigaṇṭha doctrines; AN. I, pp. 220-221 where the Licchavi Abhaya summarizes the Nigaṇṭha doctrine in much the same way as in MN. Sutta 14 above; AN. I, p. 206 which describes maliciously the "Nigaṇṭhūposatha"; AN. IV 179ff where Nātaputta dissuades Sīha from going to Buddha because the latter was an "Akiriyavāda"; AN. IV. 429 where Nātaputta is reported to have asserted: "aham antavantena ñāṇena antavantaṃ lokaṃ jānaṃ passaṃ viharāmīti", but which appears to contain some confusion since it makes Pūraṇa Kassapa also advance the claim of omniscience which is elsewhere usually associated with the Nigaṇṭha leader alone; SN. I. 66 where a Devaputta utters a *gāthā* on behalf of the doctrine of Nātaputta; SN. I. 78 where the Nigaṇṭhas are apparently distinguished from the Jaṭilas, the Acelas and the Ekasāṭakas; SN. IV. 298 where Nātaputta rejects the possibility of "avitakko avicāro samādhi" as advocated by Gotama, and declares knowledge superior to faith; SN. IV. 317-18 where a Nigaṇṭha-sāvaka summarizes the teaching of Nātaputta to Buddha as "yo koci pāṇaṃ atimāpeti sabbo so apāyiko nerayiko......adinnaṃ ādiyati....kāmesu micchā carati......musā bhaṇati......yam bahulaṃ yaṃ bahulaṃ viharati tena niyyātīti" which is then criticized.

Beside these, there are at some other places references of an indirect character. In the Mahāsīhanādasutta (MN.), for example, the description of the fourfold Brahmacariya is in spirit closely reminiscent of Jaina practice. The *gāthā* that occurs in the context, "so tatto so sīno eko bhiṃsanke vane| Naggo na caggimāsīno esanāpasuto munīti||"[22] might have been taken from a Jaina work. The Abhayarājakumāra sutta (MN.) and SN. IV. 323-25 show Nātaputta as attempting to confound Buddha by propounding clever dilemmas. The ten Nijjaravatthus in AN. V. 215 appear to be Buddhist contents poured into a borrowed framework. The definition of Niddaso Bhikkhu in AN. IV. 35 ff. "yo hi koci dvādasavassāni paripuṇṇam parisuddhaṃ brahmacariyaṃ carati"—which is criticised by Buddha, is reminiscent of the importance which the Jainas attached to twelve years of penance.

APPENDIX II. ON THE HOME OF PALI

In the commentaries the word "Pali" frequently means a "canonical text".[1] It has even been suggested that the word has been ultimately derived from "Dhammapaliyāyo" through the intermediate stages of °Pāliyāyo-Pāli.[2] As to the language of the "Pali-canon", the commentaries tell us that it is Māgadhī. Now Aśokan Māgadhī shows at least two of the three distinctive features of "literary" Māgadhī[3] viz., nominatives in *e* in place of *o*, and the use of *l* in place of *r*.[4] Both of these "Māgadhisms" are absent in canonical Pali except at a few places.[5] It is clear, thus, that the present Pali canon cannot be considered linguistically identical with the

[22] MN. I. p. 79.

[1] Dhs. A, 157, 168; Dhp. A, IV. 93. The word 'Pali' is found only in the commentaries, not in the Piṭakas (PTSD).

[2] J. Kashyap: Pāli Mahāvyākaraṇa—pp. Nine-Eleven.

[3] Grammatik. p. 23.

[4] e.g., see the Dhauli version of the First Separate Rock Edict (Sircar—Select Ins. I. pp. 41 ff), or the Barabar Hill cave Inscriptions of Aśoka (Ib. pp. 78-79).

canon said to have been compiled at Pāṭaliputra in the reign of Aśoka.

As to the basic dialect of Pali, scholars have advanced a number of conflicting identifications,[6] and though the controversy has been reviewed more than once[7] few definitive results have been achieved.

Now Dr. Barua has proved after a careful examination of the evidence that the sound-system and grammatical forms of the language of the Girnar version of Aśoka's Rock Edicts are strikingly similar to those of Pali.[8] Further, that judged by the sound-system and syntax, the language of the old Brāhmī inscriptions in the Khaṇḍagiri and Udayagiri caves is very nearly Pali.[9] This suggests that Pali represents the literary development of some Central Indian dialect. This conclusion accords very well with the traditional account of the introduction of Buddhism into Ceylon, which, we are told, was the work of Mahinda during the reign of Aśoka.[10] It may be remembered that Mahinda is supposed to have come to Ceylon from the region of Ujjenī and the west coast.[11]

---

[5] Such as in the course of DN. 2 (Sāmaññaphala°) or Kv. 1 (Puggalakathā).

[6] See Lévi—JA. 1912, s. 10, t. XX, p. 495ff; Konow—ZDMG. 1910, pp. 114ff; Grierson—Bhand. Comm. Vol. pp. 117ff; N. Dutt—Early History of the Spread of Buddhism—p. 249ff; S. K. Chatterji—Origin ard Development of the Bengali Language, I. 55ff; Oldenberg V. P. I. Intr. 1ff; PTSD—Foreword; Geiger—Pali Literatur und Sprache—pp. 1-5; Bapat. I.H.Q. 1928, 23ff; Keith. I.H.Q. 1925, 501ff; Mrs. Rhys Davids—Sakya p. 429ff.

[7] e.g., by Keith in Buddhist Studies (Law); Winternitz—Ind. Lit. II. App. II.

[8] Barua—OBI. pp. 161ff.

[9] Ib. pp. 157ff.

[10] Mahāvaṃsa p. 48.

[11] Mahāvaṃsa Chap. XIII; Malalasekara, DPPN. II. 583.

APPENDIX III. ON THE MAITRĀYAṆĪYOPANIṢAD

The Maitrāyaṇīya Upaniṣad has not been utilized in this sketch because it is extremely improbable that it should be pre-Buddhistic. The following arguments may be adduced for its lateness: (*a*) It draws at some places clearly and literally from older Upaniṣads:—2.2. (agrees literally with Ch. 8.3.4); 2.6. "yadidamadyate ......Śṛṇoti" (=Bṛ.5.9.1); 2.6—"manomayaḥ prāṇaśarīro bhārūpaḥ satyasaṅkalpaḥ....." (Ch.3.14.2); 6.3 "dve vāva Brahmaṇo rūpe mūrtaṃ caivāmūrtaṃca" (=Bṛ.3.1); 6.32—"etasya mahato bhūtasya etc." (Bṛ.2.4.10); 7.9 "three verses which repeat Kaṭh 1.2.4, Īśa.11 and Kaṭh 1.2.5 respectively.

(*b*) Its diction is generally well developed, and at one place it "reads like a passage from the Kādambarī" (Creative Period p. 127). Its verses are generally reminiscent of the Mbh.

(*c*) It indicates a developed knowledge of Sāṅkhya and Yoga using a large number of technical terms never or rarely found in the older Upaniṣads—"Kṣetrajñaḥ saṅkalpādhyavasāyābhimānaliṅgaḥ" (2.5.5.2); Buddhīndriya and Karmendriya (2.6); Sitāsita-karmaphala (2.7); "Prekṣakavadavasthitaḥ" (Ib); Prākṛtaguṇas (3.2); "guṇairhanyamānaḥ" (3.3); Rajas and Sattva (5.2); Puruṣa, Pradhāna, Triguṇa, Prakṛti, "mahadādyaṃ viśeṣāntaṃ liṅgam", "Sukhaduḥkhamohasañjñam", Vyakta, Avyakta (6.10); "Prāṇāyāmaḥ pratyāhāro dhyānaṃ dhāraṇā tarkaḥ samādhiḥ ṣaḍaṅga ityucyate yogaḥ ...." (6.18); "nāḍī suṣumṇākhyā" (6.21); Cittavṛtti (6.34.1).

(*d*) It shows its knowledge of Buddhism by the following passages "eṣa śuddhaḥ pūtaḥ *śūnyaḥ śāntaḥ nirātmā*. . . . (2.4); "tadātmanātmānaṃ dṛṣṭvā *nirātmā* bhavati nirātmakatvādasaṅkhyaḥ. . . ." (6.20); "tato *nirātmakatvameti* nirātmakatvānna sukhaduḥkhabhāgbhavati. . . ." (6.21); "*śūnyaḥ śāntādilakṣaṇaḥ*" (6.31); "*Nairātmyavādakuhakairmithyādṛṣṭāntahetubhiḥ* Bhrāmyaṃ loko na jānāti vedavidyāntaraṃ tu yat" (7.8).

ABBREVIATIONS AND BIBLIOGRAPHY

NOTE: (1) Only those works are mentioned below which have been directly referred to in the preceding pages.

(2) In case different editions of the same work are used, the difference is indicated either by a difference in abbreviation or by specification otherwise.

(3) In the following list authors and books are arranged according to the alphabetical order of the *abbreviations* used.

AB .. Aitareya-Brāhmaṇa (Ānandāśrama Sanskrit Series).

Abhidhammatthasaṅgaho with the Navanīta Ṭīkā of D. Kosambi.

Ab. K. .. L'Abhidharmakośa De Vasubandhu (traduit et annoté par Louis de la Vallée Poussin. 1923—1925).

ABORI .. Annals of the Bhandarkar Oriental Research Institute.

Agarwal, V. S., India as Known to Pāṇini, Lucknow, 1953.

Ait. A. .. Aitareya-Āraṇyaka (Ānandāśrama Sanskrit Series, 1943).

Ait. .. Aitareya-Upaniṣad. (As in Aṣṭāviṃśatyupaniṣadaḥ, ed. Wāsudev Laxman Śāstrī Paṇsikar, 7th ed. Bombay, 1930).

Ak. V. .. Abhidharmakośavyākhyā of Yaśomitra. Vols. I-III. Ed. N. N. Law. (1949).

Allchin, Bridget & Raynard, The Birth of Indian Civilization (Penguin, 1968).

Aṃtagadadasāo (Ed. Āgamodayasamiti).

AN .. Aṅguttara-Nikāya (Ed. Pali Text Society).

Aṇuttarovavāiyadasāo (Ed. Āgamodayasamiti).

AO .. Acta Orientalia.

Ap. .. Apastamba-Dharma-Sūtra, ed. G. Bühler, 2nd ed.

Ars. Up. .. Ārṣeyopaniṣad. (See below, Four Unpub. Up.)

Arthaśāstra .. Kauṭilya's Arthaśāstra (TSS edition).

Āryamañjuśrīmūlakalpa—Edited in TSS (q.v.).

ĀŚ .. Āgamaśāstra of Gauḍapāda (edited, translated & annotated by Vidhushekhara Bhattacharya, 1943).

As. .. Āyāraṃgasutta I (edited W. S. Schubring).

AS .. Atharvavedasaṃhitā (Svādhyāyamaṇḍala, Aundh, 1938).

Ātmatattvaviveka (Chowkhamba edition).

Aṭṭhasālinī (Edition in Nāgarī Characters by P. V. Bapat and R. D. Vadekar, 1942).

AUS .. Āgamodayasamiti.

Āyāraṃgasutta, Śīlāṅka's Commentary (Calcutta, 1879).

Aveling, F., Personality & Will (Cambridge, 1931).

B. .. Bhagavatī Viyāhapannatti, with the commentary of Abhayadeva (Edited by the AUS).

Baladeva Upadhyaya, Bauddhadarśana (Hindi).

Bandyopadhyaya, N. C. Economic Life and Progress in Ancient India I (Calcutta, 1945).

Barua, Pre-Buddhistic B. M. Barua, History of Pre-Buddhistic Indian Philosophy (Calcutta, 1921).

Bareau, A., Les Sectes Bouddhiques du Petit Vehicule, Saigon, 1955

Barua, B. M., Old Brahmi Inscriptions in the Udayagiri and Khandagiri caves (Calcutta, 1929).

Bhattacharya, Vidhushekhar—Pali Prakasa.

—Basic Conception of Buddhism. (Calcutta University Press).

Bāṣkala Up. .. Baṣkalopaniṣad (See below, Four Unpub. Up.).

Baud. .. Baudhāyana-Dharmasūtra, ed. L. Srinivasacharya, Mysore, 1907.

Beal, S. Catena .. A Catena of Buddhist Scriptures.

—Romantic Legend of Śākya Buddha (London, 1875).

Belvalkar, S. K., Sri Gopal Basu Mallik Lectures on Vedanta.

BG .. Bhagavadgītā.

Bhandarkar, D. R., Asoka (2nd edition).

—Lectures on Ancient Indian Numismatics.

Bhand. Comm. Vol. .. Bhandarkar Commemoration Volume.

Bhandarkar, R. G., Collected Works Vol. VI.

Bhāratīya Anuśīlana .. (Mm. G. H. Ojha Comm. Vol.).

B. I. .. Bibliotheca Indica.

Bigandet, Life or Legend of Gautama, the Buddha of the Burmese. (London, 1880).

B. L'Ec. Fr. .. Bulletin de l'école française d'Extrême Orient.

Bodhicaryāvatāra (B. I. edition).

Bose, Atindranath, Social and Rural Economy of Northern India. Vol. I (Calcutta, 1942); Vol. II (Calcutta, 1945).

BPE .. Buddhist Psychological Ethics (translation of Dhs. by Mrs. Rhys Davids, 1900).

Br. .. Bṛhadāraṇyaka-Upaniṣad. (see above, Ait.).

Brewster, E. H., The Life of Gotama, the Buddha (Kegan Paul).

Bloomfield, R. V. .. Bloomfield, M. The Religion of the Veda (New York, 1908).

BS .. Brahmasūtras (Nirṇayasāgara edition, with Śankara's Comy., Ratnaprabhā, Bhāmatī etc.).

Buddh. Car. .. The Buddhacarita of Aśvaghoṣa. Ed. E. B. Cowell, Oxford, 1893).

Buddhavaṃsa (PTS edition).

Buddhistic Studies (Edited by Dr. B. C. Law) 1931.

Buddh. Ind. .. Rhys Davids, T. W., Buddhist India (London, 1911).

Burnet, J., Early Greek Philosophy (2nd Edition).

Burnet, J., Greek Philosophy, Thales to Plato, 1943.

Burnouf .. Burnouf, E., Introduction à l'histoire du Bouddhisme Indien (Paris, 1876).

Bury, J. B., History of Greece, London, 1906.

Bu-ston .. Bu-ston—History of Buddhism Pts. I-II, tr. E. Obermiller, 1931-32.

CAH .. Cambridge Ancient History.

Carakasaṃhitā (Ed. Haridatta Śāstrī, 2nd edition, Lahore, 1940).

Carpenter, J. E., The Bible in the Nineteenth Century (1903).

Ch. .. Chāndogyopaniṣad (See above, Ait.).

Chag. Up. .. Chāgaleyopaniṣad. (See below, Four Unpub. Up.).

Conze, E., Buddhist Thought in India, London, 1962.

Chanda, R. P., Indo-Aryan Races. (1916).

Charpentier, Uttarādhya Charpentier, J., Uttarādhyayana Sūtra, Uppsala, 1922.

Chatterji, S. K., The Origin & Development of the Bengali Language, 1926.

C. H. I. .. Cambridge History of India.

C. I. I. .. Corpus Inscriptionum Indicarum.

Comm. Vol. .. Commemoration volume.

Compendium .. Compendium of Buddhist Philosophy (P.T.S. translation of Abhidhammatthasaṅgaho).

Conze, E., Buddhist Texts, (Oxford, 1954).

Cook, Zeus. Cambridge, 1914.

Coomarswamy, A. K., Living Thoughts of Gotama, the Buddha.
—Hinduism and Buddhism.
—Yakṣas Pt. I and II.

Cornford, F. M. From Religion to Philosophy.

Coster, G., Yoga and Western Psychology. (Oxford University Press).

Creative Period .. Belvalkar, S. K., and Ranade, R. D., The Creative Period of Indian Philosophy.

CSUP .. Ranade, R. D., Constructive Survey of Upanishadic Philosophy, 1926.

Cv. .. Cullavagga.

DN .. Dīgha-Nikāya (PTS edition; else, the edition is specified).

DN (Nāg. ed.) .. Dīgha-Nikāya (Pts. I & II) ed. by N. K. Bhagwat in Nāgari Characters. (First Edition).

DA .. Dīrghāgama.

Dasgupta .. Dasgupta, S. N., History of Indian Philosophy I.

Debates Commentary, PTS Translation of KV. A. (q.v.).

Deussen, PU .. Deussen P., The Philosophy of the Upaniṣads (English tr. of the Original German, 1919).

Dhp. .. Dhammapada (for the edition, see under Ud.).

Dhp. A. .. Dhammapadaṭṭhakathā (PTS edition).

Dhs. .. Dhammasaṅgaṇi (ed. Bapat and Vadekar, Poona, 1940).

Dhs. A. .. Dhammasaṅgaṇi-Aṭṭhakathā (P T S edition).

Dh. Sū. .. Dharmasūtra.

Dialogues .. Dialogues of The Buddha, tr. (of DN) by T. W. Rhys Davids and Mrs. Rhys Davids.

Dīpavaṃsa (ed. Oldenberg, London, 1879).

Divakar, R. R., Mahayogi.

Divyāv. .. Divyāvadāna (ed. Cowell and Neil).

DPPN .. Malalasekara, Dictionary of Pali Proper Names.

Dutt, Aspects .. N. Dutt, Aspects of Mahāyāna Buddhism and its Relation to Hīnayāna.

Dube, S. N., Doctrinal Controversies in Early Buddhism. (unpublished).

Dutt, S. K. .. Early Buddhist Monachism.

EA .. Ekottarāgama.

EMB .. Early Monastic Buddhism by N. Dutt (Vol. I, 1941; Vol. II, 1945).

ERE .. Encyclopaedia of Religion and Ethics.

Etudes .. P. L. Vaidya, Etudes sur Aryadeva et son catuḥśataka (Paris, 1923).

Fick, Die soziale Gliederung R. Fick, Die soziale Gliederung im nordostlichen Indien zu Buddhas Zeit, 1897.

Field, G. C., Plato and His Contemporaries.

Four Unpub. Up. .. Four Unpublished Upanishads, ed. Belvalkar, S. K., 1924.

Frauwallner, E., The Earliest Vinaya and the Beginnings of Buddhist Literature, Rome, 1956.

u-Lan, History of Chinese Philosophy I.

.. Gautama Dharma Sūtra (Ānandāśrama Ed., 1910).

Garbe, R. .. Die Sankhya Philosophie (Leipzig, 1894).

Geiger, W., Pali Literature and Language. (tr. Baṭakrishna Ghosh) —Pali Literature and Brahman.

Ghurye, G. S., Caste and Race in India.

G. Jha Comm. Vol. .. MM. Gaṅgānātha Jha Commemoration Volume.

Gilgit Mss. .. Gilgit Manuscripts Vol. III, Ed. N. Dutt.

Glasenapp, H., The Doctrine of Karman in Jaina Philosophy. (tr. from German).

Gore, C., Jesus of Nazareth (H.U.L.).

Gurwitch & Moore, Twentieth Century Sociology.

Hardayal, The Bodhisattva Doctrine (Kegan Paul, 1932).

Hardy, E., Indische Religionsgeschichte (Leipzig, 1898).

Hardy, G. H., Pure Mathematics (7th ed.).

Hauer, Die Anfänge .. Hauer, J. W., Die Anfänge der Yoga-praxis (1922).

Hegel, Logic (tr. Wallace).
—History of Philosophy (tr. E. S. Haldane).

Herzberg, The Psychology of Philosophers.

Hobson, The Theory of Functions of a Real Variable (1921).

H. O. S. .. Harward Oriental Series.

H. U. L. .. Home University Library.

Hutton, J. H., Caste in India (2nd edition 1951).

IA .. Indian Antiquary.

IC .. Indian Culture.

I. H. Q. .. Indian Historical Quarterly.

Ind. Phil. Cong. .. Indian Philosophical Congress.

Int. Cong. Or. .. International Congress of Orientalists.

Īśa. .. Īśopaniṣad (See above, Ait.).

Īśvarapratyabhijñāvimarśinī (Kashmir Series of Texts & Studies).

It. .. Itivuttaka (for the edition utilized see remarks under Ud.).

Jacobi, Die Entwicklung .. Jacobi H., Die Entwicklung der Gottesidee bei den Indern.

Jat. .. Jātakaṭṭhavaṇṇā, edited by Fausböll.

JA .. Journal Asiatique.

Jain, Jagdish Chandra Life in Ancient India as Depicted in the Jain Canons (1947).

Jaina Sūtras I, II .. S. B. E. Vol. 22 and 45.

Jaini, J. L., Outlines of Jainism, Cambridge, 1916.

James, W., Varieties of Religious Experience.

JAOS .. Journal of the American Oriental Society.

Jayaswal, K. P., Hindu Polity, Calcutta, 1924.

JBBRAS .. Journal of the Bombay Branch of the Royal Asiatic Society.

Jayatilleke, K. N., Early Buddhist Theory of Knowledge, London, 1963.

Jinanand, B., Abhisamâcârikā, Patna. 1969.

JDL .. Journal of the Department of Letters.

JGRI .. Journal of the Gaṅgānātha Jha Research Institute.

Jolly, J., Hindu Law and Custom, Calcutta, 1928.

JPTS .. Journal of the Pali Text Society.

JRAS .. Journal of the Royal Asiatic Society.

JRASB .. Journal of the Royal Asiatic Society of Bengal.

Kalpasūtra, Published, Maphat Lal, 1942.

Kalyāṇa, Yogāṅka.

Kane .. Kane, P. V., History of the Dharma-Śāstra.

Karsten, The Origins of Religion, London, 1935.

Kashyap, J., The Philosophy of Abhidhamma, 2 Vols.

Kath. .. Kaṭhopaniṣad (See above, Ait.).

Śrī Śrī Rāmakṛṣṇakathāmṛta, Śrī-Ma-Kathita, 14th edition.

Kāṭh. S. .. Kāṭhaka-Saṃhitā (Pub. Svādhyāya-Maṇḍala, Aundh).

Kāt. Śraut S. .. Kātyāyana Śrauta Sūtra (Açyuta-granthamālā).

Kaus. .. Kauṣītakibrāhmaṇopaniṣad (See above, Ait.).

Kena. .. Kenopaniṣad (See above, Ait.).

Kern, J. H. C., L'Histoire du Bouddhisme dans l'Inde. (French tr. of the original Dutch, Paris, 1901-3).

Kern, Manual .. Kern, J. H. C., Manual of Buddhism, Strassburg, 1896.

Kh. N. .. Khuddaka Nikāya.

Kh. .. Khandha.

Kimura, R., A Historical study of the Terms Hīnayāna & Mahāyāna and the Origin of Mahāyāna Buddhism. (Calcutta, 1927).

Keith, R. P. V. .. Keith A. B., Religion and Philosophy of the Veda (H. O. S.) 1925.

—B. P. .. Buddhist Philosophy (1923).

KS .. The Book of Kindred Sayings (tr. of SN by Mrs. Rhys Davids and F. L. Woodward).

Kv. .. Kathāvatthu (PTS. edition).

Kv. A. .. Kathāvatthu-aṭṭhakathā (edited in JPTS 1889).

KZ .. Kuhn's Zeitschrift.

Lamotte, E., Histoire du Bouddhisme Indien des origines, al' ere Saka, Louvain, 1958.

LV .. Lalitavistara I (Ed. Lefmann, 1902).

Laṅkāvatāra .. The Laṅkāvatāra Sūtra, Ed. B. Nanjio, .. Kyoto, 1923.

La Vallée Poussin, Dogme .. Louis de la Vallée Poussin, Le dogme et la philosophie du Bouddhisme (Paris, 1930).

Opinions .. Bouddhisme : Opinions sur l'histoire de la dogmatique, 4th ed.
—L'Inde jusqu'au 300 avant J.C.

Law, B. C., India as Described in Early Texts of Buddhism and Jainism, London, 1941.—History of Pali Literature.

Lawrence, Brother, Practice of the Presence of God. (Pub. Samuel Bagster & Sons, Ltd.).

Leumann, E., Das Aupapātika Sūtra, Leipzig, 1883.

Lutoslawski, Plato's Logic.

MA .. Madhyamāgam.

Macculoch, The Religion of the Ancient Celts.

Macdonell, A. A., Vedic Reader.

Macdonell, V. M., Macdonell, A. A., Vedic Mythology.

Mackay, E. J. H., The Indus Civilization. (London, 1935).

Mahabodhi Journal.

Mahābhāṣya (ed. Kielhorn).

Mahāyānaviṃśaka (Nāgārjuna) Ed. MM. V. Bhattacharya.

Mahāvaṃsa (PTS edition).

Mait. S. .. Maitrāyaṇī Saṃhitā (Svādhyāya-maṇḍala, Aundh).

Maitrāyaṇīyāraṇ .. Maitrāyaṇīyāraṇyaka (Pub. along with the above).

Majumdar, R. C., Corporate Life in Ancient India.

Majumdar, R. C. (ed.)The Vedic Age.

Māṇḍ. .. Māṇḍūkyopaniṣad. (See above, Ait.).

Manorathapūraṇī (PTS edition).

Manu—Mānavadharmaśāstra.

Marin-Sola, L'Evolution homogène du Dogme Catholique I & II (Deuxieme Edition, 1924).

Marshall, MIC .. Marshall, Mohenjodaro & the Indus Civilization.

Marx, K., Capital I (tr. Moore and Aveling, Allen & Unwin, 1949).

Masson-Oursel, P., L'Esquisse d'une Histoire de la Philosophie Indienne.

Masuda, J., Origin & Doctrines of Early Indian Buddhist Schools.

Mbh. ŚP. .. Mahābhārata, Śānti Parvan (Chitrashala Press, Poona).

Mclure—The Early Philosophers of Greece.

Mehta, R. L., Pre-Buddhist India.

Mem. A. S. B. .. Memoir of the Asiatic Society of Bengal.

Minayeff, Recherches Minayeff J. P., Recherches sur le Bouddhisme (Paris, 1894).

Misra, G. S. P., The Age of Vinaya (Delhi, 1972).

Mitra, P. I. .. Mitra, P., Pre-historic India (Calcutta, 1927).

MK .. Mādhyamika Kārikās of Nāgārjuna.

MKV .. Mūlamadhyamaka-kārikās de Nāgārjuna avec la Prasannapadā (Ed. L. de Vallée Poussin).

MK. V. (Cal. ed.) .. Madhyamikā Vṛtti of Chandrakīrti (Calcutta, 1894).

Mm. .. Mahāmahopādhyāya.

MN .. Majjhima-Nikāya (PTS edition, else the edition is specified).

MN (Nag. ed.) .. Majjhima-Nikāya Pt. I-II Ed. in Devanāgarī by N. K. Bhagwat, Bombay, 1937-8.

MP .. Milindapañho (Ed. R. D. Vādekar in Devanāgarī Characters, Bombay, 1940).

MP (Trenckner) .. Milindapañho, Ed. Trenckner, 1928.

MSA .. Mahāyānasūtrālaṅkāra (ed. by S. Lévi)

Müller, F. Max—Hibbert Lectures.

Muṇḍ. .. Muṇḍakopaniṣad. (See above, Ait.).

Murray, Gilbert—Five Stages of Greek Religion.

Mvg. .. Mahāvagga.

Mvu. .. Mahāvastu, edited by E. Senart, Paris.

Nāg. ed. .. Edition in Nāgarī Characters.

Nairatmyapariprccha .. JA 1928; edited separately also by Sujitkumar Mukerji.

Nanjio, Catalogue .. Nanjio, Bunyiu, Catalogue of the Chinese Translation of the Buddhist Tripiṭaka, Oxford, 1883.

Nagraj, Muni, Āgama Aur Tripiṭak, Ek Anuśīlan, Calcutta, 1969.

Nāyā .. Nāyādhammakahāo (AUS edition).

Newman .. John Henry Cardinal Newman, An Essay on the Development of Christian Doctrine (1894).

Nip. .. Nipāta.

Nirukta of Yāska (With Durgācharya's Comy.) 2 Vols.

Nyāyabhāṣya, Chowkhamba edition.

Nyāyavārtika, Chowkhamba edition.

Nyāyamañjarī, Vizianagram edition.

OC .. All India Oriental Conference.

Oldenberg, Buddha .. Oldenberg, H., Buddha, sein Leben seine Lehre, seine Gemeinde (9th German edition).

—LU .. Die Lehre der Upanishaden und die Anfänge des Buddhismus. (Göttingen, 1915).

—RV .. Die Religion des Veda (7th edition).

—WB .. Die Weltanschauung der Brāhmaṇa —texte. (Göttingen, 1919).

Pa-Chow, W., Comparative Studies in the Mahāparinibbānasutta and its Chinese Versions. (Shantiniketan, 1946).

Pañcadaśī (Bombay, 1935).

Pande, G. C., Bauddha Dharma Ke Vikas Ka Itihas (Lucknow 1963).

—, Meaning and Process of Culture (Agra, 1972).

Paṇhāvāgaraṇa (AUS edition).

Pannavaṇā (AUS edition).

Papañcasūdanī (PTS edition).

Paṭiccasam—Paṭiccasamuppāda.

Paṭisambhidāmagga (PTS edition).

Petavatthu (For the edition see under Ud.).

Piggott—Pre-historic India.

Pischel—Grammatik .. Pischel, R., Grammatik der Prakrit Sprachen. (Strassburg, 1900).

Plotinus, Select Works of, (tr. T. Taylor, Ed. G. R. S. Mead, 1912).

Praśna .. Praśnopaniṣad. (See above, Ait.).

Pratt, J. B., The Religious Consciousness, 1945.

Pratyabhijñāhṛdaya, Ed. J. C. Chatterji.

Pravāsī, Bengali Journal

Prav. sa. .. Pravacanasāra (Rāyacandraśāstramālā).

PTS .. Pali Text Society.

PTSD .. Pali Dictionary of the Pali Text Society, edited by T. W. Rhys Davids and W. Stede.

Puggalapaññatti, PTS edition.

Points of Controversy PTS Translation of Kv.

PV. .. Pramāṇavārtika (ed. with Manorathanadin's Comy. by Rahula Sankrtyayana in JBORS, 1938).

Radhakrishnan, IP .. Radhakrishnan, S., History of Indian Philosophy.

Radhakrishnan, S., (Editor) History of Philosophy, Eastern and Western.

Rāyapaseṇaijja, AUS edition.

Raychaudhuri, P H A I Raychaudhuri H. C., Political History of Ancient India (ed. 5th).

Rhys Davids, T. W., American Lectures.
—Hibbert Lectures.

Rhys Davids, Mrs. Original Gospel .. Mrs. C. A. F. Rhys Davids, What was the Original Gospel in Buddhism?

Ind. Psy. .. The Birth of Indian Psychology and its Development in Buddhism (1936).

Sakya (Kegan Paul, 1931).

Buddhism (HUL) Revised ed.

RPV .. See above, Keith, A.B.

Rhys, John, Hibbert Lectures on the Origin & Growth of Religion as illustrated by Celtic Heathendom.

Rockhill, W. W., The Life of Buddha. (Kegan Paul).

U. Vg. .. Udānavarga, London, 1883.

Rohde, Psyche, Kegan Paul, 1925.

Rosenberg, O. Die Probleme .. Die Probleme der buddhistischen Philosophie, 1924.

Roth, G., Bhikṣuṇi Vinaya, Patna, 1970.

RS .. Ṛgvedasaṃhitā (Svādhyāyamandala, Aundh).

R. S., Sāyaṇa's Comy. (Vedic Samśodhana Mandala, Poona).

s. .. Sutta.

SA .. Saṃyuktāgama.

aw, Ledi, Expositions.

Saddharmapundarīka, Ed. H. Kern and B. Nanjio, (Bibliotheca Buddhica).

Ṣaḍ. B. .. Ṣaḍviṃśa-Brāhmaṇa (Leiden, 1908).

Satkari Mookerji Felicitation Volume, Chowkhamba, 1969.

Ṣingh, M. R., Geographical Data in the Purāṇas, Calcutta, 1972.

Sam. .. Saṃyutta.

Samantapāsādikā, PTS edition.

Samavāyaṅga, AUS edition.

Śāṅ. A. .. Śāṅkhāyana Āraṇyaka (Ānandāśrama ed.).

Śāṅ. B. .. Śāṅkhāyana Brāhmaṇa (Ānandāśrama ed.).

Sāṅkhyapravacanabhāṣya of Vijñānabhikṣu, Chowkhamba ed.

Sāṅkhyasūtras with Aniruddha's comy., Calcutta, 1935.

Sansom, G. B., Japan.

Samtani, N. H., The Arthaviniścaya-Sūtra & its Commentary, Patna, 1971.

SN .. Saṃyutta Nikāya (PTS edition).

Sāratthappakāsinī, PTS edition.

ŚB .. Śatapatha Brāhmaṇa (ed. Acyutagranthamālā).

SBE .. Sacred Books of the East.

Schmidt, The Origin and Growth of Religion. (London, 1931).

Schrader, Über den Stand .. Schrader, O., Über den Stand der Indischen Philosophie zur Zeit Mahaviras und Buddhas (1902).

Siddhi .. Vijñaptimātratāsiddhi, La Siddhi de Hiuan-Tsang, traduite et annotée par L. de la Vallée Poussin (Paris, 1928-29).

Sircar, D. C., Select Inscriptions (Select Ins.) Calcutta, 1942.

Sk. .. Sūtrakṛtāṅga (ed. P. L. Vaidya).

SK .. Sāṅkhyakārikā (See below STK).

Smith, E. H. I. .. Smith V., Early History of India (4th ed.).

Sn. .. Suttanipāta (for the edition, see below Ud.).

Soderblöm, The Living God (Oxford, 1933).

Sogen, Y., Systems of Buddhist Thought (=Systems).

Spengler, O., Der Untergang des Abendlandes, 1922.

Stcherbatsky, Nirvāṇa .. Stcherbatsky, Th., The Conception of Buddhist Nirvāṇa (Leningrad, 1927).

—Central Conception Central Conception of Buddhism and the Meaning of the Word "Dharma". (1923).

—BL .. Buddhist Logic (1932).

STK .. Sāṅkhyatattvakaumudī (Chowkhamba ed.).

Sumaṅgalavilāsinī, PTS edition.

Suzuki .. Suzuki, D. T., Outlines of Mahāyāna Buddhism (1927).

—Studies in the Laṅkāvatārasūtra. (1930).

Śvet. .. Śvetāśvataropaniṣad. (See above, Ait.).

Syādvādamañjarī (Rāyacandraśāstramālā).

Sweezy, Paul M., The Theory of Capitalist Development (1952).

TA .. Taittirīya-Āraṇyaka (Ānandāśrama edition).

Tait. .. Taittirīyopaniṣad. (See above, Ait.).

Tāṇḍ. B. .. Tāṇḍyamahābrāhmaṇa (Chowkhamba edition).

Tal. B. .. Talavakāra Brāhmaṇa.

Tantravārtika (B. I. Eng. tr. by Mm. G. Jha).

Tārānātha .. Tārānātha, Geschichte des Buddhismus in Indien (Übers. Von. Schiefner. St. Petersburg, 1869).

Tattvārtharājavārtika, Sanātana Jaina Granthamālā.

Tattvārthādhigama .. Tattvārthādhigamasūtra of Umāsvāti.

T. B. .. Taittirīya Brāhmaṇa (Ānandāśrama edition).

Ṭhā. .. Ṭhāṇaṃga (AUS edition).

Thag. .. Theragāthā (PTS edition utilized when reference by verse number alone; else, the edition in Nāgarī Characters by Rāhula Sāṅkṛtyāyana, Ananda Kausalyāyana and Jagadīśa Kāśyapa, 1937).

Thig. .. Therigāthā (As above).

Thomas, Life .. Thomas E. J., The Life of Buddha.

—Thought .. The History of Buddhist Thought (Kegan Paul, 1933).

Thomson, G., Aeschylus and Athens. (1940).

TS .. Taittirīya Saṃhitā (Ānandāśrama edition).

Tattvasaṅgraha, Gaekwad's Oriental Series.
TSS .. Trivandrum Sanskrit Series.
Tylor, E. B., Primitive Culture. (1903).
U .. Uttarajjhayaṇa (AUS edition).
Ud. .. Udāna (when referencing is by page number, the edition utilized is that in Nāgarī characters by Rāhula Sāṅkṛtyāyana, Ānanda Kausalyāyana and Jagadīśa Kāśyapa, 1937).
Upadhyaya, K. N., Early Buddhism and the Bhagavadgita (Patna, 1971).
Û. Vg. .. See Rockhill.
Upadeśasāhasrī, Bombay, 1930.
Uvāsaga .. Uvāsagadasāo (Ed. P. L. Vaidya).
Up. .. Upaniṣad.
Vaikhānasadharmapraśna, TSS.
Vas .. Vāsiṣṭha-Dharma-Śāstra. (Ed. A. A. Führer, Poona, 1930).
Vbh. .. Vibhaṅga (*edited by Mrs. Rhys Davids, PTS.* 1904).
Vedāntaparibhāṣā, Haridas Sanskrit Series, Banaras, 1937.
Ved. Sāra .. Vedāntasāra, edited with notes and translation by Hiriyanna.
V. I. .. Macdonell and Keith, Vedic Index.
Vidyabhushana, S. C., A History of Indian Logic (1920).
Vigrahavyāvartanī, JBORS XXIII.
Vijñaptimātratāsiddhi, See above, Siddhi.
Vimānavatthu (For the edition see under Ud.)
VM .. Macdonell A. A., Vedic Mythology.
Vm. .. Visuddhimaggo (Ed. in Nāgari Characters by D. Kosambi).
Vin. .. Vinaya Piṭaka (PTS edition).
Vishva Bharati Quarterly.
Vivāgasuyam, AUS Edition.
Wagle, N., Society at the Time of the Buddha, Bombay, 1966.
Walleser, M. .. Der ältere Vedānta=Geschichte, Kritik und Lehre. (1910).
—Die Sekten .. Die Sekten des alten Buddhismus.
Warder, A. K., Indian Buddhism, Varanasi, 1970.
Wassiljew .. Wassiljew : Der Buddhismus Vol. I. St. Petersburg, 1860.
Welbon, The Buddhist Nirvāṇa and its Western Interpreters, Chicago, 1968.
Wheeler, M., The Indus Civilization (1953).
Winternitz .. Winternitz M., History of Indian Literature (Unless otherwise specified Vol. II is meant). Authorised English translation, 1933.
Waldschmidt, Das Mahāparinirvāṇa sūtra, 1950-51.

WZKM .. Wiener Zeitschrift für die Kunde des Morgenlandes.

Yaj. .. Yājñavalkyasmṛti.

YS .. Yogasūtras (Ed. with the commentaries of Vyāsa, Vācaspati Miśra etc. Chowkhamba S. S., 1935).

Yoga Heute, (ed.). Ursula Von Mangoldt, Otto Wilhelm Barth Verlag, 1971.

ZDMG .. Zeitschrift der Deutschen Morgenländischen Gesellschaft.

Zeller, E., Outlines of the History of Greek Philosophy, 13th Edition, tr. L. R. Palmer. (Kegan Paul, 1931).

ZVS .. Zeitschrift für Vergleichende Sprachforschung.

INDEX

ADDENDA

p. 2, fn. 17a	Nishimoto has attempted a comparative chronology of the different versions of the Vinaya and places them between 100 BC and AD 400 (quoted H. Nakamura, *Indian Buddhism, A Survey with Bibliographical Notes*, p. 51). The dating of the Pali Vinaya around AD 100 is totally unacceptable. Cf. G.S.P. Misra, *The Age of Vinaya.*
p. 4, fn. 19	*Add* 'These texts with comparisons between different versions were published from Berlin in 1950-51, 1953, 1956, 1960.'
p. 8	At the end of the first paragraph, *add* 'The most important text comparable with the Pali *Dhammapada* is the *Gāndhāri Dharmapada,* ed. J. Brough, OUP, 1962.'
p. 9, fn. 41	The objections of Oldenberg and Franke are seen to be misconceived in the light of the hypothesis that the old canonical biography of the Buddha is now found in a dispersed state—see Frauwallner, *op. cit.*, p. 42.
p. 13, fn. 53g	*Add* 'S.N. Dube, *Cross-currents in Early Buddhism* (1980)'.
p. 251, fn. 1	*Add* 'The whole concept of 'Aryan invasion', however, is now under revision—see B.B. Lal and S.P. Gupta, *Frontiers of the Indus Civilisation* (New Delhi, 1984), pp. 430ff, B.K. Thapar, "The Aryans: A Reappraisal of the Problem" in *India's Contribution to World Thought and Culture,* pp. 147ff.'
p. 253, fn. 8	*Add* 'That the Indus civilisation was non-Aryan is no longer so certain as it seemed to Marshall, Wheeler or Piggott, cf. Bhagwan Singh, *Harappa Sabhyata aur Vaidika Sahitya,* 2 Vols. 1987, *Puratattva* 6, pp. 75-76; Lal and Gupta, *op. cit.*, pp. 437-43.'
p. 257, fn. 28	*Add* 'It is not really necessary to connect *Brāhmaṇa* and *Śramaṇa* with Aryan and Pre-Aryan conceived as races. Neither spiritual nor cultural traditions

can be shown to be characteristic of any community defined by race alone where race is defined by physical features. In the case of Aryans, the definition is, moreover, linguistic, not physical. Nor, indeed, are any pure 'races' known at any time.

p. 261, fn. 50 The profound distinction between Brāhmaṇic and Śramaṇic religio-cultural traditions may be considered to have a spiritual, not an ethnic basis nor a basis in class or caste—see G.C. Pande, *Bharatiya Parampara Ke Mula Svara*, Chap. II, *Foundations of Indian Culture*, Vol. I. Indeed Indian culture needs to be conceived as a synthesis of spiritual attitudes or values, not as a mere social mosaic or ethnic museum.

p. 262, fn. 51 While the Vedic seers preferred the solitude of forests and the bulk of the people lived in villages, towns were not unkown to them—see G.C. Pande, *Foundations of Indian Culture*, Vol. II, pp. 72ff; G.S. Ghurye, *Vedic Society*.

p. 269, fn. 88 Cf. David Frawley, *Gods, Sages and Kings*, pp. 47ff.

p. 304, fn. 333 *Add* 'Vide G.C. Pande, *Foundations of Indian Culture*, Vol. I; *Encyclopaedia of Indian Philosophies*, Vol. IV.'

p. 306, fn. 336 *Add* 'Cf. G.C. Pande, *Life and Thought of Śaṅkarācārya* (1993).'

p. 317, fn. 41 *Add* 'Indian Marxist historians have sought to connect this antiritualism with economic and social changes, but they tend to assume what needs to be shown—see my article in *Bodhirasmi* (New Delhi, 1984), pp. 5-8.'

p. 371, fn. 10 *Add* 'The principal evidence for the date of Buddha is provided by various ancient traditions about the years elapsed between the *parinirvāṇa*, the Councils, and the coronation of Aśoka; about the *nirvāṇa* of Mahāvīra, and about various synchronisms. The prevailing view about the date of Buddha's *parinirvāṇa* derives primarily from the Ceylonese tradition which places the coronation of Aśoka 218 years after it. Despite minor discrepancies, this view is on the whole consistent with the main historical data, *vide* Geiger, *Mahavaṁśa* (Tr.), *JRAS*, 1909, pp. 1-34, Raychaudhuri, *PHAI* (5th ed.), pp. 213-14, 225-28, Bareau, *JA*, 1953, *'la date du Nirvana'*. An alternative tradition deriving from *Divyāvadāna*, *Kalpanā-manditikā*, *Gilgit Manuscripts*, *Avadānaśataka*, *Mañjuśrīmūlakalpa*, Vasumitra, *Samayabhedoparacana cakra* etc. places Aśoka only 100 years after *Nirvāṇa*, *vide* Lamotte, *Histoire du bouddhisme indien*, pp. 13-15. By and large Indian historical scholarship has not regarded the Indian sources of this tradition as reliable as the Ceylonese chronicles, nor have they found it reconcilable with the chronology of the political history of the times. Recently, however, the so-called 'northern tradition' about the date of Buddha's *parinirvāṇa* has been sought to be reaffirmed e.g., Nakamura, *op. cit.*, p. 213, Heinz Bechert, *Die Lebenzeit des Buddha-das älteste feststehende Datum der indischen Geschichte* (Nachrichten der Akademie der Wissenschaften in Göttingen I Philologisch-historische Klasse), 1986, No. 4. It cannot be said, however, that Prof. Bechert has discovered any new evidence bearing on the question. His arguments rest largely on a sceptical criticism of the Pali tradition—that it shows confusion about the date of Aśoka, that its succession of Patriarchs gives them uncommonly long durations, that the different lists of Kings in Puranic, Jaina and Ceylonese traditions show disagreements. To these are added some general considerations—that Ceylonese historiography tended to follow mythical synchronisms, that Buddhism in Aśoka's times does not show as much development as would be warranted by a lapse of more than two centuries since Buddha. The sources of the 'northern traditi[illegible]', however, are far more vulnerable to sceptical criticism. Texts like the *Divyāvadāna*, for example, can hardly bear comparison with the Ceylonese chronicles. The 'short chronology' would raise grave problems for the chronology of Magadhan rulers from Bimbisāra to Candragupta Maurya. The Second Council placed 100 years AB in canonical accounts should reasonably be considered pre-Aśokan in view of the non-mention of Aśoka in the Canon. The source of the 'northern tradition' may be traced to its confusion of Kālāśoka-Kākavarṇi with Aśoka and the consequent confusion of the Second and the Third Councils. On the development of early Buddhist thought and its phases Prof. Bechert's views seem rather to be simplistic on the whole. Nor can the Göttingen Colloquium be said to have advanced relevant factual research. Although it is difficult to be certain about exact dates, there can hardly be any doubt that Buddha's *nirvāṇa* took place early in the 5th rather than in the 4th century B.C.'

p. 560, fn. 12 Dr. Dube's work was published in 1980.